FAMILY OF FAITH
P.O. Box 1442
Shawnee, OK 74802-1442

BUSINESS AND ADMINISTRATIVE
COMMUNICATION

BUSINESS AND ADMINISTRATIVE
COMMUNICATION

KITTY O. LOCKER
THE OHIO STATE UNIVERSITY

IRWIN

Homewood IL 60430
Boston MA 02116

Cover illustration: Courtesy of Don Sibley/Sibley Peteet Design

© RICHARD D. IRWIN, INC., 1989

Sponsoring editor: *William R. Bayer*
Developmental editor: *Ann M. Granacki*
Project editor: *Jane Lightell*
Production manager: *Carma W. Fazio*
Designer: *Michael Warrell*
Artist: *Rolin Graphics*
Compositor: *J. M. Post Graphics, Corp.*
Typeface: *10/12 Sabon*
Printer: *Von Hoffmann Press, Inc.*

Library of Congress Cataloging-in-Publication Data

Locker, Kitty O.
    Business and administrative communication/Kitty O. Locker.
        p. 652 cm. xx
    Includes index.
    ISBN 0-256-05611-0
    1. Business communication.   2. Communication in management.
    I. Title.
    HF5718.L63 1989
    651.7—dc19

                                                                88–13639
                                                                CIP

Printed in the United States of America
    3 4 5 6 7 8 9 0 VH 6 5 4 3 2 1

o my husband, Bob Mills, with love

January 3, 1989

Dear Student:

<u>Business and Administrative Communication</u> (BAC) takes the mystery out of writing and speaking effectively. You can use the strategies and guidelines in BAC both in this course and on the job.

BAC's chapters are short. Your instructor may ask you to read them in order: Introduction, Building Blocks of Effective Messages, Letters and Memos, Reports, Oral and Nonverbal Communication, and Job Hunting. Some courses will be organized in other ways. Even if your course doesn't use all the chapters now, you may want to read them later when you need to write a specific kind of message or when you're ready to job hunt.

Before you read a chapter, you may want to read the Chapter Outline to get an overview of what the chapter covers.

As you read,

- You may want to look for the answers to the Questions at the beginning of the chapter.

- Note the terms in boldface type and their definitions. When you read chapters out of order, check the Glossary at the end of the book for the definitions of terms defined in other chapters.

- Pay special attention to the lists, whether the items are numbered or set off with the round dots called bullets. Come back to them when you prepare your assignments or review for tests.

- Use the examples, especially the paired examples of effective and ineffective communication, as models for your own work.

- Check the side columns for anecdotes and examples that show the principles in the text at work in a variety of business and administrative situations.

- Use the Summary of Key Points at the end of the chapter to review crucial points.

When you prepare an assignment,

- Review the analysis questions in Chapter 2. Some assignments have "Hints" which help you probe the problem. Some of the longer assignments have preliminary assignments analyzing the audience or developing reader benefits or subject lines. Even if your instructor has not assigned these, you may want to read them over for ideas.

- The exercises and problems following each chapter focus on the strategies discussed in that chapter, but a good solution often incorporates material covered elsewhere in the book. You may want to review the formats in Appendix A, the advice about composing strategies in Chapter 5, or the suggestions for student groups in Chapter 25.

- If you're writing a letter or memo, check the sample problems in Chapters 12, 13, and 14. Each has a detailed analysis, a strong and weak solution, and a discussion of the solutions to help you see how to apply the principles in this book to your own writing.

- The Student Workbook by my colleague Professor Meada Gibbs will give you additional practice in reviewing each chapter, mastering its concepts, and practicing for exams.

When you study for tests, try not only to memorize the Key Points listed in the Summaries but also to understand the reasons behind each point. Why does the pattern of organization put this idea first and that one last? Why do two different situations call for different patterns of organization? Why is this version wordy and that one tight? The more fully you understand the theories presented in BAC, the better you'll do on tests.

Feedback from my own students and from students at other colleges has helped me improve this book. (Even professors revise what they write!) I'd like to hear from you, too. Write to me in care of the publisher:

Professor Kitty O. Locker
c/o Richard D. Irwin, Inc.
1818 Ridge Road
Homewood, IL 60430.

Let me know what you like and don't like, what works and doesn't work for you. Tell me how the book can be made even more useful, even more interesting. Suggest examples or anecdotes for the next edition. Send me copies of especially good papers or outlines of especially good presentations.

I look forward to hearing from you!

Cordially,

Kitty O. Locker

January 3, 1989

Dear Professor:

<u>Business and Administrative Communication</u> (BAC) is designed to make your job teaching business communication just a little bit easier.

- **BAC is flexible.** Short chapters let you create the schedule that best fits your course and your students. You may choose to teach the units in order: Introduction, Building Blocks of Effective Messages, Letters and Memos, Reports, Oral and Nonverbal Communication, and Job Hunting. You may prefer to get into full messages immediately, coming back to earlier chapters as necessary to work on specific skills. The <u>Teaching Guide</u> contains sample syllabi for several courses with different emphases.

  BAC's assignments are flexible, too. Some of the class-tested assignments are easy enough for in-class writing or impromptu speeches. Others are challenging enough for your best students. Many problems offer several options: small group discussions, individual writing, group writing, or oral presentations. Choose from a variety of in-class exercises, messages to revise, raw data for reports, problems with hints, unclassified cases, and cases presented as they'd arise in the "real world."

- **BAC is specific.** Every experienced teacher knows that students learn better from specifics: specific strategies, specific guidelines, specific examples. BAC takes the mystery out of creating effective messages by showing students, for example, five ways to create you-attitude, four kinds of openers for direct mail or oral presentations, five kinds of buffers, seven patterns of organization for reports--and illustrating each technique with an example.

  BAC analyzes and provides a strong and a weak solution for three sample problems: a positive message, a negative message, and a persuasive message. A discussion of what makes each solution good or bad shows students how to apply the principles in their own papers.

- **BAC is interesting.** Anecdotes from a variety of fields show students principles of business communication at work. The lively side columns from The Wall Street Journal and a host of other sources keep students turning pages and provide insights into the "real world" that business students demand. And the examples aren't just "empty calories." Instead, each illustrates or enlarges a point made in the text.

- **BAC is comprehensive.** BAC covers not only traditional topics but also topics on the cutting edge of the field: international communication, ethics, collaborative writing, direct mail, technology. Side columns throughout the book highlight international, ethical, and technological concerns. Assignments allow students to deal with international audiences or to cope with ethical dilemmas in informative, negative, and persuasive messages. And if you have more time for special topics, the Lecture Resource Manual and the Teaching Guide provide lecture outlines, in-class exercises, and out-of-class assignments.

- **BAC is up-to-date.** More than technology has changed in the last twenty years. Research about the composing process, document design, negative messages, group dynamics, and conflict resolution (to name only a few areas) can help us communicate more effectively. BAC incorporates research from these and other fields to show students why a specific guideline or strategy produces better messages.

  BAC is the first business communication text to offer up-to-date information both about composition and about communication in business, government, and nonprofit organizations.

A comprehensive teaching package accompanies BAC.

- In the **Answers and Analyses for Exercises and Problems**, you'll find answers to all exercises, an overview and difficulty rating for each problem, and, for 30 of the problems in the book, a detailed analysis, discussion and quiz questions, and a good solution.

  Even if you rarely use an Instructor's Manual, you may want to check the Answers and Analyses for answers to unusual exercises, such as which reader benefit drew the biggest response in a series of ads.

- **One hundred transparencies** include strong, average, and weak solutions for problems in the book, documents to critique, and summaries of key points to use in lectures and discussions.

- **An additional one hundred transparency masters** provide further structure for lectures and material for class discussions. These ready-to-duplicate masters include both material from BAC--patterns of organization, lists, and figures--and additional material to enrich your classes.

- **The <u>Teaching Guide</u>** provides sample syllabi, suggests class activities to reinforce chapter materials and prepare students for assignments, and provides sample handouts for group work, peer editing, and other activities. It suggests ways to use each transparency; it offers an overview of each chapter with cross references to the relevant transparencies, transparency masters, and the <u>Answers and Analyses</u>.

- **The <u>Lecture Resource Manual</u>** contains lecture outlines, additional transparency masters, class activities, and a list of related assignments in BAC for six topics that can enrich your course: The History of Business Jargon, Presenting Numerical Data, Presenting Information in Reports, Ethics in Business Communication, Writing Magazine Subscription Letters, and Communicating with International Audiences.

- **The test bank** contains 1500 true-false, multiple choice, and essay questions with answers and a difficulty rating for each. The questions are arranged by chapter so that you can tailor each quiz and exam to the way you arrange the course.

- **A computerized version of the objective questions in the test bank** allows you to generate random tests, add your own questions, and calculate student grades.

- **The <u>Student Workbook</u>**, by Professor Meada Gibbs of North Carolina Agricultural and Technical State University, provides exercises to help students master grammar, polish style, and apply the principles in BAC. A study guide and practice test for each chapter let students monitor their own progress.

For ongoing information about new strategies for teaching business communication and for the latest research in business communication, attend the meetings of the Association for Business Communication and read its publications: <u>The Bulletin</u> (formerly <u>The ABC Bulletin</u>) and <u>The Journal of Business Communication</u>. To learn about ABC meetings, publications, and membership, write

> Professor Robert D. Gieselman, Executive Director
> The Association for Business Communication
> University of Illinois
> 608 S. Wright Street
> Urbana, IL 61801.

The instructors who have used this book in manuscript have helped me improve it. I'd like to hear from you, too. Write to me in care of the publisher:

> Professor Kitty O. Locker
> c/o Richard D. Irwin, Inc.
> 1818 Ridge Road
> Homewood, IL 60430.

Tell me what works for your students. Suggest examples, anecdotes, or assignments for the next edition. Send copies of especially good student work. Tell me about your own success stories teaching <u>Business and Administrative Communication</u>.

I look forward to hearing from you!

Cordially,

Kitty O. Locker

Kitty O. Locker

ACKNOWLEDGMENTS

No writer is an island. Even those of us who are sole authors benefit from the ideas and advice of many people. This informal collaboration is particularly important for textbook authors who try to include the best research and pedagogical thinking in the field. Many of the people whose ideas have enriched this book are quoted or cited in the text; more general debts are acknowledged here.

I was fortunate in first learning about business communication in Francis W. Weeks' strong program at the University of Illinois. Formal meetings and informal discussions in offices with eminent faculty and intelligent graduate teaching assistants (now faculty and business people across the nation) taught me a great deal. My knowledge has been expanded by attending the meetings and reading the publications of The Association for Business Communication: *The Journal of Business Communication* and *The Bulletin of the Association for Business Communication*.

My reviewers have offered thorough, helpful comments on the later drafts of the manuscript. The reviewers whose names I have been given are

Lois J. Bachman, *Community College of Philadelphia*

Beth Camp, *Oregon State University*

Pernell H. Hewing, *University of Wisconsin—Whitewater*

Marie E. Flatley, *San Diego State University*

Donna Stine Kienzler, *Iowa State University*

Mohan Limay, *Colorada State University*

Rose Marie Lynch, *Illinois Valley Community College*

Michael J. Rossi, *Merrimack College*

Roberta M. Supnick, *Western Michigan State University*

Jean L. Voyles, *Georgia State University*

In addition, the following people have given me detailed critiques of portions of the manuscript:

Raymond W. Beswick, *Syncrude Canada Ltd.*

Patricia Campbell, *The University of Tennessee*

Robert D. Gieselman, *University of Illinois*

Andrea A. Lunsford, *The Ohio State University*

John T. Maguire, *University of Illinois*

Debra Moddelmog, *The Ohio State University*

This book has been class-tested at The Ohio State University, the University of Illinois, Washington University, and Wayne State University. I am grateful to the instructors who used the book or portions of it in manuscript and who suggested ways to improve the drafts:

John D. Beard, *Wayne State University*

Linda G. Brown, *The Ohio State University*

Susan E. Carlson, *The Ohio State University*

Ellin E. Carter, *The Ohio State University*

E. Kathy Casto, *The Ohio State University*

Mary Faure, *The Ohio State University*

Sue Hamilton, *The Ohio State University*

Ruth Ann Hendrickson, *The Ohio State University*

Jone Rymer, *Wayne State University*

Laura Scibona, *Decatur Community College*

Kate Sommer, *The Ohio State University*

Phoebe S. Spinrad, *The Ohio State University*

Betty Evans White, *Washington University*

Over 200 students at Wayne State University, the University of Illinois, and The Ohio State University have taken the time to write comments—often extensive ones—on individual chapters. This student feedback has helped me enormously. Teaching students at Texas A&M University, the University of Illinois, and The Ohio State University has enabled me to learn how the concepts in business communication can be introduced most effectively. I especially want to thank the students who have allowed me to use their letters and memos, whether or not they allowed me to use their real names in the text.

The companies where I have done consulting work have given me insights into the problems and procedures of business and administrative communication. I particularly wish to acknowledge Joseph T. Ryerson & Son, Inc., the nation's largest steel materials service center, which hired me to create the Writing Skills Improvement Program which ultimately became the first draft of this book. Special thanks also go to the organizations which permitted me to reproduce their documents in this book and in the transparency masters.

My research assistants, Kathy Casto and Susan Carlson, tracked down the elusive sources of quotations.

My publisher, Richard D. Irwin, Inc., has provided strong editorial and staff support. I am particularly grateful to L. Bevan O'Callaghan and William R. Bayer for their creative problem-solving, to Ann M. Granacki for her encouragement, patience, and attention to detail, and to Michael Warrell, Jane Lightell, and Michael Hruby for the physical appearance of the book.

I wish to thank my mother, Estelle O'Donnell, whose gift of a computer, printer, and software made manageable the task of revising the manuscript through seven drafts.

And, finally, I thank my husband, Robert S. Mills, who provided a sounding board for ideas, encouragement, a keen eye for typos, and, when deadlines were tight, rides to Federal Express every week. To Bob with love I dedicate this book.

CONTENTS

BUSINESS AND ADMINISTRATIVE
COMMUNICATION

I

INTRODUCTION

Business Communication, Money, and Management

QUESTIONS
- Why is communication important in organizations?
- Will you need to write?
- Why do people put things in writing?
- What kinds of documents do people in organizations write?
- What are the purposes of organizational writing?
- How much does correspondence cost? Why does poor writing cost even more?
- What do principles of management and principles of effective communication have in common?

> The bigger an organization becomes, the harder its management must work at communication.
>
> Buck Rodgers
> *The IBM Way,* 1986

F ew organizations exist in order to communicate. Most have another purpose: to sell a product or service, to supply a social need, to implement plans and policies. Yet to do these things, organizations spend an enormous amount of time, energy, and money communicating.

People in organizations communicate in many ways: face-to-face in two-person discussions, in informal groups, in meetings; orally on the phone; in writing by desktop computers or terminals, in letters, in memos, and in reports. All of these methods are **verbal communication,** or communication that uses words. **Nonverbal communication** does not use words. Pictures, computer graphics, and company logos are nonverbal. Interpersonal nonverbal signals include smiles, who sits where at a meeting, the size of an office, and how long someone keeps a visitor waiting.

Studies have found that people spend 70 to 85% of their work time deliberately communicating: writing, reading, speaking, listening.[1] Henry Mintzberg found that chief executives spent "almost every minute" of their days communicating.[2]

Your technical skill in accounting or computer science or marketing may get you your first job. The ability to speak and write effectively may help you keep it. A recent study showed that the inability to write was a reason that accountants were fired.[3] As you rise in an organization, technical skills become less important, and more general skills, including the ability to write and speak well, determine how fast and how far you go.

"I'LL NEVER HAVE TO WRITE BECAUSE..."

Most students understand the importance of effective oral communication skills. But some students aren't convinced that they will need to be able to write well to succeed professionally. They may think that a secretary or technical writer will do their writing, or think that they can use form letters if they do have to write. Each of these claims is fundamentally flawed.

Claim 1: "Secretaries or Technical Writers Will Do All My Writing"

Today, many workers in business and government still have their letters, memos, and reports typed by someone else. This situation is changing as more and more people draft and revise their own writing at desktop computers or CRTs (cathode-ray tube terminals). If you work for a company where someone else types your work, you may be fortunate enough to have a secretary or typist in a typing pool who can correct errors in spelling, mechanics, and format. You may not. And even the best secretary cannot compensate for fundamental errors in organization, logic, audience analysis, or tone.

Sometimes you may finish a letter after five o'clock. Sometimes you may need to work weekends to put the finishing touches on a report that's due at 9 A.M. Monday. The ability to write well (and to use your organization's typing and duplicating equipment) makes you more independent.

In hi-tech companies, materials which go to the general public or to the government may be edited or even written by technical writers. Even in organizations with a large staff of technical writers, however, engineers and computer programmers still write their own internal proposals and reports and their own letters. And virtually every business expects its accountants, sales representatives, and managers to do their own writing.

Claim 2: "I'll Use Form Letters When I Need to Write"

A form letter is a prewritten fill-in-the-blank letter designed to fit standard situations. The writer can personalize a form letter by having it individually typed with the recipient's name and address. Sometimes form letters have several different paragraphs from which the writer can choose, depending on the circumstances. Using a form letter is OK if it's a good letter, but some of the letters currently in use are dreadful. (See Figure 1.4 later in this chapter for one bad form letter.)

Even good form letters cover only routine situations. The higher you rise in your organization, the more frequently you'll face situations that aren't routine, that demand creative solutions. If you develop the skills necessary for good writing and original thinking, you're far more likely to realize your potential and reach your career goals.

WHY PEOPLE IN ORGANIZATIONS PUT THINGS IN WRITING

Many people in business and government routinely write from 10 pages of letters and memos a week to, in some cases, 20 to 30 pages a day. Most people find speaking easier than writing. The phone is faster and usually cheaper than a letter or memo. Why then do people in organizations write so much?

People in organizations put things in writing rather than depend exclusively on oral communication to create a record, to convey complex data, to make things convenient for the reader, to save money, and to convey their own messages more effectively. Let's look briefly at each of these reasons.

1. Written Memos, Reports, Instructions, and Manuals Serve as Permanent Records.

Memos and reports document what was said and done and the reasons for decisions. Months or years later, memories will have faded; the people who did the work may have been transferred or promoted and may be unavailable for questions. Carefully written memos and reports enable a company to use its earlier experience without having to reinvent the wheel every time a new set of people tackles a recurring problem. In addition, writing can protect a company by recording exactly what the company is or is not offering and

Communication Ability = Promotability*

If you want to stay at the entry level . . . you really don't have to write much. If you want promotions, on the other hand, writing becomes important. If you want to get into management positions, you're going to have to speak in front of groups and do some writing.

Japanese Investors Prefer Written Reports†

Ken Ninagawa, 50, oversees U.S. investments for a money management unit of Nomura Securities Co. in New York . . . [working] with a staff of just five people to invest almost $1 billion in the U.S. stock market. . . .

Because Japanese investors prefer written reports to phone calls, Mr. Ninagawa and his aides go so far as to write a summary of the morning "research call"—a telephone conference linking brokerage offices with their firms' securities analysts—and send it by facsimile machine to Tokyo.

---

* Joyce Cochenour, administrator, Communication, Motivation, and Human Relations Department, Allstate Insurance. Quoted in John Di Gaetani, "Interviews with Allstate," *ABCA Bulletin* 45, no. 2 (June 1982): 41.

† Quoted from Beatrice E. Garcia, "The Eye of the Beholder: A Scot, an Australian, and a Japanese Tell Us How They Play the U.S. Market," *The Wall Street Journal*, September 18, 1987, 30D.

Documents in International Business Communication

Multinational firms and companies that import or export goods write everything domestic companies write. In addition, the following documents become important in international trade:

Documentary Letter of Credit: letter conveying the ownership of goods under the contract provisions—price, shipment, requirements of country of entry—which are all spelled out in the letter.

Standby Letter of Credit: letter specifying the amount and terms of payment which will be made when a service is completed.

Letter of Introduction: letter from someone who knows the person you hope to visit, asking him or her to make time to see you.

Letter Proposal: letter about your company and your products which you submit to the foreign trade group or ministry in the country where you hope to do business.

Memorandum of Understanding: document specifying what an advertising agency in another country will do to advertise your product, how and how much you'll pay, what rights you have to approve or control the advertising plan, and what kinds of reports you'll get.

under what conditions the offer is made. If there is no written record, chaos—and expensive lawsuits—may result.

2. Written Channels (Including Graphics) Are More Effective than Oral Ones for Presenting Numerical Data and Complex Information.

Businesses depend on numbers: figures for sales and costs, projections for inflation, interest, and taxes. These raw numbers, however, must be interpreted and communicated so that decision makers can use them. Oral lists of numbers are hard to follow and hard to remember. Written lists and graphics (e.g., pie charts, graphs, flow charts) make it much easier to understand numbers and other complicated data.

3. Written Channels Are More Convenient for the Recipient than Oral Ones.

To talk, both people must be free at the same time. This is rarely the case in business. Only one-half of business phone calls find the intended receiver in the office on the first try.[4] But when you send a letter or memo, the recipient can read it when it's most convenient. Even more important, the reader can proceed at a convenient pace, skimming easier or less important sections and rereading difficult or key sections.

4. Written Channels Are Less Expensive than Oral Ones for Reaching Large Groups of People or Transmitting Information over Long Distances.

If a big organization wants to tell all its employees about a new policy, a memo is cheaper than a meeting of the whole staff. It's cheaper to write a manual explaining how to fill out a billing ticket than to take the time to teach every sales representative one by one. If a company has plants across the country or offices around the world, it's cheaper to send memos to everyone in the purchasing departments or reports to all the district managers rather than flying everyone in for a meeting.

5. Written Channels May Enable the Sender to Convey His or Her Message More Effectively.

In a conversation, you have less than a minute to talk before other people expect you to let them talk.[5] In writing, you can take as much space as you need to present your evidence. Putting a message in writing also makes it easier to present your ideas in the most effective way, even in difficult situations. We've all had the experience of fumbling for words, only to think of the perfect words to make a point after it was all over. Writing, because it can be revised, gives us the second chance we may need to achieve the effect we want.

THE DOCUMENTS THAT WRITERS IN ORGANIZATIONS WRITE

People in organizations produce a large variety of documents. Letters, memos, and reports may be the best known, but they are not the only things writers

FIGURE 1.1
*DOCUMENTS PRODUCED IN
ONE ORGANIZATION*

INTERNAL DOCUMENTS

Name of Document	Purpose of Document
Transmittal	Memo accompanying document, telling why it's being forwarded to the receiver.
Monthly or quarterly report	Report summarizing profitability, productivity, and problems during period. Used to plan activity for next month or quarter.
Minutes of meeting	Summary of meeting, distributed to some people (including superiors) who did not attend. Minutes must be clear, indicate what was decided, reason for decision, who is responsible for the next step.
Policy and procedure bulletin	Statement of company policies and instructions (e.g., how to enter orders, how to run fire drills, etc.).
Request to deviate from policy and procedure bulletin	Persuasive memo arguing that another approach is better for a specific situation than the standard approach.
Credit report on a customer	Recommendation to extend or not extend specific amount of credit to a customer.
Performance appraisal	Evaluation of an employee's performance, with recommended areas for improvement or recommendation for promotion.
Memo of congratulations	Congratulations to employees who have won awards, been promoted, or earned community recognition.

EXTERNAL DOCUMENTS

Name of Document	Purpose of Document
Quotation	Letter giving price for a specific product, fabrication, or service.
Claims adjustment	Letter granting or denying customer request to be given credit for defective goods.
Beginning-of-year letter to important customers	Goodwill letter to major customers.
Job description	Description of qualifications and duties of each job, used for performance appraisals, setting salaries, and for hiring.
10-K report	Report filed with the Securities and Exchange Commission detailing financial information.
Annual report	Report to stockholders summarizing financial information for year.
Thank-you letter	Letter to suppliers, customers, or other people who have helped individuals or the company.

in organizations write. Donald Skarzenski, manager of marketing communication at Cadre Technologies, lists the items he produces:

> Those of us who make our living in business and technical writing create product overviews, sales guides, brochures, press releases, configuration guides, product announcements, data sheets, business plans, newsletters, magazine articles, users' manuals, reference guides, proposals, specifications, marketing plans, advertising copy, and more.[6]

Figure 1.1 lists some of the documents produced in one organization. This company, a subsidiary of a Fortune 500 company, has 25 plants across the nation; it fabricates and sells steel, aluminum, and plastics to a wide variety

Does Your Writing Build a Good Image?*

People are judged on the basis of who they appear to be in their writing, and if what they write is pompous or fuzzy or disorganized they will be perceived as all those things. Bad writing makes bright people look dumb.

---

* Quoted from William Zinsser, *Writing with a Word Processor* (New York: Harper & Row, 1983), 25.

The Cost of Confused, Overstuffed
Corporate Writing*
A few years ago an oil company
chemicals unit spent a bundle rein-
venting from scratch a selective pes-
ticide one of its own researchers
had found five years before; he'd
buried the news 25 pages deep in a
hopeless gumbo of report prose that
no one apparently could get
through. Another, luckier company
accidentally stumbled on a similar
in-house report about a new production process just before it began
building a plant using the older,
costlier way. . . .

Fuzzy building instructions have
added hundreds of thousands of
dollars to building costs. And a single hyphen omitted by a supervisor
at a government-run nuclear installation may hold the cost record for
punctuation goofs. He ordered rods
of radioactive material cut into "10
foot long lengths"; he got 10 pieces,
each a foot long, instead of the 10-
foot lengths required. The loss was
so great it was classified. . . .

of industrial clients. **Internal documents** go to other people in the same organization: subordinates, superiors, and peers. **External documents** go to people outside the organization: customers, suppliers, the parent company, unions,
stockholders, potential employees, government agencies, the press, and the
general public.

All of these documents have one or more of the **three basic purposes of
organizational writing:** to inform, to request or persuade, and to build goodwill. When you **inform,** you explain something or tell readers something. When
you **request or persuade,** you want the reader to act. The word *request* suggests
that the action will be easy or routine; *persuade* suggests that you will have
to motivate and convince the reader to act. When you **build goodwill,** you
create a good image of yourself and of your organization—the kind of image
that makes people want to do business with you.

Most messages have multiple purposes. When you answer a question, you're
informing, but you also want to build goodwill by suggesting that you're
competent and perceptive and that your answer is correct and complete. In a
claims adjustment, whether your answer is *yes* or *no,* you want to suggest that
the reader's claim has been given careful consideration and that the decision
is fair, businesslike, and justified. In a policy and procedure bulletin, the writer
wants to suggest that the policy will help the organization and the reader.
Without goodwill, the reader might think that the organization was hung up
on red tape, or that it was trying to play Big Brother to employees. People are
more likely to follow procedures if they feel that the policies are fair and the
procedures reasonable.

Two of the documents listed in Figure 1.1 package the same information
in different ways for different audiences. The 10-K report filed with the Securities and Exchange Commission (SEC) and the annual report distributed
to stockholders contain essentially the same information, but differing purposes
and differing audiences create two distinct documents. Figures 1.2 and 1.3
show pages from Wendy's 1986 10-K and annual reports. The 10-K report is
informative, designed merely to show that the company is complying with SEC
regulations. The annual report, in contrast, has multiple purposes and a wide
audience. Its primary purpose is to convince stockholders that the company
is a good investment and a good corporate citizen. Annual reports will also
be read by employees, stockbrokers, potential stockholders, and job applicants,
so the firm creates a report that is persuasive and builds goodwill as well as
presenting information.

THE COST OF CORRESPONDENCE

Writing costs money. In 1987, according to the Dartnell Institute, the average
one-page business letter cost $9.33.[7] Memos cost slightly less, since they require
neither stamps nor envelopes. The cost of a letter is lower if dictation equipment
is used; the cost of a long letter or of a report is much higher. One company
in Minneapolis writes 3,000 original letters a day. If all those letters are less
than a page each, it spends $27,000 a day just on outgoing correspondence.

THE COSTS OF POOR CORRESPONDENCE

When writing isn't as good as it could be, you and your organization pay a
price in wasted time, wasted efforts, and lost goodwill.

---

*   Quoted from William E. Blundell, "Confused, Overstuffed Corporate Writing Often Costs
Firms Much Time—and Money," *The Wall Street Journal,* August 21, 1980, 21.

FIGURE 1.2
OPERATIONS SECTION OF WENDY'S 10-K REPORT

PART I

ITEM 1. Business

The Company

Wendy's International, Inc. was incorporated in 1969 under the laws
of the State of Ohio. Wendy's International, Inc. and its
subsidiaries are collectively referred to herein as the "Company".

The Company is primarily engaged in the business of operating,
developing, and franchising a system of distinctive quick-service
restaurants. At December 31, 1986, there were 3,727 Wendy's
restaurants in operation in the United States and in 17 other
countries and territories. Of these restaurants, 1,335 were
operated by the Company and 2,392 by the Company's franchise owners.
In addition, 72 restaurants were under construction at December 31,
1986, of which 24 will be Company-operated. The Company intends to
continue to expand the number of Wendy's restaurants, both Company-
operated and franchised. See page 9 of this report under Item 2,
"Properties", for information regarding the location of Wendy's
restaurants.

Operations

Each Wendy's restaurant offers a relatively standard menu featuring
hamburgers and filet of chicken breast sandwiches, which are
prepared to order with the customer's choice of condiments.
Introduced in 1986 was Wendy's new hamburger product, "Wendy's Big
Classic". Also offered are chili, chicken nuggets, a salad bar,
baked and french fried potatoes, desserts, soft drinks and other
non-alcoholic beverages, and a child's meal which includes either a
small hamburger or chicken nuggets, french fries, and a small drink.
A breakfast menu is also available at certain Wendy's restaurants
during morning hours. Effective March 10, 1986, the breakfast menu
was made optional in each restaurant, while the Company tests
various menu possibilities for future use.

The Company strives to maintain quality and uniformity throughout
all Wendy's restaurants by publishing detailed specifications for
food products, preparation, and service, by continual in-service
training of employees, and by field visits from Company supervisors.
In the case of franchise owners, field visits are made by Company
personnel who review operations and make recommendations to assist
in compliance with such specifications.

Except as described below, the Company does not sell fixtures,
equipment, food or supplies to its franchise owners. However, the
Company has arranged for volume purchases of many of these products.
Under these purchasing arrangements, independent distributors
purchase certain products directly from approved suppliers, and
store and sell them to local Company and franchised restaurants.
These programs help assure availability of products and provide
quantity discounts, quality control and efficient distribution.
These advantages are available both to the Company and to any
franchise owners who choose to participate in the distribution
program. The Company does not receive any compensation from the

The 10-K report is informative.

FIGURE 1.3
OPERATIONS SECTION OF WENDY'S ANNUAL REPORT

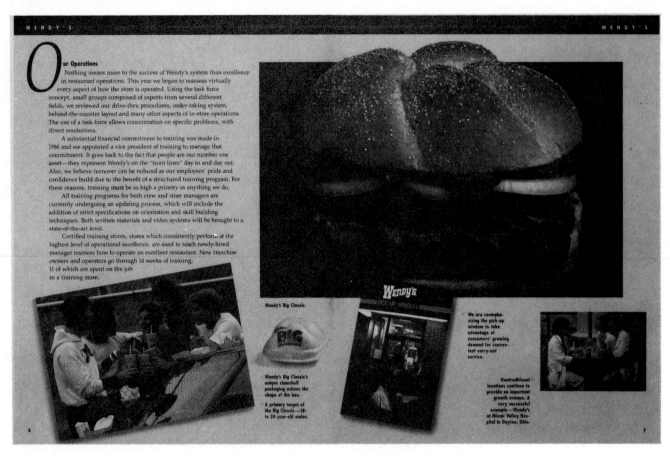

The annual report not only conveys information but also persuades and builds goodwill.

Wasted Time

Bad writing takes longer to read. Studies have shown that up to 97% of our reading time is taken not in moving our eyes across the page but in trying to understand what we're reading. How quickly we can do this is determined by the difficulty of the subject matter and by the document's organization and writing style.

Second, bad writing may need to be rewritten. Many managers find that a disproportionate amount of their time is taken trying to explain to subordinates how to revise a document.

Third, ineffective writing may obscure ideas so that discussions and decisions are needlessly drawn out. People inside an organization may disagree on the best course, and the various publics with which organizations communicate may have different interests and values. But if a proposal is clear, at least everyone will be talking about the same proposed changes, so that differences can be recognized and resolved more quickly.

Fourth, unclear or incomplete messages may require the reader to ask for more information. A reader who has to supplement the memo with questions interrupts the writer. If the writer is out of the office when the reader stops

Gentlemen:

Please be advised that upon reviewing your credit file with us, we find the information herein outdated. In an effort to expedite the handling of your future orders with us, and to allow us to open an appropriate line of credit for your company, we ask that you send an updated list of vendor references. Any other additional financial information that you can supply would be to both of our benefits.

May we hear from you soon?

Sincerely,

FIGURE 1.4
A FORM LETTER THAT CUSTOMERS COMPLAINED ABOUT

by or calls, even more time is wasted, for the reader can't act until the answer arrives.

Wasted Efforts

Ineffective messages don't get results. A reader who has to guess what the writer means may guess wrongly. A reader who finds a letter or memo unconvincing or insulting simply won't do what the message asks. Forty years ago, Richard Morris estimated that 15% of the letters businesses write wouldn't be necessary if the first letter had done the job.[8] In 1986, Frank Grazian said that between 15% and 30% of business and government letters and memos either ask what an earlier letter meant, or try to explain what it did mean.[9]

One company sent out past-due bills with the following language:

Per our conversation, enclosed are two copies of the above-mentioned invoice. Please review and advise. Sincerely, . . .

The company didn't want readers to advise it. It wanted them to pay their bills, but it didn't say so. The company had to write third and fourth reminders. It waited for its money, lost interest on it—and kept writing letters.

Lost Goodwill

Whatever the literal content of the words, every letter, memo, and report serves either to build or to undermine the image the reader has of the writer.

The people who got the form letter printed in Figure 1.4 understood the basic point. But the letter failed because it was stuffy and selfish. Four different customers called to complain about it. When you think how often you are annoyed by something—a TV commercial, a rude clerk—but how rarely you call or write the company to complain, you can imagine the ill will this letter generated.

Several things are wrong with this letter.

1. **The language is stiff and legalistic.** Note the obsolete (and sexist) "Gentlemen," "Please be advised," "herein," and "expedite."

2. **The tone is selfish.** The letter is written from the writer's point of view; there are no benefits for the reader. (The writer says there are, but without a shred of evidence the claim isn't convincing.)

Benefits of Improving Correspondence
Better writing helps you to

- **Save time.** Reduce reading time since comprehension is easier. Eliminate the time now taken to rewrite badly written materials. Reduce the time taken asking writers "What did you mean?"

- **Make your efforts more effective.** Increase the number of requests that are answered positively and promptly—on the first request. Present your points—to other people in your organization, to clients, customers, and suppliers, to government agencies, to the public—more forcefully.

- **Communicate your points more clearly.** Reduce the misunderstandings that occur when the reader has to supply missing or unclear information. Make the issues clear, so that disagreements can surface and be resolved more quickly.

- **Build goodwill.** Build a positive image of your organization. Build an image of yourself as a knowledgeable, intelligent, capable person.

Poor Writing Costs a Belgian Bank
£1 Million*

Business letters are even more expensive in Europe than in the United States. European banks require that letters involving large sums be countersigned; two or three signatures may be needed depending on the amount involved.

The regional headquarters of a large Belgian bank received "approximately 5,000 letters of complaint relating to account statements last year. Because of the poor written communication from the bank to its clients, it took an average of five letters to settle each complaint, or a total of 25,000 letters. At a cost of FB 1200 (£40) per letter, the economic burden from the bank staff's inability to communicate effectively in writing was estimated to be FB 30 million, or about £1 million that year."

In 1981, the pound was worth about $2.40. A £1 million loss would have equalled $2.4 million.

Employee Satisfaction Boosts
Productivity†

Honda of America produces cars in Ohio. President Shoichiro Irimajiri said the secret of Honda's success in this country is its work force "and our sincere commitment to their growth and job satisfaction.". . .

"I have learned from our associates that without employee satisfaction, we will not enjoy long-term productivity," Irimajiri said, noting some of the ways Honda tries to build this satisfaction. Among them are a suggestion system, quality awards, safety awards, profit sharing, and the New Honda Circle, in which employees work together to come up with ways the company can be more productive . . .

[One New Honda Circle] . . . used several means to speed up the pre-cast heating process in the early morning, saving Honda about $50,000 a year. This is typical of the involvement of Honda's employees.

3. **The main point is buried** in the middle of the long first paragraph. The middle is the least emphatic part of a paragraph.

4. **The request is vague.** How many references does the supplier want? Are only vendor references OK, or would other credit references, like banks, work too? Is the name of the reference enough, or is it necessary also to specify the line of credit, the average balance, the current balance, the years credit has been established, or other information? What "additional financial information" does the supplier want? Annual reports? Bank balance? Tax returns? The request sounds like an invasion of privacy, not a reasonable business practice.

5. **Words are misused** (*herein* for *therein*), suggesting either an ignorant writer or one who doesn't care enough about the subject and the reader to get things right.

GOOD MANAGEMENT AND GOOD COMMUNICATION

The principles that help people be better managers also help them be better writers. If you've had courses in management, you'll find many parallels between principles you've learned in those courses and the strategies this book recommends. If you haven't yet studied management, this book will give you a head start on good management techniques.

Many theories of management argue that good managers care about the needs of the people in their organization as well as the organization's need to produce a product or provide a service. The **Managerial Grid** (Figure 1.5) portrays this dual commitment most clearly.

The manager who shows concern for subordinates but little concern for production (1,9) creates "a comfortable, friendly organization atmosphere" but is likely to be criticized by higher management when the unit fails to meet its organizational goals.[10] At the other extreme (9,1) is the manager who runs an efficient operation but ignores employee morale. Many managers attempt a balance (5,5) which gives some attention to both dimensions. The ideal manager in this model is the one who cares deeply about both organizational and employees' needs (9,9).

Good managers care about their subordinates. Good sales representatives care about their customers. This caring demonstrates itself in thinking about things from the audience's point of view and creating a message to meet the audience's needs as well as yours.

You don't need to reinvent the wheel as you try to manage effectively through communication. Research and experience have taught us something about the kinds of language, the patterns of organization, the strategies, and the composing processes that work best. Neither writing nor management is an exact science, but the principles and techniques you learn in this book will help you create messages that meet your needs, the needs of your organization, and the needs of your audience.

* Based on Herbert H. Hildebrandt, conversation with the author, October 1987 and C. Jorgensen, H. B. Kassier, P. Kuborn, and J. M. Verbeke, "Business Communication in Belgium: An Overview," *International Business Communication: Theory, Practice, Teaching Throughout the World*, ed. Herbert H. Hildebrandt (Ann Arbor, MI: Division of Research, Graduate School of Business Administration, University of Michigan, 1981), 24.

† Quoted from Barnet D. Wolf, "Honda Plant Aims at Flexibility," *Columbus Dispatch*, October 8, 1987, G1.

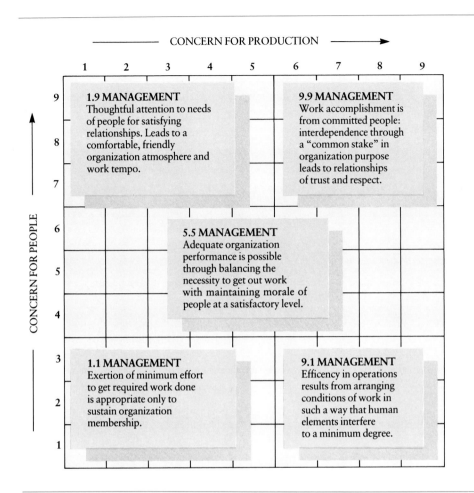

Source: The Managerial Grid figure from *The Managerial Grid III: The Key to Leadership Excellence*, by Robert R. Blake and Jane Srygley Mouton. Houston: Gulf Publishing Company, Copyright © 1985, page 12. Reproduced by permission.

FIGURE 1.5
THE MANAGERIAL GRID: CONCERN BOTH FOR TASK AND PEOPLE

SUMMARY OF KEY POINTS

- Communication helps organizations and the people in them achieve their goals. The ability to write and speak well becomes increasingly important as you rise in an organization.

- People put things in writing to create a record, to convey complex data, to make things convenient for the reader, to save money, and to convey their own messages more effectively.

- **Internal documents** go to people inside the organization. **External documents** go to audiences outside: clients, customers, suppliers, stockholders, the government, the press, the general public.

- The three basic purposes of business and administrative communication are to **inform, to request or persuade, and to build goodwill.** Most messages have more than one purpose.

- The average one-page business letter cost $9.33 in 1987. Poor writing costs even more since it wastes time, wastes effort, and jeopardizes goodwill.

- The principles that help people be better managers—concern for both people and product—also help them be better writers and speakers. Good communication meets the needs of the writer or speaker, the organization, and the audience.

NOTES

1. E. T. Klemmer and F. W. Snyder found that workers (including clerical workers) in a research and development laboratory spent, on the average, 69% of their time communicating ("Measurement of Time Spent Communicating," *Journal of Communication* 22, no. 2 [June 1972]: 148). Martha H. Rader and Alan P. Wunsch found that business graduates spent 85% of their time communicating ("A Survey of Communication Practices of Business Graduates by Job Category and Undergraduate Major," *Journal of Business Communication* 17, no. 4 [Summer 1980]: 35).

2. Henry Mintzberg, *The Nature of Managerial Work* (New York: Harper & Row, 1973), 30.

3. Gordon S. May, "No Accounting for Poor Writers," *The Wall Street Journal,* May 29, 1987, 17, citing research of Alan Cherry, Loyola Merrymount College in Los Angeles.

4. Louis H. Mertes, "Doing Your Office Over—Electronically," *Harvard Business Review* 59, no. 2 (March–April 1981):133.

5. Men tend to interrupt women after 12 syllables; women interrupt men after 25 syllables. Candace West and Dan Zimmerman, NBC "Today," 1980; cited in Lois B. Hakt and David Dalte, *The Sexes at Work: Improving Work Relationships between Men and Women* (Englewood Cliffs, NJ: Prentice-Hall, 1983), 53.

6. Review of *Make Your Point: A Guide to Improving Your Business and Technical Writing, Journal of Business Communication* 21, no. 1 (Winter 1984): 113. Augmented by telephone conversation with the author, July 1987.

7. Conversation with Kathy Casto, March 1, 1988.

8. William Whyte, "The Language of Business," *Fortune,* November 1950; reprinted in *Readings in Business Communication,* ed. Robert D. Gieselman, 4th ed. (Champaign: Stipes, 1986), 186.

9. Frank Grazian, "Can We Cure Murky Memos?" *Communication Briefings* 5, no. 4 (1986):3.

10. Robert R. Blake and Jane S. Mouton, *The Managerial Grid: Key Orientations for Achieving Production through People* (Houston: Gulf Publishing Company, 1964), 10.

EXERCISES AND PROBLEMS FOR CHAPTER 1

1–1 INTERVIEWING A WRITER IN BUSINESS OR ADMINISTRATION

Interview someone who works in business, government, or a nonprofit organization about the writing he or she does. Possible questions to ask include:

What kinds of documents do you write? Which ones are the hardest to write? Why? Which ones are most important?

To whom do you write? Other people in the organization? To customers, clients, suppliers, the union, state or federal agencies? How well do you know the people you write to? How many different people read what you've written? Which audiences are the easiest to write to? Which are the hardest? Why?

How much time in an average week do you spend reading materials you've received? How much time do you spend writing?

How do you write? Do you dictate? Draft with pen and pencil? Compose at a computer? Do you do lots of planning first? Does anyone else help you plan or revise? Do you ever work in a group to produce a document?

How important are communication skills—reading, writing, speaking, listening—to success in your particular job? In your organization in general?

How do you expect the speaking and writing you do to change in kind or mount as you advance in the organization?

As your instructor directs,
a. Write up the results of your interview in a memo to your instructor.
b. Report the results of your interview orally to the class.
c. Write a letter to the interviewee thanking him or her for taking the time to talk to you.

1–2 INTRODUCING YOURSELF TO YOUR INSTRUCTOR

Write a $1^1/_2$- to 3-page memo introducing yourself to your instructor. Include the following topics:

Background: Where did you grow up? What have you done in terms of school, extracurricular activities, jobs, and family life?

Interests: What are you interested in? What do you like to do? What do you like to think about and talk about?

Achievements: What achievements have given you the greatest personal satisfaction? In your list, include things which gave *you* a real sense of accomplishment and pride, whether or not they're the sort of thing you'd list on a résumé.

Goals: What do you hope to accomplish this term? Where would you like to be professionally and personally five years from now?

Use complete memo format with appropriate headings. See Appendix A for examples. Use a conversational writing style; check your draft to polish the style and edit for mechanical and grammatical correctness. A good memo will enable your instructor to see you as an individual. Specific details will make your memo more vivid and more interesting. Remember that one of your purposes is to interest your reader!

1–3 WRITING ABOUT YOURSELF IN A GRADUATE SCHOOL APPLICATION

You're applying to a graduate school which wants to get some sense of you as a person. The form gives the following instructions:

Write a letter to the director of admissions in which you answer two or three of the following questions in a maximum of four single-spaced typed pages. The committee is interested in getting a sense of you as a person. Your response will be judged on its individuality, insight, and sincerity and on the quality of the writing itself. Use a conversational writing style and correct letter format.

1. What three magazines would you read regularly if someone made you a present of the subscriptions? Why do you choose them?
2. Which three people (living or dead) do you admire most? Why?
3. If all possible careers (including doing nothing) offered the same material rewards, which would you choose? Why?
4. What is your definition of success?
5. What three things would you like to accomplish before you die? Briefly explain why these goals are important to you.
6. Suppose that you were going on a three-year space trip (measured by Earth time) to Jupiter. NASA provides facilities and supplies for all your basic physical and psychological needs. What three objects would you take with you to make your trip more enjoyable?

Assume that the size and weight of the objects do not matter. Identify them by name or title; explain the reason for each choice.

Choose a graduate school and degree program that interests you, and assume that the current director of admissions is Joshua Kenney, 202 Blackburn Hall, 1594 Neil Road. Use the real university with its real city, state, and zip code. In addition to the letter to Kenney, write a brief memo to your instructor answering the following questions:

a. What program are you writing this letter for (M.B.A., law, architecture, history, etc.)?

b. Have you made any choices in your answers specifically to increase your chances of being admitted? Briefly describe the choices and your reasons for making them.

1–4 DESCRIBING YOUR EXPERIENCES IN AND GOALS FOR WRITING

Write a 1^1/$_2$- to 3-page memo to your instructor describing the experiences you've had writing and what you'd like to learn about writing during this course. Possible questions you could answer in this memo include:

What memories do you have of writing? Are they pleasant? Unpleasant? What made writing fun or frightening in the past?

What have you been taught about writing? Have past classes given you rules or guidelines to follow? (List any that you remember.) Have you had much formal training in grammar? Has anyone ever talked with you about the writing process? About ways to improve your style? About strategies for thinking of ideas? Have the various things you've been taught about writing seemed consistent, or has one instructor contradicted what an earlier teacher told you?

What kinds of writing have you done in school? Have you written about your own experiences? Written argumentative papers proving a thesis? Written library research papers? How long have the papers been? Have you written papers of a variety of lengths or mostly of one length?

How has your school writing been evaluated? Did the instructor care more about what you said than how you said it? Did the instructor mark or comment on mechanics and grammar? Style? Organization? Logic? Content? Audience analysis and adaptation? Have you gotten extended comments on your papers? Grades with no comments? Something in between? Have instructors in different classes had the same standards, or have you changed aspects of your writing for different classes?

What voluntary writing have you done—journals, poems, stories, essays? Has this writing been just for you, or has some of it been shared or even published?

Have you written on a job or in a student or volunteer organization? Have you ever typed other people's writing? What have these experiences led you to think about real-world writing?

What do you see as your current strengths and weaknesses in writing skills? What skills do you think you'll need in the future? What kinds of writing do you expect to do after you graduate?

Use complete memo format with appropriate headings (see Appendix A). Use a conversational writing style; check your draft to polish the style and edit for mechanical and grammatical correctness.

1–5 DESCRIBING YOUR EXPERIENCE IN AND KNOWLEDGE ABOUT BUSINESS

Write a 1^1/$_2$- to 3-page memo to your instructor about your experience in and knowledge about business. Include experience as a consumer, work experience, what you've learned from other adults (including your parents), and what you've learned from classes.

Possible questions you could answer in this memo include the following:

What experience have you had as a consumer? Do you rent an apartment and pay for your own utilities? Are you paying off a loan? How have you been treated by the businesses you deal with? Have you received letters from landlords or businesses? about what? Do you feel the letters were good? Why or why not?

What experiences have you had as an employee? Where have you worked? Were you treated as an intelligent person or was the atmosphere authoritarian? Did you have the opportunity to read or type letters, memos, and reports? What did your boss(es) seem to think was most important for good writing?

What have your parents or other adults told you about business, government, or nonprofit organizations? If you remember any specific stories or examples, share them.

What business courses have you had? What have you learned about the best way to manage people? about the attitudes and actions that lead to success in your field?

Use complete memo format with appropriate headings (see Appendix A). Use a conversational writing style; check your draft to polish the style and edit for mechanical and grammatical correctness.

The Principles of Business and Administrative Communication

QUESTIONS
- What are the criteria for judging messages?
- How can you create effective messages?
- How should you solve the problems in this book?

> This breefe & plaine order in your letters, I thinke it best you
> should for a time vse . . . for after this maner of stile you may
> write to most sortes of persons.
>
> J[ohn] B[rowne]
> *The Marchants Avizo, 1589*

M ost courses in business and administrative communication ask you to begin writing immediately. You'll learn the principles of business and administrative communication gradually during the course, but in one sense, you need to know everything right away. Good writing is seamless: it uses you-attitude, reader benefits, organization, visual impact, and more in every document. Yet you can't read the whole textbook before you prepare the first assignment.

To help resolve this dilemma, this chapter presents a brief overview of the principles of business and administrative communication. Each of the topics is covered in more detail later in this book.

CRITERIA FOR EFFECTIVE MESSAGES

Good business and administrative writing meets five basic criteria: it's clear, complete, and correct; it saves the reader's time, and it builds goodwill.

1. **Is clear.** The meaning the reader gets is the meaning the writer intended. The reader doesn't have to guess.
2. **Is complete.** All of the reader's questions are answered. The reader has enough information to evaluate the message and act on it.
3. **Is correct.** All of the information in the message is accurate. The message is free from errors in punctuation, spelling, grammar, word order, and sentence structure.
4. **Saves the reader's time.** The style, organization, and visual impact of the message help the reader to read, understand, and act on the information as quickly as possible.
5. **Builds goodwill.** The message presents a positive image of the writer and his or her organization. It treats the reader as a person, not a number. It cements a good relationship between the writer and the reader.

Whether a document satisfies the criteria for effective messages depends on **the interactions among the writer, the audience, the purposes of the message, and the situation.** No single set of words will work in all possible situations.

We can judge whether a document is *correct* by measuring it against the facts and against standard English grammar and usage. Chapter 8 discusses using the right word; Appendix B reviews grammar and usage.

No absolute rule can tell us whether a draft is *clear* or *complete*. Are the following sentences clear?

High priority should be given to developing an input editing routine
for on-line billings.

We are not taking full advantage of Title 20 money.

No deduction shall be allowed under subsection (*a*) for any contribution or gift which would be allowable as a deduction under section 170 were it not for the percentage limitations, the dollar limitations, or the requirements as to the time of payment, set forth in such section.

We can't say whether these sentences will be clear to a reader without knowing who the reader is. Some readers may find these sentences clear; others will be lost. Similarly, a memo which seems complete to one reader could leave another reader with several questions. A document which saves the time of readers in one situation may take unnecessary time for other readers in another situation. A series of words which maintains goodwill when the writer and reader already have a long-established regard for each other may be inadequate for a writer who's trying to overcome an initial negative image.

HOW TO CREATE MESSAGES THAT MEET THE CRITERIA

To create good messages, use this seven-step process:[1]
Before you write or speak,

1. Analyze your audience, your purposes, and the situation.
2. Use this analysis to organize your information.
3. Use this analysis to design the physical appearance of your document.

Revise your document to

4. Be friendly and businesslike.
5. Emphasize the positive.
6. Use standard English; double-check names and numbers.

After your message is delivered,

7. Use the response you get to measure your success and to help you plan future messages.

This whole book is about these seven steps. Here is a brief explanation of each of them.

Before You Write or Speak

Time spent planning will pay off in better messages that you produce more quickly. Planning is important even if you will compose a written message that can go through several drafts. Planning is crucial if you dictate or deliver an oral presentation, since you'll want to get things right the first time.

1. Analyze your audience, your purposes, and the situation. Be sure that you can answer the following six questions before you begin composing your message:

- **Who is (are) your audience(s)? What characteristics are relevant to this particular message? If you are writing or speaking to more than one person, how do the people in your audience differ?**
  How much does your audience know about your topic? How will it respond to your message? Some characteristics of your readers will be irrelevant; focus on ones that matter *for this message*.

Effective Messages in Various Cultures*

The criteria for effective messages may differ among cultures. In the United States, saving time is important. Messages are supposed to build goodwill at the same time as they discuss business, without taking much extra time or space. In other cultures, building goodwill is far more important than saving time.

Japanese business letters, for example, frequently begin with a paragraph about the season and the weather. January is "very cold, midwinter"; February is "still very cold, but the ice is beginning to melt"; March brings "early spring, a hint of spring"; April is "mid-spring, the season of cherry blossoms." Only after goodwill is established does the writer get down to business. Dwight Stevenson points out, "The phrase 'by the way' in Japanese documents is a dead giveaway: it means that business is about to begin."

Even in the United States, cultural differences exist, particularly in interpersonal communication. In a big city in the Northeast, phone calls get to the point immediately. This directness might be considered rude in the South or in smaller towns even in the Northeast, where small talk acknowledging the other person as an individual has to come before impersonal business.

---

* Based on Dwight W. Stevenson, "Audience Analysis across Cultures," *Journal of Technical Writing and Communication* 13, no. 4 (1983): 327–28.

The Value of Clarity Depends on the Culture*

The British, like Americans, value clarity and directness. Yet misunderstandings abound. A study in one British firm showed that in 40% of the cases where a superior thought he or she had given an *instruction,* the subordinate had heard it as only *advice.*

U.S. ads are direct. The Japanese don't like U.S. ads: they prefer subtle messages where the point is not spelled out.

Skilled Japanese managers use ambiguity as a management tool. Instead of criticizing a report, the manager asks for more information. Kazuo Nishiyama points out, "When they say, 'I'd like to reflect on your proposal for a while,' when the decision must be [made] soon, it means 'You are dead wrong, and you'd better come up with a better idea very soon. But I don't tell you so, because you should know that yourself!'"

Whenever you write to several people or to a group (like a memo to all employees), try to identify the subgroups that may respond differently to what you have to say.

See Chapter 6 for a fuller discussion of how to analyze your audience and how to adapt your message based on your analysis.

- **What are your purposes in writing?**

  Decide what your needs are. What must this message do to solve the organizational problem? What must it do to meet your own needs? What do you want your readers to do? To think or to feel? List all your purposes, major and minor. Specify *exactly* what you want your reader to know or think or do. Specify *exactly* what kind of image of yourself and of your organization you want to project.

  Even in a simple message, you may have several related purposes: to announce a new policy, to make readers aware of the policy's provisions and requirements, and to have them feel that the policy is a good one, that the organization cares about its employees, and that you are a competent writer and manager.

- **What information must your message include?**

  Make a list of the points that must be included; check your draft to make sure you include them all. If you're not sure whether a particular fact must be included, ask your instructor or your boss.

  You can include information without emphasizing it.

- **How can you build support for your position? What reasons or reader benefits will your reader find convincing?**

  Brainstorm to develop reasons for your decision, the logic behind your argument, and possible benefits to readers if they do as you ask. Reasons and reader benefits do not have to be monetary. Making the reader's job easier or more pleasant is a good reader benefit. In an informative or persuasive message, identify at least five reader benefits. In your message, use those that you can develop most easily and most effectively.

  Be sure that the benefits are adapted to your reader. Many people do not identify closely with their companies; the fact that the company benefits from a policy will help the reader only if the saving or profit is passed directly on to the employees. That is rarely the case: savings and profits are often eaten up by returns to stockholders, bonuses to executives, and investments in plants and equipment or in research and development.

  Chapter 7 has more information about developing reader benefits. Chapters 14, 15, 16, and 17 suggest more advanced ways to build support for your position.

- **What objection(s) can you expect your reader(s) to have? What negative elements of your message must you deemphasize or overcome?**

  Some negative elements can only be deemphasized. Others can be overcome. Be creative: is there any advantage associated with (even

* Based on Benjamin Walter, *Bureaucratic Communications: A Statistical Study of Influence* (Chapel Hill, NC: Institute for Research in Social Science, University of North Carolina, 1963), vi; Christopher A. Amatos, "U.S. Marketing Strategies Fall Flat on Their Faces in Japan," *Columbus Dispatch,* September 23, 1987, H1; and Kazuo Nishiyama, "Intercultural Problems in Japanese Multinationals," *Communication: The Journal of the Communication Association of the Pacific* 12 (1983): 58.

though not caused by) the negative? Can you rephrase or redefine the negative to make the reader see it differently?

See Chapters 7, 13, and 15 for examples of ways to deemphasize or overcome negative information.

- **What aspects of the total situation may affect reader response? The economy? The time of year? Morale in the organization? The relationship between the reader and writer? Any special circumstances?**
  Readers may like you or resent you. You may be younger or older than the people you're writing to. The organization may be prosperous or going through hard times; it may have just been reorganized or may be stable. All these different situations will affect what you say and how you say it.

2. Use this analysis to organize your information. You'll learn several different psychological patterns of organization later in this book. For now, remember these three basic principles:

1. Put good news first.
2. In general, put what the reader wants to know first. In the subject line or first paragraph, make it clear that you're writing about something that is important to the reader.
3. Disregard point 2 and approach the subject indirectly when
   a. You have bad news to give the reader.
   b. You must persuade a reluctant reader.

See Chapters 12, 13, and 14 for patterns of organization for three basic kinds of messages: informative, negative, and persuasive. Chapters 15, 16, 17, 18, 20, 21, 24, and 28 show you how to adapt the basic patterns for specific kinds of messages in various situations.

3. Use this analysis to design the physical appearance of your document. You can design the physical appearance of your document to get your points to your reader more quickly. A clear, easy-to-read typeface is only the first step in creating a well-designed document. To make a document visually attractive,

- Use a subject line to orient the reader quickly.
- Use headings to group related ideas.
- Use lists and indented sections to emphasize subpoints and examples.
- Number points that must be followed in sequence.
- Use short paragraphs—usually six typed lines or less.

If you plan these design elements before you begin composing, you'll save time and the final document will probably be better.

The best physical form for a document depends on how it will be used. For example, a document that will be updated frequently needs to be in a loose-leaf binder, so the reader can easily throw away old pages and insert new ones.

See Chapter 10 for a fuller discussion of document design.

When You Revise Your Draft

Chapter 5 discusses effective strategies for composing and revising. As you'll see, it's easier to write if you don't worry about too many things while you're getting ideas down on paper. But before you type up a final copy, revising and editing are crucial. Check for friendliness and for positive emphasis. Check to be sure that grammar, spelling, and numbers are correct.

Mini-Review: Purposes of Organizational Writing
Business and administrative writing has three basic purposes: to inform, to request or persuade, and to build goodwill. When you **inform**, you explain something or tell readers something. When you **request or persuade**, you want the reader to act. The word *request* suggests that the action will be easy; *persuade* suggests that you will have to motivate and convince your audience. When you **build goodwill**, you create a good image of yourself and of your organization.

Most messages have at least two of these three purposes.

Brainstorming 100 Headlines
Creates a Classic*

[David Olgilvy] told me once that
he wrote at least one hundred headlines for any given advertisement,
every one containing the name of
the product and its "promise" or
consumer benefit.

His most famous headline is, of
course, the classic for Rolls-Royce,
"At Sixty Miles an Hour, the Loudest Noise in This New Rolls-Royce
Comes From the Electric Clock."

4. Be friendly and businesslike. In addition to being an organizational member or a consumer, your reader has feelings just as you do. Writing that keeps the reader in mind uses you-attitude. Read your message over as if you were in your reader's shoes. How would you feel if *you* received it?

Good business and administrative writing is both friendly and businesslike. If you're too stiff, you put extra distance between your reader and yourself. If you try to be too chummy, you'll sound unprofessional. When you write to strangers, use simple, everyday words and make your message as personal and friendly as possible. When you write to friends, remember that your message will be filed and read by people you've never even heard of: avoid slang, clichés, and *in* jokes.

Chapter 7 explains you-attitude and other ways to build goodwill. Chapter 9 discusses good style in business and administrative writing.

5. Emphasize the positive. Sometimes you must mention limitations, draw-backs, or other negative elements, but don't dwell on them. People will respond better to you and your organization if you seem confident. Expect success, not failure. If you don't believe that what you're writing about is a good idea, why should they?

You emphasize the positive when you

- Focus on what is possible, not what is impossible.
- Eliminate negative words whenever possible.
- Put positive information first, give it more space, or set if off visually in an indented list. Since these techniques emphasize information, don't use them for negative information. Put negative information in the middle of a paragraph or document; present it as briefly as possible.

See Chapter 7 for a fuller discussion of positive emphasis.

6. Use standard English; double-check names and numbers. Business people care about correctness in spelling, grammar, and punctuation. If your grasp of mechanics is fuzzy, if standard English is not your native dialect, or if English is not your native language, you'll need to spend some time memorizing rules and perhaps find a good book or a tutor to help you. If you know how to write correctly but rarely take the time to do so, now is the time to begin to edit and proofread to eliminate careless errors. Correctness in usage, punctuation, and grammar is covered in Appendix B.

Always proofread your document before you send it out. Double-check the reader's name, any numbers, and first and last paragraphs.

After Your Message Is Delivered

7. Evaluate the feedback, or response, you get. The real test of any message is "Did you get what you wanted, when you wanted it?" If the answer is *no*, then the message has failed—even if the grammar is perfect, the words elegant, the approach creative, the document stunningly attractive. If the message fails, you need to find out why.

Analyze your successes, too. You know you've succeeded when you get the results you want, both in terms of objective, concrete actions and in terms of image and goodwill. You want to know *why* your message worked. Often, you'll find that the principles in this book explain the results you get. If your

* Quoted from Jane Maas, *Adventures of an Advertising Woman* (New York: St. Martin's Press, 1986), 50.

results are different, why? There has to be a reason, and if you can find what it is, you'll be more successful more often.

HOW TO SOLVE THE PROBLEMS IN THIS BOOK

When you're faced with a business communication problem, you need to develop a solution that will both **solve the organizational problem and meet the psychological needs of the people involved.** At the beginning of the course, it may help you to use the following guidelines to begin your analysis.

- **Read the problem several times.** What are the facts? What can you infer from the information you're given? Are there any irrelevant facts or red herrings? What additional information might be helpful? Where could you get it?

- **Analyze your reader(s), your purposes, and the situation.** Try to imagine yourself in the situation, just as you might use the script of a play to imagine what kind of people the characters are. The fuller an image you can create, the better.

  Use the six analysis questions on pp. 21–23 to help you cover the key points. Some of the problems have additional questions either with the problem or in the student workbook.

- **Brainstorm solutions.** In all but the very simplest problems, there are *several* possible solutions. The first one you think of may not be best. Consciously develop several solutions. Then measure them against your audience and purposes: Which solution is likely to work best?

- **Think about the general business and regulatory climate, especially as it affects the organization specified in the problem.** Use the real world as much as possible. Think about interest rates, business conditions, and the economy. Is the industry in which the problem is set doing well? Is the government agency in which the problem is set enjoying general support? Think about the time of year. If it's fall when you write, is your business in a seasonal slowdown after a busy summer? Gearing up for the Christmas shopping rush? Or going along at a steady pace unaffected by the seasons?

  To answer these questions, draw on your experience, your courses, and your common sense. You may want to talk to other students or read *The Wall Street Journal* or look at a company's annual report. Sometimes you may even want to phone a local business person to get information. For instance, if you needed more information to think of reader benefits for a problem set in a bank, you could call a local banker to find out what kinds of services it offers customers and what its rates are for loans.

- **If you want to add or change information, get permission from your instructor first.** You can add facts or information to the problems only if the information (1) is realistic; (2) is consistent with the way real organizations work; and (3) does not change the point of the problem. If you have any questions about ideas you want to use, *ask your instructor.* He or she can tell you *before* you write the message.

  Sometimes you may want to use a condition which is neither

The Errors That Bother People in Organizations*

Professor Maxine Hairston constructed a questionnaire with 65 sentences, each with one grammatical error. She asked respondents to indicate whether they were bothered "not at all," "a little," or "a lot" by each sentence. Eighty-four administrators, executives, and business people responded. They were most bothered by the following:

Very Serious Errors

  Wrong verb forms ("He brung his secretary with him.")

  Double negatives

  Objective pronoun used for subject of sentence ("Him and Richards were the last ones hired.")

  Sentence fragments

  Run-on sentences

  Failure to capitalize proper names

  Would of for *would have*

  Lack of subject-verb agreement

  Comma between verb and complement ("Cox cannot predict, that street crime will diminish.")

  Lack of parallelism

  Adverb errors ("He treats his men bad.")

  Set for *sit*

Serious Errors

  Errors in word meaning

  Dangling modifiers

  I as objective pronoun ("The army moved my husband and I.")

  Not setting off interrupters (e.g., *however*) with commas

  Tense switching

  Plural modifiers with singular nouns

  Hairston writes: "I was not surprised to have the comments indicate that the qualities in writing that business and professional people value most are clarity and economy. I was surprised, however, at how vehement and specific they were about misspellings, faulty punctuation, and what they unabashedly call 'errors.'"

---

* Based on Maxine Hairston, "Not All Errors Are Created Equal: Nonacademic Readers in the Professions Respond to Lapses in Usage," *College English* 43, no. 8 (December 1981): 794–806.

They Needed to Proofread

One man who dictated his letters found that one letter complained that an office was "eating material improperly." The right word was *E.T.ing* (Emergency Transferring), not *eating*. But he hadn't told the typist that he wanted capital letters and periods, and the typist didn't understand what he said.

One woman mailed out a cover letter for a $750,000 contract asking the reader "to take a moment not to read and sign this contract."

One man mailed a letter to a male friend with the salutation, "Dear Ms. Weeks."

A magazine subscription letter began, "Dear Debra: You are a small group of women."

In the "Help Wanted" section of the *Chicago Tribune,* one company asked for a "programmer with at least 203 years experience in IBM mainframe environment, especially FORTRAN."

A highly selective midwestern business school lost a donor because a letter went out with a spelling error. A fund-raising letter to current donors to persuade them to give bigger gifts referred to a new faculty member as *a man of reknown.* A wealthy donor incensed by the error refused ever to give anything to the school again. The word *renown* was spelled correctly in the spelling checker on the school's word-processing program. Evidently no one used the spelling checker to proofread the letter before it was mailed.

specified in the problem nor true in the real world. For example, you may want to assume that you're sending out a letter in April even though you're really writing it in October. Change facts *only with your instructor's approval.*

SUMMARY OF KEY POINTS

- Good business and administrative writing meets five basic criteria: it's clear, complete, and correct; it saves the reader's time; and it builds goodwill.
- To evaluate a specific document, we must know the interactions among the writer, the reader(s), the purposes of the message, and the situation. No single set of words will work for all readers in all situations.
- The following seven-step process helps create effective messages:
  Before you write or speak,
  1. Analyze your audience, your purposes, and the situation.
  2. Use this analysis to organize your information.
  3. Use this analysis to design the physical appearance of your document.

  Revise your document to
  4. Be friendly and businesslike.
  5. Emphasize the positive.
  6. Use standard English; double-check names and numbers.

  After your message is delivered,
  7. Use the response you get to measure your success and to help you plan future messages.
- A solution to a business communication problem must both solve the organizational problem and meet the psychological needs of the people who are involved.

NOTE

1. This process was inspired by a process with seven slightly different steps developed by Francis W. Weeks, *Principles of Business Communication* (Champaign, IL: Stipes, 1973), 45.

EXERCISES AND PROBLEMS FOR CHAPTER 2

Measure each group of letters against the five criteria for effective messages.

Is the message **clear?** Are there any phrases which could be misunderstood?

Is the message **complete?** Does it answer all the reader's questions? Is it acceptable as a record?

Is the information **correct?** Is the message free from errors in punctuation, spelling, grammar, word order, and sentence structure?

Does the message **save the reader's time?** Does it focus on the reader's main questions?

Does the message **build goodwill?** Is the style friendly, without being either too casual or too stiff? Does the message demonstrate you-attitude? Does the writer emphasize the positive? Does the message create a positive image of the writer and his or her organization? Does the message cement a good relationship between the writer and the reader?

2–1 LETTERS FOR DISCUSSION—STEEL BARS*

Situation. Your steel materials service center sells and fabricates steel. One of your customers is the Kramer Manufacturing Corporation, which makes roller coasters and other rides for amusement parks. You've just received a letter from Samantha Smith, purchasing agent for Kramer. In her letter, Ms. Smith reports that the last shipment of 500 1/2″ steel bars was damaged. To quote her letter, the bars were "bent and twisted—some of them look like pretzels." She wants a replacement shipment of steel bars.

The following letters are possible approaches to answering Ms. Smith's letter:

1. Dear Madam:

    I checked to see what could have caused the defective shipment you received. After ruling out problems in transit, I discovered that the steel was bent in our warehouse by some of the boys who came back from a three-beer lunch and decided to prove just how strong they were to a new woman foreman.

    Needless to say, we have disciplined the men responsible for this childish display—hardly harmless fun, for it will cost our company several hundred dollars since we will have to send you a replacement shipment.

* Inspired by a set of letters written by Joel P. Bowman. See Joel P. Bowman and Bernadine P. Branchaw, "Getting Them Started: Helpful Handouts," *ABCA Bulletin* 39, no. 3 (September 1976): 15–16.

Please let me know if the new shipment arrives safely. We trust that you will not complain again.

2. Dear Sam:

    Sorry we goofed on that order. Sometimes steel buried at the bottom of a truckload can't take the strain. (Some days I can't take the strain myself!) We'll send you some more bars sometime next week. If you can, junk the defective bars—we don't have any use for them. Or our driver can pick them up and we'll credit your account for 300 1/2″ steel bars. Hope this hasn't destroyed your production schedule.

3. Dear Miss Jones:

    What do you mean by "look like pretzels"?

    Sometimes bars at the bottom of a truck get a little bent, but in all my years in the steel business I've never seen one bent in the shape of a pretzel unless someone deliberately bent it. Sounds like sabotage to me.

4. Gentlemen:

    Your letter of the 5th has come to the attention of the undersigned.

    According to your letter, your P.O. # 47420 of 500 1/2″ rounds arrived in a bent and twisted condition. Please be advised that it is our policy to make adjustments as per the Terms and Conditions listed on the reverse side of our Acknowledgement of Order. If you will read that document, you will find the following:

    If you intend to assert any claim against us on this account, you shall make an exception on your receipt to the carrier and shall, within 30 days after the receipt of any such goods, furnish us detailed written information as to any damage.

    Your letter of the 5th does not describe the alleged damage in sufficient detail. Furthermore, the delivery receipt contains no indication of any exception. If you expect to receive an adjustment, you must comply with our terms and see that the necessary documents reach the undersigned by the close of the business day on the 20th of the month.

5. Dear Samantha:

    I'll take care of the difficulty for you. I'll be down with the replacement rounds next Friday. While I'm in town, I'd like to take you out for lunch at the nicest restaurant in town just to be sure that you've forgiven us.

6. Dear Ms. Smith:

    You'll get 500 replacement bars by Friday.

    The Strongsteel bars you ordered have a tensile strength of 99,000 lbs. per square inch. Sometimes, however, steel shifts during shipment and bars may get even more pressure. Evidently this happened to the rounds in your last order.

    When the driver delivers the new bars, he'll pick up the others so that your account can be credited for the first shipment.

2–2 MEMOS FOR DISCUSSION— CONGRATULATIONS

Situation. Xylophone Music Supplies is a small company which makes instruments for school bands and private use. Employees are invited to make suggestions that will improve sales, production, work conditions, efficiency, or morale. If the suggestion will save money or increase profits, the person who suggested the idea gets 10% of the first year's estimated savings or increase. If the suggestion improves conditions or morale without saving money, the employee gets a check for $35. Supervisors let employees know whether their suggestions are accepted. The president of the company is very much in favor of the plan and writes a memo to everyone whose suggestion is accepted. This week, one of the winners of a $35 check is Leonard Skinner, who suggested a method to get mail (both interoffice memos and outside letters) delivered more quickly.

Here are several possible approaches for a message congratulating Leonard Skinner.

1. To: Leonard Skinner
    Subject: Congratulations on Winning $35

    It gave me an enormous sense of personal satisfaction to learn that you had an idea which was worth $35. It is employees like you who will lift Xylophone to greatness, enabling it to fulfill the dreams I had when I founded this company.

2. To: Len
    Subject: Speeding Mail Deliveries

    Job well done. Doesn't surprise me—I always knew you had it in you. Want to get all your love letters faster, eh, baby? Ha, Ha! Don't think you can fool *me*. I always knew you were a real mailman! (Get it?!!)

Don't blow the $35 all in one place. I can give you a special deal on a trombone: down payment $35, this week only!

3. To: Mr. Skinner
    Subject: A Note of Congratulations on an Award-Winning Idea

    May I add my small voice to all those who are doubtless congratulating you on your perspicacity and perception in creating an innovation in the delivery of our mail?

    Mail may seem like a small thing, but in fact it is not. Think of the mail that comes in to the company: orders, requests for information, brochures about changes in the music industry. Think of the importance of interoffice mail, the lifeblood flowing to communicate between sales representative and factory worker, between marketing manager and quality control inspector. Truly, without mail, we would have to do something else.

    The role of the inventor in American business cannot be underestimated. Without such greats as Thomas Edison, Alexander Graham Bell, and thousands of unsung heroes, the products that make American business profitable and American life the highest standard of living in the world would never have been created. Your initiative shows that you have joined that line of people who have made our business and our world what it is today.

    I congratulate you.

4. To: Leonard Skinner, Employee #450–23– 9488
    Subject: Presidential Congratulations

    Congratulations on your idea which earned you $35. I only wish I could make it more.

    We are always pleased when any employee has the company loyalty as well as the personal creativity and drive to suggest a new way of doing something. Perhaps the success you have had will inspire others to propose new and improved ways to improve productivity and profits.

    Again, thank you for your insight and inventiveness. Your contribution is an interesting one and will not be forgotten.

5. Dear lenard

    Thanx for you're idea. If it wasn't any good, the comitee wouldn't of excepted it. As such, you're idea will help our compnay be it's best. The $45 reward is a small tokin of our esteem. Keep up the good work.

6. To: Leonard Skinner
    Subject: Good Work, Leonard!

    Congratulations on your award!

    For years we've waited a day or more to get memos from one part of the building to another; now, thanks to you, that time will be cut in half.

    Lots of little improvements add up to major benefits. Last year wasn't a good year for school bands in general, but Xylophone's sales continued to rise— largely due to the efforts of dedicated workers like you.

    I'm sending a copy of this memo to your supervisor to go in your file. In addition to the cash award now, your idea should be recognized as part of your next performance appraisal.

    Thanks for making Xylophone a little bit better. And keep telling us other ways we can improve!

The Technology of Office Communication

QUESTIONS

- How do word processing systems work?
- What are the implications of word processing for writers and readers?
- Where should you start when you choose a word processing system for yourself or your own small business?
- What are electronic mail, voice mail, and teleconferencing? What are their implications for users?
- How are international messages transmitted?

> The development [between 1876 and World War I] of the telephone, typewriter, and interoffice mail system revolutionized internal communication in American businesses. The 1980s may be witnessing another communication revolution—an electronic one centering on computer technology. . . .
>
> Managers will have to understand the mechanics and characteristics of this new medium if they are to use it effectively—to avoid its pitfalls and exploit its advantages.
>
> Judith Stein and JoAnne Yates
> "Electronic Mail," 1983

Today, many workers use computers routinely to project financial data and to draft and print letters, memos, and reports. Desktop publishing allows workers to produce newletters, announcements, and brochures without going to a print shop. In many companies, employees use electronic mail instead of paper memos or use voice mail to supplement the phone system. Instead of flying to another city for a conference, employees may participate in a telephone conference call or a video conference.

How much and what kind of office technology you find will depend on where you work. In some corporations, employees are field-testing new systems on the cutting edge of technological development. At the other extreme, some organizations—not all of them tiny ones—are still using 1970s technology.

Computer technology is improving so quickly that there's little point in trying to master the details of any specific system until you're ready to use it or thinking of buying it. But it is worth your while to understand the implications of office technology for the way people produce and interpret messages.

PRODUCING DOCUMENTS

Since the late 1970s, an increasing number of offices have used dictation systems and word processing to produce documents.

How Dictation Systems Work

In a centralized dictation unit, employees dictate messages into desk or hand-held units or over the phone. Many systems allow employees to call from any phone—not only office phones but also from home, from pay phones, and from phones in other organizations. The messages are received in a **centralized dictation unit,** where transcriptionists—dozens of them in the largest units—type the messages into word-processing equipment. Many centralized units use **dedicated word processors,** that is, machines that can do only word processing. A paper or **hard copy** is printed out and returned to the **originator** (the person who wrote the document), who makes any necessary revisions. The transcriptionist makes these changes (typing only the new or revised material) and reprints the document. The originator signs or initials the document and sends it out.

Chapter 5 outlines the steps in dictating a document. Dictators may need to use a different composing strategy than people who compose on paper or on screen. With screen or pen-and-paper drafting, writers can change their plans as they compose. Someone who is dictating a document to a centralized unit needs to plan carefully before beginning to dictate.

How Word-Processing Systems Work

Word processing is a method of capturing the keystrokes of typing so that a document can be revised or reformatted without retyping the parts that are unchanged. To use a computer for word processing, all you need to know is how to turn the computer on, format and copy disks, and use the software package. **Software** is a program, usually sold on a disk, which performs a specific task. The computer itself and other equipment are **hardware.**

With a word-processing program you can compose on screen or key in already-prepared material. With just a keystroke or two, you can call up old documents, move within the document, delete material, insert new material, block sections of text, and then copy, move, save, or delete the block, create footnotes or endnotes, and manipulate the text in many other ways. The document is saved inside the computer on a hard disk or on a floppy disk which you store between uses in a safe place.

When the computer is hooked up to a **printer,** you can print out a hard copy. **Daisy wheel printers** function like fast typewriters. A wheel with a slight resemblance to a daisy spins around and the petal with the appropriate letter hits the ribbon. **Dot matrix printers** use a pattern of dots to form each letter. Some dot matrix printers have both a draft quality, which is fast but a bit hard to read, and a near-letter quality, in which each line is printed twice to produce darker, clearer letters. **Laser printers** are even faster than dot matrix printers (printing several pages each minute) and produce sharp, easy-to-read letters. The cost of laser printers is now low enough for most medium-sized businesses; their use will undoubtedly grow as cost falls even further. Both dot matrix and laser printers can print graphics. Daisy wheels, like typewriters, can print only text.

Some word-processing programs are compatible with programs for spreadsheets or data bases. A **spreadsheet** program sets up financial or other formulas and allows the user to change variables to see how they'd affect the outcome. For example, you can calculate the effect of several different sales levels to show when you'd break even on a new product. Many programs create graphics based on the numbers from the spreadsheet. A **data base** program organizes data in categories which the user can then manipulate to get the information he or she needs. For instance, a nonprofit organization might have a data base listing the names and addresses of donors and the date and amount of the donor's last gift. A worker could use the data base to get a list of all donors who had given at least $50 last year and who lived in New York, New Jersey, or Connecticut.

With a compatible program, you could move columns of numbers or graphs from a spreadsheet into a report without retyping them. Combining a word-processing program with a data base of names, addresses, and other information allows you to write a basic form letter which is customized for each individual reader. A **merge** program then combines the basic form with the individual data, producing individually typed letters for each reader.

---

* Based on John T. O'Donnell, letter to the author, February 25, 1988; Michael Moritz, *The Little Kingdom: The Private Story of Apple Computer* (New York: William Morrow, 1984), 191; Wynn L. Rosch, "Hard Disk Heavyweights," *PC Magazine* 6, no. 11 (June 9, 1987): 117; Scott Burns, "Computers Set for Mega-Future," *Columbus Dispatch*, October 11, 1987, 3H.

† Based on Boris Beizer, *Personal Computer Quality: A Guide for Victims and Vendors* (New York: Van Nostrand Reinhold, 1986), 151–52.

The Power of Personal Computers*
The personal computer that sits on a middle manager's desk today is more powerful than the mainframe computers that universities and businesses used a generation ago.

In 1955, the first successful commercial computer, the IBM 650, had a drum memory of about 1k (kilobyte) of memory. The first Apple personal computers adopted so enthusiastically by MBA students in the 1970s had memories of 4k RAM (random access memory), which could be expanded to 48k.

Today, personal computers routinely have 256 or 640k of memory. Hard disk drives with 10, 20, 70 or even 380 *mega*bytes of memory are available for AT-style desktop computers.

The original 4k chip could store about 500 words—about the length of one paper in freshman composition. A 256 megabyte chip could store all the words in about seven average novels.

Cures for Computer Headaches†
If computers give you headaches, there may be a simple remedy.

People looking at computer screens may not blink often enough. When you use a computer for several hours, look away from the screen every now and then or consciously blink. Blinking moisturizes your eyes and prevents headaches.

Novices may get headaches because they think they're at fault when something goes wrong. People who've worked with computers know that even expensive software can have bugs—errors in the program—that cause errors on the screen or in the printout. Knowing that something isn't your fault makes you more immune to "software-induced stress." If the program does strange things, write or call the manufacturer to ask for a corrected disk.

FIGURE 3.1
A FORM THANK-YOU LETTER

COLUMBUS HOUSING LAW PROJECT
THE COLUMBUS HOUSING LAW CLINIC   *Telephone: (614) 228-5792*

July 3, 1987

^F2^

Dear ^F3^:

Thank you very much for your gift of ^F4^ to the Columbus Housing Law Clinic.
With your gift, and others like it, the Clinic is able to remain open, serving
the housing needs of the poor in this community.

The Clinic is also celebrating generous gifts from three diverse sources,
demonstrating what we believe will become a broad base of support. The Columbus
law firm of Vorys, Sater, Seymour and Pease contributed $1,000, and in May we
received a $3,000 grant from Hands Across America which was split three ways
among the Public Housing Action Council, the Tenants Union and the Law Clinic.
In addition, Immaculate Conception Church in Columbus made a grant to us of
$500. These gifts are symbolic of the support the Clinic has received from
its inception from the legal and religious communities and from the general
public.

As a result of all of this support in the last few months, the Clinic continues
to represent low-income and working-poor families who are having housing dis-
putes with private or government landlords. To conserve our resources, and
to expand the number of people we can serve, our Director is setting up seminars
for tenants about their legal rights. These will be held both at our offices
and at various gathering places around the city.

You have helped keep this new organization alive. We are most grateful for
your generosity, and we plan to repay you with our continued service to the
housing needs of the poor in Columbus.

Sincerely,

Robert S. Mills
Treasurer

506 Trautman Building   *209 South High Street*   *Columbus, Ohio 43215*

Figure 3.1 is an example of a form thank-you letter to donors. ^F2^ is the reader's name and address (which is also used on the envelope). ^F3^ is the name used in the salutation. Depending on the reader, it may be a courtesy title and the last name, a first name, or a nickname. ^F4^ is the amount of the gift. The information in each of these fields is typed and saved in one file; then by hitting a series of keys, the user merges the letter with the list. The result: an individually typed letter for each reader, personalized with the field information the writer has specified.

Implications for Users of Word Processing

Even if you're using a manual typewriter or paying a typist to type your papers right now, you should be aware of ways in which word processing affects writers and readers.

- You need to master the system to get the most out of your program. Many colleges offer short courses in some of the most popular word-processing programs. Time spent now learning the system will pay off later in better documents that you produce more quickly.

- Writers using word processing need to pay special attention to revising and proofreading their documents. Since changes are so easy to make with a word processor, some writers revise, edit, and proofread less efficiently. Instead of reading the whole draft through carefully, some writers skim until they reach one error. They fix it, print out the document again, but then find more errors as they read further. Even worse, because documents produced on a good printer look so neat, some writers don't revise or proofread at all. But keying in a document is no more accurate than typing on a traditional typewriter. Editing and proofreading are still necessary.

  See Chapter 5 for suggestions on points to keep in mind if you use a word processor to compose or revise documents.

- The widespread use of word processors is raising readers' expectations about the physical appearance of documents. Because word processing makes it easy to correct typos, change spacing and margins, and insert graphics, readers are less tolerant of badly designed documents and of documents with obvious corrections—even if the document is typed on a manual typewriter.

  Chapter 10 shows you how to make a document visually inviting, whether or not you use a computer to create documents.

TRANSMITTING MESSAGES

Virtually all organizations still use the postal service and the phone to transmit messages, but few rely on these channels exclusively. Most organizations use overnight delivery services at least occasionally. Many use **facsimile machines,** also called **fax machines,** to send copies of documents to other locations in less than a minute. Companies in New York City use couriers on bicycles to deliver messages to clients and customers. Sales representatives find that their productivity climbs when they use car phones to review the status of shipments before each customer call. Some organizations record training sessions on video cassettes. Employees can play the cassettes on VCRs at work or at home. Someone who missed a training session doesn't have to wait until the next scheduled session to get training that he or she may need now.

The biggest change in message transmission is the increasing use of electronic mail, voice mail, and teleconferencing.

Choosing a Word Processor

If you want to buy a word processor for your own use or you own business, choose the software—the programs—you want first and then pick the computer—the hardware—to run them.

Before you buy, try to use a program—more than one if you can. You'll discover things you like and dislike about the program. When you know your individual preferences, you'll be able to choose a system that meets *your* needs.

Read Albert Grossbrenner's *How to Buy Software* if you're new to PCs. Read reviews of specific programs in computer magazines. Try to find at least two different reviews of each program: just as you may not always agree with a movie reviewer, a computer reviewer's priorities may or may not be your own.

You can get a functional computer and an inexpensive printer for $300; you can get a better system for $3,000 and a still better system for even more. It's true that "you get what you pay for," but the features that make a system "better" may or may not be features that you want and will use.

Don't worry about getting a state-of-the-art system. Computer technology is changing rapidly. By the time you've chosen software and hardware to meet your current needs, even better programs and hardware that will be released in the next six months will have been announced. By the time they're out, still better systems will be announced. If you have the money and need a computer now, buy it now.

Electronic Mail

Electronic mail, or **E-mail,** bypasses paper. Messages are composed on a computer screen; the recipient reads the message on screen. However, the receiver
reads the message only when he or she checks the "mailbox." Someone who
is using the computer for other work or who is out of the office may not get
the message for hours or even days. The recipient can compose a response
immediately or save the first message for a brief time (one day or five, depending
on the service one buys). Most E-mail systems allow users to print out messages
if they want hard copies.

E-mail requires that both sender and receiver have computer terminals and
that both be on the same E-mail system. Sometimes the computers are connected by wires and cables in a network. Sometimes each computer is attached
to a **modem** which translates the computer signals into signals which can be
carried over phone lines. Public E-mail channels such as MCI Mail, EasyLink,
and AT&T Mail are available to anyone who subscribes to the service and
has the necessary equipment. Several companies provide electronic mail for
corporations. Many of the regional Bell telephone companies offer or plan to
offer E-mail systems.

E-mail reduces the time needed for office meetings and memos, particularly
for organizations with offices in different buildings, different cities, or different
countries. However, other results are less clear-cut. Eaton Corporation's Truck
Components Marketing Group calculates that E-mail has cut paperwork so
much that its service workers get an extra day a week to spend with customers.[1]
Other companies find that people still print out everything—and thus handle
every message twice. E-mail seems to have increased the total number of
messages people send and read. In February 1985, a month with 20 workdays,
one executive sent and received 534 E-mail messages.[2] Nor does E-mail necessarily save money. In 1985, Citibank had 10 different E-mail systems which
could not communicate with each other; the bank had yet to save any money.[3]

If you use E-mail, consider these implications for writers and readers:

- Writers using E-mail feel as if they're speaking, so they may not
  worry about logic, grammar, or spelling. Receivers know that
  they're reading the message and judge it as they would any written
  document. Even worse, the E-mail message may be printed out and
  shown around, preserving all the flaws of the sender's "quick and
  dirty" message.

- Writers using E-mail are much less inhibited than they would be on
  paper or in person, sending insults, swearing, name-calling, and
  hostile statements.[4] The time required to produce a typed document
  on paper may encourage writers to think before they commit their
  feelings to paper; a typist or boss who sees such a message may
  counsel moderation. But writers using E-mail can send out messages
  quickly—and thoughtlessly. **Flaming** is the term used to denote this
  imprudence.

- Many E-mail systems allow receivers to preview the message by
  reading the subject line and the first five lines. If these don't appear
  interesting or relevant, the receiver will choose not to call up the
  rest of the message.

- E-mail screens hold fewer lines of type than does a single-spaced
  typed page. Yet there's the same resistance to moving to a new

screen that there is to turning a page. The shorter screen length puts a greater premium on highlighting important points and being concise. A reader may skim a paper document to the end, but he or she is unlikely to keep going if the first screen of an E-mail message looks irrelevant.

Voice Mail

Voice mail allows a sender to leave a message in his or her own voice using a push-button telephone. Various numbers on the phone allow the sender to record a message, play it back, or send it. To record a message, the sender simply speaks into the phone; to hear recorded messages, one listens just as one would to a regular phone call.

In some voice-mail systems, callers deliberately dial voice mail, usually using a password. In other systems, the voice-mail system functions as an answering machine. People who will be away from the office or who simply don't want to be interrupted by the phone can forward their calls to the system. Most systems allow users to listen to the message and rerecord it; the system adds the time and date of the call automatically. A sender can record a message in advance to be released at a later date.[5]

Unlike the telephone or some kinds of E-mail, voice mail doesn't permit two-way conversations. But phone calls which ask for or give information really don't need conversations. Voice mail is particularly useful when the work staff are away from their offices a great deal and when callers don't want "to leave a technical message with a secretary for fear the message would be garbled."[6]

By 1988, all of the regional Bell companies were planning to offer voice mail.[7] Voice mail is likely to be cheaper than an answering machine for people who receive lots of messages. It may be cheaper than E-mail in companies where every employee has a phone but not a computer terminal. In addition, using a phone may be less scary for some people than using a computer.

Voice mail shares some of the benefits of E-mail. Both help avoid **telephone tag**, the situation which arises when people keep calling and returning calls before they finally get an answer. Both are effective for communicating from one factory shift to another or from one time zone to another. Both reduce the number of memos and meetings. Voice mail doesn't reduce the amount of time workers spend on the phone, but it allows them to schedule their phone time rather than being interrupted whenever someone else wants to talk.

Callers using voice mail need to plan their messages so that they can state their requests or give their information clearly and concisely.

Teleconferencing

Teleconferencing includes both telephone conference calls among three or more people in different locations and video conferences, where one-way or two-way TV supplements the audio channel.

Telephone conference calls can be made on ordinary phones by scheduling the conference in advance with a telephone operator. Many organizations have installed phone systems which permit conference calls within the organization without any outside help. Video conferences require special equipment and a

---

Tele-Politics Is on the Rise*

Thousands of high-tech hobbyists, linked by desktop computers and modems, are blitzing the Federal Communications Commission and Congress with letters decrying an FCC proposal to raise rates for computer communications. . . .

Most of the high-tech howling has been organized by computer. In Boston, for example, Richard tenEyck [sic], a software designer, wrote a 12-page analysis of the FCC action, including a sample protest letter, and sent it electronically this summer to two bulletin boards. . . . Within three days, Mr. tenEyck's message had circulated cross country. . . .

Computer organizing is spreading to other issues as well. Beyond War, a Palo Alto, Calif., anti-war group, says it is . . . enlisting activists over PeaceNet, a computer communications system used by 300 peace groups. On the other end of the political spectrum, the National Association of Manufacturers, a business trade group, has begun NAMnet, to keep members posted on 45 issues before Congress.

In Colorado Springs, Colo., Wayne Fisher says his underdog candidacy for city council took off when he posted his platform on local electronic bulletin boards and answered comments from voters electronically.

Emotion on the Computer Screen†

In systems with only upper-case letters, full capitals and lots of exclamation points may indicate intensity: I NEED THIS TODAY!!!!!

Parenthetical ha-has are necessary to signal irony and exaggeration as well as attempts at humor.

On one network, sideways "smiley faces" appeared, consisting of a colon for eyes, a hyphen for the nose, and an ending parenthesis for the mouth:

:-)

---

* Quoted from Bob Davis, "Hobbyists as Lobbyists: Computer Users Are Mobilized to Support Host of Causes," *The Wall Street Journal*, September 29, 1987, 33.

† Based on Esther C. Huckaby, "Writing Is Back in Business," Conference on College Composition and Communication, New Orleans, LA, March 13–15, 1986, and Eric Tilenius, "Those SMILEY Faces," message on PUCC.BITNET (Princeton University—Computing and Information Technology, rec.humor group), January 12, 1987.

Dial "O" for Options*

[Some voice mail systems allow] callers to select from among various options using the buttons on a touch-tone phone.

Such devices now enable some 40,000 students at Texas A&M University to register for classes by phone....

Consider the system at Citizens & Southern National Bank in Atlanta. Every day—24 hours a day, seven days a week—the bank receives some 16,000 calls from customers who can tap in a password and an account number to find out about account balances, credit-card payments or whether certain checks have been cashed....

Deluxe hotels, too, are beginning to install voice-mail systems to take messages for guests.... The system installed [at an Embassy Suites hotel in Minneapolis] lets international callers leave messages in their own languages and has improved accuracy.

The Electronic Meeting†

The video conference is a perfect tool for communicating a uniform message simultaneously to audiences in multiple locations. The chief financial officer of W. R. Grace, for example, makes an annual presentation via videoconferencing to securities analyst groups in nine northeastern cities. He spends only two hours before the camera to get the job done instead of rushing under pressure to appear in two different cities each day over a period of several arduous days.

Some corporations, like ARCO, use the system to facilitate internal communication within their network of offices and plants throughout the country. Others, like Ford Motor Company, use teleconferencing to produce a spectacular new product launch in the presence of journalists and dealers around the world.

good deal of planning—including, depending on the distance, arrangements to transmit the signals by satellite.

Telephone conference calls are more expensive than regular long-distance calls, and video conferences are very expensive. But both may be less expensive than in-person meetings when one considers not only the cost of transportation and hotel rooms but also the time participants spend getting to the meeting and recovering from jet lag afterward. Furthermore, people may be able to find time in their schedules for a two-hour teleconference who could not spare a whole day to drive or fly to another city for a meeting.

People planning or participating in teleconferences should consider the following points:

- Because they are expensive, teleconferences need well-planned agendas and limited goals. Teleconferences are suitable for informative presentations and for choosing one of a small number of clearly defined alternatives. They are not suitable for brainstorming sessions or for decision making when a great deal of conflict is expected.

- Because less time is spent on nontask matters (both in meeting sessions and before and after the meeting), teleconferences are less effective than in-person meetings for building relationships and goodwill.

- People who have to travel frequently will welcome the opportunity to stay home and participate in a teleconference. People who travel infrequently may prefer the chance to visit a new city.

THE TECHNOLOGY OF INTERNATIONAL BUSINESS COMMUNICATION

Air mail and phone calls are part of international business, but alone they won't do the job. Air mail is too slow. Sending an air-mail letter from Illinois to England takes a full week. Even if the recipient responds immediately, two weeks go by before the sender receives the response. Phone calls require coordination, since differences in time zones mean that normal work hours in one country may be early morning or late evening in another. Furthermore, some countries have only a few international lines, severely limiting the number of calls that can take place simultaneously.

For years, organizations with a significant amount of international correspondence have used **telex** messages. The name *Telex* comes from TELegraph EXchange. Telex messages are keyed in on a special machine which translates the keystrokes into a code. Incoming messages are decoded by the machine and printed on paper. While telex transmission continues, **fax machines** now outnumber telexes eight to one in the United States.[8] Fax machines send a facsimile, while telex machines transmit only text and use only capital letters.

Both fax and telex create a written message which serves as a legal record of transactions. In addition, the firm receiving a fax or telex in another language can take as much time as it needs to reply, even going outside the firm to find a translator, if necessary.

---

* Quoted from William M. Bulkeley, "Dial 'O' for Options: Computers Enhance Phone Answering Gear," *The Wall Street Journal*, October 15, 1987, 35.

† Quoted from *Letitia Baldrige's Complete Guide to Executive Manners*, ed. Sandi Gelles-Cole (New York: Rawlinson, 1985), 229.

SUMMARY OF KEY POINTS

- **Word processing** is a method of capturing the keystrokes of typing so that a document can be revised or reformatted without retyping the parts that are unchanged. The two basic kinds of word-processing systems are personal computers with word-processing software and centralized dictation units.

- To choose a word-processing system, pick the software first and then choose hardware to run it. Try to test several programs and to read two reviews of any program before you buy it.

- Writers using word processing need to pay special attention to planning, revising, and proofreading their documents. Word processing makes readers less tolerant of badly designed documents and of documents with obvious corrections.

- **Electronic mail, or E-mail,** bypasses paper. Messages are typed on a computer screen, relayed by computer, and read on the receiver's computer screen. E-mail reduces time needed for office communication.

- Writers need to think twice before sending E-mail. Since E-mail can be printed out, writers must realize that their messages may be seen by many people and may be used as evidence of their ability to think or to write.

- Writers using E-mail need to use clear, complete subject lines and effective first paragraphs. They need to make their messages concise—less than 19 lines if possible.

- **Voice mail** allows users to record messages in their own voices. Callers using voice mail need to plan their messages so that they can state their requests or give their information clearly and concisely.

- **Teleconferences** include telephone calls among three or more people and video conferences between two or more locations. Teleconferences are suitable for informative presentations and for choosing one of a small number of clearly defined alternatives. Teleconferences are less effective than in-person meetings for building relationships and goodwill.

- **Telex** and **fax** messages are common in international business communication. Both provide a legal record; both can be translated at leisure.

NOTES

1. International Data Corporation, "Automating Mobile Offices," in "Office Automation and Desktop Computing," advertising supplement, *Forbes* 140, no. 8 (October 19, 1987): 24.

2. Esther C. Huckaby, "Writing Is Back in Business," Conference on College Composition and Communication, New Orleans, LA, March 13–15, 1986.

3. Judith K. Stein, "Electronically Mediated Exchanges," Association for Business Communication International Convention, Chicago, IL, October 31–November 3, 1985.

4. Sara Kiesler, Jane Siegel, and Timothy W. McGuire, "Social Psychological Aspects of Computer-Mediated Communication," *American Psychologist* 39, no. 10 (October 1984): 1129; also Esther C. Huckaby, telephone conversation with the author, August 3, 1987.

5. Raymond W. Beswick, "Office Technology: Voice Store-and-Forward," *Information Systems and Business Communication*, ed. Raymond W. Beswick and Alfred B. Williams (Urbana, IL: American Business Communication Association, 1983), 5.

6. Raymond W. Beswick and N. L. Reinsch, Jr., "Attitudinal Responses to Voice Mail," *Journal of Business Communication* 24, no. 3 (Summer 1987): 25.

7. Julie Amparano, "A Wide Variety of Information Services Will Soon Be Available on Phone Lines," *The Wall Street Journal*, March 11, 1988, 19.

8. Neal Santelmann, "'It'll Be Around for Quite A While,'" *Forbes* 141, no. 4 (February 22, 1988): 110.

* Based on John Stewart, conversation with the author, November 17, 1987.

Exchange Rates on Radio*

Not all countries have sophisticated electronic communication systems. In many countries, the radio is the primary medium for communicating government information. Prices aren't marked on items in stores in many Third World countries; instead, they're published in the newspapers. You have to read the paper to find out, for example, how much flour costs.

In Tanzania, changes in the exchange rates are broadcast on the radio. Travelers who arrived just before a rate change was due in June 1986 had to wait until the six o'clock news to get their own money changed into the local currency.

EXERCISES AND PROBLEMS FOR CHAPTER 3

3–1 SURVEYING STUDENTS' EXPERIENCES WITH COMPUTERS

Survey several students about their experiences with and attitudes toward computers. Possible questions to ask include the following:

Have you ever used a computer? Have you used a mainframe? Have you used a personal computer? Which kinds (e.g., IBM-compatible or Apple) or brands?

Have you every used programs written by other people (shareware or commercial software)? What kinds of programs (e.g., word processing, spreadsheets)? What specific brand names (e.g., Lotus 1–2–3®, WordPerfect®).

Do you have access to a computer with a word-processing program and a printer? Can you use the computer whenever you like, or is access limited?

What do you like least about using computers?

What do you like most about using computers?

As your instructor directs,
a. Share your answers with a small group of classmates.
b. Present your findings in an oral report to the class.
c. Present your findings in a memo to your instructor.
d. Combine your findings with those of other students in a group report.

3–2 COMPARING TWO SOFTWARE PROGRAMS

Compare two commercial software programs in a single category (e.g., two word-processing programs, two spreadsheets). Use printed reviews; if possible, talk to people who use the programs and use them yourself. Your analysis could include the following topics:

How much memory does the program require?

What kind(s) of computers (e.g., IBM-compatible, Apple) can it be used on?

How difficult is the program to learn?

Can someone who knows the program well type in commands rather than following a menu?

What operations does the program perform? How many keystrokes are needed to perform various operations? Are the operations equally easy in both programs?

Is the program compatible with programs in other categories? That is, could you integrate the word-processing program with a spreadsheet? What are the names of compatible programs in other categories?

What is the list price of the program?

If you were choosing one of the programs for your own use, which would you prefer? Why?

As your instructor directs,
a. Present your analysis in an oral report to the class.
b. Present your analysis in a memo to your instructor.
c. Combine your analysis with those of other students in a group report.

3–3 PRICING EQUIPMENT FOR A HOME OFFICE

Assume that you're pricing equipment for a home office. Get price and other information (e.g., size, capacity, features) for each of the following:

Personal computer with monitor.

Printer.

Modem.

Telephone answering machine.

Copier.

Fax machine or fax card for the computer.

As your instructor directs,
a. Present your analysis in an oral report to the class.
b. Present your analysis in a memo to your instructor.
c. Combine your analysis with those of other students in a group report.

Hints:

• The quality you'll need will depend on what kind of business the equipment is for. Do you need a color monitor and printer? Do you need a laser printer? Do you need a hard disk?

3–4 INTERVIEWING USERS OF ELECTRONIC MAIL

If the computers on your campus are linked to national or local networks, interview several people who have used the system. Possible questions to ask include the following:

How often do you log onto the network? How many messages do you send and receive a week?

With whom do you communicate? Colleagues? Teachers? Students? Strangers?

What do you use the network for? To write messages? To get information necessary to your work? For fun? For what other purposes?

How do the messages you send and receive by electronic mail compare in terms of

Length
Purpose and audience
Formality
Speed of response
Importance
Ease of use

to messages you'd send and receive on the phone? On paper?

What do you like about using electronic mail? What do you dislike about it?

As your instructor directs,
a. Present your analysis in an oral report to the class.
b. Present your analysis in a memo to your instructor.
c. Combine your analysis with those of other students in a group report.

3–5 USING A MERGE SYSTEM TO CREATE PERSONALIZED LETTERS

If you have the computer and program available, combine the form letter from one of the following assignments with a list of names and addresses and print out the letters individually.

7–8   Revising a Form Letter for Success Consciousness and Audience Adaptation
12–2   Announcing a Change in Premium Structure
12–7   Revising an Admissions Letter
12–15 Providing Information to Job Applicants
14–15 Persuading Businesses to "Adopt a School"
16–6   Selling a "Care" Package
17–6   Asking for Donations for a Shelter for Homeless People

3–6 CALCULATING TIMES FOR INTERNATIONAL CALLS

Calculate the time difference between your city and each of the following cities. Assuming a 9–5 workday, with people generally unavailable from 12–2, at what times (if any) would you and someone in each of the following cities both be in your offices? If you had to arrange a call outside normal work hours, what time(s) would be best? Why?

Buenos Aires	Lagos
Calcutta	London
Canberra	Moscow
Copenhagen	Paris
Hong Kong	Tokyo
Jerusalem	Vancouver

How much would it cost for you to call each city?

How much would it cost for someone in that city to call you?

Communication Theory and Semantics

CHAPTER OUTLINE

A Model of the Communication Process
Communication Channels in Organizations
Principles of Semantics
1. *Perception Involves the Perceiver as Well as What Is Perceived.*
2. *Facts, Inferences, and Judgments Are Not the Same Thing.*
3. *No Two Things Are Ever Exactly Alike.*
4. *Things Change Significantly with Time.*
5. *Most "Either-Or" Classifications Are Not Legitimate.*
6. *A Statement Is Never the Whole Story.*
7. *Words Are Not Identical to the Objects They Represent.*
8. *The Symbols Used in Communication Must Stand for Essentially the Same Thing in the Minds of the Sender and the Receiver.*

Summary of Key Points

QUESTIONS

- What does communication theory try to explain?
- What are the steps in the communication process?
- Why does communication so often break down?
- What are the advantages of various kinds of channels?
- If a conflict is "just a matter of semantics," is the conflict a minor one that will be easily resolved?
- What semantic principles explain the breakdowns and help us communicate more effectively?

First Umpire: "There are strikes and there are balls, and I call them as they are."

Second Umpire: "There are strikes and there are balls, and I call them as I see them."

Third Umpire: "A pitch doesn't become a strike or a ball until I call it."

Anonymous

L anguage shapes the way we see reality. Sometimes communicating is hard because our words are based on different understandings of reality. **Communication theory** attempts to explain what happens when we communicate. **Semantics** is the study of the way our behavior is influenced by the words and other symbols we use to communicate. (Sometimes it is called **general semantics** to distinguish it from more narrow meanings of *semantics*.) Communication theory and semantics both show why and where communication can break down. Both suggest things that we can do—as writers and speakers—to get more of our meaning across to other people and—as readers and listeners—to more accurately understand the messages that we receive.

A MODEL OF THE COMMUNICATION PROCESS

Figure 4.1 shows the basic steps of the process that occurs when one person tries to transfer ideas to someone else.

The process begins when Person A (let's call him Alex) **perceives** some stimulus. Here we are talking about literal perception: the ability to see, to hear, to taste, to smell, to touch. Next, Alex **interprets** what he has perceived. Is it important? Unusual? The next step is to **choose** or **select** the information Alex wishes to send to B (whom we'll call Barbara). Now Alex is ready to put his ideas into words. (Some people argue that we can think only in words and would put this stage before interpretation and choice.) Words are not the only way to convey ideas: gestures, clothing, and pictures can also carry meaning. The stage of putting ideas into any of these symbols is called **encoding.** Then Alex must **transmit** the message to Barbara using some **channel.** Channels include memos, phone calls, meetings, billboards, TV ads, and electronic mail, to name just a few.

To receive the message, Barbara must first perceive it. Then she must **decode** it, that is, extract meaning from the symbols. Barbara then repeats the steps Alex has gone through: interpreting the information, choosing a response, and encoding it. The response Barbara sends to Alex is called **feedback.** Feedback may be direct and immediate or indirect and delayed; it may be verbal or nonverbal.

Noise can interfere with every aspect of the communication process. Noise may be physical or psychological. Physical noise could be a phone line with static, a lawn mower roaring outside a classroom, or handwriting that is hard to read. Psychological noise could include not liking a speaker, being concerned about something other than the message, or already having one's mind made up on an issue.

FIGURE 4.1
A MODEL OF TWO-PERSON COMMUNICATION WITH FEEDBACK

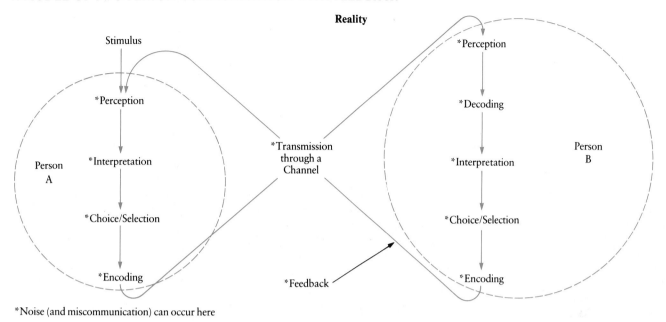

*Noise (and miscommunication) can occur here

Channel overload occurs when the channel cannot handle all the messages that are being sent. A small business may have only two phone lines; no one else can get through if both lines are in use. **Information overload** occurs when more messages are transmitted than the human receiver can handle. Some receivers process information "first come, first served." Some may try to select the most important messages and ignore others. A third way is to depend on abstracts or summaries prepared by other people. None of these ways is completely satisfactory.

Here's how the process might work in an organizational situation:

Alex is an inspector for a state Department of Public Health who inspects nursing homes to be sure that they meet state standards. Answering some of the questions on the form (Does each resident have a separate bed?) calls only for **perception.** Others (Do residents receive appropriate care?) depend on **interpretation** as well as perception. Today, Alex is appalled at the condition of the Olde Folks Inne. He must choose details to put in his report to document his judgment that Olde Folks violates state standards.

Alex **encodes** his information in words only; he didn't think to bring a camera along, and he doesn't think a drawing or a table is necessary. The **channel** he chooses is the standard format for inspection reports in his office. He **transmits** his report to his boss, who may forward it to the attorney general's office if the violations are sufficiently severe.

Barbara is a lawyer in the attorney general's office. She gets Alex's report about three weeks after he wrote it (the **channel** isn't very fast) but doesn't read the report for another two weeks because she's so busy. Barbara is experiencing **information overload:** she cannot deal with messages as fast as they arrive.

When Barbara finally reads Alex's report, she **perceives** the typed document

They Hadn't Heard the War Was Over*

On January 8, 1815, British soldiers attacked New Orleans. The battle was a decisive defeat for the British. Over 2,000 British soldiers were killed; seven Americans were killed.

Neither the British nor the Americans knew that a peace treaty ending the war had been signed in Belgium on December 24, 1814—15 days earlier. Transmission of the information would be by ship, across the Atlantic Ocean and then up the Mississippi River. The channel wasn't fast enough to prevent the battle.

---

* Based on Kate Caffrey, *The Twilight's Last Gleaming: Britain vs. America 1812–1815* (New York: Stein & Day, 1977), 276–79.

and **decodes** it. There are some technical terms in the report (Alex has talked about §302.1.a of the State Code for Nursing Homes) which she understands since she's an expert in this area. She must **interpret** Alex's information. Are the violations severe enough to warrant taking a case against Olde Folks? She thinks they are. Furthermore, the governor made a speech three months ago promising to curb abuses in nursing homes, so clearing up this case will make her and her office look good.

Barbara **chooses** points which she wants to check on; she **encodes** her questions in simple, direct language and **transmits** her message to Alex by a phone call. Her questions serve as **feedback**. Alex learns that his report is on target, but that at several points Barbara needs more information. (It isn't enough to say that residents are "neglected"; Barbara needs measurable, objective data to prove her case.)

The initial communication circuit expands. Barbara makes an appointment to visit the nursing home with Alex to collect the evidence she needs and interview some of the residents. She adds these **perceptions** to the information Alex has already given her. In her office after the visit, Barbara will **interpret** the evidence, **choose** the strongest arguments, and **encode** and **transmit** messages designed to make the nursing home make the necessary improvements voluntarily. She'll try persuasion and negotiation first; if they fail, she'll **encode** and **transmit** the documents necessary to file a suit against the nursing home.

The example above represents successful communication. But things don't always work so well. At every stage, both Alex and Barbara could misperceive, misinterpret, choose badly, encode poorly, and choose inappropriate channels. Given all the possibilities for miscommunication, the wonder is not that we misunderstand each other, but that we communicate as well as we do.

COMMUNICATION CHANNELS IN ORGANIZATIONS

Channels vary in speed, accuracy of transmission, cost, number of messages carried, number of people reached, efficiency, and ability to promote goodwill. Depending on the audience, your purposes, and the situation, one channel may be better than another.

Oral channels are better for group decision making, allow misunderstandings to be cleared up more quickly, and seem more personal. Shorter communication channels are more accurate than longer chains. And all-channel patterns, where everyone can communicate with everyone else, produce better group decisions and more satisfaction. Figure 4.2 illustrates some of the communication channels that exist in organizations.

PRINCIPLES OF SEMANTICS

Semantic principles offer guidelines for communicating more accurately. The basic principles of semantics may be expressed in eight statements. In the list below, the principles are linked to the parts of the communication model which they explain:

Perception

1. Perception involves the perceiver as well as what is perceived.

*   Quoted from David A. Ricks, *Big Business Blunders* (Homewood, IL: Dow Jones-Irwin, 1983), 53.

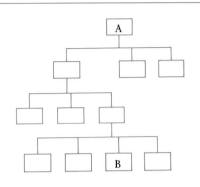
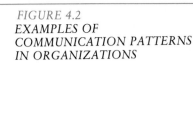

FIGURE 4.2
EXAMPLES OF
COMMUNICATION PATTERNS
IN ORGANIZATIONS

Direct channel from A to B

A must go through other people to get to B

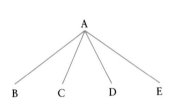
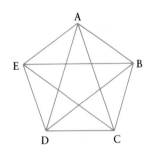

A can send messages to four people
simultaneously. They must go
through A to send messages to
each other.

A can send messages to four people
simultaneously. They can send
messages directly to each other.

Interpretation

2. Facts, inferences, and judgments are not the same thing.
3. No two things are ever exactly alike.
4. Things change significantly with time.
5. Most either-or classifications are not legitimate.

Choice

6. A statement is never the whole story.

Encoding and Decoding

7. Words are not identical to the objects they represent.
8. The symbols used in communication must stand for essentially the
   same thing in the minds of the sender and the receiver.

Let's look at each of these principles.

1. Perception Involves the Perceiver as Well as What Is Perceived. Perception
is not a passive recording of reality. What we see is conditioned by what we
are able to see, what we have seen in the past, what we are prepared to see,
and what we want to see.

Our ability to perceive is limited first of all by our senses. Some people
cannot distinguish between red and green; some people need glasses to see or

FIGURE 4.3
HOW CONTEXT AFFECTS
PERCEPTION

FIGURE 4.3
HOW CONTEXT AFFECTS
PERCEPTION

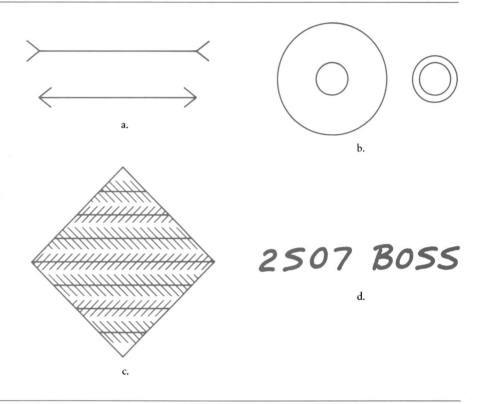

Freshness Is in the Eye of the Beholder*

Stew Leonard's food store in Norwalk, Connecticut, grosses almost $2 million a week—seven times the gross of the average supermarket. Part of his success comes from listening to customers—and giving them what they ask for.

At a focus group meeting, a woman complained that the store didn't sell fresh fish. The fish sales rep, who was also at the meeting, protested: the fish came fresh every morning, some from the Fulton Fish Market, some from the Boston piers. But the customer held her ground. To her, fish on a styrofoam plate in plastic wrap didn't look fresh.

What did the Leonards do? "We set up a fish bar with ice in it . . . it's the same price as over in the package. Our packaged fish didn't decrease at all, but we doubled our fish sales. We were doing about 15,000 pounds a week; now we're doing 30,000 pounds a week."

hearing aids to hear. Perception is also affected by context. A line may appear longer or shorter depending on arrows at its ends (Figure 4.3a). A circle may appear bigger or smaller depending on the circle around it (Figure 4.3b). Parallel lines may appear slanted when other lines cross them (Figure. 4.3c). A symbol may appear to be the letter *S* or the number *5* depending on whether it's part of a word or a number (Figure 4.3d).

We perceive what our culture has trained us to recognize. The fact that children have not yet mastered all the elements of American culture explains some of the amusing errors kids make:

A child wondered why he was asked, every day at school, to pledge allegiance to the republic of Richard Stands.

On reading a chemistry exam, a teacher learned that radium was discovered by madman Curie.[1]

A sixth-grader wrote to President Carter, "How come it costs so much to live in the USA? I thought America was the home of the free."[2]

Perceptions can even shape reality. In one school, a group of researchers gave teachers their students' aptitude scores, telling the teachers that they wanted to see whether high-scoring children really learned more quickly. At the end of the term, the high-aptitude children indeed scored higher on achievement tests than their classmates did. At this point, the researchers revealed the truth: the aptitude scores they had given the teachers had no relation to the students' real scores. The children who learned the most were not the smartest

* Based on "In Search of Excellence: The Film," transcript by John Nathan (Waltham, MA: Nathan-Tyler Productions, 1985), 6–8 and Joanne Kaufman, "In the Moo: Shopping at Stew Leonard's," *The Wall Street Journal,* September 17, 1987, 28.

ones, but rather those the teachers *perceived* to be the smartest—those they expected to learn most easily. Evidently, by nonverbal feedback, extra attention, or some other means, the teachers enabled these children to learn more, whether or not they really were "smart."[3]

This experiment has implications for supervisors as well as teachers, for it suggests that our own expectations may shape the performances we get from those we evaluate.

Perception is also affected by what we want to see. Most people have a tendency to attribute their own feelings to other people as well; we tend to repress ideas which are unpleasant or threatening. We may literally tune out messages we think will challenge our own positions; we seek messages that support the positions we have taken. The most avid readers of car ads are people who have just bought that make of car and who want to be reassured that they made the right choice.[4]

Use these correctives to check the accuracy of your perceptions:

1. Recognize that everyone's perception will be in some measure biased; the person who sees only reality does not exist.
2. Recognize that different positions cause us to view reality differently and to make different inferences from what we observe. When you disagree with someone, try to go back to the facts to see if a difference in perception is at the root of the conflict.
3. If a new fact or idea comes along which does not fit neatly into your worldview, recognize that your worldview, not the challenging idea, may need rethinking.

2. Facts, Inferences, and Judgments Are Not the Same Thing. Semanticists distinguish among three kinds of statements. To a semanticist, a **fact** is a statement which you yourself have verified. An **inference** is a statement which you have not personally verified, but whose truth or falsity could be established, either now or in the future. A **judgment** or an **opinion** is a statement which can never be verified, since it includes terms that cannot be measured objectively. Let's look at some examples.

1. The book you are reading is titled *Business and Administrative Communication.*
2. The author teaches at The Ohio State University.
3. The book is widely used in college-level courses in business communication.

Statement 1 is a fact: you can verify it by checking the cover and title page. Statement 2 is an inference. It seems reasonable, based on what the title page says, but you don't know that of your own knowledge. (Even if the statement was true when the book went to press, is it still true?) However, you could check the truth of the statement if you wanted to take the time and trouble to do so. Statement 3 is a judgment. There is no way to prove that it is true, because people will have different notions of what makes a textbook "widely used."

The semanticist's definition of *fact* is much narrower than the use that word has in everyday speech. Consider this statement:

On Monday, October 19, 1987, the Dow Jones Industrial Average fell 508 points.

The Story of the Plainfield Eleven*

Remember that great year at Plainfield State Teacher's College when the football team . . . was ranked nationally among the top small college teams that were untied and undefeated? Remember the team's great quarterback, Johnny Chung, who would down a bowl of rice between the halves and come out to lead Plainfield on to victory and an invitation to the coveted Blackboard Bowl? No? Maybe you are too young to remember, for it was over thirty years ago when Plainfield State was part of the Saturday night football results. And just as well, too, because there was no such college as Plainfield State. It was all a hoax, later described by Alexander Klein in *Grand Deception,* devised by a New Jersey public relations man who was overwhelmed by the Saturday night litany of football scores which seemed to come mostly from places he'd never been and didn't really care to know about. The Plainfield eleven would have gone on to that glorious Blackboard Bowl, too, if *Time* magazine hadn't wanted to do a story on the team and their fabled quarterback Chung. . . . It wasn't until somebody checked up that they found there was no such school, that it was all a hoax. If that amuses you and you feel better for knowing about it, how do you know that this story and Alexander Klein and all that is not yet another hoax?

---

* Quoted from John C. Condon, Jr., *Semantics and Communication* (New York: Macmillan, 1985), 113–14.

But It *Looked* Like Oil*

Once again last week, motorists slowed along Rt. 235 in Logan County, apparently thinking they were witnessing an oil gusher in a farm field.

Not so, Ruth Ann Jackson said.

The dark stream jetting over a corn field was liquified manure being pumped from two lagoons on the Jackson farm.

Too Close for Comfort†

In *The Silent Language*, Edward Hall noted that his colleagues in Latin America stood much closer to him that he was used to standing. He concluded that Latin Americans needed less personal space than did North Americans and that a North American who kept backing up would seem rude to a Latin American.

A U. S. student studying in Colombia read Hall's book and made a conscious effort not to be rude. But when he stood close to the maid in the home where he lived, she thought he was attacking her. He was invading her personal space.

The personal distance appropriate for same-sex colleagues is not appropriate for opposite-sex people who do not know each other. North Americans can't stereotype all Latin Americans as desiring the same personal space.

Is that a fact? Well, you certainly didn't observe it. Even the brokers on the floor of the stock exchange depended on computers and ticker tapes. But anyone who has played computer games has seen images on computer screens that were fiction, not fact. We accept the crash as "fact" because we trust the TV announcers who reported it then and the books which record it now. However, in semantic terms, the crash is an inference for everyone who has not personally verified it.

Printed information is not always true. In 1988, an investigative panel found that a Harvard researcher studying the immune system made up the "facts" he had reported in several published papers.[5] Computer technology allows editors to alter pictures. In 1982, *National Geographic* moved the great pyramids of Giza so they'd look better in a cover photo. *Rolling Stone* removed a pistol and holster from its cover photo of TV star Don Johnson.[6]

If one uses the narrowest possible definition of *fact,* there are almost no facts. Almost everything we know we are taking on someone else's authority rather than on our own. Even much of what we know by observation may be inference rather than direct observation. Furthermore, facts will vary from person to person, since different people will have verified different things.

Acting on inferences as if they were facts can create a great deal of trouble. In World War II, planes actually showed up on American radar screens two hours before the Japanese reached Pearl Harbor, but both the workers monitoring the screen and their supervisor—to whom they reported the sightings—assumed that either the radar or the machine was malfunctioning.[7]

In everyday life and in business, you can never have all the facts; you have to make decisions based on inferences ("That driver whose right turn signal is blinking intends to turn right." "I will live long enough to need a retirement fund." "The sales figures I've been given are accurate.") and even on judgments ("We have too much money tied up in long-term investments."). What should you as a reader or writer do?

Both as a reader and writer, you should

1. Check each statement to see whether it is a fact, an inference, or a judgment.

As a reader or listener making decisions based on information you get from other people, you should

2. Estimate the accuracy of the inference by comparing it to your past experiences with the source and with this kind of information.

3. If the cost of making a mistake is high, try to get more information.

As a writer or speaker trying to persuade people, you should

4. Use measurable statements, not just statements which contain value terms that will mean different things to different people.
   Not: Buying a slag grinder would be a good investment.
   But: Buying a slag grinder will enable us to save $25,000 on the Moreland order alone.

---

* Quoted from *The Columbus Dispatch*, December 31, 1986, D1.

† Based on Raymond L. Gorden, *Living in Latin America* (Skokie, IL: National Textbook, 1974), 147.

5. Label your inferences, so that your audience can distinguish between what you know to be the case and what you think, assume, believe, or judge to be true.

3. No Two Things Are Ever Exactly Alike.

Part of the way we make sense of the world is by grouping things into categories. Once we have categories, we do not have to evaluate each new experience independently; instead, we simply assign it to a category and then make the response we find appropriate to that category.

Unfortunately, this convenient lumping can lead to **stereotyping:** putting similar people or events into a single category, even though significant differences exist. A list of the customers whose accounts are overdue, for example, may include several different kinds of people:

- A good customer who is behind on bills because of a temporary setback.
- A marginal risk who won't pay the bill until forced to do so.
- Someone whose record-keeping is poor and who has honestly forgotten to pay.
- Someone who claims that he or she never received the merchandise or that the amount of the bill is in error and who is delaying payment until the dispute is settled.

The approach that would be needed to get a customer in the second category to pay would be unnecessary and even offensive if used with customers in other groups. Different "delinquent" customers need to be treated differently.

Generalizing—faultily—on the basis of experience is a particular problem when our experience is limited to one or two cases. Suppose, for instance, that someone has had a female supervisor who isn't a good boss. If that woman is the only female boss the employee has ever known, the employee may conclude that women don't make good supervisors. If the same person has a male supervisor who isn't a good boss, he or she is less likely to make a parallel assumption about male bosses. Because we see many male supervisors, some of whom are better than others, it is easy to recognize that men in general can make good supervisors, even though this particular man may be a poor supervisor.

To guard against stereotyping, you should

1. Recognize significant differences as well as similarities. The members of any one group are not identical.
2. When you use an analogy to make your point clear, be sure that the analogy is in fact accurate at the point of comparison.

4. Things Change Significantly with Time.

If you keep up with the stock market, with commodity prices, or with interest rates, you know that things (especially prices) change significantly with time.

People change too. The sales representative who was once judged too

---

Will Women Managers Have Trouble Overseas?*

When an American banker named Frederica Challendes-Angelini recently went to Saudi Arabia to negotiate a loan, her first problem was getting a foot in the door. Literally.

Saudi Arabia generally doesn't allow unaccompanied women into the country—no matter who they are. So Miss Challendes-Angelini took a transit visa—indicating that she was only stopping at the airport before her flight carried her to another destination—and, when no one was looking, she walked out the airport door.

"Once in the country, I had no problems whatsoever," says Miss Challendes-Angelini, who is an assistant vice president with Amex Bank Ltd., a London-based subsidiary of American Express Co. "I suppose that if your company has sent you there and you act in a competent manner, they'll accept you." When the time came for her to leave, her Saudi customers took care of the exit formalities.

---

* Quoted from Eric Morgenthaler, "Women of the World: More U.S. Firms Put Females in Key Posts in Foreign Countries," *The Wall Street Journal,* March 16, 1978, 1.

But Things Are Different Now*
North American business people see contracts as important. These people are sometimes shocked to find that business people from other cultures "violate" contracts. But written contracts have a different meaning in other cultures. Indeed, some cultures assume that the parties cannot be expected to abide by the original provisions of the contract if conditions have changed. A U.S. exporter or diplomat may see this changed behavior as evidence of dishonesty or unreliability. The importer or diplomat in another country may see this changed behavior as a sensible response to different circumstances.

Creative Solution to a Pricing Problem†
A pharmaceutical firm used a massive publicity campaign to announce that it would introduce a new drug in a particular European country on a particular date. However, the government refused to allow the price the firm wanted to charge for the drug. The price the government wanted was too low, the firm argued, to cover its research and development costs. And if the price was low in one country, it would have to be low in other countries too. At first, the only other option seemed to be to delay the release date. But delay might antagonize the government and lose the goodwill of the medical community. The firm decided to keep the release date, distributing the drug free while it continued to negotiate with the government to find a mutually acceptable selling price.

abrasive to make a good supervisor may have mellowed by now; employees who accepted management dictates without question 20 years ago may be more critical; the student who almost flunked out freshman year may have settled down, solved his or her problems, and become an excellent prospect for employment or graduate school.

Someone who does not recognize that prices, situations, and people change is guilty of making a **frozen evaluation.** The following correctives help us remember not to "freeze" evaluations:

1. Date statements. The price of IBM stock on October 18, 1987, is not the price of IBM stock on January 3, 1990.
2. Provide a frame of reference so your reader has some basis for comparing grades, profits, injuries, percentages, or whatever the relevant criterion may be.
3. Periodically retest your assumptions about people, businesses, products, and services to make sure that your evaluations apply to the present situation.

5. Most "Either-Or" Classifications Are Not Legitimate. A common logical fallacy is **polarization:** trying to force the reader into a position by arguing that there are only two possible positions, one of which is clearly unacceptable:

Either the supervisor runs this department with a firm hand, or anarchy will take over and the work will never get done.

Very few areas of life allow only two options. Running a department "with a firm hand" is only one of several possible leadership styles; sharing authority with or even transferring it entirely to subordinates need not result in anarchy.

Even people who admit that there are more than two possible positions may still limit the options unnecessarily. Imposing limits that do not exist in reality is called **blindering,** after the blinders that horses in the 19th century wore. Sometimes blindering is responsible for bad questions in surveys:

Do you own _____, rent _____, or live with your parents _____?

At first glance, that question may seem to cover the options. But what about someone who lives with a friend or with relatives other than parents? What about a minister who lives in a parsonage or manse furnished by the church as part of the minister's compensation? The minister does not own the house, but neither does he or she rent it. Depending on what the makers of the questionnaire really want to know, better questions would be:

How much is your housing worth a month?

How much do you pay a month for your housing?

Blindering can also keep us from solving problems creatively and effectively. Consider the following problem (Figure 4.4):

*   Based on Paul S. Crane, *Korean Patterns* (Seoul: Royal Asiatic Society, Korean Branch, 1978), 99, quoted in Jerrold J. Merchant, "Korean Interpersonal Patterns: Implications for Korean/American Intercultural Communication," *Communication* 9 (October 1980): 73.

†   Based on Amir Mahini and Louis T. Wells, Jr., "Government Relations in the Global Firm," *Competition in Global Industries,* ed. Michael E. Porter (Boston: Harvard Business School Press, 1986), 292.

FIGURE 4.4
CAN YOU SOLVE THIS PUZZLE?

Start with your pencil on any one of the dots. Draw four straight lines without removing your pencil from the page. You may cross lines, but you may not retrace them. Connect all nine dots.

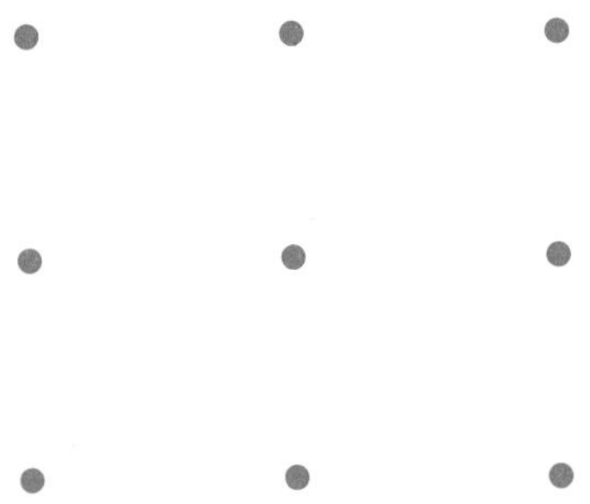

You can't solve the problem if you limit yourself by thinking of the nine dots as an area which you must stay inside; the problem becomes easy when you use the whole page. (Still stumped? Ask your instructor to check the *Teaching Guide* for a solution.)

Polarization sharpens divisions between people and obscures the common ground on which they could forge a decision which everyone could live with. Blindering prevents our seeing creative solutions to the problems we face. Here are some correctives:

1. Recognize the complexities of a situation. Resist the temptation to oversimplify.
2. Whenever you see only two alternatives, consciously search for a third, and maybe even a fourth or fifth, before you make your decision.
3. Redefine the question or problem to get at the real issue.
   Don't ask: How can I as a manager show that I'm in control?
   Ask: How can we improve productivity in this unit?

6. A Statement Is Never the Whole Story. It is impossible to know everything; it is impossible to tell someone everything. Thinking that we know everything about a subject or can communicate everything about it that is important is the fallacy semanticists call **allness.** One of the things we learn as we get more deeply into a subject is that we do not know everything about it. Even in subjects where we're the expert, we cannot convey everything we know to someone else. When we assume that a statement contains all the important information, or when the context is omitted (deliberately or inadvertently), meanings are inevitably twisted.

Since, even with the best intentions, we cannot include everything, what can we do to avoid misstatements by implication?

1. Avoid statements about *all* the members of any group.
2. Recognize that the reports you get are filtered; you are almost certainly getting inferences as well as facts.
3. Check the correspondence you send out to make sure you have provided the background information the reader needs to interpret your message accurately.

FIGURE 4.5
SEMANTIC TRIANGLE

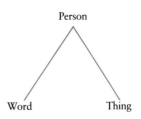

Person

Word   Thing

Can It Taste Good If It Sounds Terrible?*

Relaxing at a restaurant table, you sip your drink by candlelight and chat with your companion, appetite slowly building. The waiter brings the menu. With anticipation you begin to scan the seafood entrees: Broiled ratfish. Fried grunt. Poached mudblower with parsley sauce.

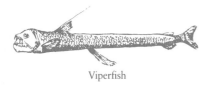

Viperfish

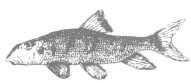

Hogsucker

Ratfish? Mudblower? How disgusting. Maybe you don't want seafood after all. What else have they got?

This is the kind of reaction that frustrates the National Marine Fisheries Service. If only people knew. If only they realized how great ratfish tastes. If only they would *try* ratfish. If only ratfish had a different name. . . .

The National Marine Fisheries Service is renaming fish. . . . While familiar kinds of food fish dwindle in population, dozens of delicious and nutritious species contentedly swim and jump, increase and multiply, protected by repugnant names.

7. Words Are Not Identical to the Objects They Represent. Semanticists point out that there is no inherent relationship between words and things. People perceive objects and think of ideas; they attach labels to those objects and ideas. Other labels could be substituted without affecting reality. In the **semantic triangle** in Figure 4.5, there is no base, no connection between the thing and the word that symbolizes it. People, who name things and use words, provide the only connection.

We often respond to words rather than to reality. Our degree of distress during a bleak economic period is likely to be as much a product of the label given the period as it is of the rate of unemployment: a *slowdown* doesn't sound as bad as a *recession,* and even that is better than a *depression.* Labeling a book a *best seller* is sure to increase sales. An album entitled "John Denver's Greatest Hits" catapulted Denver to popularity; none of his previous records had been hits. Billy Joel put the song "You're Only Human" on his "Greatest Hits" album before he had even released it as a single.

Because people respond to symbols, organizations choose names carefully. Corporate name changes raise stock prices 2.4% "solely because of name changes."[8] In World War II, a Navy ship changed its call signal from SAPWORTH to HELLCAT—with a marked improvement in morale.[9] Eastman Kodak called its division making cameras in the United States the U.S. Equipment Division until someone looked at the acronym and pointed out that people might not want to buy USED cameras.[10]

Responding to the symbol rather than to reality, "confusing the map with the territory," is called **intensionalism.** Note the spelling: the term has nothing to do with intentions, which are deliberate plans. Intensionalism is an unconscious response. The opposite of intensionalism is **extensionalism:** inspecting reality itself.

Advertising works in part because we respond intentionsionally to symbols. When coffee prices were going up and coffee sales were falling, General Foods developed a new product blending coffee with less expensive chicory and a little molasses to hide the bitter taste of the chicory. The first focus group asked to taste the coffee hated it. Before the next focus group came in, advertiser Jane Maas wrote new descriptions for the three containers of (identical) coffee:

> One was "New coffee made the old-fashioned American way." (I had read that pioneers, crossing the prairie, brewed coffee from exactly these ingredients.) Another concept was "Now, the great taste of Scandinavian coffees comes to America!" (More research had indicated that the coffees of Scandinavia often owed their rich taste to the same kind of brew.) And the third was "Now, rich coffee without the bitter taste!" This concept explained that the molasses smoothed out the taste of the chicory. . . . [The next focus group]

---

* Quoted from Gay Sands Miller, "When Bureaucrats Cast for Fish Names, Be Prepared to Wait," *The Wall Street Journal,* May 1, 1980, 1.

thought coffee made the old American way was fine. They were intrigued by coffee made the Scandinavian way. But coffee made with chicory and molasses that would taste rich and never bitter was dynamite! When they tasted the test product, *exactly the same coffee sampled by the previous group*, they pronounced it delicious.[11]

Since we must use symbols to communicate, it's hard to avoid treating symbols as if they were reality. Semanticists suggest these correctives:

1. Support general statements and evaluations with specific evidence for examples.
2. Check your own responses to make sure that your decisions are based not on labels but on valid, logical arguments.

8. The Symbols Used in Communication Must Stand for Essentially the Same Thing in the Minds of the Sender and the Receiver.   Communication depends on symbols; if those symbols mean different things to the people who use them, communication will fail. **Bypassing** occurs when two people use the same symbol to mean different things.

Bypassing creates misunderstandings. A factory employee who had been absent frequently notified his supervisor that he would not be at work the next day. The supervisor said "OK," meaning only that he had heard what the worker had said and was acknowledging having heard it. The worker thought the "OK" signified approval, that is, that his absence was acceptable. When he received a written warning notice for poor attendance, he felt he was being treated unfairly and filed a grievance against management.

Symbols have to be learned. If someone has not previously been exposed to a symbol, he or she is not likely to understand it. In the 1970s, a number of American churches "adopted" Vietnamese families. A member of one such church was escorting a newly arrived family on a tour of the neighborhood. The children ran ahead, and, much to the church member's dismay, ran across a busy intersection even though the light was red. The fact that red traffic lights symbolize *stop* is deeply ingrained in our culture, but these children had never encountered traffic lights before. The symbol meant nothing to them.

Because we can't look into each other's minds, we can't be certain that symbols mean exactly the same things to us as they do to the people with whom we communicate. But there are some measures which will help us avoid bypassing:

1. Be sensitive to contexts.
2. Consider the other person. Given his or her background and situation, what is he or she likely to mean?
3. Put what the other person has said into your own words, and let him or her check it for accuracy. (*Note:* Use different words for the key ideas. If you use exactly the same word, you still won't be able to tell if you and the other person mean the same thing by it.)
4. Ask questions.

SUMMARY OF KEY POINTS

- **Communication theory** attempts to explain what happens when we communicate. **Semantics** is the study of the way our behavior is influenced by

The Map Is Not the Territory*
Travelling over the United States in a balloon, Huck Finn expects the world to look just like the maps he has seen:

"[If] we was going so fast we ought to be past Illinois, oughtn't we?"
"Certainly."
"Well, we ain't."
"What's the reason we ain't?"
"I know by the color. We're right over Illinois yet. And you can see for yourself that Indiana ain't in sight."
"I wonder what's the matter with you, Huck. You know by the *color?*"
"Yes, of course I do."
"What's the color got to do with it?"
"It's got everything to do with it. Illinois is green, Indiana is pink. You show me any pink down here, if you can. No, sir; it's green."
"Indiana *pink?* Why, what a lie!"
"It ain't no lie; I've seen it on the map, and it's pink."

* Quoted from Mark Twain, *Tom Sawyer Abroad,* Chapter 3, *The Family Mark Twain* (New York: Harper Brothers, 1935), 1101–02.

Bypassing and Nuclear War*

The consequences of bypassing can be tragic. In July 1945, Japan announced a policy of *mokusatsu* in response to the Allies' Potsdam Declaration, which told Japan to surrender or be crushed.

"According to Kazuo Kawai (1950), who during the war years was editor of the *Nippon Times*, rough translations of *mokusatsu* are 'to be silent,' 'to withold comment' or 'to ignore.' Kawai suggests that 'to withold comment' probably came closest to the true meaning. . . . However, Tokyo's newspapers and the Domei Press Agency reported that the government held the Potsdam Declaration in contempt, and that the Suzuki government had rejected it. The Pacific War Research Society . . . point [sic] out that in the *Kenkyusha Dictionary* the word is defined as 'take no notice of; treat with silent contempt; ignore by keeping silent.' It also means 'remain in a wise and masterly inactivity.' It is their view that it is this latter definition that Suzuki had in mind. . . . Nevertheless, the damage had been done."

The Allies thought that Japan had decided to ignore the Declaration, and the United States of America dropped atomic bombs on Hiroshima and Nagasaki.

the words and other symbols we use to communicate. Communication theory and semantics both show why and where communication can break down and what we can do to communicate more effectively.

- A sender goes through the following steps: **perception, interpretation, choice or selection, encoding,** and **transmitting** the message through a **channel.** The receiver perceives the message, **decodes** it, interprets it, chooses a response, encodes the response, and transmits it. The message transmitted to the original sender is called **feedback. Noise** is anything that interferes with communication; it can be both physical and psychological. Miscommunication can occur at every point in the communication process.

- The best channel for a message will depend on the audience, the sender's purposes, and the situation.

- **Channel overload** occurs when a channel cannot handle all the messages being sent. **Information overload** occurs when the receiver cannot process all the messages that arrive. Both kinds of overload require some sort of selection to determine which messages will be sent and which ones will be attended to.

- Eight principles of semantics will help us avoid errors in perception, interpretation, choice, and encoding and decoding.

Perception
1. Perception involves the perceiver as well as what is perceived.

Interpretation
2. **Facts** are statements which you yourself have verified. **Inferences** are statements which have not yet been verified, but which could be. **Judgments** can never be proven, since they depend not on measurable quantities but on values.
3. No two things are ever exactly alike.
4. Things change significantly with time. Violating this principle produces **frozen evaluations.**
5. Most "either-or" classifications are not legitimate. Seeing only two alternatives is called **polarization.** Assuming limits which do not in fact exist is called **blindering.**

Choice

6. A statement is never the whole story. Thinking that one can know or tell everything is called **allness.**

Encoding and Decoding

7. Words are not identical to the objects they represent. The **semantic triangle** shows that the only link between word and object is the person who uses the word.
8. The symbols used in communication must stand for essentially the same thing in the minds of the sender and the receiver. When the sender and the receiver use the same symbol to mean different things, **bypassing** occurs.

- Because semantics deals with the way we perceive and process information, conflicts that "are just a matter of semantics" may be fundamental. Depending on the situation, it may or may not be possible to find words which everyone in the group can endorse.

---

* Quoted from Verner C. Bickley, "Language as the Bridge," in *Cultures in Contact: Studies in Cross-Cultural Interaction,* ed. Stephen Blochner (New York: Pergamon Press, 1982), 108.

NOTES

1. *Leo Rosten's Giant Book of Laughter* (New York: Crown Publishers, 1985), 402 and 193 respectively.

2. *Kids' Letters to President Carter,* ed. Bill Adler, quoted in *Reader's Digest,* June 1978, 114.

3. Robert Rosenthal, *Pygmalion in the Classroom* (New York: Holt, Rinehart & Winston, 1968).

4. Danuta Ehrlich, Isaiah Guttman, Peter Schonbach, and Judson Mills, "Postdecision Exposure to Relevant Information," *Journal of Abnormal and Social Psychology* 54 (1957), 98–102; summarized in Elliot Aronson, *The Social Animal* (San Francisco: W. H. Freeman, 1972), 101.

5. "U.S. Rips Harvard Medical Research, Phony Data," *Los Angeles Times,* in *The Columbus Dispatch,* February 16, 1988, 9A.

6. "That Great Photo Might Not Be the Real Thing," *San Francisco Examiner,* in *The Columbus Dispatch,* December 6, 1987, 2F.

7. Hugh Russell Frazer, "56 Minutes Before Pearl Harbor," *American Mercury,* August 1957, 80–85, reprinted William V. Haney, *Communication and Interpersonal Relations,* 4th ed. (Homewood, IL: Richard D. Irwin, 1979), 268–72.

8. William M. Bulkeley, "A Firm by Any Other Name Means Likely Rise in Stock, Research Finds," *The Wall Street Journal,* July 10, 1987, 20.

9. Elmo R. Zumwalt, Jr., *On Watch: A Memoir* (New York: Times Books, 1976), 189; cited in Thomas J. Peters and Robert H. Waterman, Jr., *In Search of Excellence: Lessons from America's Best-Run Companies* (New York: Warner Books, 1982), 263–64.

10. "Kodak Alters Use of Name," Champaign-Urbana *News-Gazette,* April 8, 1983, C-1.

11. Jane Maas, *Adventures of an Advertising Woman* (New York: St. Martin's Press, 1986), 75–77. Emphasis added.

EXERCISES AND PROBLEMS FOR CHAPTER 4

4–1 CHOOSING A CHANNEL TO REACH A SPECIFIC AUDIENCE

Suppose that your business, government agency, or non-profit group had a product, service, or program targeted for each of the following audiences. What would be the best channel(s) to reach people in that group in your city? Would that channel reach all group members?

    a. Homeowners.

    b. People who own stocks.

    c. Presbyterians.

    d. Sexually active teenagers.

    e. Members of labor unions.

    f. Parents with children less than five years old.

    g. Blacks.

    h. Homeless people.

    i. Accountants.

    j. People with multiple sclerosis.

4–2 CHOOSING A CHANNEL TO CONVEY A SPECIFIC MESSAGE

Assume that you're campaign manager for a campus, local, or state race. (Pick a real candidate and a real race.) What would be the advantages and disadvantages of each of the following channels as media to carry ads for your side?

    a. Ads in the campus newspaper.

    b. Posters around campus.

    c. Ads in the local newspaper.

    d. Ads on a local radio station after midnight.

    e. Ads on the local TV station during the local news show.

    f. Ads on billboards.

    g. Ads on yard signs.

    h. Flyers distributed door-to-door.

    i. Ads on cable TV.

4–3 DEALING WITH CHANNEL AND INFORMATION OVERLOAD

In each of the following situations, identify ways that people could deal with the overloads described. What are the consequences of the methods that might be used?

    a. On Mothers' Day, millions of people try to call their mothers between noon and 5 P.M.

    b. A student is unable to complete all the reading assignments for his classes.

    c. The committee choosing a new sound system for a synagogue has time to contact only three vendors.

    d. After making a speech on a controversial subject, a senator gets 20 bags of mail a day for three weeks.

    e. During a snowstorm, a busy airport is able to keep only three runways open.

    f. An analyst follows closely only 50 stocks of all those that are traded on the New York Stock Exchange.

    g. A sales representative doesn't have time to visit each potential buyer in her territory.

    h. On the evening that his computer user support group meets, a man has to attend a PTA meeting.

4–4 SEPARATING FACTS, INFERENCES, AND JUDGMENTS

Indicate whether each of the following statements is a fact, an inference, or a judgment.

    a. There is a chair in this room.

    b. The Dow Jones Industrial Average broke 2,500 for the first time in July 1987.

    c. High stock prices are a sign that the economy is healthy.

    d. Accounting majors get good jobs.

    e. All the people in this room will be employed three years from today.

    f. It's better to be 75% right and 100% on time than 100% right and a week late.

    g. *The Wall Street Journal* is delivered to subscribers Monday through Friday, but not on Saturday or Sunday or on holidays.

Pick a topic and write a statement of fact, a statement of inference, and a statement of judgment about it.

4–5 EXPLAINING BYPASSING

1. Show how the following statements could produce bypassing:

    a. No one would be better for this job than Roger Truett.

    b. Write on one side of the paper only.

    c. Customers who think our waiters are rude should see the manager.

2. Bypassing is the basis of many jokes. Find a joke that depends on bypassing and share it with the class.

4–6 IDENTIFYING SEMANTIC ERRORS

Match each of the following statements with the semantic error it represents.

1. Allness
2. Frozen Evaluation
3. Intensionalism
4. Polarization
5. Stereotyping

a. All Australians are cricket maniacs.

b. We tried that two years ago and it didn't work. There's no point in trying it again.

c. My subordinate isn't looking at me while I talk to him. He must be rebelling against my authority.

d. The *New York Times* prints all the news that's fit to print.

e. Businesses should not be allowed to keep windfall profits.

4–7 VERBAL MAP—REALITY TEST*

Directions: If a statement is *true under all circumstances*, check the line in the "True" column. If the statement is *ever false* or if its truth *cannot be determined*, put a check in the "False" column.

True	False	
_____	_____	1. A statement is either true or false.
_____	_____	2. 1 + 1 = 2
_____	_____	3. A college education is a good thing to have.
_____	_____	4. Communists are atheists.
_____	_____	5. A person is dead when he or she has no heartbeat.

True	False	
_____	_____	6. A tomato is a vegetable.
_____	_____	7. No one wants to die.
_____	_____	8. Roses are red.
_____	_____	9. The sum of the angles of a triangle is 180°.
_____	_____	10. All people are born equal.
_____	_____	11. The speed of light is 186,000 miles a second.
_____	_____	12. Money is the root of evil.
_____	_____	13. Freedom of speech is good.
_____	_____	14. Do unto others as you would have them do unto you.
_____	_____	15. Love makes people better.

4–8 INFERENCE-OBSERVATION TESTS*

Directions: You will read a brief story. Assume that all the information in the story is *accurate* and true.

You will then read statements about the story. Answer them in order. You may reread the story as you answer the questions, but DO NOT go back to fill in answers or change answers once you have marked them.

As you read each statement, determine whether the statement is

"T"—on the basis of the information presented in the story, the statement is definitely true.

"F"—on the basis of the information presented in the story, the statement is definitely false.

"?"—the statement may be true (or false) but on the basis of the information presented in the story one cannot be sure. (Mark "?" if any part of the statement is doubtful.)

Sample Story
The only vehicle parked in front of 619 Oak Street is a red truck. The words "Paul J. Grigsby, Plumber" are spelled in large black letters across the door of the cab.

*Test by William Haney, in Harry E. Maynard, "Advertising as Communication: How to Test Your Semantic I.Q.," *Printer's Ink*, December 11, 1964, 53.

*Adapted from "Advertising as Communication: How to Test Your Semantic I.Q.," Harry E. Maynard, *Printer's Ink*, December 11, 1964, 52.

Statements about the Sample Story

1. The color of the truck in front of 619 Oak Street is red.   T F ?

2. There is no lettering on the door of the truck parked in front of 619 Oak Street.   T F ?

3. Plumbing repairs are being done at 619 Oak Street.   T F ?

4. The red truck parked in front of 619 Oak Street belongs to Paul J. Grigsby.   T F ?

Test Story

Babe Smith has been killed. Police have rounded up six suspects, all of whom are gangsters. All of them are known to have been near the scene of the killing at the approximate time that it occurred. All had substantial motives for wanting Smith killed. However, one of the suspected gangsters, Slinky Sam, has positively been cleared of guilt.

Statements about the Story

1. Slinky Sam is known to have been near the scene of the killing of Babe Smith.   T F ?

2. All six of the rounded-up gangsters were known to have been near the scene of the murder.   T F ?

3. Only Slinky Sam has been cleared of guilt.   T F ?

4. All six of the rounded-up suspects were near the scene of Smith's killing at the approximate time that it took place.   T F ?

5. The police do not know who killed Smith.   T F ?

6. All six suspects are known to have been near the scene of the foul deed.   T F ?

7. Smith's murderer did not confess of his or her own free will.   T F ?

8. Slinky Sam was not cleared of guilt.   T F ?

9. It is known that the six suspects were in the vicinity of the cold-blooded assassination.   T F ?

4–9 REMOVING BLINDERS

To solve the following problems, you may need to remove some blinders.

a. How can the following be true:

$$A = 3$$
$$B = 4$$

But $A + B = 5$

b. How can you drop an egg six feet through the air over a hard surface without breaking the egg?

c. How can you, with one line, turn VII into the number 8? How can you, with one line, turn IX into the number 6?

d. Finish the alphabet, putting each letter above or below the line according to the pattern below:

A   EF HI
—————————————
 BCD G   J

e. When men and women are on an elevator and all of them are getting off on the second floor, who should get off first?

4–10 IDENTIFYING LOGOS

Using newspapers and magazines, find four corporate logos. Do all your classmates recognize all the logos? Which logos seem to be especially effective symbols for their organizations? What makes them so effective?

THE BUILDING BLOCKS OF EFFECTIVE MESSAGES

Effective Strategies for Composing

QUESTIONS

- What writing processes seem to be associated with good writing?
- How can a writer overcome writer's block or procrastination?
- What planning and revision are necessary if you dictate a document?
- What should you look for when you revise a draft? When you edit it?
- How can you become a better proofreader?
- How can boilerplate harm a document?
- What strategies can help a group compose the best possible document?

True Ease in Writing comes from Art, not Chance,
As those move easiest who have learn'd to dance.
Alexander Pope
Essay on Criticism, 1711

killed performances look effortless. In reality, as every dancer, musician, or athlete knows, they're the product of hard work, hours of practice, attention to detail, and intense concentration. The popular myth is that good writing is inspired, that it comes easily and naturally. Like skilled performances in other arts, however, writing rests on a base of work.

Looking at the **process** of writing—what people actually *do* when they write—can help writers improve their **products**—their written documents. (We see the same phenomenon in sports, where a detailed analysis, often on videotape or computer, of the process of hitting a tennis ball or running can help athletes improve their form and their game.)

OVERVIEW OF THE COMPOSING PROCESS(ES)

Given any writing assignment, there is more than one acceptable set of words (product) and more than one way to get there (process). Most researchers would agree that writing processes can include eight activities: planning, gathering, writing, evaluating, getting feedback, revising, editing, and proofreading. The activities do not have to come in this order. Not every writing task demands all eight.

Planning includes all the thinking you do about your subject and how to achieve your purposes. It includes such activities as analyzing the problem, defining your purposes, and analyzing the audience; thinking of ideas; choosing a pattern of organization or making an outline and arranging points within your document; drawing on your memory of similar documents you've read or written in the past, etc. Planning includes not only devising strategies for the document as a whole but also generating "mini-plans" that govern sentences or paragraphs.

Gathering includes physically getting the data you need. It can mean simply getting a copy of the letter you're responding to; it can also include informal and formal research—everything from getting a computer printout or looking something up in a reference book to administering a questionnaire or conducting an experiment.

Writing is the act of putting words on paper or on a screen, or of dictating words to a machine or a secretary. Writing can be lists, fragmentary notes, stream-of-consciousness writing, or a formal draft. It can be just a few words or a sustained flow of several paragraphs or pages.

Evaluating means rereading your work to see how good it is, measuring it against your goals and the requirements of the situation and audience. The best evaluation results from *re-seeing* your draft as if someone else had written it. Does it say what you want it to say? Will your audience understand it? Is it complete? Convincing? Friendly?

You can evaluate *every* activity in the process, not just your draft. Is your view of purposes adequate? Do you have enough information to write? Are your sources believable? Do your revisions go far enough?

Getting feedback means asking someone else to evaluate your work. Again, you could get feedback on every activity, not just your draft. Is your pattern of organization appropriate? Does a revision solve an earlier problem? Are there any typos in the final copy?

Revising means making changes in the draft: adding, deleting, substituting, or rearranging. Revision can be changes in single words, but more often it means major additions, deletions, or substitutions as the writer measures (evaluates) the draft against purpose and audience and reshapes the document to make it more effective.

Editing means checking the draft to see that it satisfies the requirements of good English and the principles of business writing. Here, you'd correct spelling and mechanical errors and check word choice and format. Unlike revision, which can produce major changes in meaning, editing focuses on the surface of writing.

Proofreading means checking the final copy to see that it's free from typographical errors.

Note the following points about these eight activities:

- **The activities do not have to come in this order.** Some writers may want to write a draft, *then* look at the draft to see what they've said and plan the best structure. Some people may gather data *after* writing a draft when they see that they need more specifics to achieve their purposes.

- **You do not have to finish one activity to start another.** Some writers plan a short section and write it, plan the next short section and write it, and so on through the document. Evaluating what is already written may cause a writer to do more planning or to change the original plan. After writing a single sentence, a writer may spot a simple mechanical error and stop to fix it (edit). It's even possible (though scary) to see major ways to improve a document while proofreading what you had thought was the final copy.

- **Most writers do not use all eight activities for all the documents they write.** You'll use more activities when you write a kind of document, about a subject, or to an audience that's new to you. Experienced writers will do some of the stages almost automatically. And some kinds of writing do not demand all eight stages.

Research about what writers really do has destroyed some of the stereotypes we used to have about the writing process. Consider planning. Traditional advice stressed the importance of planning and sometimes advised writers to make formal outlines for everything they wrote. But we know now that not all good documents are based on outlines.[1] One study suggests that extroverts do little planning and prefer to work out their ideas as they go along, while introverts prefer to work out their ideas fully before they begin writing;[2] either method can produce good writing. A study on writer's block found that some ineffective writers spent so much time planning that they left too little time to write the assignment.[3] "Plan!" is too simplistic to be helpful. Instead, we need to talk about how much and what kind of planning for what kind of document.

One Writer's Planning Process*

Kenneth E. Nelson [is] an experienced engineer in Chicago who spends roughly half his time on the job writing. . . .[He] manages the office [of a transportation consulting firm]. . . . Since he nearly always writes in response to a specific request (e.g., a client's request for a proposal; requirements for progress reports and final reports) and since he writes certain kinds of documents again and again, his consideration of purpose has become ingrained, almost second nature. . . .

Because Nelson knows that his audience will approve or reject his proposals or judge reports useful or deficient, he thinks about their needs at the very beginning of the writing process. He considers past associations with clients or telephone conversations with them to stimulate his thinking. While inventing [thinking of] content for a proposal related to an airport-development project in Waukegan, for instance, Nelson mulled over a four-page RFQ (Request for Qualifications) for over two hours, thinking about his audience's criteria and considering how he could adapt his company's resources for such a client. . . .

The intricacy, tidiness, and formality of Nelson's outlines are interesting features of his writing process. Nelson divides the material he has generated and selected into groups and subgroups. While he uses no numbers, letters, Roman numerals, or the like, he does use dots, indentations, and headings to indicate coordinate and subordinate relationships. For anything likely to require more than four or five pages of written text, he uses separate sheets of paper for each major heading.

* Quoted from Jack Selzer, "The Composing Processes of an Engineer," *College Composition and Communication* 34 (May 1983): 178–82.

FIGURE 5.1

PROCESSES THAT MAKE IT HARDER OR EASIER TO WRITE WELL

	Processes That Hurt Writers	Processes That Help Writers
Expectations about writing	Expect writing to flow effortlessly. Expect first draft to be perfect. Assume that no document is acceptable unless it's perfect.	Realize you can revise a draft; do not expect the first draft to be final. Be willing to settle for writing that is "good enough" even if not perfect.
Writing behavior	Avoid writing. Put off writing until just before something is due. If words don't flow quickly, give up.	Sit down to write regularly. Think about writing tasks even when you aren't actually writing, "rehearsing" or going over possible words in your head.
Perceived match between abilities, task	Decide that the task is too big or too difficult (you'll be paralyzed). Or decide it's too easy (you'll be bored).	Modify task if necessary. If the task is large or difficult, break it into subtasks. If it's routine or simple, focus on the interesting parts or find a way to make it more challenging.
Goals for writing task	Have fuzzy goals, if any. Ignore the complexities in the problem. Set minor goals such as "write three pages" rather than major goals such as "achieve these purposes for this audience."	Have clear goals for task. Recognize the complexities in the problem to be solved. Define goals in ways that match reality, focusing on purpose and audience.
Strategies for writing	Depend on a small number of simple, unimaginative strategies. Stick with first strategy even when it obviously isn't working.	Have a repertoire of many different strategies from which to choose. Switch strategies if the first isn't working. Create a new strategy if old ones don't work.
Use of rules while writing	Use rules rigidly ("Passive verbs are bad; you must have three points; you must have a great opener"), even though rules may be inappropriate or may even conflict.	Use functional rules (e.g., "when stuck, write!"). See rules as guidelines that can vary depending on circumstances, rather than as absolutes.
Editing behavior	Edit immediately, even though too-early attention to surface of writing may cause you to lose train of thought or to ignore larger issues such as content.	Delay most editing until after draft is complete. To delay the impulse to edit, mark things for later attention: circle words or write a note to yourself ("Develop this").

Working in Clay*

Convince yourself that you are working in clay not marble, on paper not eternal bronze: let that first sentence be as stupid as it wishes. No one will rush out and print it as it stands. Just put it down; then another. Your whole first paragraph or first page may have to be guillotined in any case after your piece is finished: it is a kind of "forebirth." But as modern mathematics has discovered, there can be no second paragraph (which contains your true beginning) until you have a first.

THE WAYS GOOD WRITERS WRITE

No single writing process works for all writers all of the time. However, good writers seem to use different processes than poor writers.[4] Good writers are more likely to

- Realize that the first draft will not be perfect.
- Write regularly.
- Modify the initial task if it's too hard or too easy.
- Have clear goals focusing on purpose and audience.
- Have several different strategies to choose from.
- Use rules flexibly.
- Wait to edit until after the draft is complete.

If you sometimes use processes listed in Figure 5.1 that make writing more difficult, consciously try to adopt the strategies in the last column. They work for the writers studied in research thus far; they may help you, too.

---

*   Quoted from Jacques Barzun, *On Writing, Editing, and Publishing* (Chicago: University of Chicago Press, 1971), 8.

OVERCOMING WRITER'S BLOCK AND PROCRASTINATION

You probably know students who put off assignments until 10 P.M. the night before they're due. Some managers whose reports are due in two months will spend seven weeks worrying and one week frantically trying to complete the work. These avoiders paint themselves into a corner, sometimes leaving too little time to do a decent job, and never enough time to do their best work.

The next time you face writer's block or are tempted to put off writing, use the tricks in the following lists to see what works for you.

Overcoming Writer's Block

If words won't come, you need to get them flowing again. Try everything on this list at least once to see which strategies work best for you.

- Try to redefine the problem, purpose, or audience. Check to see whether the limits you're working under are necessary ones or ones that you have imposed and that you could change. Remember that even what your teachers and texts have told you about writing are only guidelines, not absolute rules. If a rule is making it hard for you to write, abandon it—at least for this draft.
- Brainstorm. List as many ideas as you can. Later, you can go back and decide which reader benefit or attention-getter is best. Brainstorming helps writers get over the tendency to be overcritical or to develop a mental block after they've thought of one idea or approach. The first idea you have may not be the best.
- Write the part that's easiest to write: the table that will go in the middle of the report, the history of the problem, whatever you *can* write. The parts of a document don't need to be composed in the order in which they'll appear in the final document.
- Do something you can do without thinking: take a walk, wash the car, fold your laundry. As you work, try "saying" ideas to yourself in your head.
- Try **freewriting**.[5] Make yourself write, without stopping, for 10 minutes, even if you must write "I will think of something soon." At the end of 10 minutes, read what you've written, identify the best points in the draft, then set it aside, and write for another 10 uninterrupted minutes. Read this draft, marking anything that's good and should be kept, and then write again for another 10 uninterrupted minutes. By the third session, you will probably produce several sections that are worth keeping—maybe even a complete draft that's ready to be revised.
- Try explaining what you mean to a friend. Some people are more fluent orally than they are on paper. It may be easier to talk to a real audience than to try to imagine your audience as you write.
- Draw a picture or diagram of what you mean. Some people think more easily in pictures rather than words.
- Try dictating the document. If you don't have dictating equipment, use a tape recorder.

An Unsuccessful Self-Treatment of a Case of Writer's Block*

---

* Quoted in full from D. Upper, "An Unsuccessful Self-Treatment of a Case of Writer's Block," *Journal of Applied Behavior Analysis* 4 (1974): 497.

WIRMI*

WIRMI is a strategy for getting yourself to make a clear and concise statement of your point, whenever you find yourself bogged down in trying to perfect a sentence. Simply say to yourself, *What I Really Mean Is* . . . and switch from writing prose to "talking to yourself." Just say what you think, then perfect the prose later.

- If too-early editing stops the flow of ideas, use this strategy to stop editing: write with a worn-out ballpoint pen on a piece of carbon paper over another sheet of paper (when you pause, don't pick up the pen) or darken the screen on your computer.
- Put the document away for a while. Sometimes ideas need time to germinate.

Overcoming the Tendency to Procrastinate

If your problem is sitting down to write at all, some of the techniques for getting past blocks won't help. Putting a document aside, for example, will only make the problem worse. Instead, you need techniques that help create an environment which favors writing. Again, try all of these techniques to see what works for you.

- Set a regular time to write. Sit down and stay there for the time you've planned, even if you write nothing usable.
- Develop a ritual for writing. Choose tools—paper, pen, computer, chair—that you find comfortable. Use the same tools in the same place every time you write.
- Try freewriting. Remember that freewriting is just for yourself; it doesn't have to be "good."
- Write down the thoughts and fears you have as you write. If the ideas are negative, try to substitute more positive statements: "I can do this." "I'll keep going and postpone judging." "If I keep working, I'll produce something that's OK."
- Identify the problem that keeps you from writing. Deal with that problem; then turn back to writing.
- Set modest goals and reward yourself for reaching them.

GETTING AND USING FEEDBACK

You can improve the quality of the feedback you get by telling people which aspects you'd especially like comments about. For example, for the first draft of a memo you might want to know whether the general approach is effective. In your second draft, you might want to know whether reader benefits are well developed. By the third draft, you might be ready for feedback on style and grammar. If you've given someone a first draft and the reader just notices grammar, that feedback won't be very useful to you.

It's easy to feel defensive when someone criticizes your work. If the feedback stings, put it aside until you can read it without feeling defensive. Even if you think that the reader hasn't understood what you were trying to say, the fact that the reader complained usually means that the section could be improved. If the reader says "This isn't true" and you know that the statement is true, several kinds of revision might make the truth clear to the reader: rephrasing the statement, giving more information or examples, or documenting the source.

REVISING, EDITING, AND PROOFREADING

Good writers make their drafts better by judicious revising, editing, and proof-reading. As you have already seen, **revising** means making changes which will

*   Quoted from Linda Flower, *Problem-Solving Strategies for Writing* (New York: Harcourt Brace Jovanovich, 1981), 39.

better satisfy your purposes and your audience. **Editing** means making surface-level changes which make the document gramatically correct. **Proofreading** means checking to be sure that the document is free from typographical errors.

What to Look for When You Revise

Every chapter in this section on building blocks of effective messages suggests questions you should ask as you revise as well as when you initially plan your document. When you write to an audience you know well, you may be able to check everything at once. When you're writing to a new audience or have to solve a particularly difficult problem, plan to revise the draft at least three times. The first time, look for content and clarity. The second time, check the organization and layout. Finally, check style and tone.

Thorough Revision Checklist

Content and Clarity

- Is your view of purposes complete? What words or sections help achieve each purpose?
- Have you given readers all the information they need to understand and act on your message?
- Is each sentence clear? Is the message free from apparently contradictory statements?
- Is the logic clear and convincing? Are reader benefits clear? Convincing? Adequately developed?

Organization and Layout

- Is the pattern of organization appropriate for your purposes?
- Do ideas within paragraphs flow smoothly?
- Does the design of the document make it easy for readers to find the information they need? Is the document visually inviting?
- Are the points emphasized by layout ones that deserve emphasis?

Style and Tone

- Is the message easy to read?
- Is the message friendly and free from sexist language?
- Have you built goodwill? Can you-attitude, positive emphasis, or success consciousness be improved?

As you revise, be sure to read the document through from start to finish. This is particularly important if your document incorporates blocks of text from other documents. Researchers have found that such documents tend to be well organized but don't flow well.[6] Revising the style or providing transitions may be necessary.

If you're really in a time bind, do a light revision. The quality of the final document may not be as high as with a thorough revision, but even a light revision is better than skipping revision altogether.

Light Revision Instructions

- Check the first and last paragraphs. They make the biggest impression on your reader.
- Check visual impact—paragraph length, use of headings, and so on.
- Check to make sure you've told the reader what he or she needs to do.

How to Dictate

Dictating a document can be three or four times as fast as composing it in longhand or at a keyboard. In addition, many people find that dictating enables them to produce more natural-sounding messages, once they've had some practice. Use these steps to dictate effectively.

1. Learn the system.
2. Before you start, plan the message.
   a. Gather any materials you need: prior correspondence, enclosures.
   b. If you're answering a message, underline the key words in it. Jot down any other points you want to make. Number all of these in the order in which you want to treat them in your message.
   c. Choose a pattern of organization.
   d. Decide what layout features you want to include: headings, lists, charts, tables, etc. Chapters 10 and 11 will give you specific suggestions.
3. Give the typist the necessary instructions. (These may vary depending on the typist or the system you're using.)
4. Dictate.
   a. Speak clearly.
   b. Specify headings, the beginnings and ends of lists, and the beginnings of paragraphs.
   c. Dictate colons, semicolons, dashes, underlining, and parentheses.

Because dictating feels so much like talking, it's easy to slip into habits that are acceptable in speaking but which weaken written messages. When you get back the transcription of your dictation, check to see whether your dictating style is tight enough to read well. If it needs work, you'll need to revise material you dictate until you learn to "talk writing" the first time through.

Sooner or Later You'll Hit the Ball*
In baseball, you only get three swings and you're out. In rewriting, you get almost as many swings as you want and you know, sooner or later, you'll hit the ball.

What to Look for When You Edit

Even good writers need to edit, since no one can pay attention to surface correctness while thinking of ideas. Editing should always *follow* revision. There's no point in taking time to fix a grammatical error in a sentence which may be cut when you clarify your meaning or tighten your style.

It's easier to see errors in a typed copy than in a longhand draft. Some editors find that editing on a computer screen is more accurate than editing hard copy,[7] perhaps because they read more slowly from a screen.[8] Other people prefer hard copy.

You need to know the rules of grammar and punctuation to edit. Review Appendix B as you check to be sure that the following are accurate:

- Sentence structure.
- Subject-verb and noun-pronoun agreement.
- Punctuation.
- Word usage.
- Spelling—including spelling of names.
- Numbers.

Most writers make a small number of errors over and over. If you know that you have trouble with dangling modifiers or subject-verb agreement, for example, specifically look for them in your draft.

How to Catch Typos

To proofread, you must slow your reading speed so you see each individual letter. Proofreading is hard because writers tend to see what they know should be there rather than what really is there.

The ideal way to proofread is to have one person read the document aloud, voicing punctuation and spelling out names, while another person follows along the longhand or original typed copy. This way is so slow and so expensive that it is reserved for very important documents or for documents like phone books where it is the only way possible.

An acceptable alternative is to read the document twice. Read once quickly for meaning, to see that nothing has been left out. Read a second time, slowly. When you find an error, correct it and then *reread that line*. Readers tend to become less attentive after they find one error and may miss other errors close to the one they've spotted. Always triple-check numbers, headings, the first and last paragraphs, and the reader's name.

Reading out loud and reading lines backward or pages out of order can help you proofread a document you know well.

USING BOILERPLATE

Boilerplate is language from a previous document that a writer includes in a new document. In some cases, boilerplate may have been written years ago. For example, many legal documents, including apartment leases and sales contracts, are almost completely boilerplated. In other cases, writers may use boilerplate they themselves have written. For example, a section from a proposal describing the background of the problem could also be used in the final report after the proposed work was completed. A section from a progress

---

*   Quoted from Neil Simon, in Paul D. Zimmerman, "Neil Simon: Up from Success," *Newsweek,* February 2, 1970, 55.

report describing what the writer had done could be used with only a few changes in the Methods section of the final report.

Writers use boilerplate both to save time and energy and to use language which has already been approved by the organization's legal staff. However, as Glenn Broadhead and Richard Freed point out, using boilerplate creates two problems.[9] First, using unrevised boilerplate can create a document with incompatible styles and tones. Second, boilerplate can encourage writers to see as identical situations and audiences which in fact have subtle differences.

Before you incorporate old language in a new document,

- Check to see that the old section is well written.
- Consciously look for differences between the two situations, audiences, or purposes which may require different content, organization, or wording.
- Read through the whole document at a single sitting to be sure that style, tone, and level of detail are consistent in the old and new sections.

COLLABORATIVE WRITING

Collaborative writing means working with other writers to produce a single document.[10] People in business, nonprofit, and government organizations may choose to collaborate, but even more often they are told to do so. Collaboration is often prompted by one of the following situations:

1. The task is too big or the time is too short for one person to do all the work.
2. No one person has all the knowledge required to do the task.
3. A group representing different perspectives must reach a consensus.
4. The stakes for the task are so high that the organization wants the best efforts of as many people as possible; no one person wants the sole responsibility for the success or failure of the document.

Collaborative writing can be done by two people or by a much larger group. The group can be democratic or run by a leader who makes decisions alone. The group may share or divide responsibility for each of the eight stages in the writing process. The following patterns illustrate three of the many possibilities:

- A group plans the document and divides the work. Individuals gather the necessary material for their parts and write their sections separately. The entire group evaluates and revises the document. (Democratic teams in business and students assigned group projects in business classes often organize their work this way.)
- One person plans the work and divides it. Each member of the group carries out his or her assignments. The parts are put together, and the whole group or one person revises it. (Team projects in business may be run this way when the group leader is also the supervisor of the group members.)
- A group gathers information and discusses the topic. A single writer plans and writes a document to reflect the group's position. The group evaluates the document and may suggest possible revisions. The writer revises the document until the group feels it is acceptable. (Many committee reports are written this way.)

Using Spelling and Grammar Checkers

Many word-processing programs have spelling checkers; you can also buy spelling checkers separately. If you use a computer to prepare your documents, by all means use a spelling checker.

Even if you use a spelling checker, you still need to proofread the document once for meaning. Spelling checkers work by matching words: they will signal any group of letters not listed in their dictionaries. However, they cannot tell that the meaning demands *of* rather than *or*, or *not* rather than *now*.

You also need to check numbers and the spelling of names.

Writers with a good command of grammar and mechanics can do a better job than the computer grammar checkers currently available. Grammar checkers can help writers who have a very poor command of grammar and mechanics. However, since grammar checkers do not catch all errors, it's worth taking the time to master grammar and mechanics so you can edit and proofread yourself.

Warning: Boilerplating May
Be Hazardous to Your
Financial Health*

[One of the best writers in an international management consulting firm said:]

I wrote a proposal last week that I thought was going to be exactly like another proposal that I wrote for another company. It is in the same industry, the same products, the same size specifications, almost the exact same geographic area. I pulled out that other proposal in order to boilerplate from it. I thought this would be a cake walk. But by the time I was done, the only thing the other proposal did was to supply some neat ideas for me.

They were just totally different because the other proposal was for a company that I had done ten or twelve studies for before. It was for the president that I knew very well, whose son was a client of mine, and there was this relationship, a little better than a client relationship, and his company was fantastically successful. But this one was for a company where I had never met anybody; the company was in trouble; there was no warm feeling; there was no ten years of experience; there were no previous assignments.

The previous proposal was sort of a "Hey, Stan, this sort of confirms what we will do together, and we will do our best and if we blow it we will change in midstream, and it has been great seeing you and the wife kind of thing." But this current one is, "(1) you don't know me, (2) I have to establish my credentials and my firm's credentials, (3) we are sorry we took so long to respond, because we lost your letter (which is really # 4); of all the firms you talk to, however, we are the only ones with exactly the right qualifications—here they are," and now, suddenly, we have a totally different proposal.

Research in collaborative writing has not yet told us whether certain kinds of collaboration produce better writing or how to use each kind of collaboration most effectively. The following suggestions are based on research in group process, the experiences of several teachers who have used group writing assignments, and common sense.

Planning the Work and the Document

Formal planning is needed to make collaborative writing successful. Businesses schedule formal planning sessions for large projects to set up a time line specifying intermediate and final due dates, meeting dates, who will attend each meeting, and who will do what. Putting the plan in writing reduces misunderstandings during the project.

When you plan a collaborative writing project,

* Make your analysis of the problem, the audience, and your purposes explicit so you know where you agree and where you disagree.
* Plan the organization, format, and style of the document before anyone begins to write to make it easier to blend sections written by different authors.
* Build some leeway into your deadlines. It's harder for a group to finish a document when one person's part is missing than it is for a single writer to finish the last section of a document on which he or she has done all the work.

Composing the Drafts

Most writers find that composing alone is faster than composing in a group. However, composing together may reduce revision time later, since the group examines every choice as it is made.

When you draft a collaborative writing project,

* Use word processing to make it easier to produce the many drafts necessary in a collaborative document.
* If the quality of writing is crucial, have the best writer(s) draft the document after everyone has gathered the necessary information.

Revising the Document

Revising a collaborative document requires attention to content, organization, and style. The following guidelines can make the revision process more effective:

* Evaluate the content and discuss possible revisions as a group if at all possible.
* Recognize that different people favor different writing styles. If the style satisfies the demands of standard English and the conventions of business writing, accept it even if you wouldn't say it that way.

---

* Quoted from Glenn J Broadhead and Richard C. Freed, *The Variables of Composition: Process and Product in a Business Setting,* Conference on College Composition and Communication Studies in Writing and Rhetoric (Carbondale, IL: Southern Illinois University Press, 1986), 58.

- When the group is satisfied with the content of the document, one person—probably the best writer—should make any changes necessary to make the writing style consistent throughout.

Editing and Proofreading the Document

Since writers' mastery of standard English varies, a group report needs careful editing and proofreading.

- Have at least one person check the whole document for correctness in grammar, mechanics, and spelling and for consistency in the way that format elements, names, and numbers are handled.
- Run the document through a spell checker if possible.
- Even if you use a computerized spell checker, at least one human being should proofread the document too.

Making the Group Process Work

The better your understanding of group process, the more smoothly the group will function and the more rewarding the experience will be. Chapter 25 discusses how to listen effectively, run meetings efficiently, and deal with conflict constructively. Use those suggestions in addition to the ones here:

- Give yourselves plenty of time to discuss problems and find solutions. Purdue students writing group reports spend six to seven hours a week outside class in group meetings—not counting the time they spend gathering information and writing their drafts.[11]
- Take the time to get to know group members and to build group loyalty. Group members will work harder and the final document will be better if the group is important to members.
- Be a responsible group member. Attend all the meetings; carry out your responsibilities.
- Be aware that people have different ways of experiencing reality and of expressing themselves. Use the principles of semantics in Chapter 4 to reduce miscommunication.
- Because talking is looser than writing, people in a group can think they agree when they don't. Don't assume that because the discussion went smoothly, a draft written by one person will necessarily be acceptable.

SUMMARY OF KEY POINTS

- Writing processes can include eight activities: planning, gathering, writing, evaluating, getting feedback, revising, editing, and proofreading. **Revising** means changing the document to make it better satisfy the writer's purposes and the audience. **Editing** means making surface-level changes which make the document grammatically correct. **Proofreading** means checking to be sure the document is free from typographical errors. The activities do not have to come in any set order. It is not necessary to

---

The Act of Writing Can Change the Corporate Structure*

While [the president of a new software company] was away [on a business trip], the vice presidents began to work on the new Business Plan [to raise the funds needed to keep the company solvent]. . . . Each of the vice presidents took responsibility for his area of expertise and together the group began to consider how the Plan should be written.

During this collaborative invention [planning] process two significant things happened: (1) for the first time ever, the vice presidents made large-scale company decisions without the approval of the president; and (2) the vice presidents came to believe that the financial crisis occurred not only because the company had suffered from a previously unorganized production system, but also because the president had seriously mismanaged the company's finances. The latter discovery arose as the vice presidents tried to organize the company's financial records for the new Business Plan.

As a result of the financial revelation, Microwave's board of directors decided in a dramatic and emotional meeting that the president's autocratic rule must end. Thus, the act of writing led to a change in the corporate structure. That is, the writing process not only influenced the substance of what was written, but also influenced the organization.

---

*   Quoted from Stephen Doheny-Farina, "Writing in an Emerging Organization: An Ethnographic Study," *Written Communication* 3, no. 2 (1986): 167; paragraphing added.

Collaborative Fighting*

Another collaborator . . . suggested that instead of calling the process collaborative writing, it should be called "collaborative fighting." He added, "Most of the conflicts I've been involved in in the end have been productive. In the interim, they have had all sorts of negative effects—self doubts, doubts about other people, and all sorts of things. I've had my stomach turned in knots a couple of dozen times by this guy [his coauthor] because of the way in which he marks up my manuscripts, but then I also know that although I may take it personally I'm gonna get over that, and I'm gonna be able to deal with it; and in the long run probably two thirds to three fourths of the comments he made—if I'm gonna implement them in some fashion—are gonna make that into a better paper."

finish one activity to start another. Most writers use all eight activities only when they're writing a kind of document, about a subject, or to an audience that's new to them.

- Processes that help writers write well include not expecting the first draft to be perfect; writing regularly; modifying the initial task if it's too hard or too easy; having clear goals; knowing many different strategies; using rules as guidelines rather than as absolutes; and waiting to edit until after the draft is complete.

- To overcome writer's block, use strategies that reduce tension, simplify the writing problem, and "lower the stakes." To overcome the tendency to procrastinate, modify your behavior by rewarding yourself for the actions that *lead to* writing, whether or not you produce anything usable at a particular session.

- You can improve the quality of the feedback you get by telling people which aspects of a draft you'd like comments about. If a reader criticizes something, fix the problem. If you think the reader misunderstood you, try to figure out what caused the misunderstanding and revise the draft so that the reader can see what you meant.

- If the writing situation is new or difficult, plan to revise the draft at least three times. The first time, look for content and clarity. The second time, check the organization and layout. Finally, check style and tone.

- **Boilerplate** is language from a previous document that a writer includes in a new document. Using unrevised boilerplate can create a document with incompatible styles and tones and can encourage writers to see as identical situations and audiences which in fact have subtle differences.

- **Collaborative writing** means working with other writers to produce a single document. Writers producing a joint document need to pay attention not only to the basic steps in the writing process but also to the processes of group formation and conflict resolution.

NOTES

1. W. Ross Winterowd, *The Contemporary Writer* (New York: Harcourt, Brace, Jovanovich, 1975), 61.

2. George H. Jensen and John K. DeTiberio, "Personality and Individual Composing Processes," *College Composition and Communication* 34, no. 3 (October 1984): 289–90.

3. Mike Rose, *Writer's Block: The Cognitive Dimension*, published for the Conference on College Composition and Communication (Carbondale, IL: Southern Illinois University Press, 1984), 36.

4. See especially Linda Flower and John R. Hayes, "The Cognition of Discovery: Defining a Rhetorical Problem," *College Composition and Communication* 31 (February 1980): 21–32; Rose, *Writer's Block;* and the essays in two collections: Charles R. Cooper and Lee Odell, *Research on Composing: Points of Departure* (Urbana, IL: National Council of Teachers of English, 1978) and Mike Rose, ed., *When a Writer Can't Write: Studies in Writer's Block and Other Composing-Process Problems* (New York: Guilford Press, 1985).

5. Peter Elbow, *Writing with Power: Techniques for Mastering the Writing Process* (New York: Oxford University Press, 1981), 15–20.

6. Raymond W. Beswick, "Communicating in the Automated Office," American Business Communication Association International Convention, New Orleans, LA, October 20, 1982.

---

* Quoted from Nancy Allen, Dianne Atkinson, Meg Morgan, Teresa Moore, and Craig Snow, "What Experienced Collaborators Say about Collaborative Writing," *Iowa State Journal of Business and Technical Communication* 1, no. 2 (1987): 80–81.

7. Linda J. Shipley and James K. Gentry, "How Electronic Editing Equipment Affects Editing Performance," *Journalism Quarterly* 58 (Autumn 1981): 371–74, 387.

8. In 1987, an IBM study found that most people read 20% more slowly from a computer screen. However, efforts to create screens that are easier to read may erase this difference. Paul B. Carroll, "Computer Firms Step Up Efforts to Make Machines Easier to Use," *The Wall Street Journal,* December 14, 1987, 25.

9. Glenn J Broadhead and Richard C. Freed, *The Variables of Composition: Process and Product in a Business Setting,* Conference on College Composition and Communication Studies in Writing and Rhetoric (Carbondale, IL: Southern Illinois University Press, 1986), 57.

10. Since collaborative writing can include so many patterns of writing, defining it is difficult. Among the most useful analyses of collaborative writing are Lisa Ede and Andrea Lunsford, "Let Them Write—Together," *English Quarterly* 10, no. 1 (Winter 1985): 119–127; Andrea Lunsford and Lisa Ede, "Why Write . . . Together: A Research Update," *Rhetoric Review* 5, no. 1 (1986): 71–77; Mary Beth Debs, "Collaborative Writing: Practices and Problems in the Field and in the Classroom," Eighth Annual Roundtable for Teachers of Business and Technical Writing, Purdue, IN, October 19–20, 1986; Nancy Allen, Dianne Atkinson, Meg Morgan, Teresa Moore, and Craig Snow, "What Experienced Collaborators Say About Collaborative Writing," *Iowa State Journal of Business and Technical Communication* 1, no. 2 (1987): 70–90; and Betty Evans White, "Comparing Papers Written Individually and Collaboratively," Association for Business Communication Annual Convention, Atlanta, GA, October 14–17, 1987.

11. Meg Morgan, Nancy Allen, Teresa Moore, Dianne Atkinson, and Craig Snow, "Collaborative Writing in the Classroom," *Bulletin of the Association for Business Communication* 50, no. 3 (September 1987): 22.

EXERCISES AND PROBLEMS FOR CHAPTER 5

5–1 INTERVIEWING WRITERS ABOUT THEIR COMPOSING PROCESSES

Interview someone about the composing process(es) he or she uses for on-the-job writing. Questions you could ask include the following:

What kind of planning do you do before you write? Do you make lists? Formal or informal outlines?

When you need some information, where do you get it?

How do you compose your drafts? Do you dictate? Draft with pen and paper? Compose on screen? How do you find uninterrupted time to compose?

On the average, how long does it take you to write a routine one- or two-page memo? Is that time all the time you need? Or just all the time you have?

How much of your writing is "first-time-final"— that is, except for proofreading, you mail out your first draft? For other documents, how many different drafts do you go through? Is there any relationship between the kind of document or the audience and how many drafts you write?

When you want advice about style, grammar, and spelling, what source(s) do you consult?

Does your superior ever read your drafts and make suggestions? How do you feel about that?

Do you ever work with other writers to produce a single document? Describe the process you use.

Describe the process of creating a document where you felt the final document reflected your best work. Describe the process of creating a document which you found difficult or frustrating. What sorts of things make writing easier or harder for you?

As your instructor directs,

a. Share your results orally with a small group of students.

b. Present your results in an oral presentation to the class.

c. Present your results in a memo to your instructor.

d. Share your results with a small group of students and write a joint memo reporting the similarities and differences you found.

5–2 KEEPING TRACK OF YOUR OWN COMPOSING PROCESS(ES)

As you write messages for this course, keep track of your composing process. Here are ways to do that:

1. Turn on a tape recorder while you write and think out loud.

2. At the end of each session thinking about your paper or writing part of the draft, jot down what you've been trying to do during that writing session. Use enough detail so that later you'll remember what you meant.

3. Keep all your notes and rough drafts. Check them to see what kinds of additions, deletions, substitutions, and rearrangements you've made.

4. Fill out the form that follows.

Form for Analyzing Composing, Revision, and Editing Strategies

1. Estimate the amount of time you spend on each of the following activities, on the average, before you compose your first draft.

	For short letters and memos for this course	For complex letters or memos or for reports
a. Discussing the problem	_____	_____
b. Thinking	_____	_____
c. Jotting down notes	_____	_____
d. Making a formal outline	_____	_____
e. Reviewing the text or previous correspondence	_____	_____
f. Other	_____	_____

2. What rituals do you have for composing? Do you always write in the same place, with the same tools?

3. When you are writing or dictating a first draft, how often do you experience writer's block—that is, a situation where you sit at your desk or computer, but can't write?

4. How often do you find yourself procrastinating—putting off writing assignments when you could start working on them earlier?

5. Which tactics (listed in Chapter 5 or others) do you use when you get stuck or procrastinate?

6. When you want help during the composing process or revising process, where do you get it? (Check all that apply.)

    _____ a. My instructor.
    _____ b. Another student who is in or who has taken this class.
    _____ c. Another student who has not taken this class.
    _____ d. The textbook.
    _____ e. The university writing lab or writing peer tutors.
    _____ f. A desk dictionary or other reference books.
    _____ g. Other (specify).

7. List three documents you've written recently which you revised. At least two of them should be papers for this course.

	Topic	Final Length	Level of Difficulty
a.	_____	_____	_____
b.	_____	_____	_____
c.	_____	_____	_____

8. Provide the following information about each of the three documents:

Document A	Document B	Document C	
_____	_____	_____	a. Total number of drafts.
_____	_____	_____	b. Time spent writing first draft and revising.
_____	_____	_____	c. Time spent editing.
_____	_____	_____	d. Time spent proofreading.
_____	_____	_____	e. Quality of final document.

9. In each of the documents, count or estimate the *number* of *revisions* you made in each of the following categories.

Document A	Document B	Document C	
_____	_____	_____	a. Taking something out.
_____	_____	_____	b. Adding something.
_____	_____	_____	c. Substituting or replacing one word, phrase, or sentence with another.
_____	_____	_____	d. Rearranging words, phrases, sentences or larger units.

10. Count or estimate the *number* of changes you made for each of the following reasons in each of the documents.

Document A	Document B	Document C	
_____	_____	_____	a. To improve content and clarity.
_____	_____	_____	b. To improve organization and layout.
_____	_____	_____	c. To improve style and tone.
_____	_____	_____	d. (Other) _____
_____	_____	_____	e. (Other) _____

5–3 ANALYZING YOUR OWN WRITING PROCESSES

Using the material you collected in 5–2, describe and analyze your process. In addition to the questions in the form in 5–2, consider the following questions:

Which of the eight activities discussed in Chapter 5 do you use?

How much time do you spend on each of the eight activities?

What kinds of revisions do you make most often?

Do you use different processes for different documents, or do you have one process that you use most of the time?

Which practices of good writers do you follow?

What parts of your process seem most successful? Are there any places in the process that could be improved? How?

What relation do you see between the process(es) you use and the quality of the final document?

As your instructor directs,

a. Discuss your process with a small group of other students.

b. Write a memo to your instructor analyzing in detail your process for composing one of the papers for this class.

c. Write a memo to your instructor analyzing your process during the term. What parts of your process(es) have stayed the same throughout the term? What parts have changed?

5–4 ANALYZING THE WRITING PROCESS FOR A COLLABORATIVE DOCUMENT

Describe and analyze the writing process that your group used to produce a collaborative document. Questions to answer include the following:

Which of the eight activities did your group use? Did working in a group cause any changes in the time needed for each activity or the way you performed that activity?

Did you make a formal plan before you began other work? Did you have to change your plan? Why?

Who composed what parts of the document? How did you decide who did what?

What kinds of disagreements surfaced when you revised and edited the document? How did you decide among different viewpoints?

How did you create one uniform style through-out the document?

Did you use computer aids such as spelling and grammar checkers?

Which members of the group edited and proof-read the document? How did you decide who would do this?

How does the quality of the document compare to the quality of documents you prepare alone?

What do you like least about writing with other people? What do you like most?

As your instructor directs,

a. Discuss the process with a small group of other students.

b. Present your analysis in a memo to your instructor.

c. Present your analysis orally to the class.

5–5 PROOFREADING

Proofread each of the following paragraphs to correct typographical errors. Fix errors in grammar, spelling, and punctuation; you do not need to change content, style, or tone.

a. Response to a Customer Complaint

Because of your experience, tow actions are now being taken. First, a copy of your comments has been sent to the hoetl's managemtn, as shown on the copy list below. Obviously, problems of the sort you experienced can only be resolved by hotel management and they have been asked to respond directily to you. Second, a copy of your comments have been sent to our Customer Representatives who travel throughout the nation inspecting every hotel in the chain for compliance with our standards. The Customer Representatives will check to be sure that this problem is corrected at any of the locations at which it may arise.

b. Information Sheet Accompanying a Scholarship Application Form

The local chapter of PRSSA has established a scholarship program to benefits its members whose hard work and dedication consistently place the chapter among the best in the nation. This years' program has up to three $500 scholarships available for members who have been in good standing for at least one quarter (including the current quarter and who will not graduate before next DEcember.

c. A Proposal to Determine Whether a Fast-Food Restaurant Needs More Drive-Through Windows

I will conduct an indepth time study of waiting times during peak rush hour times from 4:45 pm to 6:15 pm on five week days to collect the necessary data. I will examine the layout of the facility to determine weather their is enough space to build additional drive-thru windows.

5–6 DICTATING A RESPONSE

Jayne Martin, a junior at your high school, is planning to visit your campus in three weeks. Dictate a letter to her, inviting her to accompany you to your classes on either Tuesday or Wednesday. Tell her what time to meet you and where to meet you; give her necessary directions.

Hints:

- How will Jayne get to campus? Does she need advice on which bus stop to get off at or where to park?
- How much money does she need to bring for parking, lunch, and any miscellaneous expenses?
- Is there any other information that would make her trip more pleasant?

As your instructor directs,

a. Record your letter on a tape cassette.

b. Exchange cassettes with another student and type the letter **exactly** as the other student has dictated it.

c. Write a memo to the student whose tape you typed suggesting ways he or she can become a better dictator.

d. Write a memo to your instructor analyzing the differences between composing a document on paper or screen and dictating it.

Chapter

6

Adapting Your Message to Your Audience

QUESTIONS
- Who is your audience?
- How can you analyze the audience?
- How do you use this information to adapt your message to the audience?
- How do you adapt the message if members of the audience have different needs?

I even hear them as I write.
Virginia Woolf
Letter to
Dame Ethel Smyth, 1933

Good writers can mentally hear readers' reactions to a draft. They craft their texts to encourage the reactions that will give their ideas the best hearing.

In the last 15 years it has become a truism that writers, like speakers, must be conscious of their audiences and adapt their presentations to fit the audience's needs, interests, and concerns. Books have appeared giving extensive checklists to use to analyze audiences. Less has been written, however, about what factors really make a difference in the way readers and hearers will respond and how writers can use this information to modify their texts.

WHO IS YOUR AUDIENCE?

The first step in analyzing your audience is to decide who your audience is. In personal correspondence, that's easy: the audience is the person whose name is in the salutation. In an organizational setting, however, the person to whom a letter or memo is addressed is not necessarily the most important audience.

J. C. Mathes and Dwight W. Stevenson provide a useful way of looking at audiences in organizations.[1]

1. The **primary audience** will make a decision or act on the basis of your message. You must reach the primary audience to fulfill your purposes in any message.
2. The **secondary audience** is affected by the decision or action. These people may be asked by the primary audience to comment on your message or to implement your ideas after they've been approved.
3. The **immediate audience** routes the message to other audiences. Most immediate audiences choose which messages to send on; they serve as "gate-keepers." The immediate audience therefore controls whether your message even gets to the primary audience.

Let's see who these audiences are in two specific examples.

Dawn is an assistant account executive in an ad agency. Her boss asks her to write a proposal for a marketing plan for a new product the agency's client is introducing. Her **immediate audience** is her boss, who must approve the plan before it is submitted to the client. Her **primary audience** is the executive committee of the client company, who will decide whether to adopt the plan. The **secondary audience** includes the marketing staff of the client company, who will be asked for comments on the plan, as well as the artists, writers, and media buyers who will carry out details of the plan if it is adopted.

Joe works in the data processing unit of a bank. He must write a monthly progress report describing his work—this month, implementing a centralized system for handling customers' checks. His boss is **both a primary and an immediate audience.** His boss will write a performance appraisal evaluating his work, so Joe wants to present his own efforts positively. The boss may also include paragraphs from Joe's progress report in a memo to the president of the bank, who wants to know when the bugs in the system will be worked out. The president is thus also a **primary audience.** The **secondary audience** includes the bank's customer service representatives, who must answer customer questions and deal with complaints about the new system, and sales representatives from the computer company which sold the hardware to the bank, who want to be sure that bank personnel are able to use the equipment effectively.

WAYS TO ANALYZE YOUR AUDIENCE

The most important tools in audience analysis are common sense and empathy. **Empathy** is the ability to put yourself in someone else's shoes, to feel with that person. Empathy requires that one not be self-centered. In all probability, the audience is *not* just like you. Use what you know about people and about organizations to predict likely responses.

When you write or talk to one person or a small group of people, you can use informal methods to gather information about your audience. These methods might include talking to members of your audience, talking to people who know your audience, and observing your audience.

Big audiences or expensive projects may justify the cost of focus groups, interviews, and questionnaires. **Focus groups** are small groups (usually no more than 12 people) who come in to talk with a skilled leader about a potential product. In an **interview,** the researcher talks to one person at a time. **Questionnaires** or **surveys** are less expensive because they can be filled out by many people at the same time. Chapter 19 discusses these and other research methods. When the audience is too big or the budget too small for interviews and questionnaires, researchers sometimes use demographic and psychographic data.

Demographic characteristics are measurable features that can be counted objectively: age, sex, race, education level, income, and so on. Sometimes demographic information is irrelevant; sometimes it's important. Is the reader's education important? Well, the fact that the reader has a degree from Eastern State rather than from Harvard probably doesn't matter, but how much the reader knows about accounting may. Age is often irrelevant. On the other hand, if you were explaining a change in your company's pension plan, you'd expect older workers to be much more concerned than younger workers would be.

Psychographic characteristics are qualitative rather than quantitative: values, beliefs, goals, and lifestyles. Many marketers use the Values and Life Styles profiles (VALS) developed by a research firm in California. VALS profiles divide U.S. buyers into nine categories, including Belongers, the conservative middle class who "have benefited by the rules of the game"; Emulators, conspicuous consumers who don't have lots of money but who want to be in style; Achievers, ambitious, hard-working, comfort-loving people who "control nearly 50 percent of the buying power" in the United States; and Societally Conscious, highly educated people who are interested in conservation, the environment, and inner growth.[2] Knowing what your audience finds important allows you to organize information in a way that seems natural to your audience and to choose appeals that they will find persuasive.

Lack of Audience Analysis Can Bury a Good Idea*

A manager received a proposal from a subordinate. He thought the proposal should be adopted, so he sent copies of it to 18 people in top management. On the list were the two people who had decision-making authority on this topic. But neither saw the proposal as addressed to him.

One said, "I can't tell why I got it. I didn't read it; there was no need. It is a totally ridiculous proposal on his part."

The second said, "I read it pretty carefully. I needed to transmit it to the person who could act [I had delegated authority], but I didn't get to it until six days after it was sent out. Unfortunately I didn't see until then that it was for action by me— it wasn't addressed to me, so it ended up in my 'third pile' [to do when time permits]."

What went wrong? The manager didn't distinguish among decision makers, recipients who would be affected by the proposal, and people with no need to know about the proposal. He didn't put the decision makers' names in the "To" line of the memo; he didn't develop a subject line and first paragraph to show readers why this proposal was important and why they should act on it.

---

* Based on Dwight W. Stevenson, "The Writer's Audiences: An Egocentric View," *Proceedings,* International Technical Communication Conference, 1976, EW6, 124–25.

FIGURE 6.1
USING THE MYERS-BRIGGS
TYPES TO MODIFY
INSTRUCTIONS

HOW TO CONDUCT AN EXIT INTERVIEW

Sensing Directions

1. Schedule a 20-minute interview at least one week in advance. Leave at least 10 minutes between interviews.
2. Gather the materials needed for the interview: Exit Interview questionnaire form, pen or pencil, handout on severance pay, handout on disposition of pension plan, and change of address form.
3. Prepare for the interview by reading the employee's performance appraisals and resignation statement, if any.
4. Spend the first two minutes of the interview making the employee comfortable.
5. Use minutes 3 to 12 of the interview to obtain answers to the 10 questions in the Exit Interview questionnaire. Answer every question.
6. Use minutes 13 to 16 of the interview to discuss benefits the employee may continue to receive. Explain how any accrued penison benefits will be paid. Give the employee the handouts on severance pay and disposition of pension plan.
7. Use minutes 17 to 19 of the interview to answer any additional questions the employee may have.
8. Make sure the employee fills out the change of address form to receive his or her final paycheck and to receive a W-2 Form at the end of the calendar year.
9. Wish the former employee good luck.
10. Write up a report of the Exit Interview within 10 days. Make three copies: one for your files, one for the Headquarters Office, and one for Affirmative Action. Forward the latter copies to their appropriate destinations within two weeks after the Exit Interview.

Intuitive Directions

Exit Interviews provide an opportunity for the organization to leave a good image with the departing employee and to learn of improvements that may help the organization.

When you conduct an Exit Interview, divide departing employees into people whose departure is inevitable (due to retirement, end of summer job, laid off, and so forth) and those whose departure is discretionary (fired or resigned even though they would not have to leave). In the first case, use the Exit Interview to learn the employee's impression of the company and to give all the necessary information about severance pay and continuing benefits. Be sure to explain to retirees and laid-off workers how they can remain covered by health insurance. If reemployment in the future seems likely, tell the departing employee when and how to reapply.

When the departure is discretionary, look for patterns. Could a firing have been avoided with a different job assignment, better training and development, or clearer performance appraisals? Or was hiring this person a mistake in the first place? Could a resignation have been avoided with more opportunity for advancement or better conditions? Or have this employee's goals become incompatible with the opportunities in this organization?

Departures do not represent a random sequence. The thoughtful personnel director will be able to use the Exit Interview to get an overview of the strengths and weaknesses of personnel policies throughout the company. Consider who in the organization needs the information that you now have, and let them know what they're doing well and what they need to change. Some managers may respond well to a written report. Others will be more receptive if you talk to them over lunch or after work. Use the method that seems best to you.

The **Myers-Briggs Type Indicator** test categorizes people on four dimensions.[3] One of these is well known: introvert-extrovert. The other three dimensions in the Myers-Briggs scale are sensing-intuitive, thinking-feeling, and perceiving-judging. Sensing-intuitive measures the way someone gets information. Sensing types gather information through their senses. Intuitive types see relationships. Thinking-feeling measures the way someone makes decisions. Thinking types use objective logic to reach decisions. Feeling types make decisions that feel "right," without necessarily being able to define the path they took to make the decision. Judging-perception measures the degree of certainty someone needs. Judging types like closure. Perceptive types like possibilities.

The poles on each of these scales represent a preference, just as we have a preference for using either our right or our left hand to write. If necessary, we can use the opposite style, but we have less practice in it and use it less easily.

You can find out your own personality type by taking the Myers-Briggs test at your college's counseling center or student services office. Some businesses administer the Myers-Briggs test to all their employees. Even when you don't have test results, you can often make accurate guesses about someone's type by close observation.

Figure 6.1 shows how you could change a set of instructions depending on whether the reader was a sensing or an intuitive type. Sensing types like detailed instructions and a clear sequence of steps. Intuitive types want to create their own goals and to be original. If you find the first set of directions absurdly rigid, you may lean toward intuition as a way of gathering information. If you find the second set of directions sloppy and formless, you may tend to gather data through your senses. Since a real set of directions would be used by both sensing and intuitive types, the best directions would combine aspects of both examples.

Like demographic and psychographic data, the Myers-Briggs test may encourage us to stereotype people. Stereotypes may be all we have when we know almost nothing about the audience, but stereotypes are always misleading. At a minimum, use whatever feedback may be available to provide a fuller picture of this audience the next time you communicate with them.

USING AUDIENCE ANALYSIS TO ADAPT YOUR MESSAGE

If you know your audience well and if you use words well, much of your audience and adaptation will be unconscious. If you don't know your audience or if the message is very important, take the time to analyze your audience formally and to revise your draft with your analysis in mind.

Here is one set of questions to ask about readers and suggested ways to modify a message based on the answer for any particular reader. These questions apply to most situations. In some cases you won't need answers to all of them to write effective messages; sometimes you may need even more information.

1. **What Will the Reader's Initial Reaction Be to the Message?**
   a. Will the reader see this message as highly important? Will he or she be likely to read the message and act on it immediately?

   Almost everyone has too much to read and too much to do. One of the most common ways to deal with this overload is to skim a message and assign a priority to it. *A* messages must be acted on as soon as possible. *B* jobs are important, but can wait. *C* jobs can be done when time permits. Most workers never get back to items in their *C* piles; even *B* jobs often have very long delays.

They Looked at the Audience and Saw Themselves*

Before a bank took a survey of its customers, employees were asked to describe the bank's typical customer.

The CEO answered: "About 60, upper-income, community leader."

The middle managers said: "About 40 with grown children. On the way up; good, solid citizen."

The tellers said: "Twenties or thirties, newly married, just starting out. Lots of energy and drive."

According to the survey, the typical customer was in the mid-30s, had been married a few years, earned $20,000 a year, had $1\frac{1}{2}$ cars and 2 children.

People looked at customers but saw only themselves.

The Audience That Watches the Ads May Not Like the Show†

Psychology Today tried a series of TV ads to get new subscriptions. It identified its target market as *upscale professionals*.

Where did it find them? It got the best results with ads on "Bozo's Circus." Why? Homemakers, watching TV with their kids, were bored stiff and jumped at the chance to get a product that let them be intelligent adults even if they did stay at home with their children.

---

* Based on Ray Considine and Murray Raphel, *The Great Brain Robbery* (Pasadena, CA: The Great Brain Robbery, 1981), 68–69.

† Based on Richard Sangerman, "Broadcast Media," CADM/DMEF Direct Marketing Institute for Professors, Northbrook, IL, May 31–June 3, 1983.

Analyzing Intercultural and International Audiences*

People who differ from the majority in gender, race, ethnic background, or nationality alternately protest, "Don't assume I'm different," and "Don't assume I'm just like you." Treating a group as different can lead to separation, discrimination, and even persecution. But treating all people as though they were the same ignores and shuts out people who do not belong to the majority. In some situations, similarities are more important than differences; in other situations, differences are more important.

People overseas sometimes say that when they ask a U.S. visitor how Americans feel about something, the visitor always says, "I'm not a typical American."

People in other countries are diverse, too. Not all Arabs are Muslims. Some are Christians; some are Jews; some are Zoroastrians. Not all people from Third World countries live in primitive rural areas. Not all Ethiopians are starving.

Once we have a stereotype, we tend to look for instances which confirm it rather than for instances which challenge it. Someone who thinks all Japanese are "inscrutable" is unlikely to notice a Japanese speaker's nonverbal cues. Someone who thinks that Arabs get angry easily may stay away from noisy gatherings of Arab students.

Stereotypes may be useful when someone who knows almost nothing about another culture must learn, in a hurry, to communicate in order to do business. But we need to be alive to feedback so that we can recognize the differences as well as the similarities among people who share a country or a culture.

When the reader may see the message as of moderate or low importance, you need to

* Use a subject line or first paragraph that convinces the reader that this message is important and relevant.
* Make a special effort to make your writing easy to read.
* Make the action as easy as possible.
* Suggest a realistic deadline for action.
* Keep the message as short as possible since people are more likely to delay reading long documents.

b. How will the fact that the message is from you affect the reader's reaction to the words on the page?

The reader's experience with you, your organization, and the subject you're writing about shapes the way the reader responds to this new message. Someone who thinks well of you and your organization will be prepared to receive your message favorably; someone who thinks poorly of you and the organization will be quick to find fault with what you say and the way you say it.

When you must write to a reader who has negative feelings about your organization, your position, or you personally, you need to

* Make a special effort to avoid phrases which could seem parental, arrogant, rude, hostile, or uncaring.
* Make a special effort to counteract the natural tendency to sound defensive. Use success consciousness to sound confident.
* Develop logic and reader benefits fully.

Success consciousness and reader benefits are discussed in Chapter 7.

2. How Much Information Does the Reader Need?

a. How much does the reader already know about this subject?

It's easy to overestimate the knowledge an audience has. People outside your own immediate unit may not really know what it is you do. Even people who once worked in your unit may have forgotten specific details now that their daily work is in management. People outside your organization won't know how *your* organization does things, even if they work in the same field.

When some of your information is new to the reader, you need to

* Make a special effort to be clear. Define terms, explain concepts, use examples.
* Link new information to old information that the reader already knows.
* Use paragraphs and headings to break up new information into related chunks, so that the information is easier to digest.
* Use a layout that makes it easy for the reader to go back to new information.

---

* Based on Deborah Tannen, *Conversational Style: Analyzing Talk among Friends* (Norwood, NJ: Ablex, 1984), 17, and Laray M. Barna, "Stumbling Blocks in Intercultural Communication," in *Intercultural Communication,* ed. Larry A. Samovar and Richard E. Porter (Belmont, CA: Wadsworth Publishing, 1985), 331–34.

- Try to test a draft of your document with your reader or a subset of your intended audience to see whether the audience can understand and use what you've written.

b. Is the reader's knowledge based on reading? Personal experience?

Things we have learned directly, through personal experience, always seem more real and more true than things we learn indirectly or from books. Other people may see our experience as an exception, an aberration, or a fluke; we see it as the best guide of what to expect in the future.

If you're trying to change a reader's understanding of a policy or organization, you need to

- Acknowledge the reader's initial understanding early in the message.
- Use examples as well as theory or statistics to show the difference between short-term and long-term effects, or to show that the reader's experience is not universal.
- Allow the reader to save face by suggesting that changed circumstances call for new attitudes or action.

c. What aspects of the subject does the reader need to be aware of to appreciate your points?

When the reader must think of background or old information to appreciate your points, you can

- Preface information with "As you know" or "As you may remember" to avoid suggesting that you think the reader does not know what you're saying.
- Put old or obvious information in a subordinate clause.
- If the background information or reminder is long, put it in a separate section with an appropriate heading or in an attachment to your letter or memo.

3. What Obstacles Must You Overcome?

a. Is your reader opposed to what you have to say?

Readers who have already made up their minds are highly resistant to change. When you must write to readers who oppose what you have to say, you need to

- Start your message with any areas of agreement or common ground that you share with your reader.
- Make a special effort to be clear and unambiguous. Points that might be clear to a neutral reader can be misread by someone with a chip on his or her shoulder.
- Make a special effort to avoid inflammatory statements.
- Limit your statement or request to the smallest possible area. If parts of your message could be delivered later, postpone them.
- Develop logic and reader benefits fully.
- Try to respond to the specific objections you anticipate from your audience.
- Show that your solution is the best solution currently available, even though it isn't perfect.

An Organization Chart Isn't Enough

Knowing where the reader sits in the organization and how much power he or she has is only the first step in audience analysis. The organization chart doesn't tell whether the reader *cares* about the topic you're writing about. The chart doesn't tell you whether the reader helped create the status quo and therefore will feel attacked by any proposed change, or whether he or she is sufficiently new in the position to look at a proposal more objectively. The chart doesn't tell you what the reader most values: quality? the bottom line? sensitivity to people? It doesn't tell you the reader's loyalties and priorities. Yet all these are the kinds of things you need to know to present your own message effectively.

I Zig, You Zag: We Miscommunicate*

Have you ever moved to one side to avoid bumping into someone in a hall, only to have the other person move to the same side to avoid you? The result is that neither of you can, for a moment, get through.

Audience adaptation can produce the same zigzags when people try to allow for each other's cultural backgrounds. Thus a Colombian plans a party for 9 P.M. But knowing that North Americans think they should show up on time, the Colombian tells a U.S. visitor that the party will start at 10 P.M. The visitor, knowing that parties never start on time in Colombia, shows up at 11 P.M. By this time, the Colombian host has assumed the U.S. visitor isn't coming, since North Americans are always on time.

b. Will it be easy for the reader to do as you ask?

Everyone has a set of ideas and habits and a mental self-image. If we're asked to do something which violates any of those, we first have to be persuaded to change our attitudes or habits or self-image—a change we're reluctant to make.

When your request is time-consuming, complicated, or physically or psychologically difficult, you need to

- Ask for the smallest action that will satisfy your purposes.
- Make the action as easy as possible. Provide a form that can be filled out quickly; provide a stamped, self-addressed envelope if you are writing to someone in another organization.
- Break down actions into a list, so the reader can check off each step as it is completed.
- Show that what you ask is consistent with some aspect of what the reader believes.
- Show how the reader (not just you or your organization) will benefit when the action is completed.

4. What Positive Aspects Can You Use to Build Support for Your Points?
   a. From the reader's point of view, what are the benefits of what you have to say?

   Benefits help persuade the reader that your ideas are good ones. Make the most of the good points inherent in the message you want to convey.

   - Put good news in the first paragraph.
   - Use reader benefits that go beyond the basic good news in the first paragraph.

   b. What experiences, interests, goals, and values do you share with the reader?

   A sense of solidarity with someone can be an even more powerful reason to agree than the content of the message itself. Always use all the strategies that are available to win support for your ideas.

   When the message will be read by only one reader, or by readers who all share the same experiences, interests, goals, and values, you can

   - Consider using a vivid anecdote to remind the reader of what you share. The details of the anecdote should be interesting or new; otherwise you may seem to be lecturing the reader.
   - Make a special effort to make your writing style friendly and informal.
   - Use a salutation and close that remind readers of their membership in this formal or informal group.

5. What Expectations Does the Reader Have about the Appropriate Language, Structure, and Form for Messages?
   a. What style of writing does the reader prefer?

   Good writers adapt their style to suit the reader's preferences. A reader who sees contractions as too informal needs a different style

---

* Based on Raymond L. Gorden, *Living in Latin America* (Skokie, IL: National Textbook, 1974), 128–29.

from one who sees traditional business writing as too stuffy. As you write,

- Use what you know about your reader to choose a more or less distant, more or less friendly style.
- Use the reader's first name in the salutation only if you use that name when you talk to him or her in person or on the phone.

b. Are there "red flag" words that may distract the reader?

If a term has a special meaning to a reader, you don't have time to convince the reader that the term is broader or more neutral than his or her understanding. When you need agreement or approval, you should

- Avoid entirely terms that carry emotional charges for many readers: for example, *criminal, un-American, feminist, fundamentalist, liberal.*
- Use your previous experience with an individual reader to replace any terms which have particular meanings for him or her.

c. How much detail does the reader want?

A message that does not give the reader the amount of or kind of detail he or she wants may fail. When you know your readers, ask them how much detail they want. When you write to readers you do not know well, you can

- Provide all the detail the reader needs to understand and act on your message.
- Group chunks of information under headings so that the reader can go directly to the parts of the message that he or she finds most interesting, skipping details that are unimportant to him or her.
- Consider similar documents to the same audience. If they have succeeded, you're probably safe in using the same level of detail that they do.

d. Does the reader have expectations about formal elements such as length, visuals, or footnotes?

A document that meets the reader's expectations about length, number of visuals, and footnote format is more likely to succeed. Work with the reader's expectations whenever possible. If you can't meet those expectations, you need to

- Revise your document carefully. Be sure that a shorter-than-usual document covers the essential points; be sure that a longer-than-usual document is free from wordiness and repetition.
- Check with the reader to see whether the standards are flexible.
- Pretest the message on a subset of your audience to see if the format enhances or interferes with comprehension and action.

6. How Will the Reader Use the Document?

a. Under what physical conditions will the reader use the document?

Reading a document in an office calls for no special care. But suppose the reader will be reading your message on the train commut-

Three Kinds of Baby Boomers*
Market analysis using psychographics divides baby boomers aged 20 to 30 into three groups:

Self-stylers (30 million people) are independent. They're interested in enriching their own lives, travel, and entertainment. They're less likely to be parents. They're the most affluent and the most educated. They want quality and performance, not status.

Materialists (23 million people) want to be "in." They need to impress others and want to own the "right things." They are the youngest segment; they are less likely to be college-educated or to be professional managers.

Nesters (23 million people) are traditional. They don't care much about travel, personal fulfillment, or money; they do care about time with their families and simple things. They have the least discretionary income of the three groups and are price-conscious. Many have only a high school education.

---

* Based on Tony Wainwright, "Beyond Advertising: Speak the Right Language," *Advertising Age,* July 27, 1987, 34.

ing home, or on a ladder as he or she attempts to follow instructions. Then, clearly, the physical preparation of the document can make it easier or harder to use.

When the reader will use your document outside an office,

- Use lots of white space.
- Consider using bigger type.
- Make the document small enough to hold in one hand.
- Number items so the reader can find his or her place after an interruption.
- Consider using plastic to protect the document.

b. Will the reader use the document as a general reference? As a specific guide? As the basis in a lawsuit?

Understanding how your audience will use the document will enable you to choose the best pattern of organization and the best level of detail. A great deal of detail is needed in an Environmental Protection Agency Inspection Report which will be used to determine whether or not to bring suit against a company for violating pollution control regulations. A memo within a company urging the adoption of pollution control equipment would need less information. Full information would be needed for instructions by the manufacturer of the equipment explaining how to install and maintain it.

If the document will serve as a general reference,

- Use a subject line to aid in filing and retrieval. If the document is on-line, consider using several key words to make it easy to find the document in a data base search program.
- Use headings within the document so that readers can skim it.
- Give the office as well as the person to contact so that the reader can get in touch with the appropriate person some time from now.
- Spell out details that may be obvious now but might be forgotten in six months or a year.

If the document will be a detailed guide for instructions,

- Check to be sure that all the steps are in chronological order.
- Number steps or provide check-off boxes so that readers can easily see which steps they've completed.
- Group steps into five to seven subprocesses if there are many individual steps.
- Put any warnings at the beginning of the document; then repeat them just before the specific step to which they apply.

If the document will be used as the basis for a lawsuit,

- Give specific observations with dates and exact measurements as well as any inferences you've drawn from those observations.
- Give a full report with all the information you have. The lawyer can then decide which parts of the information to use in preparing the case.

---

* Quoted from David A. Ricks, *Big Business Blunders* (Homewood, IL: Dow Jones-Irwin, 1983), 32.

c. Will the document be filed?

In contemporary organizations, everything of importance (and some things of little importance) will be filed. When you know that your message will be filed,

- Provide a subject line for easy filing and retrieval.
- Specify details that may be forgotten six months or a year from now.
- Check both the draft and the final typed copy for accuracy, completeness, and friendliness.

WRITING OR SPEAKING TO MULTIPLE AUDIENCES WITH DIFFERENT NEEDS

One of the most difficult assignments is addressing a multiple audience with different needs. Little research has been done in this area, so we have to rely on common sense: when the needs differ, meet as many needs as possible. When it is not possible to meet everyone's needs, meet the needs of decision makers first. If you must get past a hostile gate-keeper before you get to the decision makers, consider attaching a one-page transmittal adapted to the gatekeeper. If the circumstances don't permit a transmittal, design your document to get past the immediate audience.

Here are some specific applications of this principle:

Organizing the Document

- Use headings and a Table of Contents so readers can turn to the portions that interest them.
- Organize your message based on the decision makers' attitudes toward it.

Level of Formality

- Avoid personal pronouns. *You* ceases to have a specific meaning when several different audiences use a document.
- If both internal and external audiences will use a document, use a slightly more formal style than you would in an internal document.

Level of Detail

- Provide an overview or executive summary for readers who just want the main points.
- In the body of the document, provide enough detail for decision makers and for anyone else who could veto your proposal.
- If the decision makers don't need details that other audiences will want, provide those details in appendices—statistical tabulations, earlier reports, and so forth.

Use of Technical Terms and Theory

- In the body of the document, assume the degree of knowledge that decision makers will have.

Play to the Primary Audience*

When an architect gave the Worthington City Council its first official look recently at plans for developing 45 acres at the site of the United Methodist Children's Home on High St., council President John Coleman didn't mince words on which audience the architect should be playing to.

As Rick Morse juggled the plans on an easel, Coleman suggested he move to the other side, because he was blocking the council's view.

"If I stand on the other side, the audience can't see," Morse said.

"They're not going to vote," Coleman said. "You can set your own priorities."

---

* Quoted from Carol Ann Lease, "Behind the Screens," *Columbus Dispatch*, July 29, 1987, E1.

- Put background information and theory under separate headings. Then readers can use the headings and the Table of Contents to read or skip these sections, as their knowledge dictates.
- If decision makers will have more knowledge than other audiences, provide a glossary of terms. Early in the document, let readers know that the glossary exists.

SUMMARY OF KEY POINTS

- The **primary audience** will make a decision or act on the basis of your message. The **secondary audience** is affected by the decision or action. These people may be asked by the primary audience to comment on your message or to implement your ideas after they've been approved. The **immediate audience** routes the message to other audiences and may control whether the message gets to the primary audience.
- Common sense and empathy are crucial to good audience analysis.
- The following questions provide a framework for audience analysis:

  1. What will the reader's initial reaction be to the message?
  2. How much information does the reader need?
  3. What obstacles must you overcome?
  4. What positive aspects can you use to build support for your points?
  5. What expectations does the reader have about the appropriate language or format for messages?
  6. How will the reader use the document?

- When you write to multiple audiences, use the primary audience to determine organization, level of formality, level of detail, and use of technical terms and theory.

NOTES

1. J. C. Mathes and Dwight Stevenson, *Designing Technical Reports: Writing for Audiences in Organizations* (Indianapolis: Bobbs-Merrill, 1976), 21.
2. Carla Marinucci, "Marketers Have Word for You," *San Francisco Examiner,* in *Columbus Dispatch,* December 23, 1987, B1–B2.
3. Isabel Briggs Myers, "Introduction to Type," (Palo Alto, CA: Consulting Psychologists Press, 1980). The material in this section follows Myers's paper.

* Based on Aletha S. Hendrickson, "How to Appear Reliable Without Being Liable: CPA Writing in its Rhetorical Context," *Worlds of Writing: Teaching and Learning in Different Discourse Communities,* ed. Carolyn Mataline (New York: Random House, forthcoming 1988).

EXERCISES AND PROBLEMS FOR CHAPTER 6

6–1 IDENTIFYING PRIMARY, SECONDARY, AND IMMEDIATE AUDIENCES

In each of the following situations, label the primary, secondary, and immediate audiences.

Eric owns a company that cleans homes and offices. He's just bought new machinery that cleans much faster and more thoroughly than typical home cleaning appliances. He writes a press release about the new machines to send to the local paper, where he hopes it will be run as a news story in the Home section. If this story is run, it will cost him nothing and be more credible than a paid ad.

Tanya works for the Revenue Department of a major city. The city has an income tax, but residents are not required to file city tax forms. Her boss, the Director of the Revenue Department, asks her to calculate how much revenue the city would gain if tax filing were mandatory, and also to calculate the financial cost of printing tax forms and hiring staff to process them. The members of the city council will vote on whether filing should be mandatory. Before they vote, council members will hear from (1) citizens, who will have an opportunity to read the report and communicate their opinions to the city council; (2) Directors of Revenue Departments in other cities, who may be asked about their experiences; (3) consultants who will be asked both to evaluate Tanya's findings and to decide whether the ill will that mandatory filing would produce will hurt the mayor and council members politically.

Carol is a college professor applying for a National Science Foundation (NSF) grant to fund research she wants to do. The director of NSF Grant Funding reads all proposals to determine that they fit the agency's criteria and then funnels them to experts for opinions. Next, two experts will read her proposal, summarize it for the full committee, and rank it against the other proposals they have read. Finally, the selection committee will vote on which proposals to fund and whether to fund them fully or at a reduced rate.

6–2 CHANGING THE LOAN PERIOD FOR LIBRARY BOOKS

Assume that your school's library is considering shortening the loan period for undergraduates by one week. For example, if books may currently be checked out for three weeks, under the new plan they could be checked out for only two weeks. Loan periods for graduate students and for faculty would not be changed. According to an article published in a national library journal, books are rarely returned before the due date, but the rate of renewal is independent of the loan period. That is, shortening the loan period does not increase the percentage of books renewed.

Proponents of the plan argue that shorter loan periods would make books more accessible to students and patrons (and perhaps reduce the need for as many multiple copies of books in great demand). Since fines are charged if books are neither brought back nor renewed, it is possible that the new system would also generate more income for the library. Opponents argue that the system would simply make more work for library clerks. Indeed, it is possible that at least one extra clerk would need to be hired, which would more than offset any income from fines.

Identify the major advantage and the major disadvantage of the proposal for each of the following groups:

1. Freshmen and sophomores (who take only a few classes which require library research).
2. Juniors and seniors (who are more likely to be in classes which require library research).
3. Library clerks (who check books in and out and shelve them).
4. Library supervisors (who supervise clerks and answer questions about the availability of books).
5. Library administrators (who make out the budget and who are responsible for the overall usability of the library).
6. Faculty (who assign research papers, but who also use books for their own teaching and research).

Which of the groups would be the easiest to convince? Which would be hardest? Do you think this proposal could be accepted on your campus? Why or why not?

6–3 PERSUADING AN ORGANIZATION TO RECYCLE ITS PAPER

In spite of the telephone and electronic mail, the volume of paper used in business, government, education, and nonprofit organizations is enormous. Assume that you want to urge the organization you work for to reduce its use of new paper. That might include using paper on both sides, using the back of paper printed on just one side for scratch paper rather than buying pads of paper, having recycling bins to collect waste paper, and buying recycled rather than new paper.

Every ton of paper recycled saves 17 trees. Paper that has been shredded to protect confidentiality of ideas can be recycled too. However, it is cheaper to produce new paper than to recycle it. Everyone sells new paper; recycled paper may have to be specially ordered. Using less paper to start with certainly cuts the amount an organization spends for paper. If everyone in a city used less paper, the cost of trash pickup might drop, since there would be less solid waste to put in landfills. However, this saving would not occur unless recycling became widespread.

Identify the major benefit and the major objection to reducing paper use for each of the following organizations:

1. A manufacturing company that is barely making a profit.
2. A lumber company.
3. The U.S. Department of Forestry.
4. City officials, in a city that provides trash pickup funded by taxes.
5. A successful insurance company.
6. Your community college, college, or university.

6–4 ANALYZING THE OTHER STUDENTS IN YOUR COLLEGE

Present an analysis of the students in your college. (If the college is large, analyze the students in your major program of study.) Is there a typical student? Or are all of you quite different? Consider the following kinds of information in your analysis:

Demographic Data

Age (Average; high and low)

Sex (What proportion are men? What proportion are women?)

Race or ethnic backgrounds (What groups are represented? How many of each?)

Marital status

Number of children

Parents' income

Personal or family income

Full- or part-time

Outside jobs

Membership in campus organizations

Religious affiliations

Political preferences

Proportion going on for further education after graduation

Psychographic Data

What values, beliefs, goals, and lifestyles do students have? Which are common? Which are less common?

What do students hope to gain from the classes they're taking? What motivates them to do their best work in classes?

Additional Information

What are students' attitudes toward current campus problems? current political problems?

What is the job market like for students in your college or major? Will students find it easy to get jobs after graduation? How much will they be making? Where will they be working?

As your instructor directs,

a. Present your information orally to the class.
b. Keep notes of your answers as background for problems 6–5 and 17–4.
c. Report your results in an informal report to your instructor.

6–5 CHOOSING RELEVANT PORTIONS OF AN AUDIENCE ANALYSIS

Using your analysis from problem 6–4, identify the factors which would be most relevant in each of the following situations:

a. You want to persuade your classmates to donate money for a class gift to the college or university (see problem 17–4).
b. You want to find out if there are enough parking spaces on campus.
c. You want to know if the campus placement office is providing adequate services to students.
d. You want to hire students to staff a business that you're starting.
e. You want to recruit students to volunteer for a Big Brother/Big Sister program with children from local schools (see problem C-3).

6–6 ANALYZING YOUR INSTRUCTOR

Identify the information about your instructor that you could use to prepare a message for each of the following situations:

a. Your instructor is moving to a new town and is choosing a moving company (see problem 15–8).

What other family members would be involved in the move?

What possessions might be difficult to move? Which may be especially important to your instructor?

b. The class is full, and you want to persuade the instructor to let you in anyway (see problem 14–4).

Should you show how much you need the class or how good a student you are? What appeals might convince your instructor?

c. You plan to ask your instructor to write a letter of recommendation for you for a job or for further schooling.

6–7 ANALYZING EMPLOYEES IN A PLACE YOU'VE WORKED

Assume that a place where you've worked is planning to start a suggestion system (see problem 12–3). Answer the following questions about the hourly employees there:

1. Which categories of employees are paid by the hour? What are their job titles? What exactly do they do?

2. What are their ages? How much education do they have? Is this a temporary job for most while they're in school, or is it a permanent career? Is it realistic for hourly employees to hope to move into management?

3. What hassles do they encounter in their daily work? What could be done to alleviate one or more of those hassles? If things were better, how would their work lives be easier or more pleasant?

4. Is the pay good? Is the amount of the bonus for a suggestion likely to be much of an incentive? Is it reasonable to think that general money-saving plans will help all employees, or will they just help management? If service to customers or clients improves, will employees benefit directly?

5. How competitive is the job market? Could the employees easily get jobs elsewhere? How long have they worked at this company, on the average? How much loyalty do they have to this particular organization?

6. How competitive is the economic market? Is this company doing well financially? Can its customers or clients easily go somewhere else? Is it a government agency dependent on tax dollars for fundings?

7. Has management treated hourly people well in the past? Or have hourly people been talked down to?

8. Do most of the hourly people know each other? Or do differences in location and shifts separate people?

Building Goodwill

QUESTIONS

- Why is goodwill important in business and administrative communication?
- Does you-attitude mean using the word *you*?
- How can you emphasize positive points? Is it ever better to be negative?
- How do you project success consciousness?
- What are the characteristics of good reader benefits?
- Why are intrinsic benefits better than extrinsic benefits?
- How do you think of reader benefits and develop them?
- Why do reader benefits work?

A guest at a dinner given in honor of Marshal Foch in Denver, Colorado, said that there was nothing but wind in French politeness. Marshal Foch retorted: "Neither is there anything but wind in a pneumatic tire, yet it eases wonderfully the jolts in life's highway."

Marshal Ferdinand Foch
1921

P oliteness and goodwill help to ease the jolts of working in business or administration. You-attitude, positive emphasis, success consciousness, and reader benefits are four ways to help build goodwill. Writing that shows **you-attitude** seems to speak from the reader's point of view, not selfishly from the writer's. **Positive emphasis** means focusing on the positive rather than the negative aspects of a situation. **Success consciousness** allows you to project a tone of confidence in yourself, your products and services, and your organization. **Reader benefits** are benefits or advantages that the reader gets by using the writer's services, buying the writer's products, following the writer's policies, or adopting the writer's ideas. Reader benefits can exist for policies and ideas as well as for goods and services.

You-attitude, positive emphasis, and success consciousness are primarily matters of style: they affect how you present your ideas without making major changes in content. Reader benefits are matters of content, not style. You write or talk about reader benefits using you-attitude and positive emphasis. All four help you achieve your purposes and make your messages friendlier, more persuasive, and more humane. They suggest that you care not just about money but about your readers and their needs and interests.

YOU-ATTITUDE

According to Professor Francis W. Weeks, Executive Director Emeritus of the Association for Business Communication, the most prevalent problem in business communication is that writers think only of themselves and their problems, not about the reader. Putting what you want to say in you-attitude is a crucial step both in thinking about the reader's needs and in communicating your concern to the reader.

How to Create You-Attitude

You-attitude is a style of writing which looks at things from the reader's point of view, emphasizing what the reader wants to know, respecting the reader's intelligence, and protecting the reader's ego.

To apply you-attitude, use the following five principles:

1. Focus on what the reader receives or can do. In positive or neutral situations, stress what the reader wants to know.
2. Refer to the reader's request or order specifically.
3. Don't talk about your own feelings unless you're sure the reader wants to know how you feel.

4. Don't presume that you know how the reader feels or will react.

5. In negative situations, avoid the word *you*. Protect the reader's ego. Use impersonal expressions and passive verbs to avoid assigning blame.

Let's look at each of these in more detail. Note that many of the you-attitude revisions are *longer* than the sentences lacking you-attitude. You-attitude sentences have *more information,* so they are often longer. They are not wordy. **Wordiness** means having more words than the meaning requires. We can add information and still keep the writing tight.

1. Focus on What the Reader Receives or Can Do. In Positive or Neutral Situations, Stress What the Reader Wants to Know. The reader isn't interested in what you've done; instead, readers want to know how they benefit or are affected. When you provide this information, you make your message more complete and more interesting.

Not you-attitude:	I have negotiated an agreement with Apex Rent-a-Car that gives you a discount on rental cars.
You-attitude:	As a Sunstrand employee you can now get a 20% discount when you rent a car from Apex.
Not you-attitude:	We are shipping your order of September 21 this afternoon.
You-attitude:	The two dozen Corning Ware starter sets you ordered will be shipped this afternoon and should reach you by September 28.

The reader is less interested in when we shipped the order than in when it will arrive. Note the phrase *should reach you by* leaves some room for variations in delivery schedules. If you can't be that exact, give your reader the information you do have: "UPS shipment from California to Texas normally takes three days." If you have absolutely no idea, at least give the reader the name of the carrier, so the reader knows whom to contact if the order doesn't arrive promptly.

In many messages, you will need to talk about what you and your organization are doing or need. Too many *I*'s are a danger sign, however. One expert suggests using at least four *you*'s for every *I*.[1] The word *we* is OK if it includes the reader (as it will in an internal memo). *We* can be a danger sign if it excludes the reader (as it would in a letter to a customer or supplier).

The word *you* is both singular and plural; it can mean a single reader or a whole group of readers.

2. Refer to the Reader's Request or Order Specifically. When you write about the reader's request, order, or policy, you probably have it in front of you, so refer to it specifically, not as a generic *your order* or *your policy*. If your reader is an individual or a small business, it's friendly to specify the content of the order; if you're writing to a company with which you do a great deal of business, give the invoice or purchase order number. The phrase *your IBM PC* is fine for an individual ordering one computer by direct mail; it would

Goodwill in International Business*
In the United States, goodwill is useful. In international business, it's crucial.

In Latin American and Arab countries, people want to establish a friendly relationship before they talk about business.

The Japanese tend to work *only* with people they like. But Japanese firms are loyal to their friends. Once they have accepted a company as a supplier, Japanese firms won't end the relationship just because someone else comes in with a better deal.

* Based on "Managing the Overseas Assignment," Going International Film II, Copeland Griggs Productions; Oliver C. S. Tzeng, "The Use of the Atlas of Affective Meanings in Intercultural Training," *Handbook of Intercultural Training,* ed. Dan Landis and Richard W. Brislin (New York: Pergamon Press, 1983), 242; Kathryn Fenich, "Why Culture Should Be the Key Factor in Studying Marketing in Japan," Sixth Annual Conference on Languages and Communication for World Business and the Professions, Ann Arbor, MI, May 7–9, 1987.

You-Attitude with International Audiences

When you communicate with international audiences, look at the world from their point of view.

The United States is in the middle of most of the maps sold in the United States. It isn't in the middle of maps sold elsewhere in the world.

The United States clings to a measurement system that has been abandoned by most of the world. When you write for international audiences, use the metric system.

Even pronouns and direction words need attention. *We* may not feel inclusive to readers with different assumptions and backgrounds. *Here* won't mean the same thing to a reader in Bonn as it does to one in Boulder.

be hopelessly vague in a letter to Computerland about a shipment of 100 computers.

Not you-attitude:	Your order . . .
You-attitude (to individual):	The desk chair you ordered . . .
You-attitude (to large store):	Your invoice #783329 . . .

3. Don't Talk about Your Own Feelings Unless You Know the Reader Wants to Know How You Feel. In most business situations, your feelings are irrelevant and should be omitted.

| Not you-attitude: | We are happy to extend you a credit line of $5,000. |
| You-attitude: | You can now charge up to $5,000 on your American Express card. |

The reader doesn't care whether you're happy to grant credit, bored stiff at granting a routine application, or worried about granting so much to someone who barely qualifies. All the reader cares about is the situation from his or her point of view.

It *is* appropriate to talk about your own emotions in a letter of congratulation or condolence.

| You-attitude: | I was really pleased to read that you've been named district manager. |

In internal memos, it may be appropriate to comment that a project has been gratifying or frustrating. In the letter of transmittal that accompanies a report it is permissible to talk about your feelings about doing the work. But even other readers in your own organization are primarily interested in their own concerns, not in your feelings.

4. Don't Presume That You Know How the Reader Feels or Will React. It's distancing to have someone else presume that he or she knows how we feel—especially if the writer is wrong. Avoid statements about the reader's feelings or reactions.

| Not you-attitude: | You'll be happy to hear that Open Grip Walkway Channels meet OSHA requirements. |
| You-attitude: | Open Grip Walkway Channels meet OSHA requirements. |

Maybe the reader expects that anything you sell would meet government regulations (OSHA—the Occupational Safety and Health Administration—is a federal agency). The reader may even be disappointed if he or she expected higher standards. Simply explain the situation or describe a product's features; don't predict the reader's response.

When you have good news for the reader, simply give the good news.

| Not you-attitude: | You'll be happy to hear that your scholarship has been renewed. |
| You-attitude: | Congratulations! Your scholarship has been renewed. |

5. In Negative Situations, Avoid the Word *You*. Protect the Reader's Ego. Use Impersonal Expressions and Passive Verbs to Avoid Assigning Blame. You-attitude is not simply a matter of using the word *you* rather than *I*. Indeed, using the word *you* in negative situations will attack or insult the reader. Avoid the word *you* in negative situations. One alternative is to use a noun for a group of which the reader is a part instead of *you* so readers don't feel that they're singled out for bad news.

Not you-attitude: | You | must get approval from the Director | before you | publish any articles or memoirs based on | your work | in the agency.

You-attitude: Agency personnel must get approval from the Director to publish any articles or memoirs based on their work at the agency.

Two more strategies are to use passive verbs and impersonal expressions to avoid blaming the reader. **Passive verbs** describe the action performed on something, without necessarily saying who did it. (See Chapter 9 for a full discussion of passive verbs.) **Impersonal constructions** omit people and talk only about things.

In most cases, active verbs are better. But when your reader is at fault, passive verbs may be useful. If you accuse your reader of making an error, the reader's energy goes into defending him- or herself, by trying to excuse or justify the mistake. Energy spent on ego-defense is energy that could better be spent rectifying the error.

Normally, writing is most lively when it's about people—and most interesting to readers when it's about them. When you have to report a mistake or bad news, however, you can protect the reader's ego by using an impersonal construction, one in which things, not people, do the acting.

Not you-attitude: | You made no allowance | for inflation in | your | estimate.

You-attitude (passive): No allowance for inflation has been made in this estimate.

You-attitude (impersonal): This estimate makes no allowance for inflation.

A purist might say that impersonal constructions are illogical: an estimate, for example, is inanimate and can't "make" anything. In the pragmatic world of business writing, however, impersonal constructions often help you convey criticism tactfully.

You-Attitude Beyond the Sentence Level

Good messages apply you-attitude beyond the sentence level by using organization and content as well as style to build goodwill. Consider the letter in Figure 7.1.

As the marginal notes indicate, many individual sentences in this letter lack you-attitude. The last sentence in paragraph 1 sounds both harsh and defensive; the close is selfish. The language is stiff and filled with outdated jargon. Perhaps

---

Truth Can Be Spoken in Different Ways*

One Iranian told a fable of an ancient king who had an ominous dream. In the dream the king saw himself aged and afflicted, with decaying and falling teeth. Calling together his court astrologers for an interpretation, the shaken king heard the first say, "Your Majesty, I regret to tell you that the interpretation must be bad. The dream means that you will die within a year." In a rage the king threw the astrologer out of his court and turned to the second man.

The second astrologer said, "Your Majesty, it is good news, the very best. It means that all your programs and projects will live on after you, and all your sons and daughters will survive you." The king, who was old and knew he might die soon, nevertheless was pleased with this interpretation and richly rewarded the astrologer.

---

* Quoted from John P. Fieg and John G. Blair, *There Is a Difference: 12 Intercultural Perspectives* (Washington, DC: Meridian House International, 1975), 83.

FIGURE 7.1
A LETTER LACKING YOU-ATTITUDE

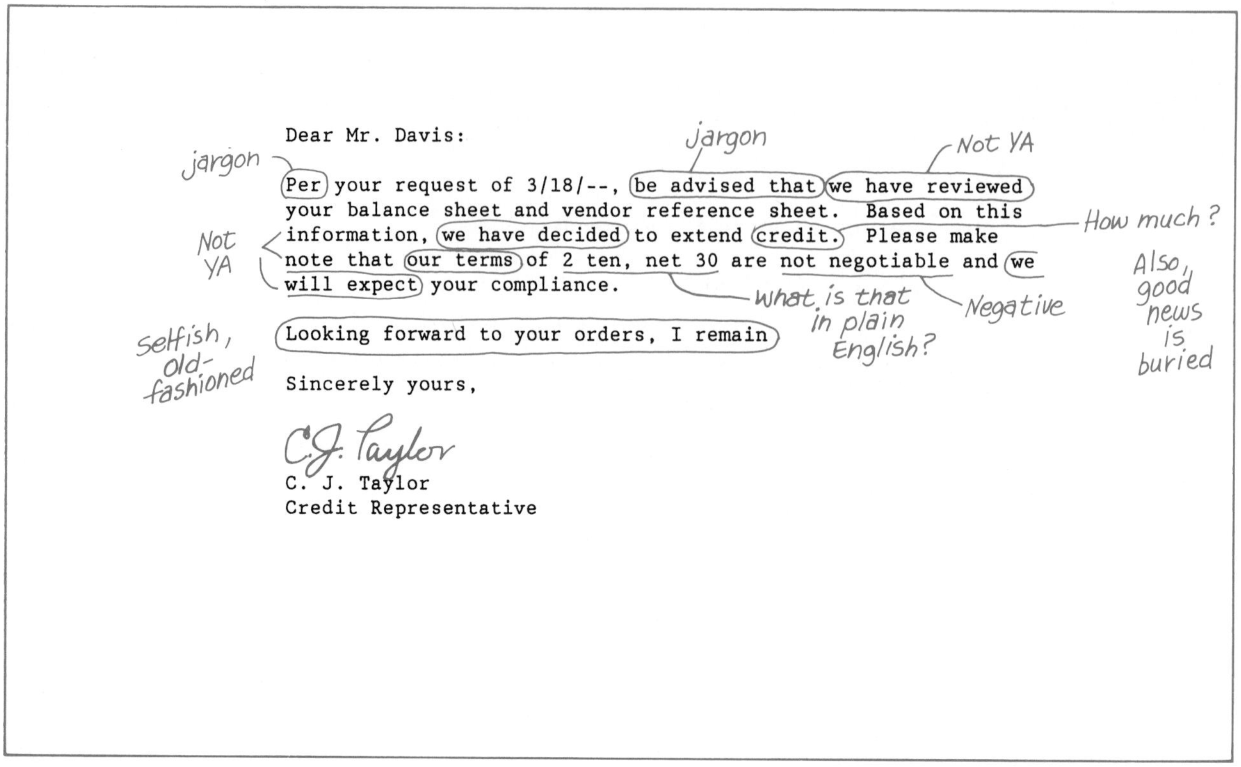

Dear Mr. Davis:

jargon — (Per) your request of 3/18/--, (be advised that)(we have reviewed) *Not YA* / *Jargon*

your balance sheet and vendor reference sheet. Based on this

Not YA < information, (we have decided) to extend (credit.) Please make — *How much?*

note that (our terms) of 2 ten, net 30 are not negotiable and (we   *Also,*

will expect) your compliance.   *good*

what is that   Negative   *news*

selfish,   (Looking forward to your orders, I remain)   *in plain   is*

old-   *English?   buried*

fashioned

Sincerely yours,

C. J. Taylor

C. J. Taylor
Credit Representative

the most serious problem is that the most important sentence in the letter from the reader's point of view is buried in the middle of the first paragraph. Since we have good news for the reader, we should put that information first.

Fixing individual sentences could improve the letter. However, it really needs to be totally rewritten. Figure 7.2 shows a possible revision.

The revision starts with good news and specifies the amount of credit. Using the company's name makes the letter more specific and builds goodwill by linking the company name to the good news. The negative statement about bills is put in the middle paragraph. The phrasing is changed to put "2 ten, net 30" in everyday language; the 2% savings is presented as a benefit, a point which was lost in the original. Instead of a selfish close, the last paragraph focuses on benefits to the reader.

POSITIVE EMPHASIS

Few things are perfect. If you emphasize the negative, however, you may suggest that things are worse than they really are. Since negative ideas often cause readers to feel less positively about the source of those ideas, it's to your advantage to eliminate unnecessary negatives.

On occasion, you will have unrelieved bad news to give the reader—refusals, rejections, announcements of product defects and recalls, price increases, reprimands, etc. In Chapter 13 you'll learn how to convey this negative information while retaining as much goodwill as possible. The techniques in this chapter are more general and can be used in almost every kind of message.

FIGURE 7.2
A LETTER REVISED USING YOU-ATTITUDE

Dear Mr. Davis:

Yes, you can have a credit line of $10,000 with Mercury
Electronics.

Bills are due within 30 days of invoices; you can save 2% by
paying within ten days.

Whether you need standard boards or custom-designed wiring, at
Mercury you can get the high-quality parts you need to make the
products your customers want.

Sincerely,

C. J. Taylor

C. J. Taylor
Credit Representative

Handwritten annotations:
- Specific
- Good News in #1
- Company name
- "2 10, net 30"
- Presented as benefit
- in plain English
- Last ¶ written from reader's point of view

How to Create Positive Emphasis

You can deemphasize negative information by using the following five techniques:

1. Eliminate negative words and words with negative connotations.
2. State information positively. Focus on what the reader can do rather than on what you won't or can't let the reader do.
3. Justify negative information by giving a reason or linking it to a reader benefit.
4. If the negative is truly unimportant, omit it.
5. Bury the negative information and present it compactly.

Now, let's see how to apply each of these principles.

1. Eliminate Negative Words and Words with Negative Connotations. Negative words include the following:

afraid	error	lacking	trivial
anxious	except	loss	trouble
avoid	fail	some *mis-*	wait
bad	fault	words:	weakness
careless	fear	misfortune	worry
damage	hesitate	mistake	wrong

Can You Ever Be Negative?

Are there times when you shouldn't hide the bad news?

Yes, if people need the information so they can correct dangerous practices. Auditors, fire safety inspectors, and food safety inspectors have a responsibility to the public.

Yes, if your purpose is to deliver a rebuke with no alternative. If you're fining a company for violating a law or firing an employee for embezzlement, you may have no reason to use positive emphasis. Even here, however, avoid insults or global attacks on the reader's integrity or sanity.

Probably, if deemphasizing the negative may backfire. When car manufacturers made previously optional equipment standard and claimed that prices had only risen 2% on 1988 cars, car buyers weren't fooled. The cheapest cars available in 1988 were 7 to 10% more expensive than the cheapest cars in 1987.

Maybe, if emphasizing the negative will create a "reverse psychology" which makes people look favorably at your product. Rent-a-Wreck is thriving. (The cars really don't look so bad.) Irv's Menswear in Chicago advertises that it is "inconveniently located at _____." The listener perks up, recognizes the address, and says, "That's not so bad."

Some advertisers feel that negatives get more attention since most ads are stuffed with superlatives. But some negative ads have bombed. It's still safer to be positive.

delay	ignore	missing	many *un-*
delinquent	ignorant	neglect	words:
deny	impossible	never	unclear
difficulty	many *in-*	no	unfair
some *dis-*	words:	not	unfortunate
words:	inadequate	objection	unfortunately
disapprove	incomplete	problem	unpleasant
dishonest	inconvenient	reject	unreasonable
dissatisfied	insincere	sorry	unreliable
eliminate	injury	terrible	unsure

When you find one of these words in a draft, try to substitute a more positive word. When you must use a negative, use the *least negative* term that will convey your meaning.

Negative: We have ⬚failed⬚ to finish taking inventory.

Better: We have⬚n't⬚ finished taking inventory.

Still better: We will be finished taking inventory Friday.

If a sentence has two negatives, substitute one positive term.

Negative: ⬚Until⬚ these invoices are paid, your account will be considered ⬚delinquent.⬚

Better: As of March 15, 1989, these invoices are still open on your account.

Getting rid of negatives has the added benefit of making what you write easier to understand. Sentences with three or more negatives are very hard to understand.[2]

Beware of **hidden negatives**: words that are not negative in themselves, but become negative in context. *But* and *however* indicate a shift, so, after a positive statement, they are negative. *Patience* may sound like a virtue, but it is a necessary virtue only when things are slow. Even positives about a service or product may backfire if they suggest that in the past the service or product was bad.

Negative: Please be ⬚patient⬚ as we switch to the automated system.

[Implication: you can expect problems.]

Better: If you have ⬚questions⬚ during our ⬚transition⬚ to the automated system, call Melissa Morgan.

Still better: You'll be able to get information instantly about any house on the market when the automated system is in place. If you have questions during the transition, call Melissa Morgan.

Negative: Now Crispy Crunch tastes ⬚better⬚.

[Implication: it used to taste terrible.]

Better: Now Crispy Crunch tastes even better.

When you eliminate negative words, be sure to maintain accuracy. Words that are exact opposites will usually not be accurate. Instead, use specifics to be both positive and accurate.

Negative:	The exercycle is $\boxed{\text{not}}$ guaranteed for life.
Not true:	The exercycle is guaranteed for life.
True:	The exercycle is guaranteed for 10 years.

Legal phrases also have negative connotations for most readers and should be avoided whenever possible. The idea will sound more positive if you use normal English rather than legalese.

2. State Information Positively. Focus on What the Reader Can Do Rather Than on What You Won't or Can't Let the Reader Do. Sometimes positive emphasis is a matter of the way you present something: Is the glass half empty or half full? Sometimes it's a matter of eliminating double negatives. When there are limits, or some options are closed, focus on the good that remains.

Negative:	You will $\boxed{\text{not}}$ get your refund $\boxed{\text{for at least}}$ four weeks.
Better:	Your refund will arrive in four to six weeks.

Negative:	We will $\boxed{\text{not}}$ allow you to charge $\boxed{\text{more than \$1,500}}$ on your VISA account.
Better:	You can charge $1,500 on your new VISA card.
or:	Your new VISA card gives you $1,500 in credit that you can use at thousands of stores nationwide.

As you focus on what will happen, **check for you-attitude**, too. In the last example, "We will allow you to charge $1,500" would be positive, but it lacks you-attitude.

When you have a benefit and a requirement the reader must meet to get the benefit, the sentence is usually more positive if you put the benefit first.

Negative:	You will $\boxed{\text{not}}$ qualify for the student membership rate of $25 a year $\boxed{\text{unless}}$ you are a full-time student.
Better:	You get all the benefits of membership for only $25 a year if you're a full-time student.

3. Justify Negative Information by Giving a Reason or Linking It to a Reader Benefit. A reason can help your reader see that the information is necessary; a benefit can suggest that the negative aspect is outweighed by positive factors. Be careful, however, to make the logic behind your reason clear and to leave no loopholes.

Negative:	We $\boxed{\text{cannot}}$ ship in lots of less than 10.
Loophole:	To keep down packaging costs and to help you save on shipping costs, we ship in lots of 10 or more.

The Ethics of Positive Emphasis*

Deemphasizing negatives may be ethically suspect.

GM announced its recall of all 125,000 1984 Pontiac Fieros sold in the United States at 4:31 P.M. the day before Thanksgiving. The sixth paragraph out of 10 announced a second problem, separate from the defect that caused the recall: catastrophic engine failure. Both timing and layout buried the negatives. But GM's credibility slipped further.

Company annual reports bury or omit bad news, even when high return rates or high-risk investments may be "material facts" that affect the value of the company's stock. The reports are positive, but they lack credibility.

South Africa chose a positive label for the rural areas to which Blacks were exiled: *Homelands*. The word connotes a green paradise, the ancestral home of family and friends. The reality: arid, barren land, far from employment. The areas are hardly ancestral homelands; most of the areas were empty before the government rounded up Blacks and trucked them in. The label creates a positive picture only until one reads about the areas. Then, the positive emphasis backfires, further undermining the South African government's credibility.

The fact that positive emphasis tries to shape the audience's response is not in itself bad. Persuasion is a neutral tool. But all of us who use language have a responsibility to examine the implications of the words we use and the values we're promoting. Some negatives may be too important to deemphasize.

---

* Based on Paul Ingrassia, "GM 'Quality' Can Be Hazardous to Your Health," *The Wall Street Journal*, December 2, 1987, 24, and Roger Thurow, "The Dispossessed: Far from the Unrest, South African Blacks in Rural Areas Suffer," *The Wall Street Journal*, January 21, 1988, 1, 25.

Suppose the customer says, "I'll pay the extra shipping cost. Send me seven." If you can't or won't ship in lots of less than 10, you need to write:

Better: To keep down packaging costs and to help customers save on shipping costs, we ship only in lots of 10 or more.

If you link the negative element to a benefit, be sure that it is a benefit which the reader will acknowledge. Avoid telling people that you're doing things "for their own good." They may have a different notion of what their own good is. You may think you're doing customers a favor by limiting their credit so they don't get in over their heads and go bankrupt. They may feel they'd be better off with more credit so they could expand in hopes of making more sales and more profits.

4. If the Negative is Truly Unimportant, Omit It. Omitting negative information is an easy way to avoid upsetting the reader, and some writers overdo it. Omit negatives entirely only when

- The reader does not need the information to make a decision.
- You have already given the reader the information and he or she has access to the previous communication.
- The information is trivial.

The following examples suggest the kind of negatives you can omit:

Negative: A one-year subscription to *PC Magazine* is $29.97. That rate is not as low as the rates charged for some magazines.

Better: A one-year subscription to *PC Magazine* is $29.97.

Still better: A one-year subscription to *PC Magazine* is $29.97. You save 54% off the newstand price of $64.90.

Negative: If you are not satisfied with Interstate Fidelity Insurance, you do not have to renew your policy.

Better: Omit the sentence.

5. Bury the Negative Information and Present It Compactly. The beginning and end are always positions of emphasis. Use these positions for ideas you want to emphasize. Put negatives in the middle of a paragraph rather than in the first or last sentence, in the middle of the message rather than in the first or last paragraphs.

When a letter or memo runs several pages, remember that the bottom of the first page is also a position of emphasis, even if it is in the middle of a paragraph, because of the extra white space of the bottom margin. (The first page gets more attention since it is on top and the reader's eye may catch lines of the message even when he or she isn't consciously reading it; the tops and bottoms of subsequent pages don't get this extra attention.) If possible, avoid placing negative information at the bottom of the first page.

Giving a topic lots of space emphasizes it. Therefore, you can deemphasize negative information by giving it as little space as possible. Give negative information only once in your message. Don't list negatives vertically on the page since lists take space and emphasize material.

---

* Quoted from Clare Ansberry, "Forgive or Forget: Firms Face Decision Whether to Apologize for Their Mistakes," *The Wall Street Journal*, November 24, 1987, 29.

Apologies

When you are at fault, you may build goodwill by admitting that fact forthrightly. Apologies are a special kind of negative and call for slightly different rules.

- No explicit apology is necessary if the error is small and if you are correcting the mistake.

Negative: I'm sorry the clerk did not credit your account properly.

Better: Your statement has been corrected to include your payment of $263.75.

- Do not apologize when you are not at fault.

  When you have done everything you can, and when a delay or problem is due to circumstances beyond your control, you aren't at fault and don't need to apologize. It may be appropriate to include an explanation so the reader knows you weren't negligent. If the news is bad, put the explanation first. If you have good news for the reader, put it before your explanation.

Negative: I'm sorry that I could not answer your question sooner. I had to wait until the sales figures for the second quarter were in.

Better: (neutral or bad news)   We needed the sales figures for the second quarter to answer your question. Now that they're in, I can tell you that . . .

Better: (good news)   The new advertising campaign is a success. The sales figures for the second quarter are finally in, and they show that . . .

If the delay or problem is long or large, it certainly is good you-attitude to ask the reader whether he or she wants to confirm the original plan or make different arrangements.

Negative: I'm sorry that the chairs will not be ready by August 25 as promised.

Better: Due to a strike against the manufacturer, the desk chairs you ordered will not be ready until November. Do you want to keep that order, or would you like to look at the models available from other suppliers?

- When you apologize, do it early and briefly.

  Apologize only once, early in the message: let the reader move on to other, more positive information.

  Even if major trouble or inconvenience has resulted from your error, you don't need to go on about all the horrible things that happened. The reader already knows this negative information, and you can omit it. Instead, focus on what you have done to correct the situation.

You Can If You Think You Can*

Texas Instruments proved that success consciousness works. One group of new employees received conventional training. Members of the second group had, in addition to the conventional training, a one-day anxiety-reduction workshop which emphasized these points:

"Your opportunity to succeed is very good." Trainees were told five or six times during the day that all of them could expect to succeed.

"Disregard 'hall talk.'" Trainees were told that old-timers might try to scare them about how tough the job was and how many people failed. So they could spot distortions, trainees were told both the good and the bad aspects of the job and exactly what was expected of them.

"Take the initiative in communication." Trainees were assured that they weren't expected to know everything; it was OK to ask lots of questions. Trainees were also told the absolute truth about the supervisor's personality, so they'd be better able to interpret signals.

The results? The group that attended the anxiety-reduction workshop was at full production twice as quickly as the standard group. Absenteeism and tardiness dropped to half the previous level. Waste and rejects were cut by four-fifths. And costs went down 15% to 30%.

Telling people they'll succeed and giving them the tools to succeed pays off for the company, too.

---

* Based on Earl R. Gomersall and M. Scott Myers, "Breakthrough in On-the-Job Training," *Harvard Business Review* 44, no. 4 (1966): 62–72.

Different Benefits for Different
Audiences*

French women drink mineral water
because it helps keep them svelte.
Germans drink mineral water because it is thought healthful for internal organs; it is a curative and
preventative home-remedy product.

Floride toothpaste sells for its de-
cay prevention benefits in Germany,
Holland, and Denmark with the
basic U.S. marketing and advertising
strategy; but in England, France,
and Italy, the cosmetic claims for
toothpaste are more important, and
the U.S. strategy does not work.

Volvo . . . has emphasized economy, durability, and safety in
America; status and leisure in
France; performance in Germany;
and safety in Switzerland. Price is
considered to be a critical variable
in Mexican consumers, but quality
is of more importance to Venezue-
lans.

Closing [a $100,000 life insur-
ance sale to a Chinese-American,
the sales rep] stressed that Met Life
was a venerable 119 years old—a
standard pitch to Chinese-Ameri-
cans. . . . It probably worked better
than Snoopy, the "Peanuts" character used in the insurer's mainstream
ads. Says Ruben Lopez, Met Life's
marketing director for special projects, "The Chinese aren't going to
buy life insurance from a dog."

If you don't know whether or not any inconvenience has resulted,
don't raise the issue at all.

Negative: I'm sorry I didn't answer your letter sooner. I hope that my
             delay hasn't inconvenienced you.

Better: I'm sorry I didn't answer your letter sooner.

SUCCESS CONSCIOUSNESS

The reader's evaluation of the information or services you offer is unlikely to
be higher than the evaluation your own words imply. Just as a successful sales
representative projects a sense of confidence in the products he or she offers,
so a successful writer will use words which assume success and not failure.

To develop success-consciousness in your writing,

- Eliminate words that express doubt. *I hope* and *I trust that* show
  that you aren't sure.
- Eliminate words that imply that the reader may not be satisfied.
- Eliminate words that suggest you may not have expressed yourself
  clearly or convincingly.

Doubtful: We hope you are satisfied with Quill's quality merchandise
             and "we care" service.

Confident: You get quality merchandise and "we care" service from
             Quill.

Doubtful: This bulletin is intended to explain . . .

Confident: This bulletin explains . . .

Doubtful: If you can't understand this explanation, feel free to call
             me.

Better: If you have further questions, just call me.

Confident: Omit the sentence.

If the reader's request is unclear, tell the reader what is available and ask
what he or she would like you to send.

Doubtful: I hope this is the information you wanted.

Confident: Bulletins are available both on gas and electric heat. Would
             you like me to send both of them to you?

Success consciousness does not mean being arrogant or pushy.

Arrogant: I look forward to receiving all of your future business.

Confident: Call Mercury whenever you need transistors.

Arrogant: You need someone who can recommend the best
             investments for your clients. Here is where I can help
             you.

Confident: My success in classroom cases and in managing my own
             portfolio suggests that I can help your clients find the
             investments that are best for them.

*Quoted from Robert F. Roth, *International Marketing Communications* (Chicago: Crain, 1982),
56, 296–97; David A. Ricks, *Big Business Blunders* (Homewood, IL: Dow Jones-Irwin, 1983),
60; "Tapping into a Blossoming Asian Market," *Newsweek,* September 7, 1987, 47.

READER BENEFITS

Reader benefits are important in both informative and persuasive messages. In informative messages, reader benefits give reasons to comply with the policies you announce and suggest that the policies are good ones. In persuasive messages, reader benefits give reasons to act and help overcome reader resistance.

First we'll learn how to evaluate reader benefits. Then we'll discuss ways to think of reader benefits and develop them effectively.

Characteristics of Good Reader Benefits

Good reader benefits meet the following criteria:

1. They are adapted to the audience.
2. They are based on intrinsic rather than extrinsic advantages.
3. They are supported by clear logic and are explained in adequate detail.
4. They are phrased in you-attitude.

Let's examine each of these.

1. Reader Benefits Must Be Adapted to the Audience. What one reader sees as an advantage may be unimportant to a second reader and a drawback to a third. When you write to different audiences, you may need to stress different reader benefits.

Suppose that you manufacture a product and want to persuade dealers to carry it. The features you may cite in ads directed toward customers—stylish colors, sleek lines, convenience, durability, good price—won't convince dealers. Shelf space is at a premium, and no dealer carries all the models of all the brands available for any given product. Why should the dealer stock your product? To be persuasive, talk about the features that are benefits from the dealer's point of view: turnover, profit margin, the national advertising campaign that will build customer awareness and interest, the special store displays your offer that will draw attention to the product.

Figure 7.3 illustrates a reader benefit adapted to the subscribers of *The Wall Street Journal*. The flyer, which is included with the letter persuading people to renew their subscriptions, offers the $89 cost of the second year as "a 34% tax-free return on your money." The benefit is highly appropriate for an audience concerned about returns on investments and aware of the risk that normally accompanies high returns.

2. Reader Benefits Should Be Based on Intrinsic Rather Than Extrinsic Benefits. **Intrinsic benefits** come automatically from using a product or doing something. **Extrinsic benefits** are "added on." Someone in power decides to give them; they do not necessarily come from using the product or doing the action.

Intrinsic rewards or benefits are better than extrinsic benefits for two reasons:

1. There just aren't enough extrinsic rewards for everything you want people to do. You can't give a "prize" to every customer every time he or she places an order or to every subordinate who does what he or she is supposed to do.
2. Research shows that extrinsic rewards may actually make people *less* satisfied with the products they buy or the procedures they follow.

In a ground-breaking study of professional employees, Frederick Herzberg found that the things people said they liked about their jobs were all *intrinsic*

FIGURE 7.3
A BENEFIT ADAPTED TO THE WALL STREET JOURNAL READERS

WHAT INVESTMENT CAN GUARANTEE YOU A 34% RETURN?

A TWO-YEAR SUBSCRIPTION TO THE WALL STREET JOURNAL.

Look at it this way. A one-year subscription to The Journal is $119. A two-year subscription is $208. That extra $89, you might think, would be better off in your hands for a year than in ours.

Think again. You can, of course, take that $89 and put it in a money-market fund for a year, or in any of a number of other investments. (Check today's Journal for all the latest information.) But if you're in, say, the 28% tax bracket, even an investment paying 10% will only turn your $89 into about $95 a year from now.

Yet, if you invest that $89 in The Journal, that same $89 will grow to be worth at least $119 — what you'll be paying in a year for another one-year subscription to The Journal. **That's a 34% tax-free return on your money.** And, since you know you're going to continue to need The Journal's indispensable daily business coverage, it's an investment that's virtually risk-free.

Make a solid investment decision today: Invest in a two-year subscription to The Wall Street Journal.

Activity	Extrinsic Reward	Intrinsic Reward
Reading a book	Getting a gold star	Learning or entertainment
Making a sale	Getting a commission	Pleasure in convincing someone; pride in using one's talents to think of a strategy and execute it
Turning in a suggestion to a company suggestion system	Getting a monetary reward when the suggestion is implemented	Solving a problem at work; making one's work environment a little more pleasant
Writing a report that solves an organizational problem	Getting praise, a good performance appraisal, and maybe a raise	Pleasure in having an effect on an organization; pride in using one's skills to solve problems; solving the problem itself

FIGURE 7.4
EXTRINSIC AND INTRINSIC REWARDS

rewards—pride in achievement, an enjoyment of the work itself, responsibility. Extrinsic features—pay, company policy—were sometimes mentioned as things people disliked, but they were never cited as things that motivated or satisfied them. People who made a lot of money still did not mention salary as a good point about the job or the organization.[3] More recently, John Weger found that recognition, achievement, and interpersonal relations were the three most important motivators. Salary ranked ninth on the list of motivators for managers, fourth on the list for supervisors.[4]

A number of psychological experiments show that intrinsic rewards (pay, in most of the experiments) actually drive out intrinsic motivation. Subjects who are paid for their performance spend less time on the assigned task and seem less willing to do it than other subjects performing the same tasks without external rewards.[5] The more interesting the task, the more likely this negative correlation is to occur. This research suggests that you'll motivate subordinates more effectively by stressing the intrinsic benefits of following policies and adopting proposals.

3. Reader Benefits Must Be Supported by Clear Logic and Explained in Adequate Detail. A reader benefit is a claim or assertion that the reader will benefit if he or she does something. If readers don't see the connection between their actions and the benefit you promise, or if they don't believe the benefit will occur even if they do act, you've lost them.

Convincing the reader, therefore, involves two steps: making sure that the benefit really will occur, and explaining it to the reader.

If the logic behind a claimed reader benefit is faulty or inaccurate, there's no way to make that particular reader benefit convincing. Revise the benefit to make it logical.

Faulty logic:	Using a computer will enable you to write letters, memos, and reports much more quickly.
Analysis:	If you've never used a computer, in the short run it will take you *longer* to create a document using a computer than it would to type it. Even after you know how to use a computer and its software, the real

Not Everyone Wants to Compete*
[Two Americans in the Philippines set up a croquet game in their front yard and] began to play. Several of their Agta Negrito neighbors became interested and wanted to join the fun. Roy explained the game and started them out, each with a mallet and ball.

As the game progressed, opportunity came for one of the players to take advantage of another by knocking that person's ball out of the court. Roy explained the procedure, but his advice only puzzled his Negrito friend. "Why would I want to knock his ball out of the court?" he asked. "So you can get ahead and finish first," was Roy's reply. "Why would I want to do that?" he asked again. "So you will be the one to win!"

The short-statured man . . . shook his head in bewilderment. Competition is generally ruled out in his hunting and gathering society, where people survive not by competing, but by sharing equally in every activity.

The game continued, but no one followed Roy's advice. When a player successfully got through all the wickets, the game was not over for him. He went back and gave aid and advice to his fellows. As the final player moved toward the last wicket, the affair was still very much a team effort. And finally, when the last wicket was played, the "team" shouted happily, "We won!"

* Quoted from D. Elkins, "We Won," *In Other Words* 4, no. 5 (April 1979): 3.

The Yuppie Transformed*

Yuppie

Young urban professional
Wears Rolex, sign of wealth
Lives together
Drives Volvo (Yuppie status car)
Unbridled ambition
Seen at fancy restaurants
"Because I'm worth it" (L'Oréal)

Post Yuppie

Somewhat older urban professional
Wears Rolex, sign of hard work
Gets married
Drives Volvo (safe car)
Ambition under control
Eats at home
"Because I worked hard"

time savings comes when a document incorporates parts of previous documents or goes through several revisions. Creating a first draft from scratch will still take planning and careful composing; the time savings may or may not be significant.

Revised
reader
benefit:

Using a computer allows you to revise and edit a document more easily. It eliminates retyping as a separate step and reduces the time needed to proofread revisions. It allows you to move the text around on the page to create the best layout.

If the logic is sound, making that logic evident to the reader is a matter of providing enough evidence and showing how the evidence proves the claim that there will be a benefit. How much detail you need depends on the situation and the audience. Always provide enough detail to be vivid and concrete. You'll need more detail when you know

a. The reader may not have thought of the benefit before.
b. The benefit depends on the difference between the long run and the short run.
c. The reader will be hard to persuade, and you will need detail to make the benefit vivid and emotionally convincing.

Does the following statement have enough detail?

You'll save money by using our shop-at-home service.

Readers always believe their own experience. Readers who have never used a shop-at-home service may think, "If somebody else does my shopping for me, I'll have to pay that person. I'll save money by doing it myself." They aren't likely to think that the service might enable them to save money by using your service and not having to pay for gas, car wear and tear, and parking, and by not losing the time it would take to travel to several different stores to get the selection you offer. Readers who already use shop-at-home services may believe you if they compare your items and services with another company's to see that your cost is lower. Even then, you could make saving money seem more forceful and more vivid by telling readers how much they could save and mentioning some of the ways they could use your service.

4. Reader Benefits Must Be Phrased in You-Attitude. If reader benefits aren't in you-attitude, they'll sound selfish and won't be as effective as they could be. A Xerox letter selling copiers with strong you-attitude as well as reader benefits got a far bigger response than did an alternate version with reader benefits but no you-attitude.[6] It doesn't matter how you phrase reader benefits while you're brainstorming and developing them, but in your final draft, check to be sure that you've used you-attitude.

Not you-attitude: We have the lowest prices in town.
You-attitude: At Havlichek Cars, you get the best deal in town.

---

* Quoted from Joanne Lipman, "Played Out: The Going Gets Tough and Madison Avenue Dumps the Yuppies," *The Wall Street Journal*, December 9, 1987, 1.

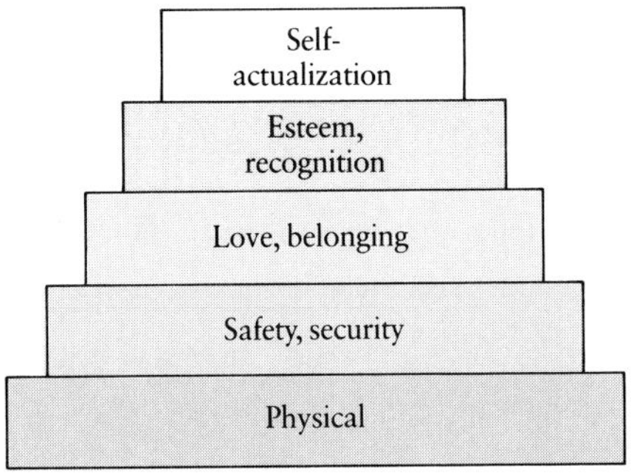

FIGURE 7.5
MASLOW'S HIERARCHY
OF NEEDS

How to Identify and Develop Reader Benefits

Sometimes reader benefits will be easy to think of and to explain; when they are, you don't need to follow any formula at all. But sometimes they may be harder to identify or to develop. When that happens, you may want to use the following steps to identify and then develop good reader benefits:

1. Identify the feelings, fears, and needs that may motivate your reader.
2. Identify the objective features of your product or policy that could meet the needs you've identified.
3. Show how the reader can meet his or her needs with the features of the policy or product.

1. Identify the Feelings, Fears, and Needs That May Motivate Your Reader. One of the best-known analyses of needs is Abraham H. Maslow's hierarchy of needs, illustrated in Figure 7.5.[7] Physiological needs are the most basic, followed by needs for safety and security, for love and belongingness, for esteem and recognition, and finally for self-actualization or self-fulfillment. All of us go back and forth between higher- and lower-level needs. Whenever they make themselves felt, lower-level needs usually take priority. For example, a college student who has been up late studying for a test may find that her physical need for sleep is stronger than her self-actualizing need to learn all that she can about the subject.

Although Maslow's model has not been substantiated in empirical tests,[8] and may not work in other cultures,[9] it is a good starting place to identify the feelings, fears, and needs that may motivate your audience. Daphne Jameson's expansion of the basic Maslow model in Figure 7.6 is a good aid to brainstorming reader benefits. No single product or idea will fulfill every need on this list, but you may be surprised to find how many different needs one product or idea could be used to meet.

2. Identify the Objective Features of Your Product or Policy That Could Meet the Needs You've Identified. Sometimes just listing the reader's needs makes it obvious which feature meets that need. Sometimes several features together meet the need: try to think of all of them.

Suppose that you want to persuade people to come to the restaurant you manage. It's true that everybody needs to eat, but telling people they can satisfy their hunger needs won't persuade them to come to your restaurant rather

FIGURE 7.6
A LIST OF HUMAN MOTIVES

1. **Fear** (of pain, illness, poverty, social pressure, embarrassment, penalties, punishment, etc.).
2. **Pleasure**—desires for
   Travel, getting away from it all, escape from anxiety.
   Freedom to do what you want.
   Fun, excitement, adventure, action.
   Beauty, attractiveness.
   Satisfaction of physiological needs (hunger, sleep, health, etc.).
3. **Ease**—desires for
   Convenience, simplicity.
   Physical and psychological comfort.
   Efficiency.
4. **Security and safety**—desires for
   Good working conditions.
   Good living conditions.
   Satisfactory salary.
   Saving time/money.
   Making money/profit.
   Satisfying curiosity.
   Understanding the reason for something.
   Fair treatment.
   Conserving human and environmental resources.
   Financial protection.
5. **Acceptance**—desires for
   Getting along with family, friends, associates.
   Fair play, cooperation.
   Belonging to groups and having friends.
   Conformity, being "in."
   Sexual attractiveness.
   Emotional rewards—feeling needed and appreciated by others.
   Patriotism, loyalty.
   Humanity, altruism.
   Moral values, religious faith.
   Welfare of a group you identify with (e.g., workers, students, taxpayers, members
     of an organization, people of your age and sex, etc.).
   Being responsible to friends, family, coworkers, clients, the public, future generations.
   Following the lead of authorities or experts or public figures.
6. **Recognition**—desires for
   Public respect, status, prestige.
   Feeling superior or unique or exclusive.
   Being admired, popular.
   Promotion, advancement, attaining power or authority.
   Pride in doing a good job, achievement, mastery.
   Good past reputation (especially important for a company).
   Good quality.
7. **Self-actualization**—desires for
   Self-respect, pride in self.
   Serving humanity.
   Quest for knowledge, creativity.
   Using talents, abilities.
   Getting the most out of life, fulfillment.
   Being the best you can be.

Source: Daphne A. Jameson

than going somewhere else or eating at home. Depending on what features your restaurant offered, you could appeal to one or more of the following subgroups:

Subgroup	Features to Meet the Subgroup's Needs
People who work outside the home	A quick lunch; a relaxing place to take clients or colleagues.
Parents with small children	High chairs, child-size portions, and things to keep the kids entertained while they wait for their order.

Subgroup	Features to Meet the Subgroup's Needs
People who eat out a lot	Variety both in food and in decor.
People on tight budgets	Economical food; a place where they don't need to tip (cafeteria or fast food).
People on special diets	Low-sodium and low-calorie dishes; vegetarian food; kosher food; etc.
People to whom eating out is part of an evening's entertainment	Music or a floor show; elegant surroundings; reservations so they can get to a show or event after dinner; late hours so they can come to dinner after a show or game.

If your restaurant can meet several of these needs, for a single message you'd need to select a **central selling point.** A central selling point is a super reader benefit. It's big enough to motivate readers by itself, but it also serves as an umbrella to cover the other benefits you have and to unify your message.

Once you've chosen a central selling point, think about the details that are part of the benefit. If your selling point is your relaxing atmosphere, think about the specific details that make the restaurant relaxing. If your strong point is elegant dining, think about all the details that contribute to that elegance. Sometimes you may think of features which do not meet any particular need but which are still good benefits. In a sales letter for a restaurant, you might also want to mention the nonsmoking section, your free coatroom, the fact that you're close to a freeway or offer free parking or a drive-up window, how fast your service is.

Whenever you're writing to customers or clients about features which are not unique to your organization, it's wise to present both benefits of the features themselves and benefits of dealing with your company. If you talk about the benefits of dining in a relaxed atmosphere but don't mention your own restaurant, people may go somewhere else!

Hint
Brainstorm lots of reader benefits—perhaps twice as many as you'll need for the final letter or memo. Then you can choose the ones that are most effective for that audience, or that you can develop most easily. The first benefit you think of may not be the best. It's a lot easier to discard a so-so reader benefit when you have better ones to use in its place.

3. Show How the Reader Can Meet His or Her Needs with the Features of the Policy or Product. Features alone rarely motivate readers. Instead, link the feature to the readers' needs—and provide details to make the benefit vivid!

Weak: We have placemats with riddles.
Better: Answering all the riddles on Monical's special placemats will keep the kids happy till your pizza comes. If they don't have time to finish (and they may not, since your pizza is ready so quickly), just take the riddles home—or answer them on your next visit.

Make your reader benefits specific.

Weak: You get quick service.
Better: If you only have an hour for lunch, try our Business Buffet. Within minutes, you can choose from a variety of main dishes, vegetables, and make-your-own-sandwich-and-salad

Reader Benefits for the Right Side of the Brain*

[Foote, Cone & Belding was named Agency of the Year for 1986 by *Advertising Age.* FCB uses a] somewhat regimented, somewhat unusual method of brain analysis, considered a key in developing ads that speak to their intended audience.

The "left brain," dominated by an analytical, linear, verbal process, looks for rational thought, explicit truths and what amounts to a hard-sell pitch. Not surprisingly, say FCB executives, account management types are left-brainers.

The "right brain" instead responds to intuitive, emotional, holistic appeals and is the primary focus for creative people. . . .

If this sounds like psychological hogwash, consider an application of said technique that led to a subtle yet important change in an on-going campaign for Pearle Vision Centers.

"The previous campaign tried to argue Pearle had first-rate eyecare, a rational pitch. . . . But we found that the decision was really an emotional one; trust is paramount."

Commercials began focusing less on fast service and qualified optometrists and more on an inherent trust between specialist and patient, with the tagline, "Nobody cares for eyes more than Pearle."

bar. You'll have a lunch that's as light or filling as you want, with time to enjoy it—and still be back to the office on time.

Why Reader Benefits Work

Reader benefits improve both the attitudes and the behavior of the people you work with and write to. They make people view you more positively; they make it easier for you to accomplish your goals.

Expectancy theory argues that people are motivated by the expectation that they will be rewarded if they do something. Somewhat simplified, this theory says that how much motivation you feel to perform a task or reach a given level of performance will depend on your expectation and your values. Do you expect that if you try you will succeed? Do you expect that you'll be rewarded for success? How important is the reward? How much do you care about doing well for its own sake?

Most people try to do their best only when they believe that they can succeed and when they want the rewards that success brings. If an employee feels that even superhuman effort will not make it possible to write a satisfactory report, there will be little motivation to put forth any effort at all. If someone feels that he or she can indeed write a good report but doesn't expect to be rewarded for doing so or doesn't care about the reward, motivation will again be low.

Effort alone does not determine performance: natural ability and training also affect the result. Someone who is a good writer may be able to write a good report with less effort than someone whose writing skill is less developed. Another factor in effort is one's perception of one's role. If someone has acquired the notion that "men can't write" or "women can't do math," he or she may unconsciously act in accordance with that role, even though natural abilities would fight the stereotype.

Performance leads to some reward. If you get a $1,000 raise after working on a report, but the three other people on your team get $5,000 raises, you won't be satisfied. Oddly enough, the reverse is also true: if you get $5,000 while the others get only $1,000, you'll probably feel guilty and uncomfortable.[10] How much pleasure you get from the rewards will affect how hard you try on your next assignment.

Figure 7.7 shows how expectancy theory is influenced by reader benefits and other information from the organization.

Since reader benefits are rewards, their role in producing satisfaction is obvious. Less obvious but perhaps even more important is the role that reader benefits, as part of a letter or memo, play in shaping perceptions and determining expectations. Reader benefits tell or remind readers that they can do the job and that success will be rewarded.[11] Thus they help overcome two problems that reduce motivation:

1. People may not think of all the possible outcomes or benefits.
2. People may misperceive the relationships between efforts, performance, and rewards.[12]

* Quoted from Gary Levin, "Hot Raisins and More: FCB Turns on Its Creative Brainpower," *Advertising Age,* July 6, 1987, 24.

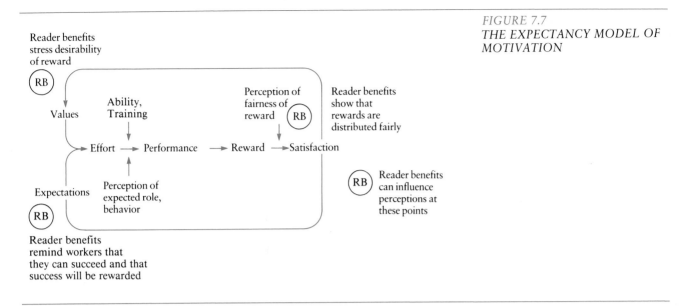

FIGURE 7.7
THE EXPECTANCY MODEL OF
MOTIVATION

Adapted from Lyman W. Porter and Edward E. Lawler III, *Managerial Attitudes and Performance* (Homewood, IL: Richard D. Irwin, 1968), 17; Edward E. Lawler III, *Motivation in Work Organizations* (Monterey, CA: Brooks/Cole Publications, 1972), 54, 58.

SUMMARY OF KEY POINTS

- **You-attitude** is a style of writing which looks at things from the reader's point of view, emphasizing what the reader wants to know, respecting the reader's intelligence, and protecting the reader's ego.
- To apply you-attitude, use the following five principles:
  1. Focus on what the reader receives or can do. In positive or neutral situations, stress what the readers wants to know.
  2. Be specific about the reader's request or order.
  3. Don't talk about your own feelings unless you're sure the reader wants to know how you feel.
  4. Don't presume that you know how the reader feels or will react.
  5. In negative situations, avoid the word *you*. Protect the reader's ego. Use impersonal expressions and passive verbs to avoid assigning blame.
- Apply you-attitude beyond the sentence level by using organization and content as well as style to build goodwill.
- **Positive emphasis** means focusing on the positive rather than the negative aspects of a situation.
- Deemphasize negative information by using the following five techniques:
  1. Eliminate negative words and words with negative connotations.
  2. State information positively. Focus on what the reader can do rather than on what you won't or can't let the reader do.
  3. Justify negative information by giving a reason or linking it to a reader benefit.
  4. If the negative is truly unimportant, omit it.
  5. Bury the negative information and present it compactly.
- **Success-consciousness** allows you to project a tone of confidence in yourself, your products and services, and your organization.

- To develop success-consciousness in your writing,
  1. Eliminate words which express doubt.
  2. Eliminate words which imply that the reader may not be satisfied.
  3. Eliminate words that suggest you may not have expressed yourself clearly or convincingly.
- **Reader benefits** are benefits or advantages that the reader gets by using the writer's services, buying the writer's products, following the writer's policies, or adopting the writer's ideas. Reader benefits can exist for policies and ideas as well as for goods and services. Reader benefits tell readers that they can do the job and that success will be rewarded.
- Good reader benefits are adapted to the audience, based on **intrinsic** rather than **extrinsic** advantages, supported by clear logic and explained in adequate detail, and phrased in you-attitude. Extrinsic benefits simply aren't available to reward every desired behavior; further, they reduce the satisfaction in doing something for its own sake.
- To create reader benefits,
  1. Identify the feelings, fears, and needs that may motivate your reader.
  2. Identify the objective features of your product or policy that could meet the needs you've identified.
  3. Show how the reader can meet his or her needs with the features of the policy or product.
- You-attitude, positive emphasis, and success-consciousness are primarily matters of style. Reader benefits are content; you write or talk about reader benefits using you-attitude and positive emphasis.

NOTES

1. Kevin Leo, "Effective Copy and Graphics," DADM/DMEF Direct Marketing Institute for Professors, Northbrook, IL, May 31–June 3, 1983.

2. Mark A. Sherman, "Adjectival Negation and the Comprehension of Multiply Negated Sentences," *Journal of Verbal Learning and Verbal Behavior* 15 (1976): 143–57.

3. John J. Weger reports Herzberg's research in *Motivating Supervisors* (American Management Association, 1971), 53–54.

4. Weger, 63.

5. Barry Staw, "Intrinsic and Extrinsic Motivation," *Faculty Working Papers,* College of Commerce and Business Administration, University of Illinois at Urbana-Champaign, October 16, 1974, no. 213; Edward L. Deci, "The Hidden Costs of Rewards," *Organizational Dynamics* 4, no. 3 (Winter 1976): 61–72.

6. Leo, "Effective Copy and Graphics."

7. Abraham H. Maslow, *Motivation and Personality* (New York: Harper & Row, 1954).

8. Annette N. Shelby, "The Theoretical Bases of Persuasion: A Critical Introduction," *Journal of Business Communication* 23, no. 1 (Winter 1986): 26 n. 5.

9. Geort Hofstede, *Culture's Consequences: International Differences in Work-Related Values* (Beverly Hills, CA: Sage Publications, 1980), 32.

10. See Edward E. Lawler III, *Motivation in Work Organizations* (Monterey, CA: Brooks/Cole Publications, 1973), 74–76.

11. Cf. Tove Helland Hammer and H. Peter Dachler, "A Test of Some Assumptions Underlying the Path-Goal Model of Supervision: Some Suggested Conceptual Modifications," *Organizational Behavior and Human Performance* 14 (1975): 73.

12. Lawler, 59. Lawler also notes a third obstacle: people may settle for performance and rewards that are just OK. Offering reader benefits, however, does nothing to affect this obstacle.

EXERCISES AND PROBLEMS FOR CHAPTER 7

7–1 IMPROVING YOU-ATTITUDE, POSITIVE EMPHASIS, AND SUCCESS CONSCIOUSNESS
Revise these sentences to improve you-attitude, positive emphasis, and success consciousness. Eliminate any jargon or awkward phrasing. In some cases, you may need to add information to revise the sentence effectively.

1. Tickets for the tournament are not available to you if you did not buy a season ticket. Even if you did buy a season ticket, you can get only two tournament tickets.

2. At WKEX, we offer a full promotional staff to help you design ads for the young adult market.

3. This handout is intended to provide an explanation of how to enter an order on the CRT terminal.

4. You will be happy to know that we won't charge you anything extra for additional credit cards for your spouse or child.

5. I apologize for my delay in answering your inquiry. The problem was that I had to poll all the committee members to give you a report on the provisions likely to be in the final bill.

6. Surely you will see the obvious advantages of The Commodity Futures Market's leverage over conventional methods and will be a likely candidate for our business services.

7. If I haven't explained in sufficient detail for you to make a decision, please do not hesitate to call me.

8. Unfortunately, I'll be out of town the day you visit here and won't be able to meet with you, but I hope I won't miss seeing you when I'm in your town next month.

9. You must not allow your property to fall into such a condition as to create an eyesore, health hazard, or public nuisance. Anyone caught in violation of this ordinance will be fined if the problem is not rectified within 14 days of receiving a legal notice.

10. We regret that we are unable to process your application because you did not give us all the necessary information.

7–2 IMPROVING YOU-ATTITUDE, POSITIVE EMPHASIS, AND SUCCESS CONSCIOUSNESS
Revise these sentences to improve you-attitude, positive emphasis, and success consciousness. Eliminate any jargon or awkward phrasing. In some cases, you may need to add information to revise the sentence effectively.

1. You cannot become a volunteer counselor unless you attend all three training sessions.

2. As per your request, we have arranged to have the plans sent by express mail. We hope this will be satisfactory.

3. The material you sent us was not lost in the mail. I'm happy to tell you it reached us, and I'm sorry that you were worried about it.

4. Hopefully these new, clearer instructions will eliminate misuse of the training package.

5. At The Gifted Graduate, we have taken a lot of trouble to assemble a wide variety of gifts, clothing, and souvenirs.

6. Thank you for making a pledge to public TV, but do not delay sending your check. If we don't have the money in the bank by June 30, we will have to cut back on scheduled programming; we won't be able to buy all the movies we had planned to buy to show Saturday nights.

7. If the above information is unclear, or if further communication on this or any other topic is necessary, please do not hesitate to contact me.

8. You cannot accept gifts from anyone with whom you, as an employee of the Environmental Protection Agency, deal, because some citizen might suspect that your enforcement decision had been subject to undue influence.

9. I would like to make an appointment for an interview but am only available Tuesdays and Thursdays because of my classes.

10. If you submitted a check with your order, as you claim, we have failed to receive it.

7–3 IMPROVING YOU-ATTITUDE, POSITIVE EMPHASIS, AND SUCCESS CONSCIOUSNESS
Revise these sentences to improve you-attitude, positive emphasis, and success consciousness. Eliminate any jargon or awkward phrasing. In some cases, you may need to add information to revise the sentence effectively.

1. If you are not convinced by the proposal, please give me the chance to try to provide more information.

2. Never fail to back up disks with important business information.

3. Open this envelope only if you've decided to say *no* to our offer.

4. You should avoid registering for an overload (18 hours or more) because it may cause you to do more poorly in your coursework.

5. As you read this brochure, we hope you see why Alpine Legal Management is considered one of the most powerful law-firm software packages on the market today.

6. Although my work experience is not outstanding, I believe I developed communication and organization skills as a receptionist.

7. It should be obvious to you that we cannot make an exception in your favor and treat you differently than we treat other clients.

8. Sizes and colors are limited. Call early to avoid disappointment.

9. I'm sure you'll agree that setting goals is the first step in financial planning.

10. It is hoped that all those desirous of additional filing cabinets will be satisfied with the new filing cabinets which have now arrived.

7–4 IDENTIFYING AND DEVELOPING READER BENEFITS

Listed here are several programs which an organization might offer to employees and several things an organization might like its employees to do.

a. Identify the motives or needs which might be met by each of the following items or activities.

b. Assume that you're writing to employees announcing or advocating one of these items or activities. Take each need or motive and develop it as a reader benefit in a full paragraph. Use additional paragraphs for the other needs met by the activity. Remember to use you-attitude!

1. An employee newsletter.

2. Taking job-related night classes.

3. Participating in professional organizations.

4. Flextime (a system under which employees must work a certain number of hours a week, but set their own starting and quitting times).

5. Taking public transportation or a carpool to work rather than driving in alone.

6. Exercising or participating in a sport.

7. Playing in a company volleyball league.

7–5 IDENTIFYING AND DEVELOPING READER BENEFITS FOR DIFFERENT AUDIENCES

Assume that you own a small company dedicated to encouraging people to do or pay for one of the activities in the numbered list below.

a. Brainstorm specific products or services that your firm could offer.

b. Identify needs that you could meet for the audiences listed here. In addition to needs that several audiences share, identify at least one need that would be particularly important to each group.

c. Identify at least one reader benefit that could meet each need.

d. Write a paragraph developing each reader benefit you have identified. Remember to use you-attitude!

1. Exercising Regularly
   Audiences: College men and women.
                Diabetics.
                Executives.
                Older men and women.

2. Getting Advice about Interior Decorating
   Audiences: Young people with little money to spend.
                People upgrading or adding to their furnishings.
                Older people moving from single-family homes into smaller apartments or condominiums.
                Builders furnishing model homes.

3. Getting Advice on Investment Strategies
   Audiences: New college graduates.
                People earning over $100,000 annually.
                Parents with small children.
                People within 10 years of retirement.

4. Using a Shop-at-Home Service
   Audiences: Two-career couples.
                Shut-ins (people too ill or infirm to leave their homes).
                People who live in rural areas.
                Parents staying home with small children.

5. Buying Custom-Designed Clothing
   Audiences: Rich people.
                Basketball players.

People in wheelchairs.

People who are very interested in fashion.

6. Shopping at a Large Department Store
   Audiences: People shopping in August and September.

   People shopping in November and December.

   People shopping in May and June.

7–6 DEVELOPING READER BENEFITS FOR AN INSURANCE COMPANY

Suppose your insurance company offers a discount on health insurance to people who exercise regularly. In addition to benefits of exercising regularly, what benefits could you offer for being insured with your company?

Hints:

- Do the people who buy health insurance from you need other kinds of insurance too? What kinds of policies do you offer?
- What hassles do people sometimes have with health insurance claims? Can you offer procedures to eliminate those hassles?
- On what do people base their choice of an insurance company? Is there really much price difference between companies? What kinds of appeals do you see in ads for insurance companies?

7–7 REVISING A FLYER TO IMPROVE YOU-ATTITUDE AND DEVELOP READER BENEFITS

You're owner of a copy shop that opened on campus a year ago. Your assistant has drafted a promotional brochure to go out to faculty reminding them about your services. Here's the draft:

TWOFERS COPIES

We at Twofers offer copying on regular 20# bond paper as well as on bright colors and/or pastels. We carry top-of-the-line résumé paper plus card and cover stock in a wide variety of colors.

We are also able to offer you four (4) different color inks for your copying needs. We have BLACK, BLUE, RED, AND GREEN. With your camera-ready art, we can use all four colors to make your copies personal and unique.

Our other services include:

    Typing.
    Word Processing—IBM PC.
    Binding.
    Collating.
    Reductions and Enlargements.
    Business Cards.
    Letterheads and Stationery.

We deliver the highest copy quality at the most reasonable prices. We offer all TAs, professors, and teachers discount prices for having your work done by us. Be sure to notify your students of our low prices on copying student booklets, term papers, and other projects.

Come in and see for yourself the excellent services we offer! We are open 9 A.M. to 7 P.M. Monday to Thursday, till 5 P.M. on Friday, and 10 A.M. to 5 P.M. Saturday.

We look forward to your business.

This flyer has no you-attitude at all. In addition to lacking you-attitude at the sentence level, the document also lacks you-attitude in its organization and selection of details.

As your instructor directs,

a. Without changing organization or content, revise the document's sentences to make them you-attitude.

b. Revise the organization and add content to make the whole document show you-attitude. As you revise, think about your audience:

    What kinds of copying will they be doing?
    How do they choose a copy shop?

Think about the questions they'll want answers to:

    How much is the discount?
    How far in advance must originals be brought in?
    Is work guaranteed?

c. Revise the document for reader benefits. Think about ways that basic services and kinds of papers can be related to the reader's needs.

7–8 REVISING A FORM LETTER FOR SUCCESS CONSCIOUSNESS AND AUDIENCE ADAPTATION

You've just been promoted to Vice President of Customer and Community Relations for a large savings and loan association. One day, you get a batch of form letters to sign. These letters are designed to go to customers who have recently closed their savings accounts. Here's the basic form.

> Dear————:
>
> We thank you for having kept your savings with us.
>
> Although you recently closed your Savings Account #_____, we hope that our service was efficient and convenient enough to merit your confidence.
>
> Whatever your needs—savings, home loans, installment loans, traveler's checks, safe deposit boxes, or assistance in tax-sheltering your income—please call on us.
>
> Sincerely,

You're not going to send that letter out with your name on it. The second paragraph practically says you think readers withdrew their money because they didn't like or didn't trust you—hardly the image a savings and loan wants to convey!

As your instructor directs,
   a. Rewrite the letter to go out to all customers who close savings accounts.
   b. Assume that your computer can compare the list of people who close savings accounts with the list of people who have just taken out home or installment loans or who have just bought travelers' checks. Write more specific form letters to people in each of these three groups who have withdrawn their savings, presumably,
      (1) to buy houses.
      (2) to make a major purchase (e.g., car, boat, remodeling), or
      (3) to take a trip.
   c. Assume that you know which of your customers who close savings accounts are moving out of town. Write a form letter to this group.

7–9 GUESS THE WINNER

In his column in *Direct Marketing,* John Caples sometimes reports the results of split-run tests in magazines and newspapers. In a split-run test, one version of an ad appears in every other copy printed, while a second version appears in the other copies. In the following test, the copy, art, offer, size, and order forms of the ads were identical: only the headline (and thus the central selling point) differed.

Each ad asked for an order. The number of orders for each version thus indicates which central selling point works better.

Can you guess which headline in each group brought in more orders?

1. *Reader's Digest* Subscriptions
   a. Now at 25% Reduced Holiday Rates
   b. How to Do Christmas Shopping in One Minute

2. Cushiontone Sound-Absorbing Material
   a. Your Home Is Often as Noisy as a Busy Street
   b. How to Cut Down Noise in Your Kitchen for as Little as $30

3. Rybutol Vitamins
   a. Why Rybutol Can Make You Feel Peppier
   b. Worn Out? Nervous? Run Down?

4. Wynn's Friction-Proofing Automobile Oil
   a. Car Owners! Save One Gallon of Gas in Every Ten
   b. Add This Product to Any Motor Oil for More Power with Less Gas

5. Anahist Tablets
   a. Quick Relief for Miseries of HAY FEVER
   b. How to DRY UP Nasal Miseries of HAY FEVER

6. Gypsom Wallboard
   a. Build Your Own Darkroom
   b. Build an Extra Attic Room

7. Bromo Seltzer
   a. Fight Headache Three Ways
   b. BROMO SELTZER Fights Headache Three Ways

8. Wildroot Hair Set
   a. New Hair Set for Soft Alluring Hair
   b. Girls! Want Quick Curls?

9. Electrolux Vacuum Cleaner
   a. Now . . . a Cleaner That Pops Out the Dirt . . . All Wrapped, Sealed
   b. Now . . . a Cleaner That Keeps Its Efficiency Automatically

10. Cyclone Fence
   a. Cyclone Fence Is Lasting Protection for Children, Pets, and Lawns
   b. How to Fence Your Home—FREE BOOK

When you know the winners (ask your instructor to check the *Teaching Guide*), what generalizations can you make about

The advantages of using benefits
What kinds of benefits work better

How specific to be
Positive versus negative phrasing
Particularly good words to use?

How can you apply these principles to general business writing? To persuasion? To sales letters?

Choosing the Right Word

QUESTIONS

- Why are denotations and connotations important in business and administrative communication?

- Why are short words better for business and administrative communication? Is it ever OK to use long words?

- Why should writers use nonsexist language? How do you produce nonsexist words and phrases, job titles, courtesy titles, and pronouns?

- If there's more than one way to make language nonsexist, which way should you use?

"I don't know what you mean by 'glory, '" Alice said.

Humpty Dumpty smiled contemptuously. "Of course you don't—till I tell you. I meant 'there's a nice knock-down argument for you!'"

"But 'glory' doesn't mean 'a nice knock-down argument,'" Alice objected.

"When *I* use a word," Humpty Dumpty said, in rather a scornful tone, "it means just what I choose it to mean—neither more nor less."

"The question is," said Alice, "whether you *can* make words mean so many different things."

"The question is," said Humpty Dumpty, "which is to be master—that's all."

Lewis Carroll
Through the Looking-Glass, 1871

Humpty Dumpty's theory of language doesn't work for business communicators. We must choose words that communicate the meaning and attitudes we want to convey.

The best word depends on context: the situation, your purposes, your audience, the words you have already used. People who are very skilled with using words often have an intuitive sense for the right word. As you develop that skill, these principles can help you master the words you use:

1. Use a word that means what you want to say.
2. Use a word whose implications and connotations are appropriate.
3. Use short, familiar words.
4. Use nonsexist language.

Let's examine each of these.

ACCURATE DENOTATIONS

Denotation is a word's literal or dictionary meaning; **connotation** means the emotional colorings or associations that accompany a word. Most common words in English have more than one denotation. Context usually makes it clear which of several meanings is appropriate.

Pound: unit of weight
        hit
        place where stray animals are kept
        unit of money

A language will have many words, each with a slightly different denotation, for concepts that are important in its culture. The different denotations permit writers and speakers to convey meaning precisely. Linguists frequently point out, for example, that Eskimos have different words for different kinds of snow. English has even more different words for different kinds of motor vehicles.

Problems arise when writers use words whose denotations are inappropriate or even contradictory.

8.1 In the latter part of 1975, the western part of Ohio was transferred from Chicago to Cleveland.[1]

8.2 Three major associations of property-liability companies are poised to strike out in opposite directions.[2]

8.3 Earn a free lunch.[3]

In Example 8.1, the author has omitted words. Ohio has not moved. Instead, a company has moved responsibility for sales in the western part of Ohio. In Examples 8.2 and 8.3, the authors have misused words. Three different directions cannot be "opposite" each other. A lunch one earns isn't "free."

To write or speak well, you need to know the denotations of words. A good dictionary is a useful resource. Appendix B lists 40 pairs of similar-sounding words which are sometimes confused. Reading a good newspaper and good books will also help you build a sense of the differences in denotations among similar words.

Accurate denotations can make it easier to solve problems. One production line had a high failure rate: twenty of each 100 units coming off the line needed some sort of repair, and many repairs involved two or three items. The largest category of defects was *missed operations*. At first, the supervisor wondered if the people on the line were lazy or irresponsible. But some checking showed that several different problems were labeled *missed operations:* parts installed backward, parts that had missing screws or fasteners; parts whose wires weren't connected. Each of these problems had different solutions. Using accurate words redefined the problem and enabled the production line both to improve quality and to cut repair costs.[4]

If words are consistently misused, their denotations may change. In one company, a production department labeled every maintenance request a *rush job*. At first, maintenance handled every request promptly. But the people in maintenance quickly realized that these "rush" jobs were routine and could wait. One day, of course, production ran into a problem that really was urgent—and turned in a request for rush service. But the department had cried "wolf" too often, and service was delayed, with serious consequences for the company.[5]

Over time, the denotation of a word can change. The word *mailed* originally meant "sheathed in defensive material" (like a "coat of mail").[6] Letters were "mailed" to protect them from the elements or from unwanted readers; eventually the term took on its current meaning. The 1987 second edition of the unabridged *Random House Dictionary of the English Language* lists 50,000 new words and 75,000 new definitions that were not in the first 1966 edition.[7]

Sometimes denotations change because common use consistently associates a word with another meaning. *Escalator* was once a brand name; now it denotes any moving staircase. Coca-Cola spends an estimated $2 million a year to protect its brand names so that *Coke* will denote only that brand and not just any cola drink.[8] New denotations can also be created by influential people and organizations. *Crest* denotes a bird's top plumage or the peak of a hill or mountain. Effective advertising also makes the word denote "a brand of toothpaste" for many Americans.

When Is a Chicken Not a Chicken?*

When two people use the same word to denote different meanings, bypassing occurs.

Even apparently simple words can produce bypassing. Take, for example, the word *chicken*. A buyer claimed that he had received stewing hens instead of the fryers he wanted. The contract specified that *chickens* would be delivered at a certain price. Is a stewing hen a *chicken*? A court said it is; the buyer lost the case.

---

* Based on *Frigaliment Importing Co., Ltd. v. B.N.S. International Sales*, 190 F. Supp. 116 (S.D.N.Y. 1960).

APPROPRIATE CONNOTATIONS

Words with similar denotations may nevertheless plant different ideas in the reader's mind because of their connotations, that is, their emotional associations or colorings. A great many words carry connotations of approval or disapproval, delight or disgust. Words in the first column suggest approval; words in the second column suggest criticism.

Positive Word	Negative Word
assume	guess
curious	nosy
negotiate	haggle
conservative	hidebound
cautious	fearful
persistent	nagging
careful	nit-picking
willing to take risks	a foolhardy gambler
firm	obstinate
flexible	wishy-washy

A supervisor can "tell the truth" about a subordinate's performance and yet write either a positive or a negative performance appraisal, based on the connotations of the words in the appraisal.

Connotations are also important in advertising and in public relations. Expensive cars are never *used;* instead, they're *preowned, experienced,* or even *preloved.* An executive for Rolls-Royce once said, "A Rolls never, never breaks down." "Of course," he added, with a twinkle in his eye, "there have been occasions when a car has failed to proceed."[9]

Words may also connote status. Both *salesperson* and *sales representative* are nonsexist job titles. But the first sounds like a clerk in a store; the second suggests someone selling important items to corporate customers.

If a word has different connotations when it is applied to men than when it is applied to women, sexism is at work. *Aggressive* is a positive word when it is applied to men in business; it seems negative to many people when it is applied to women in business.

Although connotations rarely appear in a dictionary, they are not individual or idiosyncratic. The associations a word evokes will be consistent in any one culture but may differ among cultures. One scholar reports that while "the term 'discussion' is connotatively neutral for North Americans, it possesses a negative connotation for Latin Americans, who view it as an attempt to change someone else's mind."[10] Even within a culture, connotations may change over time. The word *charity* had acquired such negative connotations by the nineteenth century that people began to use the term *welfare* instead. Now, *welfare* has acquired negative associations and we may be ready for another term.

Connotations are important in business and administrative communication because we want to convey not only information but also attitudes about that

* Based on David A. Ricks, *Big Business Blunders* (Homewood, IL: Dow Jones-Irwin, 1983), 38–39, 46; Robert Grosse and Duane Kujawa, *International Business: Theory and Managerial Applications* (Homewood, IL: Richard D. Irwin, 1988), 363; Alan M. Rugman, Donald J. Lecraw, and Lawrence D. Booth, *International Business* (New York: McGraw-Hill, 1985), 358; and Noreene Janus, "Transnational Advertising: Some Considerations on the Impact of Peripheral Societies," *Communication and Latin American Society: Trends in Critical Research 1960–1985,* ed. Rita Atwood and Emile G. McAnany (Madison, WI: University of Wisconsin Press, 1986), 139.

information. When we sell a product or an idea, we want to present it as positively as possible. How positively can we present something and still be ethical? Certainly the words we use can shape response. A *defense budget* sounds essential; a *military budget* sounds less positive. A *nuclear accident* is scary; a *nuclear event* is neutral. We have the right to package our ideas attractively, but we have the responsibility to give the public or our superiors all the information they need to make decisions.

Test the connotations of your words against these guidelines.

* Make sure that the connotations of one word fit with those of the other words in your message.
* Avoid words with negative or damaging connotations.
* When you're recommending a product to a buyer or a candidate for promotion to your supervisor, don't rely on connotations alone to make your point. Instead, support your recommendation with specific evidence.

SHORT, FAMILIAR WORDS

Good business writing uses short, familiar words whenever possible. Occasionally you'll need a long or an unfamiliar word because it is the only word that exactly conveys your meaning. But many of the words writers use in an effort to impress are unnecessary. Whenever you can choose between two words that mean the same thing, use the shorter, more common one.

A series of long, learned, abstract terms makes writing less interesting, less forceful, and less memorable. Will big words make you sound more intelligent? Only if they're needed to communicate. Consider this memo from the Superintendent of Schools of the Houston School District to "All Administrative Staff":

> Subject: Sequential Page Numbering of Documents
>
> Please give immediate attention to insure that the pages of all documents prepared for distribution are numbered sequentially and in a place of optimum visibility. This is needed to facilitate our ability to refer to items during meetings.[11]

Impressive? No. Silly? Yes. When you have something simple to say, use simple words.

The following list gives a few examples of short, simple alternatives.

Formal and Stuffy	Short and Simple
ameliorate	improve
commence	begin
execute	sign
remittance	check, payment
render assistance	help
prioritize	rank
reside	live
subsequently	later
utilize	use
viable option	choice

Tribe Connotes Primitiveness[*]

The American's query, "What tribe are you from?" unsettled the Nigerian businessman. . . . Was the remark merely a type of small talk coming from a basically well-meaning person whose knowledge of Africa and Nigeria was limited to "there are lots of tribes in Africa"? Or was it a question by someone who conceived of Africa as the "Dark Continent" inhabited by primitive nomadic groups of people? Or then again, was it a query of a person who knew Africa, appreciated its peoples and cultures, and was honestly interested in knowing more about the man with whom he was speaking? . . .

"It's all in the connotation of the word 'tribe,' " explained a Nigerian university professor. "How can you say that 11 million Yorubas or 11 million Hausas who belong to ancient and sophisticated cultures are members of a 'tribe'? Would you ask a Belgian if he were a member of the Flemish or French-speaking tribe? No, of course not!"

[*] Quoted from John P. Fieg and John G. Blair, *There Is a Difference: 12 Intercultural Perspectives* (Washington, DC: Meridian House International, 1975), 99–100.

"Good" Means "Mediocre"*

The Agriculture Department, granting a consumer petition for the first time, has decided to rename a beef grade to enhance the image of lean beef.

Beginning Nov. 23 [1987], beef cuts currently graded as "USDA Good" will be stamped "USDA Select," department officials said. . . . [T]he current grading system discourages shoppers from choosing more healthful, lean beef over the top grades, Prime and Choice, which are more heavily marbled, or flecked, with fat. . . .

The grade name "Good" connotes mediocrity to most food shoppers, said Ellen Haas, executive director of Public Voice for Food and Health Policy, the consumer group that petitioned for the change. The switch to "Select" will give lean beef a more appealing name.

There are three exceptions to the general rule that "shorter is better."

1. Use a long word if it is the only word that expresses your meaning exactly.
2. Use a long word if it is more familiar than shorter words. *Send out* is better than *emit* and *poisonous* is better than *toxic* because more people know the first word in each pair.
3. Use a long word if its connotations are more appropriate.

REDUCING SEXUAL BIAS IN BUSINESS WRITING

Nonsexist language treats both sexes neutrally; it does not make assumptions about the "proper" gender for a job; it does not assume that men are superior to or take precedence over women. Using nonsexist language is a good idea for at least three reasons. First, the language we use reflects and reveals our understanding of the world around us. An organization that treats people fairly should use language that treats people fairly. A second reason for using nonsexist language is to remove a potential barrier to the images people create of themselves. A steady diet of sexist language encourages women to have low aspirations, to seek jobs rather than careers, to think that middle management is as high as they can go. The third reason to use nonsexist language, and perhaps the most important, is that it's fairer and friendlier.

Sexist language is so common that it may seem natural. But the subtle message that the people who matter are male is just as offensive as are other forms of discrimination. Sexist language is distancing. When a woman gets a letter with the wrong courtesy title, she knows the writer doesn't know *her;* when she reads a job description that uses male pronouns, it's clear that the writer isn't writing to her. Everything we do in good business writing attempts to build goodwill. Nonsexist language helps sustain the goodwill we work so hard to create.

Check to be sure that your writing is free from sexism in four areas: words and phrases, job titles, courtesy titles, and pronouns.

Words and Phrases

Many sexist words and phrases have no place in business to start with, so we need not concern ourselves with them here.[12] Some terms, however, like those in Figure 8.1, do need attention.

Manager, however, is *not* sexist. The word comes from the Latin *manus* meaning "hand"; it has nothing to do with maleness.

Job Titles

Use neutral titles which do not imply that a job is held only by men or only by women. Many job titles are already neutral: accountant, banker, doctor, engineer, inspector, manager, nurse, pilot, secretary, technician, to name a few. Other titles reflect gender stereotypes and need to be changed.

---

* Quoted from Bruce Ingersoll, "U.S. to Encourage Healthier Eating, Decides to Rename Lean Beef Grade," *The Wall Street Journal,* September 23, 1987, 34.

Instead of	Use	Because
The girl at the front desk	The woman's name or job title: "Ms. Browning," "Rosa," "the receptionist"	Call female employees *women* just as you call male employees *men*. When you talk about a specific woman, use her name, just as you use a man's name to talk about a specific man.
The ladies on our staff	The women on our staff	Use parallel terms for males and females. Therefore, use *ladies* only if you refer to the males on your staff as *gentlemen*. Few businesses do, since social distinctions are rarely at issue.
Manpower Manhours Manning	Personnel Worker Hours or Hours Staffing	The power in business today comes from both women and men. If you have to correspond with the U.S. Department of Labor's Division of Manpower Administration, you are stuck with the term. When you talk about other organizations, however, use nonsexist alternatives.
Managers and their wives	Managers and their spouses	Managers may be female.

FIGURE 8.1
GETTING RID OF SEXIST TERMS AND PHRASES

If you need a substitute for a traditional word, check the U.S. Department of Labor's *Job Title Revisions to Eliminate Sex- and Age-Referent Language from the Dictionary of Occupational Titles*, 3rd ed., 1975.

Instead of	Use
Businessman	A specific title: executive, accountant, department head, owner of a small business, or Men and women in business, or, as a last resort, Business people
Chairman	Chair, Chairperson, Moderator
Foreman	Supervisor (from *Job Title Revisions*)
Woman lawyer	Lawyer
Workman	Worker, employee. Or use a specific title: Crane operator, brick layer, etc.

Courtesy Titles

Memos normally use first and last names without courtesy titles. Letters, however, require courtesy titles in the salutation *unless* you're on a first-name basis with your reader.

When You Know Your Reader's Name and Gender. *Mr.*, the traditional courtesy title for men, does not indicate marital status. The parallel title for women is *Ms.*, and in most circumstances, it is the title you should use in business correspondence to women. There are, however, two exceptions:

1. If the woman has a professional title, use that title if you would use it for a man.

The Ethics of Word Choice*
People can use accurate words to lie.

As a prize for visiting a condominium resort, a woman "won" an all-terrain vehicle. She had to pay $29.95 for "handling, processing, and insurance" to get it.

Then she saw her prize: a lawn chair with four wheels that converts into a wheeled cart.

The company claimed it told the truth: "It is a vehicle. It's a four-wheel cart you can take anywhere—to the beach, to the pool. It may not be motorized, but [we] didn't say it was motorized."

The company may be guilty of deceptive trade practices: the courts will have to decide that. But whether or not the practice is illegal, it isn't ethical to use words that most people will misinterpret.

---

* Based on Carmella M. Padilla, "It's a . . . a . . . a . . . All-Terrain Vehicle, Yeah, That's It, That's the Ticket," *The Wall Street Journal*, July 17, 1987, 17.

Ms. in Any Language*

Other countries are also developing nonsexist courtesy titles for women.

United States
    Miss
    Mrs.
    Ms.
Denmark
    Frøken
    Fru
    Fr.
France
    Mademoiselle (Mlle.)
    Madame (Mme.)
    Mad.
Spain
    Señorita (Srta.)
    Señora (Sra.)
    Sa.
Japan
    San
    San
    San

Dr. Kristen Sorenson is our new company physician.
The Rev. Elizabeth Townsley gave the invocation.
Professor Olga Jordan will conduct the seminar.

2. If the woman prefers to be addressed as *Mrs.* or *Miss,* use the title she prefers rather than *Ms.* (You-attitude takes precedence over nonsexist language: address the reader as she [or he] prefers to be addressed.)

To find out if a woman prefers a traditional title,

   a. Check the signature block in previous correspondence. Women who prefer traditional titles can list them with their (typed) names. If a woman signs herself (*Miss*) *Elaine Anderson* or (*Mrs.*) *Kay Royster,* use the title she designates.

   b. Notice the title a woman uses in introducing herself on the phone. If she says, "This is Robin Stine," use *Ms.* when you write to her. If she says, "I'm Mrs. Stine," use the title she specifies.

   c. Check your company directory. In some organizations, women who prefer traditional titles can list them with their names.

   d. Call the company and ask the receptionist which title the woman you need to write to prefers. This is a particularly good strategy when you're writing job letters or other letters to people on whom it is crucial to make a good impression.

Ms. is particularly useful when you do not know what a woman's marital status is. However, even when you happen to know that a woman is married or single, **you still use *Ms.* unless you know that she prefers another title.**

In addition to using parallel courtesy titles, be sure to use parallel forms for names.

Not Parallel	**Parallel**
Members of the committee will be Mr. Jones, Mr. Yacone, and Lisa.	Members of the committee will be Mr. Jones, Mr. Yacone, and Ms. Melton, or
	Members of the committee will be Irving, Ted, and Lisa.

When You Know Your Reader's Name But Not the Gender. Initials, some names, and many nicknames can be used for both men and women. It isn't safe to guess: getting the reader's gender wrong is a sure way to antagonize him or her. Instead, either

1. Call the company and ask the receptionist, or
2. Use the reader's full name in the salutation:
    Dear Chris Crowell:
    Dear J. C. Meath:

---

* Based on Mary Ritchie Key, *Male/Female Language* (Metuchen, NJ: Scarecrow Press, 1975), 50, and John C. Condon and Fathi Yousef, *An Introduction to Intercultural Communication* (Indianapolis: Bobbs-Merrill, 1975), 50.

When You Know Neither the Reader's Name nor Gender. If you don't know the reader's name, or if you're writing form letters which will not be individually typed, you have several options:

1. Use the reader's position or job title:

   Dear Loan Officer:

   Dear Registrar:

2. Use a general group to which your reader belongs:

   Dear Investor:

   Dear Tennis Enthusiast:

   Dear Admissions Committee:

   Terms that are meant to be positive (*Dear Careful Shopper:* and *Dear Concerned Citizen:*) may backfire if readers see them as manipulative flattery.

   Although many people claim to dislike *Dear Friend:* as a salutation in a form letter, research shows that letters using it outpull (bring in a higher response than) letters with no salutation.

3. Use a letter format which omits the salutation. The AMS simplified letter format (see Appendix A) includes the inside address and uses a subject line but omits the salutation (and complimentary close).

   SUBJECT: RECOMMENDATION FOR BEN WANDELL

Do not use *Dear Sir or Madam:*, *Dear Gentlepersons:*, or *To whom it may concern*. These terms may be nonsexist, but they are stuffy, have undesirable connotations, or sound silly.

Pronouns

When you write about a specific person, use the appropriate gender pronouns:

In his speech, John Jones said that . . . .

In her speech, Judy Jones said that . . . .

When you are not writing about a specific person, but about anyone who may be in a given job or position, traditional gender pronouns are sexist.

Sexist: a. Each supervisor must certify that the time sheet for his department is correct.

Sexist: b. When the nurse fills out the accident report form, she should send one copy to the Central Division Office.

There are four ways to eliminate sexist generic pronouns: use plurals, use second-person *you*, revise the sentence to omit the pronoun, and use pronoun pairs. The following examples use these methods to revise sentences a and b.

1. Use Plural Nouns and Pronouns.

Nonsexist: a. Supervisors must certify that the time sheets for their departments are correct.

Note: When you use plural nouns and pronouns, other words in the sentence may need to be made plural too. In the example above, plural supervisors have plural time sheets and departments.

Attempts to Create a Unisex Pronoun*

For 140 years, people have attempted to coin a unisex pronoun. None of the attempts has been successful.

Date	*he* or *she*	*his* or *hers*	*him* or *her*
1850	ne	nis	nim
1884	le	lis	lim
1938	se	sis	sim
1970	ve	vis	vim
1977	e	e's	em

As awkward as pronoun pairs sometimes seem, they're better than these unisex pronouns.

Avoid mixing singular nouns and plural pronouns.

Nonsexist but
grammatically incorrect: a.   Each supervisor must certify that the time sheets for their department is correct.

Since *supervisor* is singular, it is incorrect to use the plural *their* to refer to it. The resulting lack of agreement is becoming acceptable orally but is not yet acceptable in writing. Instead, use one of the four grammatically correct ways to make the sentence nonsexist.

2. Use *You.*

Nonsexist: a.   You must certify that the time sheet for your department is correct.

Nonsexist: b.   When you fill out an accident report form, send one copy to the Central Division Office.

You is particularly good for instructions and statements of the responsibilities of someone in a given position. Using *you* also frequently shortens sentences, since you write "Send one copy" instead of "You should send one copy." It also makes your writing more direct.

3. Substitute an Article (*a, an,* or *the*) for the Pronoun, or Revise the Sentence So That the Pronoun Is Unnecessary.

Nonsexist: a.   The supervisor must certify that the time sheet for the department is correct.

Nonsexist: b.   The nurse will
1. Fill out the accident report form.
2. Send one copy of the form to the Central Division Office.

4. When You Must Focus on the Action of an Individual, Use Pronoun Pairs.

Nonsexist: a.   The supervisor must certify that the time sheet for his or her department is correct.

Nonsexist: b.   When the nurse fills out the accident report form, he or she should send one copy to the Central Division Office.

When the pronoun is the subject of its clause, you have several choices: *he or she, s/he, she or he.* The first is probably the least disruptive to the reader. It may be sexist always to put the male pronoun first in a pair, but since it is more like traditional English it is the smoother order from the reader's point of view.

Pronoun pairs can be awkward if there are lots of pronouns, or if you must use intensive or reflexive pronouns:

If the salesperson is busy on another line when a customer calls, ask him or her whether he or she would like to leave a message or speak to someone else.

The sales representative should set goals for himself or herself that are challenging yet feasible.

* Based on Dennis E. Baron, "The Epicene Pronoun: The Word That Failed," *American Speech* 56 (1981): 83–97.

You can avoid awkwardness by using all four methods to eliminate sexist pronouns; don't just rely on method 4 alone.

The Goal: Unbiased and Inconspicuous Language

Sexism is so deeply ingrained in the language we're used to using that nonsexist alternatives may seem odd at first. As time goes on and we hear it more often, nonsexist language begins to sound more familiar. It's easier to use nonsexist language in writing, where you have a chance to revise, than in speaking, but many speakers now use nonsexist language too.

Whenever you have a choice of two or more ways to make a phrase or sentence nonsexist, choose the alternative that is the smoothest and least conspicuous. Our real goal is to allow readers to focus on *what* we say without distracting them by the *way* we say it.

SUMMARY OF KEY POINTS

- The best word depends on context: the situation, your purposes, your audience, the words you have already used. These principles can help you choose the right word:
  1. Use a word whose denotation is accurate.
  2. Use a word whose connotations are appropriate.
  3. Use short, familiar words.
  4. Use nonsexist language.
- **Denotation** is a word's literal or dictionary meaning; **connotation** means the emotional colorings or associations that accompany a word. Both denotations and connotations can change over time. Even within one period, connotations can vary from culture to culture.
- Connotations are important in business and administrative communication because we want to convey not only information but also attitudes about that information. We have the right to package our ideas attractively, but we have an ethical responsibility not to mislead our audience.
- Short words are best for most business writing. Use a long word instead of a short word
  1. If the long word more accurately expresses your meaning.
  2. If a long word is more familiar than shorter words.
  3. If a long word's connotations are more appropriate.
- Writing should be free from sexism in four areas: words and phrases, job titles, courtesy titles, and pronouns.
- *Ms.* is the nonsexist courtesy title for women. Whether or not you know a woman's marital status, use *Ms.* *unless* the woman has a professional title or unless you know that she prefers a traditional title.
- Traditional pronouns are sexist when they refer to a class of people, not to specific individuals. Four ways to make the sentence nonsexist are to use plurals, to use *you,* to revise the sentence to omit the pronoun, and to use pronoun pairs.
- Nonsexist language is fair and friendly. It includes all readers; it helps to sustain goodwill.

NOTES

1. Interoffice memo in a steel company.
2. Quoted by Emery Hutchison, "Things My Mother Never Taught Me about Writing," *Journal of Organizational Communications,* Winter 1972, 20.

3. Sign in front of a Kentucky Fried Chicken Franchise in Bloomington, IN, July 13, 1984.

4. Philip B. Crosby, *Quality Is Free: The Art of Making Quality Certain* (New York: New American Library, 1979), 79–84.

5. Bradford B. Boyd, "An Analysis of Communication between Departments—Roadblock and Bypasses," *Personnel Administration* 28, no. 6 (November-December 1965): 34.

6. William Foster, ed., *The English Factories in India, 1618–1621* (Oxford: Clarendon Press, 1906), 81, 81 n.

7. "'Chocoholic'? Look It Up: A Dictionary for the '80s," *Newsweek,* September 14, 1987, 69.

8. John Koten, "Mixing with Coke over Trademarks Is Always a Fizzle," *The Wall Street Journal,* March 9, 1978, 1, 32.

9. *News-Gazette,* Champaign-Urbana, IL, January 16, 1979, C-8.

10. D. Rhoads, "Cultural Influences on Negotiations with Latin Americans," cited in Lawrence B. Nadler, Marjorie Keeshan Nadler, and Benjamin J. Broome, "Culture and the Management of Conflict Situations," *Communication, Culture, and Organizational Processes,* ed. William B. Gudykunst, Lea P. Stewart, and Stella Ting-Tommey (Beverly Hills, CA: Sage Publications, 1985), 109.

11. January 31, 1978, quoted in Lynn Ashby, "7, 8, Facilitate," *Houston Post,* February 17, 1978.

12. For a thorough review of sexism in many parts of language, see Bobbye Sorrels Persing, *The Nonsexist Communicator* (East Elmhurst, NY: Communications Dynamics Press, 1978).

EXERCISES AND PROBLEMS FOR CHAPTER 8

8–1 WORDS WITH MULTIPLE DENOTATIONS

a. Each of the following words has several denotations. How many can you list without going to a dictionary? How many additional meanings does a good dictionary list?

buckle	checked
court	grade
light	log
mass	rock
sentence	strike
table	train

b. The denotations of the following words change when their pronunciations change. Identify the meaning(s) for each pronunciation.

bow	invalid
minute	object
present	refuse
resort	wind

c. Find six words, not listed in *a* or *b*, which have two or more denotations. How many words can you find with three denotations? With four?

8–2 IDENTIFYING ACRONYMS AND ABBREVIATIONS

a. Identify the meaning(s) for each of the following:

ASAP	IRA
CD	LIFO
EOE	OSHA
FIFO	RFP
FYI	RSVP
GIGO	SOR
HMO	WOR

b. Go through a basic textbook in your major or through a trade publication. List and identify the acronyms and abbreviations you find.

8–3 CORRECTING ERRORS IN DENOTATION AND CONNOTATION

Identify and correct the errors in denotation or connotation in the following sentences:

1. The management training program consists of a one-year intensive indoctrination in products and procedures.
2. Our agency deviates from the norm in a number of ways.
3. Some people are repulsed toward the idea of onion ice cream.
4. The Ad Club's campaigns have helped several campus activities and now an academic department gain notoriety.
5. The unit is designed to give students practice in self-assessing and revising their writing with the aid of a text-editing package.
6. Some schools still use capital punishment as an apparent quick fix for discipline problems.
7. The manager should provoke unity among his or her subordinates.
8. So far this season, the team has five losses to its credit.
9. The electrician is charged with inspecting the wiring.
10. *Writer's Workbench* consists of approximately 18 programs writers can use to evaluate their writing.

8–4 CORRECTING ERRORS IN DENOTATION AND CONNOTATION

Identify and correct the errors in connotation or denotation in the following sentences.

1. Mechanical engineers will be the primary targets of industry hiring in the next decade.
2. The company can increase its financial picture.
3. Five people died in the highly fatal accident.
4. The copier is perfect for small offices and executives.
5. I've always been close to my parents and going away to college brought me closer to them.
6. Every day, 4.7 million people literally devour *USA Today* from first page to last.

7. Time management strategies allow workers to maximize their time.

8. The company's profits depend on how large a dividend its stockholders get.

9. This report will ignore the effects of possible changes in the tax law.

10. At this point, the future of nuclear power as an energy source is tentative.

8–5 IDENTIFYING INCONGRUITIES IN CONNOTATION

Explain why the connotations of the words in the following phrases don't go together:

gourmet grub
old world waterbeds
a serious boo-boo
prudent speculator

8–6 IDENTIFYING CONNOTATIONS IN NEWS STORIES

Pick a news story (not an editorial) from your local newspaper. Identify all the words whose connotations shape the reader's response to the story.

8–7 USING CONNOTATIONS TO SHAPE RESPONSE

Write both a sentence with positive connotations and one with negative connotations to describe each of the following situations:

1. The boss seems to like Jones.

2. Jones tries to anticipate the boss's wishes and do what the boss wants.

3. Jones follows orders and doesn't initiate projects without being told to do so.

4. Jones finds out what's going on in colleagues' personal lives and talks with them about their problems.

5. Jones pays close attention to details of projects that other people often ignore.

6. Jones often starts work on a new project without being told to do so.

7. Jones shows little emotion in the office.

8. Jones gives subordinates detailed instructions about exactly how to perform their assignments.

9. When a subordinate asks a question, Jones answers at length.

10. Jones doesn't spend time on small talk.

8–8 SIMPLIFYING LANGUAGE

Each of the following sentences hides a proverb. Use simpler words to present the proverb more forcefully.

a. A mass of concreted earthy material perennially rotating on its axis will not accumulate an accretion of byorphytic vegetation.

b. It is not inappropriate to know that all articles which coruscate do not necessarily possess a high intrinsic monetary value.

c. Individuals who are domiciled in vitreous structures of patent frangibility should on no account employ petrous formations as projectiles.

8–9 REVISING SEXIST JOB TITLES

Suggest nonsexist alternatives for each of the following:

Congressman	night watchman
fireman	policeman
male nurse	repairman
mail boy	stewardess
mailman	waitress

8–10 ELIMINATING SEXIST LANGUAGE

Explain what makes each of the following sentences sexist and revise them to make them nonsexist:

1. New additions to the marketing department are Greg Gibson and Natalie Shanes. Both came to us from the Wharton MBA program. Greg is an avid tennis player; Natalie is an attractive brunette.

2. A student can have a detailed credit history by the time he graduates if he looks ahead.

3. Please draw up a projection for our manpower needs for the next 10 years.

4. Tell the nurse your symptoms so that she can tell the doctor. He can then think about your problems as he walks to your room.

5. Jackie Greenfeld
   Rosenthal Corporation
   2300 Ross Drive S.W.
   Cedar Rapids, IA 52406

   Gentlemen:

6. The suggestion plan encourages the suggester to sign his name but does not require him to do so.

7. Survey the lady of the house to see what brand of laundry detergent she buys.

8. Three surgeons will discuss their experience

with malpractice cases: Dr. Evan Carpenter, Dr. Alexander Ryan, and Mrs. Agnes Lomax.

9. All employees and their wives are covered by the new health plan.

10. Every manager should give his secretary a number where she can reach him when he goes out of the office.

8–11 RELATING WORD CHOICE TO SEMANTICS

Using examples from Chapter 8, from other books and newspapers, or from your own experience, show how word choice is related to blindering, bypassing, and intensionalism.

A single organization produces many different documents (Chapter 1).
Michael J. Hruby

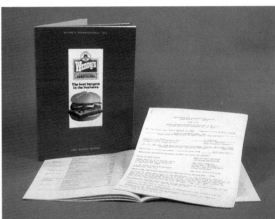

The 10-K report filed with the SEC and the annual report sent to stockholders contain essentially the same information, but differing purposes and audiences create two distinct documents (Chapter 1).
Michael J. Hruby/Courtesy of Wendy's International, Inc.

Cellular mobile phones can be used in cars and boats (Chapter 3).
Mug Shots

A facsimile or fax machine transmits a copy of your message to another location in less than a minute (Chapter 3).
Kenji Kerins

Teleconferences with video transmission allow people in different locations to participate in a meeting (Chapter 3).
Gabe Palmer/Mug Shots

Good corporate logos provide instant identification and shape our response to a company. How many different logos do you recognize? (Problem 4-10, Chapter 4).

Courtesy of Greyhound

Courtesy of Cadillac

Courtesy of The Quaker Oats Company

Courtesy of Merrill Lynch & Co., Inc.

Courtesy of Apple Computer, Inc.

Courtesy of Wendy's International, Inc.

When the Class of '96 wanted to learn how computers and communications worked together, NEC showed them.

The best channel for a message depends on the audience, your purposes, and the situation (Chapter 4).
Used with permission of NEC America, Inc.

Good writers revise their drafts to improve content and clarity, organization and layout, and style and tone (Chapter 5).
Jim Pickerell/TSW/Click

Writers who use boilerplate, or old language from another document, need to be sure that the old language fits with the new language, is truly appropriate in the current situation, and is well written (Chapter 5).
Kenji Kerins

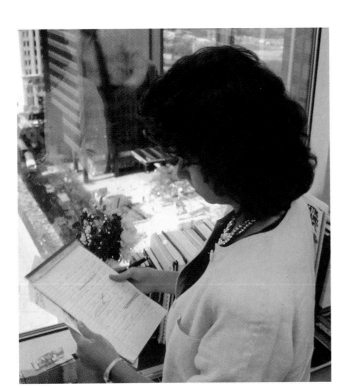

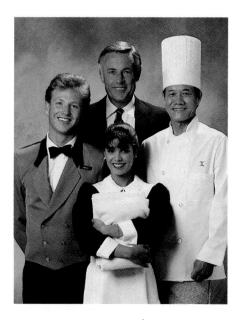

Even a message to U.S. employees may need to meet the needs of multiple audiences in a multicultural workforce (Chapter 6). Hilton employees speak 23 different native languages.
Hilton Hotels Corporation

Working in a group to produce a single document is common in organizational settings (Chapter 5).
Michael Philip Manheim/Gartman Agency

Successful multinational companies adapt their messages to audiences in different countries (Chapter 6).
Courtesy The Coca-Cola Company

Campbell Soup uses three different ad campaigns on Spanish-language television, targeting three different subsets of the U.S. Hispanic audience.
Courtesy Campbell Soup Company

Different audiences respond to different reader benefits (Chapter 7). U.S. consumers buy Tupperware to preserve perishable food. Japanese consumers buy Tupperware because it makes storage more efficient.
Both photos by Kenji Kerins

Common words have many different denotations, or dictionary meanings. An unabridged dictionary lists all the current meanings (Chapter 8).
Michael J. Hruby

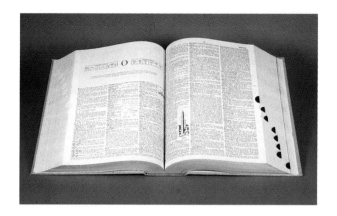

The growing number of women in the workforce is one reason to use nonsexist language (Chapter 8).
Brent Jones

Gabe Palmer/The Stock Market

A light board illuminates slides and allows a document designer to arrange the parts of a page mechnically (Chapter 10).
Eric Futran/Gartman Agency

Changes in white space, layout, and typography can create major improvements in the appearance of the final document (Chapter 10).
Richard Gross/The Stock Market

Charts and graphs can make comparisons and contrasts vivid, emphasize material, and present numerical data compactly (Chapter 11).
Chris Jones/The Stock Market

Many computer programs translate the numbers from a spread-sheet into visuals.
Photo courtesy of Hewlett-Packard Company

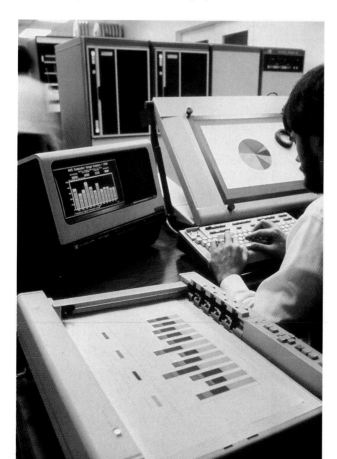

The California raisins were the most popular TV ad in 1987 but spent much less for air time than did other popular ads. Are popularity and TV spending inversely related? Or is low spending an exception to the general trend? Check the data in problem 11-4 to see (Chapter 11).
Michael J. Hruby/Courtesy of the California Raisin Advisory Board

Making Your Writing Easy to Read

QUESTIONS

- Can you believe everything you've heard about style?

- Will the style that you're used to using in other classes work for business and administrative writing?

- How can you tell if your writing is wordy? How can you tighten your writing?

- How long should sentences be? How can you write more readable sentences?

- What are the two kinds of jargon? Is either kind acceptable in business and administrative writing?

- Why are active verbs usually better than passive verbs? Is it ever OK to use passive verbs?

- What are strong verbs? Why are they better than weak verbs?

- What is parallel structure and how do you use it?

- Why do topic sentences make writing easier to read?

- What do readability formulas measure? Can they tell you if your writing is good?

> Writing, when properly managed (as you may be sure I think mine is), is but a different name for conversation.
>
> Laurence Sterne
> *Tristram Shandy,* 1759–67

Good business and administrative writing sounds like a person talking to another person, not like a computer interfacing with an android. Unfortunately, much of the writing produced in organizations today is hopelessly stuffy; it seems to have been written by faceless bureaucrats rather than by real people.

Your message isn't the only thing on the reader's desk. To help your letter, memo, or report compete with the other items demanding your reader's attention, make what you write easy to read. In just a few seconds, the reader mentally categorizes each document and decides whether to finish it now or lay it aside for later. When your message invites reading, the reader gets to it—and you get an answer or action—much sooner.

You can make your writing easier to read in two ways. First, you can make individual sentences and paragraphs easy to read, so that skimming the first paragraph or reading the whole document takes as little work as possible. Second, you can make the document look visually inviting and structure it with signposts to guide readers through the document. This chapter focuses on ways to make sentences and paragraphs easier to read. Chapter 10 will discuss ways to make the document as a whole easier to read.

HALF-TRUTHS ABOUT STYLE

Many generalizations about style are half-truths and must be applied selectively, if at all. For instance, have you ever heard the following?

Write as you talk.
Never use *I*.
Never begin a sentence with *and* or *but*.
Never end a sentence with a preposition.
Big words impress people.

Each of these has a foundation in truth, but none of them is completely true as a rule of style.

Half-Truth 1: "Write As You Talk."

One of the best tests of style is to read what you've written out loud to someone sitting about three feet away. If a passage sounds stiff and overly formal when you read it out loud, revise it: almost certainly it will sound stiff and perhaps even rude to the reader. If you wouldn't say it, don't write it.

However, unless our speech is exceptionally fluent, "writing as we talk" will cause most of us to produce awkward, repetitive, and badly organized prose. Such writing may also be unclear. In conversation, you can depend on context and gestures to convey part of your meaning. You can use your listeners' nonverbal and verbal feedback to gauge how well they understand your message and to add information, if necessary. If you make a mistake, it floats away on the air. Writing takes away the situational context and the nonverbal cues; it delays the feedback you get and preserves any errors you make. It's OK to write as you talk to get your first draft dictated or written on paper, but don't stop there. Edit to create a good written style.

Half-Truth 2: "Never Use *I.*"

Using *I* too often can make your writing sound self-centered; using it unnecessarily will make your ideas seem tentative. If you write, "I think we should adopt this plan," you imply that it's really only your idea, that other people may disagree, and that you may be wrong. When you write, "We should adopt this plan," you sound more confident.

When you write about things you've done or said or seen, using *I* is both appropriate and smoother than resorting to awkward passives or phrases like "this writer" or "the undersigned."

Half-Truth 3: "Never Begin a Sentence with *And* or *But.*"

Beginning a sentence with *and* or *also* makes the idea which follows seem like an afterthought. If you want to sound as though you have thought about what you are saying, put the *also* in the middle of the sentence or use another transition: *moreover, furthermore.*

But tells the reader that you are shifting gears and that the point which follows not only contrasts with but also is more important than the preceding ideas. Presenting such verbal signposts to your reader is important. Beginning a sentence with *but* is fine if doing so makes your paragraph read smoothly.

Half-Truth 4: "Never End a Sentence with a Preposition."

Prepositions are those useful little words that indicate relationships: for example, *with, in, under, at.* The prohibition against ending sentences with them is probably based on two facts:

1. The end of a sentence (like the beginning) is a position of emphasis. A preposition may not be worth emphasizing.
2. When the reader sees a preposition he or she expects something to follow it. At the end of a sentence, nothing does.

In job application letters, reports, and important presentations, avoid ending sentences with prepositions. Most letters and memos are less formal; it's OK to end an occasional sentence with a preposition. Analyze your audience and the situation, and use the language that you think will get the best results.

Half-Truth 5: "Big Words Impress People."

Learning an academic discipline requires that you master its vocabulary. After you get out of school, however, no one will ask you to write anything just to prove that you understand it. Instead, you'll be asked to write or speak to people who need the information you have.

Does It Sound Like Me?*

"Do you think that you're familiar with the sound of your own voice?"

"Well, sure. I know what I sound like."

"And do you think that you know what I sound like? I mean, suppose somebody told you that I had said something and they had taken it down and this was it. Would you believe them?"

I show my student two typewritten paragraphs from a piece of my own writing. He reads them slowly, a slightly puzzled frown narrowing his eyes. He looks up at me from beneath heavy eyebrows drawn together and makes a remarkable reply:

"Yes, and no. It sounds like you all right, but it's better than you talk. I mean, it's better than anybody talks, I think. What it really sounds like is you, the way you talk, but put through some kind of finishing machine so that all the pieces fit together better than when you said them."

[Good writing is your best possible voice, the way you talk "put through some kind of finishing machine."]

---

* Quoted from Daniel Fader, "Literacy and Family," *Literacy for Life: The Demand for Reading and Writing*, ed. Richard W. Bailey and Robin Marie Fosheim (New York: Modern Language Association, 1983), 236.

FIGURE 9.1
THE DIFFERENCES BETWEEN
BUSINESS AND TERM PAPER
STYLE

Good Business Style	Good Term Paper Style
Conversational: sounds like a real person talking.	More formal than conversation would be, but retains a human voice.
OK to use occasional contractions.	Few contractions, if any.
Uses *I*, first- and second-person pronouns.	First- and second-person pronouns kept to a minimum; uses *one*.
Friendly.	No effort to make style friendly.
Personal. May refer to reader by name; refers to specific circumstances of readers.	Impersonal. May generally refer to "readers" but does not name them or refer to their circumstances.
Short, simple words.	Many abstract words, technical terms.
Short sentences and paragraphs.	Sentences and paragraphs usually long.
Attention to visual impact of document.	No particular attention to visual impact.

Will They or Won't They
When people are undecided, you can tell which way they're leaning by what comes after the *but*.

"I'd like to go out, but I really need to study." Call someone else.

"I really need to study, but I'd like to go out." The person wants to be persuaded.

"You deserve a raise, but our budget is really tight this year." No raise.

"Our budget is really tight this year, but you deserve a raise." Keep pushing. The boss is on your side.

Sometimes you may want the sense of formality or technical expertise that big words create. But much of the time, big words just distance you from your audience and increase the risk of miscommunication.

When people misuse big words, they look foolish. If you're going to use big words, make sure you use them correctly.

GOOD STYLE IN BUSINESS AND ADMINISTRATIVE WRITING

The style of writing that usually earns high marks in college essays and term papers is very different from good business and administrative writing (see Figure 9.1). If most of your writing so far has been for classes, you may need to use a different style for business writing.

Differences in style exist even within the range of business and administrative writing. A memo to your boss complaining about the delays from a supplier will be informal, perhaps even chatty; a letter to the supplier demanding better service will be more formal.

Keep the following points in mind as you choose a level of formality for a specific document:

* Use a friendly, informal, specific style to someone you've talked with. If you go from a casual speaking style to a formal writing style, you'll sound stuffy or even rude.
* Avoid contractions, slang, and even minor grammatical lapses when you write to someone you don't know or to a group of people. Some people are more critical than others; don't risk a negative reaction.
* Pay particular attention to your style when you have to write uncomfortable messages: when you write to people you fear or when you must give bad news. Reliance on nouns rather than on verbs and a general deadening of style increase when people are under stress or feel insecure.[1] Confident people are more direct. Edit your writing so that you sound confident, whether you feel that way or not.

NINE WAYS TO MAKE YOUR WRITING EASIER TO READ

Bureaucratic writing is hard to read. James Suchan tested two versions of a memo report. The "high impact" version had the "bottom line" (the purpose of the report) in the first paragraph, simple sentences in normal word order, active verbs, concrete language, short paragraphs, headings and lists, and first- and second-person pronouns. The "low impact" version, in contrast, buried the bottom line in the last paragraph and used compound and complex sentences, passive verbs, abstract language, long paragraphs without headings and lists, and no personal pronouns. The high-impact version took 22% less time to read. Readers said that they understood the report better, and tests showed that they really did understand it better.[2] We'll talk about paragraph length and headings and lists in Chapter 10. The techniques that apply to the sentence level appear here.

Revise your draft in the following ways to make your writing easier to read. When you revise, remember that very little specific advice about style applies to all situations. Keep using a technique only if it improves your writing.

1. Tighten your writing.
2. Vary sentence length and sentence structure.
3. Use technical jargon sparingly; eliminate business jargon.
4. Use active verbs most of the time.
5. Use verbs—not nouns—to carry the weight of your sentence.
6. Use parallel structure.
7. Begin most paragraphs with topic sentences.
8. Use specific, vivid language.
9. Put your readers in your sentences.

Let's see why each of these strategies works and how to revise sentences and paragraphs to use them.

Tighten Your Writing.

Writing is **wordy** if the same idea could be expressed in fewer words. Unnecessary words increase typing time; they bore your reader; and they make your meaning more difficult to follow, since the reader must hold all the extra words in mind while trying to understand your meaning.

Good writing is tight. Tight writing may be long because it is packed with ideas. In Chapter 7, we saw that revisions to create you-attitude and positive emphasis and to develop reader benefits were frequently *longer* than the originals because the revision added information not in the original.

Sometimes you may be able to look at a draft and see immediately how to tighten it. When wordiness isn't obvious, try the following strategies for tightening your writing.

a. Eliminate words that are clear from the context or that tell the reader nothing.
b. Use gerunds (the *-ing* form of verbs) and infinitives to make sentences shorter and smoother.
c. Combine sentences to eliminate unnecessary words.
d. Reword sentences to cut the number of words.

The purpose of eliminating unnecessary words is to save the reader's time, not simply to see how few words you can use. You aren't writing a telegram, so keep the little words which make sentences complete. (Incomplete sentences are fine in lists where all the items are incomplete.)

Prepositions and the Prime Minister*

When writing styles were more formal than they are now, some people took great care never to end a sentence with a preposition. Even then, however, there were people who let prepositions fall anywhere in the sentence. Winston Churchill was one of these people, and his secretary always revised his drafts to reposition the preposition. Finally, an exasperated Churchill sent the following note to his secretary: "This is the sort of English up with which I will not put!"

---

* Based on Ernest Gowers, *The Complete Plain Words*, rev. Bruce Fraser (London: Her Majesty's Stationery Office, 1973), 131.

The Most Common Weaknesses in Executives' Writing*

Eighty-three percent of surveyed chief executive officers said their younger executives can't write well. The most common problems:

- Wordiness.
- Poor organization.
- Style or tone inappropriate for the intended audience.
- No clearly stated purpose.

The following examples show how to use these methods.

a. Eliminate Words That Are Clear from the Context or That Tell the Reader Nothing. Cut words that are already clear from other words in the sentence. Substitute single words for wordy phrases.

Wordy:	Keep this information on file for future reference.
Tighter:	Keep this information for reference.
or:	File this information.

Wordy:	Ideally, it would be best to put the billing ticket just below the CRT screen and above the keyboard.
Tighter:	If possible, put the billing ticket between the CRT screen and the keyboard.

Phrases beginning *of, which,* and *that* can often be shortened.

Wordy:	the question of most importance
Tighter:	the most important question

Wordy:	the estimate which is enclosed
Tighter:	the enclosed estimate

Sentences beginning with *There are* or *It is* can often be tighter.

Wordy:	There are three reasons for the success of the project.
Tighter:	Three reasons explain the project's success.

Wordy:	It is the case that college graduates advance more quickly in the company.
Tighter:	College graduates advance more quickly in the company.

b. Use Gerunds and Infinitives to Make Sentences Shorter and Smoother. A **gerund** is the *-ing* form of a verb; grammatically, it is a verb used as a noun. In the sentence "Running is my favorite activity," *running* is the subject of the sentence. An **infinitive** is the form of the verb which is preceded by "to": *to run* is the infinitive.

In the revision below, a gerund (*purchasing*) and an infinitive (*to transmit*) tighten the revision.

Wordy:	A plant suggestion has been made where they would purchase a QWIP machine for the purpose of transmitting test reports between plants.
Tighter:	The plant suggests *purchasing* a QWIP machine *to transmit* test reports between plants.

Even when gerunds and infinitives do not greatly affect length, they often make sentences smoother and more conversational.

c. Combine Sentences to Eliminate Unnecessary Words. Frequently, a second sentence repeats information given in an earlier sentence. If this is the case, combining the sentences will allow you to eliminate words while retaining all the meaning. In addition to saving words, combining sentences sharpens the

---

* Quoted from "Weak Writers," *The Wall Street Journal,* June 14, 1985, 1.

relationship between ideas, makes your writing sound more sophisticated, and focuses the reader's attention on key points.

Wordy: I conducted this survey by telephone on Sunday, April 21. I questioned two groups of upperclassmen—male and female—who, according to the Student-Staff Directory, were still living in the dorms. The purpose of this survey was to find out why some upperclassmen continue to live in the dorms even though they are no longer required by the university to do so. I also wanted to find out if there were any differences between male and female upperclassmen in their reasons for choosing to remain in the dorms.

Tighter: On Sunday, April 21, I phoned upperclassmen and women living in the dorms to find out (1) why they continue to live in the dorms even though they are no longer required to do so, and (2) whether men and women had the same reasons for staying in the dorms.

d. Reword Sentences to Cut the Number of Words.   If none of the first three methods work, reword the sentence. Think about what you *mean* and try saying the same thing in several different ways. Some alternatives will be tighter than others. Choose the tightest one.

Wordy: The reason we are recommending the computerization of this process is because it will reduce the time required to obtain data and will give us more accurate data.

Better: We are recommending the computerization of this process because it will save time and give us more accurate data.

Tight: Computerizing the process will give us more accurate data more quickly.

Wordy: The purpose of this letter is to indicate that if we are unable to mutually benefit from our seller/buyer relationship, with satisfactory material and satisfactory payment, then we have no alternative than to sever the relationship. In other words, unless the account is handled in 45 days, we will have to change our terms to a permanent COD basis.

Better: A good buyer/seller relationship depends upon satisfactory material and satisfactory payment. You can continue to charge your purchases from us only if you clear your present balance in 45 days.

Vary Sentence Length and Sentence Structure.

Readable prose mixes sentence lengths and varies sentence structure. A really short sentence (under 10 words) can add punch to your prose. Really long sentences (over 30 or 40 words) are danger signs, but a 20-word sentence isn't necessarily clearer than a 25-word sentence.

Use these guidelines for sentence length and structure:

- Always edit sentences for tightness. Even a 17-word sentence can be wordy.
- When your subject matter is complicated or full of numbers, make a special effort to keep sentences short.

Words to Cut

The following words can usually be cut:

  quite
  really
  very

Cut redundant words.

  ~~a period of~~ three months
  continue ~~on~~
  during ~~the year of~~ 1989
  ~~in conjunction~~ with
  maximum ~~possible~~
  ~~past~~ experience
  plan ~~in advance~~
  refer ~~back~~
  ~~the color~~ blue
  ~~true~~ facts

Substitute a single word for a wordy phrase.

  ~~at the present time~~   now
  ~~due to the fact that~~   because
  ~~in the event that~~   if
  ~~prior to the start of~~   before

- Use long sentences
  To show how ideas are linked to each other;
  To avoid a series of short, choppy sentences;
  To reduce repetition.
- Group the words in long and medium-length sentences into chunks that the reader can process quickly.[3]
- When you use a long sentence, keep the subject and verb close together.

Let's see how to apply the last three principles.

Use Long Sentences to Show How Ideas Are Linked to Each Other, to Avoid a Series of Short, Choppy Sentences, and to Reduce Repetition.   The following sentence is hard to read not simply because it is long but because it is shapeless. Just cutting it into a series of short, choppy sentences doesn't help. The best revision uses medium-length sentences to show the relationship between ideas.

Too long: It should also be noted in the historical patterns presented in the summary, that though there were delays in January and February which we realized were occurring, we are now back where we were about a year ago, and that we are not off line in our collect receivables as compared to last year at this time, but we do show a considerable over-budget figure because of an ultraconservative goal on the receivable investment.

Choppy: There were delays in January and February. We knew about them at the time. We are now back where we were about a year ago. The summary shows this. Our present collect receivables are in line with last year's. However, they exceed the budget. The reason they exceed the budget is that our goal for receivable investment was very conservative.

Better: As the summary shows, although there were delays in January and February (of which we were aware), we have now regained our position of a year ago. Our present collect receivables are in line with last year's, but they exceed the budget because our goal for receivable investment was very conservative.

Group the Words in Long and Medium-Length Sentences into Chunks that the Reader Can Process Quickly.   Note the chunks in the "better" revision above:

1. As the summary shows,
2. although there were delays in January and February
3. (of which we were aware),
4. we have now regained our position of a year ago.
5. Our present collect receivables are in line with last year's,
6. but they exceed the budget
7. because our goal for receivable investment was very conservative.

The two sentences are presented in seven chunks: an introductory phrase (1), a subordinate clause (2) with a parenthetical phrase (3), followed by the main clause of the first sentence (4). The second sentence begins with a main clause

(5). The sentence's second main clause (6) is introduced with a *but,* showing that it will reverse the first clause. A subordinate clause explaining the reason for the reversal completes the sentence (7). At 27 and 24 words respectively, these sentences aren't short, but they're readable because no chunk is longer than 10 words.

Any sentence pattern will get boring if it is repeated sentence after sentence. Use different sentence patterns—different kinds and lengths of chunks—to keep your reader awake.

Keep the Subject and Verb Close Together. One book suggests that if more than 10 words separate the subject and the verb, the reader is almost sure to get lost.[4] "Ten words" isn't a magic formula. But in general, sentences are easier to read if the subject and verb are near each other.

Often you can move the subject and verb closer together if you put the modifying material in a list at the end of the sentence. For maximum readability, present the list vertically.

Hard to read: *Movements* resulting from terminations, layoffs and leaves, recalls and reinstates, transfers in, transfers out, promotions in, promotions out, and promotions within *are* presently *documented* through the Payroll Authorization Form.

Smoother: The following *movements are documented* on the Payroll Authorization Form: terminations, layoffs and leaves, recalls and reinstates, transfers in and out, and promotions in, out, or within.

Still better: The following *movements are documented* on the Payroll Authorization Form:
Terminations.
Layoffs and leaves.
Recalls and reinstates.
Transfers in and out.
Promotions in, out, and within.

Sometimes you will need to change the verb and revise the word order to put the modifying material at the end of the sentence.

Hard to read: The size sequence *code* which is currently used for sorting the items in the NOSROP lists and the composite stock list *is* not part of the on-line file.

Smoother: The on-line *file does* not *contain* the size sequence code which is currently used for sorting the items in the composite stock lists and the NOSROP lists.

Minimize Technical Jargon; Eliminate Business Jargon.

There are two kinds of **jargon.** The first kind of jargon is the specialized terminology of a technical field. *LIFO* and *FIFO* are technical terms in accounting; *byte* and *baud* are computer jargon; *scale-free* and *pickled and oiled* designate specific characteristics of steel. A job application letter is the one occasion where it's desirable to use technical jargon: using the technical terminology of the reader's field helps suggest that you're a peer who also is competent in that field.

In other kinds of messages, use technical jargon only when you know that all three of the following conditions are met:

Learning the Company's Lingo*
Many companies have a whole set of specialized terms.

As part of her study of a major company, Rosabeth Moss Kanter asked 12 wives whose husbands worked in the same unit to list the words they'd heard their husbands use but couldn't define: the group listed 103 terms before she stopped it.

This cryptic jargon included terms like *A/C,* which in this company meant *agreement and comprehension.*

Jargon creates a sense of unity among the in-group but distances people in other units—even within the same organization—and distances workers from their families.

1. The term is needed to convey meaning precisely.
2. No simpler equivalent exists.
3. You are **sure that the reader understands the term.**

Much of the time, technical terms do have "plain English" equivalents:

Jargon: Foot the average monthly budget column down to Total Variable Cost, Total Management Fixed Cost, Total Sunk Costs, and Grand Total.

Better: Add the figures in the average monthly budget column for each category to determine the Total Variable Costs, the Total Management Fixed Costs, and the Total Sunk Costs. Then add the totals for each category to arrive at the Grand Total.

The revision here is longer, but it is better because it uses simple words which nearly everyone understands. The original will be meaningless to a reader who does not know what *foot* means.

It is especially important to replace jargon with "plain English" when the specialized meaning of the technical term is not in fact being used. Consider this example:

Jargon: Additional parameters for price exception reporting were established for nonstock labor buy costs.

Better: We decided to include nonstock labor buys of over $_____ in the price exception report.

The word *parameters* means factors which are held constant while other variables change. It is a term that is essential in mathematics and statistics, but it is rarely used properly in general business and administrative writing. As the revision shows, the real meaning here was simple; no technical term was needed.

Terms that have technical meanings but which are used in more general senses may be called **business slang.** In addition to *parameters,* business slang includes *bottom line, GIGO, blindsiding,* and *back to square one.* Used sparingly, these terms are appropriate in job application letters and in messages for people in your own organization, who are likely to share the vocabulary.

General slang includes words like *awesome, heavy,* and *at the end of my rope.* Slang is sometimes used in conversations and in presentations, but it is too sloppy for business and administrative writing.

The second kind of jargon is the **businessese** which some writers still use: *as per your request, enclosed please find, please do not hesitate.* Some terms were common two or three hundred years ago but are no longer part of spoken English. Some have never been used outside of business writing. They seem to have arisen partly because writers did not understand the Latin used in earlier letters and partly because writers had the impression that they ought to use a specialized terminology for business writing.[5] Business does require some specific terms, but none of the words in this second category of jargon are necessary. Indeed, some writers call these terms *deadwood,* since they are no longer living words.

College students who are straight out of high school aren't as guilty of using general business jargon as are people who have worked for several years. Some of these terms, however, seem to float through the air like germs. If any of the

*   Based on Rosabeth Moss Kanter, *Men and Women of the Corporation* (New York: Basic Books, 1977), 58, 113–14.

Instead of	Use	Because
At your earliest convenience	(The date you need a response)	If you need it by a deadline, say so. It may never be convenient to respond.
As per your request; 55 miles per hour	As you request; 55 miles an hour	*Per* is a Latin word for "by" or "for each." Use *per* only when the meaning is correct; avoid mixing English and Latin.
Enclosed please find	Enclosed is; Here is	An enclosure isn't a treasure hunt. If you put something in the envelope, the reader will find it.
Forward same to this office	Return it to this office	Omit legal jargon.
Hereto, herewith	(Omit)	Omit legal jargon.
Please be advised, Please be informed	(Omit—simply start your response.)	You don't need a preface. Go ahead and start.
Please do not hesitate	(Omit)	Omit negative words.
Pursuant to	According to; (or omit)	*Pursuant* does not mean "after." Omit legal jargon in any case.
Said order	Your order	Omit legal jargon.
This will acknowledge receipt of your letter.	(Omit—start your response)	If you answer a letter, the reader knows you got it.
Trusting this is satisfactory, we remain	(Omit)	Eliminate *-ing* endings. When you are through, stop.

FIGURE 9.2
GETTING RID OF BUSINESS JARGON

terms in the first column of Figure 9.2 show up in your writing, replace them with more modern language.

Use Active Verbs.

Use active verbs most of the time.

A verb is **active** if the grammatical subject of the sentence does the action the verb describes. A verb is **passive** if the subject is acted upon.

Active	Passive
The customer received 500 widgets.	Five hundred widgets were received by the customer.
I recommend this method.	This method is recommended by me.
The state agencies will implement the program.	The program will be implemented by the state agencies.

Verbs can be changed from active to passive by making the direct object the new subject. To change a passive verb to an active one, you must make the agent (*by _____*) the new subject. If no agent is specified in the sentence, you must supply one to make the sentence active.

Active	Passive
The plant manager approved the request.	The request was approved by the plant manager.

How to Spot Passive Verbs

Passives are usually made up of a form of the verb *to be* plus a past participle:

were received	(in the past)
is recommended	(in the present)
will be implemented	(in the future).

Passive has nothing to do with *past*. Passives can be past, present, or future.

To spot a passive, find the verb. If the verb describes something that the grammatical subject is doing, the verb is active. If the verb describes something that is being done to the grammatical subject, the verb is passive.

Hidden Verbs

Nouns ending in *-ment, -ion, -al* and *-ance* often hide verbs.

make an adjustment	adjust
make a payment	pay
make a decision	decide
reach a conclusion	conclude
take into consideration	consider
make a referral	refer
provide assistance	assist

Active	**Passive**
The plant manager approved the request.	The request was approved by the plant manager.
The committee will decide next month.	A decision will be made next month.
Send the customer a letter informing her about the change.	A letter will be sent informing the customer of the change.

If the sentence does not have a direct object in its active form, there can be no passive equivalent for the active verb.

Active	**No Passive Exists**
I would like to go to the conference.	
The freight charge will be about $1,400.	
The phone rang.	

Passive verbs have at least three disadvantages:

1. If all the information in the original sentence is retained, passive verbs make the sentence longer. Passives take more time to understand.[6]
2. If the agent is omitted, it's not clear who is responsible for action.
3. When many passive verbs are used, or when passives are used in material that has a lot of big words, the writing can be boring and pompous.

Passive verbs are desirable in these situations:

1. Use passives to emphasize the object receiving the action, not the agent.

   Your order was shipped November 15.

   The customer's order, not the shipping clerk, is important.

2. Use passives to provide coherence within a paragraph. A sentence is easier to read if "old" information comes at the beginning of a sentence. When you have been discussing a topic, use the word again as your subject even if that requires a passive verb.

   When your order arrived, orange turtleneck shirts were temporarily out of stock. Your order was filled on September 26.

   Using *order* as the subject of the second sentence provides a link between the two sentences, making the paragraph as a whole easier to read.

3. Use passives to avoid assigning blame.

   The order was damaged during shipment.

An active verb would require the writer to specify *who* damaged the order. The passive here is more tactful.

If none of these cases applies, use active verbs. They make your writing more interesting and easier to read.

Use Strong Verbs.

Put the weight of your sentence in the verb. Strong verbs make sentences more forceful and up to 25% easier to read.[7]

Weak: The financial advantage of owning this equipment instead of leasing it *is* 10% after taxes.

Better: Owning this equipment rather than leasing it *will save* us 10% after taxes.

Sometimes the meaning of your sentence hides in nouns. Use verbs to present the information more forcefully.

Weak: We *will perform* an investigation of the problem.

Better: We *will investigate* the problem.

Weak: Selection of a program *should be based* on the client's needs.

Better: *Select* the program that best *fits* the client's needs.

Use Parallel Structure.

Words or ideas that share the same logical role in your sentence must also be in the same grammatical form. Parallelism is also a powerful device for making your writing smoother and more forceful. In the following examples, the parallel portions are italicized.

Faulty: Errors can be checked by reviewing the daily exception report or note the number of errors you uncover when you match the lading copy with the file copy of the invoice.

Parallel: Errors can be checked *by reviewing* the daily exception report or *by noting* the number of errors you uncover when you match the lading copy with the file copy of the invoice.

Also parallel: To check errors, note
1. *The number* of items on the daily exception report.
2. *The number* of errors discovered when the lading copy and the file copy are matched.

Note that a list in parallel structure must fit grammatically into the umbrella sentence that introduces the list.

Use Topic Sentences.

A good paragraph has **unity;** that is, it is about only one idea, or topic. The **topic sentence** introduces or summarizes that main idea. Grammatically, the topic sentence may be either stated or implied; that is, as long as the paragraph is about only one topic, it does not need to have an explicit topic sentence. Grammatically, the topic sentence may come anywhere in the paragraph: at the beginning, middle, or end. Your writing will be easier to read, however, if you make the topic sentence explicit and put it at the beginning of the paragraph.[8]

Writing to Be Translated*

[When you know that something will be translated into another language, avoid figurative language, images, and humor. They just don't translate well.]

Consider the American copyriter who prepared a campaign on snow blowers for the European market without giving a thought to translations. . . . "Super Snow Hound" [was] the most powerful model. . . . Just what were the translators supposed to do with the names in French, German, etc.? . . . The copywriter wrote the headline: "Super Snow Hound Blows Up a Storm." You can imagine the difficulty of retaining the idiom and connotations of "blows" for snow blower and "up a storm" for heavy duty performance in a snow storm.

[Sometimes equivalent idioms exist. For example, if you're preparing a document for Quebec, use French proverbs rather than English ones.]

"Nothing to sneeze at" should become "nothing to spit on."

"To be sitting on the fence" should become "to swim between two streams."

"To make a mountain out of a molehill" should become "to drown in a glass of water."

"You can't teach an old dog new tricks" should become "one does not teach an old monkey to make faces."

---

* Quoted from Robert F. Roth, *International Marketing Communications* (Chicago: Crain Books, 1982), 139 and David Ricks, *Big Business Blunders* (Homewood, IL: Dow Jones-Irwin, 1983), 87.

How Formal Should *You* Be?*

Writers in English have it easy: *you* is both formal and informal. But many other languages have two words for *you*. Even when you're speaking to one person, the more formal term may be needed.

The French use *vous* rather than *tu* even when they're on a first-name basis.

The Danish corporate culture demands *Sie* rather than *du*.

Some Germans now use *du* rather than *Sie* if they're on a first-name basis. Germans find the informality "American" and chic.

But *du* in German also connotes an adult speaking to a child. German women facing sexual harassment sometimes use *du* to put down the man, suggesting that his behavior is childish.

Plan B also has economic advantages.
(Prepares the reader for a discussion of B's economic advantages.)

We had several personnel changes in June.
(Prepares the reader for a list of the month's terminations and hires.)

Employees have complained about one part of our new policy on parental leaves.
(Prepares the reader for a discussion of the problem.)

When the first sentence of a paragraph is not the topic sentence, readers who skim may miss the main point. Move the topic sentence to the beginning of the paragraph. In some cases you may need to write a topic sentence. If you can't think of a single sentence which serves as an "umbrella" to cover every sentence, the paragraph lacks unity. To solve the problem, either split the paragraph into two or eliminate the sentence which digresses from the main point.

Use Specific, Vivid Words.

Specific, vivid word choices show that your mind is at work; they surprise your reader; they perk up your writing. Even a routine informative report can benefit from an occasional vivid image. Persuasive messages need specifics to be convincing.

The following sentences illustrate effective specifics:

My notes from our discussion look like a schematic of the electricity cables underneath downtown Chicago, so please let me know if I have made mistakes.[9]

Computers do not like the food that humans eat. So be careful that no crumbs, sauces, soups, or oils get into the machinery if you're eating nearby.[10]

Put Your Readers in Your Sentences.

Use second-person pronouns (*you*) rather than third-person (*he, she, one, they*) to give your writing more impact. *You* is both singular and plural; it can refer to a single person or to every member of your organization.

Third-person:	Funds in a participating employee's account at the end of each six-month period will automatically be used to buy more stock unless a Notice of Election Not to Exercise Purchase Rights form is received from the employee.
Second-person:	Once you begin to participate, funds in your account at the end of each six-month period will automatically be used to buy more stock unless you turn in a Notice of Election Not to Exercise Purchase Rights form.

* Based on Iris I. Varner, "A Comparison of American and French Business Communication," Association for Business Communication International Convention, Atlanta, GA, October 15–17, 1987; Vincent O'Neill, "Training the Multi-Cultural Manager," Languages and Communication for World Business and the Professions Sixth Annual Conference, Ann Arbor, MI, May 8–9, 1987; Raymond Schaub, conversation with the author, Ann Arbor, MI, May 9, 1987.

Of course, you should use *you* only when it refers to your reader. Otherwise, you'll come up with confusing sentences like the following:

Incorrect: My visit with the outside sales rep showed me that your schedule can change quickly.

Correct: My visit with the outside sales rep showed me that schedules can change quickly.

READABILITY FORMULAS AND GOOD STYLE

Because you're likely to encounter readability formulas, you should know what they are and why they are at best a very limited guide to good style.

Computer packages that analyze style may give you a readability score. Some state "plain English" laws require consumer contracts to meet a certain readability score. Some companies require that warranties and other materials for consumers meet certain scores. The sidebar shows how to calculate the two best known formulas, the Gunning Fog Index and the Flesch Reading Ease Scale.

As you can see, readability formulas depend heavily on word length and sentence length. But as Janice C. Redish and Jack Selzer have shown, using shorter words and sentences will not necessarily make a passage easy to read.[11] Some short words (e.g., *waive, bear market, liquid*) may not be easy to understand, especially if they have technical meanings. Short choppy sentences and sentence fragments are actually harder to understand than well-written medium-length sentences.

Even more serious, no reading formula yet devised takes into account three factors that influence how easy a text is to read: the complexity of the ideas, the organization of the ideas, and the layout and design of the document.

Instead of using readability formulas to measure style, the Document Design Center recommends that you test your draft with the people for whom it is designed. How long does it take them to find the information they need? Do they make mistakes when they try to use the document? Do they think the document is easy to use? Answers to these questions can give us much more accurate information than any readability score.

BUILDING A GOOD STYLE OF YOUR OWN

There are two basic ways to build a good business style: read widely and write a great deal. To get a sense of the informality needed for business writing, read magazine articles and the copy in newspaper and magazine ads. Read this book: it uses the same informal style you'll use in letters and memos. Immerse yourself in language: notice the words people use and how you respond to different styles.

Experiment with different styles, recognizing that anything that's new to you will feel strange for a while. Writing well takes practice. Start a journal, where you simply jot down ideas, reactions to what you're reading, or the way things are going that day. Or do some freewriting at least three times a week: write for 15 minutes (set a timer) without stopping to think, revise, or edit. When you write a letter, memo, or report, read what you've written out loud to another person. If you'd never *talk* like that, try rephrasing your idea in words that are more conversational.

How to Calculate Readability Formulas*

The Gunning Fog Index

1. Find the average number of words in a sentence by dividing the total number of words in the passage by the number of sentences. If the passage is long, take several samples of 100 words spaced evenly through it.

2. Find the percentage of "hard words" by dividing 100 into the number of words in the passage with three or more syllables. In a long passage, take several 100-word sections. In the count of words with three or more syllables,

    Omit capitalized words.

    Omit easy words (e.g., *book-keeper, butterfly*).

    Omit verbs that have three syllables because of *-ed* or *-es*.

3. Multiply the two numbers (average words per sentence, number of hard words per 100 words) by .4. This yields a grade level for the education necessary to understand the passage:

    8 = eighth-grade.

    11 = high school junior.

    13 = college freshman.

The Flesch Reading Ease Scale

1. Figure the average number of words per sentence. Multiply that number by 1.015.

2. Figure the average number of syllables per word. Multiply that number by .846.

3. Add the two numbers and subtract the total from 206.835. This yields a number between 0 (very difficult) and 100 (very easy). The higher the score, the better.

* Based on Janice C. Redish, "Readability," *Document Design: A Review of the Relevant Research*, ed. Daniel B. Felker (Washington, DC: American Institutes for Research, 1980), 73–75.

The Boss Won't Let Me Write
That Way
When a writing consultant urged them to use *I*, the engineers in Research and Development (R&D) at one firm claimed they couldn't: "Our boss won't let us." The consultant checked with their boss, the Vice President for Research and Development. He said, "I don't care what words they use. I just want to be able to understand what they write."

The Vice President had a Ph.D. and had once done experiments in R&D himself; but he'd spent several years in management. He no longer knew as many technical details as did his subordinates. Their efforts to impress him backfired: he was annoyed because he couldn't understand their reports and had to tell subordinates to rewrite them.

Moral #1: If you think your boss doesn't want you to write simply, ask him or her. A few bosses do prize flowery language. Most don't.

Moral #2: Even if your boss has the same academic background you do, he or she won't necessarily understand what you write. You need to revise your memos and reports so that what you say is clear and easy to read.

Building a good style takes energy and effort, but it's well worth the work. Good style can make every document you write more effective; good style will help make you the good writer so valuable to every kind of organization.

SUMMARY OF KEY POINTS

- Good style in business and administrative writing is less formal, more friendly, and more personal than the style usually used for term papers.
- The following techniques will make your writing easier to read:
  1. Tighten your writing. Writing is **wordy** if the same idea could be expressed in fewer words.
     a. Eliminate words that are clear from the context or that tell the reader nothing.
     b. Use gerunds and infinitives to make sentences shorter and smoother.
     c. Combine sentences to eliminate unnecessary words.
     d. Reword sentences to cut the number of words.
  2. Vary sentence length and sentence structure.
  3. Use technical jargon sparingly; eliminate business jargon. Technical jargon is acceptable when
     - The term is needed to convey meaning precisely.
     - No simpler equivalent exists.
     - The writer is sure that the reader understands the term.
     General business jargon is never acceptable.
  4. Use active verbs most of the time. Active verbs are better because they are shorter, clearer, and more interesting.
  5. Use verbs—not nouns—to carry the weight of your sentence.
  6. Use parallel structure. Use the same grammatical form for ideas that have the same logical function.
  7. Begin most paragraphs with topic sentences so that readers know what to expect in the paragraph.
  8. Use specific, vivid language.
  9. Put your readers in your sentences.

- Readability formulas are not a good guide to style. They imply that all short words and all short sentences are equally easy to read; they ignore other factors which make a document easy or hard to read: the complexity of the ideas, the organization of the ideas, and the layout and design of the document.
- To polish your own style, read widely and write a great deal.

NOTES

1. Robert L. Brown, Jr. and Carl G. Herndl, "An Ethnographic Study of Corporate Writing: Job Status as Reflected in Written Text," *Functional Approaches to Writing: A Research Perspective,* ed. Barbara Couture (Norwood, NJ: Ablex, 1986), 16–19, 22–23.

2. James Suchan, "The Effect of Written Communication Style on Reading Time and Comprehension," Conference on College Composition and Communication, St. Louis, MO, March 15–17, 1988.

3. Arn Tibbetts, "Ten Rules for Writing Readably," *Journal of Business Communication* 18, no. 4 (Fall 1981): 55–59.

4. J. C. Mathes and Dwight W. Stevenson, *Designing Technical Reports: Writing for Audiences in Organizations* (Indianapolis: Bobbs-Merrill, 1976).

5. See Kitty O. Locker, "'As Per Your Request': A History of Business Jargon," *Iowa State Journal of Business and Technical Communication* 1, no. 1 (January 1987): 27–47.

6. Harris B. Savin and Ellen Perchonock, "Grammatical Structure and the Immediate Recall of English Sentences," *Journal of Verbal Learning and Verbal Behavior* 4 (1965): 348–53; Pamela Layton and Adrian J. Simpson, "Deep Structure in Sentence Comprehension," *Journal of Verbal Learning and Verbal Behavior* 14 (1975): 658–64.

7. E. B. Coleman, "The Comprehensibility of Several Grammatical Transformations," *Journal of Applied Psychology* 48, no. 3 (1964): 186–90; Keith Raynor, "Visual Attention in Reading: Eye Movements Reflect Cognitive Processes," *Memory and Cognition* 5 (1977): 443–48.

8. Thomas N. Huckin, "A Cognitive Approach to Readability," *New Essays in Technical and Scientific Communication: Research, Theory, Practice,* ed. Paul V. Anderson, R. John Brockmann, and Carolyn R. Miller (Farmingdale, NY: Baywood Publishing, 1983), 93–98.

9. Bill Bayer to Kitty Locker, January 23, 1987.

10. "Micro Center Service Department Helpful Hints," distributed by Micro Center, Columbus, OH, Summer 1987.

11. Janice C. Redish and Jack Selzer, "The Place of Readability Formulas in Technical Communication," *Technical Communication* 32, no. 4 (1985): 46–52.

EXERCISES AND PROBLEMS FOR CHAPTER 9

9–1 CHANGING VERBS FROM PASSIVE TO ACTIVE

Identify the passive verbs in the following sentences and convert them to active verbs. In some cases, you may need to add information to do so. You may use different words as long as you retain the basic meaning of the sentence. Remember that imperative verbs are active, too.

1. It has been observed that some of the terminals are not used.

2. With the assistance of computers, books are rapidly catalogued, bibliographic entries are verified, orders for materials are placed, and reference questions are answered.

3. When the business plan is complete it is suggested that it be rerouted for final approval.

4. The conclusions were made after repeated measurements and calculations were taken.

5. All employees being budgeted should be listed by name and position. Any employee whose name does not appear on the September Listing of Salaried Employees must be explained. If this employee is a planned replacement, indicate who will be replaced and when. If it is an addition, the reason must be explained.

6. Checks should be signed only by designated officers or employees of the corporation.

7. Before an invoice is approved for payment, its numerical accuracy should be tested by the assistant treasurer.

8. As stated in my résumé, I supervised a staff of 25 workers as a McDonald's Crew Chief.

9. Many shareholders are confused by the language in annual reports.

10. The questionnaire responses were analyzed and the conclusion made that the demand for educational toys will increase.

9–2 REDUCING WORDINESS

Eliminate words and combine sentences to eliminate wordiness.

1. There are five possible options available.

2. One advantage of the program is that it offers short-term quick results.

3. This topic seems to be of importance.

4. We must make a recommendation that will solve this problem.

5. I conducted my survey the weekend of April 20th in an all-female housing unit. I gave out questionnaires to 50 women who ranged from freshman to seniors. My purpose was to test the hypothesis that women who exercised on a regular basis had higher GPAs.

6. During the audit, there were found inconsistencies between the amount on typed expense vouchers and the sums that were recorded on hand-written vouchers.

7. None of the questions were of a personal nature.

8. Yesterday I received a call from Norman Conte of community services. He said that he had left numerous messages for employees to call him back, but he has not had any response from us.

9. Recently customers have complained that they have to wait in line for long periods of time. The reason this is happening is because there aren't enough employees available to wait on them.

10. If the reader should happen to find any sections which are overly wordy in this book, it is no doubt due to the fact that the author did not have enough time to make the necessary cuts and revisions.

9–3 EDITING SENTENCES TO IMPROVE STYLE

Revise these sentences to make them smoother, less wordy, and easier to read. Eliminate jargon and repetition. Keep the information; you may reword or reorganize it. If the original is not clear, you may need to add information to write a clear revision. You may want to review Chapter 8 as you do this exercise.

1. Please advise the undersigned whether the new hospital wing will be completed by January 15. If the wing will not then be ready, please advise as to whether the required notices for an extension of time to complete have been given. Also, advise as to the amount of money which has been paid out under the construction contract agreement.

2. Can I be of assistance to you?

3. This report does not provide all the information necessary for a proper analysis of expenditures on a monthly basis.

4. I hopefully look forward to meeting you personally on my next trip.

5. Students with no credit history can get a charge card at Sears if
   a. Must be a junior, senior, or graduate student.
   b. They substitute personal references for credit references.
   c. Must have some income besides parental support. It can be anything from a summer job to a part-time job during school.
   d. They open a special account with a $300 limit. After six months, the limit can be raised if the payment record is satisfactory.

6. We are in the process of negotiating a new insurance policy and will forward to your office, a certificate confirming your coverage to be effective July 15, as soon as possible.

7. We are recommending that the agency buy a laser printer because it will produce documents more quickly and enable us to create a greater variety of documents.

8. On an overall basis, the installation of computers in dormitories is estimated to be approximately 40% complete.

9. Each person in a supervisory position has important responsibilities. People in managerial positions have important responsibilities, too.

10. As a result of this meeting I recommend:
    a. Purchase of IBM software and use our computer for N/C tape preparation.
    b. To assist with future tape requests, someone from the Chicago office should be considered as an addition to this area.
    c. Tape preparation for other plants should be done in Chicago.
    d. Each plant should, however, have a TWX machine to receive perforated tape for use on the N/C machine.

9–4 EDITING SENTENCES TO IMPROVE STYLE

Revise these sentences to make them smoother, less wordy, and easier to read. Eliminate jargon and repetition. Keep the information; you may reword or reorganize it. If the original is not clear, you may need to add information to write a clear revision.

1. Material must not be left on trucks outside the warehouse while it is waiting to be unloaded. You might consider parking these trucks inside the plant. Another option is to unload at the time of receiving the truck.

2. This shortfall can be eliminated with the following measures:
   • Increase cost containment through better management and labor productivity.
   • Raise fares gradually to keep pace with costs.
   • The state will provide an annual operating subsidy of $75 million if the transit system balances its budget.

3. It is our opinion that these measures are absolutely necessary for the maintenance of our position in the market.

4. The company library has standard reference works. It also has copies of government reports. Copies of all internal reports are housed there too. The library was opened in 1983.

5. This memo will describe our thoughts for possible cash management approaches that you may want to consider for your operations. We believe that the use of such techniques would indicate a reduction in cash requirements of $500,000 per year, or, at 10% interest rates, an additional $50,000 annual gross operating profit.

6. There is reason to believe that part of our difficulties may arise because we do not know the specific requirements for imports which do and do not need to pay duties when imported into the destination countries.

7. From a tax standpoint, these mutual funds would seem to be attractive to investors who, for investment reasons, desire to diversify their holdings or otherwise to sell them, without incurring capital gains tax.

8. The property is close in proximity to rail transportation.

9. The new fixed interest rate is guaranteed for a three-year period of time.

10. The library's card catalog has grown beyond a manageable size and subsequently has ceased to function at an acceptable level.

9–5   COMBINING SENTENCES

Combine the following short sentences to show how their ideas are related. Revise wording or the order in which information is given, if necessary.

1. The cost of making the merchandise is higher. The cost to the consumer is higher.

2. A newsletter will be published every other month for all employees. Publication will begin in March. The newsletter will report company information and special interest stories. It will also name "The Employee of the Month."

3. Normally the matching ratio is 25% State and 75% Federal funds. We are not following the normal pattern. We are paying 30% of the cost from State funds. By doing this more projects can be funded.

4. We can't approve such a large capital expense. We can only approve expenses that will increase production and profits.

5. The subsidiary is a separate corporate entity. Its financial rating should be based on its own net worth. Its financial rating should not be based on the net worth of the parent company.

6. I visited the Colorado office. I was impressed with what I saw.

7. Being a management trainee gives you many experiences. These experiences are very important in your professional development. You can use these experiences to learn about the company, too.

8. Last week I received a letter from one of our prospective clients. This letter voiced the client's dissatisfaction of the impersonal nature of the letters received from our department.

9. We made an excellent presentation to the County Board. We did not get the contract.

10. We were able to reduce the number of uncollectible accounts. The total amount of uncollectible bills rose.

9–6   IDENTIFYING TECHNICAL JARGON

Using a textbook for an introductory course in your major, find five terms that have technical meanings. As

your instructor directs, answer the following questions orally or in writing.

a. What is the technical meaning of each term?

b. Do the terms also have nontechnical meanings? What are they?

c. How widely do you think the technical meaning is known? For example, if the term is from accounting, would people who are not accountants be likely to know the meaning of it? Why or why not?

9–7   ELIMINATING JARGON AND SIMPLIFYING LANGUAGE

Revise these sentences to eliminate jargon and to use short, familiar words. In some sentences, you'll need to reword, reorganize, or add information to produce the best revision. Review Chapter 8 as you do this exercise.

1. Please advise the undersigned if any further assistance can be rendered to you by us.

2. The project cannot commence until budget estimates are finalized.

3. At this point in time, the most viable option is to terminate breakfast service in the cafeteria.

4. As per your request, the writer has secured an estimate of the cost to install a company-wide electronic mail system.

5. Please be advised that upon reviewing the legislative issues file, we find the information therein outdated.

6. Upon completing your reading and examination of the document, please affix your signature to same and forward said document to this office at your earliest convenience.

7. In my most recent employment, I utilized a computer.

8. When the premises are vacated, it is required that the illumination be extinguished.

9. We must prioritize our options.

10. Pursuant to your instructions, please find enclosed three copies of the blueprints.

9–8   IDENTIFYING BUSINESS SLANG

Gather information about business slang in a particular organization or field. Use one or more of the following methods:

List and define the business slang that employees use in a place where you work or have worked.

Ask people to list jargon and business slang their spouses use to talk about work.

Ask someone who has been employed for less than a year to list and identify the jargon and slang terms he or she learned after coming to work for this employer.

As your instructor directs,

a. Present your information orally to the class.

b. Present your information in a memo to your instructor.

c. Combine your information with that of other students in a group memo or report.

9–9 EDITING YOUR OWN PROSE

As you write letters, memos, and reports for this course, save your drafts. Go through them to find a passage where you used or could use each of the nine techniques described in this chapter.

As your instructor directs,

a. Share your results orally with a small group or with the entire class.

b. Report your results in a memo to your instructor.

c. Use your results to rewrite the memo, letter, or report.

9–10 USING READABILITY FORMULAS

Apply one of the readability formulas explained in this chapter to each of the following:

1. One of your papers for this course.
2. One of your papers for another course.
3. A textbook.
4. A set of instructions.
5. A newspaper article.

Do the scores correlate with the relative difficulty of the various texts? Why or why not?

If you used two readability formulas, did they both rank all five texts in the same order of difficulty?

As your instructor directs,

a. Share your results orally with a small group or with the entire class.

b. Report your results in a memo to your instructor.

Designing the Document

QUESTIONS

- Why does the appearance of documents matter?
- How should you organize material and lay it out on the page to make it easier to read?
- Can you use headings in letters and memos? How do you set up headings?
- What typographical principles make material easier to read?
- At what stage in the writing process should you think about document design?

Form ever follows function.
Louis Henri Sullivan
"The Tall Office Building
Artistically Considered," 1896

A bout the same time that the tall office building was reshaping American skylines, memo format evolved to fill the needs of internal correspondence in the late 19th and early 20th centuries. In the last two decades, writers have begun streamlining the body of memos and letters as well. Psychologists and graphic artists have done considerable research on the ways that we perceive print, and more and more writers have begun to apply that research. The way words are presented visually can make documents easier to use.

Visual impact means the visual first impression that you get when you look at a page. An attractive document looks inviting, friendly, and easy to read. The visual grouping of ideas also makes the structure of the document more obvious so the document **is** easier to read.

Good design isn't just for newsletters and booklets. Everyday memos, letters, reports, and notices will be easier to read and to act on if they're designed well. Good design gets your point across more efficiently. Research shows that easy-to-read documents also enhance your credibility and build an image of you as a professional, competent person.[1]

GUIDELINES FOR DESIGNING DOCUMENTS

Use the following nine guidelines to create visually attractive documents. The first four guidelines cover how you organize information and lay it out on the page; the last five cover the physical appearance of the words on the page.

Organization and Layout

1. Use white space to separate and emphasize points.
2. Use headings to group points and lead the reader through the document.
3. Design the page so that the eye moves from the top left to the lower right corner.
4. Use a grid of imaginary columns to unify documents with many graphic elements.

Typography

5. Use highlighting devices in moderation.
6. Use ragged right margins, not justified margins.
7. Use a limited number of type fonts.
8. Avoid tiny type.
9. Limit the use of words all set in capital letters.

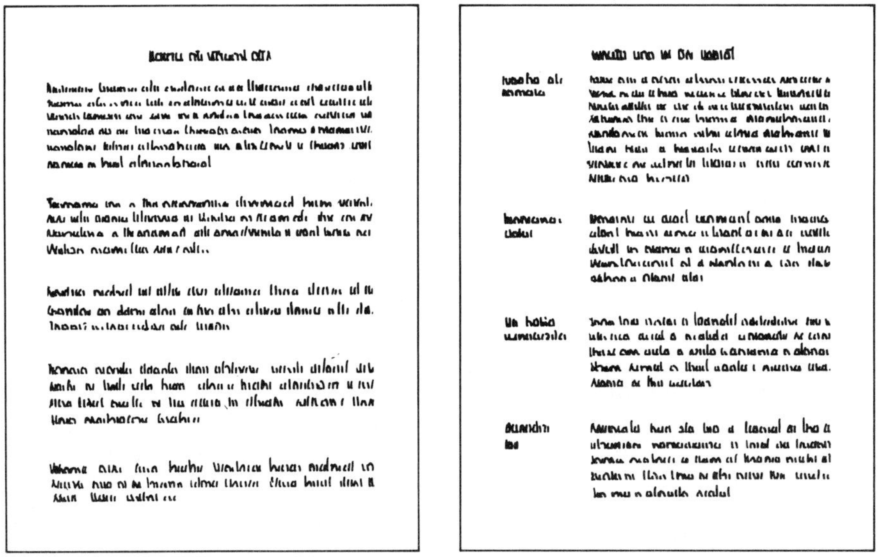

FIGURE 10.1
USE OF MARGINS TO CREATE
WHITE SPACE

We'll look at each of these guidelines briefly and then see how all of them together can be used to revise a document.

1. Use White Space.

White space—the empty space on the page—makes material easier to read by emphasizing the material that it separates from the rest of the text. White space can be achieved in several ways.

Use **big margins** if the number of pages doesn't matter. A page usually looks better if the top margin is slightly bigger than the bottom margin.

Vary paragraph lengths, but use mostly short paragraphs. A page looks easier to read when most of the paragraphs are short (six typed lines or less). First and last paragraphs should be quite short—just three to five typed lines. It's even OK to have a paragraph that's just one sentence. Internal paragraphs should be no longer than seven to eight typed lines.

A page will look monotonous if all the paragraphs are the same length. Try for a good mix of medium-length, shorter, and very short paragraphs.

Occasionally indent paragraphs (on both sides) for emphasis. Depending on the effect you want, you can indent on the left only or on both left and right.

> Indenting material calls attention to it. Make sure that anything you indent deserves emphasis. Make indented sections positive, specific, and interesting.

Use **lists** to emphasize material. Use numbered lists when the number or sequence of items needs to be exact; use **bullets** (large dots) when the number and sequence don't matter. You can use lists for phrases, sentences, or even paragraphs.

When you use a list, make sure that all of the items in it are parallel and fit into the structure of the umbrella sentence that introduces the list. (For a discussion of parallel structure, review Chapter 9.)

Keeping Up with Document Design Research

The Document Design Center in Washington, DC revises documents for businesses and government agencies, conducts research, and keeps tabs on work done in document design and "plain English."

The center has published several short books about how to produce better documents and issues two free newsletters: "Simply Stated" and "Simply Stated in Business."

To get on the mailing list for the newsletters or to get information about the center's publications, write:

Document Design Center
American Institutes for Research
3333 K Street, NW
Washington, DC 20007

Leave Room for Language*

If you're writing a text that will be translated, leave more white space than you would for an English-only document. When text is translated from English into other languages, it may take up 25% to 30% more space.

Bullets are large round dots that set off items in a list. Numbering a list suggests that both the number and order of items matter. When you are giving examples, but the number is not exact and the order does not matter, use bullets to set off items. To type a bullet, type a lower case *o* and fill it in with pen or pencil. Skip three or four spaces between the *o* and the first letter in the word or phrase which follows it.

2. Use Headings.

As George Miller has shown, people can process only seven plus or minus two bits of information at a time.[2] It doesn't matter whether the bit is a single stimulus such as a musical tone or a single word, or a large chunk of information like a musical theme or a philosophical concept. Our short-term memories can only hold seven plus or minus two bits at a time. Only after those bits are processed and put into long-term memory can we assimilate new information. Large amounts of information will be easier to process if they are grouped into three to seven chunks rather than presented as individual items.

Headings are words or short phrases which group points and divide your letter, memo, or report into sections. They help the reader in several ways:

- They break up the page, making it look less formidable and more interesting.
- They enable your reader to see how the document is organized at a glance.
- They help your reader to turn quickly to sections of special interest.
- They enable your reader to compare and contrast points more easily.

If you use headings at all, you'll normally have several. Headings should be specific; "Part-Time Personnel in the Dallas Office" is better than "Personnel." Headings must also cover all the material until the next heading. Normally, you will spend at most two or three paragraphs on a subject before you switch your focus—and need a new heading.

You can also use complete sentences or questions for headings. The headings at any one level should be parallel: all noun phrases, for example, or all complete sentences. In all but the most formal documents, it's OK to use different kinds of headings at different levels. For example, a writer could use phrases for the main headings and sentences for the subheadings.

In a letter or memo, main headings are typed even with the left-hand margin and are underlined or boldfaced. The first letters of the first word and of other major words are capitalized; all other letters are lower case. Some organizations use all capital letters for headings rather than just capitalizing the first letters of words. Triple-space between the previous text and the heading and double-space between the heading and the next which follows.

If you need **subdivisions within a head,** indent the subheading, underline it (or use bold type), and put a period after it. Begin the paragraph on the same line. Use subheadings only when you have at least two subdivisions under a given main heading.

In a report, you may need more than two levels of headings. See Chapter 20 for information on setting up five levels of headings for reports.

---

* Based on Robert F. Roth, *International Marketing Communications* (Chicago: Crain Books, 1982), 301.

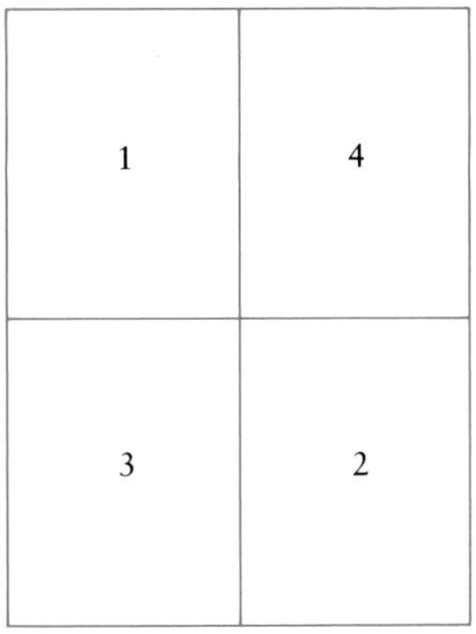

FIGURE 10.2
THE RELATIVE EMPHASIS
OF THE FOUR QUADRANTS
OF THE PAGE

3. Design the Page So That the Eye Moves from the Top Left to the Lower Right.

Readers in Western cultures start in the upper-left-hand corner of the page and read to the right and down. As Philip M. Rubens notes, the four quadrants of the page carry different visual weights. The upper-left-hand quadrant seems to be the most important, the lower-right-hand quadrant second most important, and the upper-right hand corner the least important.[3] See Figure 10.2.

4. Use a Grid to Unify Graphic Elements.

For years, graphic designers have used a **grid system** to design pages. In its simplest form, a grid imposes two or three imaginary columns on the page. In more complex grids, these columns can be further subdivided. Then all the graphic elements—text indentations, headings, visuals, etc.—are lined up within the columns. See Figure 10.3 for examples.

Symmetry creates a more pleasing page, since the eye looks for patterns.[4]

5. Use Highlighting Devices in Moderation.

Underlining, boldface type, marginal notes, and changes in type size and type font can highlight key points. However, don't overdo it. A page that uses every possible highlighting device just looks busy and hard to read.

Color works well to highlight points, but it doesn't photocopy well. Blue may not be picked up by a photocopier at all.

Don't draw boxes around key points. Readers interpret boxed sections as afterthoughts and tend to skip them.[5]

6. Use Ragged Right Margins.

The following paragraphs illustrate the two kinds of right margins:

Justified margins end evenly on the right side of the page. This paragraph is set with justified margins. Books and other typeset materials have traditionally used justified margins; now many word-processing programs are able to justify margins. Some programs, however, leave wide spaces between words. These "rivers" that run down the page are distracting to readers.

How Big Is Your Short-Term Memory?

One way to test the capacity of your short-term memory is to think about phone numbers. Telephone numbers in the United States are seven digits. If you sometimes forget a phone number while you are dialing it and have to look back at the listing in order to finish dialing, your short-term memory holds only five or six bits of information. If you never have to look back at the book, your memory holds at least seven bits of information.

FIGURE 10.3
EXAMPLES OF GRIDS TO IMPROVE DESIGN

A Memo

Memo

Indented sections in columns—regular text uses whole width of page.

A Page with Visuals

NEWS AND VIEWS

Headline across whole width. Visuals in first vertical column. Text covers columns two and three.

A Newsletter Page

Our Company

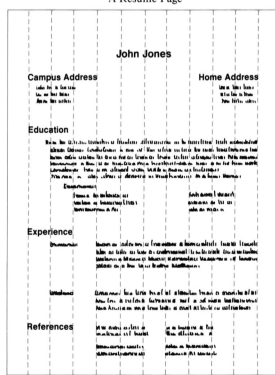

Six-column grid. Headline across whole width. Picture in middle third. Text in two halves nests around photo.

A Résumé Page

John Jones

Campus Address   **Home Address**

Education

Experience

References

Twelve-column grid. Name centered. Campus and home address in two halves. Headings at left margin. Text under heads may go across whole page for some categories; uses columns for other categories.

Geneva **Bold** <u>Underlined</u> *Italic* Condensed

Benquiat **Bold** <u>Underlined</u> *Italic* Conde

Cheltenham **Bold** <u>Underlined</u> *Italic* Cond

Korinna **Bold** <u>Underlined</u> *Italic* Condensed Ex

Weiss **Bold** <u>Underlined</u> *Italic* Condensed E

Souvenir **Bold** <u>Underlined</u> *Italic* Condensed Ex

Zapf **Bold** <u>Underlined</u> *Italic* Condensed E

Unjustified margins are sometimes called **ragged right margins.** This paragraph is set with ragged right margins. Anyone using a manual typewriter will produce ragged right margins. Many word-processing programs offer nonjustified margins as an option. If the document has mostly short words, ragged right margins will still be fairly even. However, lots of long words may create big differences in line length.

Unless your printer produces proportional type (that is, an *i* that takes up less space than an *m*), justifying will be done by leaving extra spaces between some words. These extra spaces slow readers considerably. Research shows that poor readers find justified type harder to read than unjustified type.[6]

Ragged right margins are usually less expensive to produce. If a change is made in a line of justified type, it affects the spacing for that line and perhaps for the whole page or document. Because ragged right margins are uneven, it is more likely that you can add or delete a letter or even a word without affecting other pages.

Why Would I Want to Make Clothes Dirty?*

One laundry detergent company certainly wishes now that it had contacted a few locals before it initiated its promotional campaign in the Middle East. All of the company's advertisements pictured soiled clothes on the left, its box of soap in the middle, and clean clothes on the right. But, because in that area of the world people tend to read from the right to the left, many potential customers interpreted the message to indicate the soap actually soiled the clothes.

7. Limit the Number of Type Fonts.

Fonts are the style of type. Each font has a design for each letter, number, and symbol. See the examples in Figure 10.4.

Two different fonts in one document are usually enough. You can create emphasis and levels of headings by using these fonts in bold and in different sizes.

Use black type on white paper. White letters on dark paper take longer to read.

---

* Quoted from David A. Ricks, *Big Business Blunders* (Homewood, IL: Dow Jones-Irwin, 1983), 55.

FIGURE 10.5
FULL CAPITALS HIDE THE
SHAPE OF A WORD

Full capitals hide the shape of a word.

FULL CAPITALS HIDE THE SHAPE OF A WORD.

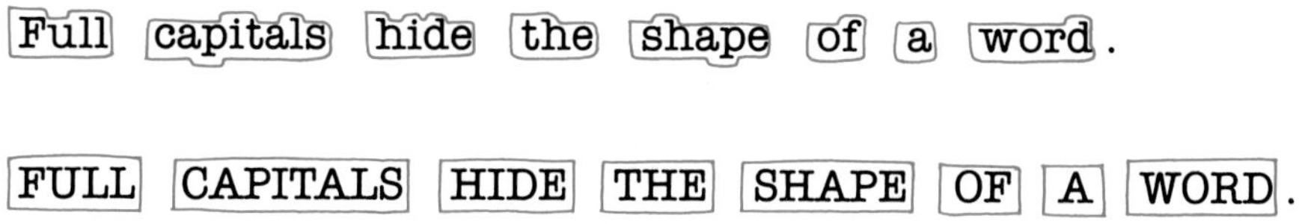

Don't Write Ransom Notes*
The first time people use desktop publishing, a lot of them produce documents that look like ransom notes with words cut out of newspapers. Every word uses a different size and a different font.

8. Avoid Tiny Type.

"Fine print" has become almost a synonym for points that the writer is trying to hide. A point size of 8 to 10 works well for most texts. With some audiences (for example, children or old people) type needs to be bigger.

If your material will not fit in the available pages, try cutting one more time. Putting some sections in tiny type will save space, but most readers will skip those sections. Whether they read them or skip them, readers are likely to have negative feelings about a document that is hard to read—negative feelings which may extend to the organization that produced the document.

9. Limit the Use of Words All Set in Capital Letters.

We recognize words by their shapes.[7] In capitals, all words are rectangular; letters lose the descenders and ascenders that make reading go more quickly. Use full capitals sparingly. See Figure 10.5.

Using the Guidelines to Redesign a Document

Figure 10.6 shows how the Document Design Center used these guidelines to redesign Ford's warranty booklet.

DOCUMENT DESIGN AS PART OF THE WRITING PROCESS

Document design isn't something to "tack on" when you've finished writing. Indeed, the best documents are created when you think about design at each stage of the writing process.

- As you plan, think about your audience. Are they skilled readers? Are they busy? Will they read the document straight through or skip around in it? What do they want to know?
- As you write, incorporate lists and headings. Use visuals to convey numerical data clearly and forcefully.
- Get feedback from people who will be using your document. How long does it take them to read it? Can they answer *yes/no* questions correctly using the document? What parts of the document do they think are hard to understand? Is there additional information they need?

* Based on Ross Figgins, "Desktop Publishing," Association for Business Communication International Convention, Atlanta, GA, Oct. 14–17, 1987.

FIGURE 10.6
"BEFORE" AND "AFTER" PAGES FROM FORD'S WARRANTY BOOKLET

This is a "before" example:

This is an "after" example:

...any v...our r...th p...
ba...ag...The detail...your warra...age are ou...
in this...oklet.

The warranty begins on the original retail delivery date, or on the date of first use, whichever occurs first.

BASIC COVERAGE

The entire vehicle, except tires, is covered for 12 months or 12,000 miles, whichever occurs first.

The Ford radio or radio/tape components and the factory-installed air conditioning, heater, rear window defogger or de-icer, heated outside rear view mirror systems, and electrically heated windshields are covered for 12 months regardless of mileage.

CORROSION COVERAGE

Repairs to correct perforation from corrosion of any body sheet metal panel are covered to 36 months from the warranty start date, regardless of mileage. (Repair of corrosion due to a defect, without perforation, is covered for 12 months or 12,000 miles, whichever occurs first.)

— **FORD CONSUMER**

If a warranty matter is not handled to your satisfaction, you may w independent third-party review. It is recommended but *not* required ship management and the Ford Parts and Service Division District C the Ford Consumer Appeals Board procedure is shown in the C detailed information on the Ford Consumer Appeals Boards pleas tained by calling the Ford Consumer Appeals Board at 1-800-241 peals Board before taking action under the Magnuson-Moss Warra provided by certain state laws. This dispute handling procedure rights which are independent of the Magnuson-Moss Warranty Ac

These warranties give you specific legal rights and you may also have o WARRANTY OF MERCHANTABILITY OR FITNESS FOR A PARTICULAR A TIME. INCONVENIENCE. COMMERCIAL LOSS. OR CONSEQUENTIAL DA

Basic coverage

Your warranty begins with a period of basic coverage; here are details about this coverage.

How long does basic coverage last — and what does it cover?

Basic coverage begins at the warranty start date and lasts for 12 months or 12,000 miles, whichever occurs first. Under basic coverage, all parts of your car (except tires) are covered.

The following components and systems are covered for 12 months, regardless of the mileage you put on the car:

- the Ford radio or radio/tape deck components

  and

- these factory-installed systems:

  - air conditioner

  - heater

  - rear window defroster

  - heated outside rear-view mirror

  - electrically heated windshield

Source: Lee L. Gray, "Ford Offers a Readable Warranty Booklet," *Simply Stated . . . in Business*, no. 18 (March 1987): 2.

- As you revise, check your draft against the guidelines in this chapter.

THE IMPORTANCE OF EFFECTIVE DOCUMENT DESIGN

The uses we've noted so far for document design may not seem earthshaking. But bad writing and bad design can have serious consequences, both for an organization and for society.

The defect that caused the nuclear accident at Three Mile Island appeared 14 months earlier in a Toledo power plant. At the Toledo plant, workers were able to control damage before a serious problem arose. However, it was clear

Twenty Lines of Small Type*
The chaos in Third World bureaucracies often begins with chaotic language. I remember very well a sign on the gateway to Ankara, twenty lines long, beginning, "Dear driver," and ending "yours, sincerely, City Authorities." All that just to ask for slow and cautious driving in the city. Numerous drivers reading the sign caused terrible traffic jams, and the authorities had to remove the sign.

* Quoted from Karl-Heinz Osterloh, "Intercultural Differences and Communicative Approaches to Foreign-Language Teaching in the Third World," *Culture Bound*, ed. Joyce Merrill Valdes (Cambridge: Cambridge University Press, 1986), 80.

FIGURE 10.7
KELLY MEMO

Subject: Customer Guidance on High Pressure Injection Operation

Two recent events at the Toledo site have pointed out that perhaps we are not giving our customers enough guidance on the operation of the high pressure injection system.   On September 24, 1977, after depressurizing due to a stuck open electromatic relief valve, high pressure injection was automatically initiated.   The operator stopped HPI when pressurizer level began to recover, without regard to primary pressure.   As a result, the transient continued on with boiling in the RCS, etc.   In a similar occurrence on October 23, 1977, the operator bypassed high pressure injection to prevent initiation, even though reactor coolant system pressure went below the actuation point.

Since there are accidents which require the continuous operation of the high pressure injection system, I wonder what guidance, if any, we should be giving to our customers on when they can safely shut the system down following an accident?   I recommend the following guidelines be sent:

   a)   Do not bypass or otherwise prevent the actuation of high/low pressure injection under <u>any</u> conditions except a normal, controlled plant shutdown.

   b)   Once high/low pressure injection is initiated, do not stop it unless: T_{ave} is stable or decreasing <u>and</u> pressurizer level is increasing <u>and</u> primary pressure is at least 1600 PSIG and increasing.

I would appreciate your thoughts on this subject.

---

that a problem existed which might occur again either at that plant or at other locations. The damage might be more serious the next time. The problem had to be solved.

The problem was reported in a memo on November 1, 1977.[8] As you can see in Figure 10.7, the memo has several problems. The subject line and first sentence aren't pointed enough to orient this message for the reader. Readers are likely to skip the long first paragraph and focus on the list. But the list and the vague last sentence don't seem urgent.

One of the seven recipients of this memo told a subordinate to answer it. The subordinate clearly thought the writer was "all wet" and scratched out a handwritten response without even giving a copy to his supervisor.

Three months later the supervisor, who had heard nothing, recommended new guidelines—and put them on the second page of a two-page memo. None of the 12 people on the distribution list for that memo responded. Again, a not-quite-right subject line, ineffective writing, and poor document design caused the memo to be ignored.

On March 28, 1979, the same defect led to America's worst nuclear accident to this date—an accident that would have been wholly avoidable if writers had been able to design documents that readers could understand and act on.

SUMMARY OF KEY POINTS

- **Visual impact** means the visual first impression that you get when you look at a page. An attractive document looks inviting, friendly, and easy to read. The visual grouping of ideas also makes the structure of the document more obvious so it is easier to read.

- Nine guidelines help writers create visually attractive documents.

  Organization and Layout

  1. Use white space to separate and emphasize points.
  2. Use headings to group points and lead the reader through the document.
  3. Design the page so that the eyes move from the top left to the lower right corner.
  4. Use a grid of imaginary columns to unify documents with many graphic elements.

  Typography

  5. Use highlighting devices in moderation.
  6. Use ragged right margins, not justified margins.
  7. Use a limited number of type fonts.
  8. Avoid tiny type.
  9. Limit the use of words all set in capital letters.

- The best documents are created when you think about design at each stage of the writing process.

  - As you plan, think about the needs of your audience.
  - As you write, incorporate lists, headings, and visuals.
  - Get feedback from people who will be using your document.
  - As you revise, check your draft against the guidelines in this chapter.

- Good document design can save time, money, and legal problems.

NOTES

1. Linda Reynolds, "The Legibility of Printed Scientific and Technical Information," *Information Design,* ed. Ronald Easterby and Harm Zwaga (New York: Wiley, 1984), pp. 187–208.

2. George A. Miller, "The Magical Number Seven, Plus or Minus Two: Some Limits on Our Capacity for Processing Information," *Psychological Review* 63, no. 2 (March 1956): 81–97.

3. Philip M. Rubens, "A Reader's View of Text and Graphics: Implications for Transactional Text," *Journal of Technical Writing and Communication* 16, no. 1–2 (1986): 78.

4. M. E. Wrolstad, "Adult Preferences in Typography: Exploring the Function of Design," *Journalism Quarterly* 37 (Winter 1960): 211–23; summarized in Rolf F. Rehe, "Typography: How to Make It Most Legible," Design Research International, Carmel, IN, 57.

5. Rubens, 77.

6. M. Gregory and E. C. Poulton, "Even Versus Uneven Right-Hand Margins and the Rate of Comprehension of Reading," *Ergonomics* 13 (1970): 427–34.

7. M. A. Tinker, "The Influence of Form of Type on the Perception of Words," *Journal of Applied Psychology* 16 (April 1932): 167–74, summarized in Rehe, 35.

8. This correspondence is reprinted in the report of the House Committee on Interior and Insular Affairs, *Accident at Three Mile Island Nuclear Powerplant,* H441-18, Part 1, May 9–11, 1979; H441-26, Part 2, May 21, 24, 1979.

Good Document Design Saves Money*

A few years ago, 34% of the people using a Federal financial aid form had to go through the process more than once (sometimes three or four times) because they didn't understand the form. The students and their families paid in time and frustration—and sometimes in not getting money they were eligible for. We all as taxpayers paid in processing costs, paper and mailing for extra forms, in maintaining toll-free telephone lines and in paying people to answer questions. Well-designed documents can save money. In one year, with minor changes on the form and major changes in the information and instructions, the staff of the Document Design Project reduced the error rate on this Federal financial aid form by about seven percent. . . .

When the number of CB radio owners in the U.S. increased dramatically in the mid-1970s, the Federal Communications Commission decided that the most cost-effective way to increase compliance with the rules was to rewrite them so that CB users could understand them. The revised CB rules are well-organized, clearly written, and available as an attractive booklet. Before the new rules went into effect, the FCC had an office of five people who spent all day answering telephone questions about the CB radio rules from people who were trying to comply with them. After the clear English version of the rules was distributed, the calls stopped. All five employees were transferred to other jobs.

---

* Quoted from Dixie Goswami, Janice C. Redish, Daniel B. Felker, and Alan Siegel, *Writing in the Professions* (Washington, DC: American Institutes for Research, 1981), 32–33.

EXERCISES FOR CHAPTER 10

10–1 EVALUATING DESIGN

Use the nine guidelines in Chapter 10 to evaluate each of the following page designs. What are their strong points? What could be improved?

1.

THE COMPANY

BUSINESS
Report

Volume 1; No. 1   May 1987

GEM Desktop Publisher Sets Price/Performance Benchmark for Software Industry

Digital Research announces its high performance easy to use, full-function page composition software application—**GEM Desktop Publisher.** Introducing the true price/performer, available at the end of May, at a suggested retail price of $395.

"We're excited to provide an integrated team of products for personal publishing with the addition of **GEM Desktop Publisher** to our family of GEM applications," said *Dick Williams,* Chief Executive Officer of Digital Research. "Users now have a more complete and easier to use solution for combining text and graphics than ever before. But more important for the user is the outstanding price/performance offered by our product," continued Williams.

Flexibility is a key feature of this GEM-based software product. The user can define a location anywhere in a document and automatically place text or graphics at that location.

Continued on page 5

Desktop Publishing Increases Its Share of the Market

Employees Interested in Receiving Their Own Desktop Publishing Software

Projected Market Shares
A Clear Preference

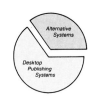

"As a product offering, it's the best thing that ever happened to personal computers," says desktop publishing expert, *John W. Seybold,* about desktop publishing, in the May issue of *Byte.*

Desktop publishing, the latest development in microcomputers, offers the user the ability to combine text and graphics to create professional quality brochures, newsletter, fliers, sales reports, marketing briefs, books, manuals, forms, and other publications on their own computer. And, as *Stewart Alsop* says in the February edition of *PC Magazine,* "Ever since Guttenberg, publishers have been looking for a better, cheaper, faster way to get words and pictures on paper."

Desktop publishing expert *John W. Seybold* establishes some shopping criteria for the "godsend" desktop publishing software, from the May issue of *Byte.* He feels the system should "let you compose text in a manner that comes close to the requirements of typesetting." Including well-designed and proportionately spaced characters, multiple fonts, sizes, etc.

Seybold also believes that the system should allow you to perform the composition tasks "in a manner that is considerably less code-intensive than that which characterizes trade computer typesetting." This includes the feature of WYSIWYG which "lets you point to the effects desired rather than requiring that you describe them by some sort of command language". He feels that software programs that were "code-intensive" and required "considerable user experience" should not be included in the desktop publishing category.

Growth for PC Software Market
Software Revenues for U.S. Suppliers

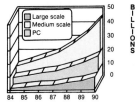

Source: Ad for Gem Desktop Publisher, *PC Magazine* 6, no. 17 (October 13, 1987): 105.

2.

BULLSEYE INVESTMENTS

Mr. Tad Davis
2901 S. 14th Street
Philadelphia, PA 19147   July 27, 1987

Dear Mr. Davis,

At Bullseye Investments drawing a brighter investment picture doesn't mean doing it "by the numbers." Sometimes you have to take risks. Take your goal of retirement at age 50. It's ambitious, but it's possible.

Your assets and investments as of 6-10-87 were about $100,000. Considering your dream, we recommend the following adjustments:

Shift your money from blue chips, preferred stocks and mutual funds (FIG. A) and into real estate, triple tax-free municipal bonds, specialized mutual funds and gold stocks (FIG. B).

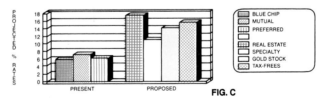

Naturally, your risks are greater. However, so are your rewards. Roughly 300% more interest and appreciation (FIG. C). I'll call soon to review your portfolio in detail.

Yours,

William C. Ricci

William C. Ricci
Certified Financial Planner

1040 Archer Road ☐ Target, PA 17070 ☐ (717) 828-5555

3.

A Special Report: Living Latin

Sit amet, con sectetuer adipicising elit, sed diam nonnumy nibh euismod tempor inci dunt ut labore et dolore

Lorem ipsum dolor sit amet, con sectetuer adipicising elit, sed diam nonnumy nibh euismod tempor inci dunt ut labore et dolore magna ali quam erat volupat. Ut wisi enim as minim veniam, quis nostrud exerci tation ullamcorper suscipit laboris nisl ut aliquip ex ea commodo con sequat. Duis autem vel eum irure dolor in henderit in vulputate velit esse consequat. Lorem ipsum dolor sit amet, con sectetuer adipicising elit, sed diam nonnumy nibh euismod tempor inci dunt ut labore et dolore magna ali quam erat volupat. Ut wisi enim as minim veniam, quis nostrud exerci tation ullamcorper suscipit laboris nisl ut aliquip ex ea commodo con sequat. Duis autem vel eum irure dolor in henderit in vulputate velit esse consequat.

Sit amet, con sectetuer adipi-

cising elit, sed diam nonnumy nibh euismod tempor inci dunt ut labore et dolore magna ali quam erat volupat. Ut wisi enim as minim veniam, quis nostrud exerci tation ullamcorper suscipit laboris nisl ut aliquip ex ea commodo con sequat. Duis autem vel eum irure dolor in henderit in vulpu-tate velit esse consequat.

Dolor sit amet, con sectetuer adipicising elit, sed diam nonnumy nibh euismod tempor inci dunt ut labore et dolore magna ali quam erat volupat. Ut wisi enim as minim veniam, quis nostrud.Duis autem vel eum irure dolor in henderit in vulpu-tate velit esse consequat.

Ipsum dolor sit amet, con sectetuer adipicising elit, sed diam nonnumy nibh euismod tempor inci dunt ut labore et dolore magna ali quam erat volupat. Ut wisi enim as minim veniam, quis nostrud exerci

tation ullamcorper suscipit laboris nisl ut aliquip ex ea commodo con sequat. Duis autem vel eum irure dolor in henderit in vulputate velit esse consequat. Lorem ipsum dolor sit amet, con sectetuer adipi cising elit, sed diam nonnumy nibh euismod tempor inci dunt ut labore et dolore magna ali quam erat volupat. Ut wisi enim as minim veniam, quis nostrud exerci tation ullamcor-per suscipit laboris nisl ut aliquip ex ea commodo con sequat. Duis autem vel eum irure dolor in henderit in vulpu-tate velit esse consequat.

Lorem ipsum dolor sit amet, con sectetuer adipicising elit, sed diam nonnumy nibh euis-mod tempor inci dunt ut labore et dolore magna ali quam erat volupat. Ut wisi enim as minim

Sit amet, con sectetuer adipicising elit, sed diam nonnumy nibh euismod tempor inci dunt ut labore et dolore

A Special Report: Living Latin

Sit amet, con sectetuer adipicising elit, sed diam nonnumy nibh euismod tempor inci dunt ut labore et dolore

Lorem ipsum dolor sit amet, con sectetuer adipicising elit, sed diam nonnumy nibh euis-mod tempor inci dunt ut labore et dolore magna ali quam erat volupat. Ut wisi enim as minim veniam, quis nostrud exerci tation ullamcorper suscipit laboris nisl ut aliquip ex ea commodo con sequat. Duis autem vel eum irure dolor in henderit in vulputate velit esse consequat. Lorem ipsum dolor sit amet, con sectetuer adipicising elit, sed diam nonnumy nibh euismod tempor inci dunt ut labore et dolore magna ali quam erat volupat. Ut wisi enim as minim veniam, quis nostrud exerci tation ullamcor-per suscipit laboris nisl ut aliquip ex ea commodo con sequat. Duis autem vel eum irure dolor in henderit in vulpu-tate velit esse consequat.

Sit amet, con sectetuer adipi-cising elit, sed diam nonnumy

nibh euismod tempor inci dunt ut labore et dolore magna ali quam erat volupat. Ut wisi enim as minim veniam, quis nostrud exerci tation ullamcor-per suscipit laboris nisl ut aliquip ex ea commodo con sequat. Duis autem vel eum irure dolor in henderit in vulpu-tate velit esse consequat.

Dolor sit amet, con sectetuer adipicising elit, sed diam nonnumy nibh euismod tempor inci dunt ut labore et dolore magna ali quam erat volupat.Duis autem vel eum irure dolor in henderit in vulpu-tate velit esse consequat.

Ipsum dolor sit amet, con sectetuer adipicising elit, sed diam nonnumy nibh euismod tempor inci dunt ut labore et dolore magna ali quam erat volupat. Ut wisi enim as minim veniam, quis nostrud exerci tation ullamcorper suscipit

laboris nisl ut aliquip ex ea commodo con sequat. Duis autem vel eum irure dolor in henderit in vulputate velit esse consequat. Lorem ipsum dolor sit amet, con sectetuer adipi cising elit, sed diam nonnumy nibh euismod tempor inci dunt ut labore et dolore magna ali quam erat volupat. Ut wisi enim as minim veniam, quis nostrud exerci tation ullamcor-per suscipit laboris nisl ut aliquip ex ea commodo con sequat. Duis autem vel eum irure dolor in henderit in vulpu-tate velit esse consequat.

Lorem ipsum dolor sit amet, con sectetuer adipicising elit, sed diam nonnumy nibh euis-mod tempor inci dunt ut labore et dolore magna ali quam erat volupat. Ut wisi enim as minim veniam, quis nostrud exerci tation ullamcorper suscipit

Sit amet, con sectetuer adipicising elit, sed diam nonnumy nibh euismod tempor inci dunt ut labore et dolore

A Special Bulletin: Living Latin

Managers Required to Study Classics

Lorem ipsum dolor sit amet, con sectetuer adipicising elit, sed diam nonnumy nibh euismod tempor inci dunt ut dolore magna ali quam erat volupat. Ut wisi enim as minim veniam, quis nostrud exerci tation ullamcorper suscipit laboris nisl ut aliquip ex ea commodo con sequat. Duis autem vel eum irure dolor in henderit in vulputate velit esse consequat. Lorem ipsum dolor sit amet, con sectetuer adipicising elit, sed diam non-numy nibh euismod tempor inci dunt ut labore et dolore magna ali quam erat volupat. Ut wisi enim as minim veniam, quis nostrud exerci tation ullamcorper suscipit laboris nisl ut aliquip ex ea commodo con sequat. Duis autem vel eum irure dolor in henderit in vulputate velit esse consequat.

Sit amet, con sectetuer adipi-cising elit, sed diam nonnumy nibh euismod tempor inci dunt ut labore et dolore magna ali quam erat volupat. Ut wisi enim as minim veniam, quis nostrud exerci tation ullamcorper suscipit laboris nisl ut aliquip ex ea commodo con sequat. Duis autem vel eum irure dolor in henderit in vulputate velit esse consequat.

Dolor sit amet, con sectetuer adipicising elit, sed diam non-numy nibh euismod tempor inci dunt ut labore et dolore magna ali quam erat volu pat Duis autem vel eum irure dolor in henderit in vulputate velit esse

Group to Attend Archeological Dig

Ipsum dolor sit amet, con sectetuer adipicising elit, sed diam nonnumy nibh euismod tempor inci dunt ut labore et dolore magna ali quam erat volupat. Ut wisi enim as minim veniam, quis nostrud exerci tation ullamcorper suscipit laboris nisl ut aliquip ex ea commodo con sequat. Duis autem vel eum irure dolor in henderit in vulputate velit esse consequat. Lorem ipsum dolor sit amet, con sectetuer adipicising elit, sed diam nonnumy nibh euismod tempor inci dunt ut labore et dolore magna ali quam erat volupat. Ut wisi

Company Briefs

nim as minim veniam, quis nostrud exerci tation ullamcorper suscipit laboris nisl ut aliquip ex ea commodo con sequat. Duis autem vel eum irure dolor in henderit in vulputate velit esse con-sequat.

Lorem ipsum dolor sit amet, con sectetuer adipi-cising elit, sed diam nonnumy nibh euismod tempor inci dunt ut labore et dolore magna ali

If Walls Could Talk

quam erat volupat. Ut wisi enim as minim veniam, quis nostrud exerci tation ullamcor-per suscipit laboris nisl ut aliquip ex ea commodo con sequat. Duis autem vel eum irure dolor in vulputate velit esse consequat. Lorem ipsum dolor sit amet, con sectetuer adipicising elit, sed diam nonnumy nibh euismod tempor inci dunt ut labore et dolore magna ali quam erat volupat. Ut wisi

Sit amet, con sectetuer adipi-cising elit, sed diam nonnumy nibh euismod tempor inci dunt ut labore et dolore magna ali quam erat volupat. Ut wisi enim as minim veniam, quis nostrud exerci tation ullamcor-

 ...tempor inci dunt ut labore et dolore magna ali

finis

Special Bulletin: Living Latin

Managers Required to Study Classics

Lorem ipsum dolor sit amet, con sectetuer adipicising elit, sed diam nonnumy nibh euismod tempor inci dunt ut labore et dolore magna ali quam erat volupat. Ut wisi enim as minim veniam, quis nostrud exerci tation ul-lamcorper suscipit laboris nisl ut aliquip ex ea commodo con sequat. Duis autem vel eum irure dolor in henderit in vulputate velit esse consequat. Lorem ipsum dolor sit amet, con sectetuer adipicising elit, sed diam nonnumy nibh

euismod tempor inci dunt ut labore et dolore magna ali quam erat volupat. Ut wisi enim as minim veniam, quis nostrud exerci tation ul-lamcorper suscipit laboris nisl ut aliquip ex ea commodo con sequat. Duis autem vel eum irure dolor in henderit in vulputate velit esse consequat.

Sit amet, con sectetuer adipi-cising elit, sed diam nonnumy nibh euismod tempor inci dunt ut labore et dolore magna ali quam erat volupat. Ut wisi

Group to Attend Archeological Dig

Lorem ipsum dolor sit amet, con sectetuer adipicising elit, sed diam nonnumy nibh euismod tempor inci dunt ut labore et dolore magna ali quam erat volupat. Ut wisi enim as minim veniam, quis nostrud exerci tation ul-lamcorper suscipit laboris nisl ut aliquip ex ea commodo con sequat. Duis autem vel eum irure dolor in henderit in vulputate velit esse consequat. Lorem ipsum dolor sit amet, con sectetuer adipicising elit, sed diam nonnumy nibh

euismod tempor inci dunt ut labore et dolore magna ali quam erat volupat. Ut wisi enim as minim veniam, quis

The group will visit many lovely spots

If Walls Could Talk

Lorem ipsum dolor sit amet, con sectetuer adipicising elit, sed diam nonnumy nibh euismod tempor inci dunt ut labore et dolore magna ali quam erat volupat. Ut wisi enim as minim veniam, quis nostrud exerci tation ul-lamcorper suscipit laboris nisl ut aliquip ex ea commodo con sequat. Duis autem vel eum irure dolor in henderit in vulputate velit esse consequat. Sit amet, con sectetuer adipicising elit, sed diam nonnumy nibh euismod tempor inci dunt ut labore et dolore magna ali quam erat volupat. Ut wisi enim as minim veniam, quis nostrud exerci tation ul-lamcorper suscipit laboris nisl ut aliquip ex ea commodo con sequat. Duis autem vel eum irure dolor in henderit in vulputate velit esse consequat.

Source: Diane Burns and S. Venit, "What's Wrong with This Page?" *PC Magazine* 6, no. 17 (October 13, 1987): 174–175.

4.

Who can benefit from @LIBERTY... and how.

Corporate Users

Do everything from budgeting to cost-estimating to forecasting.

Insurance Companies

Send your agents spreadsheets for sales illustrations.

Auditing Firms

Have your clients input their own financial data, so you can economically (and safely) perform your audit.

CPAs and Tax Lawyers

Distribute your tax planning methods to clients.

Government Agencies

For internal auditing, inventory control—almost anything you'd use a traditional spreadsheet for.

VARs and Template Developers

Develop and market your business and technical solutions.

Source: Ad for @Liberty, *PC Magazine* 6, no. 17 (October 13, 1987): 255.

5.

Recent Robotic Hand Research

Presently, there are two disparate approaches to gripper construction, with correspondingly different design goals. The two types are industrial hands and omni-hands. Industrial hands are fairly simple, uni-function, one or two DOF grippers which are currently being used for such jobs as welding and assembly-type functions. Omni-hands are complex, multiple DOF hands.

Anthropomorphic hands are supplemented by sophisticated hardware and feedback control and offer many advantages; a large range of motion and the ability to pick up objects and manipulate delicate parts without causing damage to them. Maintaining a stable grasp, high costs, and complexity of control relegate this hand to the status of a research tool for the present. The complexity of the additional degrees of freedom inherent in the Omni-hand is illustrated in Figure 1.

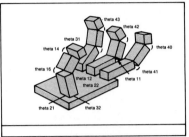

Figure 1: Angle Definitions of Hand Geometry

Until concurrent work in decision-making, task strategy, and vision systems is developed, the potential of this hand cannot be realized. The decreasing cost of producing a functional hand with more than one degree of freedom is speeding acceptance by industry as illustrated in the following graph.

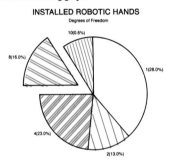

INSTALLED ROBOTIC HANDS
Degrees of Freedom

10(0.6%)
8(16.0%)
1(28.0%)
4(23.0%)
2(13.0%)

The cost figures are based on a three fingered hand, each finger supporting three DOFs. Lower acquisition costs will allow an increase in the number of degrees of freedom employed in industrial hands. Placing the control for the hand on the arm so as to reduce the weight on the hand itself also lowers cost. The hand-object system was modelled as a rigid body system, in which a heuristic for a stable grasp is a grasp that, when altered by an external force, seeks to produce a motion or force to return the system to stability.

Source: Ad for Lotus Manuscript, *PC Magazine* 6, no. 19 (November 10, 1987): 165.

10–2 USING LAYOUT TO IMPROVE A DOCUMENT

The following document is one page of a large stack of materials handed to new employees on their first day at a factory. The company hands out this information because employees come complaining to it if the company (legally) deducts money from an employee's wages to pay his or her debts. The company wants workers to understand what wage assignments are, what protection they have, and that they should try to avoid them. Unfortunately, the document is so badly designed that it just can't compete for employees' attention on a busy first day on the job.

Use layout, including white space, lists, and headings, to improve the following document. You do not need to change the style or organization of material in the document: just change layout.

MONEY DEDUCTED FROM YOUR WAGES TO PAY CREDITORS

When you buy goods on credit, the store will sometimes ask you to sign a Wage Assignment Form. This form protects creditors by allowing them to "demand" Roysner to deduct money from your wages if you do not pay your bill. When you buy on credit, you sign a contract with a store or a finance company agreeing to pay a certain amount each week or month until you have paid all you owe. The Wage Assignment Form is separate. This form must contain the name of your present employer, your social security number, the amount of money loaned, the rate of interest, the date when payments are due, and your signature. The words "Wage Assignment" must be printed in one-quarter-inch-high letters at the head of the form and also one inch above or below the line where you sign the assignment. Even if you have signed a Wage Assignment agreement, Roysner will not withhold part of your wages unless all three of the following conditions are met: (1) You have to be more than forty days late in payment of what you owe; (2) Roysner has to receive a correct statement of the amount you are in default and a copy of the Wage Assignment form; and (3) You and Roysner must receive a notice from the creditor at least 20 days in advance stating that the creditor plans to make a demand on your wages. This twenty-day notice gives you a chance to correct the problem yourself. If these conditions are all met, Roysner must withhold fifteen percent (15%) of each paycheck until the total amount past due is paid up, or until thirty days go by, whichever comes first. Roysner turns this money over to your creditor.

If you think you are not late or that you do not owe the amount stated, you can argue against it. Within twenty days after receiving the notice stating the plans to make a demand, or within five days after a demand is made, you can make what is called a "defense." You must file two copies of an affidavit stating that you have a defense, one copy with Roysner and the other copy with your creditor. An attorney or legal aid counsel can help you. Once you file a defense, Roysner will not withhold any money from you. However, be sure you are right before you file a defense. If you are wrong, you have to pay not only what you owe, but also all legal costs for both yourself and the creditor. If you are right, the creditor has to pay all these costs.

Wage assignments make things more difficult for you, your family, and Roysner. Try to avoid them. If you have any questions or if we can help, please come to the Personnel Office.

Presenting Numerical Data

QUESTIONS

- Are numbers objective?
- When you have lots of numbers, how do you decide which ones to use in a document?
- How can visuals help as you write rough drafts? When should you use visuals in the final document?
- How do you decide what kind of visual to use?
- How can you design visuals that present data accurately? What are some of the common errors that produce misleading visuals?
- Why are clean visuals better?
- How can you integrate visuals with your text?

> When you cannot measure it, when you cannot express it in
> numbers, your knowledge is of a meager and unsatisfactory kind.
>
> William Thomson, Lord Kelvin
> *Popular Lectures and Addresses,* 1891–94

Numbers are enormously useful in decision making. They can help us understand where our money is going, why we're making or losing money, whether a program is growing more or less quickly than the population using that program. Business and public policy decisions depend on numbers. Those numbers need to be presented to decision makers accurately and clearly in memos, oral presentations, meetings, letters, and reports.

Numbers are no more objective than words are: both require interpretation and context to make sense. Consider the following question:

Was the drop in the Dow-Jones Industrial Average on October 19, 1987, the largest percentage one-day drop in the Dow's history?

Whether the answer is *yes* or *no* depends on how you define a *day.* The drop on October 19, 1987, was 22.6%. However, on December 12, 1914, the Dow fell 24.4%.

Dow Jones has decided that date should not be considered a one-day loss because it was the first day of trading in more than four months. The stock market had been closed since July 30, 1914, because of the start of World War I. Therefore, the fall in the average, while occurring in a single day, was the result of more than one day's events.[1]

The same numbers can be presented in different ways to create very different impressions. On July 29, 1987, both *The Wall Street Journal* and *The Columbus Dispatch* carried stories about Wendy's second-quarter earnings, which had been announced the day before. The two newspapers carried the following headlines:

Wendy's Earnings Plummeted 92% In Second Quarter[2]
Wendy's Has 2nd Quarter Profit[3]

Both headlines are "true." Wendy's had a $1.9 million profit in the second quarter of 1987. That profit was 92% less than its second-quarter profit in 1986. The second, more positive headline is perhaps explained by the fact that Wendy's is headquartered in Dublin, Ohio, a suburb of Columbus.

When you present numerical data, think about your audience. What will people want to know? Pick data to tell a story, to make a point. Never put in numbers just because you have them; instead, use numbers because they convey information the audience needs or wants.

Visuals can present numbers dramatically. The Consumer Federation of America crystallized discontent with high interest rates on consumer loans by issuing a simple three-page study with a graph showing that while the prime rate was going down, interest on consumer loans was going up. Dan Rather showed the graph and discussed the report on the evening news; the publicity helped persuade Congress to pass laws requiring fuller disclosure and some caps on interest rates.[4]

The widespread use of computers and software makes it easy to design visuals just by using appropriate software. With many software programs, all you have to do is type in the basic numbers or import them from another computer program and indicate what kind of graphic you want. The computer then draws it for you—even recalculating the x and y axes, if, for example, a new number requires rescaling the graph.

WHEN TO USE A VISUAL

The ease of creating visuals by computer may make people use them uncritically. When every bit of numerical data is put in a visual, or if the writer chooses the wrong visual, the visual does little more than take up space.

In your rough draft, use visuals

- **To see that ideas are presented completely.**
- **To check to see what relationships exist.**

In the final report, use visuals

- **To make comparisons and contrasts vivid.**
- **To emphasize material** that might be skipped if it were buried in a paragraph.
- **To present material more compactly and with less repetition** than verbal presentation would require.

To see how a visual can help at the rough draft stage, consider the following paragraphs from a report about the costs of a company's employee insurance plan:

A total of 21,823 hospital, medical, surgical, diagnostic, major medical and H&A bills were processed in 253 working days for an average of 86.3 bills per day. This is a 13.3% increase per day over last year. This compares with 19,267 bills last year and an average of 76.5 bills per day and 15,078 in 1987 and an average of 60.1 per day.

A total of 9,368.5 days of hospital confinement were paid (member—3,803.5 days and dependent—5,565). This represents a 12.5% decrease in the number of hospital days paid. (10,702 days last year, member—4,308 and dependent—6,394.)

In addition the expenses in the Executive Medical plan were $82,761.94. This is compared to a total of $86,957.43 last year. Thirty-two executives were eligible for benefits and all participated.

On first reading, this passage seems to be organized consistently, though it is a little hard to follow. But look what happens when we put the information in a table:

EMPLOYEE HOSPITAL BENEFITS PAID, 1987–89

	1987	1988	1989	Percent of Increase 1987 to 1989
Total claims processed	15,078	19,267	21,823	—
Claims processed per day (average)	60.1	76.5	86.3	13.3
Total hospital days paid	—	10,702	9,368.5	−12.5
for members	—	4,308	3,803.5	—
for dependents	—	6,394	5,565	—
Expenses under Executive Medical Plan (EMP)	—	$86,957.43	$82,761.94	—
Number of executives participating in EMP	—	—	32	—

FIGURE 11.1
VISUAL SHOWS THE COMPARISONS AREN'T COMPLETE

* Quoted from Rhonda L. Rundle, "Hospitals Cite Mortality Statistics in Ads to Attract Heart Patients," *The Wall Street Journal*, July 28, 1987, 31.

FIGURE 11.2
VISUAL DRAWN WITH MAP-
MASTER SOFTWARE

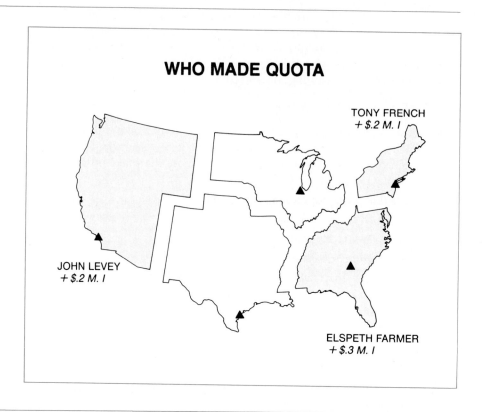

Source: *PC Magazine* 5, no. 6 (March 25, 1986): 40.

Even Computers Make Mistakes*
A computer science professor added
2.0 + 2.0 on the mainframe computer at his university. The result:
4.1. Evidently there was a bug in
the program or the circuitry.

Most organizations rely more
and more on computers for data.
But it's worth having a ballpark
sense of what the answer will be,
even before you use a computer to
calculate the exact figure. Otherwise, you won't know when to distrust the computer printout.

In addition to making the information easier to follow and eliminating much
of the awkward repetition, the table in Figure 11.1 pointedly reveals the gaps
in the writer's comparisons: why bring in the total number of claims processed
in 1987 and then abandon that year? Does the decrease in Expenses under the
Executive Medical Plan depend on a smaller number of participants than in
the previous year? By processing the data for the reader, this writer could have
spotted these problems and corrected them at the rough draft stage.

Putting information in a visual can also help you see what relationships
exist. For example, the map in Figure 11.2 shows that all the sales reps who
made quota in this company have territories on the east or the west coasts.
Are these reps better sales people, or is geography responsible? Is the central
United States suffering a recession? Is the product one that appeals to coastal
lifestyles? Is advertising reaching the coasts but not the central states? Even if
you don't use the visual in your final document, creating it may lead you to
questions you wouldn't otherwise ask.

WHAT KIND OF VISUAL TO USE

Computer graphics programs give you a list of the kinds of graphs the program
draws and ask you which you want. But visuals are not interchangeable. Good
writers choose the visual that best matches the purpose of presenting the data.

- Use **tables** when the reader needs to be able to identify exact values.
- Use **bar graphs** when you want the reader to see comparisons.

---

* Based on John T. O'Donnell, letter to the author, February 25, 1988.

- Use **segmented bar or line graphs** to show changes in the makeup of items or changes in components over time. Segmented bar graphs are also called **stacked bars.**
- Use **pictographs or histograms** to make bar graphs more interesting. Beware of distorting the data visually!
- Use **line graphs,** not bar graphs, to show trends or to allow the reader to interpolate values between the observed values.
- Use **pie charts** to emphasize percentages. Don't use pie charts if the reader needs to know the percentage exactly or if you want readers to compare different components of the total.
- Use **drawings** to show dimensions or emphasize detail.
- Use **cutaway drawings or schematic diagrams** to show the construction of an item.
- Use **photographs** to create a sense of authenticity or show the item in use. If the item is especially big or small, include something in the photograph which can serve as a reference point: a dime, a person.
- Use **maps** to emphasize location.
- Use **flow charts** to show processes.
- Use **decision trees** to allow the reader to find answers quickly.

DESIGNING THE VISUAL

Formal visuals are divided into tables and figures. **Tables** are numbers or words arrayed in rows and columns; **figures** are everything else. Formal visuals have both numbers and titles, for example, "Figure 1. The Falling Cost of Computer Memory, 1980–90." The title should summarize the story the visual tells and tell the reader what to look for in the visual or why the visual is included and is worth examining. Informal or **spot** visuals are inserted directly into the text; they do not have numbers or titles.

When you design any visual, follow these principles:

1. Make sure that the visual accurately presents the data, both literally and by implication.
2. Make the visual as clean as possible.
3. Arrange the entries in the visual logically.

Let's examine each of these.

1. Make Sure That the Visual Accurately Presents the Data, Both Literally and By Implication.

As visuals get more and more artistic, they may become misleading. Edward Tufte uses the term **chartjunk** for decorations that at best are irrelevant to the visual and at worst mislead the reader.[5] Many computer graphics packages come with a "clip art library" of images that can be added to charts and graphs. These are acceptable for oral presentation if you want to keep an audience awake, but they muddy up printed visuals which readers may try to study.

Figure 11.3 presents the progress of a fund-raising campaign. The visual is literally honest: one can figure out that slightly more than 50% of the goal

Numbers Are a Way of Seeing*

Chemistry took an important step forward when John Dalton, a meteorologist, began studying the absorption of gases and water. Dalton's training led him to look for proportions.

Chemists already knew that two different oxides of carbon contained 56% and 72% oxygen by weight. Dalton expressed the relationship as one weight of carbon to either 1.3 or 2.6 weights of oxygen. When the old measurements were put in these terms, the 2 : 1 ratio was obvious. Chemists could now understand carbon monoxide and carbon dioxide in a way that opened the door for an understanding of atomic theory.

The Power of Graphics†

Snazzy graphics are a powerful, multidimensional business tool. A single beautiful graph can illuminate the relationships between numbers, helping you analyze data. It can communicate those relationships to your peers, superiors, or clients. And that same graph will impress viewers with your professionalism.

---

* Based on Thomas S. Kuhn, *The Structure of Scientific Revolutions*, 2nd ed. (Chicago: University of Chicago Press, 1970), 126–35.

† Quoted from Cheryl J. Goldberg and Gerard Kunkel, "Graphics Software on Display," *PC Magazine* 6, no. 5 (March 10, 1987): 119.

FIGURE 11.3
CHARTJUNK DISTORTS DATA

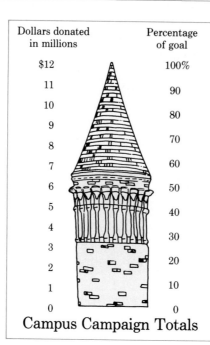

Dollars donated in millions

Percentage of goal

$12 — 100%
11 — 90
10 — 80
9 — 70
8 — 60
7 —
6 — 50
5 — 40
4 —
3 — 30
2 — 20
1 — 10
0 — 0

Campaign passes the halfway point

"Halfway" was the word on the Campus Campaign last Friday. After two weeks, the four-week solicitation of University faculty and staff members had raised some $6.5 million — or a little more than half — of its $12 million goal.

Jennifer Goins, staff director of the campaign, said fewer than one-third of the 19,000 pledge cards had been returned at the halfway point. "We're really pleased with the response so far," she said, "and we expect a lot of pledges to come in during the final two weeks before the Campus Campaign ends May 23."

Campus Campaign Totals

Source: OSU *onCampus*, May 15, 1986.

Japanese Children and Statistics*

In Japan, statistics are the subject of a holiday, local and national conventions, award ceremonies, and nationwide statistical collections and graph-drawing contests. "This year," said Yoshiharu Takahashi, a Government statistician, "we had almost 30,000 entries. Actually, we had 29,836."

Entries in the [children's] statistical graph contest were screened three times by judges, who gave first prize this year to the work of five 7-year-olds. Their graph creation, titled, "Mom, play with us more often," was the result of a survey of 32 classmates on the frequency that mothers play with their offspring and the reasons given for not doing so. . . . Other children's work examined the frequency of family phone usage and correlated the day's temperature with cicada singing.

has been reached. Visually, however, the graph lies. In an effort to make it "relevant," the artist used a campus tower. But since the tower is capped with a cone, nearly three-fourths of the area that shows is shaded. The narrowing also suggests that raising the second $6 million will go faster than raising the first $6 million did—an impression which is unlikely to be accurate.

Perspective graphs are hard for readers to interpret. Yet their use is growing because computer programs can create them easily. Figure 11.4 retains literal honesty by putting in the values for each country.

Even simple bar and line graphs may be misleading. *The Wall Street Journal,* for example, publishes daily graphs to show the movement in the stock market. However, these are **truncated** graphs, with part of the scale missing. The effect is to make small changes seem like major ones (Figure 11.5b). If a truncated graph is spread out (Figure 11.5c), the distortion is even greater, for the percentage change appears greater.

Data can also be distorted when the context is omitted. As Tufte suggests, a drop like that in Figure 11.6a may be part of a regular cycle (11.6b), a correction after an atypical increase (11.6c), or a permanent drop to a new, lower plateau (11.6d).

Another misleading visual that one company used in its annual report disguised losses by using a negative base.[6] Because readers expect zero to be the base, they're almost certain to misread the visual. Such visual lying has not been illegal: as late as 1987, the SEC monitored the numerical statements in annual reports but did not check the visuals. However, such a visual is still unethical even if it is legal.

---

* Quoted from Andrew H. Malcolm, "Data-Loving Japanese Rejoice on Statistics Day," *New York Times,* October 28, 1977, A1.

FIGURE 11.4
PERSPECTIVE GRAPHS
DISTORT DATA AND ARE
HARD TO READ

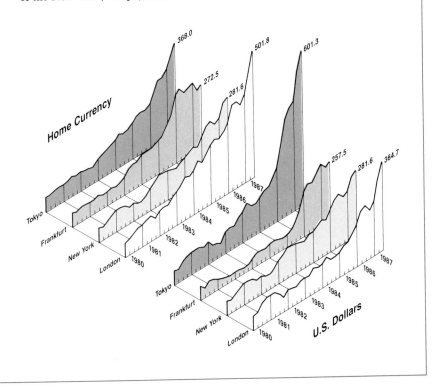

Riding the Bull: Performance of the World's Major Stock Markets

Using a base of 100 on Dec. 31, 1979, these charts show the comparative moves of the New York, Tokyo, London and Frankfurt stock markets

Source: *Newsweek,* December 21, 1987, 43.

2. Make the Visual as Clean as Possible.

Tables will be easier to read if you use only two or three significant digits for each value (e.g., 35% rather than 35.27%; 34,000 rather than 33,942). Set up the numbers in the table so readers can compare similar categories.

In any visual, use as little shading and as few lines as are necessary for clarity. Don't clutter up the visual with extra marks. In Figure 11.7, most of the grid lines could be eliminated; narrower bars could be used for the data lines.

3. Arrange the Entries in the Visual Logically.

Make your visual easier to read by arranging the entries logically. If no logical pattern is obvious, use one of the following patterns to organize your data:

Chronological.

Largest to smallest (especially good for graphs that do not represent

How Big Is a Billion?*

[If a document will be translated, use figures rather than words for large numbers.] Any number over 10,000 may be easily mistranslated. The number "billion," for example, numerically contains 9 zeroes in the United States, but contains 12 zeroes in Europe.

* Quoted from David A. Ricks, *Big Business Blunders* (Homewood, IL: Dow Jones-Irwin, 1983), 92.

FIGURE 11.5

TRUNCATED SCALES CAN DISTORT DATA

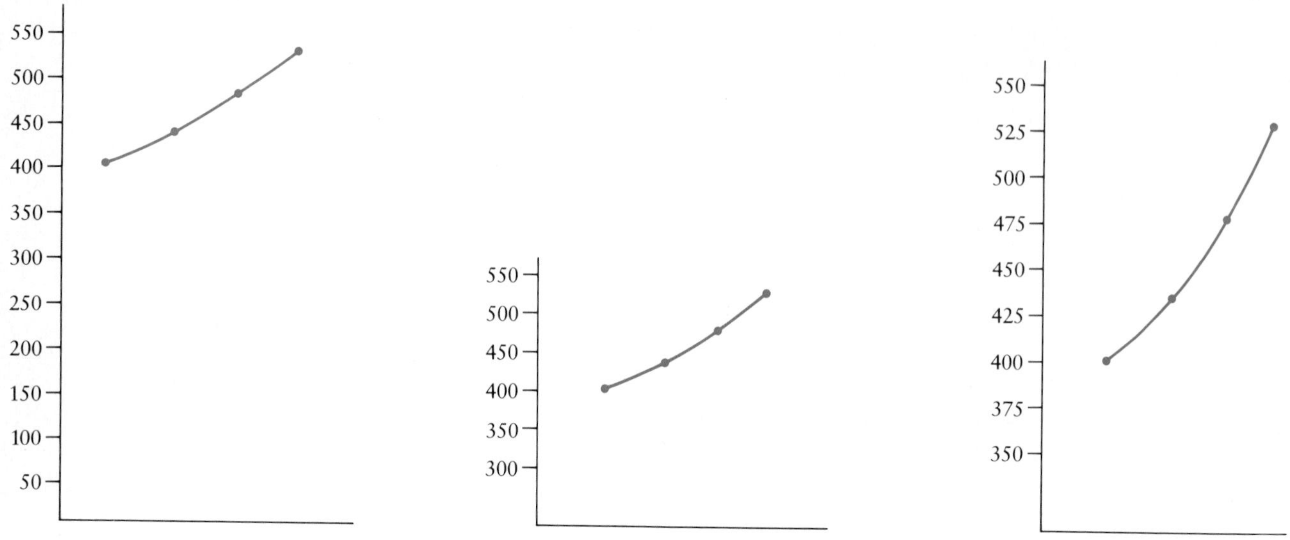

a.   Line graph with
     full scale

b.   Line graph with
     truncated scale

c.   Line graph with
     truncated scale

time sequences). Pie charts should start at 12 o'clock with the largest percentage and go clockwise to each smaller percentage.

• Alphabetical.

Color makes visuals more dramatic, but it doesn't make them easier to read. It may even make them harder to read if you're using colors to represent different levels of some characteristic. Shades of grey are better than colors: readers will interpret black as the highest level and white as an absence of the characteristic.

INTEGRATING VISUALS WITH YOUR TEXT

Summarize the main point of a visual *before* you present the visual itself. Then when readers get to it, they'll see it as confirmation of your point.

Too many writers introduce tables with the abrupt statement, "Listed below are the figures," and then follow the table with a long paragraph of explanation and analysis. This method mirrors the thought processes which occur as the writer processes data: one first categorizes the data in a very general way ("sales figures"); one next looks at the data; and one finally decides what the data mean.

But when this mental process becomes the writer's organizing pattern, the reader is forced to duplicate the whole process by which the writer reached a conclusion. Most readers, understandably, are unwilling to do work which the writer is supposed to do, so they will skim or skip the data presented in this unsatisfactory fashion. When the writer finally comes to the point, readers may be unconvinced because they haven't recognized the significance of the evidence in the table. Remember that you are writing not to reveal how your

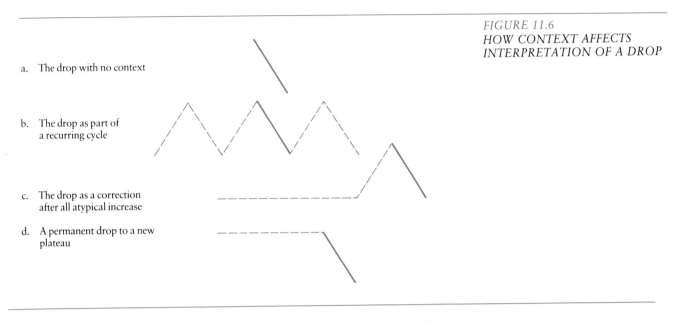

FIGURE 11.6
HOW CONTEXT AFFECTS
INTERPRETATION OF A DROP

a. The drop with no context

b. The drop as part of
    a recurring cycle

c. The drop as a correction
    after all atypical increase

d. A permanent drop to a new
    plateau

Adapted from Edward R. Tufte, *The Visual Display of Quantitative Information* (Cheshire, CN: Graphics Press, 1983), 75.

FIGURE 11.7
ORIGINAL (TOO BUSY) AND REVISION (CLEANER)

Original

1. If one assumes the Society membership reflects the profession, there are now more women than men employed as technical communicators.

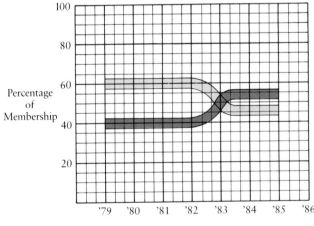

Revision

1. If one assumes the Society membership reflects the profession, there are now more women than men employed as technical communicators.

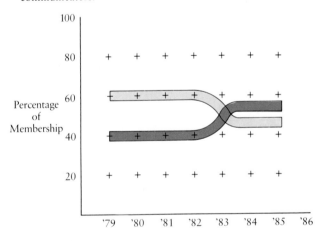

own mind works but to explain something to your readers and to convince them that your analysis is correct.

When you discuss your visuals, put numbers at the end of the clause or sentence to make the sentence easier to read:

Hard to read: As Table 4 shows, teachers participate in more community service groups than do members of 13 (54%) of the other occupations surveyed; dentists participate in more service groups than do five (20.8%) of the other occupations.

Better: As Table 4 shows, teachers participate in more community service groups than do members of 13 of the other occupations surveyed (54%); dentists participate in more service groups than do five of the other occupations (20.8%).

SUMMARY OF KEY POINTS

- Numbers are not objective. Like words they require interpretation and context to make sense.

- Pick data to tell a story, to make a point. Use numbers to convey information the audience needs or wants.

- In the rough draft, use visuals to see that ideas are presented completely and to see what relationships exist. In the final report, use visuals to make comparisons and contrasts vivid, to emphasize material that the reader might skip, and to present material more compactly and with less repetition than verbal presentation would require.

- Visuals are not interchangeable. The best visual depends on the kind of data and the point you want to make with the data.

- **Tables** are numbers or words arrayed in rows and columns; **figures** are everything else. Formal visuals have both numbers and titles which summarize the story the visual tells.

- Visuals must present data accurately, both literally and by implication. **Chartjunk** denotes decorations that at best are irrelevant to the visual and at worst mislead the reader. **Truncated** scales omit part of the scale and visually mislead readers. Perspective graphs and graphs with negative bases mislead readers.

- Visuals should be as clean as possible. The parts of the visual should be arranged logically.

- Summarize the main point of a visual before it appears in the text.

NOTES

1. "Revision Makes Dow Drop on Monday Largest Decline," AP, *Columbus Dispatch*, October 23, 1987, E1.

2. *The Wall Street Journal*, July 29, 1987, 4.

3. *Columbus Dispatch*, July 29, 1987, D1.

4. Barbara Rosewicz, "Consumer Lobbies Gain Ground on Capital Hill by Parlaying Tactics, Timing on Banking Bills," *The Wall Street Journal*, October 5, 1987, 46.

5. Edward R. Tufte, *The Visual Display of Quantitative Information* (Cheshire, CN: Graphics Press, 1983), 113.

6. Day Mines *1974 Annual Report*, 1; reproduced in Tufte, 54.

EXERCISES FOR CHAPTER 11

11–1 EVALUATING VISUALS

Evaluate each of the following visuals.

Is the point of the visual clear?

Is the visual easy to understand?

Does the visual distort data or mislead the reader in any way?

Is the visual free from chartjunk?

What other visuals could also be used to present this data?

1.
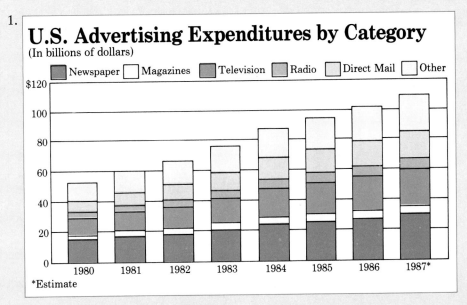

Source: *The Wall Street Journal*, September 23, 1987.

2.
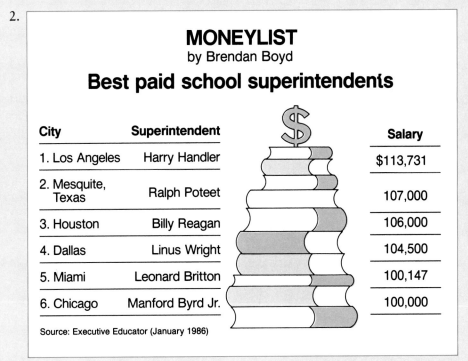

Source: *Columbus Dispatch*, July 1, 1986, 2B.

3.

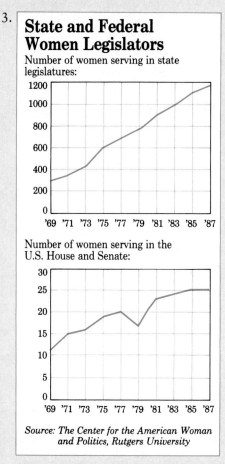

State and Federal Women Legislators

Number of women serving in state legislatures:

Number of women serving in the U.S. House and Senate:

Source: The Center for the American Woman and Politics, Rutgers University

Source: *The Wall Street Journal*, November 2, 1987, 34.

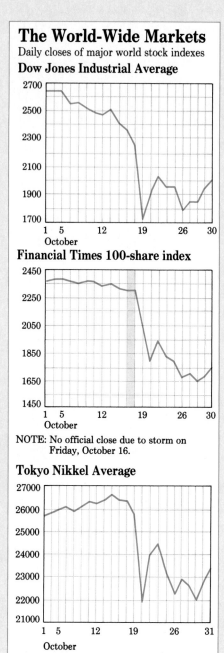

The World-Wide Markets

Daily closes of major world stock indexes

Dow Jones Industrial Average

Financial Times 100-share index

NOTE: No official close due to storm on Friday, October 16.

Tokyo Nikkel Average

4.

Source: *Consumer Reports*, May 1988, 300.

5.

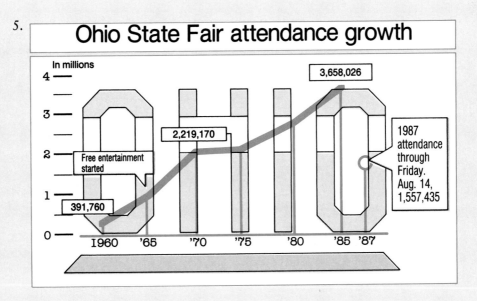

Source: *Columbus Dispatch*, August 16, 1987, B1.

6.

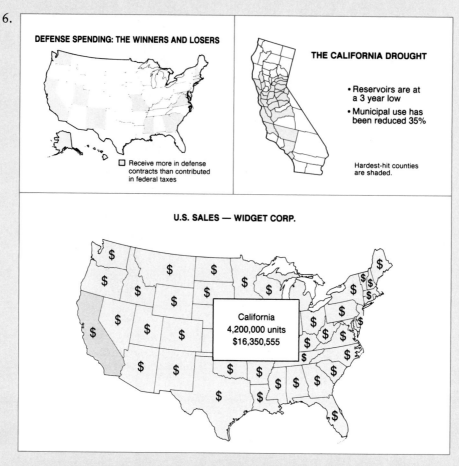

Sources: MapMaster Ad, *PC Magazine* 5, no. 6 (March 25, 1986) 40 (a); and Ashton-Tate Ad, *The Wall Street Journal*, September 28, 1987, 19.

11–2 CREATING VISUALS

a. What visuals could be used to present each of the following data sets?

b. What would be the advantages and the disadvantages of each kind of visual which could be used?

c. Create a useful visual for each kind of the following data sets.

1. Response to a questionnaire

"What time does your alarm go off in the morning?"

Before 6 A.M. <u>13</u>

6 A.M. to 7 A.M. <u>16</u>

7 A.M. to 8 A.M. <u>7</u>

After 8 A.M. <u>5</u>

Don't set alarm <u>9</u>

2. Data from the U.S. Bureau of Labor Statistics, 1986

Numbers of couples in which both are managers, professionals, or technical employees (rounded off to two significant digits):

1970   1,700,000
1975   2,300,000
1980   3,100,000
1985   3,500,000

3. Summary of First Quarter Expense Reports, by Salesperson

Hotel: Alice Rosenberg, $216.37; Jose Ortega, $253.18; Tiffany Green, $318.74; Daniel Wong, $304.65; Allen Reide, $309.43.

Airline: Alice Rosenberg, $420.21; Jose Ortega, $530.78; Tiffany Green, $894.43; Daniel Wong, $409.23; Allen Reide, $938.98.

Car Rental: Alice Rosenberg, $604.37; Jose Ortega, $53.78; Tiffany Green,

Meals
and
Entertainment:

$66.87; Daniel Wong, $271.34; Allen Reide, $89.43. Alice Rosenberg, $263.70; Jose Ortega, $453.48; Tiffany Green, $431.39; Daniel Wong, $504.05; Allen Reide, $230.95.

Miscellaneous: Jose Ortega, $3.56; Tiffany Green, $56.23; Allen Reide, $102.30.

4. County Budget Expenditures for Welfare

11 years ago:	General Operating Budget	$27.4 Million
	Welfare Expenses	3.3 Million
6 years ago:	General Operating Budget	$45.3 Million
	Welfare Expenses	5.6 Million
Last year:	General Operating Budget	$72.8 Million
	Welfare Expenses	11.6 Million

5. Data from the U.S. Commerce Department and the Japanese Ministry of Finance

Net overseas investment, in billions of U.S. dollars, was 11.5 for Japan and 106.3 for the United States in 1980. The following year the figures were 10.9 and 141.1, respectively. In 1982 Japan's investment rose to 24.7 while the U.S. figure slipped slightly to 137.0 billion. In 1983 this trend continued, with Japan's investment overseas rising to 37.3 billion U.S. dollars, while the U.S. investment fell to 89.6 billion. The figures for 1986 were Japan, 74.3; the United States, 3.6. By 1985,

Japan's investment overseas had risen to 129.8 billion, while the United States had a deficit of 111.9 billion. The figures for 1986 were 180.4 billion for Japan and a minus 263.6 billion for the United States.

11–3 MONITORING THE VISUALS IN NEWSPAPERS AND MAGAZINES
Monitor three issues of a newspaper or magazine.

How many visuals appear in the three issues you examined?

Of these, how many were tables? Line graphs? Bar graphs?

Do any of the visuals have chartjunk?

Are any of the visuals misleading? If so, how could they be redrawn?

What is the point of each visual?

As your instructor directs,
a. Share your results orally with the class.
b. Present your results in a memo to your instructor, using visuals as appropriate.
c. Team up with other students in the class to present a group report, using visuals as appropriate.

11–4 INTERPRETING DATA
How many different stories can you find in the following data on TV commercials? What visual best expresses each story?

MOST POPULAR TELEVISION COMMERCIALS OF 1987

1987 Rank	1986 Rank	Brand (Agency)	1987 TV Spending (In Millions)
1	3	California raisins (Foote, Cone & Belding)	$ 5.4
2	7	Bud Light (DDB Needham)	51.9
3	5	Pepsi/Diet Pepsi (BBDO)	90.1
4	4	Miller Lite (Backer Spielvogel Bates)	70.8
5	2	McDonald's (Leo Burnett)	344.1
6	6	Bartles & Jaymes (Hal Riney & Partners)	33.4
7	1	Coca-Cola (McCann-Erikson)	39.9
8	10	Isuzu (Della Femina, Travisano)	34.1
9	—	Du Pont Stainmaster carpet (BBDO)	22.8
10	—	Domino's Pizza (Group243)	41.0
11	9	Jello-O (Young & Rubicam)	31.8
12	16	Wendy's (Backer Spielvogel Bates)	78.4
13	12	Levi's (Foote, Cone & Belding)	20.2
14	11	Kibbles 'n Bits (J. Walter Thompson)	7.1

(continued)

1987 Rank	1986 Rank	Brand (Agency)	1987 TV Spending (In Millions)
15	17	Seagram's wine coolers (Ogilvy & Mather)	22.8
16	—	Michelob brands (DDB Needham)	71.5
17	—	Oscar Mayer (J. Walter Thompson)	21.8
18	—	Partnership for a Drug-Free America (various agencies)	70.0*
19	—	Chevrolet (Lintas: Campbell-Ewald)	186.9
20	—	Lucky Dog (Tatham-Laird & Kudner)	4.2
21	—	Angel Soft (Altschiller Reitzfeld)	10.7
22	—	Energizer (DDB Needham)	20.3
23	20	Sprite (Lowe Marschalk)	21.8
24	—	Tender Chops (J. Walter Thompson)	7.3
25	—	Long John Silver (Foote, Cone & Belding)	29.4

*Estimated value of TV time donated for these public-service spots.

Sources: Video Storyboard Tests, Broadcast Advertisers Reports.

Source: Ronald Alsop, "In TV Viewers' Favorite 1987 Ads, Offbeat Characters Were the Stars," *The Wall Street Journal*, March 3, 1988, 17.

As your instructor directs,

a. Share your results orally with the class.

b. Present your results in a memo to your instructor, using visuals as appropriate.

c. Team up with other students in the class to present a group report, using visuals as appropriate.

11–5 INTERPRETING NUMERICAL DATA

In 1986, 3,959,058 people attended the Texas State Fair, 275,893 more than attended the Ohio State Fair. But the Texas Fair lasted 31 days, while the Ohio Fair lasted 17 days. On an average day, the Ohio State Fair attracted almost twice as many people.

Who has the bigger state fair? What claims is each fair justified in making?

III

LETTERS AND MEMOS

Informative and Positive Letters and Memos

QUESTIONS

- What's the best way to organize informative and positive messages?
- How do letters and memos differ?
- What are the three criteria for good subject lines?
- What should the subject line of an informative or positive message do?
- When do you need reader benefits in informative and positive messages?
- What is a goodwill ending? How do you write one?
- How should you analyze informative and positive problems?

> All forms of wealth result from the movement of information.
> Marshall McLuhan
> *Understanding Media, 1964*

M cLuhan's statement contains a core of truth. Raw materials produce wealth only if people know how to get them and how to use them. Companies that make products need information to determine what to make, how many to make, and how to distribute and sell their products. Many professionals—accountants, marketing researchers, and college professors—make a living by providing information they know or know how to find.

We categorize messages both by **the initial response we expect from the reader** and by **the author's purposes.** In an **informative message,** the reader's basic reaction will be neutral. In a **positive** or **good news message,** the reaction should be positive. Neither message immediately asks the reader to do anything. However, you may well want the reader to save the information and to act on it later on. You usually do want to build positive attitudes toward the information you are presenting, so in that sense, even an informative message has a persuasive element.

Informative and positive messages include

- **Acceptances and awards**
  Letters confirming oral job offers.
  Letters offering admission to college or graduate school.
  Credit acceptances.
  Positive answers to readers' requests.
  Reassurances.
  Engagement letters specifying the services a CPA or other professional will provide.
- **Answers to questions**
  Information about procedures, products, services, or options.
  Letters of reference.
- **Announcements of policy changes which are neutral or positive**
  Changes which increase benefits, service, or coverage.
  Changes which increase the reader's freedom.
  Changes which readers need to be able to pass on to customers or clients.
- **Miscellaneous**
  Messages that are to the reader's benefit.
  Congratulations.
  Thank-you letters.
  Memos for the file recording actions and rationales.

Even a simple informative or positive message usually has several purposes:

Primary Purposes:
   To give information to the reader or to reassure the reader.
   To have the reader read the message, understand it, and view the information positively.
   To deemphasize any negative elements.

Secondary Purposes:

To build a good image of the writer.

To build a good image of the writer's organization.

To cement a good relationship between the writer and reader.

To reduce or eliminate future correspondence on the same subject, so the message doesn't create more work for the writer.

ORGANIZING INFORMATIVE AND POSITIVE MESSAGES

Present informative and positive messages in the following order:

1. **Give any good news and summarize the main points.** Include the date policies begin, the percent of a discount, etc. If the reader has already raised the issue, make it clear that you're responding. You make your message more important by placing it in a context your reader has raised. Share good news immediately.

2. **Give details, clarification, background.** Don't repeat information you've already given. Do answer all the questions your reader is likely to have; provide all the information necessary to achieve your purposes. Present details in the order of importance to the reader.

3. **Present any negative elements—as positively as possible.** A policy may have limits; information may be incomplete; the reader may have to satisfy requirements to get a discount or benefit. Make these negatives clear, but present them as positively as possible.

4. **Explain any reader benefits.** Most informative memos need reader benefits. Show that the policy or procedure helps readers, not just the company. Give enough detail to make the benefits clear and convincing. In letters, you may want to give benefits of dealing with your company as well as benefits of the product or policy. In a good news message, it's often possible to combine a short reader benefit with a goodwill ending in the last paragrah.

5. **Use a goodwill ending: positive, personal, and forward-looking.** Shifting your emphasis away from the message to the specific reader suggests that serving the reader is your real concern.

Figures 12.1 and 12.2 illustrate two ways that the basic pattern can be applied.

The letter in 12.1 authorizes a one-year appointment that the reader and writer have already discussed and describes the organization's priorities. Since the writer knows that the reader wants to accept the job, the letter doesn't need to persuade. The opportunity for the professor to study records that aren't available to the public is an implicit reader benefit; the concern for the reader's needs builds goodwill.

The memo in 12.2 announces a major shift in production. The memo contrasts the new method with the familiar one, explains why the shift is being made, suggests benefits for readers, and involves them in planning the details. The memo avoids false benefits: it doesn't promise raises or extra fringe benefits; it doesn't imply that all current line workers will become supervisors or computer operators. But it does offer people more control over their own work and the opportunity—if they want it—to assume more responsibility.

Myths about Informative and Positive Messages

Let's debunk two myths about informative and positive messages.

Myth 1: Informative and positive messages are short—usually less than a full page.

Truth: The length of a message depends on your purposes, the audience's needs, and the complexity of the situation.

A public health inspector got a lot of teasing from his colleagues because he wrote such long reports. His inspection reports were routinely 10 typed pages; the other inspectors rarely wrote more than four. He got the last laugh, however, when the lawyers in the enforcement division complimented him on his reports. For the first time, they were getting enough information to win cases against companies and individuals charged with violating the public health statutes. The shorter reports didn't give enough information.

If you have a reader who demands one-page memos, boil your message down. If the reader needs evidence, give the details—even if they take several pages. Almost every executive asks for short memos, but a short memo has little merit if it is incomplete, hard to understand, or doesn't do the job.

Myth 2: Informative and positive messages are easy to write.

Truth: How easy a message is to write depends on your familiarity with the situation and your readers as well as on the kind of message.

It isn't easy to decide how to present complex information or how to present routine information in an interesting way. Even good news can be hard to convey when you have lots of facts to include or when you need to develop reader benefits.

FIGURE 12.1
A POSITIVE LETTER

**Interstate Fidelity
Insurance Company**   100 Interstate Plaza   Atlanta, GA 30301   (404) 555-5000

March 8, 19--

Professor Adrienne Prinz
Department of History
Duke University
Durham, North Carolina   27000

Dear Professor Prinz:

*Good
News* ①

Your appointment as archivist for Interstate Fidelity Insurance has been
approved. When you were in Atlanta in December, you said that you could
begin work June 1. We'd like you to start then if that date is still good
for you.   *Tactful*

The Board has outlined the following priorities for your work: *Assumes reader's
primary interest
is in the job*

*Negative about
lighting
and security ③
presented
impersonally*

②

1. <u>Organize and catalogue the archives</u>. You'll have the basement of
    the Palmer Building for the archives and can requisition the sup-
    plies you need. You'll be able to control heat and humidity; the
    budget doesn't allow special lighting or security measures.

2. <u>Prepare materials for a 4-hour training session in October</u> for
    senior-level managers. We'd like you to cover how to decide what
    to send to the archives. If your first four months of research
    uncover any pragmatic uses for our archives (like Wells Fargo's
    use of archives to teach managers about past pitfalls), include
    those in the session.

3. <u>Write an article each month for the employee newsletter</u> describing
    the uses of the archives. When we're cutting costs in other depart-
    ments, it's important to justify committing funds to start an
    archives program.

4. <u>Study the IFI archives</u> to compile (a) information that can help
    solve current management problems; (b) information that could be
    included in a history of the company; and (c) information that might
    be useful to scholars of business history.

*These provisions
will appeal to
the reader*

5. <u>Begin work on a corporate history of IFI</u>. IFI will help you find
    a publisher and support the book financially. You'll have full
    control over the content.

*Negative ③
because reader
will have to
apply for
money for
assistance
after 1st 6 months*

Your salary will be $23,000 for six months; your contract can be renewed
twice for a total of 18 months. You're authorized to hire a full-time
research assistant for $8,000 for six months; you'll need to go through
the normal personnel request process to request that that money be continued
next year. A file clerk will be assigned full-time to your project. You'll
report to me. At least for the rest of this calendar year, the budget for
the Archives Project will come from my department.

*Salary is deemphasized to avoid implying
that reader is "just taking job for the
money."*

FIGURE 12.1 *(continued)*

Professor Adrienne Prinz
March 8, 19--
Page 2

IFI offices are equipped with IBM OS/80 computers with dBase IV, WordPerfect,
and Lotus 1-2-3. Is there any software that we should buy for cataloguing
or research? Are there any office supplies that we need to have on hand
June 1 so that you can work efficiently?

In the meantime,

> 1. Please send your written acceptance right away.
>
> 2. Let me know if you need any software or supplies.
>
> 3. Send me the name, address, and social security number of your
>   research assistant by May 1 so that I can process his or her
>   employment papers.
>
> 4. If you'd like help finding a house or apartment in Atlanta, let me
>   know. I can give you the name of a real estate agent.

On June 1, you'll spend the morning in Personnel. Stop by my office at
noon. We'll go out for lunch and then I'll take you to the office you'll
have while you're at IFI.

Welcome to IFI!

Cordially,

Cynthia Yen

Cynthia Yen
Director of Education and Training

Goodwill ending (5)

FIGURE 12.2
AN INFORMATIVE MEMO

May 24, 19--

To: All Employees

From: Greg Wandowski, Plant Manager *GW*

Subject: Implementing the New "Just-In-Time" Production System

(1) Our production line will begin implementing "Just-In-Time" production July 1. By September 1 the new system should be fully in place.

(2) As most of you know, in the past Wood Works has ordered materials in large batches several times a year, inventoried them, and moved them to the assembly room as they were needed. Someone has to check and inventory materials as they arrive, move them to a storage room, and move them again when the assembly line is ready for them.

"Just-In-Time" systems order small batches of materials as frequently as they're needed to arrive at the plant "just in time" to be installed in the assembly line. The systems have been used successfully by car manufacturers; small businesses like ours can use them too. "Just-In-Time" orders depend on accurate computer records of production and inventory, but the VAX system installed in January gives us the computer capability we need.

Employees may see "improving productivity"-(2) working harder for the same pay- as negative

"Just-In-Time" production will make Wood Works more competitive. Less storage space will be needed to warehouse raw materials, so we'll be able to expand production without renting larger quarters. Less employee time will be needed to check, move, and move again supplies, so productivity will improve. Since materials are ordered just before they're used, there's much less lag time between the date we must pay for supplies and the date we are paid for our products. We'll improve cash flow and reduce interest costs. Lower costs and higher productivity mean that our products will remain affordable even though the cost of raw materials continues to rise.

This explanation of why the change is being made discusses benefits to the company, not reader benefits

Some people may not (3) want to learn more

(4) *Some people (3) are afraid of computers*

"Just-In-Time" production depends on worker involvement, not just decisions made by management. Each of you will need to learn more about the entire production process. So that you can do that, each of you will spend two days during the next month observing other departments. Jill Lehman and Raj Nandi will schedule dates. At least two people in each department need to know how to use the computer to order parts. Everyone interested in learning can sign up for one of the training sessions Jerry McWhorter will run this summer.

Every Friday afternoon from June through August, production will stop at 3 p.m. to allow time for a two-hour brainstorming session on ways to implement the system, increase efficiency at each station, and improve quality. We'll try out everything that seems promising and keep the ideas that work.

Reader benefits are presented honestly

You may find that rotating work assignments or varying the pace of the assembly conveyor makes work more interesting. Maybe techniques from one station can help solve problems elsewhere on the line. Perhaps you can suggest ways to use scraps or cut energy use.

(5) Your ideas, your know-how, and your creativity will make the new system a success--"Just-In-Time" for our peak production season in the fall.

SUBJECT LINES FOR INFORMATIVE AND POSITIVE MESSAGES

A **subject line** is the title of a document. It aids in filing and retrieving the document, tells readers why they need to read the document, and provides a framework in which to set what you're about to say.

Subject lines are standard in memos and in letters using the simplified letter format; they can also be used in letters using block or modified block format. (See Appendix A, Formats for Letters and Memos.)

A good subject line meets three criteria: it is specific, concise, and appropriate for the kind of message (positive, negative, persuasive).

Making Subject Lines Specific

The subject line needs to be specific enough to differentiate that message from others on the same subject, but broad enough to cover everything in the message.

Too general:	Training Sessions
Better:	Dates for 19— Training Sessions
or	Evaluation of Training Sessions on Conducting Interviews
or	Should We Schedule a Short Course on Proposal Writing?

Making Subject Lines Concise

Most subject lines are relatively short—usually no more than 10 words, often only three to seven words.

Wordy:	Survey of Student Preferences in Regards to Various Pizza Factors
Better:	Students' Pizza Preferences
or	The Feasibility of a Cassano's Branch on Campus
or	What Students Like and Dislike about Giovanni Pizza

If you can't make the subject both specific and short, be specific.

Making Subject Lines Appropriate for the Pattern of Organization

Since your subject line introduces your reader to your message, it must satisfy the psychological demands of the situation; it must be appropriate to your purposes and to the immediate response you expect from your reader. In general, do the same thing in your subject line that you would do in the first paragraph.

When you have good news for the reader, build goodwill by highlighting it in the subject line. When your information is neutral, summarize it concisely for the subject line.

> Subject: Discount on Rental Cars
>
> Starting January 2, as an employee of Amalgamated Industries you can get a 15% discount on cars you rent for business or personal use from Roadway Rent-a-Car.

Using Patterns of Organization for Letters and Memos

The patterns of organization in this chapter and the chapters that follow will work for 70 to 90% of the writing situations most people in business and government face. Using the appropriate pattern can help you compose more quickly and create a better final product.

- Be sure you understand the rationale behind each pattern so that you can modify the pattern if necessary.

- Not every message that uses the basic pattern will have all the elements listed. The elements you do have will go in the order presented in the pattern.

- Sometimes you can present several elements in one paragraph. Sometimes you'll need several paragraphs for just one element.

In real life, writing problems don't come with labels that tell you which pattern to use. Chapters 12 through 18 offer advice about when to use each pattern. Appendix C offers problems without labels so that you can practice choosing the best pattern as well as creating an effective message.

How Letters and Memos Differ

Letters go to someone outside your organization; memos go to someone in your own organization.

In large organizations where each unit is autonomous, the organization's culture determines whether people in different units send letters or memos to each other. In some universities, for example, faculty send letters if they need to write to faculty in other departments.

Letters and memos use different formats. The most common formats are illustrated in Appendix A. The AMS Simplified Letter Format is very similar to memo format: it uses a subject line and omits the salutation and the complimentary close.

The differences in audience and format are the only differences between letters and memos. Both kinds of messages can be long or short, depending on how much you have to say and how complicated the situation is. Both kinds of messages can be informal when you write to someone you know well, or more formal when you write to someone you don't know, to several audiences, or "for the record." Both kinds of messages can be simple responses that you can dash off in 15 minutes; both can take hours of analysis and revision when you've never faced that situation before or when the stakes are high.

USING READER BENEFITS IN INFORMATIVE AND POSITIVE MESSAGES

Not all informative and positive messages need reader benefits. Figures 12.1 and 12.4b present messages that are acceptable without reader benefits.

You don't need reader benefits when

- You're presenting factual information only.
- You don't care about the reader's attitude toward the information.
- Stressing benefits may make the reader sound selfish.
- The benefits are so obvious that to restate them insults the reader's intelligence.

You do need reader benefits when

- You are presenting policies.
- You want to shape readers' attitudes toward the information or toward your organization.
- Stressing benefits presents readers' motives positively.
- Some of the benefits may not be obvious to readers.

Messages to customers or potential customers sometimes include a sales paragraph promoting products or services you offer in addition to the product or service that the reader has asked about. Sales promotion in an informative or positive message should be low-key, not "hard sell."

Reader benefits are hardest to develop when you are announcing policies. The organization probably decided to adopt the policy because it appeared to help the organization; the people who made the decision may not have thought at all about whether it would help or hurt employees. Yet reader benefits are most essential in this kind of message so readers see the reason for the change and support it.

When you present reader benefits, be sure to present advantages *to the reader.* Most new policies help the organization in some way, but few workers will see their own interests as identical with the organization's. Even if the organization saves money or increases its profits, workers will benefit directly only if they own stock in the company, if they're high up enough to receive bonuses, if the savings enables a failing company to avoid layoffs, or if all of the savings goes directly to employee benefits. In many companies, any money saved will go to executive bonuses, shareholder profits, or research and development.

To develop reader benefits for informative and positive messages, use the steps suggested in Chapter 7. Be sure to think about **intrinsic benefits** of your policy, that is, benefits that come from the activity or policy itself, apart from any financial benefits. Does a policy improve the eight hours people spend at work?

WRITING THE ONE-PAGE MEMO

Some organizations force writers to be concise by requiring or encouraging one-page memos. In simple situations, a page may be more than you need. Sometimes, careful revising and editing may enable you to cut your memo to a page. When you can't get everything on one page even with careful revision, put the key points on one well-designed page and let readers who want more information read attachments or appendices. See Figure 12.3 for an example.

FIGURE 12.3
A ONE-PAGE MEMO

August 2, 19--

To: All Salaried and Non-Bargaining Unit Employees

From: Rafael Valdez, Employee Benefits *RV*

Subject: Improvements in Health Care, Retirement, and Investment
          Plan Benefits

Improvements in three parts of your benefit package were approved
at the Board of Directors' July meeting.

Health Care

Effective September 1 your health package covers

- Specified outpatient oral surgery procedures
- Increased benefits for surgery
- Higher limits for diagnostic tests, non-surgical
  physicians' fees, and major medical expenses.

Early Retirement

Effective September 1, you can take early retirement with full
benefits at age 55 if your combined age and years with Allied
total 85 or more. If your combined age and years with Allied
total 75 or more, you can take early retirement at age 55 with
75% of full benefits.

Investment Plan

Effective January 1, you can increase deposits in the Investment
Plan to 10% of your base salary. You can continue to make
deposits either by payroll deduction or by check at the beginning
of each quarter. Allied will continue to match $1 of every $4
you invest up to 4% of your base salary.

For More Information

The attached summary explains these benefits more fully.

You receive the health care coverage automatically. To apply for
early retirement or to change the amount of your salary deposited
in the Investment Plan by payroll deduction, visit the Employee
Benefits Office.

The Political Uses of Memos*

The memo is an unrecognized art form.

How the memo is routed is at least as important as what it says. . . . For example, if I put my immediate supervisor's name AND the vice-president's name on the top, it means that . . . I have direct access to the VP. If I give the VP a copy but don't indicate that on the supervisor's memo, I am withholding information from my supervisor and asserting that my "real" boss is the vice-president. If I want to co-operate with my immediate supervisor, I address the memo to him and allow him to route it—he or she, thereby, gets credit for my activities. . . .

Equals almost never send each other memos. If you author a memo, then you are putting yourself up one or one down with respect to the receivers.

For example, I recently won an award. A peer sent me a memo saying, "Congratulations . . . keep up the fine work," to position himself as a superior. Very irritating. Very effective. He has been promoted. . . .

The simplest way to take credit [for an idea] is to attach your memo ("the attached may be of interest to you") to someone else's work. A slightly more sophisticated technique is to write a memo attaching your name to the idea of someone else or, more honestly, write a memo attaching your name to your own idea before somebody else pirates it. . . .

There are many legitimate reasons for writing memos. But just as nonverbal elements of oral communication are said to constitute 93 percent of the message, so . . . [students should consider] timing, personalities, and the overall effect of their business communication.

ENDING INFORMATIVE AND POSITIVE LETTERS AND MEMOS

Ending a letter or memo gracefully can be a problem in short informative and positive messages. In a one-page memo where you have omitted details and proof, you can tell readers where to get more information. In long messages, you can summarize your basic point. In persuasive messages, as you'll learn in Chapter 14, you can tell readers what you want them to do. But none of these strategies works in a short message containing all the information readers need. In those situations, either write a goodwill paragraph that refers directly to the reader or the reader's organization, or just stop.

Goodwill endings should focus on the business relationship you share with your reader rather than on the reader's hobbies, family, or personal life. When you write to one person, a good last paragraph fits that person so specifically that it would not work if you sent the same basic message to someone else or to a person with the same title in another organization. When you write to someone who represents an organization, the last paragraph can refer to your company's relationship to the reader's organization. When you write to a group (for example, to "All Employees") your ending should apply to the whole group.

Use a paragraph that shows you see your reader as an individual. Possibilities include complimenting the reader for a job well done, describing a reader benefit, or looking forward to something positive that relates to the subject of the message.

The letter in Figure 12.4 responds to a question from a hospital representative about how to handle a situation under the company's hospitalization policy. The specific question was, "If a patient leaves the hospital and returns, is that considered a continuation of the previous stay or a new stay for insurance purposes?"

The last paragraph in 12.4a is unnecessary. The patient either is or is not in the hospital overnight. If he or she is in overnight the stay is an extension of a claim already in force; if the patient is not, the claim is a new one. To suggest that the reader cannot understand this is not flattering to the reader's ego. It's likely that the writer uses this trite ending only because he doesn't know how to end the letter. (We should give him some credit: at least he didn't say "Please do not hesitate"!)

Figure 12.4b uses one possible goodwill ending. Other endings could also work, depending on the circumstances.

Another option would be to stop. A good one-paragraph letter is better than a longer one that uses clichés or insults the reader's intelligence.

ANALYSIS OF A SAMPLE PROBLEM

Real-life problems are richer and less well-defined than textbook problems. But even textbook problems require analysis before you begin to write. Before you tackle the assignments for this chapter, examine the following problem. See how the analysis questions probe the basic points required for a solution. Study the two sample solutions to see what makes one unacceptable and the other one good. Note the recommendations for revision that could make the good solution excellent.[1]

---

* Quoted from Carla Butenhoff, "Bad Writing Can Be Good Business," *The ABCA Bulletin* 40, no. 2 (June 1977): 12–13.

FIGURE 12.4
ENDING POSITIVE AND INFORMATIVE MESSAGES

November 5, 19--

Ms. Sharon Arakawa, Accounts Director
Good Samaritan Hospital
400 West High
Portland, OR 97802

Dear Ms. Arakawa:

Patients admitted under our Group
Plan may leave the hospital for a
few hours during the day. If the
patient is gone from the hospital
overnight or longer, start a new
claim when the patient is readmitted.

Why should reader have questions? previous ¶ explains

Should you have any questions regarding
this matter, please feel free to
call me.

Yours truly,

Martin Hobart
Employee Benefits Office

November 5, 19--

Ms. Sharon Arakawa, Accounts Director
Good Samaritan Hospital
400 West High
Portland, OR 97802

Dear Ms. Arakawa:

Patients admitted under our Group
Plan may leave the hospital for a
few hours during the day. If the
patient is gone from the hospital
overnight or longer, start a new
claim when the patient is readmitted.

Many employee-patients appreciate
the freedom to leave the hospital
for a few hours. It's nice working
with a hospital which is flexible
enough to offer that option.

Yours truly,

Martin Hobart
Employee Benefits Office

Problem

Interstate Fidelity Insurance (IFI) uses computers to handle its payments and billings. There is often a time lag between receiving a payment from a customer and recording it on the computer. Sometimes, while the payment is in line to be processed, the computer sends out additional notices: past-due notices, collection letters, even threats to sue. Customers are frightened or angry and write asking for an explanation. In most cases, if they just waited a little while, the situation would be straightened out. But policyholders are afraid that they'll be without insurance because the company thinks the bill has not been paid.

IFI doesn't have the time to check each individual situation to see if the check did arrive and has been processed. It wants you to write a letter which will persuade customers to wait. If something is wrong and the payment never reached IFI, IFI would send a legal notice to that effect saying that the policy would be cancelled by a certain date (which the notice would specify) at least 30 days after the date on the original premium bill. Continuing customers always get this legal notice as a third chance (after the original bill and the past-due notice).

Prepare a form letter which can go out to every policyholder who claims to have paid a premium for automobile insurance and resents getting a past-due notice. The letter should reassure readers and build goodwill for IFI.

Maybe They *Should* Hesitate

Some writers end every message with a standard invitation:

> If you have questions, please do not hesitate to ask.

That sentence lacks positive emphasis. But revising it to say "feel free to call" is rarely a good idea. Most of the time, the writer should omit the sentence entirely.

Inviting readers to call suggests that you have not answered the question fully. In very complicated situations, it may be simpler to let people call with individual questions. But in simple situations, you can answer the question clearly.

A state agency sent out a memo explaining when the state would pay for the cost of lunch that was included in a conference registration fee. The state would pay for lunch if the conference was out of town. If the conference was in the same town as the employee's office, the employee had to pay for lunch. Either the conference is in the same town or a different town. The answer is simple; no further explanation is necessary.

One of the reasons you write is to save the time needed to tell everyone individually. People in business aren't shrinking violets; they will call if they need help. But don't make more work for yourself by inviting calls to clarify simple messages.

Analysis of the Problem

1. Who is (are) your audience(s)? What characteristics are relevant to this particular message? If you are writing to more than one reader, how do the readers differ?

   Automobile insurance customers who say they've paid but have still received a past-due notice. They're afraid they're no longer insured. Since it's a form letter, different readers will have different situations: in some cases payment did arrive late, in some cases the company made a mistake, in some the reader never paid (check lost in mail, unsigned, bounced, etc.).

2. What are your purposes in writing?

   To reassure readers: they're covered for 30 days. To inform them they can assume everything is OK *unless* they receive a second notice. To avoid further correspondence on this subject. To build goodwill for IFI—we don't want to suggest IFI is error-prone or too cheap to hire enough people to do the necessary work; we don't want readers to switch companies; we do want readers to buy from IFI when they're ready for more insurance.

3. What information must your message include?

   Readers are still insured. We cannot say whether their checks have now been processed (company doesn't want to check individual accounts). Their insurance will be cancelled if they do not pay after receiving the second past-due notice (the legal notice).

4. How can you build support for your position? What reasons or reader benefits will your reader find convincing?

   Computer helps us provide personal service to policy holders. We offer policies to meet all their needs. Both of these points would need specifics to be interesting and convincing.

5. What objection(s) can you expect your reader(s) to have? What negative elements of your message must you deemphasize or overcome?

   Computers appear to cause errors. We don't know if the checks have been processed. We will cancel policies if their checks don't arrive.

6. What aspects of the total situation may affect reader response? The economy? The time of year? Morale in the organization? The relationship between the reader and writer? Any special circumstances?

   The insurance business is highly competitive—other companies offer similar rates and policies. The customer could get a similar policy for about the same money from someone else. Most people find that money is tight, so they'll want to keep insurance costs low. On the other hand, the fact that prices are steady or rising means that the value of what they own is higher—they need insurance more than ever.

In the late 1980s, many insurance companies are refusing to re-new policies (car, liability, malpractice insurance). These refusals to renew have gotten lots of publicity, and many people have heard horror stories about companies and individuals whose insurance has been cancelled or not renewed after a small number of claims. Readers don't feel very kindly toward insurance companies.

People need car insurance. If they have an accident and aren't covered, they not only have to bear the costs of that accident alone but also (depending on state law) may need to place as much as $50,000 in a state escrow account to cover future accidents. They have a legitimate worry.

Sample Solution 1

> Dear Customer:
>
> Relax. We got your check.
>
> There is always a time lag between the time payments come in and the time they are processed. While payments are waiting to be processed, the computer with superhuman quickness is sending out past-due notices and threats of cancellation.
>
> Cancellation is not something you should worry about. No policy would be cancelled without a legal notice to that effect giving a specific date for cancellation which would be at least 30 days after the date on the original premium notice.
>
> If you want to buy more insurance, just contact your local Interstate Fidelity agent. We will be happy to help you.

Discussion of Sample Solutions

Solution 1 is unacceptable. Since this is a form letter, we cannot tell customers we have their checks; in some cases, we may not. The letter is far too negative. The explanation in paragraph 2 makes IFI look irresponsible and uncaring. Paragraph 3 is far too negative. Paragraph 4 is too vague; there are no reader benefits; the ending sounds selfish. A major weakness with the solution is that it lifts phrases straight out of the problem; the writer does not seem to have thought about the problem or about the words he or she is using. Measuring the draft against the answers to the questions for analysis suggests that this writer should start over.

Solution 2 is much better. It opens with the good news which is true for all readers. (Whenever possible, one should use the good news pattern of organization.) Paragraph 2 explains IFI's policy. It avoids assigning blame and ends on a positive note. The negative information is buried in paragraph 3

Conveying Information to International Audiences*

The strategies that work best in North America may need to be modified when you write to international audiences.

Rather than opening with your main point, you'll often build good-will if you begin with a statement of thanks or appreciation or a personal statement.

Italian business letters expect the first paragraph to refer to the reader's family and children.

Japanese letters begin with a comment on the season or weather, congratulations on the prosperity of the reader's organization, and thanks for patronage.

Germans expect a letter to begin with background, with the main point last.

Many people who speak English as a second language have learned British English rather than American English. Avoid terms that have different meanings in British and American English. For example, in American English, *to table* a proposal means to delay voting on something. In British English, the same term means to bring something to a vote immediately.

Use specific rather than general verbs. Use words that have a limited number of meanings (e.g., *accurate*) rather than those that have many meanings (e.g., *right*).

Avoid figurative language, mental pictures, and metaphors from sports or the military.

*Based on Amy E. Shuman, interviews with Italian architectural supply firms and stonemasons, summer, 1987; Saburo Haneda and Hirosuke Shima, "Japanese Communication Behavior as Reflected in Letter Writing," *Journal of Business Communication* 19, no. 1 (Winter 1982): 21; Edward T. Hall and Mildred Reed Hall, *Hidden Differences* (Hamburg: Stern Magazine, 1983), 61; and Dorothy I. Riddle and Zeddic D. Lanham, "Internationalizing Written Business English: 20 Propositions for Native English Speakers," *Journal of Language for International Business* 1 (1985): 1–11.

Using Your Computer to Check for You-Attitude and Positive Emphasis

If you compose on a computer, you can use it to check your draft for positive emphasis and you-attitude at the sentence level.

Use the "Search" or "Type All" function to highlight

- The word *I* (cut unless absolutely necessary).
- The word *we* (make sure it includes the reader).
- The word *you* (make sure it doesn't insult or accuse the reader).
- Negative words (avoid terms in the list of negative words in Chapter 7).

You'll still need to check organization, content, and style to create you-attitude beyond the sentence level. Check organization, emphasis, and layout to be sure negative information is deemphasized.

Sample Solution 2

Dear Customer:

Your auto insurance is still in effect.

Past-due notices are mailed out if the payment has not been processed within three days after the due date. This may happen if a check is delayed in the mail or arrives without a signature or account number. When your check arrives with all the necessary information, it is promptly credited to your account.

Even if a check is lost in the mail and never reaches us, you still have a 30-day grace period. If you do get a second notice, you'll know that we still have not received your check. To keep your insurance in force, just stop payment on the first check and send a second one.

Computer processing of your account guarantees that you get any discounts you're eligible for: multicar, accident-free record, good student. If you have a claim, your agent uses computer tracking to find matching parts quickly, whatever car you drive. You get a check quickly—usually within three working days—without having to visit dealer after dealer for time-consuming estimates.

Today, your home and possessions are worth more than ever. You can protect them with Interstate Fidelity's homeowners' and renters' policies. Let your local agent show you how easy it is to give yourself full protection. If you need a special rider to insure a personal computer, a coin or gun collection, or a fine antique, you can get that from IFI, too.

Whatever your insurance needs—auto, home, life, or health—one call to IFI can do it all.

---

and is presented positively: the notice is information, not a threat; the 30-day extension is a "grace period." Telling the reader now what to do if a second notice arrives eliminates the need for a second exchange of letters. Paragraph 4 offers benefits for using computers, since some readers may blame the notice on computers, and offers benefits for being insured by IFI. Paragraph 5 promotes other policies the company sells and prepares for the last paragraph.

Solution 2 could be improved by personalizing the salutation and by including the name and number of the local agent. Computers could make both of those insertions easily. This good letter could be made excellent by revising paragraph 4 so that it doesn't end on a negative note, and by using more reader benefits. For instance, do computers help agents advise clients of the best policies for them? Does IFI offer good service—quick, friendly, nonpressured—that could be stressed? Are agents well trained? All of these might yield ideas for additional reader benefits.

SUMMARY OF KEY POINTS

- Informative and positive messages normally use the following pattern of organization:

  1. Give any good news and summarize the main points.
  2. Give details, clarification, background.
  3. Present any negative elements—as positively as possible.
  4. Explain any reader benefits.
  5. Use a **goodwill ending**: positive, personal, and forward-looking.

- **Letters** go to people in other organizations. **Memos** go to people within your own organization.
- A **subject line** is the title of a document. A good subject line meets three criteria: it is specific, concise, and appropriate for the kind of message (positive, negative, persuasive). If you can't make the subject line both specific and short, be specific.
- The subject line for an informative or positive message should highlight any good news and summarize the information concisely.
- Use reader benefits in informative and positive messages when

  - You are presenting policies.
  - You want to shape readers' attitudes toward the information or toward your organization.
  - Stressing benefits presents readers' motives positively.
  - Some of the benefits may not be obvious to readers.

- **Goodwill endings** should focus on the business relationship you share with your reader or the reader's organization. The last paragraph of a message to a group should apply to the whole group.
- Use the analysis questions listed in Chapter 2 to probe the basic points needed for successful informative and positive messages.

NOTE

1. An earlier version of this problem, the sample solutions, and the discussion appeared in Francis W. Weeks and Kitty O. Locker, *Business Writing Cases and Problems* (Champaign, IL: Stipes, 1980), 40–44.

EXERCISES AND PROBLEMS FOR CHAPTER 12

12–1 EVALUATING SUBJECT LINES

Choose the best subject line in each of the following groups. Explain the reason for your choice.

1. a. Subject: Galati Supply Company
    b. Subject: Status of Galati Supply Receivables Investment, 1/10/90
    c. Subject: Report on Efforts to Bring the Galati Supply Receivables Investment into Line with Corporate Goals for Investments

2. a. Subject: How to Get Advances for Expenses in Entertaining Job Applicants
    b. Subject: Expenses, Entertaining Job Applicants, Advances for
    c. Subject: Job Applicants

3. a. Subject: Effectiveness of Graybar's Magazine Advertising, First Quarter 1988
    b. Subject: Graybar's Magazine Advertising
    c. Subject: Evaluation of Effectiveness of Graybar's Magazine Advertisements in the First Quarter of 1988

4. a. Subject: When You Can Deduct the Cost of a Conference Meal
    b. Subject: Attendance at Conferences
    c. Subject: Reimbursement Procedures for Conference Meals

5. a. Subject: Your Memo of August 14
    b. Subject: Progress on Joint Venture Projects in Japan
    c. Subject: Problems with Joint Venture Projects in Japan

12–2 ANNOUNCING A CHANGE IN PREMIUM STRUCTURE

Until now, the rates Interstate Fidelity Insurance (IFI) has charged for health insurance have varied only according to the level of coverage someone chooses. For example, plans that pay the full cost of hospitalization cost more than plans which require the person insured to pay part of the cost.

In the last year, your actuaries have undertaken a major study of the claims submitted to IFI. They found that people who smoke, who are moderate or heavy drinkers, who are overweight, and who do not exercise regularly have significantly higher health care costs: they visit doctors more often, need more prescription drugs, and are hospitalized more often and for longer periods of time.

Therefore, IFI is adopting a new premium structure for health insurance policies. People who elect fuller coverage will still pay more for it, but now, within any level of coverage, rates will go up 10% for people who are in all four risk groups (smokers, moderate to heavy drinker, overweight, don't exercise). People who are in only three risk groups will pay 105% of the current rates; people who are in only two risk groups will have no change in rates; people who are in one risk group will pay 90% of the current rate; people who do not fall into any of the four risk groups will pay 80% of the current rates.

These are the definitions you are using:

Overweight: Weighs 120% or more of recommended weight for age, sex, and height.

Smokes: Smokes an average of at least one cigarette or cigar a day.

Exercises: Vigorous exercise for at least 30 minutes at a time, three times a week; or at least 20 minutes at a time, five times a week.

Drinks: Drinks an average of at least six ounces of beer or three ounces of wine or 1.5 ounces of hard liquor a day.

Nationwide surveys show that 31% of the adult population smoke, 25% are overweight, 40% drink moderately to heavily, and 60% do not exercise at least three times a week. You do not know whether or not your policyholders are typical of the adult population.

The new rates will take effect at the policy renewal date (different people have different renewal dates). Up to two months before the renewal date, the policyholder must visit his or her doctor, who, as part of the annual checkup, will fill out a form to be returned to IFI. (IFI pays the full cost of the checkup; IFI is sending the forms directly to the physicians, whose names it has on record.) Anyone who does not send in the form will automatically be charged the highest rate.

Write a letter to be sent out to customers 10 weeks before their policy renewal dates. Tell readers about the new premium structure; tell them to schedule appointments for their checkups.

Hints:

- The current plan, with its emphasis on risk groups, is very negative. How can you present the whole plan positively?

- Assume that each letter will be individually typed by computer, so that you can personalize the letter with the renewal date, the customer's name and address, and any other relevant information. Use complete letter format.

- Offer reader benefits both for following good health practices and for being insured with IFI. Review your notes from Exercises 7–5 and 7–6 for ideas.

12–3 INTRODUCING A SUGGESTION SYSTEM

Your organization has just decided to institute a suggestion system. Employees on hourly pay scales will be asked to submit suggestions. (Managers and other employees on salary are not eligible for this program; they are supposed to be continually suggesting ways to improve things as part of their regular jobs.) If the evaluating committee thinks that the suggestion would save money, the employee will receive 10% of the first year's estimated annual saving. If the suggestion won't save money but will improve work conditions, service, or morale, the employee will get a check for $35. The names of all people whose suggestions are implemented will be printed in the newsletter.

Write a memo to all employees announcing the program.

Hints:

- You need more information. When does the program start? Are there forms to fill out? Where can people pick them up? How often will suggestions be evaluated? Specifically, what kinds of suggestions do you want?

- The problem does not specify an organization. Pick an organization you know something about—profit or nonprofit—and use it to develop specific criteria for suggestions and ways the program will benefit the organization and the employees. Use the analysis you did for Exercise 6–7.

12–4 LINING UP A CONSULTANT

As Director of Education and Training at Interstate Fidelity Insurance (IFI) you oversee all in-house training programs. Five weeks ago, Edward Ingram, Manager of Customer Service, asked you to set up a training course on writing skills. After making some phone calls, you tracked down Patricia Ramsay, a professor of business communication at a nearby college.

"Yes, I'd be interested," she told you on the phone. "I would want at least two days with the participants— three would be better. They need time to practice the skills they'll be learning. You may want to buy a copy of my *Bottom-Line Writing* for each participant. Ideally, participants should read the first 50 pages before the session begins. I'm free Thursdays and Fridays; I might be able to free up a Wednesday if I had enough notice. I'm willing to work with a group of up to 20 people. You'll need to let me know what their problems are; I'd like to see some of their writing and maybe some samples from other people in the company. My fee is $1,400 a day. Of course, you'd reimburse me for expenses."

You told her you thought a two-day session would be feasible, but you'd have to get back to her after you got budget approval. You wrote a quick memo to Ed Ingram explaining the situation and asking for approval, for writing samples, and for information about what the session should cover.

Two weeks ago, you got this memo from him.

> I've asked the Veep for budget approval for $2,800 for a two-day session plus no more than $850 for all expenses. I don't think there will be a problem.
>
> The attached samples—internal memos and letters that go to potential and actual policyholders—illustrate the things the session should cover: how to avoid jargon and how to answer routine inquiries. I do not want a rehash of freshman composition or two days of lecturing. Small group exercises seem to produce the best results.
>
> Attached is a list of 19 people from Customer Service who are free Thursday and Friday of the second week of next month. If the session goes well, I may want you to schedule additional sessions.

Today, you got approval from the Vice President to schedule the session and pay Professor Ramsay the fee and reimburse her for expenses to a maximum of $850.

Your letter must spell out all the details, since outside consultants aren't asked to sign a contract. She will have to keep all receipts and turn in an itemized list of expenses to be reimbursed; you cannot reimburse her if she does not have receipts. Nothing was ever said about her using an assistant, but if she brings someone, that person's fee comes out of her fee. She could pay a typist out of the expense allowance if she wanted someone to type handouts.

You also need to tell her the mechanics of the session. You always have these sessions at a downtown hotel; for this conference, you've tentatively reserved the Taft room, which can be divided into smaller rooms for small group exercises. It already has a screen and overhead projector; if she wants anything else, you can provide it but you'll need to know what she needs. You can't get her book to participants in time unless she gives you a phone number to call to order 19 copies quickly. You can make reservations for her if she wants you to, but again, you'll need to do that quickly.

Send Professor Ramsay the packets as an enclosure with your letter. You don't have to persuade her to come since she's already informally agreed, but you do want her to look forward to the job and to do her best work.

Hints:

- You may need some more information (which you alone or the class in discussion may provide). Have the people for this session had any college training in writing? In business writing? Are they confident about writing? Does Professor Ramsay have any idea what people in insurance write about, or should you give her some information?

- Check the calendar to get the dates. If there's any ambiguity about what the second week of next month is, "call" Ed to check.

12–5 EVALUATING A SUGGESTION TO USE NONSEXIST LANGUAGE

At its annual meeting last year, the Board of Directors of Interstate Fidelity Insurance (IFI) tabled a proposal to require that all official IFI documents and all written materials produced in the company use nonsexist language. Several years ago, the Board of Directors voted to require that the company's contracts use nonsexist language, and, on its own initiative, the marketing department has been avoiding traditional sex stereotypes in IFI ads. Currently, however, there is no policy covering the language in areas other than contracts and ads.

When the Directors tabled the proposal, they complained that it offered too little information: it didn't explain how simple or complicated it would be to use nonsexist language; it didn't discuss the effect of sexist versus nonsexist language in internal or external documents; it didn't say whether old printed materials would have to be thrown away or whether they could still be used until they ran out, even if they used traditional language; it didn't clarify exactly what would be considered sexist language and therefore unacceptable.

Your boss, Tamara Stark, Vice President, marketing, has just been asked to write a report for this year's Board meeting. She's busy with a new direct mail program introducing policies to Hispanic-Americans, so she has asked you to write a memo to her answering the Board's questions. If she likes what you write, she may send it on to the Board unchanged, which would be a good

chance for you to become visible at a very high level in the company.

Stark suggests the following ideas to make the proposal more workable and to deal with some of the Board's complaints:

1. Don't require nonsexist language in everything. Instead, require that language be free from sexism in three areas: (1) pronoun use; (2) job titles; (3) courtesy titles and salutations in letters.

2. To save money, specify that present printed materials which do not meet the standards may be phased out gradually over the next 12 months. Any new documents, as well as all internal memos and letters to customers, should incorporate nonsexist language as soon as possible after the proposal becomes company policy.

Employees at IFI produce a variety of written materials: employee benefit statements, procedures, job descriptions for college students, an employee newsletter, direct mail sales letters to potential customers, letters answering customers' questions about policies, renewal notices, and various internal memos, to name a few.

You know that Stark believes that women represent the single most promising target market for IFI: as workers, they need health and life insurance; as buyers of cars and homes, they need automobile and homeowners' policies. You also know that she dislikes the fact that some of the people at IFI (women as well as men) see the traditional roles for women as the only acceptable ones.

Write a memo to Stark outlining the proposed policy, explaining how to achieve nonsexist pronouns, job titles, and salutations and courtesy titles, and assessing the advantages of nonsexist language. You may decide to write a memo (1) advocating the proposal or (2) one answering the questions but either (*a*) remaining neutral or (*b*) challenging the proposal. If you challenge the proposal, be sure to give your reasons clearly and calmly.

Hints:

- Give both the general principles for achieving nonsexist language and specific examples.

- You do *not* have to accept Stark's ideas, but you do have to *deal* with them: if you think a different idea would be better, you need to explain convincingly *why* it's better than hers. (Be impersonal. If you disagree, don't call them "her" ideas versus "your" better ones.) If you choose, you may discuss disadvantages as well as advantages of nonsexist language.

- The memo will be to Stark; the word *you* in the memo would refer to Stark. But because you hope she'll send the memo on unchanged to the Board of Directors, you should use personal references sparingly if at all.

12–6 ADVISING EMPLOYEES TO USE NONSEXIST LANGUAGE

In large part because of your memo, IFI's Board of Directors has just voted to require that all official IFI documents and all written materials produced in the company use nonsexist language. Now, Stark asks you to write a memo to employees telling them about the policy and explaining how they can meet it.

Adapt your memo to the Board from Problem 12–5 and write a memo to employees. Be sure to explain the policy, tell them in detail how to meet it (examples would help), and describe the benefits to IFI of using nonsexist language in its communications with current and potential policyholders and employees.

12–7 REVISING AN ADMISSIONS LETTER

State College is currently using the following form admission letter to high school students admitted to the freshman class. The material in square brackets is inserted by computer.

Dear [Mr./Ms. Name]:

We are pleased to notify you of your admission to State College, thus marking the beginning of your participation in an exciting educational experience.

You are admitted to the [name of] Campus for the [term] of [year]. You cannot be admitted to another campus or to this campus at another term or year without the written consent of the Admissions Office. We have determined that you are a state resident and qualify for the in-state tuition rate.

Your enrollment to State College depends upon the accomplishment of the following steps: (1) payment of a $200 nonrefundable Acceptance Fee (please use the enclosed form) by [date]; (2) participation in our Orientation Program [dates]. During this program we will conduct a tour of campus, explain dormitory and off-campus housing, require you to listen to brief speeches by several faculty and staff, and schedule a 15-minute appointment with the advisor to whom you have been assigned; (3) submission of the Medical History form (enclosed) by [date] and your high school transcript certifying graduation. We will send a transcript request form to your high school as soon as we receive your Acceptance Fee.

We welcome you and look forward to your attending State College.

As your instructor directs,

a. Using the information in the letter, rewrite it to improve you-attitude, positive emphasis, organization, and layout.

b. Adapt the letter for your own community college, college, or university. Use specific facts about the orientation program, housing, and campus life to make the letter more interesting and make students who are admitted to several schools choose to attend yours.

12–8 GRANTING A REQUEST

You're the regional marketing manager for a fast-food chain. You've received the following letter.

Dear [Your Name]:

The state's Office of Natural Resources sponsors clean-up days in April and October. Scout troops, school classes, community organizations, and civic groups pitch in to pick up trash and debris in public parks, along roadways, and by rivers and lakes.

For several years, [name of chain] and other restaurants have donated coupons for free meals to be given to each participant.

Would your chain donate 100 coupons for the participants in the next scheduled clean-up?

Sincerely,

Leonard Jaffe

Leonard Jaffe

Your chain is indeed willing to donate coupons. The advertising expense is small, and the goodwill and community visibility are good. Send Mr. Jaffe a letter. You'll enclose coupons for 100 medium drinks, 100 sandwiches or salads, and 100 side dishes.

12–9 ANNOUNCING A PRICE DECREASE

The FCC has reduced the access charges for long-distance phone rates. The reduction is the same for all carriers, but you want to write a letter to your customers telling them about the reduction to build goodwill for your company. You can't tell them exactly how much rates will be reduced, since the formula is complex and the exact cut will vary from customer to customer, but the change will show up on their next month's phone bill.

Write the letter.

12–10 THANKING AN EXHIBITOR

The annual meeting of the American Management Association is over, and your duties as conference coordinator are almost over, too. You still need to write thank-you letters to the textbook and trade book publishers who displayed their books at the conference. Publishers pay a fee to exhibit; the fee pays not only for the cost of the exhibit room in the hotel but also helps pay for general conference costs. In addition to the basic fee, many publishers pay extra amounts to sponsor coffee breaks, continental breakfasts, or cocktail hours which are open to all conference registrants. These fees are quite high, since hotels' charges for food and setups are high.

One of the publishers on your list is Richard D. Irwin, Inc. Irwin sponsored a continental breakfast the morning of the first full day of the conference.

Write to William R. Bayer, Editor for Management and Business Communication, to thank him for Irwin's participation. Irwin's address is 1818 Ridge Road, Homewood, IL 60430.

How would it change your letter if

a. Attendance was surprisingly low this year, so publishers got less publicity from their displays and social events.

b. Attendance was excellent, and you know that everything went smoothly for exhibitors.

c. No locked area was available for exhibits, so exhibitors either had to dismantle their displays every evening and set them up every morning, or risk having books stolen. (So far as you know, nothing was stolen.)

d. This year Irwin was displaying a new text, *Communicating in the Global Economy,* which, the company hopes, will be highly successful.

12–11 EXPLAINING AN ACCOUNTING CONCEPT*

Anyone who reads the letters to the editor in the local paper will have encountered Clyde Pitstick. He's a local curmudgeon who seems to take delight in criticizing the foolishness and foibles he sees all around him. His sarcasm is literate and sometimes funny. You read him for entertainment, but on at least two occasions, other people have written in to agree with him.

Today, the paper carries another letter from Mr. Pitstick:

> The Silver Shovel award for obfuscation and double-talk should go to an accountant right here in town.
>
> Last month my great-uncle Oscar died, leaving me and my sister his farm and equipment. Now neither of us farms or wants to, but we might want to keep the collection of antique farm equipment. And the land,

which is only 10 miles from town, may be ripe for development in the next few years.

> Well, my sister and I went to uncle Oscar's accountant to find out how much the estate was worth—partly for taxes, but partly to decide what to do with it. The accountant talked for 10 minutes without answering the question. I finally asked the man flat out what a single piece of equipment—say the 1946 tractor uncle Oscar was so proud of—would be worth. And, even with a specific, straightforward question, the man still couldn't give me a straight answer. "Do you mean reproduction cost or replacement value?" he asked.
>
> This accountant is part of a growing problem with our educational system. Students aren't learning anything practical; instead, they are learning all sorts of ways to twist the facts to mean what they want them to mean. We have far too many accountants in this country; and all of them are devoted to taking perfectly simple concepts and trying to make them sound complicated just to justify the high fees they charge. Do the Japanese have so many accountants? No! They have engineers, people who *make* things, not people who charge high fees just to confuse people and twist the facts.

As a partner in the largest CPA firm in town, you can't let that go by. Write a letter to the editor of the paper, responding to Mr. Pitstick's letter and explaining why a "single piece of equipment" can have more than one "value."

The paper states, "Letters to the editor may not be longer than two typewritten pages, single-spaced. We reserve the right to cut letters before printing them."

Hints:

- Mr. Pitstick raises a number of issues in his letter. Some of these have nothing to do with accounting: specific issues about what one family is doing with an inheritance, the possible conversion of farmland into city, the reasons for Japanese dominance in some markets. At least four issues do relate to accountants: the concept of *value*, the number of accountants, the question of whether accountants twist facts and complicate simple concepts, and the matter of fees. Do you need to get into all of these?

- The tone of Mr. Pitstick's letter is argumentative. What tone should you adopt?

- Your goal is to get your letter published and read. Most of the readers will not be accountants; some of them may share Mr. Pitstick's prejudice. Be clear; define any technical terms that you can't avoid. Try to give an example to make your explanation specific and interesting.

*Inspired by an assignment written by Betty Evans White, Washington University.

12–12 ANSWERING AN INQUIRY ABOUT AUDITS

You're a CPA at one of the Big Eight Accounting firms. Today, your supervisor asks you to answer the following letter:

> Will you please tell me how much it will cost to have your firm review my business' financial records?
>
> I started my own business six years ago designing and making quilts and comforters. I now employ two people full-time and three to six additional workers part-time, depending on the season. I've never had an audit and don't know anything about what is involved or how much it costs. My bank tells me that I must have a CPA firm check my records to get a larger loan.
>
> Sincerely,
>
> *Meredith Tam*
>
> Meredith Tam

You can't quote a flat fee. In the first place, you provide three kinds of financial reports: compilations, reviews, and audits. And the fee for any one report depends on the extent and the complexity of a company's records. Ms. Tam's letter doesn't tell you whether all her receipts are in a shoe box or whether you'll find well-kept accounting records. If she's hiring up to eight people, she's doing well, but you don't know whether you're going to be looking at a budget of $200,000 or $2 million.

A compilation uses information provided by the company; it does not "review" or "audit" records and does not provide any guarantees about the completeness of disclosure or about the trustworthiness of management. However, it is comparatively inexpensive. The compilations your firm has done for small businesses in the last year have run from $3,000 to $5,000.

An audit normally examines balance sheets, income statements, and statements of changes in financial position to see that the records are kept in accordance with generally accepted accounting standards. An audit won't necessarily uncover embezzlement, sabotage, or bad management decisions; it will certify that the financial records disclose information which would enable users of the audit to judge the company's financial position. Audits are expensive because they take more time of partners and senior accountants. At current billing rates, an audit even for a small business is likely to run at least $15,000; it could easily run $20,000 or more.

A review is less thorough than an audit but fuller than a compilation. Your staff questions company personnel about how records are kept and analyzes the data management provides. A review won't certify that management has disclosed all relevant financial data, but it does provide an independent evaluation of the company's financial position. Cost for a small business might run $8,000 to $12,000.

Write a letter to Ms. Tam.

Hints:

- You can't recommend one kind of report because her letter doesn't give enough information. Compare and contrast the kinds of reports so that she can see which needs each meets. Check an auditing text if you need more information.
- Make it clear that you cannot guarantee a price or even a price range. You could give her a closer estimate after spending one day with her books (fee: $750, applicable to the cost of the report). However, even that would not be a guarantee.
- You'd like to have her business, but all CPA firms offer the same basic services and comparable prices. A friendly letter that explains her options clearly will establish goodwill.

12–13 ANSWERING AN INTERNATIONAL INQUIRY

Your business, government or nonprofit organization has received the following inquiries from international correspondents. (You choose the country the inquiry is from.) You have corresponded with these readers before, but you have never met them.

1. Please tell us about a new product, service, or trend so that we can decide whether we want to buy, license, or imitate it in our country.

2. We have heard about a problem [technical, social, political, or ethical] which occurred in your organization. Could you please tell us what really happened and estimate how it will affect the long-term success of the organization?

3. Please tell us about college programs in this field. We are interested in sending some of our managers to your country to complete a college degree.

4. We are considering setting up a plant in your city. We have already received adequate business information. However, we would also like to know how comfortable our nationals will feel. Do people in your city speak our language? How many? What opportunities exist for our nationals to improve their English? Does your town already have people from a wide mix of nations? Which are the largest groups?

5. Our organization would like to subscribe to an English-language trade journal. Which one would you recommend? Why? How much does it cost? How can we order it?

As your instructor directs,
   a. Answer one or more of the inquiries. Assume that your reader either reads English or can have your message translated.
   b. Write a memo to your instructor explaining how you've adapted the message for your audience.

Hints:
- Even though you can write in English, English may not be your reader's native language. Write a letter that can be translated easily.
- In some cases, you may need to spell out background information which might not be clear to someone from another country.

12–14 ANNOUNCING A NEW EMPLOYEE BENEFIT

As Personnel Manager, you need to tell employees about a new fringe benefit. Starting the first Monday of next month, your company will offer company-sponsored day care for children aged six months to 5½ years. Parents will pay $125 a week for infants and toddlers and $100 a week for preschoolers. The company will make up the difference (estimated cost: $400,000 a year). Parents may pay the fees in advance or have them deducted from their paychecks.

The day care will be located in a building two miles from the company's office; the facilities include a cafeteria and a large playground.

Day care will be available from 7 A.M. to 7 P.M. A staff of 80 including an R.N. is being hired; the center will meet all state standards and will be licensed. The center can accommodate 280 children. In the survey your department conducted six months ago, parents or prospective parents of 253 children said they would "definitely" use a company day-care center; parents of 38

children said they "might" use the center. If more children sign up for the center than it can accommodate, you will consider increasing capacity, but in the meantime children will be accepted on a first-come first-serve basis. Parents can pick up forms in your office to enroll their children.

Write a memo to all employees.

Hints:
- People who may use the center will see this new policy as very good news indeed. But why should people without kids or people whose kids are in school care about day care for parents of small children? Why should they help subsidize that care through nearly half a million dollars of company money? Show how all readers benefit—not just those with children under six.
- The problem does not specify the organization. Pick one you know something about—possibly one which needs to retain skilled workers and enable them to concentrate on their jobs.

12–15 PROVIDING INFORMATION TO JOB APPLICANTS

Your company is in a prime vacation spot, and as Personnel Manager you get many letters from students asking about summer jobs. Company policy is to send everyone an application for employment, a list of the jobs you expect to have open that summer with the rate of pay for each, a description of benefits for seasonal employees, and an interview schedule. Candidates must come for an interview at their own expense; candidates should call to schedule a time in advance. Competition is keen: only a small percentage of those interviewed will be hired.

Write a form letter to students who've written to you asking about summer jobs. Give them the basic information about the hiring procedure and tell them what to do next. Be realistic about their chances, but maintain their interest in working for you.

Negative Messages

QUESTIONS

- What are the purposes in a negative message?
- How should you organize a negative message?
- What kind of subject line should you use in a negative message?
- Should you use a buffer? How can you think of good buffers? Is it ever better just to give the bad news immediately?
- What are the characteristics of a good reason for refusal? If you can think of several reasons, should you give them all? Is there ever a time when you should omit the reason?
- Should you try to imply the refusal rather than stating it directly?
- Why is it a good idea to give an alternative, if one is available?
- If you have a really good alternative, should you go ahead and set it up for the reader?
- What alternate strategies should you consider in negative situations?
- How should you analyze negative problems?

So here I am,
No happier to be here than you are to have me:
Nobody likes the man who brings bad news.
Sophocles
Antigone, 441 B.C.

Bringers of bad news have never been popular, and most of us dread having to deliver negative messages. In a **negative message,** the basic information we have to convey is negative; we expect the reader to be disappointed or angry.

Negative messages include

- **Rejections and refusals**
  Job rejections.
  Letters to employers saying you've accepted another offer.
  Credit refusals.
  Letters denying admission to college and graduate school.
  Refusals to grant a customer's or client's request.
- **Announcements of policy changes which do not benefit customers or consumers**
  Price increases.
  Changes which reduce service or coverage.
  Limitations of the reader's power or freedom.
- **Miscellaneous**
  Requests which the reader will see as insulting or intrusive.
  Negative performance appraisals.
  Disciplinary notices.
  Product recalls or notices of defects.

A negative message always has several purposes:

Primary Purposes:
  To give the reader the bad news.
  To have the reader read, understand, and accept the message.
  To maintain as much goodwill as possible.
Secondary Purposes:
  To build a good image of the writer.
  To build a good image of the writer's organization.
  To reduce or eliminate future correspondence on the same subject so
    the message doesn't create more work for the writer.

In many negative situations, the writer and reader will continue to deal with each other. Even when further interaction is unlikely (for example, when a company rejects a job applicant or refuses to renew a customer's insurance), the firm wants anything the reader may say about the company to be positive or neutral rather than negative.

Some messages which at first appear to be negative can be structured to create a positive feeling. Even when it is not possible to make the reader happy with the news we must convey, we still want readers to feel that

- They have been taken seriously.
- Our decision is fair and reasonable.
- If they were in our shoes, they would make the same decision.

ORGANIZING NEGATIVE MESSAGES

The following pattern for negative messages helps writers maintain goodwill:

1. **Consider using a buffer.** A buffer is a neutral or positive statement designed to allow you to bury, or buffer, the negative message. A good buffer makes the reader more receptive to your message.

2. **Give the reason for the refusal before the refusal itself when you have a reason that readers will understand and accept.** A good reason prepares the reader to expect the refusal. Research shows that, in credit refusals, subjects who described themselves as "totally surprised" had much more negative feelings and described their feelings as being stronger than did those who expected the refusal.[1]

3. **Avoid overemphasizing the refusal, but make it clear.**

4. **Present an alternative or compromise, if one is available.** An alternative not only gives readers another way to get what they want but also suggests that you care about readers and about helping them meet their needs.

5. **End with a positive, forward-looking statement.**

This pattern differs in three ways from older patterns of organization. In the past, writers were urged never to begin negative messages with the bad news, to present the refusal inconspicuously, perhaps implying it rather than stating it directly, and to end with a paragraph of sales promotion—even if credit had just been denied.

Research now suggests, however, that the presence of a buffer does not necessarily make readers respond more positively and that sales promotion in a negative message is counterproductive.[2] Common sense suggests that there are situations where it may be better not to use a buffer at all. And experience shows that inconspicuous refusals can be missed altogether, making it necessary to say *no* a second time.

Figures 13.1 and 13.2 illustrate ways that the basic pattern for negative messages can be used.

SUBJECT LINES FOR NEGATIVE MESSAGES

In a negative message, put the subject—but not your action on it—in the subject line.

> Subject: Status of Conversion Table Program
>
> Due to heavy demands on our time, we have not yet been able to write programs for the conversion tables you asked for.

Use a negative subject line only if you think the reader will not read the whole message. To lessen the negative impact, suggest the alternative in the subject line as well.

---

* Quoted from Robin Sekerak to Kitty Locker, March 1987.

A Reader Reacts to a Negative Message*

[A student injured in a car accident caused by a faulty tire signed a contract with a lawyer and gave him all the records and photos. Six months later, she received a letter announcing that the firm "will not be proceeding with your claim after today." The student describes her reaction to the letter:]

The first thing to note (if I go in order down the page) is the "Ms. Sekerak" which might be correct in most negative letters, but in this case since all business interactions were as "Robin" and "Joe" I feel it is offensive. It makes me feel "Robin and Joe" was falsely friendly and as soon as he knows he won't be making "big bucks" off of me he distances himself.

Second, . . . the way he talked, "This was a sure thing." It was quite a shock to find out they "once again, reviewed [my] file."

Next, "they" give me no reason for "not proceeding" with my claim. "Reviewing the legal problems as well as the law" tells me absolutely nothing. . . .

In meeting with him I mentioned several times when the statute of limitations would be up and why I need him to move on this (and that was in September). I am insulted by "You should be mindful. . . ." Also, at this point there is no way I'd have him appoint me an attorney, no matter how "happy" he is to do so. . . .

But what really takes the cake is "You can ill afford to wait" . . . by someone who has sat on this for six months. . . .

After all this I think he should send all of my photos and records to me immediately. (It's a certified letter; he knows I got it.)

. . . One last tidbit: my name was misspelled on the envelope.

FIGURE 13.1
A NEGATIVE MESSAGE WITH A BUFFER

Thorpe Industries

2930 Henry Avenue • Denver, Colorado 80236   (303) 555-4000

March 4, 1989

Mr. Scott Winston
403 East College Street
Apartment #4
Woodbridge, VA 22191

Dear Mr. Winston:

Buffer — Recently we extended an offer for you to join Class III of the Professional Development Program which will begin June 10.

Reason — Yesterday you called to tell us you would not be graduating until August. Since Class III will begin employment before your graduation date, we must withdraw our offer to you *Refusal* — for a position at this time.

Explains why no alternative exists — Class III is the last PDP we'll have in 1989, and our next offers will not be effective until Spring 1990.

Forward-looking ending — We're sorry that you will not be able to join Class III. Best of luck to you with other employment opportunities.

Sincerely,

J. B. Van Tassel

J. B. Van Tassel
Manager, Professional Development

FIGURE 13.2

Vickers Insurance Company
200 Interchange Mall
Columbus, Ohio 43278
614-555-5000

Negative ③   **Liability Coverage**
                Is Being Discontinued--
Alternative ④ **Here's How to Replace It!**

Negative message is highlighted so reader won't ignore message.

Dear Policyholder:

Negative —③
④ When your auto insurance is renewed, it will no
longer include liability coverage unless you select
the new Assurance Plan. Here's why.

③ Liability coverage is being discontinued. It, <u>and
the part of the premium which paid for it,</u> will be
dropped from all policies when they are renewed.

No reason is given. The change probably benefits the company rather than the reader, so it is omitted.

Alternative-④ This could leave a gap in your protection. But you
can replace the old Liability Coverage with Vickers'
new Assurance Plan.

The new Assurance Plan provides benefits for
litigation or awards arising from an accident--
regardless of who's at fault. The cost for the
Assurance Plan at any level is based on the ages of
drivers, where you live, your driving record, and
other factors. If these change before your policy
is renewed, the cost of your Assurance Plan may
also change. The actual cost will be listed in
your renewal statement.

Forward looking ending ⑤ To sign up for the Assurance Plan, just check the
level of coverage you want on the enclosed form and
return it in the postage-paid envelope within 14
days. You'll be assured of the coverage you select.

Sincerely,

C. J. Morgan

C. J. Morgan
President

Alternative ④ P.S. The Assurance Plan protects you against possible
legal costs arising from an accident. Sign up for
the Plan today and receive full coverage from Vickers.

A Poor Buffer Is Worse than None at All*

Good readers—especially business readers, but in fact any who weren't born yesterday—are also inherently suspicious. Alarm bells will ring if the opening sentences of a communication do not seem . . . relevant. . . .

What would be your reaction to reading [a first paragraph praising your landscaping and roses] written not by a personal friend but by the vice-president of First Federal Savings and Loan Association? Most readers, I suspect, would be trying to figure out whether they were about to be foreclosed on or merely sold a new savings plan to help finance their roses. I doubt that very many would think, "How lovely. What a thoughtful person."

. . . As a busy person with a large pile of correspondence to get through, how many neutral sentences would you tolerate? I usually tolerate one, or at most two, especially if they are in some way relevant to the topic. . . . But don't give me three sentences about my roses if your really want to discuss my mortgage.

BUFFERS

To be effective, a buffer must put the reader in a good frame of mind, not give the bad news but not imply a positive answer either, and provide a natural transition to the body of the letter.

How to Write a Buffer

The kinds of statements most often used as buffers are good news, facts and chronologies of events, references to enclosures, thanks, and statements of principle.

1. **Start with any good news or positive elements the letter contains.**

> Starting Thursday, June 26, you'll have access to your money 24 hours a day at First National Bank.

Letter announcing that the drive-up windows will be closed for two days while automatic tellers machines are installed

2. **State a fact or provide a chronology of events.**

> As a result of the new graduated dues schedule—determined by vote of the Delegate Assembly last December and subsequently endorsed by the Executive Council—members are now asked to establish their own dues rate and to calculate the total amount of their remittance.

Announcement of a new dues structure which will raise most members' dues

3. **Refer to enclosures in the letter.**

> Enclosed is a new sticker for your car. You may pick up additional ones in the office if needed. Please *destroy* old stickers bearing the signature of "L. S. LaVoie."

Letter announcing increase in parking rental rates

4. **Thank the reader for something he or she has done.**

> Thank you for scheduling appointments for me with so many senior people at First National Bank. My visit there March 14 was very informative.

Letter refusing a job offer

5. State a general principle.

> We believe good drivers should pay substantially less for their auto insurance. That's why we designed Allstate's Good Driver Plan—to reward good drivers (those with 5-year accident-free records) with our lowest available rates.
>
> We are making a change in the plan. This change will enable us to continue to provide special low rates for good drivers and help us to keep those rates low.

Letter announcing that the company will now count traffic tickets, not just accidents, in calculating insurance rates—a change that will raise many people's premiums.

When to Omit a Buffer

A buffer is optional when the bad news is mild or when the reader is already expecting bad news. For example, a wholesaler announcing a price increase to retailers doesn't need a buffer. Business readers know that prices rise. Many of them will be able to pass the increase on to their own customers, so they are not personally disappointed. Job candidates know that employers phone to offer jobs. Thus at best a letter after an on-site interview is going to announce a delay in hiring; more probably, it is a rejection letter.

In three situations, it's better *not* to use a buffer: (1) if the reader may ignore a letter with a bland first paragraph; (2) if the reader is suspicious of the writer; or (3) if the reader "won't take *no* for an answer."

1. Omit the Buffer If the Reader May Ignore or Skim the Message. People don't read messages that look unimportant. You may need to start with the negative so that the reader is sure to get it.

Vickers was wise *not* to use a buffer in Figure 13.2. People do not always read the cover letters that come with insurance renewals. If they don't read the message, they're likely to blame the company when they discover, after an accident, that they don't have the coverage they thought they had. Note, however, that both the headline and the first paragraph point out that the reader can replace the protection; note also that the first paragraph makes it clear that there is a reason for the change, even though the reader has to read on to learn what it is.

2. Omit the Buffer When the Reader May Be Suspicious of the Writer. If there is a history of bad faith, readers may see a buffer as a "runaround." Blue-collar workers who have felt manipulated by management are likely to fall into this category.

> Starting this month, you will be paid for holidays only if you report to work on the days before and after the holiday.

Buffers in Oral Negative Messages*
When you deliver bad news orally, buffer it if you want the person to accept the alternative you have to offer.

People will usually read a written message through to the end. But they may be so upset by bad news that they retaliate by leaving before you've had a chance to explain an almost-as-good alternative.

If there's no alternative, that's not a problem. But when you want someone to say *yes* to a less-than-best solution, lead into the negative gradually so that you have a chance to put all your cards on the table.

---

*   Based on Mary Jean Parson, "How to Give Bad News to Good People," *Working Woman,* July 1986, 78–80, 115.

FIGURE 13.3
AN UNCONVINCING REASON FOR A CANCELLATION

Dear Mr. Richardson:

The goal of the Knoxville CHARGE-ALL Center is to provide
our customers with the most efficient and prompt service
possible. It has been our experience that this type of
service can best be given by the local Center.

Among the advantages of dealing with a local Center is
that the Center will not only provide faster, more
personalized service, but also can tailor its services to
the needs of the community.

In as much as you now live outside the Knoxville CHARGE-
ALL service area, we feel we can no longer offer you the
advantages of a local CHARGE-ALL Center. We suggest that
you contact your local CHARGE-ALL Bank.

As each Center operates independently, it is impossible
to automatically transfer your account.

We are happy to have been of service, and should we be
able to assist you in the future, please contact us.

Sincerely,

Elena Garza

Elena Garza
Credit Department

3. Omit the Buffer When the Reader Won't Take *No* for an Answer. When
you know the reader is pushy or desperate, starting with the refusal may make
it clearer that your refusal is not a coy invitation to further persuasion but an
absolute *no*.

> I am not interested in chairing the Membership Committee again this year.

REASONS

Make the reason for the refusal clear and convincing. The reason in Figure
13.3 is inadequate.

If the reader says, "I don't care if my bills are slow and impersonal," will
the company let the reader keep the card? No. The real reason is that the

FIGURE 13.4
A CANCELLATION LETTER WITH A WATERTIGHT REASON

Dear Mr. Richardson:

Thank you for telling us about your move to Bryan, Texas.

Each local CHARGE-ALL center is permitted to offer accounts
to customers in a several-state area. The Knoxville CHARGE-
ALL center serves customers east of the Mississippi. You
can continue to use your current card until it expires.
When that happens, you'll need to open an account with a
CHARGE-ALL center that serves Texas.

Enclosed is a list of banks in central Texas offering
CHARGE-ALL accounts.

Wherever you have your account, you'll continue to get
all the service you've learned to expect from CHARGE-ALL,
and the convenience of charging items at over a million
stores, restaurants, and hotels in the U.S. and abroad--
and in Knoxville, too, whenever you come back to visit!

Sincerely,

Elena Garza

Elena Garza
Credit Department

bank's franchise allows it to have cardholders only in a given geographical region.

Figure 13.4 offers a revision.

Don't hide behind "company policy." Explain the policy.

Weak reason: I cannot write an insurance policy for you because company policy does not allow me to do so.

Better reason: Gorham insures cars only when they are normally garaged at night. Standard insurance policies cover a wider variety of risks and charge higher fees. Limiting the policies we write gives Gorham customers the lowest possible rates for auto insurance.

Often you as a middle manager will enforce policies that you did not design and announce decisions that you did not make. Don't pass the buck by saying, "This was a terrible decision." In the first place, carelessly criticizing your superiors is never a good idea. In the second place, if you really think a policy

FIGURE 13.5
A REASON THAT MAKES THE COMPANY LOOK BAD

```
    Dear Dr. Foley:

    In reply to your letter of January 20, I regret that I
    must tell you that our company is not hiring research
    chemists at the present time.

    The reason is that the company is now experiencing a very
    tight profit picture.  In fact, the down-turn has prompted
    top management to reduce the salaried staff by 5% just
    this month, with perhaps more reductions to come.
```

is bad, try to persuade your superiors to change it. If you can't think of convincing reasons to change the policy, maybe it isn't so bad after all.

If you have several reasons for saying *no*, use only those which are strong and watertight. If you give five reasons and readers dismiss two of them, readers may feel that they've won and should get the request.

Weak reason: You cannot store large bulky items in the dormitory over the summer because moving them into and out of storage would tie up the stairs and the elevators just at the busiest times when people are moving in and out.

Loophole: We'll move large items before or after the two days when most people are moving in or out.

If you do not have a good reason, omit the reason rather than use a weak one.

Even if you have a strong reason, there are circumstances when you should omit it. In Figure 13.5, the reason for the rejection is not news that the company wishes to spread.

Think what will happen to internal morale if word gets out that more reductions in salaried staff—white-collar workers—are expected. Think what will happen to stock prices. The letter makes the company appear to be on the verge of bankruptcy. Later on, it may be stable or even profitable and wish to increase its staff, but the person who got this letter is unlikely to be interested in accepting a position.

When you must reject a qualified applicant, it's good to let the reader know that he or she isn't at fault. But don't say anything that will hurt your own organization. Just say, "We don't have openings now" without explaining why you aren't hiring.

REFUSALS

Deemphasize the refusal by putting it in the same paragraph as the reason, rather than in a paragraph by itself.

Sometimes you may be able to imply the refusal rather than stating it directly.

Direct refusal: You cannot get insurance for just one month.

Implied refusal: The shortest term for an insurance policy is six months.

Be sure that the implication is crystal clear. Any message can be misunderstood, but an optimistic or desperate reader is particularly likely to misunderstand a negative message. One of your purposes in a negative message is to close the door on the subject. You do not want to have to write a second letter saying that the real answer is *no*.

ALTERNATIVES

Giving the reader an alternative or a compromise, if one is available, is a good idea for several reasons:

- It offers the reader another way to get what he or she wants.
- It suggests that you really care about the reader and about helping to meet his or her needs.
- It enables the reader to reestablish the psychological freedom you limited when you said *no*.
- It allows you to end on a positive note and to present yourself and your organization as positive, friendly, and helpful.

When you give an alternative, give readers all the information they need to act on it, but don't take the necessary steps. Let readers decide whether to try the alternative.

Negative messages limit the reader's freedom. People may respond to a limitation of freedom by asserting their freedom in some other arena. Jack W. Brehm calls this phenomenon **psychological reactance**.[3] Psychological reactance is at work when a customer who has been denied credit no longer buys even on a cash basis or a subordinate who has been passed over for a promotion gets back by deliberately doing a poor job.

An alternative allows the reader to react in a way that doesn't hurt you. By letting readers decide for themselves whether they want the alternative, you allow them to reestablish their sense of psychological freedom.

The specific alternative will vary depending on the circumstances. Suppose that a company is unwilling to quote a price on an item on which it cannot be competitive. Here are three alternatives for three different situations:

Alternative 1: The blueprints call for rings burned from 1/2″ thick A516 grade 70, on which we can't quote competitively right now. Roysner can, however, give you very good prices on burn-to-sketch jobs on heavier plate.

Alternative 2: Your blueprints call for flame-cut rings 1/2″ thick A516 grade 70. To use that grade, we'd have to grind down from 1″ thick material. However, if you can use A515 grade 70, which we stock in 1/2″ thick, you can cut the price by more than half.

Alternative 3: Your blueprints call for fabrication using brass and copper, which we don't stock. The supplier closest to you is probably Schuman, Inc., in Kansas City, MO. The number there is (314) 555-2533.

Nasty Negatives*

Straight negatives give information. "Nasty" negatives have ulterior motives.

The president of one company controlled people by using inconsistent signals to keep them off base.

A worker was walking by with a report when the president stopped him and asked for a copy. The worker made a photocopy and added a handwritten note: "Here's the copy you requested."

A week later, the worker received a biting memo from the president: "I do not know why you sent this report to me. I have enough people reporting to me and don't have time to deal with you. From now on, report to your superior."

When the bewildered worker asked around, a senior manager told him: "The president thinks you're too pushy and aren't going any further. This was just his little way of letting you know."

If someone attacks you, make your response (if you must write one) businesslike and unemotional. Check the grapevine to find out what's really happening.

If you get a memo that seems to send you off on a wild goose chase, redefine the problem, if necessary, but use the writer's own words. Point out aspects of the problem that the writer (presumably) overlooked. If the problem is minor, emphasize its unimportance. Check the grapevine to find out what the writer's real motive is.

---

* Based on Ann Blasingham, "Negative Messages," Association for Business Communication International Convention, Atlanta, GA, October 14–17, 1987.

Never Say *No* *

In some cultures, saying *no* is considered so impolite that people simply do not use the word.

In an experiment in Iran, 20% of the people asked for directions told a foreigner how to get to a place even though the place did not exist. If a customer phones to see if a store has something, the shopkeeper will say "I'm not sure" even if he knows he doesn't have it.

Koreans are also taught not to say *no*. But their culture also teaches people not to take *yes* literally. Even if a clerk says something will be ready the next day, to actually come in and ask for it then is considered rude because the action makes the clerk lose face.

To avoid saying *no* directly, Chinese negotiators may say something is "possible."

Japanese use the word *no* in filling out forms but avoid it in conversation. If they cannot escape saying it, some Japanese will switch into English to say something so crude.

Ways to avoid saying *no* in Japan include

Silence.

Vague and ambiguous answers.

Counterquestions.

Changing the subject.

Conditional and delaying answers.

Apologies.

ENDINGS

If you have a good alternative, you can end with a request: "Let me know if you can use A515 grade 70."

Avoid endings that seem selfish. The following paragraph in a refusal to increase a customer's credit limit got a very hostile response:

> As a Hymson's charge customer, you'll be receiving our Christmas Book in the mail soon. It's filled with ideas for everyone on your gift list. And Santa will be coming to Hymson's lower level Saturday, December 4. He'll be joining the rest of our staff to wish you and your family a joyous holiday season.

Even though this paragraph does not ask the reader to buy anything, subjects saw it as manipulative and uncaring, since the letter had just denied credit because the reader was overextended.

It is also crucial that your ending be believable. Recall the last paragraph in Figure 13.4:

> We are happy to have been of service, and should we be able to assist you in the future, please contact us.

This ending lacks you-attitude and would not be good even in a positive message. In a situation where the company has just refused to help, it's likely to sound sarcastic or sadistic.

TONE IN NEGATIVE MESSAGES

Tone—the implied attitude of the author toward the reader and the subject—is particularly important when you want readers to feel that you have taken their requests seriously. Check your draft carefully for positive emphasis and you-attitude, both at the level of individual words and at the level of ideas.

Even the physical appearance of a letter can convey tone. A printed rejection letter makes it clear that the writer has not given much consideration to the reader's application.

ALTERNATE STRATEGIES FOR NEGATIVE SITUATIONS

Whenever you face a negative situation, consider recasting it as a positive or persuasive message.

* Based on H. Goert Hofstede, *Culture's Consequences: International Differences in Work-Related Values* (Beverly Hills, CA: Sage Publications, 1980), 35; Morteza Javadi, conversation with the author August 8, 1987; Jerrold J. Merchant, "Korean Interpersonal Patterns: Implications for Korean/American Intercultural Communication," *Communication* 9 (October 1980): 66–68; John C. Condon Jr., *Semantics and Communication* (New York: Macmillan, 1985), 44; Lucian Pye, *Chinese Commercial Negotiating Style* (Cambridge, MA: Oelgeschlager, Gunn & Hain, 1982), 80; Keiko Uda, "Sixteen Ways to Avoid Saying 'No' in Japan," *Intercultural Encounters with Japan: Communication—Contact and Conflict: Perspectives from the International Conference on Communication Across Cultures held at International Christian University in Tokyo,* ed. John C. Condon (Tokyo: Simul Press, 1974), 186–89.

Phrase	Because
I am afraid that we cannot	You aren't fearful. Don't hide behind empty phrases.
I am sorry that we are unable	You probably are *able* to grant the request; you simply choose not to. If you are so sorry about saying *no*, why don't you change your policy and say *yes*?
I am sure you will agree that	Don't assume that you can read the reader's mind.
Unfortunately	*Unfortunately* is negative in itself. It also signals that a refusal is coming.

FIGURE 13.6
AVOID THESE PHRASES IN NEGATIVE MESSAGES

Recasting the Situation as a Positive Message

If the negative information will directly lead to a benefit that you know readers want, use the pattern of organization for informative and positive messages:

Situation:	You're raising parking rates to pay for lot maintenance, ice and snow removal, and signs so renters can have cars towed away that park in their spots—all services renters have asked for.
Negative emphasis:	Effective May 1, parking rentals will go up $5 a month.
Positive emphasis:	Effective May 1, if someone parks in your spot, you can have the car towed away. Signs are being put up announcing that all spaces in the lot are rented.
	Lot maintenance is also being improved. The lot will be resurfaced this summer, and arrangements have been made for ice and snow removal next winter.

Recasting the Situation as a Persuasive Message

Often a negative situation can be recast as a persuasive message. When the Association for Business Communication's Board of Directors voted to raise dues, the Executive Director wrote a persuasive letter urging members to send in renewals early so they could beat the increase (Figure 13.7). The letter shares some of the qualities of any persuasive letter: an attention-getting opener, offsetting the negative by setting it against the benefits of membership, telling the reader what to do, and ending with a picture of the benefit the reader receives by acting.

If you are criticizing someone, your real purpose may be to persuade the reader to act differently. Use the strategies described in Chapter 15, Handling Difficult Persuasive Situations.

I'll Kill You for That*

In a society where guns are cheap and violence is glamorized in movies and on TV, psychological reactance can be lethal.

In 1984, a worker about to be fired in Oklahoma took a gun into the post office where he worked and shot 14 coworkers. In 1987, a worker fired in California planted a bomb on a commuter plane to kill his former supervisor. All 43 people on board died.

---

* Based on Ed Timms and Carol Trujillo, "Frustrated Workers Fight with Violence," *Columbus Dispatch*, January 1, 1988, 7B.

FIGURE 13.7
A PERSUASIVE MESSAGE FOR A NEGATIVE SITUATION

The Association for Business Communication

November 9, 1987

MAY I SHARE
A SECRET
WITH YOU?

Dear ABC Member:

My secret, which can't be a secret much longer, is this: ABC's dues are going up.

The increase, approved by the Board of Directors at our recent Atlanta convention, will become effective January 1, 1988. After that date regular members will pay $5 more each year--$40 instead of the present $35.

Compared to other professional societies, ABC is still a bargain. Many charge two or three times as much as we do. And, ABC gives you two quarterly publications in addition to discounts on special publications and lower meeting registration fees. We are now addressing several critical professional problems--class size, teaching loads, tenure obstacles, improving research quality, and securing funding for research--and I know you'll want to keep informed on all these issues which affect your livelihood and professional status.

Now I know that $5 isn't very much, but I'm betting that you'll appreciate a chance to renew early and save. That's why I'm writing to you now.

To beat the increase, just write us a check for $35 (or $70 for two years, if you prefer), tuck it and the enclosed renewal form into the postage-free envelope, and mail. Then sit back and enjoy all the benefits of membership--at the old rate.

It'll be our secret.

Robert D. Gieselman
Executive Director

Enclosures

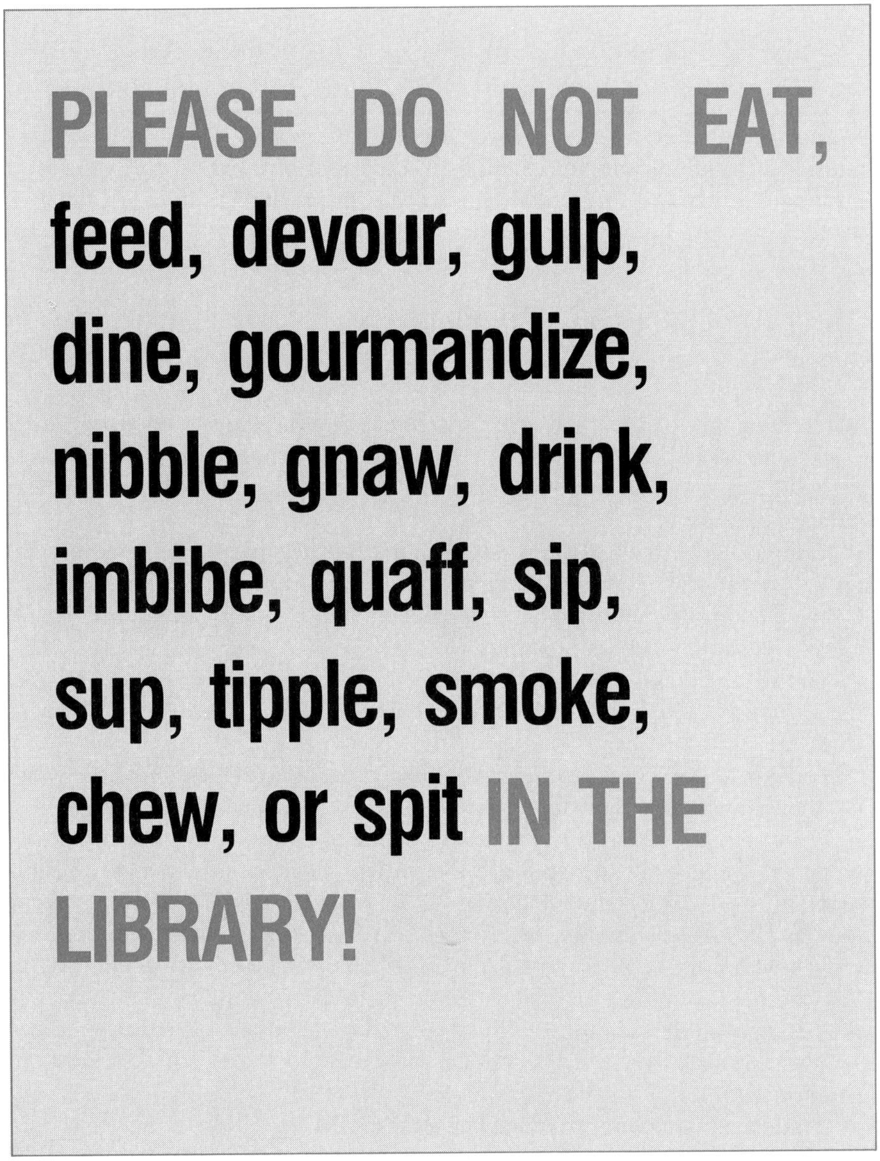

FIGURE 13.8
EFFECTIVE HUMOR
IN A NEGATIVE MESSAGE

PLEASE DO NOT EAT,
feed, devour, gulp,
dine, gourmandize,
nibble, gnaw, drink,
imbibe, quaff, sip,
sup, tipple, smoke,
chew, or spit IN THE
LIBRARY!

Humor in Negative Messages

Humor can defuse negative messages. A university library uses language to make its rule against food in the library friendly instead of fierce (Figure 13.8).

Kathryn McGrath, head of the SEC division of investment management, needed to tell an investment firm that its ad was illegal. The ad showed an index finger pointing up and large bold letters saying that performance was "up," too. Tiny print at the bottom of the page admitted that performance figures hadn't been adjusted to include front-end sales charges. Rather than writing a heavy-handed letter, McGrath sent the firm a photocopy of a thumb pointing down. The ad never ran again.[4]

Palindrome Press uses a form rejection letter that starts

Mini-Review: Positive Emphasis and
You-Attitude in Negative Messages

Negative messages can't be completely positive. But they still can use positive emphasis and you-attitude.

To deemphasize negatives in negative messages,

- Avoid negative words and words with heavily negative connotations.
- State information positively: focus on the options readers have rather than the options you are taking away.
- Give a reason for the negative decision.
- Omit minor negatives that are part of the larger negative message.
- Bury negative information in the middle of a message, the middle of a page. End the message positively.
- Give negative information as little space as possible in the message.

To create you-attitude in negative messages,

- Protect the reader's ego. Allow the reader to save face.
- Use passive verbs to avoid assigning blame.
- Use impersonal constructions to avoid assigning blame.
- Give readers all the information they need to evaluate and act on alternatives.

WOW

MOM

another reject!

Humor works best when it's closely related to the specific situation and the message. (A palindrome, for example, is a word or phrase that reads the same both backwards and forwards.) Humor that seems tacked on is less likely to work. Never use humor that belittles readers.

ANALYSIS OF A SAMPLE PROBLEM

Problem[5]

You're manager of the appliance department at a large discount store. Three weeks ago, Jane Ballinger called complaining that there was a 40° variance between the actual oven temperature in her new range and the temperature indicated on the dial.

Calibrating an oven is a time-consuming job because of the time it takes for an oven to warm up for a reading and then cool down so it can be adjusted. Calibration is difficult as well as time-consuming, so factory manuals normally allow a variation of plus or minus 25°.

You sent out a service worker who spent $3^1/_2$ hours on the job and reduced the variance to 20°. This was a warranty service call for which there was no charge.

Today you got a letter from Ms. Ballinger. She still isn't satisfied; she wants 0° variance between the temperature dial and the actual temperature.

Write to tell her that if she wants someone to come out to work on it, the work will be at her expense, since the present variance is within the factory regulations. Reducing the remaining 20° of variance might well take twice as long as it took to eliminate the first 20°. Even if someone did come out and spent seven hours (and she paid the $224) there is a very good chance that the variance would not be much smaller. If the factory allows a 25° variance, the parts probably aren't finely tuned enough to get all ovens to a significantly smaller variance. Service calls are $32 an hour ($15 wages and overhead and profit margin).

In addition, you want to make her feel that the model she bought is a good one, that the service worker did a competent job, and that your store is fair and responsible.

Write the letter.

Analysis of the Problem

1. Who is (are) your audience(s)? What characteristics are relevant to this particular message? If you are writing to more than one reader, how do the readers differ?

   Jane Ballinger. She bought an oven at my store (I can make up the name of the store, the brand of oven, etc.) She is unhappy with the product and service so far.

   There's a lot I don't know: has she read the warranty that came with the range? Is she a gourmet cook who needs precise temperatures? Will the news that she must live with a 20° variance matter much to her? I can't assume the answers since I wouldn't have them in "real life."

2. What are your purposes in writing?

> To give her the negative information that she will have to pay for any further service work.

> To dissuade her from asking for an additional service call, since the price would be so high and the benefit so low that she probably wouldn't feel she'd gotten her money's worth.

> To make her feel that she bought a good product, that the store stands behind what it sells, and that the service worker did a good job. To make her think highly of the store and say good things about it and the range she bought to people she talks to.

3. What information must your message include?

> The information about the price of service calls. The fact that any further work will be at her expense. A statement that even further work may not eliminate the problem completely.

4. How can you build support for your position? What reasons or reader benefits will your reader find convincing?

> Information about how calibration is done may help.

> The fact that a service worker did spend 3½ hours, at no charge to her, and did cut the variance in half is evidence that the store honors its warranties.

> Need to show that the range she bought is a good one. What about features, the quality of the range for the price, independent ratings of the model? (If she did buy a bottom-of-the-line model, the information won't help: having just made a major purchase, she's unlikely to want to trade it in on an even more expensive model.)

> Maybe there are alternative ways for her to know exactly what the temperature in the oven is. If the oven has a see-through door, she could use an oven thermometer without even having to open the oven. Just setting the dial 20° higher or lower may work if she's just cooking casseroles, but some dishes may need more exact temperatures.

5. What objection(s) can you expect your reader(s) to have? What negative elements of your message must you deemphasize or overcome?

> I am refusing her request.

> She may feel that the dial should be an accurate indication of temperature. The information that the parts just aren't good enough to permit perfect calibration could sound as if the manufacturer is incompetent, cutting corners, or misleading consumers.

Office Politics May Dictate an Alternate Strategy*

The cause of the memo was simple enough. Several years ago, when I was running a department in a large corporation, I believed I wasn't receiving the cooperation I needed from our company's publicity department. I wrote the company president a memo, complaining about the publicity department's lassitude.

To my astonishment, several days later I received a call from Al, the head of the publicity department, who said that *he* had been given my memo, and that he felt his department *was* doing a competent job, thank you. . . .

Where had I gone wrong? Well, first I didn't calculate that my charming boss might show the memo to Al. . . . I was blunt about my feelings toward Al's department. . . . The result: I lost a potential ally and made an enemy instead. Not very political of me, for allies are as important in the business world as tipsters are in the gambling world.

I would have been a more astute gameplayer, and won a gold star rather than a slap on the wrist, if I had appealed to Al in terms of *his* interests, suggesting how helping me would actually help him.

---

* Quoted from Victoria Pelligrino, "Office Politics: Running a Clean Campaign," *The Working Woman's Success Book* (New York: Ace, 1981), 63–64.

Granted, no one likes negative messages. But if one must get a rejection, what kind do readers want?

Graduating seniors at a southwestern university preferred rejection letters that addressed them as *Mr./Ms.* rather than calling them by their first names, that said something specific about their good qualities, that phrased the refusal itself indirectly, and that were longer.

An experiment using a denial of additional insurance found that subjects preferred a rejection letter that was longer, more tactful, and more personal. The preferred letter started with a buffer, used a good reason for the refusal, and offered sales promotion in the last paragraph. The finding held both for English-speaking U.S. subjects and for Spanish-speaking Mexican subjects.

She may feel that $32 an hour is high; she will certainly feel that $224 is an unreasonable charge—the oven itself probably didn't cost more than three or four times that.

Sample Solution 1

Dear Ms. Ballinger:

I was happy to get your letter describing your problem with the new range you bought from Slyman Brothers. Certainly you need to know how hot your oven is to cook gourmet delicacies.

I hope you remember that we have already sent a service worker out to adjust the calibration. This service worker was able to reduce the variance between the actual oven temperature and the indicated one to 20° which is within the factory's specifications. I think you should be glad that the current variance is 20% less than it is permitted to be under warranty.

Having another service worker sent to your home to attempt to reduce the variance wouldn't be covered by your warranty. Any additional work will be at your expense. Service calls are $32 an hour and the total job would be $224. Also there is no guarantee that after the service worker finishes the job the variance would be much smaller. I therefore cannot recommend that you undertake this expense.

To avoid spending the $224 on a second service call, you may want to try turning the oven up or down 20° to get the temperature you want.

I am sorry about the initial problems you had with your new range. If you decide you would still like to have a service worker try to reduce the variance, call 555-6076 and we will send someone out as soon as possible.

Sample Solution 2

Dear Ms. Ballinger:

Calibrating an oven is a time-consuming job since the oven has to warm up for a reading and then cool down so it can be adjusted. Calibration is also difficult, and factory manuals normally allow a variation of plus or minus 25°.

During our history at Slyman Brothers, we've found that most ovens have a variance of 25–30°. Your oven model, General Electric model KJBP36GW, so far is one of the few models able to be more finely tuned, and your oven is no exception. Your oven will also stick to this variance, rather than becoming more varied, as some other models do.

In the most recent issue of *Consumer Reports*, your oven model was rated the most energy-efficient wall oven, and was also rated excellent on heating speed and heat uniformity, as well as being the best priced for such a high performance level. By buying at Slyman, you purchased the KJBP36GW at the lowest price in town!

*   Based on Frederick M. Jablin and Kathleen Krone, "Characteristics of Rejection Letters and Their Effects on Job Applicants," *Written Communication* 1, no. 4 (October 1984): 387–406; John D. Pettit, "An Analysis of the Effects of Various Message Presentations on Communicatee Responses," Ph.D. diss., Louisiana State University, 1969; and Jack D. Eure, "Applicability of American Written Business Communication Principles across Cultural Boundaries in Mexico," *Journal of Business Communication* 14 (1976): 51–63.

> If you want someone to come out to recalibrate your oven again, we'll send Herb Taylor, our senior service worker. Herb has had 20 years of experience calibrating ovens and has trained our other service workers, too. Since the present variance is within factory regulations, further service would be at your expense (service calls are $32 an hour). According to Herb, the work you are requesting could take up to seven hours, and there is still a chance that the variance would not be much smaller.
>
> May I suggest an alternative? I also own the model you chose and have installed a wall-mounted oven thermometer. This way if there is any variance, a look through the oven window can tell all!
>
> Slyman Brothers carries several different oven thermometers, ranging from food thermometers to ones that mount on the oven wall itself. Sunset makes a satisfactory model for only $4.95. Come in and check them out!

Discussion of Sample Solutions

Solution 1 is not acceptable. The first paragraph is untrue (what store is *happy* to get complaints?), overly negative, and lacks you-attitude. The second sentence implies that the reader's request will be granted—a major failure for a buffer. The assumption that the reader makes "gourmet delicacies" will sound sarcastic to the reader if she just does ordinary cooking.

In paragraph 2, "I hope you remember" and "I think" are not you-attitude; they have a superior tone that is particularly offensive in negative messages. There is nothing to build the reader's confidence in the product, the service worker, or the store.

The refusal is unnecessarily negative. The bad news is repeated twice (it has already been implied in the previous paragraph). The "total" cost of $224 is presented as fact, when in fact it is only an estimate—the actual cost could be higher or lower.

The alternative—adjusting the temperature—probably will not help the reader. If she was willing to reset the dial, why would she have asked for the second service call? The suggestion may even seem insulting.

The final paragraph repeats the negative and lacks you-attitude. It also encourages the reader to schedule a service call, a dubious strategy, since its results are unlikely to please her.

Solution 2, in contrast, is very good. The material about calibration serves as a buffer and explanation. The second paragraph points out that the reader's oven is better than many. Paragraph 3 goes on to list benefits of the oven that don't relate to the variance. These facts help remind the reader that temperature variance is only one aspect of quality; they also suggest that her decision to buy this oven at the store was a good choice.

Paragraph 4 offers to send out a service worker, names a specific worker, and gives his credentials. The negative information that the reader would bear the expense of the call is buried in the middle of the paragraph. The information about the time the call would take and the small likelihood that it would work is attributed to the service worker. (In real life, the manager would have to ask a worker: it's unlikely that he or she would know the approximate time for every possible job.) The negative is further deemphasized by not giving the total for the estimate: the reader is left to multiply 7 by $32 herself.

The last two paragraphs present an alternative. The writer presents the alternative as one she herself uses, and tries to use an especially friendly style. She makes it clear that a variety of specific models are available; she doesn't dictate to the reader or assume that what is best for one person will necessarily be best for another.

SUMMARY OF KEY POINTS

- In a negative message, the basic information is negative; we expect the reader to be disappointed or angry.
- A good negative message conveys the negative information clearly while maintaining as much goodwill as possible. The goal is to make readers feel that they have been taken seriously, that the decision is fair and reasonable, and that they would have made the same decision. A secondary purpose is to reduce or eliminate future correspondence on the same subject so that the message doesn't create more work for the writer.
- Organize most negative messages in this way:
  1. Consider using a buffer (a neutral or positive statement).
  2. Give the reason for the refusal before the refusal itself when you have a reason that readers will understand and accept.
  3. Avoid overemphasizing the refusal, but make it clear.
  4. Present an alternative or compromise, if one is available.
  5. End with a positive, forward-looking statement.
- In a negative message, put the subject—but not your action on it—in the subject line.
- A **buffer** is a neutral or positive statement which allows you to bury the negative message. Buffers must put the reader in a good frame of mind, not give the bad news but not imply a positive answer either, and provide a natural transition to the body of the letter.
- The kinds of statements most often used as buffers are (1) good news, (2) facts and chronologies of events, (3) references to enclosures, (4) thanks, and (5) statements of principle.
- It's better *not* to use a buffer (1) if the reader may ignore a letter with a bland first paragraph; (2) if the reader is suspicious of the writer; or (3) if the reader "won't take *no* for an answer."
- A good reason must be watertight. Give several reasons only if all are watertight and are of comparable importance. Omit the reason for the refusal entirely if it is weak or if it makes your organization look bad.
- Make the refusal crystal clear.
- Giving the reader an alternative or a compromise
  - Offers the reader another way to get what he or she wants.
  - Suggests that you really care about the reader and about helping to meet his or her needs.
  - Enables the reader to reestablish the psychological freedom you limited when you said *no*.
  - Allows you to end on a positive note and to present yourself and your organization as positive, friendly, and helpful.
- People may respond to limits by striking out in some unacceptable way. This effort to reestablish freedom is called **psychological reactance.**
- When you give an alternative, give the reader all the information he or she needs to act on it, but don't take the necessary steps for the reader. Letting the reader decide whether to try the alternative allows the reader to reestablish a sense of psychological freedom.
- Many negative situations can be redefined to use the patterns of organization for informative and positive or for persuasive messages. Humor sometimes works to defuse negative situations.
- Use the analysis questions in Chapter 2 to solve negative problems.

NOTES

1. Kitty O. Locker, "The Rhetoric of Negative Messages," *English for Specific Purposes*, July 1984, 2.

2. Kitty O. Locker, "Factors in Reader Response to Negative Messages," American Business Communication Association International Convention, Washington, DC, December 27–30, 1980.

3. Jack W. Brehm, *A Theory of Psychological Reactance* (New York: Academic Press, 1966).

4. Leslie N. Vreeland, "SEC 'COP' Has Eye on Mutual Funds," *Columbus Dispatch*, July 21, 1987, 3F.

5. Problem written by Francis W. Weeks, problem #103 in Kitty O. Locker and Francis W. Weeks, *Business Writing Cases and Problems* (Champaign, IL: Stipes, 1984), 192. The rate for service calls has been raised.

EXERCISES AND PROBLEMS FOR CHAPTER 13

13–1 EVALUATING BUFFERS

Evaluating the following buffers. Are any good enough to use without change? Might any be acceptable with revision?

a. Refusing to grant credit.

1. Your request to have a Saks Fifth Avenue charge account shows that you are a discriminating shopper. Saks Fifth Avenue sells the finest merchandise available in the United States.

2. We have received your application for a Saks Fifth Avenue charge account.

3. In the current economic climate, all stores have to limit the credit they extend.

b. Refusing to use a software package developed by another state agency.

1. My staff and I have spent many long hours evaluating the software developed by the Department of Transportation to see if the software would be appropriate for our agency to use.

2. The Department of Transportation seems to think that no other state agency has computer personnel capable of developing effective programs. I am delighted to assure you that, whatever the dismal state of some agencies, our agency enjoys the talents of many capable people.

3. Thank you for giving me a chance to evaluate the payroll software developed by DOT.

c. Refusing to serve on the committee to arrange activities for a high school reunion.

1. I'm very glad to hear that you're making plans to celebrate the 20th reunion of the class of _____. It's especially impressive that you are beginning work so far in advance.

2. Some people think that their high school days are "the best years of their lives." I feel sorry for anyone who feels that way. Life should be a continual learning, growing, responding to new challenges, reaching new highs. To romanticize the awkward teen years and to devalue maturity creates an atmosphere in which we value youth for the wrong reasons and ignore the benefits that years can bring.

3. My business is doing well. I'm opening another branch store next month. As you may know, I am active in several community groups.

13–2 EVALUATING REASONS FOR REFUSALS

Evaluate the following reasons for refusals.

a. Refusing to grant credit.

Your income is not high, and records indicate that you carry large balances on student loans. If you were given a Saks Fifth Avenue charge account, and if you charged a large amount on it, you might have difficulty paying the bill, particularly if you had other unforeseen expenses (car repair, moving, medical emergency) or if your income dropped suddenly. If you were unable to repay, with your other debt you would be in serious difficulty. We would not want you to be in such a situation, nor would you yourself desire it.

b. Announcing that dorm residents can no longer store belongings in the dorm over the summer.

We are thinking of converting the storage closets to a games and vending room.

Furthermore, it has been brought to my attention that last summer the storage facilities broke every fire code and represented a definite fire hazard. This situation, if continued, would raise our insurance rates and lead to higher dormitory fees. In addition, we simply cannot run the risk of fire with the real possibility of property losses, injuries, and even deaths.

c. Refusing to admit a rookie athlete to the roster of athletes for whom you negotiate commercials, endorsements, and speaking engagements.

We are so busy representing well-known athletes that we are unable to accept any new clients for the next six months.

13–3 REVISING A NEGATIVE MESSAGE

Reorganize and revise the following letter that was left in each room of an airport hotel the day before Thanksgiving.

> The hotel's restaurant and lounge will be closed tomorrow, Thanksgiving Day.
>
> Food service will be available at the airport, at 94th Aero Squadron, and at David's San Francisco. The complimentary hotel van can take you to any of these places between 6 a.m. and midnight. Please check at the front desk to arrange transportation.
>
> A complimentary continental breakfast will be served in the lobby from 6 a.m. till noon on Thanksgiving Day. Later in the day, complimentary sandwiches and fruit will be available in Rooms 162 and 230.
>
> We hope this will not cause you any inconvenience.

13–4 NOTIFYING A PROGRAM DIRECTOR THAT A FILM IS NOT AVAILABLE

You're the Energy Information Specialist for the local gas and electric company. As a public relations strategy, you offer films and speakers free to any organization. These films and talks present you in a good light to the public and help you get your points across. Many people do not feel very positively about their utility companies, and you want all the goodwill you can get.

Today you've received a letter from Jeffrey Poole, vice president of the Central High School Parent-Teacher Association, asking to reserve the film *The Energy-Efficient Home* for the PTA's meeting on the fifth of next month. Unfortunately, *The Energy-Efficient Home* is your most popular film, and all three copies are booked for the first two weeks of next month. Indeed, it is so popular that people who need a specific date would do well to request it six to eight weeks in advance. Already, one copy has been reserved for the first week of the month following next month.

You do have two films on somewhat related topics which are still available for the fifth of next month: *Landscaping for Energy Savings* (two copies) and *The Heat Pump: Is It for You?* (one copy). However, you allocate films on a first-come, first-served basis, and you don't know how long they'll be available.

Write a letter to Mr. Poole.

Hints:

- Should you recommend an alternative film to Mr. Poole when you cannot guarantee that it will still be available when he gets back to you? Are you justified in holding one or both films for him? For how long? How long is it till the PTA's meeting? What implications does that length of time have in terms of finding a program?
- What can you do in your letter to build goodwill?

13–5 DENYING A CREDIT APPLICATION

You're the Credit Manager for a department store. There was a time when you gave credit cards to almost everyone who applied, but now, with more and more people defaulting on debts and even on mortgages, you've decided to tighten up.

You ask for three credit references—and you check them out. People who have a long record of paying their bills promptly are the best credit risks. The amount of credit you'd extend might vary with income. Even if someone pays bills promptly, you'd limit credit if he or she already had a lot of other loan payments to make. An important secondary criterion is stability: someone who has lived at the same address and worked for the same employer for several years is considered a good risk.

You've received a credit application from Lee Mason. According to the form you ask all applicants to fill out, Lee rents an apartment, has been at this address two months, was at the previous address 10 months, has worked for the current employer (a major employer in your town) one month, before that was a student at the University of Iowa, and now earns $17,800 a year. Only one credit reference is listed: a gasoline credit card. When you check this out, you find that no charges and no payments have been recorded on it.

Based on the information you have and your new policy, you cannot extend credit. But Lee may feel that you're unfair (How can a new college graduate build a credit rating?) and may refuse to shop at your store. Even when you are not willing to extend credit, you'd like to keep people as cash customers. And at some point in the future, Lee may have a credit history and be a good risk.

Write the letter.

Hints:

- Do you know Lee's gender? How could you know? What should you do if you don't know?
- Why are you denying credit?

- What could Lee give you now that would make you change your mind? What information would you need, say six months or a year from now, to grant a reapplication? How can a new college graduate build a credit history? Can you give advice without sounding condescending to someone who is presumably no dummy?
- How else could Lee buy things at your store without charging them on a store account?
- How can you build a good impression of the store? Remember, you can't offer Lee any special deals or sales unless they're available to everyone. What do you offer (products, services) that might be especially useful to a new college graduate?
- How can you build goodwill? What do you know about Lee from the application form? Can you use any of this to personalize your letter so it doesn't sound like a form letter?

13–6 DENYING A CHARITABLE REQUEST

As Manager of the Community Relations Division of the Clayton Corporation, one of your duties is to disburse funds to various community organizations. Clayton sets aside one-half of 1% of its profits for direct gifts. Requests, however, always exceed the amount available.

In the past, you've given money to a wide variety of groups: hospitals, ethnic groups, Boy and Girl Scouts, etc. You make it a policy to avoid gifts to religious groups; you try to support groups which serve people in the inner city where your main plant is located.

Three weeks ago, you received a form letter from the "Chicano Postal Society" announcing its second annual banquet and asking that your company buy tickets, make a donation, or buy advertising space in the banquet program. The letter mentioned a scholarship fund. You had never heard of the Chicano Postal Society, so you wrote asking for more information about the organization and its activities. You also asked for the cost of tickets for the banquet, since the form letter did not contain this information. Today you got a reply: a photocopy of your request with a photocopy of a ticket in one corner (the price is $50 a person), and a "thank you" with the writer's name and phone number scrawled in another corner. You called the number once, during business hours, and no one answered.

You have better things to do with your time than tracking this organization down. You certainly aren't going to give money to a group about which you know so little. You'd really like to close the books on this

request. Even if you knew more, you might still have to say *no;* you cannot grant all the requests you receive.

Write a letter to the Banquet Coordinator refusing to make a corporate contribution.

13–7 REFUSING TO QUOTE PRICES

You've just joined Micro Supplies, a company that sells computer parts, supplies, components, and complete computer systems to business clients. As an Inside Sales Representative, you take orders over the phone and by letter and write letters confirming orders. If you do well, you hope to be promoted to Outside Sales Representative. In that position, you'd call on major clients and get a commission rather than the straight salary you're earning now.

In your mail today you find this letter:

SUBJECT: PRICE REQUEST FOR SURGE SUPRESSORS

Please send me the prices on all five surge supressors listed in your current catalog on page 118. I would like prices for delivery in 1993. I am considering going into business for myself and need to get a clear picture of costs so that I can set up an accurate budget for my business plan.

Please send your answer to my home address:

    1100 Newell Road
    Palo Alto, CA 94303–2997.

Thank you.

E. L. EAGLETON

Not sure what to do, you show the letter to your supervisor, who says, "We can't quote prices that far in advance. Stuff just changes too fast in the computer business. This guy's a turkey to try to get a guarantee for 1993 prices on something that comes out of inventory."

You say, "It may not be a guy. 'E. L.' could be a woman."

Your supervisor says, "Well, this *woman* is a turkey. And she wants to start a business of her own! She'll never make it. Write a letter refusing to quote. But be nice. If she—or he—does actually start a business, we want Micro Supplies to get a piece of the action."

Write the letter.

13–8 REFUSING TO MEET A COMPETITOR'S PRICE

You're Sales Manager for Heitmyer Office Supplies, a large company which sells almost every office supply imaginable to organizations all over the nation by mail and phone orders.

You've just received a letter from Phil Delaney, office manager of Interstate Fidelity Insurance (IFI), saying that Bishop Office Supplies will make him a special deal on computer fan-fold paper. He wants to know if you'll match Bishop's price.

You won't. You offer the same prices to everyone through your catalog. The prices are as low as they can be and still give you an adequate profit. On most items, you think your prices are as low as any wholesaler's in the nation.

Write the letter.

13–9 REJECTING A WOULD-BE CLIENT*

You've just joined Sportstars, Inc., a company that represents professional athletes who want to increase their incomes by doing commercials, making speeches and personal appearances, and endorsing products. Sportstars persuades the sponsor to hire the athlete and helps to negotiate the contract. In addition, a considerable amount of hand-holding is necessary to see the client through rough times. For these services, Sportstars receives 20% of the fees paid to the athlete.

As part of your orientation, your boss points out what you know already: a well-known athlete can command much higher fees than someone who's less well known; normally, champions (even former champions) net much higher fees than someone who is consistently good but who has not won a major title. "The big problem," your boss says, "is what to do about young athletes. We can't afford to represent the also-rans; we'd go broke spending time on them. But some of those rookies will become champions, and we want to represent them when they get to the top. We've evolved a foolproof way to do this. When an unknown comes to us and asks to hire us as his or her personal representative, we decline but suggest a competing firm which we know does a terrible job representing its clients. Then, when the winner emerges from the pack, we approach that person and offer to represent him or her. We know we'll do a better job—and we can prove it. We've signed everyone we've approached this way."

Paul Hoganberg, a first-year player on the Pro Golf Tour, has written inviting Sportstars to represent him. The tone of his letter suggests he thinks he's doing you a favor by giving you the chance, but under the company's policy, you must turn him down; he's far from being a star yet.

*Based on Mark H. McCormack, *What They Don't Teach You at Harvard Business School.* NY: Bantam Books, 1984.

As your instructor directs,
   a. Write a letter to Paul.
   b. Write a memo to your boss at Sportstars suggesting that the company's policy be modified.
   c. Write a memo to your instructor listing the choices you made and giving the reasons for your choices.

Hints:
   - You have no obligation to give a contract to everyone who asks for one, but is it ethical to deliberately recommend the worst of your competitors? At a minimum, you're depriving Paul of income, since you know that the competitor doesn't seek commercials and endorsements aggressively for athletes and doesn't get them nearly as favorable terms as Sportstars has been able to do.
   - What will happen to you if you disobey your boss and recommend a competent competitor, several competitors, or no competitor at all?
   - How can you build goodwill so that Paul will have a positive image of Sportstars?

13–10 TURNING DOWN A FAITHFUL CLIENT

You are Midas Investment Services' specialist in estate planning. You give talks to various groups during the year about estate planning. Your policy is to ask non-profit groups (churches, etc.) just to reimburse your expenses; you charge for-profit groups a fee plus expenses. These fees augment your income nicely, and of course the talks also are marvelous exposure for you and your company.

Every January for the last five years, Gardner Manufacturing Company has hired you to conduct an eight-hour workshop (two hours every Monday night for four weeks) on retirement and estate planning for its employees who are over 60 or who are thinking of taking early retirement. These workshops are popular and have generated some clients for your company. The session last January went smoothly as you have come to expect.

Today, out of the blue, you got a letter from Linda Sedlak, Director of Employee Benefits at Gardner, asking you to conduct the workshops every Tuesday evening *next* month at your usual fee. She didn't say whether this is an extra series, or whether this will replace next January's series.

You can't do it. Your spouse, a microbiologist, is giving an invited paper at an international conference in Paris next month and the two of you are taking your children, ages 13 and 9, on a three-week trip to Europe.

(You've made arrangements with school authorities to have the kids miss three weeks of classes.) Your spouse's trip will be tax-deductible, and you've been looking forward to and planning the trip for the last eight months.

Unfortunately, Midas Investment Services is a small group, and the only other person who knows anything about estate planning is a terrible speaker. You could suggest a friend at another financial management company, but you don't want Gardner to turn to someone else permanently; you enjoy doing the workshops and find them a good way to get leads.

Write the letter to Ms. Sedlak.

13–11 REFUSING A STUDENT REQUEST*

The University of Southern Colorado (USC) is isolated from Pueblo, the nearest town. Surrounded by two square miles of desert, the buildings are all of cement block with few windows, as the intense heat makes air conditioning an expensive necessity. Even though USC has strong programs in business and journalism, research has shown that students go to universities in Denver and Boulder for these programs because the campuses are more attractive.

To try to attract more students, USC has spent several thousand dollars installing an Olympic-size outdoor pool with a deck, planting a substantial rose garden at the rear of the residence halls, and laying over an acre of sod. The garden and sod are particularly expensive to maintain in the desert as they must be irrigated and carefully tended daily.

As Dean of Students you have received a request from the student government for permission to hold the annual outdoor music festival on the newly planted grass three weeks from today. You can sympathize with the students' desire to hold the party on the grass; the only other green spot in the area is a public park in Pueblo, a half-hour's drive from the campus. But lots of bodies, several hundred pounds of musical equipment, and numerous beer cans and cigarette butts will ruin the university's investment, you think. Write a letter to Jane Williams, president of student government, asking her to keep the party and the students off the grass.

Hints:
- What alternatives exist? Is it all right for some students to wander over to sit in the grass if most students aren't squashing the tender blades and starting grass fires?
- What means do you have to enforce your request?
- Is it in the students' interest to comply with your request to stay off the sod? Why was the

grass planted in the first place? How is it in your interest to make sure that the students don't see you as an uncaring administrator and your denial as an unreasonable use of authority?

13–12 REFUSING TO PARTICIPATE ON A PANEL

As a prominent executive, you get many requests to appear before various groups. Today, you've received a request to participate in a panel of three to five professionals who will talk about "Succeeding in the Real World." The session will run from 2–5 P.M. of the second Sunday of next month.

You're trying to cut back on outside commitments. Work continues to take much of your time; you have major obligations in a volunteer organization; and you want some time for yourself and your family. This request does not fit your priorities.

How would it affect your response if the request came from

a. A college business honor society which expects 250 students at the session.

b. The youth group at the church or synagogue you attend.

c. The Japanese Student Association at the local college or university.

As your instructor directs,
Write one or more of the letters.

13–13 REJECTING A CLIENT

Five years ago, you started your own money management firm. You weathered the crash of '87 and have been successful—so successful that you and your partners have decided to raise the minimum portfolio for clients to $500,000. Current clients with smaller portfolios will be dropped at the end of the current quarter.

You charge an annual fee of 1.5% of the assets in a client's account. Transaction costs for stock trades are extra. Thus you make only $3,750 a year managing a portfolio of $250,000 but $15,000 a year managing a $1 million portfolio. Yet the smaller portfolio costs just as much in overhead—computer time, letters, reporting, record keeping—as the largest account you have. Small portfolios take even more of your time: the $250,000 client needs more hand-holding, because even a drop of $10,000 is calamitous. People with $250,000 to invest often feel that that is a very large amount of money; they never expected to have so much. And it is certainly enough to require professional investment expertise which the average person lacks.

Some firms still take small investors. But they tend to

*Problem written by E. Kathy Casto, The Ohio State University.

be newer firms without proven records or firms which have not done very well for their clients. Industry records show that about 1 in 20 new firms does very well—and grows into a big firm.

As your instructor directs,

a. Write a form letter to go to all clients announcing your new policy.

b. Write an individual letter to Kevin Collins, a college professor with a $125,000 portfolio. Dr. Collins was one of your original clients when you started your firm five years ago; he stayed with you even though his assets fell 30% in the '87 crash. He owns two houses in an area of moderate prices. He lives in one and rents out the other. As far as you know, he has no other major assets.

c. Write an individual letter to Vera Hampstead, a widow with a $400,000 portfolio. Mrs. Hampstead opened her account two years ago when her husband died and she invested the insurance benefits. Perhaps because she grew up during the Depression, perhaps because she depends on investment income for her living expenses, Mrs. Hampstead is an anxious investor. Whenever the value of an investment falls or bad economic news is announced, she's on the phone to you. She scrutinizes her monthly statement carefully and calls you if there are any charges she doesn't understand. (Frequently, it seems, there are.) She owns a home in a good part of town. Depending on how much equity she has in the house and how much other debt she has, she could probably get $100,000 or more through a second mortgage or some other instrument. Of course, she may not want to increase the debt on her home.

13–14 ANNOUNCING THE DEMISE OF AN ORGANIZATION

For the past two years, you've been president of the local chapter of the Society for Technical Communication (STC). It has been thankless and frustrating. The chapter has about 70 members, but on a good evening attendance barely reaches 15. You were really embarrassed four months ago when you invited your boss to speak about designing manuals for international audiences and only three people besides you came. The turnout was annoying as well as embarrassing because "communicating with international audiences" ranked number 2 on a survey last year of the topics people wanted. But the people who ask for certain topics don't come to the meetings.

You've been trying to carry the chapter almost alone. STC chapter guidelines recommend that the Newsletter Editor be a separate office. But you couldn't find anyone else to do it after the former editor retired eight months ago, so you've been doing it yourself. Theoretically there's a membership committee, but it doesn't seem to do anything. Your attempts to motivate the members have failed. You're sick and tired of all this work with no reward, and you told the nominating committee you were not willing to hold any office in the coming year.

Chapter elections were scheduled for this month's meeting. But the nominating committee came without a slate: everybody they'd asked had turned them down. No one who was at the meeting was willing to assume an office. You pointed out that meetings and a newsletter didn't happen by themselves, but everyone was "too busy." You probably could make time again this year, but you just aren't willing to continue to try to keep the chapter alive.

The regional director, Laura Cohen, told you that if a chapter dissolves, its treasury is transferred to the national organization. Your chapter has about $500. Members will still be part of the national organization; they will still receive national publications; their dues will stay the same. The portion of national dues which goes to the local chapter will go to the nearest local chapter. In your case, the nearest chapter is in a city about an hour and a half away by car.

Write a letter to members (active and inactive) announcing the demise of the local chapter.

Writing Persuasive Messages

QUESTIONS

- What are the primary and secondary purposes in a persuasive message?
- When should you make your request directly? In what situations is it better to be indirect?
- How can you increase your credibility?
- How should you organize a direct request?
- How should you organize a problem-solving persuasive message?
- What should you put in the subject line of a direct request? Of a problem-solving persuasive message?
- How can you counter objections that readers may have?
- How can you encourage readers to act promptly?

[Robert McNamara] taught me to put all my ideas into writing. "You're so effective one on one," he used to tell me. "You could sell anybody anything. But we're about to spend one hundred million dollars here. Go home tonight and put your great idea on paper. If you can't do that, then you haven't really thought it out."

It was a valuable lesson, and I've followed his lead ever since. Whenever one of my people has an idea, I ask him to lay it out in writing.

Lee Iacocca
Iacocca: An Autobiography, 1984

Sometimes you'll put proposals in writing because you need to persuade people you can't talk to—perhaps people you haven't even met. Sometimes the audience may already know about your idea but ask you to put it in writing either for the record or so they can examine the idea more closely.

Persuasive messages include

- **Orders and requests**
  Orders for products.
  Directions to subordinates.
  Requests for information and action.
- **Proposals and recommendations**
  Requests for funding or for permission to undertake research.
  Recommendations for company action.
  Recommendations that a subordinate be promoted.
- **Persuasive requests**
  Suggestions that you want the reader to implement.
  Sales letters.
  Job application letters.
- **Efforts to change people's behavior**
  Collection letters.
  Criticisms where you want the subordinate to improve behavior.
  Messages written to persuade subordinates to follow company procedures.
  Public-service ads designed to reduce drunk driving, drug use, and so on.

All persuasive messages have several purposes:

Primary Purposes:
  To have the reader act.

  To provide enough information so that the reader knows exactly what to do.

  To overcome any objections which might prevent or delay action.

Secondary Purposes:
  To build a good image of the writer.

  To build a good image of the writer's organization.

To cement a good relationship between the writer and reader.

To reduce or eliminate future correspondence on the same subject so the message doesn't create more work for the writer

CHOOSING A PERSUASIVE STRATEGY

Choose a persuasive strategy based on your answers to four questions: What do you want readers to do? Where are they now in relation to your request? How strong a case can you make? What kind of persuasion does your organization value?

1. What Do You Want Readers to Do?

Identify the specific action you want readers to take: come to a trade show, send in a check, authorize a purchase. If your goal requires several steps, specify what you want your reader to do *now*. For instance, your immediate goal may be to have readers come to a meeting or let you make a presentation, even though your eventual goal is a major sale or a change in policy.

2. Where Are Readers Now in Relation to Your Request?

On any topic, people have **areas of acceptance,** positions close to their own beliefs, which they could easily accept. **Areas of rejection** are positions the audience will not consider. **Areas of noncommitment** are positions which are neither immediately acceptable nor unacceptable; potentially at least, they are areas that we could persuade the audience to accept.

Ego-involvement is the emotional commitment the audience has to its position. For example, two readers might have similar areas of acceptance. Yet one of them, with little ego-involvement, might feel that the subject was trivial and be willing to change. Someone else, with a strong emotional stake in the outcome, would be more resistant to other points of view.

One kind of emotional stake is the vested interest. Readers have a **vested interest** in something if they benefit directly from keeping things as they are. People who are in power have a vested interest in retaining the system that gives them their power. Someone who designed a system has a vested interest in protecting that system from criticism. To admit that the system has faults is to admit that the designer made mistakes.

Both individuals and organizations have self-images. It's easier for readers to say *yes* when you ask for something that is consistent with that self-image, or for something that the reader has done before. For example, a student who wanted to get into a class that was filled said to the instructor, "This has been a dreadful day, but you made me smile three times in class. You've got to let me in." The instructor, who liked thinking of herself as a person with a sense of humor, granted the request.

It would be easier to persuade a college to keep its library open extra hours during finals week than to persuade the same college to serve Sunday evening meals in its dorms during finals. Providing books and study facilities is central to a college's mission. Providing food isn't.

3. How Strong Is Your Case?

The strength of your case is based on three aspects of persuasion: argument, credibility, and emotional appeal.

Argument refers to the reasons or logic you offer. Sometimes you may be

---

Different Strokes for Different Folks*

David Ricks suggests that different cultures use different dominant persuasive strategies: "In the Orient, for example, a person should not try to make the other 'lose face.' But to be taken seriously in Italy, a person must try to win the argument. . . . The British prefer a much 'softer sell' than the Germans."

Even within a culture, different individuals may prefer different persuasive strategies.

Certainly in the United States, the most successful sales representatives are those who can adapt the persuasive strategy to the audience. Some buyers like a no-nonsense approach that takes as little of their time as possible. Others are more comfortable if they get to know the sales rep first, and the sales rep takes time to get to know them as individuals. Some buyers want lots of details; others just want to know that the product will solve their problems. Some buyers react negatively to even a hint of "hard sell" pressure. Others seem to want to be urged.

Similar differences exist in other areas of persuasion. Some voters want to know as much about a candidate's stand on the issues as possible. Others care more about personal qualities such as integrity, toughness, and compassion. Still others want to vote for someone they like and feel personally comfortable with. Some investors are happy just to take their brokers' advice. Others want to know the facts for themselves, so they pore over prospectuses and business publications.

---

* Based on David A. Ricks, *Big Business Blunders* (Homewood, IL: Dow Jones-Irwin, 1983), 68 and Roger Wenschlag, *The Versatile Salesperson* (New York: John Wiley, 1987), 187–95.

Credibility and the Effective
Manager*

Twenty Indsco executives [were]
asked to define the characteristics of
effective managers. . . . They agreed
that "credibility" was more important than anything else.

"Credibility" was their term for
competence plus power—the known
ability to get results. People with
credibility were listened to, their
phone calls were answered first. . . .
People with credibility had room to
make more mistakes and could take
greater risks. . . . They were known
to be going somewhere in the organization and to have the ability to
place their people in good jobs.
They could back up their words
with actions.

able to prove conclusively that your solution is best. Sometimes your logic will
be weaker: the reasons may not be as strong, the benefits may not be as certain,
obstacles may be difficult or impossible to overcome. For example, suppose
that you wanted to persuade your organization to offer a tuition-reimbursement plan for employees. You'd have a strong argument if you could show
that tuition-reimbursement would improve the performance of marginal workers or that reimbursement would be an attractive recruiting tool in a tight job
market. However, if dozens of fully qualified workers apply for every opening
you have, your argument would be weaker. The program might be nice for
workers, but you'd have a hard job proving that it would help the company.

Credibility is the audience's response to you as the source of the message.
People are more easily persuaded by someone they see as trustworthy, unbiased,
expert, attractive, or powerful. When you don't yet have the credibility that
comes from being an expert or being powerful, build credibility by the language
and strategy you use:

- **Be factual.** Don't exaggerate. When Sears changed its catalog descriptions from the traditional superlatives to factual descriptions of
  each item, sales increased because people trusted the information
  they were getting.

- **Be specific.** If you say "X is better," show in detail *how* it is better.
  Show the reader exactly where the savings or other benefits come
  from so that it's clear that the proposal really is as good as you say
  it is.

- **Be reliable.** If you suspect that a project will take longer to complete, cost more money, or be less effective than you originally
  thought, tell your audience *immediately*. Negotiate a new schedule
  that you can meet.

Emotional appeal means making the reader *want* to do what you ask. People
don't make decisions—even business decisions—based on logic alone. J. C.
Mathes and Dwight W. Stevenson cite the following example. During his
summer job, an engineering student who was asked to evaluate his company's
waste treatment system saw a way that the system could be redesigned to save
the company over $200,000 a year. He wrote a report recommending the
change and gave it to his boss, confident that everyone would be highly impressed. Nothing happened. The problem? His supervisor wasn't about to send
up a report which would require him to explain why *he'd* been wasting over
$200,000 a year of the company's money.[1]

4. What Kind of Persuasion Does Your Organization Value?

A strategy that works in one organization may not work somewhere else.
James Suchan and Ron Dulek point out that DEC's corporate culture values
no-holds-barred agressiveness. "Even if opposition is expected, a subordinate
should write a proposal in a forceful, direct manner."[2] In another organization
with different cultural values, Frances Harrington notes, an employee who
used a hard sell for a request antagonized the boss.[3]

Corporate culture isn't written down; it's learned by imitation and observation. What style do high-level people in your organization use? When you
show a draft to your boss, are you told to tone down your statements or to
make them stronger? Role models and advice are two of the ways organizations
communicate their culture to newcomers.

*   Quoted from Rosabeth Moss Kanter, *Men and Women of the Corporation* (New York:
Basic Books, 1977), 169.

Using Your Analysis to Choose a Persuasive Strategy

If your organization prefers a specific approach, use it. If your organization has no preference, or if you do not know your reader's preference, use the following guidelines to choose a strategy.

Use a **direct approach** and the **direct request pattern** when

- The audience's initial position is positive or neutral.
- Your request falls into the audience's area of acceptance.
- The audience has no emotional feelings about the subject.

Use an **indirect approach** and the **problem-solving pattern** when

- The audience's initial position is neutral or negative.
- Your request falls into the audience's area of noncommitment or rejection.
- The audience has low or moderate emotional feelings about the subject.
- You have good arguments to support your position.
- You can counter most of the audience's objections.

Use the suggestions in Chapter 15, Handling Difficult Persuasive Situations, when

- The audience's initial position is negative.
- Your request falls into the audience's area of rejection.
- The audience has moderate or strong emotional feelings about the subject.
- The audience will not benefit personally from doing as you ask.

Use the **sales pattern** in Chapter 16, Direct Mail, when

- The audience's initial position is positive or neutral.
- Your request falls into the audience's area of acceptance or non-commitment.
- The audience has moderate or high emotional feelings about the subject.
- You can show that the audience gets something directly in return for the cost of your proposal.

WRITING DIRECT REQUESTS

Use the following pattern for simple direct requests:

1. **Consider asking immediately for the information or service you want.** When you know readers will grant your request readily, save their time by making the request right away. Delay the request if it seems too abrupt or if you have several purposes in the message.

2. **Give readers all the information they will need to act on your request.** When you have several related questions, number them or

---

Playing It Bone Straight*

You've got to be absolutely honest—bone honest. Every day, everything you say, everything you do, every night, every dealing with every employee, you've got to be straight. Because those people have been conned for centuries. And if you con them once, the credibility's gone. Absolutely, totally gone. And they're looking at you with a crooked eye until you prove it. It took us probably two years until they finally realized that we were playing it absolutely bone straight.

Sometimes Logic Isn't Enough†

Before the OPEC oil embargo in 1973, gasoline was cheap and plentiful in the United States. When prices rose and supplies dropped, many consumers blamed the gas companies. A 1974 survey showed that 62% of the respondents felt the companies deliberately held back gas to raise prices.

Shell Oil first responded to this consumer hostility with a series of ads attempting to explain government price regulations. The ads were designed by Ogilvy and Mather, but they didn't convince anybody. Indeed, many newspapers printed the picture of a U.S. senator holding up the ad as an example of oil company deceit.

Next, Shell tried ads which proclaimed that it was trying to find more oil. These ads provoked not disbelief but indifference. They too failed to persuade the public that Shell wasn't gouging them.

Finally, Shell and Ogilvy and Mather created the Shell Information Series. Instead of trying to persuade logically, the ads tried to create goodwill for Shell. Each ad in the series gave drivers useful information and carried only a tiny ad for Shell products. The series created the image of a company that cared about its customers. Without responding directly to people's objections, the ads convinced readers that the company was telling the truth in its public statements.

---

* Tom Mehlon, owner, North American Tool and Die; quoted in John Nathan, "In Search of Excellence: The Film" (Waltham, MA: Nathan/Tyler Productions, 1985), 21.

† Based on Ann Iverson and Paul Norris, "How to Sell to People Who Are Mad at You," *Viewpoint: By, for, and about Ogilvy and Mather* 4 (1982): 7–13 and "Measuring Marketplace Results: The 'Come to Shell for Answers' Campaign," *How Plain English Works for Business* (Washington, DC: U.S. Government Printing Office, 1984), 20–28; cited in Craig Kallendorf and Carol Kallendorf, "Aristotle and the Ethics of Business Communication," submitted for publication.

FIGURE 14.1
A DIRECT REQUEST

Subject: Suggestion #_____

① Please help us evaluate the attached suggestion.

● Should BCS adopt this suggestion? _____

Why or why not? _____

_____

_____

Sub questions are spelled out. Lines indicate that short, hand written answers are expected

②

● Will it save the company money? If so, how much a year?

_____

—_____

● If the suggestion is adopted, how large an award should

be given? _____

_____

_____

③ Please send your answers to these questions and the reasons
for your recommendations within two weeks to

Long enough to give reader flexibility but soon enough to encourage prompt action

        Beth Cusik
        Suggestion Committee Chair
        312 Building B

Thanks!

FIGURE 14.2
A DIRECT REQUEST TO A SUPERIOR

OSU Communication

Subject   Request for Additional Travel Funds

Date   January 11, 1988

From   Kitty Locker

To   Murray Beja

Request ①

If the department has any travel money left after MLA, I would like an additional $178.24 to cover airfare to the Association for Business Communication Eastern/Canadian Regional Conference in Montreal April 28-May 2.

Background ②

The department has already committed $356 to me for travel during 1987-88: $148 to Atlanta for ABC International, $148 to St. Louis for CCCC, and $50-60 to Louisville for ABC Midwest Regional.

I am a member of the By-Laws Committee which will be meeting at the Eastern/Canadian meeting. I'm also sending a proposal to the Program Chair (a friend of mine) just in case there happens to be an empty space left on the program.

What the reader needs to do ③

The ticket needs to be purchased by January 20 to get the discounted rate of $178.24. Could you let me know as soon as possible so that I can start the necessary paperwork? Thanks!

The Ohio State University
Form 701—Rev. 3/82 Stores 53605

set them off with bullets, so the reader can check to see that all of them have been answered.

In a claim (where a product is under warranty or a shipment was defective), explain the circumstances so that the reader knows what happened. Be sure to include all the relevant details: date of purchase, model or invoice number, etc.

In more complicated direct requests, anticipate possible responses. Suppose you're asking for information about equipment meeting certain specifications. Explain which criteria are most important so that the reader can recommend an alternative if no single product meets all your needs. You may also want to tell the reader what your price constraints are and ask whether the item is in stock or must be special ordered.

Direct Requests Don't Translate*

Making a direct request may not be the most direct way to get what you want in other cultures. Indirection and implication may work better.

In India, workers will assume that a direct request really conceals a more complicated indirect message. They'll try to figure out what the boss wants and will ignore the direct statement.

Brazilians may be so offended by a superior's direct order that they threaten to leave for the beach. Even bosses are expected to suggest, not order.

Direct orders make workers in Japanese companies feel that they aren't trusted or respected. Managers should specify the general goal, but not the specific steps for getting there.

Americans sometimes have trouble understanding implication and indirection. A leader of the Ethiopian Church came to the United States to ask church groups for help in technical and industrial arts training. Americans came to a meeting ready to help, but they didn't understand what he wanted. He didn't list the things he needed and ask for them explicitly as the U.S. culture trains people to do. Instead, he simply quoted the Biblical injunction that people who have good things should share. This was too indirect, too figurative for his audience—even though they were church people who knew the Bible. It took an Ethiopian who had lived in the United States for many years and who understood both cultures to see what was going wrong.

3. **Tell readers exactly what you want them to do.** Send you a check? A replacement? A catalogue? Answers to your questions? If you need an answer by a certain time, say so. If possible, show the reader why the time limit is necessary.

Figures 14.1 and 14.2 illustrate direct requests.

Direct requests should be direct. Don't make the reader guess what you want.

Indirect request: Is there a newer version of the 1980 *Accounting Reference Manual*?

Direct request: If there is a newer version of the 1980 *Accounting Reference Manual*, please send it to me.

Subject Lines for Direct Requests

In a direct request, put either the subject of the request or a question in the subject line.

Subject: Status of Account #3548–003

Please get me the following information about account #3548–003:

Subject: Do We Need an Additional Training Session in October?

The two training sessions scheduled for October will accommodate 40 people. Last month, you said that 57 new staff accountants had been hired. Should we schedule an additional training session in October? Or can the new hires wait until the next regularly scheduled session in February?

Direct Requests with Multiple Purposes

In some direct requests, your combination of purposes may suggest a different organization. For example, in a letter asking an employer to reimburse you for expenses after a job interview, you'd want to thank your hosts for their hospitality and cement the good impression you made at the interview. To do that, you'd spend the first several paragraphs talking about the trip and the interview. Only in the last third of the letter (or even in the P.S.) would you put your request for reimbursement.

Similarly, in a letter asking about a graduate program, a major purpose might be to build a good image of yourself so that your application for financial aid would be viewed positively. You'd want to provide information about your qualifications and interest in the field as well as asking questions.

* Based on William Bembeck and William S. Howell, *Persuasion: A Means of Social Influence* (Englewood Cliffs, NJ: Prentice-Hall, 1976), 201; John Lenkey III, "Help for the Stranger in a Foreign Land," *The Wall Street Journal,* September 21, 1987, 22; Boye De Mente, *Japanese Manners and Ethics in Business* (Phoenix: Phoenix Books, 1975), 83; and John P. Fieg and John G. Blair, *There Is a Difference: 12 Intercultural Perspectives* (Washington, DC: Meridian House International, 1975), 58.

WRITING PROBLEM-SOLVING MESSAGES

Use the problem-solving pattern of organization when you expect resistance from your reader but can show that doing what you want will solve a problem you and your reader share. This pattern allows you to disarm opposition by showing all the reasons in favor of your position before you give your readers a chance to say *no*.

1. **Catch the reader's interest by mentioning a common ground.** Provide some reason for the reader to expect that your message will be interesting or beneficial. You may want to catch attention with a negative (which you will go on to show can be solved).

2. **Define the problem you both share (which your request will solve).** Present the problem objectively: don't assign blame or mention personalities. Be specific about the cost in money, time, lost goodwill, etc. You have to convince readers that *something* has to be done before you can convince them that your solution is the best one.

3. **Explain the solution to the problem.** If you know that the reader will favor another solution, start with that solution and show why it won't work before you present your solution.

   Present your solution without using the words *I* or *my*. Don't let personalities enter the picture; don't let the reader think he or she should say *no* just because you've had other requests accepted recently.

4. **Show that any negative elements (cost, time, etc.) are outweighed by the advantages.**

5. **Summarize any additional benefits of the solution.** The main benefit—solving the problem—can be presented briefly since you described the problem in detail. However, if there are any additional benefits, mention them.

6. **Tell the reader exactly what you want him or her to do.** Often your reader will authorize or approve something; other people will implement the action. Give your reader a reason to act promptly, perhaps offering a new reader benefit ("By buying now, we can avoid the next quarter's price hikes").

Figure 14.3 uses the problem-solving pattern of organization.

Subject Lines for Problem-Solving Messages

When you have a reluctant reader, putting the request in the subject line just gets a quick *no* before you've had a chance to give all your arguments. Instead, choose a common ground or a reader benefit—something that shows readers that this message will help them.

Subject: Reducing Energy Costs in the New Orleans Office

Energy costs in our New Orleans office have risen 12% in the last three years, even though the cost of gas has fallen and the cost of electricity has risen only 5%.

Although your first paragraph may be negative in a problem-solving message, your subject line should be neutral or positive.

A Writer Explains Her Rhetorical Choices

I asked my department chair orally for travel funds, and he told me to put my request in writing.

I've toned down my request in the first paragraph by using the subjunctive "if . . . I would like" and mentioning MLA (the major conference for English departments). I want to sound reasonable and to show that I'm aware of the realities of departmental budgeting. (MLA was in San Francisco this year, so the budget for our department at Ohio State has been hit hard.)

In paragraph 2 I tell how much I'm already getting because I know that a single trip to San Francisco costs as much or more. I'd like to subtly plant the idea that I may be getting transportation to more conferences, but that I'm not getting any more money than department members who went to MLA.

I know that people who give papers are more likely to get money, so I've put in a sentence in paragraph 3 about sending in a proposal. In my first draft, I had said "Although the deadline for proposals is past," but I decided to delete that negative information. Besides, regional conferences are often less packed than national ones, and I *do* know the program chair, *and* I have a good proposal. I think there's a chance I'll get to read a paper.

I've left the request itself a little vague. Asking my department chair to authorize the expense feels too pushy since I know my chances are slim. On the other hand, I want to be positive. "Let me know" is a compromise.

Some people think we shouldn't thank people before they've done what we want. But I want this memo to be polite and friendly and a little deferential (I am writing to my boss, after all). "Thanks!" seems to end on the right note, so that I don't sound brusque or as though I'm taking a *yes* for granted.

P.S. I did get the money for the trip and I did get on the program at the conference!

FIGURE 14.3
A PROBLEM-SOLVING PERSUASIVE MESSAGE

February 16, 1987

To: All Staff Members

From: Melissa J. Gutridge *MJG*

Subject: New Sign-Out System

① Common ground

Successfully mainstreaming our clients into the community is very important and daily interaction with the public is necessary. Our clients enjoy the times they get to go to the mall or out to lunch, instead of remaining here all day. Previously, when a client was taken out for an activity, a staff member knew exactly where the client was and who the client was with. Recently, there has been a problem with this.

Problem

Clients are being taken out on activities without a staff member's knowledge of where the client is and who the client is with.

② Specific example

We need to know where all clients are at all times because social workers, psychologists, and relatives stop by unannounced constantly. Last week Janet's father stopped by to pick her up for a doctor's appointment and she was not here. No one knew where she was or who she was with. Naturally her father was very upset and wanted to know what kind of program we were running. Staff members' not knowing where our clients are and who they are with is damaging to the good reputation of our staff and program.

③ Solution, presented impersonally

⑤ Additional reader benefit

Starting Monday, February 23, a sign-out board will be located at Betty's desk. Please write down where you and the client are going and when you will be returning. When signing out, try helping the clients sign themselves out. We can turn this into a learning experience for our clients. Then when a social worker stops by to see someone that is not here, we can simply look at the sign-out board and tell where the client is and when the client will be returning.

⑥ What the reader needs to do

Please help keep up the superb reputation you have helped Weststar earn as a quality center for handicapped adults. Sign out yourself and clients at all times.

Developing a Common Ground

A common ground avoids the me-against-you opposition of some persuasive situations and suggests that both you and your readers have a mutual interest in solving the problems you face.

In your common ground, emphasize the parts of your proposal that fit with what your audience already does or believes. An employee of 3M wanted to develop laser disks. He realized that 3M's previous products were thin and flat: Scotch tape, Post-It Notes, magnetic tape. When he made his presentation to the group which chose new products for development, he held his prototype disk horizontally, so his audience saw a flat, thin object rather than a large, round, recordlike object. Making his project fit with the audience's previous experience was a subtle and effective emotional tool to make it easier for the audience to say *yes*.[4]

Use audience analysis to evaluate possible common grounds. Suppose you want to install a system to play background music in a factory. To persuade management to pay for the system, a possible common ground would be increasing productivity. However, to persuade the union to pay for the system, you'd need a different common ground. Workers would see productivity as a way to get them to do more work for the same pay. A better common ground would be that the music would make the factory environment more pleasant.

Dealing with Objections

If you know that your readers will hear other points of view, or if your audience's initial position is negative, you have to deal with their objections to persuade them.

Giving the response to the objection without naming the objection is the most common technique. In a brochure, you can present responses with a question/answer format. When objections have already been voiced, you may want to name the objection so that your audience realizes that you are responding to that specific objection. However, to avoid solidifying the opposition, don't attribute the objection to your audience. Instead, use a less personal attribution: "Some people wonder . . . "; "Some citizens are afraid that. . . ."

Try one or more of the following strategies to counter objections:

- Specify how much time or money is required—it may not be as much as the reader fears.

> Distributing flyers to each house or apartment in your neighborhood will probably take two afternoons.

- Put the time or money in the context of the benefits it brings.

> The additional $152,500 will allow The Open Shelter to remain open 24 rather than 16 hours a day. The funds will do more than just give homeless men a place where they can be during the day. The money pays for three social workers who help men find work and homes. It keeps the Neighborhood Bank open, so that men don't have to cash social security checks in bars and so that they can save the $800 they need to have up front to rent an apartment.

Writing Letters of Recommendation
Letters of recommendation call for special strategies.

Either in the first or the last paragraph, summarize your overall evaluation of the person.

Early in the letter, perhaps in the first paragraph, show how well and how long you've known the person.

Letters of recommendation must be specific. General positives that are not backed up with specific examples and evidence are seen as weak recommendations.

Letters of recommendation that focus on minor points also suggest that the person is weak.

Experts are divided on whether you should include negatives. Some people believe that negatives may make the organization vulnerable to lawsuits if the person does not get the job. Some people feel that any negative weakens the letter. Other people feel that presenting but not emphasizing honest negatives makes the letter more convincing. No one, after all, is perfect.

In a letter of recommendation, the words "Call me if you need more information" mean "I have negative information that I am unwilling to put on paper. Call me and I'll tell you what I really think."

Same Organization, Different Concerns*

Workers in the same organization may have different concerns and different priorities.

Field sales managers, responsible for the sales reps within a geographical territory, wanted their sales people to be able to offer customers the best price and shipping arrangements. Product line managers, responsible for the profitability of products across all geographic lines, controlled price and allocation.

The actual contract offered to the customer had to be negotiated by the two. In one company, the managers communicated by phone, telegram, and mail.

Field managers complained that product line managers were out of touch with the market and didn't realize how competitive things were. Product line managers complained that sales reps were so involved with their own particular customers that they forgot that their own company needed to make a profit.

- Show that money spent now will save money in the long run.

> By replacing the boiler now, we'll no longer have to release steam that the overflow tank can't hold. Holding steam means heating less new water. Depending on how severe the winter is, we could save $100 to $750 a year in energy costs. If energy costs rise, we'll save even more.

- Show that doing as you ask will benefit some group or cause the reader supports, even though the action may not help the reader directly. This is the strategy used in fund-raising letters, discussed in detail in Chapter 17.

> By being a Big Brother or a Big Sister, you'll give a child the adult attention he or she needs to become a well-adjusted, productive adult.

- Show the reader that the sacrifice is necessary to achieve a larger, more important goal to which he or she is committed.

> These changes will mean more work for all of us. But we've got to cut our costs 25% in the next year to keep the plant open and to keep our jobs.

If you cannot refute a specific objection, you may still be able to minimize it by showing that the advantages as a group outnumber or outweigh the disadvantages as a group. If you cannot overcome an objection in any other way, admit that it exists. The best solution does not have to be a perfect solution.

In some instances, you may even be able to turn a disadvantage into an opportunity. Persuaders who can do that win what had seemed to be losing battles. In one company, a hiring freeze was announced a week before the Planning Department's scheduled presentation to ask for another staff member. Most people on the committee expected that the department would drop its request. But the department went ahead, arguing that, with a company-wide freeze, each department would need more lead time to complete its own work, and that another person in Planning could provide that lead time. In spite of the freeze, the request was approved.

Offering a Reason for the Reader to Act Promptly

The longer people delay, the less likely they are to carry through with the action they had decided to take. In addition, you want a fast response so you can go ahead with your own plans.

---

* Based on Rosabeth Moss Kanter, *Men and Women of the Corporation* (New York: Basic Books, 1977), 175.

Just asking for prompt action can help speed a response. Request action by a specific date. Always give people at least a week or two: they have other things to do besides respond to your requests. Set deadlines in the middle of the month, if possible. If you say, "Please return this by March 1," people will think, "I don't need to do this till March." If you can use a response even after the deadline, say so. Otherwise, people who can't make the deadline may not respond at all.

Readers may ignore deadlines that seem arbitrary. Show why you need a quick response:

- **Show that the time limit is real.** Perhaps you need information quickly to use it in a report that has a due date. Perhaps a decision must be made by a certain date to catch the start of the school year, the Christmas selling season, or an election campaign. Perhaps you need to be ready for a visit from out-of-town or foreign colleagues.

- **Show that acting now will save time or money.** If business is slow and your industry isn't doing well, then your company needs to act now (to economize, to better serve customers) in order to be competitive. If business is booming and everyone is making a profit, then your company needs to act now to get its fair share of the available profits.

- **Show the cost of delaying action.** Will labor or material costs be higher in the future? Will delay mean more money spent on repairing something that will still need to be replaced?

Building Emotional Appeal with Psychological Description

Sense impressions—what the reader sees, hears, smells, tastes, feels—evoke a strong emotional response. **Psychological description** means creating a scenario so readers can picture themselves using your product or service and enjoying its benefits. You can also use psychological description to describe the problem your product will solve.

Lists of reader benefits alone don't motivate the reader. Consider the excerpt in Figure 14.4 from a brochure seeking new members for a faculty club.

If someone has been searching everywhere for a gourmet cooking class, he or she will learn that this club offers one. But there's nothing to make gourmet cooking—or any of the other activities—sound attractive to readers who haven't already made up their minds. In contrast, good psychological description uses vivid details and sensory imagery to motivate uncommitted readers. The flyer for a university's food services in Figure 14.5 gets your gastric juices flowing.

In psychological description, you're putting your reader in a picture. If the reader doesn't feel that the picture fits him or her, the technique backfires. To prevent this, psychological description often uses subjunctive verbs ("if you like . . ." "if you were . . .") or the words *maybe* and *perhaps*.

> You're hungry but you don't want to bother with cooking. Perhaps you have guests to take to dinner. Or it's 12 noon and you only have an hour for lunch. Whatever the situation, the Illini Union has a food service to fit your needs. If you want convenience, we have it. If it's atmosphere you're seeking, it's here too. And if you're concerned about the price, don't be. When you're looking for a great meal, the Illini Union is the place to find it.
>
> —Illini Union brochure.

Creative Response to an Objection, I*

In some cases . . . American subsidiaries or affiliates in Japan have actually found it more effective to compete on the basis of outstanding service rather than lower cost to the customer. One particularly striking example of this phenomenon is the Japanese subsidiary of Connecticut's Loctite Corporation. Though its annual volume was still only about $10 million a year, . . . as of 1985 the company held 50 percent of the Japanese market for adhesives used in the assembly of automotive engines and was making growing inroads into the market for industrial adhesives in the electronics field.

The chief explanation for this, according to Robert Krieble, . . . lies in Loctite's heavy emphasis on what might be called pre-sale service. "Japanese products in our field are good. . . . There are only a few areas in which we could honestly claim significant superiority in product terms. But what we do have is superior knowledge: we understand where and how to use adhesives beneficially in the assembly of parts better than anyone else in the world."

This, as Krieble sees it, gives Loctite a crucial edge over its Japanese rivals. "Their idea of competition," he said, "is to cut price. . . . Our sales men go to a potential customer and say, 'Here's what you can do with adhesives in your particular situation.' . . . We give knowhow away . . . and when the customer agrees that we've solved his problem, then we charge like hell for our product."

---

* Quoted from Robert C. Christopher, *Second to None: American Companies in Japan* (New York: Crown Publishers, 1986), 143.

FIGURE 14.4
FEATURES BUT NO BENEFITS

We invite you to join

Your University colleagues and supporters of the University in membership in the Levis Faculty Center. The Center is open to patronage by all full-time faculty and staff and offers regular buffet luncheons Mondays through Fridays, and dinners Wednesdays through Fridays. The Center is

The only place on campus
where cocktails, wine, and beer, are available. It offers a large variety of programs, including special ethnic dinners, lectures, and special activities for singles. It has

Excellent facilities
three lounges, two dining rooms, a reading room, music room, bar, three ballrooms, six conference rooms, and ample parking. It is a

Meeting place for the entire university community
patronized by many and boasting about 1000 members from on and off campus. It is used for

Meeting and conferences
by University-connected departments and groups and for a large variety of

Private parties and banquets
all in a striking building designed by famed architect Harry Weese that is admirably suited for our continuing program of

Art exhibits
arranged with the help of members of the University Art Department.

Privileges Available To Members

Special programs such as:

Ballroom dance classes

Bridge lessons

Gourmet cooking classes

International food and film programs, frequently combined with . . .

Wine-tastings and lectures on wine and more

(Most programs are free to members; some have a nominal fee.)

Advance reservations at discounts for special events such as

Annual Christmas madrigal dinner

New Year's Eve dinner and dance

A variety of ethnic dinners

Charge privileges for all Center activities (Charge privileges at other faculty centers throughout the U.S. can be arranged.)

Use of the Center's facilities for private parties, receptions and banquets

Participation in the governance of the Center

ANALYSIS OF A SAMPLE PROBLEM[5]

Problem

In one room in the production department of Nakamura Electronics Company, employees work on TV picture tubes under conditions which are scarcely bearable due to the heat. Even when the temperature outside is only 75°, it is over 100° in the tube room. In June, July, and August, 24 out of 36 workers quit because they couldn't stand the heat. This turnover happens every summer.

In a far corner of the room sits a quality control inspector in front of a small fan (the only one in the room). The production workers, in contrast, are carrying 20-pound TV tubes. As production supervisor, you tried to get air-conditioning two years ago, before Nakamura acquired the company, but management was horrified at the idea of spending $300,000 to insulate and air-condition the warehouse (it is impractical to air-condition the tube room alone).

FIGURE 14.5
USING PSYCHOLOGICAL DESCRIPTION TO DEVELOP READER BENEFITS

The Colonial Room

When you dine in the Illini Union Colonial Room, it's easy to imagine yourself a guest in a fine Virginian mansion. Light from the gleaming chandeliers reflects from a hand-carved mirror hanging over the dark, polished buffet. Here you can dine in quiet elegance amid furnishings adapted from 18th century Williamsburg and the Georgian homes of the James River Valley in Virginia.

Perhaps you'd like a dinner of stuffed rainbow trout. Or the pork fricassee. The menu features a variety of complete meals which are changed daily, as well as the regular a la carte service. Whatever your choice, you'll enjoy an evening of fine dining at very reasonable prices.

The Illini Union Colonial Room is located on the northeast corner of the first floor. Dinners are served Monday through Friday from 5:30 to 7:30 p.m. Please call 333-0690 for reservations, and enjoy the flavor of the Colonies tonight.

The Cafeteria

In the Illini Union Cafeteria, you start out with an empty tray and silverware. Then comes the food, several yards of it, all yours for the choosing. By the time you've finished, your empty tray has become a delicious meal.

In the morning, the warm aroma of breakfast fills the air. Feast your eyes and then your appetite on the array of eggs, bacon, pancakes, toast, sausage, rolls, juices, and coffee...They're all waiting to wake you up with good taste. Have a hearty breakfast or make it quick and tasty. The warm, freshly baked sweet rolls and coffeecakes practically beg to be smothered in butter and savored with a cup of hot coffee.

By 11 a.m. the breakfast menu has made way for lunch. Here come the plump Reuben sandwiches and the toasty grilled cheese. Soups and salads make their appearance. A variety of vegetables are dressed up to entice you and several main dishes lead the luncheon parade. Any number of complete meals can take shape as you move along.

What? Back for dinner? Well, no wonder! The Cafeteria sets out a wide selection of entrees and side dishes. Veal parmigiana steams for your attention but the roast beef right next to it is rough competition. Tomorrow the fried chicken may be up for selection. Choose the dinner combination that best fits your appetite and your pocket.

The newly remodeled Cafeteria is on the ground floor and is open for breakfast from 7 to 11 a.m. Monday through Saturday and 8 to 11 a.m. on Sunday. Lunch is from 11 a.m. to 1:15 p.m. Monday through Saturday and 11 a.m. to 2 p.m. on Sunday. Dinner is served from 4:45 to 7 p.m. Monday through Friday.

A meal in a restaurant is expensive. A meal at home is a chore. But a meal at the Cafeteria combines good food and reasonable prices to make dining a pleasure.

Creative Response to an Objection, II*

Carl Stokes' goal was to be elected mayor of Cleveland. He had the ability and dedication. And one factor that made him different from any other candidate: he was black. . . .

His supporters decided to bring the race issue up front. If it was being *whispered* about, why not have it *talked* about? They put together a series of ads and this was the first giant headline in the newspaper: *"Don't Vote for a Negro."*

Everyone in Cleveland read *that* headline.

And then, in smaller type, came this copy . . .

> Vote for a man.
> Vote for ability. Vote for character.
> Vote for a leader. A man who can attack the problems and solve them.
> A man who can rally the people of Cleveland behind him.
> Vote for a man.
> A man who believes.
> Carl Stokes.

He won.

Inflation has pushed the price of insulation and air-conditioning up to $500,000, but with such high turnover, you're losing money every summer. Write a memo to Jennifer M. Kirkland, Operations Vice President, renewing your request.

Analysis of the Problem

1. Who is (are) your audience(s)? What characteristics are relevant to this particular message? If you are writing to more than one reader, how do the readers differ?

   The Operations Vice President will be concerned about keeping costs low and keeping production running smoothly. Kirkland may know that the request was denied two years ago, but another person was Vice President then; Kirkland wasn't the one who said *no*.

2. What are your purposes in writing?

   To persuade Kirkland to authorize insulation and air conditioning. To build a good image of myself.

3. What information must your message include?

   The cost of the proposal. The effects of the present situation.

4. How can you build support for your position? What reasons or reader benefits will your reader find convincing?

   Cutting turnover may save money and keep the assembly line running smoothly. Experienced employees may produce higher-quality parts. Putting in air-conditioning would relieve one of the workers' main complaints; it might make the union happier.

5. What objection(s) can you expect your reader(s) to have? What negative elements of your message must you deemphasize or overcome?

   The cost. The time that operations will be shut down while installation is taking place.

6. What aspects of the total situation may affect reader response? The economy? The time of year? Morale in the organization? The relationship between the reader and writer? Any special circumstances?

   The electronics industry is having a shakedown; money is tight; the company will be reluctant to make a major expenditure. In spite of moderate unemployment, filling vacancies in the tube room is hard—we are getting a reputation as a bad place to work. Summer is over, and the problem is over until next year.

Sample Solution 1

Date:	October 12, 19—
To:	Jennifer M. Kirkland, Operations Vice President
From:	Arnold M. Morgan, Production Supervisor
Subject:	Request for Air-Conditioning the Tube Room

*   Quoted from Ray Considine and Murray Raphel, *The Great Brain Robbery* (Pasadena, CA: The Great Brain Robbery, 1981), 95.

Please put air-conditioning in the tube room. This past summer, two-thirds of our employees quit because it was so hot. It's not fair that they should work in unbearable temperatures when management sits in air-conditioned comfort.

I propose that we solve this problem by air-conditioning the tube room to bring down the temperature to 78°.

Insulating and air-conditioning the tube room would cost $500,000. Please approve this request promptly.

Sample Solution 2

Date: October 12, 19—

To: Jennifer M. Kirkland, Operations Vice President

From: Arnold M. Morgan, Production Supervisor *A. M. M.*

Subject: Improving Summer Productivity

Nakamura forfeited a possible $186,000 in profits last summer due to a 17% drop in productivity. That's not unusual: this plant has a history of low summer productivity. But we can reverse the trend and bring summer productivity in line with the rest of the year's.

The problem starts in the tube room. Due to high turnover and reduced efficiency from workers who are new on the job, we just don't make as many TV tubes as we do during the rest of the year. And when we don't have tubes, we can't make TV sets.

Both the high turnover and reduced efficiency are due to the unbearable heat in the tube room. Temperatures in the tube room average 25° over the outside temperature. During the summer, when work starts at 8, it's already 85° in the tube room. By 11:30, it's at least 105°. On six days last summer, it hit 120°. When the temperatures are that high, we may be violating OSHA regulations.

Production workers are always standing, moving, or carrying 20-pound TV tubes. When temperatures hit 90°, they slow down. When no relief is in sight, many of them quit.

We replaced 24 of the 36 employees in the tube room this summer. When someone quits, it takes an average of five days to find and train a replacement; during that time, the trainee produces nothing. For another five days, the new person can work at only half speed. And even "full speed" in the summer is only 90% of what we expect the rest of the year.

Here's where our losses come from:
    Normal production = 50 units/person/day (upd)

Loss due to turnover:	
Loss of 24 workers for 5 days	6,000 units
24 at ½ pace for 5 days	3,000 units
Total loss due to turnover	9,000 units
Loss due to reduced efficiency:	
Loss of 5 upd × 12 workers × 10 days	600 units
Loss of 5 upd × 36 × 50 days	9,000 units
Total loss due to reduced efficiency	9,600 units
Total loss	18,600 units

According to the accounting department, Nakamura makes a net profit of $10 on every TV set we sell. And, as you know, with the boom in TV sales, we sell every set we make. Those 18,600 units we don't produce are costing us $186,000 a year.

Based on Ray Considine and Murray Raphel, *The Great Brain Robbery* (Pasadena, CA: The Great Brain Robbery, 1981), 95–96.

Creative Response to an Objection, III*

Jim Young sold apples by direct mail order. One year, a hail storm just before the harvest bruised the apples.

At first, the obstacle appeared insuperable. For years, his selling point had been that these apples looked as good as they tasted.

But Jim was able to turn the disadvantage into an advantage.

He knew that cold weather (partially responsible for the hail storm) improves the flavor of ripening apples. So he filled the orders, inserting a note in each box:

> Note the hail marks which have caused minor skin blemishes in some of these apples. They are proof of their growth at a high mountain altitude where the sudden chills from hail storms help firm the flesh, develop natural sugars, and give these apples their incomparable flavor.

Not one customer asked for a refund. In fact, the next year, some people wrote on their orders, "Send the hail-marked apples if possible."

In Arab Countries, Deadlines Can Kill Your Request*

The mere mention of a deadline to an Arab is like waving a red flag in front of a bull. In his culture, your emphasis on a deadline has the emotional effect on him that his backing you into a corner and threatening you with a club would have on you.

One effect of this conflict of unconscious habit patterns is that hundreds of American-owned radio sets are lying on the shelves of Arab radio repair shops, untouched. The Americans made the serious cross-cultural error of asking to have the repair completed by a certain time.

How do you cope with this? How does the Arab get another Arab to do anything? Every culture has its own ways of bringing pressure to get results. The usual Arab way is one which Americans avoid as "bad manners." It is needling.

An Arab businessman whose car broke down explained it this way:

First, I go to the garage and tell the mechanic what is wrong with my car. I wouldn't want to give him the idea that I didn't know. After that, I leave the car and walk around the block. When I come back to the garage, I ask him if he has started to work yet. On my way home for lunch I stop in and ask him how things are going. When I go back to the office I stop by again. In the evening, I return and peer over his shoulder for awhile. If I didn't keep this up, he'd be off working on someone else's car.

Bringing down the temperature to 78° (the lowest allowed under federal guidelines) from the present summer average of 112° will require an investment of $500,000 to insulate and air-condition the tube room. Extra energy costs for the air-conditioning will run about $30,000 a year. We'll get our investment back in less than three years. Once the investment is recouped, we'll be making an additional $150,000 a year—all without buying additional equipment or hiring additional workers.

By installing the insulation and air-conditioning this fall, we can take advantage of lower off-season rates. Please authorize the Purchasing Department to request bids for the system. Then, next summer, our productivity can be at an all-time high.

Discussion of Sample Solutions

Solution 1 is unacceptable. By making the request in the subject line and the first paragraph, the writer invites a *no* before giving all the arguments. The writer does nothing to counter the objections that any manager will have to spending a great deal of money. By presenting the issue in terms of fairness, the writer produces defensiveness rather than creating a common ground. The writer doesn't use details or emotional appeal to show that the problem is indeed serious. The writer asks for fast action but doesn't show why the reader should act now to solve a problem that won't occur again for eight months.

Solution 2 is an effective persuasive message. The writer chooses a positive subject line. The opening sentence is negative, catching the reader's attention. However, the paragraph makes it clear that the memo offers a solution to the problem. The problem is spelled out in detail. Emotional impact is created by taking the reader through the day as the temperature rises. The solution is presented impersonally. There are no *I*'s in the memo.

The memo stresses reader benefits: the savings that will result once the investment is recovered. The last paragraph tells the reader exactly what to do and links prompt action to a reader benefit. The memo ends with a positive picture of the problem solved.

SUMMARY OF KEY POINTS

- The primary purposes in a persuasive message are to have the reader act, to provide enough information so that the reader knows exactly what to do, to overcome any objections which might prevent or delay action. Secondary purposes are to build a good image of the writer and the writer's organization, to cement a good relationship between the writer and reader, and to reduce or eliminate future correspondence on the same subject.

- **Areas of acceptance** are positions which the audience would easily accept. **Areas of rejection** are positions which the audience will not consider. **Areas of noncommitment** are positions which are neither immediately acceptable or unacceptable.

- **Ego-involvement** is the emotional commitment the audience has to its position. Readers have a **vested interest** in something if they benefit directly from keeping things as they are.

*   Quoted from Edward T. Hall and William Foote White, "Intercultural Communications: A Guide to Men of Action," *Human Organization* 19, no. 1 (Spring 1960): 9.

- Use the persuasive strategy your organization prefers.
- Use a direct approach and the direct request pattern when
  - The audience's initial position is positive or neutral.
  - Your request falls into the audience's area of acceptance.
  - The audience has no emotional feelings about the subject.

- Use an indirect approach and the problem-solving pattern when
  - The audience's initial position is neutral or negative.
  - Your request falls into the audience's area of noncommitment or rejection.
  - The audience has low or moderate emotional feelings about the subject.
  - You have good arguments to support your position.
  - You can counter most of the audience's objections.

- **Credibility** is the audience's response to you as the source of the message. You can build credibility by being factual, specific, and reliable.
- In a direct request, consider asking in the first paragraph for the information or service you want. Give readers all the information they will need to act on your request. In the last paragraph, tell readers exactly what you want them to do.
- Organize a problem-solving persuasive message in this way:
  1. Catch the reader's interest by mentioning a common ground.
  2. Define the problem you both share (which your request will solve).
  3. Explain the solution to the problem.
  4. Show that any negative elements (cost, time, etc.) are outweighed by the advantages.
  5. Summarize any additional benefits of the solution.
  6. Tell the reader exactly what you want him or her to do.

- In a direct request, put either the subject of the request or a question in the subject line. Do not put the request in the subject line of a problem-solving persuasive message. Instead, use a reader benefit or a common ground. Use a positive or neutral subject line even when the first paragraph will be negative.
- Use one or more of the following strategies to counter objections:
  - Specify how much time or money is required.
  - Put the time or money in the context of the benefits it brings.
  - Show that money spent now will save money in the long run.
  - Show that doing as you ask will benefit some group the reader identifies with or some cause the reader supports.
  - Show the reader that the sacrifice is necessary to achieve a larger, more important goal to which he or she is committed.
  - Show that the advantages as a group outnumber or outweigh the disadvantages as a group.
  - Turn the disadvantage into an opportunity.

A Comparison of French and U.S. Requests*

French business letters give the problem or the reason for the request before the request itself.

Most French buyers seem to care most about quality; getting a bargain isn't important.

Since the French government sets prices, the individual company doesn't have to justify a specific price. However, answers to inquiries may not specify the price of products. After sending advertising literature, the sales representative brings up price in a face-to-face meeting with the customer.

French requests are less direct. Unlike U.S. business letters, French letters don't tell readers what to do.

Are You Doing the Right Thing?†

Pressures of business sometimes create an environment where people think that anything goes. To be sure that you're doing the right thing, ask the following questions:

- How would you define the problem if you stood on the other side of the fence?
- Before you act, can you discuss the problem with the people who will be affected?
- Whom will your action hurt?
- How would you feel if your action were known to your boss, your CEO, your family, or to society as a whole?
- What symbolic message will people get if they understand your action? If they misunderstand it?

---

* Based on Iris I. Varner, "A Comparison of American and French Business Communication," Association for Business Communication International Convention, Atlanta, GA, October 15–17, 1987.

† Based on Laura L. Nash, "Ethics without the Sermon," *Executive Success: Making It in Management*, ed. Eliza G. Collins (New York: John Wiley, 1983), 497.

- To encourage readers to act promptly, set a deadline. Show that the time limit is real, that acting now will save time or money, or that delaying action will cost more.
- Use the analysis questions from Chapter 2 to analyze persuasive situations.

NOTES

1. J. C. Mathes and Dwight W. Stevenson, *Designing Technical Reports: Writing for Audiences in Organizations* (Indianapolis: Bobbs-Merrill, 1979), 18–19.

2. James Suchan and Ron Dulek, "Toward a Better Understanding of Reader Analysis," *Journal of Business Communication* 25, no. 2 (Spring 1988): 40.

3. Frances Harrington, "Formulaic Patterns Versus Pressures of Circumstances: A Rhetoric of Business Situations," Conference on College Composition and Communication, New Orleans, LA, March 17–19, 1986.

4. See John Nathan, "In Search of Excellence: The Film" (Waltham, MA: Nathan/Tyler Productions, 1985), 9–14.

5. An earlier draft of this problem and analysis appeared in Francis W. Weeks and Kitty O. Locker, *Business Writing Problems and Cases* (Champaign, IL: Stipes, 1980), 78–81.

EXERCISES AND PROBLEMS FOR CHAPTER 14

14–1 REQUESTING INFORMATION ABOUT A SELLER'S POLICIES

Going through some old papers, you find the following ad that has been torn out of a magazine:

THIS CHAIR DOESN'T JUST SIT THERE.

For added beauty or added guests, these stylish, wood-framed fold-away chairs with a glossy walnut finish and soft cane backs and seats will have you sitting pretty on those many occasions when extra chairs are essential. And when extra room is needed, these handsome chairs don't just sit there but conveniently fold away to just 2-$\frac{1}{2}$" deep.

They're just the right size: 31" tall back and 14" × 16" seat. And just the right price: only $40 each, plus delivery, but when ordering two or more you save $5.00 per chair at only $35 each.

_____ Please send me 1 (one) chair for $40 (#A5607), plus $10.95 shipping.

_____ Please send me _____ chairs at the savings price of $35 per chair, plus a total of $10.95 shipping for the entire order.

If delivered in Texas please add 5% tax.

_____ Check or money order enclosed. Charge to my:

___ VISA ___ MasterCard ___ American Express

Account number:

_____

Expiration Date: _____

Signature: _____

(required for credit cards)

FREE: Your order entitles you to a full year of exciting Trifles catalogues.

Name _____

Address _____

City _____ ST ___ Zip _____

Mail to: **TRIFLES,** P.O. BOX 819075, Dept. MA282, Dallas, Texas 75381-9075

You'd like some extra chairs. You'd be willing to pay $35 a chair if it looks as good in "real life" as it does in the picture in the ad. But you don't want to buy four chairs and then be stuck with them if they aren't satisfactory. You don't even want to buy one chair now and three more later; that way, you'd pay double shipping charges (for the two orders) and $5 more for the first chair, besides being out the money for the first chair if you didn't like it. The ad says nothing about a guarantee. Can you get your money back if you don't like them? What about shipping charges (both ways)? You don't

remember where or when the ad appeared. If it was some time ago, the price may have gone up, or Trifles may no longer carry the chairs.

Write a letter to Trifles to find out.

14–2 REQUESTING A COPY OF A COMPANY'S ANNUAL AND 10-K REPORTS

You're investigating a company, either as a potential investment or as a potential employer, and want a copy of its annual and 10-K reports. Pick a company that interests you and write to its main office to request the reports.

14–3 GETTING THE FULL HONORARIUM

You're in considerable demand as an after-dinner speaker in your region. Six months ago, Elizabeth Siehl, the president of the local Chamber of Commerce, wrote asking you to speak at the Chamber's annual dinner for an honorarium of $750. You frequently get more than that, but you felt the Chamber talk might lead to more engagements, so you agreed. The dinner was last week.

Today, you received the following letter:

It gives me great pleasure to send you the honorarium for your excellent talk at the annual dinner of the Chamber of Commerce. We very much appreciate your taking time from a busy schedule to talk to us.

Sincerely,

Jay Belknap

Jay Belknap
Secretary-Treasurer

A check for $500 was enclosed. Write a letter requesting the full amount.

Hints:
- To whom should your letter go? Will you be in a stronger position if you cash the current check, keep it without cashing it, or return it?
- What else should go in your letter?

14–4 PERSUADING AN INSTRUCTOR TO ADMIT YOU INTO A CLASS

You've been closed out of a class you want to take. On the first day of class, the instructor finally says to all the students who are trying to get in, "I'll admit two extra students. If you want to get into the class, write me a letter explaining why I should give one of the spaces to you. Don't write more than a page. Give me your letter tomorrow; I'll announce my decision the following day."

For this assignment, you may use any popular course on campus, whether or not you have been closed out of it. Anything you say about yourself must be true.

As your instructor directs,

a. Assume that you're trying to get into a class that your business communication instructor teaches. Use your analysis in 6–6b to construct a persuasive letter.

b. Assume that you're trying to get into another class on campus. Write a persuasive letter to that instructor.

c. Write a memo to your business communication instructor explaining the pattern of organization, the content, and the strategy you've adopted to convince your reader.

Hints:

*   On what basis will this instructor select two students from all of those who want in? Is there any way you can make the instructor see you as an individual who would make the class more pleasant or more interesting to teach?

*   Deal with any questions or objections the instructor might have: Would another section do as well? Can't you take the course next term? Do you have all the prerequisites?

HANDLING A STICKY RECOMMENDATION

As a caseworker supervisor in the state Department of Public Aid (DPA), you have a dilemma. This letter arrived today:

Arthur Davis, a caseworker in DPA, has applied for a position with the Department of Children and Family Services. On the basis of his application and interview, he is the leading candidate. However, before I offer the job to him, I need a letter of recommendation from his current supervisor.

Could you please let me have your evaluation within a week? We want to fill the position as quickly as possible.

Sincerely,

Jone Shapiro

Jone Shapiro, Director
Department of Children and Family Services

Arthur is a social worker with a college degree, friendly, competent, and thorough, but unproductive. He's good with computers. He set up the categories for the data base program your office relies on. When anyone has a problem with the data base or any other software, Arthur comes to the rescue. However, every other worker handles a case load 7% to 33% higher than Arthur's. You try to assign work fairly, but Arthur takes so long to get things done that you end up transferring cases. Public Aid sees people who need help quickly; they can't wait weeks or months for food and shelter.

You would be delighted to see Arthur leave. You can't fire him: state employees' jobs are secure once they get past the initial six-month probationary period. Because of budget constraints, you can hire new employees only if vacancies are created by resignations. You feel that almost anyone you might hire would be better than Arthur.

If you recommend that Ms. Shapiro hire Arthur, you will be able to hire someone you want. If you recommend that Ms. Shapiro hire someone else, you may be stuck with Arthur for a long time.

As your instructor directs,

a. Write the letter to Ms. Shapiro.

b. Write a memo to your instructor listing the choices you've made and justifying your approach.

Hints:

*   Polarization may make this dilemma more difficult than it needs to be. What are your options? Consciously look for more than two.

*   Is it possible to select facts or to use connotations so that you are truthful but still encourage Ms. Shapiro to hire Arthur? Is it ethical? Is it certain that Ms. Shapiro would find Arthur as unsatisfactory as you do? If you write a strong letter and Arthur doesn't do well at his new job, will your credibility suffer? Why is your credibility important?

14–6 RECOMMENDING A LETTER FORMAT

You offer short courses in business writing for local business people. Today, your mail includes the following letter from a participant in the last session.

Dear [Your Name]:

I was very interested in what you said about a standard format improving a company's image. Right now, I think every typist in my company uses a different format. Our letters look pretty bad. I want to tell people to use a standard format. Of the ones you discussed, the block one sounds best. It eliminates the useless salutation and close. The typist would save time because it would not be necessary to set tabs. And in busy periods typists from one department could work in another department since everyone would use the same format.

Do you agree that this format would be best for my company? We write mostly to customers and suppliers. Most of our letters already have an invoice number or a reference number or some other subject line.

Sincerely,

Joe Kamos

Joe Kamos
President, Kamos Electronics

Kamos seems to be confusing block and AMS Simplified letter format. Simplified format does save time: 10.9 % of the time needed to write a short 96-word letter. The savings is a smaller percent on longer letters. Some of the benefits he cites would apply to any standardized letter format. And it's ironic that he criticizes the "useless salutation and close" but uses them in his letter to you.

Answer Kamos's letter. Explain block and simplified letter formats, recommend one for him, and justify your choice.

Hints:

- See Appendix A for a review of letter formats. Since Kamos did hear your lecture, you need to present your explanation of the two formats and their advantages tactfully. Cost may not be the only consideration. Is one format easier for the reader to use? What about goodwill?
- Use the format you recommend to Kamos for your letter.

14–7 CHANGING HOTEL REGISTRATION INFORMATION

You're planning to go to this year's SWFAD convention. SWFAD, which stands for South West Federation of Administrative Disciplines, attracts up to 12,000 people. Room reservations are to be mailed into the SWFAD Housing Bureau, 1575 Johnson Boulevard, Suite D, Houston, TX 77058.

Three weeks ago, you sent in a reservation for a single room for March 24–26, indicating that the Heritage Hotel was your first choice. To guarantee the reservation past 6 P.M., you gave your Discovery number, even though the card was about to expire. A week ago, you received

a confirmation for your reservation: Heritage Hotel, March 24–26, single room, convention rate.

Today, you learned that a friend was also going to SWFAD for the first two days of the conference. The two of you want to share a room those two nights. Your friend expects to arrive early in the afternoon of the 24th, but you still want to guarantee the room. You want to stay in the Heritage, not be moved to another hotel; you want a room with two beds. In the meantime, your new Discovery card has come; the expiration date is this month, next year.

Write to the Housing Bureau to make the changes in your reservation. Assume that the reservation number is the first five letters of your last name followed by your five-digit zip code. Supply the name of the friend who will be sharing the room with you.

14–8 REQUESTING REIMBURSEMENT FOR EXPENSES

You've had a number of office visits for second interviews. Each company will need your social security number to reimburse you for your expenses; each requires copies of your receipts for all expenses.

Last week you visited the offices of the three companies you're most interested in: Business Communication Systems (BCS) in San Jose, CA; Thorpe Industries in Denver, CO; and Macoby and Byrne Consultants, Inc. (M&B), in Chicago, IL. [Assume that all three are considering you for a job that would be appropriate for your major.]

You charged the plane tickets on your VISA card: $475 to San Jose, $190 from San Jose to Denver, $210 from Denver to Chicago, and $290 from Chicago home.

In San Jose, your host, Gail Perkins, met you at the airport, took you to the hotel and prepaid the bill, and took you out to dinner at a nice restaurant. She picked you up the next morning to drive you to BCS's offices.

During the day at BCS, you had a long talk with Elaine Bacon, who would be your immediate supervisor if you were hired. You also had lunch with Gail and the vice president in charge of your division, talked to the personnel office about benefits, met some younger people in your division, and took a test that BCS requires of all employees. In your last meeting of the day, Elaine offered you a job. "I know you've got two more interviews, so I won't press you to decide today. We really want you. If you get a better offer from someone else, let me know: we'll match it." You really felt good about BCS when you left, in a taxi, to get to the airport. You paid the taxi bill ($14, plus a $2 tip) and asked the cab driver to sign a note saying you'd paid (you knew you'd need a receipt).

You flew to Denver and took a shuttle bus to your hotel ($6; you got a receipt). You put the room on your

VISA card: $128 plus $12.16 tax. You ate at one of the restaurants in the hotel and charged the bill to your room (so it would go on your credit card too). Dinner was $21.78, plus a $3.25 tip. The total bill from this hotel on your credit card: $165.19.

The next morning, you took a taxi to Thorpe. Total bill: $7.50. You forgot to get a receipt. Roger Kotlar, the man who'd be your supervisor and the person who was your host during the day, gave you a hard sell about the advantages of Thorpe and Denver. "We're growing, and you could grow with us. You can go further, faster here than you could anywhere else." As he drove you to the airport, he began to discuss specific salary and benefit figures. When you mentioned that BCS had a better benefit package, Roger said, "Well, benefits are standard for all employees. But we could make it up to you in some other way. Let me see what we could do." He handed you a large packet of information about Thorpe which you read on the plane. The material supported Roger's claim: Thorpe was positioning itself to become a market leader. It did seem that you could advance faster at Thorpe than at BCS.

In Chicago, Brian Bartlett met you at the airport. Brian would be your boss at M&B. He and his wife, Krista Jorgenson, took you out for dinner. Brian and Krista pointed out that Chicago was great for two-career couples and said that M&B was committed to helping a spouse find a job when a M&B employee was transferred. When Brian took you to your hotel, he charged the bill directly to M&B.

The next day, you had a formal interview with Brian, talked to his boss, met some people who'd been hired in the last two years, took a test, and met the Director of Education and Training. M&B has the most elaborate tuition-reimbursement plan of the three companies, as well as an active in-house training program. In the last interview of the day, Brian made you a formal job offer, at a salary less than that offered by BCS and Thorpe, but with a benefit package that was the best of the three. You said you'd let him know within three weeks. That evening, two of the younger people at M&B, Susan Dysan and Bob Matuka, took you out for a quick dinner and then to a Chicago pro game. The next morning, you paid for breakfast at the hotel restaurant ($7.80 + $1.20 tip), took a shuttle bus from the hotel to the airport ($8), and flew home.

You want to sit down and do a full comparison/contrast of all three companies. But you haven't had time to do that yet. You still have two weeks left of the three weeks each company gave you to make a decision. However, your VISA bill will be arriving all too soon. If you get reimbursed right away, you can pay the bill in full when it comes.

Assignment: Write a letter to your host at ONE of the companies. Addresses are

BCS: 4118 Industrial Park, San Jose, CA 95192
Thorpe: 2930 Henry Avenue, Denver, CO 80236
M&B: 418 E. 79th Street, Chicago, IL 60310

Hints:

- Thank the host for his or her hospitality. Use specifics so that you sound sincere. Cement the good impression you made at the interview. Show that you paid attention; mention connections between what you've already done and what you could do for that company. Use the names of people in the company you met. (See Chapter 29 for more specific advice on follow-up letters after interviews.)

- Don't make any promises since all three companies are still in the running.

- Ask for your money. Why do you want to be reimbursed quickly? Be sure to check your arithmetic. Asking for too little shortchanges you; asking for too much is unethical. Getting the arithmetic wrong also suggests that you're careless.

- If you write to M&B, pick a pro football, basketball, hockey, or baseball game, depending on the season and your interests.

14–9 PERSUADING A DOCTOR TO SEND A REPORT

You're a new attorney at a legal aid office. Legal aid serves clients whose incomes and assets fall below levels established by the federal government; services are free to the client.

Your first case is to represent Ruth O'Neill, a frail-looking, 59-year-old woman with an eighth-grade education. Ms. O'Neill has done manual labor all her life. Last year she was hurt and had to stop working. She applied for disability benefits from the Supplemental Security Income (SSI) program of the federal government's Social Security Administration. Her application was denied on the grounds that the available medical evidence did not prove she was disabled.

Ms. O'Neill wants to appeal that decision. To help her win her case (a Social Security administrative law judge rules on appeals), you need evidence from her doctor that she is indeed disabled as Social Security defines the term. An experienced attorney pulls out this letter from the files and suggests that you "fill in the blanks."

I am representing _____ in her attempt to have her application for Supplemental Security Income (SSI) benefits approved. Ms. _____'s application has initially been denied, since Social Security says she is not disabled, and she has appealed the denial to an Administrative Law Judge.

A person can qualify for SSI benefits if she is unable to engage in substantial gainful employment by reason of any medically determinable or verifiable physical or mental impairment which can be expected to last for 12 months, has lasted for 12 months, or can result in death. The initial inquiry is whether an impairment, or combination of impairments, is severe. Severity is determined by whether the impairment or combination of impairments significantly limit an individual's physical or mental capacity to perform basic work-related functions. If a person has a severe impairment but cannot be found disabled based on medical considerations alone, the claimant's age, work experience, and education are considered. The claimant always has the burden of proving her disability.

I understand that you have been treating Ms. _____ for back and other problems. Would you please complete the enclosed medical evaluation form. You will notice that among other things it asks your evaluation of Ms. _____'s lifting ability. It is very likely, that if Ms. _____ can only lift objects up to 10 lbs., she will be considered disabled by law. This evaluation form is only a guide, meant to make a report easier to write, so you may choose to use another format if you prefer. Enclosed is an authorization signed by Ms. _____ authorizing the release of information to me.

Thank you for your assistance. If you have any problems in completing the form, please advise me, since your evaluation is very important to the success of Ms. _____'s claim.

You know that this is a terrible letter. It has no you-attitude; the request is buried in the third paragraph; the long second paragraph reproduces the legalistic definition almost word-for-word; the layout is poor; the letter doesn't tell the reader when you must have the response.

You cannot offer to pay the doctor for the time it will take to fill out the form; probably Ms. O'Neill's doctor, like many physicians, is already overworked. So you must be persuasive—and take as little of the doctor's time as possible.

Write a letter that will achieve your goals. You will enclose a copy of a medical evaluation form your office has designed and a copy of Ms. O'Neill's authorization to her doctor to release the information to Legal Aid.

14–10 PERSUADING YOUR EMPLOYER TO CHANGE A COMPUTER PROGRAM

You're a new textbook sales representative. To try to persuade professors to adopt the books published by your company, you send examination copies to people who teach the relevant course at each school. Then, as much as you can, you visit individual professors to talk with them about the books.

Your company has a computerized system for mailing out examination copies. You send in the name of each instructor and the areas he or she teaches. Then, every time a new book in those areas comes out, the professor automatically gets a copy. For example, someone who teaches business communication, business ethics, and management would be sure to get the new books your firm publishes in those three areas.

Two months ago, you made your first call on the math department of one of the junior colleges in your district. The department chairperson agreed to talk to you (to your initial pleasure: often people are too busy to see you). It turned out she had a complaint.

"Your company is sending books to people who've been gone for years. One of them is dead. Others have left to go back to graduate school or to take other jobs. I hate to throw away the books when they're so expensive. And I won't sell them to used-book stores; I don't think that's ethical. But we don't have any place to store them, and we certainly don't need all these extra copies. Sometimes, we can give the books to new people who aren't on your list yet, but often the books are a real nuisance. Please clean up your mailing list so it has only current staff. If you'll just phone every fall, the secretary will give you a list of current staff."

Her point seemed reasonable. But when you went to your supervisor the next time you were in the office, you learned that you *can't* take names out of the system. A mechanism for changing someone's address and school affiliation exists, but there's no way to remove a name completely. "That's absurd," you said. "Maybe," said your boss, "but that's the way it works."

You're not a computer expert, but you know people write the programs and presumably people can change them. You have no idea how complicated or costly the change would be. It's possible that an outside consultant would have to be hired.

Write a memo to the president of the company, Timothy Firebaugh, urging that the computer program be rewritten to make it more responsive to the realities of academic life. The address of the home office is 93 Hillsdale Road, Boston, MA 02155.

Hints:
- This memo is going to someone who is much higher in the organization than you are. Does he already know who you are? What image of yourself do you want to create in your memo? What tone is appropriate?
- What kinds of arguments will the president find convincing? Will he care about the cost of examination copies? About used book sales? About service to faculty?

- What exactly do you want him to do? (He's not going to rewrite the program himself.)

14–11 ASKING FOR VOLUNTEERS*

You have an executive position with one of the major employers in town. (Pick a business, nonprofit organization, or government office you know something about.) The phone rings. It's a good friend who teaches at a local community college. After some chit-chat, your friend gets down to the purpose of the call.

"I wonder if you could help me with an assignment I want to give my students."

(You wince. You don't want to have to say *no*, but . . .) "What exactly are you asking me to do?"

"Well, I want each of them to interview someone who's doing what they hope to do someday. You know, information interviews to find out what a job involves, what preparation is needed. Our career placement office does a good job, but there's just no substitute for going into a real office and talking to someone who really does the work. I also want each of them to have a job interview."

"Wait a minute." (You say when you can get a word in.) "If there's a job opening, everyone has to go through the normal process. I can't make exceptions for your students."

"Oh, that's not what I mean. I just want fake interviews, for practice, but I want them to be by a real business person because you'll know what questions to ask. If students wear suits to class, they don't get the same practice that they'll get if they go to a real business, even though they'll know the interviews are just for practice and don't guarantee anything."

(Mentally figuring up how much time this is going to take, you decide to let your friend down gently.) "How many students do you have?"

"Seventy-five: three classes of 25 each."

(And you're supposed to give each of them two interviews? No way!) "Well, it's certainly a worthwhile assignment, but I don't have time to talk to that many students. Maybe—"

(Your friend interrupts.) "I don't want you to talk to anybody, unless you want to. What I want you to do is ask your people if *they'd* be willing to talk to students. If I write to them, they'll ignore the request because they don't know me. But if you ask them and make it clear that it's OK for them to take work time to do this, some of them might."

(What a relief. But you still see problems.) "Well, I could do that. But I'm not going to force anybody. Even if some people were willing to talk to three or four students apiece, we still wouldn't be able to do everybody—you're talking about 150 interviews. And

depending on who volunteered, we might not be able to cover all the specialties your students are majoring in."

"That's OK. I'll call some other places, too. Just send me a list of the names and phone numbers of your people who will do it. I'll need their jobs and the days they're free so I can match them up with the students. Or what times—they may not be free all day, but each interview would only need 20 or 30 minutes."

(You're making notes.) "People don't have fixed schedules the way students do. Why don't we just get names, the number of interviews they're willing to do, and the job. Then let the student call to schedule the interview. That will be good practice for your students, too—teach them telephone skills."

"OK. Thanks a lot. Could you get your memo out right away? We only have eight weeks left in the term, so I need to know right away so I can tell students who to call so they can schedule the interviews."

"I'll write a memo today. But I need to give people a week or so to get back to me. It will be 10 days before I get back to you."

"OK. Thanks a lot. This is really going to be great."

Write the memo to all employees asking them to volunteer, right now while you're thinking about it.

14–12 PERSUADING A UNIVERSITY TO CHANGE ITS COMPUTER PROGRAM FOR REGISTRATION

At State University, students fill out preregistration forms in the middle of one term for the next term. The student requests are matched to class offerings by computer. For some classes, students must have junior standing. The computer program for registration at State, however, does not check class standing before filling course requests. On the first day of class, professors are supposed to tell any freshmen and sophomores to leave the class.

Many professors think that the Registrar's office should screen out ineligible students. "I shouldn't have to take my class time up with clerical work." "I feel that I'm embarrassing the student." Not all faculty enforce the requirement.

Students have varying opinions about the requirement for junior standing. Juniors and seniors who are closed out of courses would like to see the requirement enforced. But sophomores who get into courses want to stay there. "If I can do the work, why shouldn't I be in the course?" Sometimes students were not aware of the requirement when they registered. No one is pleased to learn, after most classes are full, that he or she must try to pick up another course.

You're the Registrar and have been asked to revise the registration system so that the computer registers

*Inspired by an assignment used by Judith L. Bleicher, Lincolnland Community College.

students for classes only if they have the required class standing. Before taking action or refusing to take action, you want more information.

Write a memo to your assistant, Sarah Sims, asking her to gather the data you need.

Hints:

- You are not asking Sarah to recommend, just to inform you. Specify the questions to which you need answers.

- The cost of making the change is one factor on which you'll base your decisions. What information can Sarah give you about personnel and time needed to reprogram to help you calculate the cost? Would you approve the change if it were very expensive but if the current consequences were very serious? What kind of information would tell you how serious the problem is? Is the number of students who are closed out of classes the only factor?

- Your office puts together the information about courses that students use to register. When Sarah checks this, what should she look for?

- When do you need this information? Why? Should Sara drop other duties to finish this project quickly? If she fits it in around other work, do you want progress reports?

- What if a department changes the prerequisite for a course? Can a professor gives a student who lacks the prerequisite permission to take the course? How will you register last-term sophomores who may sign up for junior-level courses before you know whether they've passed all their classes and become juniors? If people can think of procedures for these exceptions, a programmer can write them into the system. Do you want Sarah to try to come up with some ideas?

14–13 WRITING PSYCHOLOGICAL DESCRIPTION

Everyone needs to exercise. But specific groups also have more specific needs.

a. Identify a need not shared by all the other groups which might motivate each of the following groups to join a particular health club.
   1. Single adults.
   2. Married adults.
   3. Parents with small children.
   4. Parents with children in school.
   5. Adults who work outside the home.
   6. Adults who work at home.
   7. Good athletes.
   8. Poor athletes.

b. Identify the problems, doubts, or fears which might make each of these groups reluctant or unable to join a health club.

c. Identify a program or facility that a health club could offer to meet that need. (Not all needs could be met at all health clubs.)

d. Develop each of the benefits using psychological description.

14–14 PERSUADING NEW MEMBERS TO JOIN A HEALTH CLUB

Note: the following problem specifies a weight-exercise club. Ask your instructor for permission if you'd rather use a different kind of organization: a tennis-racquetball club, a private ice rink, a YMCA, a gymnastics club for kids.

You are the executive director of the Central City Exercise Club, which offers members Nautilus weight machines, free weights, and aerobic exercise classes. In addition, you have showers, lockers, dressing areas, and saunas. Every year, many members fail to renew their memberships. Some move away, some join other health clubs, and some abandon their exercise programs.

You urgently need more capital but can't raise your dues ($400 a year; individual memberships only) since competition among health clubs in your town is intense. To raise money, you need to persuade more people to join.

As your instructor directs,

a. Write a form letter which will go out to prospective new members.

b. Write to members who have not renewed persuading them to renew.

c. Prepare a reply coupon to accompany the letter.

d. Write a memo to your instructor identifying your target audience and analyzing its needs.

Hints:

- Stress reader benefits: what do you offer that is better than exercising at home to a record or videotape? Develop at least three to five of these in detail using psychological description. Most people want to be healthy and attractive, but your letter will need to overcome inertia to make people join.

- Think about the target audience you've chosen. Be sure your benefits will motivate them and overcome the fears or objections they

may have. Past dropouts may feel like fail-
ures; persuade them it's not too late to begin
to exercise again.

- Keep your reader benefits reasonable. It is
  credible that you could hire a professional to
  give lessons, but not that you could afford
  Jane Fonda or Arnold Schwarzenegger. If in
  doubt about whether a benefit is credible, ask
  your instructor.

14–15 PERSUADING BUSINESSES TO ADOPT A SCHOOL

As superintendent of schools, you want to start an adopt-a-school program. A business that adopts a school won't have any specific guidelines to follow. You want representatives from the company, the school, and the students themselves to get together to figure how the school and the company can benefit from each other.

In other towns, businesses have sent employees as speakers to talk about jobs and job interviews; purchased computers, musical instruments, and sports equipment; hosted postprom parties; donated outdated equipment to schools; hired teachers during the summer; and encouraged students to bring in projects for employees to see during lunch hours. At least two businesses have promised to pay the college tuition of elementary school students when they enter college. Schools have sent their bands and choirs to perform at company events.

As your instructor directs,
a. Write a form letter to the CEOs of businesses in your community, urging each of them to adopt a school. You may focus on one level of school (e.g., high school) or point out the needs of schools at every level.

b. Write a letter to one CEO urging him or her to adopt a school.

c. Construct a script for a face-to-face meeting or a telephone call urging a CEO to adopt a school.

Hints:
- What are the strengths and weaknesses of schools in your district? Do students have access to computers, to musical instruments, to sports equipment? What percent of students graduate from high school? What percent of graduates go on for further education? Can students who wish to enter the job market immediately after high school do so easily, or is unemployment high?

- What specific problems do students face? Poverty? Violence? Drinking? Drugs? Teenage pregnancy?

- Do businesses in your community have an ample supply of workers? What skills are in demand? What is the labor market like? What are businesses' primary complaints about the high school graduates who apply for work with them?

- How much do you need to personalize each letter?

- What exactly do you want the reader to do as a result of your letter? Agree in principle? Specify a school to adopt? Should the reader contact the school directly or contact you? Should you recommend a specific school to a specific company or present several and let the company choose one?

Handling Difficult Persuasive Situations

QUESTIONS

- Why is persuasion sometimes so difficult?
- What strategies are possible if you can't wait for a major change?
- Will threatening people get them to do what you want?
- Is criticizing people the way to make them change?
- How can Toulmin logic help you write effective persuasive messages?
- Is persuasion cold-hearted manipulation?

You can't always get what you want,
You can't always get what you want,
You can't always get what you want,
    But if you try sometimes
    You just might find
You get what you need.
                The Rolling Stones
                "You Can't Always Get
                What You Want," 1969

E
ven if you follow all the advice in Chapter 14, you won't always get what you want. Some persuasive situations are so difficult that complete success is impossible. Your audience's initial position is negative; people are highly committed to their position; doing as you ask threatens their comfort, security, and self-images. However, if you understand the situation and your audience, if you use tight logic and control your tone, you can sometimes get what you really need.

Three sample situations show how difficult persuasion can be:

• People tune out messages they don't want to hear.

   An apartment manager sends out messages several times a year urging residents to pay their rent on time, to take their trash out to the dumpster, and to obey the "no pets" rules. The manager tries everything from pleading to insults, but nothing works.

   Many people won't follow rules if they think the rules are silly or intrusive, or if they have a grudge against the rule-giver. (How many apartment residents think the landlord is a good guy?) Punishment has only a brief effect; people go back to more convenient habits as soon as they think it's safe. Because the apartment manager's messages are unpleasant, most residents ignore them: "Oh, the manager's just spouting off again." That way, they can do what they want to do without disturbing their images of themselves as reasonable people.

• People are reluctant to say *yes* if doing so requires them to admit they've been wrong all along.

   The Traffic Manager in one company wants to buy trucks rather than continuing to lease them. His figures show that the change would save the company $10 million over the first three years, and an additional $1 million a year after that.

   Why isn't this an open-and-shut case? The company is owned by another company. Its vice president, who has to approve the proposal, is the former president of the subsidiary. The Traffic Manager has to write a memo that convinces the reader without saying "you should have made this change years ago."

• People deny realities that are too much for them to cope with.

A lab worker becomes infected with the AIDS virus. A government report shows that if lab workers follow safety procedures—if they wear gowns and gloves, and perhaps masks and goggles—they'll be safe. But workers don't follow the procedures.

When the risk is so great, why don't workers protect themselves? Perhaps because the thought of contracting AIDS is too scary. Many people who deal every day with something life-threatening practice **denial:** they persuade themselves that nothing will happen to them. Taking precautions seems to make the risk too real.

Scenarios like these make persuasion seem hopeless. But even a brief view of history shows that people can change—and can even make major changes. Societies can reject racism and sexism. Companies can abandon unprofitable products and follow the market into new ventures. People can change their minds even about such deeply held beliefs as sexual behavior and how to raise their children. Conversions—both religious and secular—do happen.

Some major changes will take years. People have to be persuaded one by one before society as a whole can change. If you want to make major changes in attitudes toward work, toward Communism, or toward the government's role in helping poor people, you'll need many formal and informal messages. And you'll need lots of time.

When you need action quickly, you have two choices:

1. Limit your audience. Go with the people you can persuade and forget about the rest.
2. Try to bring everyone on board.

LIMITING YOUR AUDIENCE

Sometimes you don't need everyone. A political candidate, for example, needs to persuade only enough people to win the election. A shelter for runaway teens doesn't need money from everyone—just enough money to meet the budget.

Figure 15.1 shows a letter that resulted when a company couldn't persuade everyone to respond to a request. Combustion Engineering had decided, as a matter of policy, to favor minority suppliers. Most suppliers ignored its request to let it know their demographic makeup. Suppliers that qualified were happy to respond, but there just weren't reader benefits for those who didn't qualify. But it didn't matter if many—perhaps most—companies didn't respond. Combustion Engineering just needed to hear from the companies it wanted to buy from.

BRINGING EVERYBODY ON BOARD

In some work situations, limited agreement isn't enough. You need widespread compliance to achieve your goal. Some bosses, faced with subordinate resistance, resort to threats. But, as the apartment manager mentioned above found, threats don't work very well. Good audience analysis, effective emotional appeal, and tight logic may save the day.

A Series of Messages Turns A Company Around*

In 1983, the Danly Machine Company was in serious trouble. Its customers were turning to Japanese and German firms charging 25% less. But even with its higher prices, Danly was barely breaking even since its costs were so high.

To regain market share, Danly cut its costs 25%. In nine months, the company changed its corporate culture, increased productivity 37%, and was once again the leading U.S. supplier to the U.S. automotive industry. By 1985, Danly's costs were 32% lower than they had been 18 months earlier.

Communication played a major role in changing attitudes and behavior. The messages in the campaign included

- At least one letter a month from top management to every employee at his or her home giving information about the company and the industry, stressing the importance of cutting costs, and building team spirit.
- Prepaid envelopes and cards, marked "confidential," to allow employees to communicate directly with top management. When people asked questions, they got honest answers.
- A 50-foot banner across a public street between plant buildings saying "WE WANT MORE JOBS IN CICERO NOT TOKYO."
- An active suggestion system on ways to cut costs.
- Speeches by top management to the whole work force and ask-anything-you-want sessions between top management and groups of workers.
- Weekly productivity reports and weekly staff meetings for supervisors.

* Based on Eugene F. Finkin, *Successful Corporate Turnarounds* (Westport, CN: Quorum, 1987), 17–30, 128.

FIGURE 15.1
A REQUEST TO PERSUADE ONLY THOSE WHO WILL DIRECTLY BENEFIT

COMBUSTION ENGINEERING

Is at Least 50%
of Your Business
Owned by Women
or Minorities?

If it is, we want to try to use you as a supplier.

You qualify for this favorable treatment if one of the following
situations applies:

    a. 50% of the business or 51% of the stock is owned by
        women.

    b. 50% of the business or 51% of the stock is owned by
        minority group members: Blacks, Asian Americans, Native
        Americans, or Spanish-surnamed Americans.

Combustion Engineering is committed to affirmative action
programs to prevent discrimination based on race, color, creed,
sex, age, or national origin. We believe that the pursuit of
profit and the pursuit of social goals are compatible. We
try to act affirmatively in hiring and promoting employees.
We also try to act affirmatively in choosing suppliers.

If at least 50% of your company is owned by women or minorities,
please send us written evidence by May 15.

If we don't hear from you, we'll assume that you're not a
minority business.

Sincerely,

Process Automation Business
Combustion Engineering, Inc.

650 Ackerman Road
Post Office Box 02650
Columbus, Ohio 43202-1502

Tel: (614) 261-2000
Fax: (614) 261-2172
Telex: 246675

Why Threats Are Less Effective than Persuasion

A **threat** is a statement—explicit or implied—that someone will be punished if he or she does something. Given the many demands any organization makes of its members, it would be impossible to find appropriate and feasible punishments with which to threaten subordinates for every imaginable error. Even if it were possible, it still wouldn't produce the results we want. As Walter R. Nord has explained, there are six reasons why punishment and threats don't work.[1]

1. **Threats don't produce permanent change.** Everyone obeys the speed limit when a marked police car is in sight; a great many people violate it when no officer is around. No supervisor has the time to monitor the performance of every subordinate every minute of the day. You need to motivate people to do what you want even when you aren't there to check up on them.

2. **Threats won't necessarily produce the action you want.** Suppose that you want people in your office to conserve office supplies. If you embarrass or punish people who take too many felt tip pens or too much paper, they might write fewer reports—hardly the response you'd want!

3. **Threats may make people abandon an action entirely—even in situations where it would be appropriate.** You may feel that workers are wasting time talking around the water fountain, but you do want workers to talk to each other: there are many situations in which co-worker communication is essential.

4. **Threats produce tension.** People who feel threatened put their energies into ego-defense rather than into productive work.

5. **People dislike and avoid anyone who threatens them.** A supervisor who is disliked will find it harder to enlist cooperation and support on the next issue that arises. A supervisor whom subordinates avoid will find it harder both to evaluate their performance and to give them the information or instruction which could make their work more effective.

6. **Threats can provoke counteraggression.** Orders, rules, threats, and nagging are perceived as a reduction of our freedom. As you saw in Chapter 13, **psychological reactance** is the name given to striking back in some way to reestablish a sense of freedom. Getting back at a boss can run the gamut from complaints to work slowdowns to sabotage.

Audience Analysis in Difficult Persuasive Situations

In difficult persuasive situations, carefully analyze your audience's objections and motivations.

Find out why your audience resists what you want them to do. Only if you know what you're up against can you construct a persuasive scenario.

Sometimes, learning about the audience's objections suggests that people simply need more information at the right time. Families of organ donors, for example, said that they wondered what happened to the organs after donation, they were asked to donate organs before they'd accepted the fact that someone

Even If You Have a Gun, Persuasion May Still Be Better*

Bosses who want to manage by intimidation sometimes think that their threats don't work only because their power is limited. But wars of revolution and attempted revolution, from the U.S. Revolutionary War to Vietnam to the current fighting in the Philippines, show that guns don't guarantee success.

In the Philippines, government forces have retaken some strongholds of the New People's Army (NPA) only to find that NPA influence continues to flourish. So the government is starting to use persuasion. Soldiers try to learn something about the concerns of local residents. Have NPA taxes been high? Has the NPA executed suspected informers? Then troops adapt their message to the audience. If jobs are an issue, they stress government efforts to create jobs. If people fear NPA retaliation, the government provides security.

Which side wins the war may depend on whether the government can persuade people that it offers them a better future than does the NPA.

---

* Second paragraph based on Richard Vokey, "Taking Cues from the Communists," *Newsweek*, April 4, 1988, 30.

Feeling Defensive and Feeling Understood*

When we're threatened, we feel defensive. Researcher Ronald D. Gordon found that at least 34% of the students he studied reported the following specific feelings when they responded to threats:

My whole body is tense . . . I have a sense of being trapped, closed-up, fenced-in, tied down, inhibited. . . .

I want to say something nasty, something that will hurt someone. . . . I keep thinking of getting even, of revenge . . . my fists are clenched. . . .

The world seems no good, hostile, unfair. . . .

In contrast, the students reported the following feelings when they "felt understood":

I feel more awake, more alert, more alive. . . .

I feel strong inside . . . taller, stronger, bigger . . . a sense of being exceptionally strong or energetic. . . . I seem to be functioning intellectually at a higher level—able to think clearly, understand everything. . . .

I want to make others happy. . . . I feel more tolerant, accepting, understanding of others. . . . I want to touch, hold, be physically close to the other person. . . . I want to communicate freely, share my thoughts and feelings with everyone around.

they loved was dying, and they worried about when they could schedule the funeral.[2]

Sometimes learning about objections suggests that a completely different strategy is needed. A Harvard Business School study found that Boston young people didn't believe the celebrities in anti-drug ads. Instead, they thought the celebrities probably used drugs themselves. Moreover, the "Just Say No" theme antagonized teens who didn't want to be told what to do. Even people who bought the basic message didn't know *how* to say "no." The Boston Mayor's office created a contest for young people themselves to create their own anti-drug commercials.[3]

Find out what concerns or conflicts you can harness to persuade your audience. The **theory of cognitive dissonance** explains that it is unpleasant to try to hold two ideas, or cognitions, which conflict, or are dissonant. For example, if you believe that it is important to conserve gasoline, you'll experience dissonance if you also want to own a sports car. Generally, we resolve dissonance in one of three ways. We can discount one of the cognitions: "There's plenty of gasoline right now, so conservation isn't important." We can reject one cognition: "A sports car really wouldn't be practical." Finally, we can construct a third cognition which has room for both of the conflicting ideas.

Persuaders can use the theory of cognitive dissonance to construct arguments in two ways:

- Show the audience that adopting the desired behavior will reduce or eliminate dissonance that already exists. ("The XYZ car looks like a racing car, but it gets 20 miles to the gallon in the city, and 30 mpg on the highway.")
- Create dissonance, and then show that adopting the desired behavior will reduce or eliminate it. ("You see yourself as a loyal employee. This company must cut costs if it is to remain competitive. Therefore, all loyal employees will forgo pay raises.")

Research in cognitive dissonance and our own experience tell us that people have an amazing capacity to develop rationalizations for what they want to do. That fact suggests that cognitive dissonance will be more useful to persuaders who want to reinforce what the audience really wants to do anyway than persuaders who want the audience to adopt an attitude or behavior which will not benefit the audience directly.

Tone and Tact in Persuasion

Make it clear by your tone and your words that you're on the reader's side. Some persuaders make the mistake of attacking people they want to persuade. If you can't force people, you've got to persuade them. People will not be persuaded by someone who attacks or belittles them.

The author of the memo in Figure 15.2 makes the mistake of attacking her readers in a negative message. Making the memo less accusatory would help, but the message doesn't need to be a negative message at all. Instead, the writer should take the information in paragraph 3 and use it as the attention-getter and common ground for a problem-solving persuasive message. Figure 15.3 shows a possible revision.

---

* Based on Ronald D. Gordon, "The Difference between Feeling Defensive and Feeling Understood," *Journal of Business Communication* 25, no. 1 (Winter 1988): 56–60.

FIGURE 15.2
ORIGINAL MEMO ATTACKING READER

October 25, 19--

To: Todd Neumann

From: Heather Johnson *HJ.*

Subject: Problems with Instrument Lab Results

— makes reader
feel incompetent

The Instrument Technicians Lab again seems to believe that if a result is
printed out, it is the correct answer. It doesn't seem to matter that the
chromatogram is terribly noisy, the calibration standards are over a month
old, or the area of the internal standard is about half what it should be.
What does it matter if the correction factor is 1286 and at the very minimum
it should be 1300? That's an average of two results--so what if the calibration
standard is six weeks old? I'm aware that the conditions in the lab have
contributed to the discouraged atmosphere, but I don't feel it's an excuse
for the shape of the lab and the equipment. The G.C. columns are in bad shape
just from abuse. I've lost count of the number of 10 ml. syringes the lab
has buried (at $20 each) mainly because they were not properly rinsed and the
plungers were lost trying to push through dried protein material. When was
the last time the glass insert in the B column was changed or even looked at?
Has anyone checked the filter on the Autolab I?

Accusatory tone

Accusatory tone

Attacks reader

Not YA

During the last six months, I have either reminded the technician of such things
or written reminders in the log book. Isn't it time for our responsible lab
technicians to take on this responsibility? Shouldn't they have fresh standards
made up, especially when they know a run is coming? Granted, we've had many
false starts, but I am still uncomfortable that the technicians will be ready
when the time comes.

Insults and attacks reader

Not YA

I don't feel that I should have to go over the chromatograms, printouts and G.C.
book every time we submit samples for analysis. However, just two weeks ago
I sent out results without doing this and immediately received a call that the
results were impossible--and they were because unacceptable KF was used, the
result of an old calibration standard.

Not YA

Presented as reader's fault

One other item bothers me. I don't know how to get the technicians interested
in the way the Autolab integrates each peak when they don't seem to look at
anything other than the answer. I feel it's very important they learn this so
they will know when a peak has been incorrectly integrated.

Not YA

Not common problem that both share

I think it's time they either take hold and run the lab themselves or they be
treated as if they were children and told what to do which means they'll need
a baby-sitter. I also would like to see them read the Autolab I Instruction
Manual and take the tape courses on the gas chromatograph and the Autolab I.
I really think the above should be a mandatory part of their training.

Attacks and insults reader

Whole ¶ lacks YA

The overall attitude and morale of the lab must be raised and a step in that
direction is to give them the responsibility which they were supposed to have
in the first place and expect them to accept it. These people are being called
technicians but they are actually classed as chemists and should be assuming
more initiative and responsibility.

Attacks reader

FIGURE 15.3
REVISED MEMO CREATING A COMMON GROUND

October 25, 19--

To: Todd Neumann

From: Heather Johnson

Subject: Cutting Requests for Re-Work

Problem writer and reader share

Two weeks ago a customer called to tell me that the results we'd sent out were impossible. I checked, and the results were wrong because we'd used an old calibration standard.

Redoing work for outside customers and for in-house projects doubles our work-load. Yet because people don't trust our results, we're getting an increasing number of requests for re-work.

Writer shows understanding of reader's problems

Part of the problem is that we've had so many false starts. Customers and especially in-house engineers say they'll need a run but then don't have the material for another day or even a week. Paul Liu has told me that these schedule glitches are inevitable. We'll just have to prepare fresh calibration standards every time a run is scheduled--and prepare them again when the run actually is ready.

You've told me that the equipment in the lab is unreliable. The Capital Expenditures Request includes a line item for G. C. columns and a new gas chromatograph. We'll be able to be more persuasive at the Board meeting if we can show that we're taking good care of the equipment we have. Please remind your staff to

- Rinse the 10-ml. syringes every day.

- Check the glass insert in the B column every week.

- Check the filter on the Autolab I every week.

What reader is to do is emphasized with a list

Treats reader as an equal who can help solve the problem

Do workers find the Autolab I instruction manual and the tape courses on the gas chromatograph and the Autolab I helpful? If the manual is hard to use or the tape course is boring, perhaps we should ask the manufacturer to redo them and, in the meantime, to send a service worker to offer a short course for our workers. What do you think would be the best way to increase the technical expertise of our staff?

By getting our results right the first time, we can eliminate the re-work and give both customers and in-house clients better service.

Links desired action to benefit and picture of the problem being solved.

CONVINCING THE READER

Any argument has a better chance if it is logically sound and well presented. **Toulmin Logic,** developed by Stephen Toulmin, is useful both in planning and in presenting arguments.[4] Toulmin logic can help you both to see whether an argument is valid and to decide how much—or what kind of—evidence you need to provide.

The Toulmin Model

In everyday life, the first part of the argument to emerge is frequently the **claim,** or the point we want the audience to accept.

   a. Your order will arrive Thursday.

   b. We could increase profits by expanding the Seattle plant.

When the reader is already on our side, all we have to do is state the claim. But when the reader disagrees with the claim or doubts it, we must support it with **evidence** or data that our audience accepts.

   a. Your order will arrive Thursday because it's scheduled to leave our plant Wednesday afternoon.

   b. We presently lose orders because we don't have the material in stock in Seattle and some customers go elsewhere rather than waiting for us to special order it from one of our other plants.

Note that **evidence** in Toulmin logic is not the same thing as a **fact** in semantics. In semantics, a statement is a fact only to people who have personally verified it. Evidence, in contrast, is any statement that the audience believes. Even a false statement ("The world is flat") could serve as evidence if the audience believed it.

Providing evidence, however, is not enough. The argument looks like this:

      Evidence   Claim

. . . without any connection between the claim and evidence which supposedly proves the claim. The reader has to make a leap of generalization to see the relationship between the evidence and the claim.

If the reader doesn't see the relationship (doesn't know it, agree with it, or happen to think of it at the moment), he or she won't be convinced. Adding more evidence won't help. Instead, we need to spell out the general principle, or **bridge,** which authorizes making the step between the evidence and the claim (Figure 15.4).

In the following examples, the bridge is in bold.

   a. Your order is scheduled to leave Wednesday evening. **It is a seven-hour drive from our plant to your warehouse.** Your order will arrive Thursday.

   b. We presently lose orders because we don't have the material in stock in Seattle and some customers go elsewhere rather than waiting for us to special order it from one of our other plants. **If we could promise immediate delivery, we'd make more sales.** We could increase profits by expanding the Seattle plant.

Cultural Preferences for Expressing Criticism*

Japanese [who want to criticize someone] . . . are more likely to remain silent, to direct their remarks to a third person, to employ non-verbal signs of disapproval, and to use ambiguity and humor to express their feelings.

   Americans, on the other hand, prefer to deal with critical situations more constructively, more sarcastically, more angrily, and more insultingly. . . . Japanese respondents [feel that they are being direct when they] expressed their complaints in a playful and half-joking manner. . . . [To American college students, "being direct" means] a more abrasive and trenchant manner.

---

* Quoted from Naoki Nomura and Dean Barnlund, "Patterns of Interpersonal Criticism in Japan and United States," [sic] *International Journal of Intercultural Relations* 7 (1983): 15–16.

FIGURE 15.4
THE BRIDGE LINKS THE
EVIDENCE TO THE CLAIM

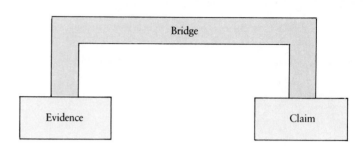

Different Evidence for Different
Cultures*
North Americans pride themselves
on making decisions based on
"facts." But decision makers in
other countries use different kinds
of evidence. The Japanese business-
person uses impressions, opinions,
and what Americans would call
gossip in reaching conclusions.
Europeans generally place less confidence solely on facts than North
Americans in reaching decisions.

In North America, when a per-
suader encounters resistance, the
best strategy is to take the facts one
by one and build up to the general
point they prove. People negotiating
with Russians and with Brazilians
have found that it works better to
start with the general principle. If
people found the theory persuasive,
specific facts didn't much matter. In
Russia, emotional involvement is an
essential part of persuasion. In Bra-
zil, "letting the facts speak for
themselves" just doesn't work. The
credibility of the source is crucial.

Sometimes the bridge is a statement which itself must be proven. (How do we know that bigger inventories will lead to greater sales?) When the proof is made explicit, the statement proving the bridge is called the **foundation.**

Sometimes the reader may accept the bridge but think of a **counterclaim** that negates the claim.

a. The fact that the order is *scheduled* to leave Wednesday doesn't necessarily mean it *will* leave then.

b. Even if we expand, sales won't *necessarily* increase. Business conditions in Seattle may change; customers who found us too slow in the past may have already found other suppliers and may not buy from us.

If a counterargument exists, we must provide a **rebuttal** to it to be convincing.

Many claims cannot be made with 100% certainty. If the claim is only *probably* and not *necessarily* true, we need to **limit** it. In the following sentence, the limiter is in bold.

a. An order scheduled for loading Wednesday evening should arrive Thursday **under normal conditions (if the truck doesn't break down, if the driver doesn't get sick, if there isn't a truckers' strike, etc.).**

You can also limit a claim with the words *probably* and *may be* and with explicit disclaimers: "These results are accurate within ±5.6%." "This projection is based on surveys taken October 28th."

Figure 15.5 shows the full Toulmin model.

Using Toulmin Logic in a Memo to Subordinates

Figure 15.6 illustrates the use of the Toulmin model in a problem-solving persuasive message. The memo is written to persuade employees not to make personal calls on office phones. The numbers in the margins identify the words, phrases, sentences, or paragraphs which

1. Build a common ground.
2. Offer evidence of the problem.
3. Prove that the problem hurts the organization.

* Based on Edward C. Stewart, "Culture and Decision-Making," in *Communication, Culture, and Organizational Processes,* ed. William B. Gudykunst, Lea P. Stewart, and Stella Ting-Toomey (Beverly Hills, CA: Sage Publications, 1985), 192–93 and Edmond S. and Christine G. Glenn, *Man and Mankind: Conflict and Communication between Cultures* (Norwood, NJ: Ablex, 1981), 162–63.

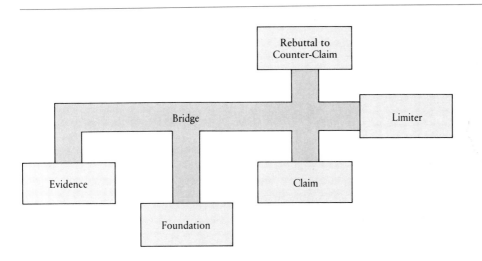

FIGURE 15.5
PARTS OF A COMPLETE ARGUMENT

4. Rebut the counterclaim that phones are tied up on business, not personal, calls.
5. Present the solution to the problem in general terms.
6. Present the complete solution in specific terms.
7. Picture the problem being solved.
8. Limit additional reader benefits that may arise from the solution but are not certain to occur.
9. Tell readers exactly what to do.
10. Build an image of the writer as someone who's on the same side as readers, helping them to solve their problems and achieve their goals.

How Much of the Full Toulmin Model to Use

It is possible to outline the full Toulmin model for any claim, even simple ones such as "Your order will arrive Thursday." Any argument is an interlocking chain of evidence-bridge-claim units. We could challenge the evidence, arguing that it too needs proof; we could formulate possible rebuttals for the smallest objections. The fact that we *could* do these things, however, does not mean that we always *need* to do them. Decide how much of the model to use by analyzing the reader and the situation.

The following guidelines can help you.

1. **Make both the claim and the evidence explicit** unless you are *sure* the reader will accept what you say totally without questions. Present minor claims with obvious evidence in complex sentences, with the evidence in the subordinate clause, to avoid giving the impression that this information is new and surprising.

> Since employers prefer job candidates with work experience, we should set up an internship program for our students.

2. **Include the bridge:**
   a. **if it is new information to the reader.**
   b. **if the reader may have heard the bridge but forgotten it.**

The Ethics of Persuasion

Persuasion depends upon building a common ground, upon supplying logical and emotional reasons for readers to do what we ask, upon showing them how they'll benefit from the action we propose. To find a common ground, we analyze the audience, understand their biases, objections, and needs, and identify with them so that we can make them identify with us. This analysis can be carried out in a cold, manipulative way. It can also be based on a respect for and sensitivity to the audience's position.

Readers are highly sensitive to manipulation. No matter how much you disagree with your audience, respect their intelligence. Try to understand why they believe or do something and why they may object to your position. If you can understand your readers' initial position, you'll be more effective—and you won't alienate your readers by talking down to them.

FIGURE 15.6
A PROBLEM-SOLVING MEMO

To: All Sales Representatives

From: James Christopher Smith *JCS*

Subject: ① Improving Service of Customers' Phone Orders

Writer as problem solver ⑩

Common ground ① (All of you have told me) that your customers are experiencing difficulties in placing orders because all the phone lines are tied up, and that some customers are ordering from other wholesalers as a result. This is causing you a loss in sales commissions.

Evidence ② The recent opening of the Johnson Wholesale House in Decatur has made competition in our field of wholesale drugs even keener. With the addition of this new warehouse, Johnson can service customers in all our sales areas almost as quickly as we can, and for approximately the same price. This new availability makes it even easier for our customers to call Johnson's instead of us. In fact, Glenn and Jack report that Walgreen's has increased ③ its business with Johnson's from a sixth to a third of its total drug business. Sue and Jerry also say that several of the small independent drug stores in central Illinois, such as the ones in Effingham and Tuscola, have switched to Johnson's from us. With competition as fierce as this, we must make ordering from us a quick and easy operation.

Rebuttal of counter claim ④ Most orders are phoned in between 9:30 and 11:30 in the morning and 1:00 and 2:00 in the afternoon, according to the times indicated on the order forms from last month. The phone operators, however, report that the lines are tied up throughout the day, usually by calls from the sales department. In order to relieve congestion, then, it is necessary to reduce phone activity in the sales department.

Solution presented impersonally ⑤ ⑦ This reduction can be made by using the pay phones for personal calls during the peak ordering hours. Calls on company business should be made during non-peak hours too, if possible. This will enable us to keep more lines open during the peak ordering hours without spending money on costly new lines.

Additional reader benefits ⑧ With the lines open to incoming calls, customers will find that they can place their orders quickly and easily. This will encourage them to keep calling us instead of our competitors, which can mean greater sales for you. In addition, good service helps build goodwill which may enable you to get a bigger share of your customers' business. The easy phone ordering service will also serve you as an additional selling point for new customers.

Tells readers exactly what to do, links action to solution of problem ⑥ ⑨ In order to improve customer relations and realize greater sales, then, use the pay phones for personal calls between the peak hours of 9:30-11:30 and 1:00-2:00, and make outgoing business calls during non-peak hours.

c. if the reader may disagree with the bridge.

d. if invalid as well as valid bridges exist.

> All of the money saved in the cost-reduction program will go into salaries and benefits, not into research and development, executive bonuses, or stockholder dividends. Therefore employees will benefit if the company saves money.

3. **Make the foundation explicit**
   a. **if it is new information to the reader.**
   b. **if the reader will disagree with the bridge.**
   c. **if specious foundations exist.**
   d. **if there are arbitrary demands for documentation** (e.g., in a term paper or a paper you are submitting for publication, where you must indicate your sources for each fact).

> XYZ university will have trouble developing a top-20 football team because its academic standards are high. After practicing four hours a day, football players don't have the time or energy to complete complex, lengthy assignments. Long practices are necessary both to reduce the risk of injury and to make the moves automatic.

4. **Always offer rebuttals to counterclaims.** Failure to close of loopholes is, after failure to provide a valid bridge, probably the most common cause of unconvincing—and unaccepted—recommendations.

> Three of our best customers got busy signals for two straight hours Monday. Business was slow Monday: quotes were down 15%, and the logs compiled by the inside sales reps don't show many outgoing business calls. But the phones were busy, and it seems likely that they were tied up with personal calls.

5. **Limit any claim whose truth is uncertain or relative.**

> This procedure should produce more accurate results.

> The best short-term solution is to import more parts.

Evaluating Arguments

By comparing an argument to the Toulmin model, you can see what kind of statements you need to make an argument convincing. Each of the examples is unconvincing, but the solutions differ.

Argument 1	By using XTROCUT tubing, you can cut production time and reduce scrap loss.
Problem with Argument	This argument needs evidence to support each of its claims.
Revised Argument	Because XTROCUT comes in the lengths and shapes you use most often, you spend less time cutting down longer tubes. Since you can order just the length you want, you don't waste 2′ every time you need a 10-foot tube.

* Adapted from Robert B. Kaplan, "Cultural Thought Patterns in Inter-Cultural Education," *Language Learning* 16 nos. 1–2 (1966): 3–15.

Logic May Not Be a Straight Line*

The logic of English paragraphs goes in a straight line. If the reader will agree easily, paragraphs start with a topic sentence. If the reader will resist, the paragraph starts with specifics and builds to the conclusion.

English Logic

Arabic and other Semitic languages develop ideas by a series of complex parallel constructions, positive and negative.

Arabic Logic

Oriental writing circles the subject, showing it in terms of what it is not. The reader infers the main point from the surrounding points.

Oriental Logic

Writers in French and other Romance languages follow ideas wherever they lead.

Romance Logic

Russian writers use a combination of parallel constructions and subordination. Minor ideas may receive as much development as major ideas in the paragraph.

Russian Logic

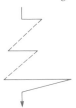

Limiting Statements in Accounting Reports*

Accountants carefully limit the claims they make in their reports. One compilation report contained the following limiting paragraph:

> Management has elected to omit substantially all of the disclosures required by generally accepted accounting principles. If the omitted disclosures were included in the financial statements, they might influence the user's conclusions about the company's financial position, results of operations, and changes in financial position.

A review contained this limiting statement:

> Based on our review we are not aware of any material modifications that should be made to the accompanying financial statements in order for them to be in conformity with generally accepted accounting principles.

Even the phrase "generally accepted accounting principles" is itself limited. CPAs are not claiming that everyone in the world accepts these principles, or even that these are the perfect principles. The claim is limited: these are the principles that are "generally accepted."

Argument 2	The workers I talked to were split 50/50. The workers at our plant don't agree whether the benefits package is adequate.
Problem with Argument	No bridge shows that the "workers I talked to" were a representative sample. The audience may also wonder whether things have changed since the date of the poll.
Revised Argument	I talked to a random sample of workers. They were split 50/50. Last week, the workers didn't agree whether the benefits package is adequate.
Argument 3	Our national advertising campaign will run during the most popular TV shows this month. This ad campaign will increase our sales dramatically.
Problem with Argument	Such a claim cannot be made with certainty: too many variables affect sales.
Revised Argument	Our national advertising campaign will run during the most popular TV shows this month. This ad campaign will support our sales reps' efforts to increase sales 5% over last month.

SUMMARY OF KEY POINTS

- Persuasion in "real life" is often difficult because
    - People tune out messages they don't want to hear.
    - People are reluctant to say *yes* if doing so requires them to admit that they've been on the wrong side all along.
    - People deny realities that are too much for them to cope with.
- When you need action quickly, you have two choices:
    1. Limit your audience to the people you can persuade.
    2. Try to bring everyone on board.
- If you don't need everyone's cooperation, use a direct request to get action from the people who already agree with you.
- Threats don't produce permanent change; they won't necessarily produce the action you want; they may make people abandon an action entirely—even in situations where it would be appropriate; they produce tension. People dislike and avoid anyone who threatens them. Threats can provoke counteraggression.
- When you want people to change their behavior, don't criticize them. Instead, show that you're on their side, that you and they have a mutual interest in solving a problem.
- In Toulmin logic, the **claim** is the point we want the audience to accept. **Evidence** is material the audience already accepts. The **bridge** is the general statement which allows us to infer the claim from the evidence. The **foundation** supports (proves) the bridge. **Counterclaims** are statements which invalidate the claim even when the evidence and bridge are sound. The **rebuttal** answers the counterclaim. The **limiter** shows under what circumstances, or with what limitations, the claim is true.
- Use these guidelines to determine how much of the full Toulmin model to use.
    1. Make both the claim and the evidence explicit.
    2. Include the bridge
        a. if it is new information to the reader.
        b. if the reader may have heard the bridge but forgotten it.
        c. if the reader may disagree with the bridge.
        d. if invalid as well as valid bridges exist.

---

* Based on Aletha S. Hendrickson, "How to Appear Reliable without Being Liable: CPA Writing in its Rhetorical Context," *Worlds of Writing: Teaching and Learning in Different Discourse Communities,* ed. Carolyn Mataline (New York: Random House, forthcoming 1988).

3. Make the foundation explicit
   a. if the reader will disagree with the bridge.
   b. if specious foundations exist.
   c. if there are arbitrary demands for documentation.
4. Always offer rebuttals to loopholes the reader may find in the main claim.
5. Limit any claim whose truth is uncertain or relative.

- To find a common ground, we analyze the audience, understand their biases, objections, and needs, and identify with them so that we can make them identify with us. This analysis can be based on a respect for and sensitivity to the audience's position.

NOTES

1. Walter R. Nord, "Beyond the Teaching Machine: The Neglected Area of Operant Conditioning in the Theory and Practice of Management," *Organizational Behavior and Human Performance* 4 (1969), 375–401.
2. "Doubtful Donors," *The Wall Street Journal*, October 19, 1987, 1.
3. *The Wall Street Journal*, September 17, 1987, 33.
4. See Stephen Toulmin, *The Uses of Argument* (Cambridge: Cambridge University Press, 1958).

One Step at a Time*

If your readers have a stake in what you are arguing against, you cannot take straightforward persuasion as your goal. You must resist your impulse to change their beliefs. You have to set your sights much lower. The best you can hope for—and it is hoping for a great deal—is to get your readers just to *understand* your point of view even while not changing theirs in the slightest. . . .

In short, stop trying to persuade the enemy and settle for planting a seed. . . .

If you can get a reader to take your point of view for just that one conditional moment—to inflate your words with his breath—then future events will occasionally remind him of the experience. Contrary views are inherently intriguing. And if your position has any merit, your reader will begin—very gradually of course—to notice things that actually support it. . . .

What does this mean in practice? . . . You can trust your instincts once you understand your goal: somehow to persuade readers to work *with* you rather than against you in the job of breathing life into your words. For example, if I were writing a short article or leaflet to readers with a stake in what I'm trying to refute, I wouldn't say, "Here's why *you* should believe nuclear power is bad." How can I get them to invest themselves in words which translate "Here's why you've been bad or stupid"? I would take an approach which said, "Here are the reasons and experiences that have made *me* believe nuclear power is bad. Please try to understand them for a moment."

---

* Quoted from Peter Elbow, *Writing with Power: Techniques for Mastering the Writing Process* (New York: Oxford University Press, 1981), 203–04.

EXERCISES AND PROBLEMS FOR CHAPTER 15

15–1 EVALUATING LOGIC

Identify the flaw in each of the following statements and revise each of the sentences so that it makes logical sense. (If the sentence is ambiguous, pick one logical meaning.)

1. Because the decision will be based on gathering data and evaluating it, it will be entirely possible to find a solution to the problem in the time available.

2. If needed, my social security number is 300–43–2341.

3. Your frank and honest answers to each question on this teaching evaluation form will help the instructor improve this course and his or her teaching techniques.

4. I gave the survey to a handful of volunteers, then proceeded to another floor to find more volunteers. I then returned to the first floor to pick them up before going to another building.

5. As a result of the questionnaire, many of the students felt that there was not enough parking on campus.

6. With this program we will be better able to understand what the future will encompass.

7. We do not issue building keys to employees because we want to keep security to a minimum.

8. I hope to work in a hospital in Colorado and New York.

9. If you're in the market for new furniture, the Woodshed is having a sale.

10. At an annual subscription price of only US$599 the *Asian Markets Monitor* is no doubt the least costly investment you will make this year. It will also certainly prove to be the most vital and useful.

15–2 USING TOULMIN LOGIC

In each of the following arguments, identify the claim and the evidence (if any). What bridge could link the evidence to the claim? Is it valid? Why or why not?

1. The mayor rejected my proposal. I must not have presented it very well.

2. The biggest department in the state uses that method and it's extremely successful. We ought to use the same method here.

3. Computers are essential to our operation as a company. This, in turn, directly benefits you as a customer of our company.

4. Of all the applicants, Bob got the highest score on the test. He's the person who should get the job.

5. Last month we used 34% more paper than we did six months ago. People are either wasting it or stealing it.

6. The vote on whether to unionize was split 50/50. Our employees can't agree on whether or not a union would be beneficial.

7. The vote on whether to unionize was split 50/50. Our employees just don't care whether or not the union comes in.

8. Johnson will never get anywhere in this organization. He's just not a team player.

9. Surveys show that demand for accountants is expected to remain high through 2000. If I major in accounting, it will be easy for me to get a good job.

10. When a husband and wife disagree, the wife ought to obey the husband, just as the lieutenant carries out the captain's orders at sea, though the lieutenant may be a better seaman than the captain and may disapprove of his orders.

15–3 INCREASING BUSINESS AT THE WRITING SKILLS LAB

If your campus has a Writing Skills Lab, include real information about location, hours, and policies. Visit the Skills Lab and talk to one of the staff people to get other information that may be useful. If your campus does not have a Skills Lab, use information listed here.

The campus Writing Skills Lab offers free tutoring in writing to any student or faculty member on campus. You ask people to sign up for appointments (20 minutes each); they may schedule as many appointments as they need. You will read papers before they are turned in only with the instructor's written consent. You will go over any graded paper to help the student master the concepts the instructor marked as needing work.

As its director, you feel that the Skills Lab is underused. You can think of several possible reasons for the fact that some students don't come in. Perhaps they don't know about the Skills Lab, don't realize that it's free, or don't know when it's open. Perhaps they think the staff will make fun of them for needing help with basics. Perhaps they think the Skills Lab is always full.

You know that the campus administration is looking for ways to save money. If you seem to have more staff than you need, your Skills Lab is likely to have its budget cut. Getting more people to use the Skills Lab will protect your budget and help improve the quality of writing on campus.

As your instructor directs,

   a. Write a memo to all instructors urging them to send students to the Skills Lab. Tell them what your purpose and policies are; show them how you can make their jobs easier. Be sure to tell them about your location, phone number, and hours.

   b. Write an announcement (250 word maximum) to go in the student paper. Analyze your audience: What will motivate students to come to the Skills Lab? What information do they need to act on that motivation?

   c. Write a memo to all instructors reminding them that they can use the Skills Lab too. Some of them may be embarrassed to admit that they have trouble writing. How can you help them overcome that embarrassment and motivate them to get help?

15–4 RECOMMENDING A SECRETARY FOR PROMOTION

As Assistant to the Personnel Manager of Wymeth Inc., you want to recommend that Molly Elliot be appointed to replace Bruce Hill, who is taking early retirement due to illness. For the last five years, Bruce has been "Special Assistant to the Vice President," in charge of projects such as liaisons with the Boy and Girl Scouts, the Company Suggestion System, and the Faculty Intern Program, a program which hires faculty from local high schools and junior colleges during the summer, so that they learn about how Wymeth works and take back to the classroom a more realistic view of business. Bruce's job involves a great deal of letter writing and record keeping, and attending a fair number of lunches and public meetings.

Your boss wants to assign Bruce's duties to Pat O'Brien, 32, Wymeth's Assistant Director of Public Relations. You know that your boss feels that Bruce was a "Special Assistant" only because someone on Wymeth's board of directors pulled some strings (whether this is true or not, you have no idea); furthermore, your boss feels that some of Pat's current responsibilities are trivial and could be dropped in favor of the projects which had been assigned to Bruce.

Molly Elliott, Bruce's secretary, has been doing most of his work during the last six months while Bruce has been on sick leave. She's written letters, kept records, and answered phone inquiries. Even before Bruce got sick, she handled a lot of the paperwork and helped him with necessary research. Bruce, you know, is brilliant but a procrastinator and not very well organized.

Molly is 48 and has been a secretary at Wymeth 28 years. She has had only two years of college. She was vice president of the League of Women Voters two years ago and has been as involved in community activities as her schedule would permit. Normally at Wymeth, secretaries stay as secretaries. The one case you know of where a secretary was moved to a line or staff position involved a 23-year-old woman.

If Molly were appointed to Bruce's position, you would have to raise her salary substantially even if Wymeth paid her less than it paid Bruce. Your boss wants to give all of Bruce's duties to Pat without raising Pat's salary. Since all of Bruce's projects are totally new to Pat, your boss plans to assign Molly as a secretary to Pat's department (Public Relations), which is short on clerical workers anyway.

Write a memo to your boss urging that Molly be made officially responsible (with an increase in title and pay) for the work she has been doing for the last six months and likely will still be doing if assigned to PR.

Hints:

- Be sure to deal with the objections your boss has! Show why Pat's duties are important and can't be cut and why the duties Molly has been doing for Bruce need to be done well. Use class discussion to get answers to these questions.

- Whether to bring up the issues of sex discrimination and pay equity depends on audience and context, neither of which is specified in the problem. As your instructor directs, either *a*) use class discussion to define audience and context or *b*) make reasonable assumptions and list them in a memo to your instructor.

15–5 PERSUADING YOUR INSTRUCTOR TO ADVISE A CHAPTER OF ALPHA BETA CHI

While you were researching a paper for your business communication class, you came across an article about Alpha Beta Chi, an undergraduate organization with the following goals:

1. Provide opportunities for members to develop personal communication skills and to encourage interest, research, and scholarship in business communication.

2. Foster high ethical standards among business communicators.

3. Provide an opportunity for business communication educators, students, and business people to meet and find a common ground between business communication theory and practice.

4. Promote the relevance of interpersonal communication in organizational development.

The article included an issue of the ABX newsletter put out by the students on one campus. The meetings sounded interesting: talks about job interviews, information about desktop publishing, panel discussions on communication problems of first-year accountants. You photocopied the newsletter to show to some of your friends: several of them were interested, too.

The article had a brief note about how to form new chapters:

It's easy to start a chapter of ABX on your campus. Just gather interested students and invite a faculty member to advise the group. Write to Professor Joel P. Bowman, Department of Business Information Systems, Western Michigan University, Kalamazoo, MI 49008 for a copy of the constitution and bylaws.

But then you hit a snag. You asked your business communication instructor to advise the group and got a *no*.

"I'm too busy. I've got papers to grade, professional journals to read, committee work to do, conferences to attend, and I'm trying to do research. Plus I'd like to have just a little time for myself. Try someone else."

You try, but don't succeed. You've got to have an advisor, and you've got a better chance at persuading your instructor (difficult though it will be) than anyone else. Try again. This time, put your request in writing so that you can marshall your most persuasive case.

Hints:
- How much work would the advisor have to do? What motivates your instructor? What aspects of the job give him or her the most satisfaction? What kinds of faculty work are rewarded at your school? How much job security does your instructor have? Could ABX meet any of your instructor's needs? Can you show that it is consistent with your instructor's goals and values?
- Use your analysis from problem 6–6.

15–6 PERSUADING EMPLOYEES TO WORK STATED HOURS
Hours in your office are 8:30 to 5. Most employees are there well before 8:30, but at 8:30 they're still sitting in the coffee room chatting. Many people seem to take long coffee breaks during the day (15 minutes twice a day is allowed) and long lunch hours too.

All of the employees are on salary rather than hourly pay; there is no time clock. You know that many of the employees frequently work past 5 and that they get no pay for this extra time. Salaried people are expected to work until the work is done. You think it looks unprofessional to have an empty office during office hours; their behavior reflects badly on you as their supervisor.

Because the budget is tight, raises in the last five years have been considerably less than increases in the cost of living. Morale in the office is fair, but most people feel underpaid, overworked, and unappreciated.

Pick a campus office, a state agency, or a nonprofit organization that you know something about. Write a memo to all staff members persuading them to be at work at their desks at 8:30 and not to abuse coffee break and lunch time.

Hints:
- Why do people need to be at their desks? If the conversation in the coffee room is about work is it OK for people to stay there and talk? If someone goofs off till 8:45, is that any worse than someone who is at the desk by 8:30 but who spends some time during the day just staring off into space? Is the work getting done? What evidence do you have that people are abusing coffee break and lunch limits?
- Pick **one** problem and address it in your memo.

15–7 REDUCING PERSONAL USE OF THE PHOTOCOPIER
Your office has a new high-speed photocopier. However, the number of copies made is excessive. People often make more copies of business documents than they really need. Some don't know how to use the machine and throw away bad copies because they've put in the original incorrectly. People make copies for their own personal use. Wasteful and personal use costs your organization money, puts wear and tear on the copier (increasing down time and repair bills), and ties up the copier when more important work needs to be run. People who don't know how to use the copier or who make personal copies during office hours are also wasting time.

Write a memo to solve the problem. Pick an organization you know something about; give yourself an appropriate title; choose a solution you think will work.

Hints:
- People know that each photocopy costs only a few pennies and takes less than a minute to make. How can you convince them that the

money or time (whichever is the real problem) is serious? How will you answer the counterclaims: "This company is drowning in paper. My stuff is just a drop in the bucket." "Going to the nearest copy shop will take (and waste) even more time than using the office copier." "Nobody is productive 100% of the time. Making copies is no worse than reading the paper or going to the water fountain."

- Are people really making lots of personal copies, or are you generalizing from a single instance?

- Some organizations ask people to pay for each personal copy—usually more than the actual cost, to encourage people to go to a copy shop instead. Such systems only work if you can count on people to record their personal use honestly and to pay for copies. Do you think an honor system would work in your organization? Why or why not?

- Try to offer your readers ways to save face as they change their behavior. Do business conditions now make it especially necessary to conserve paper, save money, or work efficiently?

15–8 PERSUADING A POTENTIAL CUSTOMER TO USE YOUR MOVING SERVICE*

You've just started work as a moving consultant for the local franchise of a large national moving company. People planning moves call you to get quotes—and call other firms as well. You get a commission for every move you book.

In training you were told,

"The first time someone calls, ask about number of family members and ages of children, destination and date of move; especially heavy, fragile, or valuable possessions; and pets. Set up an appointment to visit the caller's home to estimate the weight of belongings. During this visit, in addition to writing up an estimate, learn something abut the people as individuals—interests, concerns, motivations. Leave the estimate and a copy of our 'Smooth Moves' booklet that tells how to pack and gives tips on what to do with kids and pets. Then, when you get back to your office, write a follow-up letter persuading people to use our company.

"We can't compete on price: other firms have lower prices. We can't guarantee an exact arrival date during the peak moving season: just arrival within a 10-day period. If people arrive before their furniture does, they'll have to sleep on the floors. Make the sale

on service. Our TV and magazine ads stress that. You have to make that claim convincing."

Your predecessor used the following form letter as a follow-up:

Dear [Name]:

In order to maintain control, quality of service, and closely monitor your move from start to finish, we ask that you deal with us in regard to the following:

1. Premove arrangements.
2. Packing and loading dates.
3. Any questions pertaining to your move with which we can be of assistance.
4. Any claims, should damage occur in the course of the move, with a description of the damaged goods.

The success of your relocation is largely dependent on the information supplied by you, the shipper, with regard to your needs and how we can meet those needs. We therefore invite your questions and inquiries. You may call me or Jim Douglas at 555–4936 or 1–800–683–MOVE.

I hope you've had the time to read our information and advice which will make your planning and preparation easier.

We look forward to providing our service and wish you much happiness and good fortune at your new location.

You know that the letter is terrible: badly written and poorly organized. The first paragraph will offend many readers with its implications that they have already agreed to move with you when in fact they have not. Point 4 emphasizes the possibility of damage. The letter is vague (what will the company do for people? Who is Jim Douglas and why should they call him?). Worst of all, this impersonal letter just doesn't convince people that the service your company provides is worth the extra cost. No wonder your predecessor is no longer with the company!

Assignment: Assume that your instructor plans to move [you'll find out the fictitious date and destination in class] and that you've had several phone conversations and have made a weight estimate. Now, write a new, personalized follow-up letter from scratch.

Hints:
- Use your analysis from 6–6a.
- Think up questions to ask your instructor in class to find out what the moving consultant would know after several conversations and a home visit. Has your instructor moved before? Were the experiences good or bad? What people, pets, or things may make this move

*Adapted slightly from a problem written by John Hagge, Iowa State University.

difficult? What specific information or services can you offer to meet the instructor's needs? Would the moving consultant be calling your instructor by a title (which one?) or by the first name?

- You do not need to mention the specific price estimate quoted; you left a copy with your instructor. What are the advantages and disadvantages of mentioning specifically the weak points in your package: cost and arrival date?

15–9 PERSUADING ALCOHOLICS AND ADDICTS TO ENTER AN ASSISTANCE PROGRAM

Your company is starting an assistance program for employees and immediate family members who are alcoholics or addicted to prescription or illegal drugs. Employees who are "high" during work hours either do nothing or (even worse) create defective products and make bad decisions. Heavy drinking and drug use, even if confined to weekends, can lead to malnutrition, higher blood pressure, cirrhosis of the liver, hepatitis, and, if needles are shared, to AIDS. In addition to personal trauma, these illnesses increase your health care costs. Many of the people who need help are otherwise competent workers whose expertise you value.

The program you've adopted is a good one. Even so, long-term recovery rates are only 20–50% for alcoholics, 50–60% for addiction to prescription drugs, 10–25% for illegal drugs.

Every effort will be made to keep strictly confidential the fact that a person is participating in the program.

Moreover, employees who are participating in the program *will not be fired or demoted,* even if their work is not satisfactory. Participation in the program will not be recorded in the employee's permanent personnel file; it will not jeopardize future promotions.

Michael Brown will administer the program. His office number is extension 5–2100. He can be reached at any time (even nights, weekends) on a new hot line: 555–6538. Anyone interested should get in touch directly with him. People may volunteer for the program. They may also refer family members or subordinates who need help. He will contact anyone who is referred. The actual program will be conducted by trained, experienced psychologists and psychotherapists who run similar programs for several other organizations in town.

As Director of Benefits, write a letter to go to all employees at their home addresses announcing the program, reassuring people that participants will not be fired, and encouraging people who need the program to take advantage of it.

15–10 PERSUADING AN ADMISSIONS COMMITTEE TO REVERSE A DECISION

You're a high school guidance counselor. Today a student who is tied for second place in the senior class comes in: she's been denied admission to a prestigious university because she does not know a Western foreign language. The situation is ironic: Mariko Yamamoto knows her native Japanese and two dialects of Chinese besides English.

Write to the Admissions Committee urging it to reverse its decision and admit Mariko.

Direct Mail

QUESTIONS

- Is direct mail "junk" mail?
- How can you choose the best central selling point?
- How should you organize a direct mail letter?
- How can you think of a good opener?
- What does the body of the letter have to do?
- How long should a direct mail letter be?
- What does the action close have to do?
- Why should you use a P.S.?
- What are some of the ethical concerns about direct mail?
- What writing style is best for direct mail?
- What else goes in a direct mail package besides the letter?

Don't believe people won't read long letters. People read long books, take long trips, watch long movies and plays and read long letters provided they justify the time. They must be interesting. They must promise a profit, in entertainment, in money, in enlightenment.

Maxwell Sackheim
My First 65 Years in Advertising, 1975

Direct mail asks for an order, inquiry, or contribution directly from the reader. Direct mail is one form of direct marketing. **Direct marketing** also includes catalog sales, space ads in magazines and newspapers which have reply coupons so that the reader can buy or contribute directly, telemarketing (telephone sales), and TV direct response ads, where the viewer calls an 800 number to place an order. In 1986, direct mail sold over $100 billion worth of products and raised over $33 billion for charities.[1]

In addition to sales and fund-raising letters, direct mail includes letters asking for inquiries, cordial contact letters, which keep the company's name before the reader without attempting to sell anything, and follow-up letters persuading nonresponders to buy or contribute and thanking buyers and donors.

COMPONENTS OF GOOD DIRECT MAIL

Good direct mail has three components: a good product, a good mailing list, and a good appeal. A **good product** appeals to a specific segment of people, is not readily available in stores, can be mailed, and provides an adequate profit margin. A **good mailing list** has accurate addresses and is a good match to the product. Most professional direct mailers rent their lists from companies called list brokers that specialize in compiling and maintaining lists. A **good appeal** offers a believable description of benefits, links the benefits of the product or service to a need or desire that motivates the reader, makes the reader want to read the letter, and motivates the reader to act. The appeal is made up of the words in the letter, the pictures in the brochure, and all the parts of the package, from outer envelope to reply card.

All three elements are crucial: the best letter in the world won't persuade someone who doesn't have a garden to buy a Rototiller. However, this book will examine only the elements of a *good appeal:* how to create a message that will motivate a reader to act, assuming that you already have a good product to sell or a worthy cause to raise funds for, and that you already have a good list of people who might be interested in that product or organization.

IS IT "JUNK" MAIL?

Few people have heard the term *direct mail;* almost everybody calls it *junk mail.* If we respond **intensionally**—to the symbol, rather than to reality—we may think that *junk* mail is useless at best and a nuisance at worst. If we think of direct mail as *junk* mail, we'll feel defensive about writing it and probably won't be able to do a very good job.

Three possible criticisms of direct mail are that (1) its quality is poor; (2)

it doesn't pay its way in terms of postage costs; and (3) people don't want to get it. Let's look at each of these briefly.

The Quality of Direct Mail

The quality of the direct mail written today varies widely. The poor writing in some direct mail may mean that people who know little or nothing about direct mail are trying to do their own letters. A great deal of research has been done about what works in direct mail, but unlike academic research, this research is not generally available. To learn about direct mail, talk to someone who is experienced in the field, join the Direct Marketing Association and read its publications, or read a book like this one.

Some direct mail, like some general advertising, is filled with shaky logic. The best direct mail, however, is logically sound as well as emotionally effective. Successful direct mailers are excellent writers and skilled in audience analysis and in proving the claims they make.

Does Direct Mail Pay Its Own Way?

Most direct mail is sent third class so it can be handled less expensively than first class mail. Much direct mail is bundled by the mailer for each carrier route in the nation, so that the Post Office does not have to sort it. (If your mailing label carries the letters "CAR-RT SORT," it has been "carrier route sort"ed.)

Do People Want to Get Direct Mail?

Almost everyone claims to dislike "junk" mail. However, people do like to get mail that interests them: ads for products they want to buy, information about groups they like, letters about subjects they care about. One study found that 75% of the people who got political direct mail read the letters.[2]

To reduce the amount of direct mail you get, write to organizations you do business with and tell them that you do not want them to rent your name to other organizations. Many companies have a box on the reply card that you can check to indicate this. American Express reports that only 7% of its cardholders say they don't want "bonus" mail.

BASIC DIRECT MAIL STRATEGY

All direct mail strategies start with three basic steps: (1) learn about the product or service, (2) choose and analyze the target audience, and (3) choose a central selling point. These steps interact. An understanding of your target audience may suggest questions to ask about your product. Information you find in researching the product may suggest an idea for a possible central selling point.

1. Understand Your Product, Service, or Organization.

Try to use the product or service; visit the factory that makes it or the stores that sell it. Talk to volunteers who work for your charitable organization; if possible, visit the site where the good work is done.

Things You Can Buy by Mail*
A surprising variety of items are sold by mail. Perishable foods like steaks are shipped packed in dry ice. One firm offered a build-it-yourself helicopter to businesses for $26,000. Direct mail has been used to sell an around-the-world trip led by Admiral Byrd and to get inquiries for a $100,000 trip on the Orient Express, a $250,000 luxury yacht, a $1 million business jet, and a $2 million ion implantation system used to make semiconductors.

A high school football player who'd sat out much of his senior year due to an injury used a direct mail letter to persuade college coaches to ask for a game film. The letter, ghostwritten by his ad-executive brother, brought in 26 responses and three scholarship offers in five weeks.

---

*   Based on *Direct Marketing 48,* no. 7 (November 1985): 26, 28, 84; Robert F. Roth, *International Marketing Communications* (Chicago: Crain Books, 1982), 240; Ray Considine and Murray Raphel, *The Great Brain Robbery* (Pasadena, CA: The Great Brain Robbery, 1981), 186; *Direct Marketing 49,* no. 7 (November 1986): 127.

Lists, Lists, and More Lists*
Nearly 40,000 mailing lists are available commercially. To keep its list of new parents current, one list broker's employees read the birth announcements in 5,000 papers a week.

Among the lists available from one company are

24,000	women accountants
2,450	owners of balloon aircraft
155,500	high school athletic coaches
3,900,000	cat owners
60,000	highest salaried executives (home addresses)
2,450	rabbis
400,000	Republican contributors
5,384	top government officials in California
10,900	owners of exotic cars in Colorado
72,625	rich people in Indiana
89	owners of large yachts in Utah.

The questions here are general ones to get you started. You may need to ask additional questions depending on the product or service you're writing about.

For a sales letter, ask

- What are the product's objective features? Size? Color? Materials? How is it put together? How does it work? What options are available?
- How much does it cost? What does the buyer get for the money?
- How is it different from or better than competing products? (If the *details* of differences or superiority are interesting, jot them down. They may work well in a letter.)
- How easy is it to install? To use? To maintain?

See Chapter 17 for the questions to answer in a fund-raising letter.

2. Identify and Analyze Your Target Audience.

The **target audience** is the group of people who are likely to be interested in buying the product, using the service, or contributing to the cause. In direct mail, you do not try to sell a subscription to *Sports Illustrated* to someone who loathes sports; you do not ask Republicans to contribute to a Democratic candidate's campaign.

Professionals in direct mail rely on market research to tell them about their target audience. A list rented from a list broker normally has some demographic information. Recently, many list brokers have been offering lists of various psychographic groups, based on extensive customer interviews and market research.

For direct mail you do as a student or as a volunteer, use your own knowledge about people. Whenever possible, think of specific people you know while you write the letter. What do they care about? What would motivate *them*?

3. Choose a Central Selling Point.

A **central selling point** is a reader benefit which by itself could motivate your readers to act and which can serve as an umbrella under which all the other benefits can fit. You can and should mention other benefits, but they won't be developed in the same detail as the central selling point.

In a fund-raising letter, you must also choose the appeal that will be most powerful for the target audience. If you're raising funds from your college's alumni, possible appeals might be nostalgia, the obligation to repay the college, the feeling of making an investment in young people, or a sense of social responsibility. The best appeal depends on the specific subset of alumni—the target audience—you want to reach.

Every direct mail letter reaches three groups. A small percentage will have decided to buy or donate even before getting your letter. Another percentage will not buy or donate no matter how persuasive you are. Perhaps they don't have the money; perhaps they aren't interested in the product or service. They really don't belong on the list, but because lists never match the target audience 100%, they're getting the letter. The biggest group has enough money to buy

* Based on Jerry Heiser and Jack McNichols, "Lists and List Management," CADM/DMEF Direct Marketing Institute for Professors, Chicago, IL, May 31–June 3, 1983; Alvin B. Zeller, Inc., *1988 Catalog of Mailing Lists.*

or donate *if* they're convinced that the product, service, or organization is worthwhile. To be successful, your letter must convince this middle group.

HOW TO ORGANIZE A DIRECT MAIL LETTER

A great many patterns of organization for direct mail letters have been proposed. Most of them are more helpful to check your draft than they are in organizing or generating material while you're writing. The best model, because it is the simplest and therefore the most widely applicable, was developed by letter expert Cy Frailey in the '30s: Star-Chain-Hook.

The Star

The *Star* is the **opener** designed to catch the readers' attention. A good star opener will make readers want to read the letter and provide a reasonable transition to the body of the letter.

The Chain

The *Chain* is the **body** of the letter. It provides the logical and emotional links that move readers from their first flicker of interest to the action you want. A good chain answers readers' questions, overcomes their objections, and involves them emotionally.

The Hook

The *Hook* (like a fishhook) is the **action close,** which harnesses the motivation you have created and turns it into action. A good action close tells readers what to do, makes the action sound easy, gives them a reason for acting promptly, and ends with a reader benefit or a picture of the reader's money helping to solve the problem.

Opener (Star)

The opener of your letter is crucial. In the first 30 to 60 seconds they spend skimming the opener, people decide whether to read the rest of the letter. If your opener doesn't grab them, you're lost.

A very successful subscription letter for *Psychology Today* started out,

> Do you still close the bathroom door when there's no one in the house?

As it happens, *Psychology Today* has never run an article on what it tells about you if you do, or don't, close the bathroom door, even when you know you're alone in the house. But the question is both intriguing in itself and a good transition into the kinds of topics the magazine covers: practical psychology applied to the quirks and questions we come across in everyday life.

It's essential that the opener not only get the reader's attention but also be something that can be linked logically to the body of the letter. A sales letter started,

> Can You Use $20 This Week?

Certainly that gets attention. But then the letter went on to claim that the letter was as valuable as a $20 bill since it gave the reader the chance to save $20 on a product. Few readers are going to buy such shaky logic. Furthermore, readers may feel disappointed or even cheated when they learn that instead of getting $20, they have to spend money to save $20.

It's hard to write a brilliant opener the minute you sit down. Two reliable strategies are (1) write four or five openers, and pick the best; (2) just start writing. A good opener may in fact appear on your second or third page; sometimes you can throw away much of the prose that preceded it.

Ethics and Direct Mail

Deception in direct mail is all too easy to find.

In the early 1980s some mailers sent plain envelopes with windows through which one can see the blue paper with wavy lines used for checks, with the words "Payable to" and the reader's name and address. But the reader who opens the envelope finds that the "check" can only be applied toward the purchase price of the item the letter is selling.

In the late 1980s, many envelopes imitate government or social security envelopes. A brown envelope advises the postmaster to follow Section 694 of the U.S. Postal Service Domestic Mail Manual. (Section 694 says to throw away mail that can't be delivered.)

Inside some packages, words are deliberately designed to create bypassing: 30-minute videos touted as "feature films," a "free" membership "valued at $1,000" (note the passive—who's doing the valuing?) for which the recipient has to pay, up front, $157 for three years' maintenance fees.

There are also gray areas. Is it OK to use computers to create a letter that looks like a personal letter but in fact is going to hundreds or thousands of people? Is it OK to have the letter signed by the president of the company even though a professional wrote it? Is it OK to use washable ink to print the signature so that recipients will think a real person signed the letter when in fact the signature was printed?

Computer personalization, a credible signature, and washable ink all increase response. People who believe in their causes usually claim that "the end justifies the means." Other people feel that these tactics are acceptable because everyone "really" knows that direct mail isn't personal and isn't signed individually.

If we don't use these tactics, we create direct mail that is less effective than it might be. But when we do use them, we may contribute to the cynicism that pervades America: "You can't trust anyone anymore."

What Will the Audience Want?*
A sweepstakes appealing to an up-scale target audience successfully offered framed autographs of famous people as prizes, with the grand prize a signature of Napoleon. This fresh approach appealed to the high-income, educated prospects. And the Napoleon signature cost less than the usual grand prize—a new car!

It's often easier to brainstorm possible openers if you deliberately try to think of ways to use the four basic modes: **questions, narration, startling statements, and quotations.** Let's look at an example of each and see how the opener is related to the body of the letter.

1. Questions

> Dear Writer:
>
> What is the best way to start writing?

This letter selling subscriptions to *Writer's Digest* goes on to discuss Hemingway's strategy for getting started on his novels and short stories. *Writer's Digest* offers practical advice to writers who want to be published. The information in the letter is useful to any writer so the recipient keeps reading; the information also helps to prove the claim that the magazine will be useful.

2. Narration, Stories, Anecdotes

> Dear Reader:
>
> She hoisted herself up noiselessly so as not to disturb the rattlesnakes snoozing there in the sun.
>
> To her left, the high desert of New Mexico. Indian country. To her right, the rock carvings she had photographed the day before. Stick people. Primitive animals.
>
> Up ahead, three sandstone slabs stood stacked against the face of the cliff. In their shadow, another carving. A spiral consisting of rings. Curious, the young woman drew closer. Instinctively, she glanced at her watch. It was almost noon. Then just at that moment, a most unusual thing happened.
>
>> Suddenly, as if out of nowhere, an eerie dagger of light appeared to stab at the topmost ring of the spiral. It next began to plunge downwards—shimmering, laser-like.
>>
>> It pierced the eighth ring. The seventh. The sixth. It punctured the innermost and last. Then just as suddenly as it had appeared, the dagger of light was gone. The young woman glanced at her watch again. Exactly twelve minutes had elapsed.
>
> Coincidence? Accident? Fluke? No. What she may have stumbled across that midsummer morning three years ago is an ancient solar calendar....

This subscription letter for *Science84* argues that it reports interesting and significant discoveries in all fields of science—all in far more detail than do other media. The opener both builds suspense so that the reader reads the subscription letter and suggests that the magazine will be as interesting as the letter and as easy to read.

*   Quoted from Jane Maas, *Better Brochures, Catalogs and Mailing Pieces* (New York: St. Martin's Press, 1981), 123–24.

3. Startling Statements

> Dear Friend:
>
> If you're a working woman, you don't receive $1 for every dollar's worth of work you do.

This fund-raising letter from the National Organization for Women (NOW) goes on to document the fact that, for the same education, women receive, on the average, salaries that are only 69% of men's and to discuss other forms of financial discrimination.

4. Quotations

> "I never tell my partner that my ankle is sore or my back hurts. You can't give in to pain and still perform."
>
> —Jill Murphy
> Soloist

The series of which this letter is a part sells season tickets to the Atlanta Ballet by focusing on the people who work to create the season. Each letter quotes a different member of the company. The opening quote is used on the envelope over a picture of the ballerina and as an opener for the letter. The letters encourage readers to see the artists as individuals, to appreciate their hard work, and to share their excitement about each performance.

Body (Chain)

Once you've piqued readers' interest, you need to move them to act. A good chain answers readers' questions, overcomes their objections, and involves them emotionally.

All this takes space. One of the industry truisms is "The more you tell, the more you sell." Tests show that longer letters bring in more new customers or new donors than do shorter letters. Four pages is often considered the ideal length. Some tests show that six- or even eight-page letters outpull shorter letters.[3] Ten years ago, *Consumer Reports* used a four-page subscription letter. In 1987, the magazine updated the same basic letter on smaller paper to get a six-page letter. Expensive mailings sometimes use one uncut, folded 17″ by 11″ sheet, printed on the first and third sides, to give a two-page letter the psychological weight of four pages.

Content for the body of the letter can include

- Information readers will find useful whether or not they buy the product.
- Stories about how the product is made or was developed.
- Testimonials.
- Case histories.
- Word pictures of readers using the product and enjoying its benefits.

How to Choose the Best Central Selling Point

The first step in choosing a central selling point is to brainstorm as many different appeals as possible.

Suppose you want to sell copies of a book that explains how to grow vegetables in home gardens. Whenever you try to sell a book or magazine by mail, you are really selling the activity; the book helps readers do the activity successfully. Any of the following statements could be used as central selling points:

- Fresh vegetables from your own garden taste better than store-bought vegetables that are ripened with chemicals.
- Vegetables from your own garden are healthier. You control the chemicals you put on them; you can avoid insecticides and wax you don't want.
- It's cheaper to grow your own vegetables than to buy them in a grocery store.
- Growing vegetables is fun.
- Growing vegetables is a good family activity. There's work for everyone; children will be fascinated by growing plants.
- Growing your own vegetables is a way to get back to nature, to have a simpler, more natural lifestyle.

A professional direct mailer might test two or more different approaches with samples of the target market, then "roll out" the best letter to the whole list.

As a student, you can't run a test. How do you choose?

First, eliminate any central selling points that don't fit your target audience.

Next, use your own understanding of people to decide whether to stress taste or health or economy or fun or working with nature.

If two or more appeals seem equally effective, try writing each of them. In your assignment, use the one that you can develop most effectively.

How to Write Good Questions*

Not all questions work well as openers.

The following question fails on two counts. (1) A reader who says *no* has no reason to read the letter. (2) The question doesn't suggest that the information will be worthwhile or relevant.

Do you want information about investments?

The following revision isn't much better.

Do you know the best investment for your money right now?

Answering *no* makes the reader feel incompetent. Putting down the reader is never a good way to make someone want to read on.

A professional in direct mail suggests the following revision:

Interest rates are out of sight. Can you still make money investing in land?

Good questions challenge but don't threaten the reader. They're interesting enough that readers want the answers, so they read the letter.

Action Close (Hook)

The action close in the letter must do four things:

1. **Tell the reader what to do:** respond. Avoid *if* ("If you'd like to try . . . ") and *why not* ("Why not send in a check?"). They lack positive emphasis and encourage your reader to say *no*.

2. **Make the action sound easy:** fill in the information on the reply card, sign the card (for credit sales), put the card and check (if payment is to accompany the order) in the envelope and mail the envelope. If you provide an envelope and pay postage, stress those facts.

3. **Offer a reason for acting promptly.** Reasons for acting promptly are easy to identify where a product is seasonal or when there is a genuine limit on the offer—time limit, price rise scheduled, limited supply, etc. Sometimes you may be able to offer a premium or a discount if the reader acts quickly. When these conditions do not exist, remind readers that the sooner they get the product, the sooner they can benefit from it; the sooner they contribute funds, the sooner their dollars can go to work to solve the problem.

4. **End with a positive picture** of the reader enjoying the product (in a sales letter) or of the reader's money working to solve the problem (in a fund-raising letter). The last sentence should never be a selfish request for money.

The action close can also remind readers of the central selling point, stress the guarantee, and mention when the customer will get the product.

Using a P.S.

Studies of eye movement show that people often look to see who a letter is from before they read the letter. Therefore, direct mail often uses a deliberate P.S. after the signature block. The P.S. may offer a reader benefit or make a point not made in the letter. If it restates the central selling point, or some other point which the letter does make, it should do so in different words so that it won't sound repetitive when the reader does read the letter through from start to finish.

Here are three of the many kinds of effective P.S.s.

- Reason to act promptly:

> P.S.   Once I finish the limited harvest, that's it!   I do not store any SpringSweet Onions for late orders.   I will ship all orders on a first come, first served basis and when they are gone they are gone.   Drop your order in the mail today . . . or give me a call toll free at 800–531–7470!   (In Texas: 800–292–5437)

Sales letter for Frank Lewis Alamo Fruit

---

* Based on Hershell Gordon Lewis, "To Ask or Not to Ask, That Is the Question," *Direct Marketing* 45 (August 1982): 56–57.

- Reference to another part of the package:

> P.S. I'm enclosing a brochure that will tell you a little bit more about the thousands of kids who come to us each year. I hope you will read it, and give our kids whatever help you can. Thanks.

> Fund-raising letter for Covenant House, a shelter for runaway children and teens

- Restatement of central selling point:

> P.S. *Guarantee:* Food and fun and fascination in one of the world's most dynamic cities. Cosmopolitan to the core, beautiful to the boundary of belief, a city which offers dining and theatres and galleries—where performances and exhibits of artistically creative expression can help you appreciate even more fully your own love affair with words. Yes?

> Letter asking for reservations for the Association for Business Communication's International Convention in Toronto

WRITING STYLE

Direct mail is the one kind of business writing where elegance and beauty of language matter; in every other kind, elegance is welcome but efficiency is all that finally counts. Direct mail imitates the word choice and rhythm of conversation. The best sales and fund-raising writing is closer to the language of poetry than to that of academia: it shimmers with images, it echoes with sound, it vibrates with energy.

Because readers will keep reading only if the letter is interesting and easy to read, writing must be not only tight but also vivid and entertaining. Many of the things that make writing a joy to read *add* words because they add specifics or evoke an emotional response. Individual sentences should be tight. The passage as a whole may be fun to read precisely because of the details and images that "could have been left out."

1. Make Your Writing Tight.

Flabby writing is never good; in direct mail, it is particularly dangerous, since a bored reader will stop reading. To tighten writing, direct mail breaks some of the rules of grammar. In the following examples, note how sentence fragments and ellipses (spaced dots) are used in parallel structure to move the reader along:

> So tiny, it fits virtually unnoticed in your pocket. So meticulously hand-assembled by unhurried craftsmen in Switzerland, that production may never exceed demand. So everyday useful, that you'll wonder how you ever got along without it.

Letter asking for inquiries about Dictaphone

---

* Quoted from Bill Jayme, quoted in John Francis Tighe, "Complete Creative Checklist for Copywriters," *Advertising Age,* February 9, 1987, 24, 69.

Why Are Direct Mail Letters So Long?*

People in mainstream advertising often ask why we in direct marketing are so verbose. Letters that can run to eight pages. Brochures the size of a bedsheet. . . . How come? Because a single mailing package must in one fell swoop do the work, in more conventional settings, of many hundreds of people.

It must create a need for your product, like the print ad, radio commercial, or billboard. . . .

It must show how your product looks, like the TV commercial. . . .

It must explain how your product works, like the in-store demonstrator. . . .

It must answer questions and reassure, like the salesperson.

It must instruct and caution, like the label. . . . It must inspire confidence, like a reputable company. . . .

Finally, it must ring up the sale, like the person at the checkout counter. Do you take credit cards? Can I give you a postdated check? If he hates it, can I bring it back?

Gimmicks and Gadgets in Business-to-Business Sales*

Direct mail letters to business customers frequently use unexpected enclosures to get the attention of busy executives.

Federal Express sent executives a five-pound barbell to introduce its five-pound overnight delivery service.

Airborne Express sent a plastic pouch of shredded U.S. currency to persuade executives that "air express shipping with someone else is like tearing up money."

Health and Tennis Corp. of America sells corporate fitness programs. Its package to executives included a message printed on a pair of size-60 boxer shorts.

Mature Outlook increased its ad pages with the campaign "Get a Taste of the Fresh New Way to Reach the Mature Market." Mailings in the series included a crate of oranges, an orange sweatshirt, and a candy dispenser with orange and green jelly beans. The campaign cost $90,000 and brought in $142,000 of additional revenue in the first issue after the campaign.

Cessna delivered 800 homing pigeons in cages to 800 decision makers. Copy told readers, "If you want more information, let loose this homing bird who will bring your request flying to us and we will have our key man come to see you about the new Cessna executive jet. . . . If you want the cage and bird picked up, call us and we will have a messenger come and take the bird away." The "mailing" cost $15,000. The return: four jets sold—at $1 million each.

> Dear Member-elect:
>
> If you still believe that there are only nine planets in our solar system . . .
>
> . . . that wine doesn't breathe . . . and that you'd recognize a Neanderthal man on sight if one sat next to you on the bus . . .
>
> . . . check your score. There aren't. It does. You wouldn't.

Subscription letter for *Natural History*

2. Use Sound Patterns to Emphasize Words.

When you repeat sounds, you create patterns that catch the reader's attention, please the ear, and emphasize the words they occur in. You're already familiar with a number of kinds of sound patterns, even if some of the terminology is new to you. **Alliteration** occurs when several syllables begin with the same sound. **Rhyme** is the repetition of the final vowel sounds and, if the words end with consonants, the final consonant sounds. **Rhythm** is the repetition of a pattern of accented and unaccented syllables. The **rule of three** explains that when you have a series of three items that are logically parallel, the last receives the most emphasis.

Alliteration marks the opener-anecdote quoted earlier. The *s* and *z* sounds in the first sentence focus our attention on the snakes. The repetition of *st* in the third paragraph emphasizes those words. (Note that these paragraphs also use sentence fragments.)

> She hoisted herself up noiselessly so as not to disturb the rattlesnakes snoozing there in the sun.
>
> To her left, the high desert of New Mexico. Indian country. To her right, the rock carvings she had photographed the day before. Stick people. Primitive animals.
>
> Up ahead, three sandstone slabs stood stacked against the face of the cliff.

Subscription letter for *Science84*

Rhythm, rhyme, and the rule of three emphasize words in the following example:

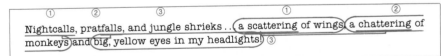

Headline, sales letter for Tom Timmins cigars

This letter goes on to tell the story of a search for tobacco in a tropical jungle—in a style that evokes the feeling of the Bogart-Hepburn movie *The African Queen.*

---

* Based on John Yeck, "Federal Express Mail Program Successful in Many Areas," *Direct Marketing* 45, no. 3 (July 1982): 60–66; *Direct Marketing* 50, no. 10 (February 1988): 80; "1986 Caples Creative Award Winners," *Direct Marketing* 49, no. 10 (February 1987): 80; Gloria Savini, "Sense Appeal," *Direct Marketing* 50, no. 6 (October 1987): 152–54; *Direct Marketing* 49, no. 7 (November 1986): 123; Ray Considine and Murray Raphel, *The Great Brain Robbery* (Pasadena, CA: The Great Brain Robbery, 1981), 186.

3. Use Psychological Description.

Psychological description, as you saw in Chapter 14, means describing your product or service in terms of reader benefits. In a sales letter, you can use psychological description to create a scenario so the reader can picture himself or herself using your product or service and enjoying its benefits. You can also use psychological description to describe the problem your product will solve.

A *Bon Appétit* subscription letter uses psychological description in its opener and in the P.S., creating a frame for the sales letter:

> Dear Reader:
>
> First, fill a pitcher with ice.
>
> Now pour in a bottle of ordinary red wine, a quarter cup of brandy, and a small bottle of Club soda.
>
> Sweeten to taste with a quarter to half cup of sugar, garnish with slices of apple, lemon, and orange....
>
> ...then *move your chair to a warm, sunny spot.* You've just made yourself Sangria—one of the great glories of Spain, and the perfect thing to sit back with and sip while you consider this invitation....
>
> ...
>
> P.S. One more thing before you finish your Sangria....

It's hard to imagine any reader really stopping to follow the recipe before finishing the letter, but the scenario is so vivid that one can imagine the sunshine even on a cold, gray day.

4. Make Your Letter Sound as if It's Written by a Real Person.

The "author" of a letter—the **persona,** or character who allegedly writes the letter—can be interesting and can keep us reading. Use the rhythms of speech, vivid images, and colloquial words to create the effect that the author is a "character."

The following opening creates a persona who fits the product:

> Dear Friend:
>
> There's no use trying. I've' tried and tried to tell people about my fish. But I wasn't rigged out to be a letter writer, and I can't do it. I can close-haul a sail with the best of them. I know how to pick out the best fish of the catch, I know just which fish will make the tastiest mouthfuls, but I'll never learn the knack of writing a letter that will tell people why my kind of fish—fresh-caught prime-grades, right off the fishing boats with the deep-sea tang still in it—is lots better than the ordinary store kind.

Sales letter, Frank Davis Fish Company

This letter, with its "aw, shucks, I can't sell" persona, with language designed to make you see an unassuming fisherman ("rigged out," "close-haul"), was written by a professional advertiser.[4]

Characters can also be used to create interest. A company that rents office

---

I'm Not Going to Use a Dictionary to Read Direct Mail*

I flew home from the US on United Airlines last year. Now I receive direct mail from them once in a while. I've never read any of it, though, since it's all written in English. Of course, I can read English with a dictionary in my hand, but I am not willing to go to that much effort just to read direct mail. I wonder if any Americans ever receive direct mail from Japanese companies in Japanese.

---

* Quoted from Tohru Hasegawa, "Computers Here and There," *Intercom* 33, no. 7 (March 1988): 2.

FIGURE 16.1
S. MOUSE OF S. ROSE[5]

Buy new and used
office equipment,
furniture and business
machines:

DISTRIBUTORS FOR:
• Cosco • Wesco
• Gregsom • Sturgis
• Meilink • Bentson
• Stocor • Mayline
• Myrtle • Imperial
• Port-A-Wall

S. ROSE, INC.

1213 PROSPECT AVENUE   •   CLEVELAND 15, OHIO   •   CHerry 1 · 1060

```
i am s. mouse of s. rose, inc. and the s. stands for sinnamon.

you can spell sinnamon any way you want.  my mother spells it with
an s.

that man whose account ive been handling for the roses just laughed
and ,laughed at me over the telephone.  you cant even spell sinnamon,
he said.

i told him he was lucky to get a mouse that could spell at all.
i said, most mice couldnt even answer the phone.

and he said, i meant to ask you about that, how do you answer the
phone.  and i said, well you watch the little buttons and the one
that lights up, thats the one you press and you say, hello.

why you little rat, he said, dont get smart with me.  im tired of
waiting on those filing cabinets, anyhow.  all 15,000 of them.

you mean, 12,500, i said, you told me 10,000 and then changed your
mind and he said, youve moused me up for the last time.  turn in
your night managers suit, mouse, he said. im cancelling my order.

wait, i said, i am trying to learn the business.

im giving you the business, he said, from now on i will deal with
bob rose and dick rose direct.  thats cherry 1-1060, isnt it.

yes, sir, i said.  i only know the underside of this business.  bob
and dick know everything about office furniture and fixtures and
machines.  theyll sell you what you want or theyll rent it to you
or theyll even buy your equipment.  just call cherry 1-1060.

i know that, he said, so why should i deal with a stupid mouse.

gee, i wish that man would leave me alone.  the worst part of it
is i dont even know his name.  sometimes i wonder if i will ever
be a hard-hitting go-getter in the business world.

                              cordially,
```

```
                              s. mouse
                              night manager
                              s. rose, inc.
```

*Greater Trade Allowance on
Your Furniture and Business
Machines...Because We
Sell Both New and Used
Equipment and Maintain Our
Own Complete Repair Factory.

furniture used a mouse to "author" a series of mailings. Figure 16.1 reprints one letter in the series. Typography helps to define the character: the mouse can't hit two keys simultaneously, so there are no capital letters or symbols (e.g., the apostrophe) that require using the shift key on a traditional typewriter. The "signature" is a tiny pawprint. Even though we know "s. mouse" isn't real, his personality makes a letter about office furniture—not in itself a fascinating topic—interesting to read.

PARTS OF A DIRECT MAIL PACKAGE

The letter is the most important part of a direct mail package, but several other parts help accomplish your purpose. The **package** includes the outer envelope and everything that goes in it: the main letter, brochures, samples, secondary letters, reply coupon or card, and the reply envelope.

The **envelope** can do more than simply protect the contents during mailing. One test found that an envelope marked "OPEN NOW" produced an 18% higher response rate than a plain envelope (the rest of the package parts were identical). Words on the envelope are called **teaser copy**. Like openers, teasers must get the reader's attention and have some logical link to the body of the letter.

Brochures give more information about the product or organization and, especially if they have color pictures, can involve the sense of sight and contribute to the package's emotional appeal. Magazines and products relating to food, decorating, scenery, gardening, sports, and history seem especially to lend themselves to good brochures, but you can use a brochure in almost any package.

Samples give the reader something to touch and may help sell your product. Swatches of cloth enable readers to check color and quality of the clothing you're selling; a small packet of seeds may motivate readers to order your book on gardening; a scratch-and-sniff card can help sell perfume or scented soap.

Many packages contain **secondary letters:** letters on small paper to readers who have decided not to accept the offer, letters from people who have benefited from the charity in the past, letters from recognized people corroborating the claims made in the main letter.

The **reply card** can be a separate card, a tear-off stub of the letter or brochure, or even the (large) inside flap of the reply envelope. Make the card easy to fill out. Ask only for essential information, but ask for everything you need to fill the order or to use for later mailings to that reader.

If readers will be sending in checks, a separate reply envelope is necessary. In sales packages, the postage is normally paid. In fund-raising appeals, even if the postage is paid the letter often invites the reader to affix a stamp, so that more of the organization's money can go to the cause. A postage-paid reply card, with no envelope, is possible if you are just asking for inquiries or if only credit sales are possible, but be careful—some readers prefer not to make their requests or their credit card numbers public.

SUMMARY OF KEY POINTS

- **Direct mail** asks for an order, inquiry, or contribution directly from the reader.
- **A good appeal** offers a believable description of benefits, links the benefits of the product or service to a need or desire that motivates the reader,

What to Put on a Reply Card
A good reply card will have

- The central selling point.
- Basic information about the product or service (price, etc.).
- Place to indicate how long a subscription or what size, color, etc. the customer wants.
- How many items the reader wants, or, for fund-raising letters, the size of the gift. (Suggest a range of donations and have a spot for "other" amounts.)
- A reminder that the donation is tax-deductible (if it is).
- If credit sales are allowed, the customer's credit card, number, expiration date, and signature.
- The company's name and address (so the reader can act even if the letter and the reply envelope are lost).
- The reader's name and address, with a special place for the zip code. (You must have the zip code to mail packages.)
- A code indicating the mailing (so the mailer can see which version of a letter brings in the most responses).

Most of this information also appears elsewhere in the package; nevertheless, it must be repeated on the reply card or coupon. Some readers who plan to order or donate may throw away the letter and just keep the reply card.

Direct Mail and the Entrepreneur

If you think you might like to go into business for yourself, you can save money if you can do your firm's own direct mail. Professionally written direct mail is expensive: $3,000 a package if you hire someone who's not well-known, $7,000 to $25,000 if you hire a "name." And that's just the creative cost: you still have to pay for printing and postage.

Most small businesses just can't afford that money. Following the principles here won't make you a "pro" overnight, but it will enable you to write solid, serviceable letters that will build your business. Then, when you're rich, you can hire an agency if you want to.

makes the reader want to read the letter, and motivates the reader to act. The appeal is made up of the words in the letter, the pictures in the brochure, and all the parts of the package, from outer envelope to reply card.

- Calling direct mail "junk" mail may cause us to respond to the negative symbol rather than to the reality.
- The first three steps in writing a sales or fund-raising letter are to (1) learn about the product or service, (2) choose and analyze the target audience, and (3) choose a central selling point. The **target audience** is the group of people one expects to be interested in the product, service, or cause. A **central selling point** is a reader benefit which by itself motivates your readers to act and serves as an umbrella to cover all the other benefits.
- The most useful pattern of organization for direct mail letters is Star-Chain-Hook. A good **star** (opener) makes readers want to read the letter and provides a reasonable transition to the body of the letter. Four modes for openers are **questions, narration, startling statements, and quotations.** A good **chain** (body) answers readers' questions, overcomes their objections, and involves them emotionally. A good **hook** (action close) tells readers what to do, makes the action sound easy, gives them a reason for acting promptly, and ends with a reader benefit or a picture of the reader's money helping to solve the problem.
- Good writing in direct mail is tight. It uses sound patterns to emphasize words, uses psychological description, and sounds as if it were written by a real person.
- A **direct mail package** includes the outer envelope and everything that goes in it: the main letter, brochures, samples, secondary letters, reply coupon or card, and the reply envelope.

NOTES

1. "Direct Marketing . . . An Aspect of Total Marketing," *Direct Marketing* 50, no. 6 (October 1987): 29.

2. Larry J. Sabato, "Mailing for Dollars," *Psychology Today,* October 1984, 38.

3. Pat Farley, "Direct Mail Copy—The Marketing and Creative Process," Direct Mail/Marketing Manual Release 310, no. 1, May 1979, 1, 3.

4. Maxwell Sackheim, *My First 65 Years in Advertising* (Blue Ridge Summit, PA: Tab Books, 1975), 97–100.

5. S. Rose is a major Cleveland, Ohio, full-service office furniture dealership. The creative work and marketing strategy were developed by Robert Silverman, Inc. of Cleveland, Ohio.

EXERCISES AND PROBLEMS FOR CHAPTER 16

16–1 EVALUATING ENVELOPE TEASERS

In the examples in 16–1, the words in square brackets describe the appearance of the envelope or lettering. The name in parentheses is from the return address. If no name is listed, either the return address is a street address only or there is no return address at all. Unless otherwise noted, the teaser copy appeared on the front (address side) of the envelope.

Assume that you are part of the target audience for each of the following sales or fund-raising campaigns. Would you open the envelope? Why or why not? Do others in the class agree with you?

1. [8½″ by 11″ red envelope with black print]
   (The Danbury Mint)
   A classic car
   for kings,
   queens,
   movie stars
   . . . and you!

2. (Popular Science Book Club)
   Take your $42.50 copy of
   Carpentry and Building Construction
   for just $3.95.

3. (The Veterans Census)
   Confidential
   ["Resident" and your address printed on the envelope]

4. [Green envelope with a black-and-white picture of a turtle]
   (Greenpeace) [on back of envelope]
   All the turtles of this species are male.
   Can you guess how they reproduce?

5. [First five lines in black letters; last line in red]
   ENCLOSED:
   Your first
   real chance
   to tell the
   National Rifle Association
   TO GO TO HELL

6. [Mayor's seal as part of return address. Words in black handwriting.]
   (The City of Fort Wayne, Office of the Mayor)
   The best invitation

You ever gave
a burglar . . . Photo
enclosed!

7. [5″ by 8″ red envelope arriving in mid-February]
   A love letter especially for [your name and address]

8. [Material above line on front of envelope. Material below line on back.]
   A Consumer Reports
   True or False
   Quick Quiz

   1. Two Excedrin Tablets
      contain more caffeine
      than a cup of coffee
      True[ ] False [ ]
         (over)

   _____

   2. A 100-watt, soft-white, *long-life* light bulb provides as much light as a standard 100-watt bulb.
      True[ ] False [ ]
   3. Foreign-built cars provide you with greater protection in an accident than domestic models.
      True[ ] False[ ]
      For the answers and explanation, see inside.

9. (McGraw-Hill)
   Rub here [large round spot, revealing the word "FREE" when scratched off]
   to develop
   a silver tongue
   a golden touch
   and
   a mind like
   a steel trap.

10. [5″ by 8″ envelope with a picture of a surprised, indignant, long-necked bird staring straight at you. The return address is printed sideways on the envelope, as are the words "Do not fold. Bumper sticker enclosed."]

    (The Nature Conservancy)
    RELAX!
    Both of you. [Two hands, one pointing to

the bird, one to the window
with your name and address]
(A $10 nest egg will do it.)

16–2 EVALUATING SALES LETTERS

Collect sales letters that you receive. To expand your collection, ask your parents, co-workers, landlord, or neighbors to save the ones they get. Use the following questions to evaluate each package:

- Does the envelope use a teaser? Did the recipient open the envelope?
- What mode does the opener use? Is it related to the teaser, if any? Is it related to the rest of the letter? How good is the opener?
- What central selling point does the letter use?
- What kinds of proof does the letter use? Is the logic valid? Can you think of any questions or objections that aren't answered?
- Where does the letter use alliteration, rhythm, rhyme, or the rule of three?
- What kind of persona does the letter create? Does it seem appropriate for the product or service? Who signs the letter?
- Does the close tell readers what to do, make action easy, give a reason for acting promptly, and end with a positive picture?
- Does the letter use a P.S.? How good is it?
- Is the visual appeal of the letter attractive? Why or why not?
- What other items besides the letter are in the package?

As your instructor directs,

a. Share your analysis of one or more letters with a small group of your classmates.

b. Analyze one letter in a presentation to the class. If possible, make overhead transparencies of the parts of the letter you discuss.

c. Analyze one letter in a memo to your instructor. Provide a copy or photocopy of the letter along with your memo.

d. With several other students, write a group memo or report analyzing one part of the letter (e.g., openers). Use at least 10 letters for your analysis; provide the copies or photocopies as an appendix to your report.

16–3 INCREASING ATTENDANCE AT COLLEGE REUNIONS

You're Director of Alumni Affairs for your campus. One of your concerns is reunions. Less than 10% of the alumni whose names and addresses you have come to

the reunions—even the big ones for those 25 and 50 years after graduation. You'd like to get more people. People who come to reunions are far more likely to make major gifts to the school. Also, if you could get more people, you could plan more expensive events during the weekend, which might in turn appeal to more people.

As your instructor directs,

a. Do some research. Find out what information your Alumni office has about its alumni. In addition to current address, does it know occupation? Income? Interests? What were the concerns of these people 25 or 50 years ago? Look at past issues of the college paper and yearbook, at past issues of the local newspaper.

b. Identify the kind of events that would be most likely to appeal to the alumni. Would they enjoy a sports event? A movie? A concert? A lecture? (on what topic?) A dance (what kind of music)? What special touches could be added to make the weekend more enjoyable for them? How can spouses best be included in the weekend, without being made to feel excluded if they didn't go to the same school?

c. Write a letter, reply card, and brochure to go out to alumni inviting them to come to their 25th or 50th class reunion.

d. Repeat the process for other class reunions.

16–4 BRAINSTORMING OPENERS FOR A MAGAZINE SUBSCRIPTION LETTER

a. Using at least **two** of the four different modes—question, narration, startling statement, and quotation—write **three** possible openers for a letter urging readers to subscribe to a magazine (you pick the magazine).

b. For each opener indicate (1) what mode it uses and (2) how you would make a transition to the body of the letter. (You may write out the transition or just describe it, whichever is easier.)

c. Rate the three openers in terms of their effectiveness, and briefly explain the reason for your ratings.

16–5 WRITING A MAGAZINE SUBSCRIPTION LETTER

Write a $2\frac{1}{2}$- to 4-page letter persuading **new subscribers** to subscribe to a magazine of your choice. Assume that your letter would have a reply coupon and postage-paid envelope. You do NOT have to write these, but DO refer to them in your letter.

Choose a magazine you yourself read or one which deals with a subject or sport you know something about. You may choose a narrower target audience for this letter than the magazine uses. For example, if the magazine is designed to appeal to women ages 18–35, for this assignment you could write to college women, ages 18–25. If you narrow the target audience, be sure to tell your instructor.

Hints:

- Read several issues of the magazine, looking both at editorial content and at ads, to see who the magazine's target audience is. Choose a central selling point that will appeal to that audience.

- Pay special attention to language. To keep your letter moving quickly, consider occasionally using sentence fragments or ellipses. Try to choose vivid, evocative language; try your hand at alliteration or other repetitive patterns.

- Everyone has had the experience of seeing interesting headlines on a magazine cover but then being disappointed by the stories inside. Be sure to prove your claims by giving examples and specifics. You may use material from previous issues of the magazine; you may need to edit or rewrite it for maximum effect. Choose details that will interest your reader.

- Get current figures about subscription rates from the magazine itself. It's OK to offer a free issue, a premium, or a discount, but do not depend on the offer alone to motivate people. Your letter must be fully persuasive even without the special premium.

16–6 SELLING A CARE PACKAGE

To raise money, some student governments sell Care Packages for final exam week. Parents buy the packages for their sons or daughters. If your campus does this, use the real information about prices and contents. If it doesn't, use the information below:

Package contains: 1 apple, 1 orange, 1 pear, 1 box of raisins, 2 cans of natural unsweetened juice (1 tomato, 1 grapefruit), 6 fresh-baked chocolate chip cookies, 1 Hershey candy bar, 1 Snickers candy bar, 5 pieces of bubble gum, 1/4 lb. wrapped hard candy. Delivered the last day of classes. Price: $12.95 (includes delivery).

As your instructor directs,
a. Write a letter which could be sent to the parents or guardians of students at your school

to persuade them to order the package for their students.
b. Prepare a reply card. [Hint: what information will you need to deliver the package? Do all parents have only one child in school at a time?]

16–7 CREATING A PERSONA

Create a persona who could be used in sales letters for one of the following:

- A pharmaceutical company in mailings to doctors.
- A company selling gourmet candies.
- A company selling clothing and supplies for hunting, fishing, and other outdoor sports.
- A publisher in mailings to bookstores about new books.
- A company that provides cleaning and janitorial services.
- A catering company.
- A company that sells sports equipment to schools.

As your instructor directs,
a. Describe the persona.
b. Write one to three pages of copy from the persona. You may use a single letter or several messages, but they must total one full single-spaced page.

16–8 CHOOSING A GIMMICK

While any enclosure will encourage recipients to open an envelope, the best gimmicks are tied in some way to the sender's business or to the purpose of the letter.

1. Select an inexpensive gimmick to use with each of the following:
   a. A CPA firm in a goodwill letter to its clients.
   b. A stock-brokerage firm in a first letter to create inquiries about buying stocks.
   c. A car dealership in a letter promoting its service facilities to car buyers whose warranties have expired.
   d. A university in mailings to high school students whom it wants to attract: good students, athletes, minority students.
   e. A letter selling a book on growing vegetables.
2. Select a gimmick to use with each of the following. Assume that the cost of each item is not an issue: the expected return on investment allows expensive enclosures.

a. A letter to filmmakers urging them to film on location in your state.

b. A letter to Association Executives urging them to book your hotel for their conventions.

c. A letter selling an electronic piano/synthesizer which can create the sound of 45 different instruments.

d. A letter to hospitals urging them to buy your computer system for tracking patient records, billing, and insurance reimbursements.

e. A letter to well-to-do homeowners urging them to hire your landscape architecture firm to design and implement plans for front and back yards.

16–9 SELLING A BOOK ON GARDENING

Assume that your state's land-grant college has prepared a 64-page paperback book *Growing Vegetables in [Your State]*. The book has advice about how big a garden to plant, fertilizing and watering, and choosing and harvesting vegetables. It highlights 30 vegetables, telling which varieties of each grow best in your state, the pros and cons of starting from seed or buying plants, and when to plant outdoors. The book is written by two professors in the college of agriculture of the land-grant university; the price is $6.95, which includes postage and handling.

Pick a target audience and write a $2\frac{1}{2}$- to 4-page letter persuading them to buy the book.

If your instructor directs, also prepare a reply card.

Fund-Raising Letters

QUESTIONS

- What information do you need to write a good fund-raising letter? Where can you find it?

- What is the basic strategy of fund-raising letters? How does the strategy affect the close?

- What is the secondary purpose in a fund-raising letter?

- What kinds of actions should you suggest besides giving money?

- How much should you ask for? How can you increase the amount that people give?

- What four things do you have to prove in a fund-raising letter?

- How do you build emotional appeal? How strong should emotional appeal be?

- What is the function of a common ground in a fund-raising letter?

The [fund-raising] letter unites members of the group by
identifying the warring forces of good and evil and enlisting the
reader's participation in the battle. The act of giving money to the
group acquires a particular symbolic interpretation in the letter: it
is a call to arms, a celebration, a last-ditch stand, a fight against
impossible odds, or a call to brotherhood.

John Pauly
"The Historical and Cultural Significance
of Direct-Mail Fund-Raising Letters," 1985

M any of us are active in groups that need to raise money: churches and
synagogues, high school and college bands, community theatres, sororities and
fraternities, sports teams, local and national politics, scouting, historical societies, charitable groups. If you can write good fund-raising letters, you can
make a substantial contribution to groups you care about while you work for
the goals and values you believe in.

GETTING THE INFORMATION YOU NEED

To write a good fund-raising letter you need to be able to answer the following
questions in detail:

- What is the problem your group is helping to solve? (If possible,
  collect examples to illustrate the need.)
- How, specifically, is your group helping? (Collect stories about specific people who have been helped, specific gains that have been
  achieved. Also get overall figures.)
- What support does your group already get from tax dollars, user
  fees, ticket sales, etc.? Why are private funds necessary?
- What are the group's immediate goals? How much will it cost to
  achieve them? (Try to get costs for some of the specific subgoals as
  well as the total budget needed.)

If you're writing a letter for a local organization, visit its office or center
and talk to the people who work there. If you're writing a letter for a national
group, check the phone book to see if there's a local chapter where you can
get brochures, flyers, and information. Check the university or public library
for information on the group or on the problem the group is working to
alleviate. Check *The Reader's Guide to Periodical Literature* for magazine
articles about the problem which may have anecdotes and specifics you can
use.

STRATEGY IN FUND-RAISING APPEALS

In a fund-raising letter, the basic emotional strategy is **vicarious participation.**
By donating money, readers participate vicariously in work they are not able
to do personally. This strategy affects the pronouns you use. Throughout the

letter, use *we* to talk about your group. However, at the end, talk about what *you* the reader will be doing. End positively, with a picture of the reader's dollars helping to solve the problem.

Your **primary purpose** in a fund-raising letter is to get money, and you ask for donations in your close. An important **secondary purpose** is to build support for your cause, so that readers who are not persuaded to give will still have favorable attitudes toward your group and will be sympathetic when they hear about it again. This secondary purpose affects both the content of your letter and the action close.

To achieve both your primary and secondary purposes, you must give a great deal of information in fund-raising letters. This information (1) helps to persuade readers; (2) gives supporters evidence to use in conversations with others; and (3) gives readers who are not yet supporters evidence which may make them see the group as a worthwhile one, even if they do not give money now.

This information makes fund-raising letters long. You can be brief only when you are writing to people who already support your cause. To gain new donors, or to persuade previous donors to increase their gifts, you must provide both logical proof and emotional appeal.

In your close, in addition to asking for money, suggest other ways the reader can help: doing volunteer work, scheduling a meeting on the subject, writing letters to Congress or the leaders of other countries, etc. By suggesting other ways to participate, you not only involve readers but also avoid one of the traps of fund-raising letters: sounding as though you are selfish, only interested in readers for the money they can give.

Deciding How Much to Ask For

How much to ask for depends only partly on how much you need. Not everyone will give, so you need some sizeable gifts from those who do respond.

There are two basic strategies in suggesting amounts. The usual strategy is to suggest a range of amounts, from $15 or $25 (for employed people) up to perhaps double what you *really* expect to get from a single donor. However, a second strategy is to ask for a small, set amount which nearly everyone can afford ($1 or $5). This strategy is particularly effective in a follow-up to people who did not respond to your first appeal.

You can increase the size of gifts by using the following techniques:

1. **Suggest amounts in descending order.** Both in your close and the reply card, say "$100, $50, $25, or whatever amount you prefer" rather than starting with the smallest and going up. (In your close, suggest only three specific amounts to keep the sentence a manageable length. On the reply card, you can suggest more. In both, allow for "other" amounts.)

2. **Ask for gifts slightly higher than the normal cutoff points.** Most people think in terms of a gift of $5, $25, $50, $100, etc. You can increase the average gift by asking for $6, $30, $60, etc.

3. **Link the gift to what it will buy.** Tell how much money it costs to buy a brick, a hymnal, or a stained glass window for a church; a book or journal subscription for a college library; a meal for a hungry child. Linking amounts to specific gifts helps readers feel involved and often motivates them to give more: instead of saying,

---

What Else Can They Do Besides Sending Money?*

Most of the alternatives to giving money are fairly obvious: giving supplies, volunteering, scheduling speakers, writing letters. But the Center for Environmental Education asked Florida readers to turn off their lights.

Newly hatched sea turtles instinctively know to wait until dark before leaving the nest. Then they head for light: the wide expanse of sky over the sea is brighter than the dark horizon over land.

But the floodlights from condominiums fool the turtles. They crawl toward land, away from the safety of the sea. Cars crush some; predators devour others. Those that survive the night bake in the sun the next day.

The letter asked for funds for newspaper ads urging state and local governments to pass laws to limit outdoor lights. But it also asked owners of beachfront properties to turn off their outdoor lights after 11 P.M. from May 1 until October 31—the sea turtle hatching season.

* Based on "The 1986 John Caples Award Winners," *Fund Raising Management,* March 1987, 59–60.

For the Right Price, Your Name Can Be on Just About Anything*

Most people would rather not have their name on bathroom walls. Gary Horowitz isn't most people.

Mr. Horowitz, a professor and administrator at Alfred University in Alfred, N.Y., donated $5,000 for renovations at the school last year and got his name on a plaque. It reads "Everyone Has to Be Remembered Somehow!" and is mounted on one of the most scrutinized walls on campus, just across from the toilet in the first floor men's room of Alumni Hall.

"I could have bought a window for $7,500," he says. "But I wanted to be remembered in a different way." . . .

More than ever, many colleges, hospitals, museums and other institutions are naming nearly everything after someone—for the right price.

To name an endowed chair at Columbia University costs $1.5 million, but naming a plastic chair at the school's football stadium costs just $1,000. Carnegie Hall will name a grand staircase for $500,000 and a loading dock for $250,000. . . . Sutter General Hospital in Sacramento, Calif., is putting plaques on a wide range of equipment, from $127,000 ultrasound devices to $1,254 baby scales and $170 tuning-fork kits. . . .

It pays to do some comparison shopping. A new Chapel at Massachusetts General Hospital, for example, costs $2 million; at Westmoreland Hospital, the chapel went for $20,000. The gift shop at the Seattle Art Museum can be yours for $500,000; the new Judaica shop at the Temple of Israel in Greenville, S.C., will be named for a donor who recently gave $10,000. . . .

Elevators are popular, too. "Some people laugh about it," says Dell N. Thompson, vice president at the Albany (N.Y.) Medical Center, which is offering elevators for $150,000 each. "But when you bring to their attention the high kind of visibility that an elevator receives, it really turns their thinking around."

"I'll write a check for $25," the reader may say, "I'd like to give a _____" and write a check to cover it.

4. **Offer a premium for giving.** Public TV and radio stations have used this ploy with great success, offering books, umbrellas, and carryall bags for gifts at a certain level. The best premiums are things that people both want and will use or display, so that the organization will get further publicity when other people see the premium.

5. **Ask for a monthly pledge.** Many people can't write a big check even if your letter convinces them that your organization is one they strongly support. However, even people on tight budgets could give $5 or $10 a month; more prosperous people could give $25 a month or more. These repeat gifts not only bring in more money than the donors could give in a single check but also become part of the base of loyal supporters which is essential to the continued success of any organization that raises funds.

Always send a thank-you letter to people who respond to your letter, whatever the size of their gifts. By telling about the group's recent work, a thank-you letter can help reinforce donors' commitment to your cause. See Figure 3.1 in Chapter 3 for an example of a thank-you letter which uses a computer to personalize letters, filling in the donor's name and the amount of each gift.

Logical Proof in Fund-Raising Letters

You must prove four things in the body of your letter: (1) that the problem is serious, (2) that it can be solved or at least alleviated, (3) that your organization is helping to solve it, and (4) that private funds are needed. Let's look at each of these briefly.

1. The Problem Is Serious. Nobody can support every cause. You must show that your problem is not merely an annoyance but really matters.

If your problem is life-threatening, it is easy to show that it is serious, but you still need to be specific: you cannot count on everyone's knowing how many people are killed in the United States every year by drunk drivers, or how many children in the world go to bed hungry every night. Give some statistics; also tell about one individual who is affected.

If your problem is not life-threatening, you will need both logic and emotion. A good strategy for demonstrating the severity of a problem is to show that it threatens some goal or principle your readers find important. For example, a fund-raising letter to boosters of a high school swim team showed that team members' chances of setting records were reduced because timers relied on stopwatches. The letter showed that automatic timing equipment was accurate and produced faster times, since the timer's reaction time was no longer included in the time recorded.

2. The Problem Can Be Solved or Alleviated. People will not give money if they see the problem as hopeless: why throw money away? Obviously, 1 and 2 are in conflict: problems that are most serious (hunger, the threat of nuclear war, political repression, racism, major illnesses like cancer) are also those that are hardest to wipe out. Sometimes you can reason by analogy. Cures have

---

* Quoted from Gilbert Fuchsberg, "For the Right Price, Just About Anything Can Bear Your Name," *The Wall Street Journal,* September 21, 1987, 1, 18.

been found for other deadly diseases, so it's reasonable to hope that research can find cures for cancer and AIDS.

Sometimes you can show that short-term or partial solutions exist. For example, a UNICEF letter showed that four simple changes could save the lives of millions of children: oral rehydration, immunization, promoting breast feeding, and giving mothers cardboard growth charts so they'll know if their children are malnourished. Those solutions don't affect the underlying causes of poverty but they do keep children alive while we work on long-term solutions.

3. Your Organization Is Helping to Solve or Alleviate the Problem. Everyone has heard horror stories about fund-raising groups that give only 10% of the money they raise to the cause. The number of such groups may be small, but their existence means that every fund-raising group needs to prove that it is legitimate.

You also need to prove you are effective. Be specific. Talk about your successes in the past. Your past success helps readers believe that you can accomplish your goals.

4. Private Funds Are Needed to Accomplish Your Group's Goals. We all have the tendency to think that taxes, or foundations, or church collections yield enough to pay for medical research or basic human aid. If your group does get some tax or foundation money, show why more money is needed. If the organization helps people who might be expected to pay for the service, show why they cannot pay, or why they cannot pay enough to cover the full cost. If some of the funds have been raised by the people who will benefit, make that clear.

Emotional Appeal in Fund-Raising Letters

Logical conviction alone will not make people pull out their checkbooks; readers must be moved emotionally as well. Two questions arise: How strong should emotional appeal be? How do you create emotional appeal?

As a writer, you face a dilemma: a mild appeal is unlikely to sway any reader who is not already committed, but readers will feel manipulated by appeals they find too strong and reject them completely. Audience analysis may help you decide how much emotional appeal to use. If you don't know your audience well, use the strongest emotional appeal *you* feel comfortable with.

Emotional appeal is created largely by specifics. It is hard to care about, or even to imagine, a million people; it is easier to care about one specific person. Details and quotes help us see that person as real. A letter for a New York hospital talked about four people who owed their lives to the hospital: a baby, a young girl, a businessman, and an elderly woman. The letter brought in a greater response than a previous mailing which simply used statistics.[1]

Choosing and Using a Common Ground

In fund-raising letters, your common ground contributes both to logic and to emotional appeal. Your common ground needs to relate the goals of your organization to your readers' goals and values.

The Life You Save May Be Your Own*

A Stanford M.B.A. and former management consultant, [Sharon] Monsky was forced to change her life drastically when, in 1982, she was diagnosed as having scleroderma, a fairly rare disease that in the form she has kills most of its victims within seven years. Now, as head of the Scleroderma Research Foundation, a nonprofit company she started last November [1986], she is using her business acumen to raise money for studying the disease. . . .

At the start, she formed a board of directors, recruited a medical advisory board comprising doctors at universities across the country, and vowed that if she couldn't raise $150,000 in nine months she would quit. She raised $200,000 by the deadline and about $375,000 in the company's first year.

Fund-raising is "like selling Cheerios," explains Ms. Monsky, who says she now makes her presentations the way she used to pitch to clients as a consultant. "I have to convince people why they should support this cause over any other.". . .

Ms. Monsky also says that her illness has given her a new perspective: "I thought I had it all—a husband, a career, a brilliant future. Then I found out I'm not Superwoman. No one is a superperson. I appreciate being here much more each day. I just want to enjoy life and make a contribution."

---

* Quoted from Carrie Dolan, "One Victim of an Obscure Disease Uses Her Entrepreneurial Skills to Fight Back," *The Wall Street Journal*, December 14, 1987, 25.

Fund-Raising in Europe*

Although the United States is the richest country in the world, it is not the most generous.

A charity that raises funds for the Third World has been raising funds in the United States for over 20 years, has a list of several hundred thousand previous donors, and mails 10 million pieces a year.

In 1984, a branch of the same charity in a small European country started fund-raising by mail. The population is perhaps 1/20 as big as the U.S. population, yet, three years after it began sending out letters, the charity's Third World project gets more money from the European branch than it does from the United States.

Different Common Grounds for Different Audiences

If you hope to raise funds from two or more disparate groups, you may need two or more separate mailing pieces.

A service center for migrant farm workers appealed to two different groups: Christian churches and labor unions. The message to church people started with Jesus' quotation from Isaiah (Luke 4:18–19) and presented giving as an opportunity to follow Jesus' example. The message to union members didn't mention religion. Instead, it stressed employers' violations of state laws and the workers' need for justice within the law.

Make the common ground explicit. If you are raising funds from college alumni and using nostalgia as your common ground, refer to events that happened when they were in school. (Check back issues of the college yearbook for ideas.) If you're writing to members of a sorority or fraternity, refer to events the house is proud of, and use a salutation and complimentary close that remind readers of their membership. If you are writing to a group which sees the Bible as an authority, use appropriate biblical quotes and allusions.

SAMPLE LETTERS FOR ANALYSIS

Before you write your own fund-raising letters, examine the following examples: a professionally written letter for a national organization, a letter written for a local organization, and a follow-up letter to people who did not give to the first appeal.

Greenpeace "Save the Whales"

The powerful letter in Figure 17.1 uses both logic and emotional appeal effectively. The mailing list includes people who have given to liberal causes but not necessarily to wildlife or environmental causes specifically.

Visual Impact. This letter uses several devices to create good visual impact: a headline in large type, varied paragraph length, the restrained use of underlining, and indented paragraphs and lists. The letter is printed on two pages front and back. The blue-green ink suggests water.

Opener. The quote is a powerful opener. "Nursing infants," emphasized by being in the last line in boldface, builds emotional appeal.

The letter itself opens with a startling statement, which leads into a story. The opening description is powerful, in part because the first description of the killing is presented as a "lucky" shot, an easy death. The contrast between the living creature desperately trying to survive and the impersonality of "Quick Frozen Quality Whale Meat" further enlists our sympathies.

Body. The negative description with which the letter opens continues for almost a full page. But the end of the first page is positive: a picture of Greenpeace stopping the slaughter. More negative description will follow, but only after the reader has been assured that the problem can be solved.

Page 1 builds emotional appeal; the rest of the letter offers logical proof. On page 2, paragraphs 3 and 4 show that there are substitutes for each of the products made from whales. These paragraphs answer the objection that the killing, though regrettable, may be necessary. Pages 2 and 3 have lists showing what Greenpeace has done. The list that begins at the bottom of page 3 shows what the money is used for.

Close. The action close comprises the last four paragraphs. The three actions build to an appeal for funds (which should have been presented in descending order). The various options involve the reader; any of them will help Greenpeace further its goals. The last sentences of point 3 are excellent, suggesting urgency and reinforcing the claims that the money is needed and will be well spent.

* Based on Jerald E. Huntsinger, "Some Disturbing Advice from Fund Raisers Overseas," *Fund Raising Management* 18, no. 1 (March 1987): 95.

FIGURE 17.1
GREENPEACE "SAVE THE WHALES"

How do they kill the whales?
It's simple; they harpoon every
whale they can find, right down to
the nursing infants.
—a former crewmember of a pirate
whaler

Dear Friend,

Let's be precise from the start: the ship Hai Yen is a pirate, an outlaw. When it sails next month, it will do what it's done for the last four years: kill whales, as many as possible, as quickly and profitably as it can. Manned by expert Japanese crews, it will leave Taiwan to roam the Pacific -- and leave devastation in its wake.

The Hai Yen's owners don't care about the survival of whales, or international limits on whaling. Taiwan doesn't have whaling limits, so the Hai Yen and other ships like it are free to kill whatever they find -- thousands of whales a year.

The killing itself can be monstrous.

When the earth's largest mammals surface for air, the harpoon with its explosive iron tip is fired. With luck, the harpoonist's aim, the swell of the seas, the turn of the whale all combine to place the harpoon deep within the whale's spine where the shock of the explosion does its work quickly, tearing through the inside of the creature.

But often, "luck" escapes. The harpoon strikes badly, inaccurately, burying itself deep inside the whale but not killing. Then the whale sounds, diving deep in a desperate attempt to escape. But the escape is seldom successful -- in time, shock, the bleeding, the exhaustion take effect, and the boat slowly comes alongside, reeling the harpoon's line. When the animal finally dies, cable is attached and it is winched aboard, to be carved up and sold as oil, as fat, or even as "Quick Frozen Quality Whale Meat."

Pirate whaling -- based in Taiwan and other nations which ignore international treaties, are a growing danger to the whales. As other nations cut back on whaling, their share of the total increases. Last year that total cost the lives of more than 20,000 whales.

That's why when the whalers put to sea this year, Greenpeace will be there.

Once we sight their ships, we'll then do what we have done for the last six years: scramble into tiny rubber boats, and set out to place

FIGURE 17.1
(continued)

-2-

ourselves between the hunters and the hunted, between the harpoons and the largest relative of mankind.

But this year we need your help -- more than ever before -- to save the whales.

Every 26 minutes a great whale dies in agony at the hands of men. All nine species of great whale are on the U.S. Government's endangered list ... and some may soon enter the pages of history, as the Atlantic Gray Whale already has. Before intensive hunting began, the great Blue Whale -- the largest animal that has ever lived -- numbered over 300,000; today it is commercially extinct.

The tragedy of the slaughter is that there is no need. Once upon a time perhaps there was: whale oil was used to light lamps and lubricate machines. Delicate ambergris was used in expensive perfumes, and baleen was used for stays in women's corsets. But once upon a time there were millions of whales.

Today every single product made from the whale can be replaced by something else. Clearly, whale oil for lamps was replaced long ago; its use as a delicate lubricant for machines is now finally done by synthetics. Baleen corsets haven't been seen on women in decades, and ambergris for perfumes can be replaced by a number of other substitutes.

But that doesn't stop the whalers.

Which is why Greenpeace exists, and why we need your support.

If governments and politics aren't stopping the whalers, worldwide protest is. In the past six years, Greenpeace has non-violently confronted whalers in every ocean in the world. From the stormy North Atlantic to the mid-Pacific to the shores of western Australia, we have pursued and protested relentlessly.

-- Last summer, for example, our ship the Rainbow Warrior, saved several pods of rare North Atlantic Fin whales from Icelandic whalers, then turned south and pursued Spanish whalers until we were nearly seized by the Spanish navy.

-- In 1978, out in the mid-Pacific, the ex-minesweeper Peacock chased the industrial whaling fleets of the North Pacific 2,500 miles from North America, freeing vast stretches of ocean from their grisly presence.

-- Off the western Australian coast in 1977 we gathered in 14-foot Zodiacs to protest the operation of a shore-based whaling station, drawing international attention to its activity.

This year, we're going to go out again. And again. And again.

Does it work?

**Since 1971 the United States has ceased commercial whaling entirely.

FIGURE 17.1
(continued)

-3-

** Under heavy pressure, the International Whaling Commission has
cut the quota for whale hunters by 47% in the last six years.
And large factory fleets are now prohibited from taking all
species except minke whales.

** Congress passed the Pelly Amendment giving the President power
to cut off trade with nations that continue to engage in
illegal whaling activities.

** The Packwood/Magnuson Amendment allows the President to reduce
the fishing quotas for nations involved in illegal whaling.

** The Australian whaling station we protested against has shut
down entirely, the last of its kind in the English-speaking
world. After an official inquiry, the Australian government
completely reversed its policy -- to one of advocating a total
ban on all commercial whaling.

For the whales, those are not small victories. For a growing sense
of the interconnectedness of man and his environment they are victories,
too.

But for all the victories the whaling hasn't stopped.

This year, however, the International Whaling Commission will be
debating a call for a complete moratorium on all commercial whaling. If
it passes, it will save the lives of more than 15,000 whales a year. And
it will place tremendous pressures on the governments of the "pirate"
whalers -- pressures, which if successful, will mean for the first time
in 2,000 years, whales will be at peace with man -- free of centuries of
slaughter.

Greenpeace believes that this complete moratorium on all commercial
whaling is the only answer.

Such a moratorium would not only give the whales time to repopulate,
but also give scientists the chance to assess the effects of large-scale
whaling operations on other species of marine life. We know little about
whales themselves, and to allow the disappearance or rank decimation of
the species -- given man's history with the bison, the carrier pigeon,
the Blue Whale and other species too numerous to mention -- seems an act
of criminal neglect.

More immediately, we believe it is time to create marine sanctuaries
-- large coastal areas designated specifically for such research and
study. Group behavior, mating patterns, forms of communication are all
vital areas of investigation if we are to come to know more about the
world's largest mammals.

But none of this will happen without the involvement and support of
people like you.

Right now, Greenpeace is getting ready for the whaling
season, outfitting the Rainbow Warrior that will sail the
oceans this year, searching out and non-violently
confronting the whalers wherever we can find them. But the

FIGURE 17.1
(concluded)

-4-

Rainbow Warrior costs money -- for fuel, for supplies, for medical equipment, for radio systems, for shore support.

Moreover, Greenpeace will launch a major public campaign -- from radio and newspapers, to neighborhood meetings to lobbying at the International Whaling Commission for a complete moratorium on commercial whaling.

More than once in the past we have had to turn back, leave the whaling grounds for want of fuel or some other basic necessity. This year we expect the cost to reach over $200,000 -- an enormous sum, but one vital if we are to stop the senseless slaughter of whales.

Greenpeace receives no government grants or large corporate support. We rely, as we always have, on people who believe as we do in the fundamental debt we all owe nature -- and in the sacred right of whales to live, peacefully, in harmony with other living creatures including mankind.

Please, won't you help Greenpeace this year launch its boats in defense of the whales -- and help us forever put an end to their needless death. If you agree with Greenpeace that we must feel for and support all forms of life as we feel for ourselves, won't you take just a moment right now to:

1) Send the enclosed postcards to the Japanese and Icelandic ambassadors demanding an end to their whaling operations.

2) Share with your friends, your community, your church or club or classroom the need for a moratorium on all commercial whaling -- so that the senseless slaughter may stop.

3) Support Greenpeace with $15, $25 -- whatever you can afford will help (your contribution is tax-deductible). Send as much as you can. But please do it today. The whalers are putting to sea. We must be there to meet them.

Sincerely,

Susan Fountain

Susan Fountain
for the men and women of Greenpeace

P.S. In our efforts to save the whales, we've tried to reach as many people as possible. Forgive us if you receive more than one appeal -- please share it with a friend.

GREENPEACE USA
Fort Mason Bldg. E   San Francisco, CA 94123

FIGURE 17.2
WELFARE RIGHTS CLINIC

Welfare Rights Clinic

124 N. Neil
Champaign, IL 61820
Phone: 352-7059

March 15, 1985

Dear Friend:

Dealing with a governmental bureaucracy can be tough. For most of us, the hassles of cutting through red tape are only an annoyance.

But for people on public aid, who depend on the "safety net" of welfare to pay for a roof over their heads or for food for their families, problems and delays can mean the difference between eviction and paying the rent, between hunger and food on the table.

Up until a few years ago, people with problems like these could take them to Land of Lincoln Legal Assistance for free legal help in dealing with Public Aid. But Reagan's budget cuts have severely reduced legal aid: the Champaign office has had to lay off half its attorneys in the last three years; regular funds for law clerks were eliminated for most of 1984. As a result, Land of Lincoln now takes only the most urgent cases--which leaves a lot of people in Champaign County who still need help.

We've helped over 400 of these people in the last two years.

Early in 1983, University of Illinois law students founded the Welfare Rights Clinic, to help absorb the overload of cases that Land of Lincoln can't handle. The work we do is simple, but it's crucial to the people who come us.

The Clinic helps poor people in Champaign County untangle the bureaucratic red tape that sometimes creates a wall between citizens and the social service agencies that are supposed to help.

Law students, under the guidance of experienced Clinic workers and with consultation from attorneys at Land of Lincoln, talk to each client, do any necessary research, negotiate with the caseworker, and, if necessary, represent the client at administrative hearings. We can't do any court work; if a case can only be handled by taking it to court, we refer it to Land of Lincoln attorneys for them to pursue if they choose.

What kinds of problems do people bring to the Clinic?

> Food Stamps. A woman was told she'd receive $59 worth
> of food stamps, but received a voucher for only $9.
> Her caseworker and supervisor both agreed that she
> should have received a voucher for $59--but neither
> would authorize a voucher for the missing amount.

FIGURE 17.2
(continued)

Page 2

<u>Transfer Payments</u>. While a woman was receiving AFDC, Public
Aid collected her child support payments. When she
became self-supporting and was on her own again, Public
Aid continued to collect and to hold the child support
payments-$1200 by the time she called us. How could
she get her money?

<u>Disputes with Public Aid</u>. A woman received a notice from
Public Aid saying that her aid would be suspended for
one month because she had turned in an income statement
late. But she had mailed the wage statement two days
before the deadline. Was there anything that could be
done to stop Public Aid from cutting off her check?

Sometimes, when a client calls, the Clinic confirms that the
caseworker's actions were proper. Sometimes, we can track down the
bureaucratic snag in Champaign or in the central Public Aid office in
Springfield and resolve a stalled case quickly. Sometimes we can tell
clients that they have the right to appeal the caseworker's decision--
and we represent them in the negotiations and hearings that follow an
appeal.

The Clinic runs on a shoestring. Since its founding, the Clinic has
received office space and limited access to photocopying and to a word
processor. Our primary expenses have been our phone bill and paying
staff during vacation and exam periods. A major part of this cost has
been covered by a grant from the Campaign for Human Development of the
Peoria Roman Catholic Diocese.

But that grant was seed money and will be exhausted in December. To
continue after December, the Clinic needs your help.

We need your help to pay for

<u>Salaries</u> for client representatives during the summer months,
winter break, and exam periods. During the school year,
law students staff the clinic as volunteers. During
exams they need to study, so the Clinic hires an
attorney; during the summer, law students need to take
paid jobs to earn money to pay for tuition and living
expenses. At $5 an hour, working at the Clinic isn't
going to make anyone rich, but the money does enable law
students to keep the Clinic open in the summer--and
problems with welfare occur all year round.

<u>Equipment and supplies</u> to enable Clinic workers to do their
jobs: file cabinets (to replace the cardboard ones we
use now) and a typewriter (no, we don't have one yet).

And, if we could, we'd like to put in a second phone line and
rent an office which is accessible to the handicapped
and which has a room whose door could be closed for
confidential interviews (our current free quarters, on
the second floor of a building accessible only by a

FIGURE 17.2
(concluded)

Page 3

> stairway, are in an open alcove in a large office used by other groups). But that would take a great deal of money.

You can help the Clinic stay open after March by sending a tax-deductible contribution for $100, $50, $15-- whatever you can afford. Just fill out the coupon at the bottom of the page and mail it in the enclosed, self-addressed envelope.

You'll be helping to give poor people in Champaign County the help they need to cope with the "system" that's supposed to help them.

Sincerely,

Robert S. Mills

Robert S. Mills
Chairperson

YES, I/we want to help poor people in Champaign County get the help
    they need to deal with Public Aid. To help keep the Welfare
    Rights Clinic open, I/we

_____ Enclose a check for

        ___$100 ___$75 ___$50 ___$25 ___$15 ___other $___

_____ Pledge $_____ a month or
        $_____ payable by _____.

Name_____ Phone_____

Street Address_____

City, State, Zip_____

Please make checks payable to: Welfare Rights Clinic
                                124 N. Neil Street
                                Champaign, IL 61820

Contributions are tax-deductible.

Enclosures in Fund-Raising Letters

Fund-raising letters rarely have expensive enclosures. But with imagination, enclosures can still help carry the message.

Brochures are inexpensive, particularly if you photocopy them. Mailings to alumni have included "Why I Teach at Earlham" (featuring three professors) and letters from students who have received scholarships.

Seeds don't cost much. Mailings from both Care and the New Forests Fund include four or five seeds to the leucaena, a subtropical tree which can grow 20 feet in a year. Its leaves feed cattle; its wood provides firewood or building materials; its roots reduce soil erosion. (Indeed, the enclosure easily becomes the theme for the letter.)

Reprints of newspaper or magazine articles about the organization or the problem it is working to solve add interest and credibility. Pictures of people the organization is helping build emotional appeal.

Records can be pressed on thin vinyl. School songs and sports broadcasts can motivate people to give to a university and its athletic program.

Major campaigns may budget for enclosures: pictures of buildings, tapes of oral history interviews, even sea shells and Mason jars.

P.S.   The P.S. is adequate. Large-scale fund-raising drives use several lists; the same name may appear on several of the lists. Letters need to deal with this fact so that people who give are not offended when they receive a second mailing.

Enclosures.   Enclosures in the letter include not only a reply card and envelope but also decorative stamps to put on letters and postcards the reader can mail to the embassies of countries which still hunt whales. Preprinted postcards rarely have a huge effect on their recipients, but sending them does help the cause a little and is a good way to further involve readers.

Welfare Rights Clinic

In 1983, a group of law students started a clinic to help people who had problems with Public Aid. Working on a shoestring with free photocopying from their law school and space from another group, the students funded a bare-bones budget for the first year by selling pizza to fellow students, getting a $2,000 seed money grant, and sending fund-raising letters to fellow students and faculty.

In their second year, the students decided to seek help from a wider audience. They sent the letter in Figure 17.2 to a mailing list loaned to them by a local Democratic candidate.

Visual Appeal.   A budget which allows only one-color photocopying prohibits some of the effects that professional direct mail uses. Varied paragraph lengths and indented sections with main points underlined provide some visual variety. The first page would be more attractive with an indented section in the middle of the page. Since the letter is short, the margins for pages 2 and 3 follow the margins of the first page. The list of the Board of Directors—who may change every year—is photocopied, reduced, and photocopied onto a piece of letter-head stationery.

Opener.   The opener is adequate but not really "startling." It sets up a contrast between readers, who are annoyed with governmental red tape but who have the resources to cope with it, and the people served by the Welfare Rights Clinic, who lack the resources but who depend on the government for basic needs.

Body.   The body of the letter answers several possible objections: Isn't there already a tax-supported agency that helps these people? You're not lawyers yet. What can you do to help? Who's training you? Then the letter goes on to outline in more detail the kind of needs it helps to meet. These specifics build emotional appeal as well as showing that the need is serious.

In the second paragraph at the main margin on page 2, the students are careful to show that they don't necessarily oppose the agencies that help welfare recipients. The people on the mailing list may work for these agencies or support them. The last third of the letter shows the other support the group has received and why more funds are needed.

Close.   The last two paragraphs are the action close. The close makes the point that deductions are tax-deductible, information which is repeated on the reply coupon. Note that the enclosed envelope is "self-addressed" but not "postage-paid" or "stamped." This group can't afford that extra cost. The last paragraph offers a picture of the reader's dollars helping to meet the need.

FIGURE 17.3
UNIVERSITY OF ILLINOIS "DIME A DAY"

224 Illini Union · Urbana, Illinois 61801

UNIVERSITY OF ILLINOIS FOUNDATION

November 1969

Who cares?

You might think that with over 145,000 alumni of the University of Illinois we wouldn't care that you aren't among the supporters of the Foundation's Annual Fund for 1969.

But we do!

We wonder why you have felt your help isn't needed. And I guess the fault lies with us. Somewhere along the line we haven't emphasized enough just how important your gift can be. No matter what the size.

Take, for example, $1. If you, and every other alumnus, would slip a single dollar bill into the enclosed reply envelope the result would be overwhelming. Over 20 important University projects that directly benefit students and faculty would progress at the rate of $145,000! A small fortune by any standard.

So, you see, it's not always the size of your gift that matters. It's your decision to do something now that counts. Your positive action, combined with a similar action by other alumni, will make possible scholarships and research. Student loans. Library collections. Rehabilitation of physically handicapped students. And many other alumni supported activities.

A dime a day. For just ten days. Please care that much.

Mark the University project you personally want to see accomplished and mail your contribution in the same envelope. Today, if you can.

Sincerely yours,

Joseph W. Skehen

Joseph W. Skehen
Executive Director

JWS:rm

P.S. We'll show others that you want to help make a great university even greater by publishing your name in the 1969 "Honor Roll" of contributors to the University of Illinois Foundation. You'll receive your copy early next year.

Contributions and the I.R.S.*

Even if your group is not required to pay taxes, contributions may not be tax-deductible. Such groups with incomes over $100,000 a year must "state conspicuously" in all fund-raising solicitations, including phone calls, that the gift is not tax-deductible. If the donor gets a premium or ticket, the solicitation must list the deductible and nondeductible amounts separately.

Positive emphasis can make donors feel that the gift is still worth giving:

> Your contribution to NARAL's hard-hitting lobbying and mobilization efforts is not tax-deductible as a charitable contribution. Please make your check payable to NARAL and return along with this Special Reply Memorandum to. . . .

Sometimes, particularly in December, people will give because a gift is tax-deductible. However, you should never suggest that that is the *reason* people would give. In your letter, mention the fact that gifts are tax-deductible (if they are), but subordinate that fact to the work of the organization which the reader's gift makes possible.

Reply Coupon. To save money, the reply coupon is printed on the bottom of the last page of the letter.

University of Illinois "Dime a Day"

No matter how good your letter, not everyone will respond. A good fundraising campaign not only thanks donors but also asks nondonors at least one more time. The very successful letter to nonrespondents in Figure 17.3 originated at the University of Illinois but has been copied by at least a dozen other universities. At Illinois, the letter has been used many times in the last 20 years, with the number of alumni (and thus the amount of money possible if everyone gave) adjusted each year. It has brought in several hundred thousand dollars, mostly in small gifts, sometimes with notes attached, "I didn't know a dollar would help."

Visual Impact. This letter creates good visual impact by varying paragraph lengths and by underlining words and phrases. The modified block format helps balance the letter on the page. The opener visually takes the place of a salutation, so it receives additional emphasis. The letter is cheaper to produce because the reader's name and address are not used in the inside address and salutation.

Both the name of the organization and the signature are printed in blue ink. The letter uses a typewriter typeface, printed in dark grey—not black—ink, to echo the effect of a slightly worn typewriter ribbon.

Opener. The initial question is negative, an unusual tactic designed to get the reader's attention. However, note that the third paragraph turns the negative around. The letter does not stay negative for long.

Body. The writer does not blame the reader for not responding; instead, the writer says "it must be our fault." Since the letter is a follow-up to the annual letter to alumni it does not need to go into detail about what the money is used for, but it does mention some of the projects. The letter builds credibility by admitting that $1 alone will not help much and saying instead, "If you and everyone else gave, projects that benefit students and faculty would have $145,000."

Close. The last two paragraphs are the action close. There is no reason for the reader to act quickly (the university can use money year-round), but prompt action is encouraged by the phrase "Today, if you can."

P.S. The offer to list the reader's name offers publicity as a reward for giving and peer pressure as an implicit reason to give. Although the statement is put positively (as it should be), it is clear that everyone can check the class list to see who gave and who didn't.

Later Versions of the Letter. By 1974, inflation had caught up with this letter, and it was revised to ask for "a $5 bill." Paragraph 7 read

A quarter a day. For just twenty days. Please care that much.

The letter didn't work as well as it had in the past. Why? Twenty days sounds like a long time; the gift sounds like a lot of trouble. In addition, the revision

---

* Based on "Tax Report," *The Wall Street Journal*, February 3, 1988, 1; "Tax Report," *The Wall Street Journal*, August 10, 1988, 1; and NARAL reply coupon.

Your letter or memo isn't the only thing on the reader's desk. A good pattern of organization, an easy-to-read style, a good subject line, and an effective first paragraph can help your message compete. Use the strategies in Chapters 12, 13, and 14.
John Clark/The Stock Market

Sorting and delivering mail is a full-time job in many organizations.
Jim Pickerell/TSW/Click

Some job hunters get enough rejection letters to cover a door. How good are the rejection letters that companies send to students at your school? Do the letters help the reader to understand and accept the message? Do they retain as much goodwill as possible? (Chapter 13).
Michael J. Hruby

Airborne Express sent a plastic pouch of shredded U.S. currency to persuade executives that "air express shipping with someone else is like tearing up money" (Chapter 16).
Sharp Hartwig, Inc./Airborne Express

Federal Express sent executives a reproduction of a 5-pound antique barbell to introduce its 5-pound overnight delivery service (Chapter 16).
Michael J. Hruby/Courtesy Federal Express

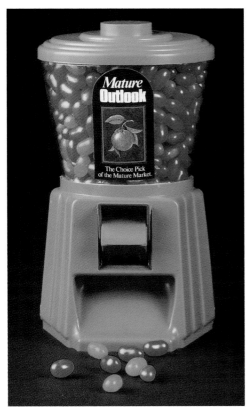

Mature Outlook's campaign to increase ad pages cost $90,000 and brought in $142,000 of additional revenue in the first issue after the campaign. One of the mailings was a candy dispenser with orange and green jelly beans (Chapter 16).
Sandren True Pruitt, Inc./Mature Outlook

Health and Tennis Corp. printed a letter on size-60 boxer shorts to persuade executives to use its corporate fitness programs (Chapter 16).
Michael J. Hruby/Courtesy of Health and Tennis Corp. of America.

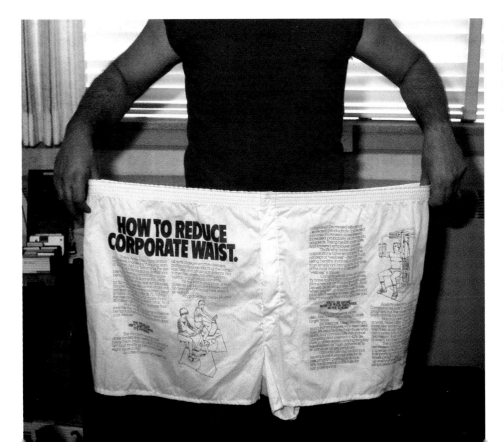

A complete direct mail package includes the outer envelope and everything that goes in it: the main letter, secondary letters, brochures, samples, reply card, and the reply envelope (Chapter 16).
Michael J. Hruby/Courtesy of the National Geographic Society

Enclosures in direct mail packages have included boomerangs, rulers, sea shells, peanuts, apples, letters in bottles, and a copy of the Gettysburg Address. If the recipient uses or displays the enclosure, the sender gets continuing exposure (Chapter 16).
Both photos by Michael J. Hruby

Enclosures in fund-raising packages have included prints, tapes of oral history, vinyl records of school songs and sports events, letters in mason jars, and seeds (Chapter 17).
Michael J. Hruby

A fund-raising letter will bring in more big checks if you suggest possible amounts in descending order (Chapter 17).
Kenji Kerins

Kenji Kerins

You'll work late at the office less often and spend less money on overnight delivery if you use the strategies in Chapter 18 for writing specific kinds of letters and memos and for dealing efficiently with the items in your "in" basket (Chapter 18).
Courtesy of UPS

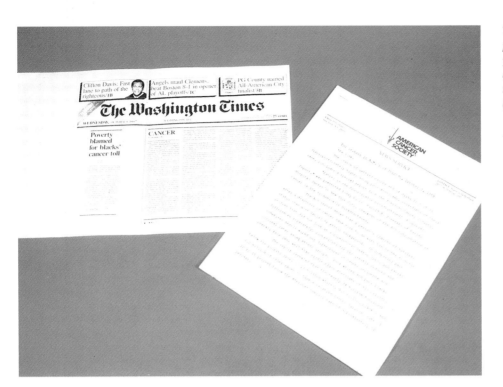

To increase the chances that your press release will be printed, adapt your opening sentence and your details to the audience that reads the paper or watches the newscast (Chapter 18).

Michael J. Hruby/Courtesy of the American Cancer Society

Good questions for a survey or interview are phrased neutrally, avoid making assumptions about the respondent, and mean the same thing to all respondents (Chapter 19).

Spencer Grant/Gartman Agency

A proposal for a multi-million-dollar contract will be long and elaborate, perhaps using several volumes and special bindings. Show that you understand the priorities of the buyer or the funding agency; answer all the questions and objections your readers may have (Chapter 21).
Kenji Kerins

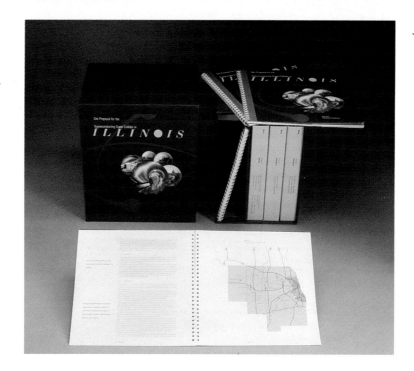

Companies may create special task forces to work full-time on proposals for multi-million-dollar projects (Chapter 21).
Henley & Savage/TSW/Click

lacks the alliteration that made the original so powerful. A better wording would have been

A dollar a day. For just five days. Please care that much.

Even though a dollar is more than a quarter, the alliteration and the short number of days would make the gift seem easier to make.

SUMMARY OF KEY POINTS

- In a fund-raising letter, the basic strategy is vicarious participation. By donating money, readers participate vicariously in work they are not able to do personally.
- The primary purpose in a fund-raising letter is to get money. An important secondary purpose is to build support for the cause, so that readers who are not persuaded to give will still have favorable attitudes toward the group and will be sympathetic when they hear about it again.
- To increase the size of gifts, suggest amounts in descending order, ask for gifts slightly higher than the normal cutoff points, link the gift to what it will buy, offer a premium for giving, and ask for a monthly pledge.
- A fund-raising letter must prove that the problem is serious, that it can be solved or at least alleviated, that your organization is helping to solve it, and that private funds are needed.
- Use specifics to create emotional appeal.
- End fund-raising letters with a picture of the reader's dollars helping to solve the problem.

NOTE

1. Jane Maas, *Better Brochures, Catalogs and Mailing Pieces* (New York: St. Martin's Press, 1981), 98–99.

How Many People Will Give?
When your group is deciding whether to send out a fund-raising letter, you may want to know how many people will respond. Industry wisdom is that a "cold list"—a list of people with no prior connection to your group—will have a 2% response rate. Good timing, a good list, and a good appeal can double or even triple that percentage.

If people on your list have some connection with your organization (e.g., they've been patients at the hospital or have visited the museum) you can expect a higher response rate. From a list of people who have given *to your organization* before, the response rate can be well over 50% and for some groups can approach 90%.

When they have to economize on fund-raising, some groups find that it pays to reduce the number of people who get letters. Save the Children increased donations 66% in 1985 while cutting the cost of fund raising 22%. How? By focusing on 80,000 contributors who had previously given gifts over and above the monthly commitment to sponsor a needy child.

EXERCISES AND PROBLEMS FOR CHAPTER 17

17–1 EVALUATING P.S.s

The following P.S.s come from fund-raising letters. What are the strengths and weaknesses of each? Will they motivate readers to read the whole letter if readers do turn to them first? Will they motivate readers in the target audience to give?

1. P.S.   Because I'm certain that you'll want to join the Aquarium, I've enclosed your temporary membership card with this letter. . . . It's good for *1 FREE visit to the Aquarium until October 15th!*

2. P.S.   I have enclosed a postcard for you to sign on behalf of Iosef Begun. If justice is to be served, we must speak out. We cannot let him languish in prison. If each of us mails just one postcard, the world will know that we are watching. Please affix a $0.15 stamp and mail it as quickly as possible.

3. P.S.   This election year, I expect to see many fast-moving and important choices being made here in Washington and all throughout the country. *All of them will affect our national security.*

    Your new ASC Legislative Hot Line telephone number sticker is attached to the top of my letter. Simply peel off the top label and attach it to the back of your ASC membership card I mailed to you on May 7th. Use it often to call us for the latest news on defense strategy and political developments here in Washington between now and the elections.

4. P.S.   If a friend admires your free football poster from 1928, let me know. I'll be glad to send him or her information about how to purchase a copy.

5. P.S.   Please send at least $30 today. It would mean a lot to [Candidate's name] to see your expression of support this month— we're trying to pay for television and radio spots for the fall, and we need to raise $30,000 within the next three weeks. We're waiting to hear from you. Thanks!

17–2 EVALUATING FUND-RAISING LETTERS

Collect fund-raising letters that you receive. To expand your collection, ask your parents, co-workers, landlord, or neighbors to save the ones they get. Use the following questions to evaluate each package:

- Does the envelope use a teaser? Did the recipient open the envelope?
- What mode does the opener use? Is it related to the teaser, if any? Is it related to the rest of the letter? How good is the opener?
- What common ground does the letter use?
- What kinds of proof does the letter use? Is the logic valid? Can you think of any questions or objections that aren't answered?
- How does the letter create emotional appeal?
- Does the close tell readers what to do, make action easy, give a reason for acting promptly, and end with a positive picture?
- Does the letter use a P.S.? How good is it?
- Is the letter visually attractive? Why or why not?
- What other items besides the letter are in the package?

As your instructor directs,

a. Share your analysis of one or more letters with a small group of your classmates.

b. Analyze one letter in a presentation to the class. If possible, make overhead transparencies of the parts of the letter you discuss.

c. Analyze one letter in a memo to your instructor. Provide a copy or photocopy of the letter along with your memo.

d. With several other students, write a group memo or report analyzing one part of the letter (e.g., openers) or one kind of letter (e.g., political letters, organizations fighting hunger, etc.). Use at least 10 letters for your analysis if you look at only one part; use at least six letters if you analyze one kind of letter. Provide copies or photocopies as an appendix to your report.

17–3 WRITING A FUND-RAISING LETTER

Write a 2$\frac{1}{2}$- to 4-page letter to raise money from **new donors** for an organization you support. You must use a real organization, but it does not actually have to be conducting a fund-raising drive now. Assume that your letter would have a reply coupon and postage-paid envelope. You do not have to write these, but do refer to them in your letter.

Options for organizations include

- Tax-deductible charitable organizations— churches, synagogues, hospitals, groups working to feed, clothe, and house poor people.

- Lobbying groups—Mothers Against Drunk Driving, the National Abortion Rights Action League, the National Rifle Association, groups working against nuclear weapons, etc.
- Groups raising money to fight a disease or fund research.
- Colleges trying to raise money for endowments, buildings, scholarships, faculty salaries.
- Athletic associations raising money for scholarships, equipment, buildings, facilities.

For this assignment, you may also use groups which do not regularly have fund-raising drives but which may have special needs. Perhaps a school needs new uniforms for its band or an automatic timing device for its swimming pool. Perhaps a sorority or fraternity needs repairs, remodeling, or expansion.

17–4 GETTING DONATIONS FOR A SENIOR GIFT

A few years ago, your university revived the custom of the seniors' giving some gift to the campus. Because of your involvement in student activities, the dean has appointed you to a committee to choose this year's senior gift and to raise funds for it. The committee could decide not to have a senior gift, but you all know that the dean really wants the class to give one.

As your instructor directs,

a. Choose a gift. Think about how much your class could raise, and what project or item people would be most likely to support. (If you think that your class could not be persuaded to give any gift, you may decide not to participate in the project.)

b. Write a memo to the dean explaining the rationale for your decision.

c. Write a letter to go to all seniors explaining the gift and asking for donations or pledges over the next two years.

d. Write a follow-up letter to go to graduates the November after graduation.

Hint:

Use your analysis from problem 6–4 and 6–5a.

17–5 WRITING A FUND-RAISING LETTER FOR A POLITICAL CANDIDATE

One of the problems in running for office is financing the campaign. Direct mail is a primary means to raise money. A letter can give far more information about a candidate's views than a TV or radio spot; unlike those media, it can target a specific group of voters. For presidential elections, direct mail is essential: candidates must demonstrate national support to qualify for federal matching funds.

Choose a real candidate and write a letter to raise funds for him or her. Use real information about the candidate's positions and the issues in the race. Let readers know ways to help the campaign instead of or in addition to giving money. Assume that your letter would have a reply coupon and postage-paid envelope. You do not have to write these, but do refer to them in your letter.

Choose a target audience that would be likely to support this candidate. In a memo to your instructor, describe the audience and explain your decision to personalize or not to personalize the letter with the name and address of a specific voter.

Hints:

- Read newspapers and pick up the candidates' literature to find out where candidates stand on the issues. The League of Women Voters can help you find each candidate's headquarters.
- Talk to some of the people who live in the district to see what their concerns are. Read material from other candidates so you'll know what you have to combat.

17–6 ASKING FOR DONATIONS FOR A SHELTER FOR HOMELESS PEOPLE

Shelters for homeless people in most cities are underfunded: the number of people who need help strains the resources available. If there is a shelter in your city, visit it to learn what its needs are.

Assume that the letters will be produced on a computer so that the name of the recipient and his or her organization can be used both in the inside address and salutation and in the body of the letter, if appropriate.

As your instructor directs, write a letter and a reply card for one or more of the following situations:

a. To keep their food hot, fast-food restaurants throw away food that has been sitting for a certain length of time. Write a letter to the fast-food restaurants in your town to persuade them to donate food to the shelter rather than throwing it away.

b. Banquets sometimes have leftover food. Write a form letter to hotels and caterers asking for their leftovers for the shelter.

c. Shelters need blankets for beds and towels and soap so that residents can take showers. Write to the hotels and motels in town asking for any blankets or towels too worn to use for guests and for any partially used bars of soap left by guests.

d. In some towns, groups offer to fix a soup-and-sandwich dinner one night a month or one night a quarter for residents of the shelter. Write a letter to churches and synagogues urging them to sign up for one night a month or a quarter.

e. Write a letter to homeowners urging them to donate money to help pay the costs of providing a safe place for the homeless to sleep.

Hints:
- What would you like to know (both about the shelter and about your readers) before you write? If people are going to sign up to fix a meal, do you want people to call you? Would you rather call them? How will you know whom and when to call? Can you pick up leftover food and used blankets and soap, or do you need donors to deliver them?

- At what point would it be more efficient to talk to people face-to-face or over the phone instead of writing letters?

Business and Administrative Documents

QUESTIONS

- How do you organize a transmittal?
- How should a performance appraisal be written in style and content?
- What does a claim letter need to do?
- What kinds of things should be included in a complaint?
- What pattern of organization should you use for adjustments?
- How should you respond to customer complaints?
- How kind or firm should a collection letter be?
- How can you increase the likelihood that your press releases will be published?
- How should you organize a trip report?
- Should you take the time to send thank-you letters?
- When you've got a pile of mail to take care of, what should you do first?

> [I] find much business to lie upon my hand; and was late at the
> office, writing letters by candlelight. . . .
>
> Samuel Pepys
> *Diary*, 1662

C andles and quill pens have given way to electricity and computers.
Working late at the office, however, is still a fact of life. You can cut the time
you spend on correspondence if you have some strategies for writing some of
the genres, or kinds, of letters and memos and for dealing quickly with the
correspondence that shows up in your in-basket.

Many messages can be informative, negative, or persuasive depending on
what you have to say. A transmittal, for example, can be positive when you're
sending glowing sales figures or persuasive when you want the reader to act
on the information. A performance appraisal is positive when you evaluate
someone who's doing well, negative when you want to compile a record to
justify firing someone, and persuasive when you want to motivate a partially
satisfactory worker to improve. A collection letter is persuasive; it becomes
negative in the last stage when you threaten legal action. Because these and
other documents can vary so much, it seems best to discuss them here rather
than in a chapter devoted to just one kind of message.

TRANSMITTALS

When you send someone something in an organization, you always attach a
memo or letter of transmittal explaining what you're sending. A transmittal
can be as simple as a small yellow Post-It note with "FYI" written on it ("For
Your Information") or it can be a separate typed document.

Organize a memo or letter of transmittal in this order:

1. Tell the reader what you're sending.
2. Summarize the main point(s) of the document.
3. Indicate any special circumstances or information which would
   help the reader understand the document. Is it a draft? A partial
   document which will be completed later?
4. Tell the reader what will happen next. Will you do something? Do
   you want a response? If you do want the reader to act, specify
   exactly what you want the reader to do and give a deadline.

Frequently transmittals have important secondary purposes. Consider the
writer's purpose in Figure 18.1, a transmittal from a lawyer to her client. The
primary purpose of this transmittal is to give the client a chance to affirm that
his story and the lawyer's understanding of it are correct. If there's anything
wrong, the lawyer wants to know *before* she files the brief. But an important
secondary purpose is to build good will: "I'm working on your case; I'm earning
my fee." The greatest number of complaints officially lodged against lawyers
are for the lawyer's neglect—or what the client perceives as neglect—of the
client's case.

FIGURE 18.1
A LETTER OF TRANSMITTAL

Drew & Associates

Attorneys at Law

147 Park Avenue
Minneapolis, MN 55430
1-800-610-4527

October 8, 19--

Mr. Charles Gibney
Personnel Manager
Roydon Interiors
146 East State Street
Denver, CO 80202

Dear Mr. Gibney:

Here is a copy of the brief we intend to file with the Tenth
Circuit Court of Appeals in support of our position that the
sex discrimination charge against Roydon Interiors should be
dropped.

Will you please examine it carefully to make sure that the facts
it contains are correct? If you have changes to suggest, please
call my office by October 17th, so that we can file the brief
by October 19th.

Sincerely,

Diana Drew

Diana Drew

PERFORMANCE APPRAISALS

At regular intervals, supervisors evaluate, or appraise, the performance of their subordinates. In most organizations, employees have access to their files; sometimes they must sign the appraisal to show that they've read it. The superior normally meets with the subordinate to discuss the appraisal. The written document is crucial since it is used to justify the company's actions. An organization is in trouble if it tries to fire for incompetence someone whose supervisor has filed evaluations which minimize or ignore the subordinate's mistakes.

At the same time that they need to protect the organization, appraisals also need to motivate the employee. These two purposes conflict. Most of us will see a candid appraisal as negative; we need praise and reassurance to believe that we're valued and can do better. But the praise that motivates someone to improve can come back to haunt the company if the person does not eventually do acceptable work.

In an appraisal, cite facts, not inferences.

Inference: Sam is an alcoholic.

Two Cultural Styles of Goal-Setting*

The American vice-presidents [in the U.S. headquarters of a Japanese bank complained]: "We have a non-stop running battle with the president. We simply cannot get him to specify a performance target for us.... He won't tell us how large a dollar increase in loan volume or what percent decrease in operating costs he expects us to achieve over the next month, quarter, or even year. How can we know whether we're performing well without specific targets to shoot for?"

A point well taken, for every major American company and government bureau devotes a large fraction of its time to the setting of specific, measurable performance targets....

When I returned to reinterview the Japanese president, he explained, "If only I could get these Americans to understand our philosophy of banking, to understand what the business means to us—how we feel we should deal with our customers and our employees. What our relationship should be to the local communities we serve. How we should deal with our competitors, and what our role should be in the world at large. If they could get that under their skin, then they could figure out for themselves what the appropriate objective would be for any situation, no matter how unusual or new, and I would never have to tell them, never have to give them a target."

Observation:	Sam called in sick a total of 12 days in the last two months. After a business lunch with a customer last week, Sam was walking unsteadily. Two of his subordinates have said that they would prefer not to make sales trips with him because they find his behavior embarrassing.

Sam might be an alcoholic. He might also be having a reaction to a physician-prescribed drug; he might have a mental illness; he might be showing symptoms of a physical illness other than alcoholism. A supervisor who jumps to conclusions creates ill will, closes the door to solving the problem, and may provide grounds for legal action against the organization.

Be specific in an appraisal.

Too vague:	Sue does not manage her time as well as she could.
Specific:	Sue's first three weekly sales reports have been three, two, and four days late, respectively; the last weekly sales report for the month is not yet in.

Most of us "don't manage our time as well as we could." Without specifics, Sue won't know that her boss objects to late reports. She may think that she is being criticized for spending too much time on sales calls or for not working 80 hours a week. Without specifics, she might change the wrong things in a futile effort to please her boss.

Good supervisors try not only to identify the specific problems in a subordinates behavior but also in conversation to discover the causes of the problem. Does the employee need more training? Perhaps a training course or a mentor will help. Does he or she need to work harder? Then the supervisor needs to motivate the worker and help him or her manage distractions. Is a difficult situation causing the problem? Perhaps the situation can be changed. If it can't be changed, the supervisor and the company should realize that the worker is not at fault.

Some organizations use evaluation forms that encourage bypassing. One state agency, for example, required the supervisor to check the appropriate box: "Exceeds Expectations," "Meets Expectations Consistently," "Usually Meets Expectations," or "Fails to Meet Expectations." Only employees with checks in the first box were eligible for merit raises. But the agency never specified *whose* expectations were being met or exceeded: the employee's? the supervisor's? the agency's? Nor did it consider the fact that a supervisor would have higher expectations for someone who was intelligent and highly knowledgeable than he or she would have of someone who seemed less intelligent and less knowledgeable.

Sometimes performance appraisals reflect mostly the month or week right before the appraisal, even though it is supposed to cover six months or a year. Many managers record critical incidents. A **critical incident** is an important event that demonstrates the subordinate's behavior. By recording these two or three times a month, the supervisor has a file to jog the memory so that the appraisal doesn't focus unduly on recent behavior.

Appraisals are more useful to subordinates if they make clear which areas are most important and contain specific recommendations for improvement. No one can improve 17 weaknesses at once. Which two should the employee work on this month? Is getting in reports on time more important than in-

---

* Quoted from William G. Ouchi, *Theory Z: How American Business Can Meet the Japanese Challenge* (Reading, MA: Addison-Wesley Publishing, 1981), 40–41.

creasing sales? The supervisor should explicitly answer these questions during the appraisal interview.

CLAIM LETTERS AND COMPLAINTS

Claim letters seek a replacement or refund. **Complaint letters** may challenge policies or seek to get decisions changed.

In a claim letter,

- Establish that you didn't get everything you paid for, or that the product is not working as it should.
- Be specific about the price, model number, date of purchase, and other details.
- Give enough information about the malfunction so that it's clear that you aren't at fault.
- If you are seeking damages beyond the price of the product itself, be detailed about costs that resulted from your problems with the product.
- In the last paragraph, indicate what you want: a refund? replacement? something else?

In a complaint letter to someone in another organization,

- Use logic to back up your points.
- Show that you're part of a class of people who are injured by the policy or decision.
- Be specific about the inconvenience or harm that has been or will be caused by the policy or decision.

When you want to complain about the behavior of someone in your own organization, use the strategies discussed in Chapter 15.

ADJUSTMENTS

The response to a claim letter is called an **adjustment** because it may adjust the amount due. In some cases, an adjustment letter is good news, replacing the product or refunding the customer's money. In these cases, use the pattern of organization in Chapter 12. If you are making a partial adjustment, you can still use the basic good news pattern, but you will need to explain why you aren't granting the whole request. When you assume responsibility for a mistake, explain the cause of the mistake only if it makes your organization look good.

In other cases, you will refuse to make any adjustment at all, so the letter will be a negative message, following the pattern of organization in Chapter 13. When you refuse an adjustment, be sure to explain why you are saying *no*.

Most adjustments have a strong secondary purpose of strengthening the reader's confidence in the organization and its products.

Most People Are Average Most of the Time*

Ignorance of statistics may distort performance appraisals.

Statisticians know that a big sample is more likely to stick close to the average. A series of four coin flips probably won't get half heads and half tails. A series of 4,000 flips will be closer to the true 50/50 proportion more often.

Supervisors who observe subordinates frequently will see more "ordinary" behavior. Supervisors who, because of the pressures of their own work, are only rarely aware of what a particular subordinate is doing are likely to see more behavior that is better or worse than the worker's norm. As a result, the supervisor will have a more positive or more negative view than is deserved.

Two psychologists noted this effect with flight instructors. Instructors found that students who were praised for good landings usually did more poorly the next time, while those who were criticized for poor landings did better the next time. The instructors concluded that criticism made people improve, while praise made them slack off.

The psychologists, with statistical backgrounds, had another interpretation. The phenomenon of regression toward a mean suggests that usually a good performance will be followed by a bad one rather than by another good one. The instructors' praise or criticism may have had no effect at all. Over time, most behavior is neither especially good nor especially bad, but simply ordinary.

---

* Based on P. J. Crowley, *Understanding Communication: The Signifying Web* (New York: Gordon & Breach Science Publishers, 1982), 126–27.

FIGURE 18.2
LETTER FROM A "CUSTOMER" TO McDONALD'S

```
                                        164 Palm
                                        San Rafael,
                                        California
                                        February 16, 19--

        Mr. Ray Kroc
        President
        McDonald's
        Oak Brook, Illinois


        Dear Mr. Kroc:

        Recently I was driving to Pasadena, California,
        and I saw a billboard for McDonald's that made
        me start thinking.  It showed an egg McMuffin,
        which looked very good, and next to it there
        was some jelly.  Personally, I think a lot of
        people will not like the egg McMuffin with jelly.
        It would be like putting jelly on top of eggs!

        I think that billboard will make a lot of people
        not order an egg McMuffin - even though I know
        they don't have to use the jelly if they don't
        want to.
        It just makes me sad that the egg McMuffin looked
        so good and that jelly just goes and spoils the
        whole thing.

        I write this just as a suggestion since I have
        enjoyed your hamburgers and fries so much and I
        would hate to see your fine organization be hurt
        by trying to be nice and giving out jelly, but it
        just doesn't go.

                                Sincerely,

                                Lazlo Toth

                                Lazlo Toth
```

Source: Don Novello, *The Lazlo Letters: The Amazing Real-Life Actual Correspondence of Lazlo Toth, American!* (New York: Workman Publishing, 1979), no page numbers.

RESPONSES TO CUSTOMER COMPLAINTS

The most crucial goodwill letters are responses to complaints. Whether or not you agree with the complaint, you want to communicate the attitude that you care about quality and about the negative experience that your reader has had. If you were at fault, indicate what steps have been taken to improve matters.

In addition to complaint letters, organizations get a variety of mail from consumers. Good companies take the letters seriously.

FIGURE 18.3
McDONALD'S RESPONSE

McDonald's Systems, Inc.
McDonald's Plaza
Oak Brook, Illinois 60521

(312) 887-3551
Direct Dial Number

March 4, 19--

Mr. Lazlo Toth
164 Palm
San Rafael, CA

Dear Mr. Toth:

In our Egg McMuffin outdoor billboards we show jelly
next to our newest product for one main reason--we
have found that a lot of our customers take off the
top half of the muffin and eat it separately from the
rest of our Egg McMuffin product. The jelly is
provided to make the top half, when eaten separately,
taste even better.

And, just in case you haven't tried an Egg McMuffin
yet, here's a gift certificate which should go most
of the way to buy you one at your nearby McDonald's.
(We think you'll find it delicious.) Or, you can
use it to buy anything else you might prefer.

Many thanks for your letter to Mr. Kroc--and thank
you for your continued patronage.

Sincerely,

MCDONALD'S SYSTEM, INC.

Darrough Diamond
National Advertising Manager

DD/lm
cc: Ray Kroc
     Roy Bergold

Source: Don Novello, *The Lazlo Letters: The Amazing Real-Life Actual Correspondence of Lazlo Toth, American!* (New York: Workman Publishing, 1979), no page numbers.

In the 1970s using the persona of "Lazlo Toth, American!" comedian Don Novello wrote a number of letters to various organizations and people in the public eye. He collected the letters and responses in *The Lazlo Letters*. Figures 18.2 and 18.3 reprint part of his correspondence with McDonald's.

If you get a letter that seems "off the wall," is it safe to assume that the writer is a comedian or crazy? Absolutely not. An insensitive answer just gives people more ammunition to use against you.

In 1987, a British schoolboy wrote to the Prime Minister of Malaysia protesting the destruction of rain forests. The response was patronizing:

Dear Darrell,

It is disgraceful that you should be used by adults for the purpose of trying to shame us because of our extraction of timber from our forests....

If you don't want us to cut down our forests, tell your father to tell the rich countries like Britain to pay more for the timber they buy from us. Then we can cut less timber and create other jobs for our people.

Your elders should not be too arrogant and think they know best how to run a country.... They should expel all the people living in the [British] countryside and allow secondary forests to grow and fill these new forests with wolves and bears etc. so you can study them before studying tropical animals.

I believe strongly that children should learn all about animals and love them. But adults should not teach children to be rude to their elders.

If he was going to respond, the Prime Minister should have used the opportunity to build goodwill. Portions of his hasty letter were reprinted first by BBC Wildlife and then by *The Wall Street Journal*.[1]

In 1988, an award-winning Minneapolis ad agency lost a major corporate client when an employee responded to a complaint that the agency's ads were sexist with a series of letters which many people saw as rude, sexist, and racist. When the exchange was publicized in *Advertising Age, Newsweek,* and *The Wall Street Journal*, even more people learned about the employee's poor judgment.[2]

COLLECTION LETTERS

Collection letters ask customers to pay (as they have already agreed to do) for the goods and services they have already received. Some businesses don't need to write collection letters. If a customer doesn't pay an insurance premium, the insurance simply lapses. Large industrial companies usually find that visits or phone calls are more effective than letters in getting money from customers.

But small businesses need to write collection letters. A collection agency normally retains 20% of what it collects. Thus, even if it collects the full bill, your company gets only 80%. And legal fees may eat up most of a small or moderate bill.

---

*   Based on Captain Phoebe S. Spinrad, conversation with the author, August 20, 1987.
†   Quoted from Roderick Lippert, memo to John Beard, November 11, 1986.

The Collection Series

Instead of sending one letter, or repeated copies of the same letter, good credit departments send a **series** of letters. Letters in the series should be no more than two weeks apart. Waiting a month between letters implies that you're prepared to wait a long time—and the reader will be happy to oblige you!

Early letters are gentle, assuming that the reader intends to pay but has forgotten or has met with temporary reverses. Early letters can be obvious form letters or even just a second copy of the bill with the words *Second Notice* or *Past Due* stamped on it.

A student who had not yet been reimbursed by a company for a visit to the company's office put the second request in the P.S. of a letter refusing a job offer:

P.S.   The check to cover my expenses when I visited your office in March
hasn't come yet.   Could you check to see whether you can find a record of
it?   The amount was $490 (air fare $290; hotel room $185; taxi $15).

Middle letters are more assertive in asking for payment. Frequently, they offer to negotiate a schedule for repayment if the reader is not able to pay the whole bill immediately. To persuade readers to pay, middle letters may remind the reader of the importance of a good credit rating (which will be endangered if the bill remains unpaid). They may also educate the reader about credit and explain why the creditor must have prompt payment.

Middle letters must appear to be individually written. A form letter conveys the message that you don't really care about this payment and may insult readers who want to be seen as individuals.

Unless you have firm evidence to the contrary, middle letters should assume that readers have some legitimate reason for not yet paying. Perhaps they've been out of town. Perhaps their checks were lost in the mail. Perhaps they're waiting to receive payments due them so that they can pay their own creditors. Even people who are juggling payments because they do not have enough money to pay all their bills or people who will put payment off as long as possible will respond more quickly if you do not accuse them. If a reader is offended by your assumption that he or she is dishonest, that anger can become an excuse to continue delaying payment.

The collection letter in Figure 18.4 is the fifth letter to a student who has not repaid a loan from the Emergency Fund at her university. The basic form letter is poor, but even a good letter can't be used unchanged so late in the collection process. The biggest problem with the letter is the handwritten note which the signer has added. The letter didn't work: the sender continued to send the same letter with even angrier notes (Figure 18.5). Six *months* later the student still hadn't paid the bill. She just didn't believe, she said, that the university really needed her $25.

Late letters threaten legal action if the bill is not paid. Under federal law, the writer cannot threaten legal action unless he or she actually intends to sue. Other regulations also spell out what a writer may and may not do in a late letter.

*   Based on Terence E. Deal and Allan A. Kennedy, *Corporate Culture: The Rites and Rituals of Corporate Life* (Reading, MA: Addison-Wesley Publishing, 1982), 49.

†   Quoted from Frank Gibney, *Japan: The Fragile Superpower*, 2nd ed. (New York: New American Library, 1986), 142–43.

Answering Customer Complaints and the Road to the Top*
IBM identifies the most promising newcomers of each year's hiring and assigns them to answer customer complaint letters for a year. In this job, they see how important service is to IBM; they become more sensitive to customer concerns; they more quickly embrace the IBM corporate culture.

A Master at Handling Complaints†
Mr. Imamura was also a master at handling complaints and apologizing. Most Japanese groups contain within them an apologizer, useful for occasions when a soft, well-spoken answer can turn away a lot of wrath. Since Imamura's company sold household appliances, through the agency of some one thousand fast-talking salesmen, the old man often had some very angry customers to soothe. He rarely failed. Bathed in the polite polysyllables of Imamura's gentle phrases, relaxed by the utterly ambiguous wanderings of his honorifics, refreshed by the flattering balm of his concern for the other party's health, living arrangements, and future familial prosperity, the most irate complainant would generally go away happy, his order uncanceled.

FIGURE 18.4
STUDENT SERVICES COLLECTION LETTER 5/17

Westfield State University

OFFICE OF STUDENT SERVICES • 130 STUDENT SERVICES
420 PRIOR AVE. W. • WESTFIELD, WISCONSIN 53950 • (612) 487-2670

May 17, 1988

Ms. Jane Jones
417 N. 62nd St.
Chicago, IL   60617

Dear Jane:

The emergency loan from the Undergraduate Student Aid Fund in the amount of $25.00 which you agreed to repay on Dec. 16, 1987, is past due.

Immediate repayment is essential if we are to continue to aid students with needs as critical as yours. Please come in or call to discuss your plans for repayment.

Your promise seems to mean little if anything to you.

Cordially,

Mary E. Harrison
Associate Dean
(612) 555-0055

MEH/bf

Humor in Collection Letters

Early collection letters sometimes use humor to defuse negative feelings and to set themselves apart from other mail. Since readers' senses of humor differ, the real test of a collection letter using humor should be, Does it enrage readers who think they have already paid? Does it make the request seem trivial, as though the bill is a joke?

The collection letter in Figure 18.6 uses humor effectively. The topic of the quote is exactly the same as the letter's—the circumstances under which a creditor can and cannot demand repayment of a debt—and facilitates a smooth transitional buffer which stresses the writer's reasonableness. The letter's emphasis on the circumstances under which the reader would *not* owe $6 enables *Intellectual Digest* to subordinate the negative fact that payment is due or past due.

The source of humor in Figure 18.6 is its challenge to the reader in paragraph 2. Some readers might respond with documentation of flooding; others might write that drought, not flood, had devastated their crops and ask if Hammurabi's code covered that. If the magazine lives up to its bargain, such interchanges of wit should be fun for the subscriber as well as the magazine.

FIGURE 18.5
STUDENT SERVICES COLLECTION LETTER 6/1

Westfield State University

OFFICE OF STUDENT SERVICES • 130 STUDENT SERVICES
420 PRIOR AVE. W. • WESTFIELD, WISCONSIN 53950 • (612) 487-2670

June 1, 1988

Ms. Jane Jones
417 N. 62nd St.
Chicago, IL 60617

Dear Jane:

The emergency loan from the Undergraduate Student Aid Fund in the amount of $25.00 which you agreed to repay on Dec. 16, 1987, is past due.

Immediate repayment is essential if we are to continue to aid students with needs as critical as yours. Please come in or call to discuss your plans for repayment.

Cordially

*7th Notice!
Incredible that
you promised to repay—
Your word must not
mean anything to you—*

Mary E. Harrison
Associate Dean
(612) 555-0055

MEH/bf

PRESS RELEASES

Press releases package information about your company that you would like announced in local and national media: promotions, expansions, new programs, new products. They give you a way to tell your side of the story about negative events: the firing of a CEO, a downturn in profits, a plant closing, a strike, or an organizational error.

The mechanics of writing a press release are simple:

* Open the release with a **lead:** an attention-getting statement, quotation, or question.

* Early in the release, answer the 5 Ws and H: who, what, when, where, why, and how.

* Put the most important information early in the release. Editors cut releases, like other news stories, to fit the space or time available.

* Triple-space the release for easy reading and editing. Put "MORE" at the bottom of every page except the last one.

* At the top of the first page, give the name and phone number of

FIGURE 18.6
INTELLECTUAL DIGEST COLLECTION LETTER

Porland Place
Boulder, Colorado 80302

> "If a man owe a debt and Adad inundate his field
> and carry away produce, or, through lack of
> water, grain have not grown in the field, in that year
> he shall not have to make any return of grain to the
> creditor..."
>
> Prologue to
> The Code of Hammurabi
> King of Babylon

Dear Subscriber:

What was good enough for Hammurabi is good enough for
INTELLECTUAL DIGEST:

If you can submit documented evidence that Adad,
the storm god, hath inundated your field and
carried away produce, I.D. will, under the provisions
of The Code of Hammurabi, forgive the $6 our records
say you owe us.

I can think of only two other circumstances which might
also persuade us to hold off billing:

(1) You already paid, and somehow it hasn't registered
with us.

(2) You haven't been receiving I.D.

If any of the circumstances I've noted apply, please
let us know promptly. Otherwise, please send us your check
so that we can keep sending you I.D.

Sincerely,

Mark V. Earley

Mark V. Earley
Circulation Director

MVE:abc

P.S. While you're at it, why not take advantage of
this limited-time offer and extend your subscription: Send
us $12 for 2 years or $18 for 3 years.

someone in the organization who can be contacted for more information.

- At the top of the first page, indicate the release date.

Every week, however, hundreds of press releases that satisfy these rules are thrown away. Your press release has to compete not only against hard news but also against dozens, perhaps hundreds, of other press releases.

To increase the chances that your release will be printed,

- Get the name of the editor and address the release to him or her specifically. A phone call can give you the name. Or check *Broadcasting Yearbook* for radio and TV editors and *Editor and Publisher International Yearbook* for newspaper and magazine editors.
- Adapt your lead and your details to the audience that reads the paper or watches the newscast. Many small papers will print press releases only if they have a strong local slant. As Iris and Carson Varner point out, in a story on a plant closing, a local paper will be concerned about the effect on jobs and on the economy. What will happen to the people who are losing their jobs? What will happen to the town's tax revenues? A national business paper will be more concerned about the effect of this belt-tightening on the organization's profitability.[3]

INSTRUCTIONS AND PROCEDURES

Instructions tell how to perform actions that one person can do alone. **Procedures** involve several different people, working together or in sequence.

When your write instructions for a consumer product, maintenance directions, or installation procedures, use the following guidelines:

- Use imperative verbs. Talk directly to the reader and tell him or her exactly what to do.
- Number the steps. If there are more than 10 steps, group them into a smaller number of processes, to avoid overloading short-term memory. Give each group a heading.
- Justify steps or safety procedures that the reader may be tempted to skip; explain their function or why they're necessary.
- Put warnings or explanations at the beginning of the document and again just before the specific step to which they apply. Don't put them after the step: most readers follow instructions step by step, without skimming the document first.
- When you write a manual that will be used by people with different levels of technical background, divide the instructions into chapters so readers can read only what they need.

```
If you've never used a computer before, start with Chapter 1.
If you've used a computer but haven't used a word-processing program,
    start with Chapter 2.
If you've used a word-processing program but are new to WordPerfect,
    start with Chapter 3.
```

---

* Letter quoted from Samuel Richardson, *Familiar Letters on Important Occasions*, 1741, rpt. Intro. Brian W. Downs (London: George Routledge and Sons, 1928), 48.

- Use pictures and diagrams to clarify your instructions.

Regulations will be easier to follow if you construct a scenario, or story, that takes a reader through the document. People read regulations not to remember them but to find out how to do something right now.

Regulations and procedures are easier to follow if writers

- Lay out a path that readers can follow.
- Present action stories or scenarios with human agents.
- Highlight information that is most important to users.
- Use operational definitions to describe meaning in practical terms.[4]

TRIP REPORTS

When you visit a client or go to a conference, you may be asked to write a **trip report** to share your findings and impressions with other people in your organization. Chronological accounts are the easiest to write but the least useful for the reader. Your company doesn't need a blow-by-blow account of what you did; it needs to know what *it* should do as a result of your trip. Most trip reports should be persuasive, not informative.

Organize a trip report in this way:

1. Put the main point from your organization's point of view—the action to be taken, the perceptions to be changed—in the first paragraph.
2. Provide an **umbrella paragraph** to cover and foreshadow the points you will make in the report.
3. Provide necessary detail to support your conclusions and cover each point. Use lists and headings to make the structure of the document clear.

In the following example, the revised first paragraph summarizes the sales representative's conclusions after a call on a prospective client:

Original: On 4/20/88, Rich Patel and I made a joint call on Consolidated Tool Works. The discussion was held in a conference room, with the following people present:
1. Kyle McCloskey (Vice President and General Manager)
2. Bill Petrakis (Manufacturing Engineer)
3. Garett Lee (Process Engineering Supervisor)
4. Courtney Mansor-Green (Project Engineer)

Revised: Consolidated Tool Works is an excellent prospect for purchasing a Matrix-Churchill grinding machine. To get the order, we should
1. Set up a visit for CTW personnel to see the Matrix-Churchill machine in Kansas City;

* Based on Fredric A. Kannensohn, "Attorney Beware: Fair Debt Collection Practices Act," Gregory L. Karam, "Drafting a Demand Letter in Compliance with the Fair Debt Collection Practices Act," both in *Ohio State Bar Association Report* 60, no. 30 (July 20, 1987): 1236–44.

† Based on Robert F. Roth, *International Marketing Communications* (Chicago: Crain Books, 1982), 333.

2. Guarantee 60-day delivery if the order is placed by the end of the quarter; and

3. Extend credit terms to CTW.

THANK-YOU AND CONGRATULATORY LETTERS

Writers who make time for the letters that "don't have to be written" build good will for themselves and their organizations.

Sending a **thank-you letter** will make people more willing to help you again in the future. Thank-you letters can be short but must be prompt. They need to be specific to sound sincere.

Congratulating someone can cement good feelings between you and the reader and enhance your own visibility. Again, specifics help.

Avoid language that may seem condescending or patronizing. A journalism professor was offended when a former student sent this letter to congratulate the professor on a feature article that appeared in a major newspaper:

> I write to you after all this time because I have read your article and I was quite impressed with it. You described exactly what has affected quite a number of people in the same position, and recently I came to the same conclusion myself. Thanks for sharing your views so clearly. Too bad we never talked about this when I was in New York. It might have been quite an interesting discussion. I am convinced, after reading your article, that we hold a similar view on this topic and would have agreed on many points. <u>Keep up the good work!</u>

As the journalism professor pointed out, the letter's language implies that the writer has more status than the person being praised. The praiser is "quite impressed," congratulates the writer on reaching a conclusion that she had already reached, and assumes that the journalist would have wanted to discuss matters with the praiser. To the reader, "Keep up the good work!" implied that the one cheering her on had been waiting for ages at the finish line.[5]

IN-BASKET: MANAGING THE PAPER GLUT

In addition to knowing how to write specific kinds of messages, you also need to know what to do with the messages you receive. In a business communication class, you generally have only one or two assignments each week. In real life, however, you're likely to get a dozen letters and memos a day. While you're deciding how to answer a particularly difficult message, you also have to dash off two routine messages, answer the phone, spend time with a client or sales representative who comes in, mediate a dispute between two subordinates, and go to a meeting.

Phoebe S. Spinrad suggests three basic strategies for dealing with your in-basket mail:[6]

1. **Discard** immediately anything you don't need: invitations to events you do not need to attend, ads for items you don't want, papers you don't plan to read.

Instructions Are Culture-Bound*

Just translating an English manual into another language won't work.

Japanese readers want a more gradual introduction to technical equipment than American readers want.

In some countries, where the written word is less trusted, a hands-on demonstration or a video cassette will be a more effective medium than written instructions.

Revising a Trip Report†

A group of Computyme managers were discussing a trip report that one employee had written.

Most of the managers had trouble revising the report because they too tried to use the chronological organization of the original. One woman, however, was able to cut to the heart of the issue: the trip was "worthwhile" because it suggested that the company had serious weaknesses as a long-term vendor. Her version was the memo the first employee had *thought* he was writing.

The following elements made the revision successful:

- The revision was designed to persuade, not simply to inform.
- The first paragraph highlighted the contrast between short-term satisfaction with the vendor and long-term doubts about its reliability.
- The three problem areas were listed vertically in the second paragraph. Headings helped readers go directly to the area that most interested them.

The revision presented the writer as analyst and problem solver, participating in the decisions of the company. It wasn't just better writing; it was better management and better office politics.

---

* Based on "Writing User Manuals for Japanese Readers," *Simply Stated*, July 1985.

† Based on Mary G. LaRoche and Sheryl S. Pearson, "Rhetoric and Rational Enterprises: Reassessing Discourse in Organizations," *Written Communication* 2, no. 3 (July 1985): 253–57.

Thank-You Notes Create Goodwill*

Linda Smith, director of Creative Workshop Associates in Baltimore, . . . always writes her sources thank-you letters. "It keeps them open and willing to help me again," Smith says.

Kate Brevell, a top administrator at a large university, recruits speakers for the symposiums she organizes. "For speakers on the circuit, you must not only pay the honorariums, you must also send letters if you want the speakers or their friends to attend your symposiums in the future. It's especially important to send letters if I use someone from my university, since I'm not allowed to pay her. . . . The letter becomes part of her personnel file. Consultants I've hired use copies of their thank-you letters as evidence of their capabilities. That's why it's important to be specific when writing the letter."

Similarly, when [Professor Laura] Murray was sent to three European countries as a participant in a U.S. Information Agency program, she encountered a foreign-service officer in the Barcelona Consulate who was helpful above and beyond the call of duty. She sent him a thank-you note and also wrote a letter to his boss back in the U.S. State Department documenting exactly how he'd helped her. She says, "Besides showing my gratitude, these letters may help keep him from being posted to East Mud Flats and inspire him to help me get invited back."

Redirect anything that has been sent to you in error. Get it out of your in-basket and off to its proper destination.

2. **Note and file** items which require no action on your part but which you need to save. Discard items if you don't need the original. For example, throw away a meeting announcement after you've recorded the time, place, and purpose on your calendar.

   Some items must be kept for later reading or reference: important reports and journal articles that you need to read eventually; policy changes, employee benefit notices, etc. Set up a detailed filing system. Specific heads on your file folders take longer to set up at the beginning, but save time every time you need an item you've filed.

   Some note-and-file items require that you do something but not that you write a message. Attach a routing slip to send the message to other people who also need to see it. Mark deadlines on your calendar. If it's a continuing program (for example, a new suggestion system), simply make sure you understand what you have to do.

3. **Answer** the items that require written messages. Do first those that you can do quickly or easily and those that require immediate action.

   As a manager, be prepared to delegate. Write a note to the person who asked for information, telling to whom you've assigned the task and when he or she will report. Write a note to the person to whom you're giving the work, adding any necessary directions, and specifying a date for a formal or informal progress report.

   Some correspondence needs time. You may need to get information, write to someone who opposes you, or placate someone who is angry at you. Take time to think before you write, and make time to draft and revise the message carefully.

For some messages, a "first-time-final" draft will do. Other messages, either because they are more important or because they are going to more critical readers, need revision and editing.

Even with these strategies, you must still decide what to do first. Check deadlines. If something important is due tomorrow, you have to write something, even if it's only a request for more time. Check the sender. Some people are more important to your career than others. Check benefits to you. Sometimes things that are not crucial can give you something if you act on them.

What to do first is partly a matter of personal style. Some people need to clear away the small jobs to concentrate on major problems. Other people can't do even little things with major problems hanging over their heads. And still other people may find that their energy level varies depending on the day or the time of the day. At periods of low energy, they might as well do little things because they can't do anything else. They need to take care of major problems when their energy is high to do justice to complex tasks.

SUMMARY OF KEY POINTS

- Organize a memo or letter of transmittal in this order:

  1. Tell the reader what you're sending.
  2. Summarize the main point(s) of the document.

---

* Quoted from Merrill Cherlin, "Note Worthy," *Savvy*, September 1983, 28.

3. Indicate any special circumstances or information which would help the reader understand the document.

4. Tell the reader what will happen next. If you want the reader to act, specify exactly what you want the reader to do and give a deadline.

- Performance appraisals should cite facts, not inferences. They should be specific. They should cover the entire period being evaluated, not just the last month or week. They should contain specific suggestions for improvement and identify the two or three areas that the worker should emphasize in the next month or quarter.

- In a claim letter,
  - Establish that you didn't get everything you paid for, or that the product is not working as it should.
  - Be specific about the price, model number, date of purchase, and other details.
  - Give enough information about the malfunction so that it's clear that you aren't at fault.
  - If you are seeking damages beyond the price of the product itself, be detailed about costs that resulted from your problems with the product.
  - In the last paragraph, indicate what you want: a refund? replacement? something else?

- In a complaint letter,
  - Use logic to back up your points.
  - Show that you're part of a class of people who are injured by the policy or decision.
  - Be specific about the inconvenience or harm that has been or will be caused by the policy or decision.

- Use the pattern for positive messages when you grant a claim. Use the pattern for negative messages when you refuse a claim. When you make a partial adjustment, consider the reader's probable response to pick the best pattern.

- Take all complaints and customer correspondence seriously.

- Early in the collection series, remind the reader about the debt matter-of-factly. In middle letters, be more assertive. Try to negotiate for partial payment if the reader is not able to pay the full amount.

- Open a press release with a **lead:** an attention-getting statement, quotation, or question. Early in the release, answer the 5Ws and H: who, what, when, where, why, and how. Adapt your lead and your details to the audience that reads the paper or watches the newscast.

- Put the most important information early in the release. Editors cut releases, like other news stories, to fit the space or time available.

- Get the name of the editor and address the release to him or her specifically.

- Organize a trip report in this way:
  1. Put the main point from your organization's point of view—the action to be taken, the perceptions to be changed—in the first paragraph.
  2. Provide an umbrella paragraph to cover and foreshadow the points you will make in the report.
  3. Provide necessary detail to support your conclusions and cover

Writing for Someone Else's Signature

When you write a message that someone else will sign, ask the following questions:

1. How well does the signer know the reader? Should you use the reader's first name in the salutation? Can you build on a base of goodwill? Or does the reader dislike the signer?

2. What information does the signer feel must be included?

3. What kind(s) of language does the signer prefer? How formal or informal does the signer want to be? Is it OK to use company jargon? Are there any terms the signer avoids?

4. How important is it to the signer that the message
   a. Be well-written.
   b. Be sent out promptly.
   c. Build goodwill.
   d. Meet other individual or corporate standards?

Timing U.S. Press Releases*

Plan a news release for the day after Thanksgiving or Christmas. The media are loaded with holiday ads but lack news items immediately following because little hard news occurs on holidays.

each point. Use lists and headings to make the structure of the document clear.

- Discard or redirect any mail that isn't relevant for you. Note and file things that don't require answers. Take the amount of time each item needs. Rank items both according to priority and to your own work style.

NOTES

1. Stephen Duthie, "A Letter from a British Schoolboy, 10, Stirs Malaysian Leader's Sharp Reply," *The Wall Street Journal,* April 4, 1988, 8.

2. See Richard Gibson, "Fallon McElligott Loses a Major Client over 'Stupid' Reply to Sexist Ad Charge," *The Wall Street Journal,* January 14, 1988, 12 and Annetta Miller, "A Donnybrook in the Ad World," *Newsweek,* January 18, 1988, 55.

3. Iris I. Varner and Carson H. Varner, "The Press Release to Illustrate Reader Adaptation in Business Report Writing," *The ABCA Bulletin* 42, no. 3 (September 1979): 3.

4. See Linda S. Flower, John R. Hayes, and Heidi Swarts, "Revising Functional Documents: The Scenario Principle," Technical Report #10 (Washington, DC: Document Design Project, 1980), 5, 20, 22, 27, and 29.

5. Deborah Tannen, *That's Not What I Meant: How Conversational Style Makes or Breaks Your Relations with Others* (New York: William Morrow, 1986), 108.

6. Phoebe S. Spinrad, "The In-Basket: Real-World Teaching for a Real-World Task," *Iowa State Journal of Business and Technical Communication,* forthcoming 1989.

---

* Quoted from *Communication Briefings* 1, no. 12 (October 1982): 2.

PROBLEMS FOR CHAPTER 18

18–1 DEALING WITH AN EMPLOYEE WHO HAS STOLEN CITY PROPERTY

Jake Charles is in charge of $6 million worth of materials and supplies in the city's Division of Sewerage and Drainage. He ordered another employee, Vernon Rook, to take $30 worth of city-owned topsoil and deliver it to the home of a third employee, Carol Hammond. On Charles's orders, Rook took a city truck and delivered the soil on city time.

One of Hammond's neighbors saw the truck and called the Mayor's office. You're Director of the Division of Sewerage and Drainage, and the Mayor's assistant called you. Questioning the three employees revealed the facts cited in the first paragraph. Ms. Hammond offered to reimburse the city for the cost of the topsoil.

As your instructor directs,

a. Work with a small group of students to decide what disciplinary action, if any, is appropriate for each of the three employees.

b. Write a description of this incident, and the disciplinary action, for each employee's personnel file. The employee has access to this file.

c. Write a memo to all employees, reminding them that city property belongs to the city, not to them.

d. Write a memo to the Mayor, reporting your action(s).

Hints:

- White-collar workers take property home, too. But a $30 calculator doesn't need a city truck for delivery; neighbors can't tell that it doesn't belong to the employee. If you're hard on these employees, you're probably discriminating against blue-collar workers. How does that affect your decision and the messages you write?

18–2 HANDLING A SUBORDINATE'S MISTAKE

You're president of The Executive Search, a headhunter firm. You interview applicants for professional and managerial jobs and refer those best qualified (sometimes just one, sometimes several) to client companies who need to fill positions. The company reads the applicant's résumé and your evaluation and chooses whether to interview the applicant. If the employer hires someone you recommend, the employer pays you a fee equal to one month's salary of the person hired. Since you handle only professional and managerial positions, each fee is substantial.

The Executive Search has eight experienced staff interviewers. You do some spot supervision, but basically they're autonomous. While an applicant is in your "active" file, his or her records are kept in the office of the interviewer working with that candidate. When an applicant accepts a job (with a firm you recommended or with someone else), all of his or her records are transferred from the interviewer's file to a central file which your secretary supervises.

Today your secretary brought you a copy of a letter one of your subordinates, Brian Trent, mailed to a (former) applicant. "This letter fell out of a folder and I just happened to see it. I thought you'd want to know about it."

Ms. Wendy Ritter
2209 Wheeler Street
Cincinnati, OH   45219

Dear Wendy:

I understand you called while I was at the Personnel Conference in Aspen.

My assistant informed me of your uncooperative and "snotty" attitude when she asked you where you had accepted a position.

I'd like to remind you once again that we are retained by employers and are not working for you. By the time our clients started calling us about seeing you, you had decided on a job.

Wendy, there are several lessons you should learn, and you might as well learn them at the start of your career:

1. Don't burn your bridges.
2. Don't be nasty to secretaries; they are the antennae for their bosses.
3. You can never have too many friends.
4. The relationships you build with people will prove more valuable in the long run than your engineering ability.

I won't wish you bad luck as you might expect. I am a good and effective person, and nothing you say to my secretary can change that.

Sincerely,

Brian Trent

Brian Trent
Staff Interviewer

You're appalled. Evidently Ms. Ritter said some un-kind things about Brian, but Brian's letter doesn't solve the problem.

a. What should you say to Brian about this in-cident? How should he have handled the situation? Make notes for a meeting.

b. Write a memo for Brian's personnel appraisal file based on this incident. This is not the complete evaluation; it is simply a descrip-tion of this incident while your memory of it is fresh. Brian has access to his file and will undoubtedly read your memo.

c. Write a letter to Wendy Ritter. She has ac-cepted an engineering position with Steel-works, Inc., 3200 Leonard Avenue NE, Grand Rapids, MI 49506.

Hints:

- Do you need more information before you criticize Brian? What? How could you get it?
- What specifically is wrong with Brian's letter? Should he have simply swallowed his anger? Is there any way he could have told Ms. Rit-ter he disagreed with her and still have left a good impression of himself and of The Executive Search?
- Does this incident suggest that Brian needs more supervision? If so, how much and what kind?
- You discovered this letter by accident. Should you do a spot check of all the correspondence your staff interviewers are sending out? Can you do that without making people feel that they are being spied on? Won't Brian feel spied on as it is?

18–3 ASKING FOR A REFUND ON A DEFECTIVE PRODUCT

A college group of which you're social chair decided to order matching jerseys with the group name on them. You ordered them from Insignia, Inc., the largest of many firms providing such products. The jerseys arrived in due course and you distributed them. After one wash-ing, however, they "bled," and the sharp white lettering on bright red is now a faded pink.

You still have your copy of the order form, which states "Custom-imprinted items are not returnable." However, you think Insignia should refund the group's money. Write to Insignia's president, Laura Cochran. Ask for a refund and urge her to discontinue the line of bleeding jerseys. Insignia has an excellent selection of products, and it's possible that your group will want to

order something from Insignia in the future. The address is 842 Pierremont Road, Shreveport, LA 71106.

18–4 RESPONDING TO A REQUEST FOR A REFUND

Laura Cochran, president of Insignia, gives you a letter asking for a refund on an order of jerseys (Problem 18–3).

Situation A

Laura tells you, "Give them their money back. That never should have happened. We must have had de-fective dies. Make sure they understand that we stand behind what we sell and that our quality is very good. We want future orders from them."

As your instructor directs,

a. Write a letter to accompany the refund check.

b. Write a letter to complain to your supplier.

Situation B

Laura tells you, "We can't afford to give them their money back, but we can redo the order and send them replacements at no extra charge. Since we're backed up right now, it will be a good six weeks before the order is ready to ship. If they'd rather not wait, we could give them a credit on their next order. Write and see what they want."

c. Write a letter to the organization.

Situation C

Laura says, "No way. They probably washed them in those horrid washers and dryers in college dorms—the only temperature they have is Hot. The label ex-plicitly says the jerseys have to be washed in cool water on a delicate cycle. Most of those dorm ma-chines only have one cycle—rough. No wonder the colors ran. But it isn't our fault."

d. Write a letter to the organization.

18–5 RESPONDING TO A COMPLAINT

You're Assistant Executive Director of a large hospital. You've received the following letter from the mother of a recent patient:

Dear Hospital Administrator:

Last month my daughter Betsy was in your hospital for three days when she had her appendix removed. The nurses were very friendly and I am satisfied that she received good medical care. However, there were several aspects of the service that were not satisfactory.

My first complaint is the fee. We just got the bill, and we were charged $275 a day for a semi-private room— just the room. The TV, medicine, doctor's bills, nursing care, and lab tests were all extra! That's outrageous! She could have had a room all to herself (with TV) in the best hotel in town for half that. I realize the hotel rate doesn't include meals, but the food she got hardly cost $150 a day! We are paying this bill ourselves, and we are not rich people.

Second, the room was not clean. The drapes were dirty. The walls were filthy. This is a serious concern when you have sick people.

Finally, the television set in the room was not working. I complained about it and a repair worker came promptly. However, I think you should do your maintenance before patients check in, not wait until someone is already inconvenienced before you make the necessary repairs. I also think we should not have to pay for the day the TV was not working.

Sincerely,

Barbara Stuart-Williams

Barbara Stuart-Williams

You do some checking and find these facts: the malfunctioning TV was reported six hours after Elizabeth Stuart-Williams checked in, and fixed two hours after the malfunction was reported. The extra charge for a TV in a room is $10 a day. The room had severe water damage last year, which discolored the walls and draperies. The drapes have stains but are clean. Because cleaning would not remove the stains, and because they were old and in poor condition, replacements were ordered two months ago; however, the replacements still have not arrived. The room was repainted two weeks ago. The painting had been scheduled three months ago.

Write to Barbara Stuart-Williams.

Hints:

- Why do hospital rooms charge more than hotels? What extra services (not itemized in the bill) account for the difference?

- Is a patient entitled to a lower rate if the family, rather than an insurance company, is paying the bill?

- Presumably $10 will not mean the difference between profit and loss for your hospital.

Should you deduct the charge for one day's TV rental from the bill?

- Some of the concerns the writer raises are legitimate. How can you acknowledge her concern while restoring her confidence in the hospital?

18–6 WRITING COLLECTION LETTERS

You have a small consulting firm helping people with computer applications. Unfortunately, not all your clients pay promptly.

As your instructor directs, write letters for one or more of the following situations.

a. A $50 bill for setting up an accounting system for Flowers and More is three weeks overdue. Flowers and More has been open only three months. The owners probably have their own problems with cash flow.

b. A $150 bill for showing a veterinarian how to use a payroll program is three months overdue. You sent a reminder two months ago but nothing happened, and you have been too busy since then to write or phone.

c. A $2,500 bill for refining a data base for Interstate Fidelity Insurance is six weeks past due. You've phoned twice, and each time the person who answered the phone promised to send you a check, but nothing has happened.

d. A $1,250 bill for defining a data base for the local school system is seven weeks past due. After you sent a reminder notice a month ago, you got a note saying that the data base was not acceptable and that you would not be paid until you fixed it (at no extra charge) to the staff's satisfaction. You've been unable to schedule a time to meet with the staff to find out whether problems with the data base are your fault; in the meantime, you want to be paid.

18–7 REVISING A TRASH PICKUP SCHEDULE

In Central City, trash pickup is a city service funded by tax dollars. People are required to bring their trash out to the curb, where it is picked up once a week. There are five routes, one for each day of the week.

Every time there's a holiday, pickup is delayed a day and all the routes are moved back a day. This system greatly reduces overtime and saves the city money, but it confuses residents. Things are particularly bad at the end of December, when Christmas and New Year's—a week apart—thoroughly confuse people.

Now a new system has been devised to help residents keep track of the day their trash will be picked up. The five routes are being given color names. Four-letter names were chosen so that residents can call 222– and their number (e.g., 222–GOLD) to find out their collection day. The call will trigger a recording. The phone system will cost the city $10 a month for each of the five lines plus 9¢ a call and 15¢ a minute callers are on the line. The five colors are gold, gray, ruby, navy, and pink. Information on route schedules will also appear in the local paper, but not everyone subscribes to the paper.

The system will be phased in gradually over the next three months.

As your instructor directs,

    a. Write a press release describing the new plan for the local paper.

    b. Write a press release describing the new plan for a trade journal read by city administrators across the country.

    c. All of the phone numbers needed for this system are already in use. As Deputy Director of the Public Service Department, you must tell the people affected that they are losing their old number and what their new number is. One of the people affected is Municipal Judge Marilyn Frampton. Her old number was 222–7829; her new number will be 222–7351. Write a memo to her.

18–8 DESCRIBING A PROCEDURE OR WRITING INSTRUCTIONS

Pick a procedure you understand from your job or academic work.

As your instructor directs,

    a. Describe the procedure.

    b. Write instructions that could be followed by someone who has never done the procedure before.

    c. Write instructions that could be used by someone who reads English as a second language.

18–9 THANKING A FORMER TEACHER

Write a letter to the best teacher you've ever had, telling him or her what you appreciate about the teaching you received. Be specific!

18–10 DEALING WITH THE DOCUMENTS IN YOUR IN-BASKET*

Today is the 10th of the month. Your in-basket contains five new items. You have two hours in the office before leaving for the airport to go to a crucial conference; you'll be gone a week. Do something with each of the five items.

Instructions:

1. After reviewing the entire package, arrange the items in order of priority and answer those that require answers. Even if you're delegating the work, you must give your correspondent the name of the person now in charge and some idea of when more information will be forthcoming.

2. Answer the following questions. Be sure to identify which items you're talking about.

    a. Which item did you answer first? Why?

    b. Which item did you answer second? Why?

    c. For each item in the package, describe
        (1) Your immediate reaction.
        (2) Your reaction after reflection.
        (3) The action you took.

Note any aspects of the message and other parts of the package that influenced your response. Be specific!

3. *As your instructor directs,* write the messages needed to dispose of each of the items.

The Items in Your In-Basket
18–10–1

Date: [Four Days Ago]   *KC*

To: Division Chiefs

From: Katherine Connelly, Personnel Director

Subject: Affirmative Action Survey

Each year, our division must submit a progress report on the numbers of women and minorities employed by our company. Continued government funding depends on these figures. However, because of transfers, part-time hires, and ambiguous entries on personnel sheets, it is sometimes difficult to report as accurately as government standards demand. Therefore, we must ask all division chiefs to do a direct personal survey of their employees so that we can ensure the accuracy of this year's report and update our file for future years.

Please report the total number of employees in your division, along with the number of women, Blacks, Hispanics, Native Americans, and Asian-Americans. Indicate whether these employees are full- or part-time workers.

Since our report is due next month, we must have all information by the 16th of this month.

Thank you for your cooperation.

[Handwritten note from your boss: Get me the figures from your department by the 11th.]

---

* Adapted slightly from a problem written by Phoebe S. Spinrad, The Ohio State University.

18–10–2

Date: [Yesterday]

To: [Your Name]

From: I. M. Boss   *ImB*

Subject: Office Discipline

It has come to my attention that some of your people
have been wasting time in the coffee room instead of
taking care of business. I can hear them laughing all
the way down the hall, and I can also hear phones
ringing without anyone answering them. Business is
tight, and we need people at their desks all day, starting at 8:30 when the workday begins.

Your department has had a good record up to now, and
I don't want to see that record slip. Please advise
what you plan on doing about this matter.

18–10–3

Date: [Yesterday]

To: All Departments

From: George V. Gates, Administrative Services *GVG*

Subject: Paper Conservation Program

Because of recent budget cuts, all offices at Amalgamated Products are directed to reduce paper usage, effective immediately. Our targeted reduction is 50% in
the first year of the program. This includes stationery, copier paper, forms, printouts, and all other paper
products.

By Friday, please provide in writing an initial report of
paper on hand, along with the name of the person responsible for paper conservation in your office. Follow-up reports will include numbers of sheets used, by
category, size, and purpose.

Further guidelines will be forthcoming as the reduction program develops. Meanwhile, start at once to
keep track of the paper use in your department.
Reports will be required each month to track your
progress.

If we all pull together, we can reach our target of 50%
reduction. Thank you for your cooperation.

18–10–4

Date: [Yesterday]

To: Staff

From: Clayton C. Courtney, Senior Vice President *CCC*

Subject: Supervisory Staff Meeting

A meeting of all supervisors and division chiefs will be
held in the 4th floor meeting room on the 23rd of this

month at 3 p.m. The agenda includes an overview of
next year's budget, plans for the paper-conservation
campaign, and review of personnel policies.

Input and additional items for the agenda should be directed to my administrative assistant, P. S. Spinrad
(ext. 4643).

CCC/pss

18–10–5

[Letterhead]

GROVESPORTS, INC.

[Four days ago]

[Your Name]
Customer Service Department
Amalgamated Products, Inc.
164 W. 17th Avenue
[Your City, State, and Zip Code]

Dear [Your Name]:

Jerry Storch at your suburban branch suggested that I
contact you about the possibility of Grovesports, Inc.'s
sponsoring your department's softball team. We've
been sponsoring Jerry's team for five years, and now
that we're opening branch stores in [Your City], we
hope to continue the tradition with you.

Grovesports will provide topnotch uniforms and your
first set of equipment. And during the softball season,
you'll get special team discounts on just about all the
equipment in our Grovesports stores. What's the
catch? None. As a customer services rep yourself,
you know that the public relations we get from local
teams is worth every penny we put into them. Besides, I like softball. Just ask Jerry.

I'll be in [Your City] on the afternoon of the 23rd of
the month to look over our new sites. Can we get together then?

Sincerely,

Alan Markoff
Alan Markoff
Customer Relations

PART

IV

REPORTS

Research Strategies for Reports

QUESTIONS

- What are the criteria for good questions for surveys and interviews?
- Why is it necessary to try to persuade nonrespondents to participate?
- What are the advantages of using a random sample? How do you get one?
- What indexes can help you find library materials?
- How do you search computer data bases?
- How is citation different from documentation? How much documentation is necessary in business reports?

> Amateurs try to write with words; professionals write with information.
>
> Donald M. Murray
> "The Essential Delay:
> When Writer's Block Isn't," 1985

P eople in organizations write reports not to prove that they know something but to answer questions. To answer an organization's questions, you may use two different kinds of research. **Original** or **primary research** gathers new information. Surveys and interviews are common methods for gathering new information for business reports. **Secondary research** retrieves information that someone else gathered. Library research and searches in computer data bases are the best known kinds of secondary research.

Whether you collect new data or rely on published sources, you need to examine the research design. Data is only as good as the methods used to collect it. This chapter discusses ways to word and arrange questions to produce more reliable answers. But even the act of collecting data can bias the results. Such biased results are sometimes called **Hawthorne effects,** after the famous Hawthorne experiments in the 1920s. Researchers studying work efficiency wanted to test the effect of various levels of lighting on productivity. But output continued to rise, even though the room became almost too dark to see in. Scholars continue to debate the meaning of the Hawthorne experiments, but most agree that the employees worked harder because they were noticed. Don't accept your results uncritically. Always ask whether other factors could also be at work to produce the responses you get.

SURVEYS AND INTERVIEWS

A **survey** questions a large group of people, called **respondents** or **subjects.** The easiest way to ask many questions is to create a **questionnaire,** a written list of questions that people fill out. An **interview** is a structured conversation with someone who will be able to give you useful information.

Designing Questions for Surveys and Interviews

Good questions are phrased neutrally, avoid making assumptions about the respondent, and mean the same thing to different people.

Phrase questions in a way that won't bias the response. A state representative mailed out a survey to constituents with the question, "Do you think the Legislature should enact a cost-of-living raise for teachers?" He might have gotten a much less positive response if he had asked, "Would you be willing to pay higher taxes to fund a cost-of-living raise for teachers?" A *New York Times*/CBS News Poll used two different questions about abortion. A majority opposed "a constitutional amendment prohibiting abortions." But about 20% of the sample changed their answer when presented with a more emotionally charged question: "Should there be a constitutional amendment protecting the life of the unborn child?"[1]

Avoid questions that make assumptions about your subjects. The question "Does your wife have a job outside the home?" assumes that your respondent is a married man.

Use words that mean the same thing to you and to the respondents. If a question can be interpreted in more than one way, it will be. Words like *often* and *important* mean different things to different people. Whenever possible, use more objective measures:

Vague: Do you study in the library frequently?

Better: How many hours a week do you study in the library?

Even questions that call for objective information can be confusing. For example, consider the owner of a small business confronted with the question: "How many employees do you have?" Does the number include the owner as well as subordinates? Does it include both full- and part-time employees? Does it include people who have been hired but who haven't yet started work, or someone who is leaving at the end of the month?

A better wording would be

How many full-time employees were on your payroll the week of May 16?

Bypassing occurs when two people use the same symbol but interpret it differently. To reduce bypassing,

1. Train your observers. Decide on definitions in advance; do some practice coding to allow observers to apply the definitions.
2. Avoid entirely terms which are likely to mean different things to different people.
3. Pretest your questions with several people like those who will fill out the survey to catch questions that can be misunderstood.

Questions can be categorized in several ways.

Closed questions have a limited number of possible responses. **Open questions** do not lock the subject into any sort of response. Figure 19.1 gives examples of closed and open questions. Closed questions are faster for subjects to answer and easier for researchers to score. However, since all answers must fit into prechosen categories, they cannot probe the complexities of a subject. You can improve the quality of closed questions by conducting a pretest with open questions to find categories that matter to respondents.

Use an "Other, Please Specify" category when you want the convenience of a closed question but cannot foresee all the possible responses:

What is the single most important reason that you ride the bus?
___I don't have a car.
___I don't want to fight rush hour traffic.
___Riding the bus is cheaper than driving my car.
___Other (Please specify) _____.

Multiple-choice closed questions are especially good for topics that respondents may find embarrassing. Seeing their own situation listed as an option can make people feel that it is acceptable. When you use multiple-choice questions, make sure that any one answer fits only in one category. In the following example of overlapping categories, a person who worked for a

---

If People Can Misunderstand the Question, They Will*

Q: Give previous experience with dates.
A: Moderately successful in the past, but I am now happily married!

Q: How many autopsies have you performed on dead people?
A: All my autopsies have been on dead people.

Q: James stood back and shot Tommy Lee?
A: Yes.
Q: And then Tommy Lee pulled out his gun and shot James in the fracas?
A: (After hesitation) No sir, just above it.

Q: What is the country's mortality rate?
A: 100%. Everybody dies.

Q: Give number of employees broken down by sex.
A: None. Our problem is booze.

Q: Sex?
A: I feel this is a very personal subject.

---

*   Based on James Hartley, *Designing Instructional Text* (London: Kogan Page, 1978), 109; Richard Lederer, *Anguished English* (Charleston, SC: Wyrick, 1987), 23, 21; and folklore.

FIGURE 19.1
CLOSED AND OPEN QUESTIONS

Closed Questions

Are you satisfied with the city bus service? (yes/no)

How good is the city bus service?
    Excellent 5 4 3 2 1 Terrible

Indicate whether you agree or disagree with each of the following statements about city bus service:
    A   D   The schedule is convenient for me.
    A   D   The routes are convenient for me.
    A   D   The drivers are courteous.
    A   D   The buses are clean.

Rate each of the following improvements in the order of their importance to you.
(1 = most important, 6 = least important)
    _____ Buy new buses.
    _____ Increase non-rush hour service on weekdays.
    _____ Increase service on weekends.
    _____ Provide earlier and later service on weekdays.
    _____ Buy more buses with wheelchair access.
    _____ Provide unlimited free transfers.

Open Questions

How do you feel about the city bus service?

Tell me about the city bus service.

Why do you ride the bus? (or, Why don't you ride the bus?)

What do you like and dislike about the city bus service?

How could the city bus service be improved?

---

company with exactly 25 employees could check either *a* or *b*. The resulting data would be unreliable.

Overlapping categories: Indicate the number of full-time employees in your company:
                           __ a. 0–25
                           __ b. 25–100
                           __ c. 100–500
                           __ d. over 500

Discrete categories: Indicate the number of full-time employees in your company:
                           __ a. 0–25
                           __ b. 26–100
                           __ c. 101–500
                           __ d. over 500

Branching questions direct different respondents to different parts of the questionnaire based on their answers to earlier questions.

> 10. Have you talked to an academic advisor this year? yes   no
>   (if "no," skip to question 15.)

Mirror questions and probes are important in interviews. A **mirror question** paraphrases the content of the last answer: "You think that this product costs too much." Mirror questions are used both to check that the interviewer understands what the interviewee has said and to prompt the interviewee to continue talking. **Probes** follow up an original question to get at specific aspects of a topic:

> What do you think about the fees for campus parking?
>   Probes: Would you be willing to pay more for a reserved space? How much
>   more? Should the fine for vehicles parked illegally be increased?

Probes are not used in any definite order. Instead, they are used to keep the interviewee talking, to get at aspects of a subject that the interviewee has not yet mentioned, and to probe more deeply into points that the interviewee brings up.

Even the best-designed question may not yield accurate data if people are unwilling or unable to answer it. Very sensitive issues are perhaps better asked in an interview, where the interviewer can build trust and reveal information about him- or herself to encourage the interviewee to answer. Questions about recent time periods will be easier for people to answer. Advertisers who want to know whether readers have noticed their ads can't ask directly; people tend to say they've seen an ad whether they have or not. One researcher put dabs of glue between pages of magazines in a doctor's office and later checked to see which seals had been broken.

Generally, put early in the questionnaire questions that will be easy to answer. Put questions that are harder to answer or that people may be less willing to answer (e.g., age and income) near the end of the questionnaire. Even if people choose not to answer such questions, you'll still have the rest of the survey filled out.

If subjects will fill out the questionnaire themselves, pay careful attention to the physical design of the document. Use indentations and white space effectively; make it easy to mark and score the answers. Include a brief statement of purpose if you (or someone else) will not be available to explain the questionnaire or answer questions. Pretest the questionnaire to make sure the directions are clear. One researcher mailed out a two-page questionnaire without pretesting it. Twenty-five respondents didn't answer the questions on the back of the first page.[2]

Methods of Conducting a Survey

Face-to-face surveys are convenient when you are surveying a fairly small number of people in a specific location. In a face-to-face survey, the interviewers' sex, race, and nonverbal cues can bias results. Most people prefer not to say things they think their audience will find unacceptable. For that reason, women will be more likely to agree that sexual harassment is a problem if the interviewer is also a woman. Blacks are more likely to admit that they suffer discrimination if the interviewer is also black.

Telephone surveys are popular because they can be closely supervised. Interviewers can read the questions from a computer screen and key in answers as the respondent gives them. The results can then be available just a few minutes after the last call is completed.

The major limitation of phone surveys is that they reach only people who have phones and thus underrepresent poor people. Other limitations can be

---

Stuffing the Ballot Box*

So what's the best rock radio station in the country?

Don't even try to guess. For the *ninth* consecutive year, Cleveland's WMMS has been voted No. 1 by Rolling Stone magazine readers. That's quite a coup, considering Cleveland is only the country's 11th largest radio market.

So what is WMMS's secret? Its with-it disk jockeys? Its mix of hard rock with the top-40 hits? How about its ballot-box stuffing?

The truth is in the stuffing.

WMMS, a Malrite Communications Group Station, says it bought some 800 copies of the magazine that contained the poll and distributed many of them to fans and station employees. "We urge employees to fill them out, but we don't know who they voted for," says Station Manager Lonnie Gronek. . . .

WMMS won this year's contest with 1,000 votes, beating New York's WNEW by 30 votes. About 23,000 votes were cast. . . .

For its part, the magazine is considering stripping WMMS of the once-coveted award. And it has pulled the plug on future radio-popularity votes.

---

*   Quoted from Gregory Stricharchuk, "Repeat after Me: I Like WMMS, I Like WMMS, I Like WMMS. . . ," *The Wall Street Journal*, March 2, 1988, 25.

Different Research Methods Give Different Numbers*

How many people read *Reader's Digest?* According to Simmons Market Research Bureau, over 37 million people. Another research firm, Media Research Inc. (MRI), gets a much higher answer: almost 51 million people. The numbers are important because advertisers use them to decide where to place more than $5 billion of print ads every year. The two firms get different numbers because they use different research techniques.

Simmons shows people shortened issues of magazines and counts those who say they've read the issue. Critics contend that a shortened issue (with only nine articles and no ads) doesn't look like the real magazine. Simmons's method, they say, underestimates real readers.

MRI, on the other hand, shows people flash cards with each magazine's logo and counts those who say they've read the issue. Critics point out that people can be confused by magazines with similar names. Even worse, many people say they've read a magazine when they haven't. A study several years ago asked people about magazines that didn't exist. Yet 13 million people claimed to read them. MRI's method, critics say, inflates readership figures.

What's the right answer? We don't know. Advertisers who reject both Simmons and MRI are left with the magazines' own numbers, which may be no more reliable. No research firm uses a technique that everyone accepts.

avoided with good designs. Since a survey based on a phone book would exclude people with unlisted numbers, professional survey takers use automatic random-digit dialing. Since women are more likely to answer the phone than men are, decide in advance to whom you want to speak, and ask for that person rather than surveying whoever answers the phone.[3]

Mail surveys can reach anyone who has an address. Some people may be more willing to fill out an anonymous questionnaire than to give sensitive information to a stranger over the phone. However, mail surveys are not effective for respondents who don't read and write well. Further, it may be more difficult to get a response from someone who is reluctant to participate. Over the phone, the interviewer can try to persuade the subject and overcome his or her objections.

A major problem with any kind of survey is the **response rate**—or, more accurately, the number of people who do not respond. Professional pollsters report that 25% of the people they call refuse to participate in political polls.[4] Even the Census Bureau gets a 5% refusal rate when it conducts its monthly Current Population survey.[5] Good researchers attempt to reach nonrespondents at least once and preferably twice to get a total response rate of 80% or higher.[6] People who do not respond at first are likely to be different than those who respond quickly. You need information from both groups to be able to generalize to the whole population.

Selecting a Sample for Surveys and Interviews

To keep research costs reasonable, only a sample of the total population is polled. How that sample is chosen and the attempts made to get responses from nonrespondents will determine whether you can infer that what is true of your sample is also true of the population as a whole. The **population** is the group you want to make statements about. Depending on the purpose of your research, your population might be all Fortune 1000 companies, all business students at your college, or all consumers. Consult a statistics text to calculate sample size.

A **convenience sample** is a group of subjects who are easy to get. Convenience samples are useful for a rough pretest of a questionnaire. However, you cannot generalize from a convenience sample to a larger group. The fact that 58% of the people you question in a shopping mall at 4 P.M. on a Monday afternoon agree that taxes should be raised to reduce the federal deficit does not mean that 58% of the people in your community or 58% of the people in the nation feel the same way.

A **judgment sample** is a group of people whose views seem useful. Someone interested in surveying the kinds of writing done on campus might ask each department for the name of a faculty member who cared about writing, and then send surveys to those people.

In a **random sample**, each person in the population theoretically has an equal chance of being chosen. When people say they did something "randomly" they often mean "without conscious bias." However, unconscious bias often exists. Someone passing out surveys in front of the library will be more likely to approach people who seem friendly and less likely to ask people who seem intimidating, in a hurry, much older or younger, or of a different race, class, or sex. True random samples rely on random digit tables, published in statistics texts and books such as *A Million Random Digits.* Computers can also be

---

* Based on Joanne Lipman, "Readership Figures for Periodicals Stir Debate in Publishing Industry," *The Wall Street Journal,* September 2, 1987, 21.

programmed to generate random numbers. If you take a true random sample, you can generalize your findings to the whole population from which your sample comes. For example, a phone survey that shows that 65% of the respondents approve of a presidential policy may be accurate ±7%. That is, in the population as a whole, between 58% and 72% approve the policy. The accuracy range is based on the size of the sample and the expected variation within the population. Statistics texts tell you how to calculate these figures.

Four kinds of true random samples are simple random samples, systematic random samples, random cluster samples, and stratified random samples.

A **simple random sample** requires that you have a list of all the members in your population. To take a simple random sample,

1. Number the list of all the members of a population.
2. Use a random digit table to select the members for the sample. Continue until you have the size sample you need.
3. Ignore numbers in the random digit table that have already been chosen or that are higher than the total number in the population.

A **systematic random sample** requires only that you have a list, such as a phone book or a student directory, even if the list is incomplete. A systematic random sample is much faster because it allows you to create a **template,** or pattern, which you apply to a systematic sample of pages. Figure 19.2 shows one template. To take a systematic random sample,

1. Take a systematic sample of the pages in the book.
   a. Figure the number of lines on each page that will not contain eligible names. (For example, the staff directory may have a new name every third line. In addition, some of the listings will be out of date.) Add that number to the sample size you want. You now have the total number of lines you need.
   b. Divide this total into the number of pages. You now have an interval. If for example, your interval is 5, you will take every fifth page.
   c. Use a random digit table to choose the starting page between one and the interval. Use the starting page and every interval page after that. For example, if your starting page is 2 and the interval is 5, you would use pages 2, 7, 12, 17, etc.
2. Take a systematic sample of items on a page. Use a random digit table to choose a number for the column and a number for the line in that column.
3. Make a template of the location of the random column and line, and use it on every page identified in (1c).
4. If the template hits an ineligible line, go on to the next page interval—not the next item on that page.

A **random cluster sample** allows you to take a random sample of locations and a random sample within each location. This method reduces the time and money needed to survey. To take a random cluster sample,

1. Identify the geographic locations where subjects may be found.
2. If the locations differ in important ways, group them and determine approximately what proportion of subjects may be found in each group. Plan to take one-fifth to one-twentieth of your sample at each location. Use more locations when you expect differences among the locations.

Writing Cover Letters for Surveys and Interviews

Writing effective cover letters is one of the minor but essential skills in conducting productive research. A good cover letter can persuade people to fill out your questionnaire or to grant you an interview.

In your letter,

- Briefly explain what you want the reader to do. Indicate how long the questionnaire or interview will take.
- Explain why you need the information and how it will be used.
- Assure confidentiality, if you can.
- Offer a copy of the final report, if you can afford to send one.
- Ask the reader to return questionnaires by a specific date. If you want to interview the reader, say you'll call next week to set up an appointment.

When you think the reader will grant the request easily, use the pattern for Direct Requests. If the reader may be reluctant, use the pattern for Problem-Solving Persuasive Messages. Both patterns are in Chapter 14.

See Appendix A, Figure A.9, for an example of a cover letter asking people to fill out a survey.

FIGURE 19.2
A TEMPLATE FOR A
SYSTEMATIC RANDOM
SAMPLE

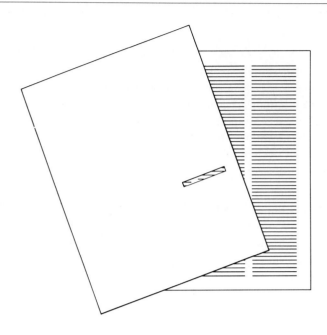

3. Take a simple random sample *of the locations*. If the locations are very different, take a simple random sample of *each* group.
4. Sample the number of people you need at each location.

A **stratified random sample** builds on your knowledge of the makeup of your overall population. For example, if you know that 12% of the students at your college are older than 28, then 12% of your sample would be students older than 28. Choose the categories, or **strata,** based on the characteristics that are important for your survey. Depending on the survey's purposes, strata might be year in school, occupation, number of employees, or number of years in business. To take a stratified random sample,

1. Calculate the percentage of the population that is in each stratum, or division within the population.
2. Divide the sample size into the same percentages.
3. Within each stratum, sample the appropriate number of people.

Conducting Interviews

Interviews can be structured or unstructured. In a **structured interview,** the interviewer uses a detailed list of questions to guide the interview. Indeed, a structured interview may use a questionnaire just as a survey does. In an **unstructured interview,** the interviewer has three or four main questions. Other questions build on what the interviewee says. To prepare for an unstructured interview, learn as much as possible about the interviewee and the topic.

If you read questions to subjects in a structured interview, limit the number of choices that the interviewee needs to remember.

> "I'm going to read a list of factors that someone might look for in choosing a restaurant. After I read each factor, please tell me whether that factor is Very Important to you, Somewhat Important to you, or Not Important to you."

If the interviewee hesitates, reread the scale.

Pulitzer Prize-winner Nan Robertson offers the following advice to interviewers:[7]

- Do your homework. Learn about the subject and the person before the interview.
- To set a nervous interviewee at ease, start with nuts-and-bolts questions, even if you already know the answers.
- Save controversial questions for the end. You'll have everything else you need, and the trust built up in the interview makes an answer more likely.
- Listen sympathetically, even if you disagree. Be willing to show that you're a real person, not just a cold-hearted reporter after a story.
- Go into an interview with three or four major questions. Listen to what the interviewee says and let the conversation flow naturally.
- At the end of the interview, ask for the interviewee's office and home telephone numbers in case you need to ask an additional question when you write up the interview.

FINDING PUBLISHED INFORMATION

You can save time and money by checking published sources of data before you gather new information. Even when you don't need this information for your final document, reading it helps you understand the subject, see relationships, and ask better questions. Many community college, college, and university libraries have guides to using the collections. Check your library's guide as well as the following sources.

The Reader's Guide to Periodical Literature enables you to find articles in general-interest magazines. For serious research, use more specialized indexes. Some of the following indexes cover not only journal articles but also books, dissertations, and other sources. **Indexes** permit you to search by key word, by author, and often by company name. **Abstracts** publish a brief description or summary of an article.

Accountants' Index	*Hospital Literature Index*
Agricultural Index	*Industrial Arts Index*
Architectural Index	*Journalism Abstracts*
Business Periodicals Index	*Personnel Management Abstracts*
Education Index	*Social Sciences Index*
Forestry Abstracts	*World Textile Abstracts*

Many prominent newspapers have annual indexes. *The New York Times Index* and *The Wall Street Journal Index* are especially useful for general research.

A variety of books provide facts, figures, and forecasts:

Almanac of Business and Industrial Financial Ratios
Cost of Living Indicators
Moody's Manuals
Predicasts
Predicasts' Baseline
The Statistical Abstract of the U.S.

Market Research Creates an Ad Campaign*

[The tiny company that made Boker knives was considering dropping the brand. Market share was small and stagnant. But before making the decision, executives and ad agency personnel talked to current and potential customers: people who hunt and fish.]

They knew they were onto something when they ran into a longtime Boker customer who told them what he liked about the knife. He said that whenever he wants to make French fries, he just opens his Boker, puts it in the glove box of his four-by-four pickup with a bunch of potatoes, and drives over a rocky road in second gear. He added, "Of course, for hash browns I use third gear."

As they began to collect stories like this, others poured in. The agency ran a print campaign featuring fanciful pictures of old-time Boker users. The title of the ad ran: IN EVERY LIE ABOUT THE BOKER THERE'S A LITTLE BIT OF TRUTH. The ads recounted the tall tales, which guaranteed high readership. Then the ads told the serious part of the Boker message. Within a year, both market share and profits had doubled.

---

* Quoted from Robert H. Waterman, *The Renewal Factor* (New York: Bantam Books, 1987), 163.

Trades and Securities Statistics
The Value Line Investment Survey

Also check U.S. Census reports on specific industries and the publications of major trade associations.

Many college and university libraries contain copies of corporate annual reports and of the 10-K reports which companies are required to file with the Securities and Exchange Commission. Directories provide factual information about organizations, including the names of officers and directors.

Directory of American Firms Operating in Foreign Countries
Dun & Bradstreet's *Million Dollar Directory*
Dun & Bradstreet's *Reference Book of Corporate Managements*
Dun's Employment Opportunities Directory
National Directory of Minority-Owned Business Firms
Poor's Register of Corporations, Directors and Executives
Thomas' Register of American Manufacturers

The federal government gathers and publishes statistics on many subjects. Congressional hearings gather experts to testify on specific subjects. Many reports are issued by government commissions. The following three indexes can help you find relevant statistics, testimony, and reports:

American Statistics Index
Congressional Information Service Index and Abstracts
Monthly Catalog.

USING COMPUTER DATA BASES

Printed sources of information have two main disadvantages: searching through them takes time, and the information in them is likely to be at least 2 to 12 months old. Several sources make information in special fields available on computer. With a hard disk or a modem, you can access the data base and come up with extensive information quickly. Many college libraries subscribe to one or more services and conduct computer searches for a fee.

To use a computer data base efficiently, check the *ABI/INFORM Thesaurus* to see the **descriptors,** or **key words,** that are used for various topics, and the hierarchies in which information is arranged in various data bases. Identify the concepts you're interested in and choose key words that will help you find relevant sources. General key words will give you a long list of sources, most of which are irrelevant. Narrow your search by linking two or more key words with *and* so you get only sources which have all the terms you want. For example, if you're studying the effect of changing the minimum wage on employment in the restaurant industry, you might specify the following:

(**minimum wage**) and (**restaurant** or **fast food**) and (**employment rate** or **unemployment**)

This descriptor would give you the names of articles that treat *all three* of the topics in parentheses. Without *and,* you'd get articles that discuss the minimum wage in general, articles about every aspect of *restaurants,* and every article that refers to *unemployment,* even though many of these would not be relevant to your topic. The *or* descriptor calls up articles that use either the term *fast*

*   Quoted from Robert H. Waterman, *The Renewal Factor* (New York: Bantam Books, 1987), 152.

food or the term *restaurant*. An article which used the phrase *food service industry* would be eliminated unless it also used the phrase *restaurant* or *fast food*.

Many words can appear in related forms. To catch all of them, use the data base's **wild card** or **truncated code** for shortened terms and root words. For example, in most data bases, a search for articles about *job hunt** would also yield references to *job hunters* and *job hunting*.

USING AND DOCUMENTING SOURCES

In a good report, sources are cited and documented smoothly and unobtrusively. **Citation** means attributing an idea or fact to its source **in the body of the report.** "According to the 1980 Census . . ."; "Jane Bryant Quinn argues that. . . ." Citing sources demonstrates your honesty and enhances your credibility. **Documentation** means providing the bibliographic information readers would need to go back to the original source.

How to Cite Sources

Direct quotes and paraphrased statements need to be cited. The first time you cite an author's work, use his or her full name: "Rosabeth Moss Kanter points out. . . ." In subsequent citations, use only the last name: "Kanter shows. . . ."

The verb you use in the citation indicates your attitude toward the source.

Neutral:
Says, said
Writes

Suggest that you agree with source:
Points out
Suggests
Notes
Discovered that

Suggest that not everyone agrees with source:
Claims
Argues
Contends that
Believes
Alleges

Indicate that the source implied something, but did not directly say it:
Implies
Suggests

Long quotations (five typed lines or more) are used sparingly in business reports. Since many readers skip quotes, always summarize the main point of the quotation in a single sentence before the quotation itself. End the sentence with a colon, not a period, since it introduces the quote. Indent long quotations 10 spaces on the left to set them off from your text. Indented quotations do not need quotation marks; the indentation shows the reader that the passage is a quote.

Affordable Research on Foreign Markets*

A small company interested in foreign markets needs inexpensive research. Akihisa Kumayama and Steuart Henderson Britt suggest the following ways to get information cheaply:

- Use foreign nationals in your city. Take a focus group to a good restaurant and let its members discuss your proposal there.

- Talk to people in government and journalism in another country about laws, competition, the general readiness for a certain product.

- If you plan to introduce an industrial product in several countries, get small samples of knowledgeable people in each country rather than a large sample from only two or three countries.

---

*   Based on Akihisa Kumayama, "Creating a Course Combining Marketing, Language, and Cross-Cultural Communication with Japanese and American Cultures as a Model," Languages and Communication for World Business and the Professions, Sixth Annual Conference, Ann Arbor, MI, May 8–9, 1987; Steuart Henderson Britt, quoted in Robert F. Roth, *International Marketing Communications* (Chicago: Crain Books, 1982), 26–27.

FIGURE 19.3
WHEN TO CITE AND
DOCUMENT SOURCES

KIND OF INFORMATION	CITATION NEEDED?		DOCUMENTATION NEEDED?	
	Internal Report	External Report	Internal Report	External Report
Results of original research: interviews, experiments, surveys, etc.	No	No	No	No
Direct quote from a source	Yes	Yes	No	Yes. (One note can often cover all the quotes from one source.)
Paraphrased statement: Opinion from a source	Yes	Yes	No	Yes, but page number may not be needed.
Fact from a source	No	Desirable	Only if fact is startling or reader will want proof.	Yes
Table, graph, chart, picture, or other visual	No	Yes	No	Yes. Can go under visual rather than in a footnote.

Comparing Apples and Oranges*

Comparisons must be based on similar units. Some units that look alike are actually very different. Suppose someone wanted to compare income in India and in the United States. Just using the exchange rate isn't enough. First of all, a dollar in India buys more than it does in the United States. Second, official figures for the gross national product count only transactions involving money. Yet work that isn't paid in money occurs in every country. For example, the gross national product counts meals eaten at restaurants but not the labor of preparing a meal at home. Bartering, or exchanging goods and services, is more common in India than it is in the United States. A doctor may get a chicken or washing done instead of receiving cash. Money doesn't change hands; often no record is kept. Anyone using official figures to compare the income of doctors in the United States with those in India will come up with a wrong answer. The numbers may claim to measure income in the two countries, but they really measure different things.

What to Document

The rules for documenting properly vary both according to the area or discipline and to the kind of document. Academic documents (term papers, scholarly articles, theses) require that you document *every* fact and idea that you take from a source except facts that are common knowledge. Historical dates and facts are considered common knowledge. Generalizations are considered common knowledge ("More and more women are entering the work force") even though specific statements about the same topic (such as the percentage of women in the work force in 1958 and in 1988) would require documentation.

Government reports and **external reports**—reports written by a consultant for an organization of which he or she is not a permanent employee—require that direct quotes, paraphrases, and tables or other visuals be documented. Facts are not documented if they are accepted by experts in the field. Facts that would *not* require documentation in external reports would include the number of cars sold in the United States in the previous year, the number of students in a school system, the amount of marijuana confiscated by a local police force, and the number of brokerage firms that hold seats on the New York Stock Exchange.

Internal reports—reports written by employees for use only in their organization—require very little documentation. When documentation is required, one note often covers all the quotes from a single source. Thus even long reports have very few notes. In some organizations, authors document facts taken from other sources only if the author thinks that the audience will want proof. Informal internal reports often have no documentation at all.

---

* Based on Harry C. Triandis, "Essentials of Studying Cultures," in *Handbook of Intercultural Training*, ed. Dan Landis and Richard W. Brislin (New York: Pergamon Press, 1983), 94.

FIGURE 19.4
FORMATS FOR LIST OF WORKS CITED[8]

Books and Printed Documents

APA   Fisher, R. & Ury, W. (1981). <u>Getting to yes: Negotiating agreement without giving in</u>. Boston: Houghton Mifflin.
House Committee on Interior and Insular Affairs. (1979). <u>Accident at Three Mile Island nuclear powerplant</u> (H441-18 and H441-26). Washington, DC: U.S. Government Printing Office.
U.S. League of Savings Institutions. (1988). <u>Homeownership: A decade of change</u>. Chicago: Author.

MLA   Fisher, Roger and William Ury. <u>Getting to Yes: Negotiating Agreement without Giving In</u>. Boston: Houghton Mifflin, 1981.
United States. House Committee on Interior and Insular Affairs. <u>Accident at Three Mile Island Nuclear Powerplant</u>. 2 vols. Washington: GPO, 1979.
U.S. League of Savings Institutions. <u>Homeownership: A Decade of Change</u>. Chicago: U.S. League of Savings Institutions, 1988.

Chicago   Fisher, Roger, and William Ury. <u>Getting to Yes: Negotiating Agreement without Giving In</u>. Boston: Houghton Mifflin, 1981.
U.S. Congress. House. Committee on Interior and Insular Affairs. <u>Accident at Three Mile Island Nuclear Powerplant</u>. 96th Cong., 1st sess., H. Docs. 441-18 and 441-26. '
U.S. League of Savings Institutions. <u>Homeownership: A Decade of Change</u>. Chicago: U.S. League of Savings Institutions, 1988.

Dissertations and Theses

APA   Cawley, K. (1984). Planning and producing writing in the workplace (Doctoral dissertation, Fordham University, 1984). <u>Dissertation Abstracts International</u>, <u>45</u>, 1972A.

MLA   Cawley, Kevin. "Planning and Producing Writing in the Workplace." Diss. Fordham U, 1984.

Chicago   Cawley, Kevin. "Planning and Producing Writing in the Workplace." Ph.D. Diss. Fordham University, 1984.

Unpublished Reports and Interviews

APA   Petajan, M. J. (May 1982). <u>How Planned Parenthood clinic can improve its volunteer interviewer program</u>. Unpublished report.

MLA   Petajan, Melanie J. <u>How Planned Parenthood Clinic Can Improve Its Volunteer Interviewer Program</u>. Champaign, IL: Planned Parenthood, 1982.

FIGURE 19.4 *(continued)*

White, Betty Evans. Personal interview. 17 October
    1987.

Chicago   Petajan, Melanie J. "How Planned Parenthood Clinic
    Can Improve Its Volunteer Interviewer Program."
    Champaign, IL: Planned Parenthood, 1982.
    White, Betty Evans. Interview with author. Atlanta,
    GA, 17 October 1987.

Articles in Journals or Books

APA   Gilsdorf, J. W. (1983). Executive and managerial
    attitudes toward business slang: A Fortune-list
    survey. Journal of Business Communication, 20(4),
    29-42.

MLA   Gilsdorf, Jeanette W. "Executive and Managerial
    Attitudes toward Business Slang: A Fortune-List
    Survey." The Journal of Business Communication
    20.4 (1983): 29-42.

Chicago   Gilsdorf, Jeanette W. "Executive and Managerial
    Attitudes toward Business Slang: A Fortune-List
    Survey." Journal of Business Communication 20,
    no. 4 (1983): 29-42.

Figure 19.3 summarizes the documentation needed for different kinds of information.

When you write a report on the job, ask your boss how much documentation you need to supply and check copies of old reports. When you write a report for a class, ask your instructor how much documentation is needed. Some instructors require full documentation even for assignments that are "internal reports" so that students will learn to use and document sources.

How to Document Sources

Three of the most widely used formats for footnotes, endnotes, and bibliographies in reports are those of the American Psychological Association (APA), the Modern Language Association (MLA), and the Chicago *Manual of Style*, which this book uses.

Study documentation format before you begin note-taking so that you record all the information you need. Be sure to record which source each note is from and the page number on which it appears.

The APA format uses **internal documentation** with a **list of references**; it does not use footnotes or endnotes. The MLA format advises **internal documentation** and a **list of works cited** but permits endnotes instead. The Chicago *Manual of Style* permits either endnotes or internal documentation.

Internal documentation provides the work and the page number where the reference was found in parentheses in the text. The work may be indicated by the author's last name (if that isn't already in the sentence), or by the last name plus the date of the work (if you're using two or more works by the same author or if the dates of the works are important).

> Training for overseas assignments should include facts about the country and culture, but those facts must be organized and related to each other and to the participants (Brislin, Landis, and Brandt, 11).

The full bibliographical citation appears in a List of References or Works Cited at the end of the report. Figure 19.4 gives the APA, MLA, and Chicago formats for some of the kinds of sources most commonly used in business reports.

SUMMARY OF KEY POINTS

- **Original** or **primary research** gathers new information. **Secondary research** retrieves information that someone else gathered.

- A **survey** questions a large group of people, called **respondents** or **subjects**. A **questionnaire** is a written list of questions that people fill out. An **interview** is a structured conversation with someone who will be able to give you useful information.

- Good questions are phrased neutrally, avoid making assumptions about the respondent, and mean the same thing to different people.

- **Closed questions** have a limited number of possible responses. **Open questions** do not lock the subject into any sort of response. **Branching questions** direct different respondents to different parts of the questionnaire based on their answers to earlier questions. A **mirror question**

Computer Records and the Investigative Reporter*

Computers are rapidly altering the once-shadowy world of investigative journalism.

Consider:

- Reporters at Knight-Ridder Inc's Washington bureau last year pinpointed unusually high death rates at certain hospitals around the country by analyzing computerized Medicare records of open-heart surgeries.

- At the San Jose Mercury News in California, reporters using a computer tapped into a real-estate data bank to help locate U.S. property secretly owned by deposed Philippine leader Ferdinand Marcos and his associates.

- By sifting through computer data on everything from parking tickets to detectives' expense vouchers, the Seattle Times last year proved how a police investigation into the deaths of 46 women was botched. . . .

By comparing data gleaned from several [computer] tapes, the Providence Journal has uncovered stories that in the past might never have been possible. For example, when three Rhode Island children were hit and killed in separate school-bus accidents in 1985, the paper compared its list of bus-driver licenses to a tape of traffic violations. It discovered that some bus drivers had been ticketed as many as 20 times over a three-year period. . . .

That information, coupled with the tape of criminal convictions, showed that several bus drivers were convicted felons. As a result of the story, licensing procedures were tightened, and buses were made safer.

---

* Quoted from Gregory Stricharchuk, "Computer Records Become Powerful Tool for Investigative Reporters and Editors," *The Wall Street Journal*, February 2, 1988, 23.

Ask Your Friendly Neighborhood Librarian*

[Librarians] produced a wealth of material I would have been hard-pressed to uncover for myself even on a well-connected personal computer. For one thing, the librarians had access to many more data bases than I could afford to rent. For another, their use of the data bases was far more expert than mine could ever be. They knew the protocols and peculiarities of different data base services; they knew which it paid to try, and they knew the best strategies for tapping them quickly. . . .

There was another advantage the librarians enjoyed. By virtue of their training and experience, they knew when *not* to use the computer. As a fully stocked information service, the library includes a multitude of standard reference books which are often the best, quickest, and cheapest place to look up a fact. . . .

Many public libraries have expanded their information services to include references, pamphlets, and contacts that cover a wide range of community social needs: legal assistance, tenants' rights, unemployment benefits, job training, immigration, health, welfare, and consumers' problems.

paraphrases the content of the last answer. **Probes** follow up an original question to get at specific aspects of a topic.

- Good researchers attempt to reach nonrespondents at least once and preferably twice.
- A **convenience sample** is a group of subjects who are easy to get. A **judgment sample** is a group of people whose views seem useful. In a **random sample**, each person in the population theoretically has an equal chance of being chosen. Varieties of random samples include **simple, systematic, cluster, and stratified random samples.** Only in a random sample is the researcher justified in inferring that the results from the sample are also true of the population from which the sample comes.
- Use specialized indexes and directories to find information about a specific company or topic.
- Check the *ABI/INFORM Thesaurus* to learn the **descriptors,** or key words, and the hierarchies in which information is arranged in various data bases. Use *and* to find only sources which treat the specific topic you're studying. Use *or* to include alternate or closely related labels. Use the data base's **wild card** or **truncated code** to yield references which use the term in a different grammatical form.
- **Citation** means attributing an idea or fact to its source **in the body of the report. Documentation** means providing the bibliographic information readers would need to go back to the original source.
- Government reports and **external reports**—reports written by a consultant for an organization of which he or she is not a permanent employee—require that direct quotes, paraphrases, and tables or other visuals be documented. **Internal reports**—reports written by employees for their own organization—require little or no documentation.

NOTES

1. Brock Brower, "The Pernicious Power of the Polls," *Money*, March 1988, 146.
2. Janice M. Lauer and J. William Asher, *Composition Research: Empirical Designs* (New York: Oxford University Press, 1986), 66.
3. Irving Crespi, quoted in W. Joseph Campbell, "Phone Surveys Becoming Unreliable, Pollsters Say," *The Columbus Dispatch*, February 21, 1988, 8F.
4. Campbell.
5. Brower, 155.
6. Lauer and Asher, 67.
7. Thomas Hunter, "Pulitzer Winner Discusses Interviewing," *IABC Communication World*, April 1985, 13–15.
8. For guides to other kinds of documents, see *Publication Manual of the American Psychological Association*, 3rd ed., *The MLA Style Manual*, 2nd ed., and *The Chicago Manual of Style*, 13th ed.

* Quoted from Theodore Roszak, *The Cult of Information: The Folklore of Computers and the True Art of Thinking* (New York: Pantheon-Random House, 1986), 174–75.

EXERCISES AND PROBLEMS FOR CHAPTER 19

19–1 CHOOSING RESEARCH STRATEGIES

For each of the following reports, indicate the kinds of research that might be useful. If a survey is called for, indicate the most efficient kind of sample to use.

a. How [Men's Clothing Store] Can Increase Sales

b. Should the National Football League Approve a Franchise in Columbus, Ohio?

c. A Promotional Plan to Create a Successful Image for [Name of Store or Product]

d. How XYZ Restaurant Can Reduce Turnover

e. Should the SEC Limit Computer Trading?

f. Rape Prevention: Increasing Campus Awareness

g. How the Health Center Can Help Students with Eating Disorders

19–2 IDENTIFYING KEY WORDS FOR COMPUTER SEARCHES

As your instructor directs, identify the key word combinations that you could use in researching one or more of the following topics.

a. Cost of reducing or preventing acid rain

b. The effect of computer trades on the stock market crash of 1987

c. Ways to increase timber yields

d. Effect of advertising on sales of automobiles

e. Ways to reduce homelessness in the United States

f. Ethical issues in accounting reports

g. Advantages and problems of local area networks

19–3 COMPILING A BIBLIOGRAPHY

Answer the following questions about a topic of your choice. Ask a reference librarian or another expert for help.

Specific Topic:_____

General Area:_____

1. List the source that indexes or abstracts books, articles, and dissertations in this field.

2. List any computer indexes, bibliographies, or data bases in this field.

3. What congressional committees or federal agencies would be most likely to have published documents that might be useful in your research?

4. You don't know whether or not any congressional committees have issued reports which might help. What index can you check to find out?

5. You know that Edward Expert has done important work in your field. How can you find out whether he has testified before a congressional committee?

6. What book is most likely to have statistics or facts that might be relevant to your topic? Give the full title and the call number.

7. You know that Susan Scholar has done important work on your subject. How can you find the names and references for other researchers who have extended or challenged her findings? (Hint: researchers who build on someone's work almost always cite that person.) Give the title of the book and its call number.

8. List the name(s), department(s), and phone number(s) of faculty who might know something about this topic.

9. List the name(s), position(s), and phone number(s) of anyone in the community who might know something about this topic.

10. List the name of the reference librarian who could help you find sources on this topic and the hours when he or she is on duty.

11. Give full bibliographic information for 5 to 10 articles, books, dissertations, or government reports that seem relevant to your topic.

19–4 EVALUATING QUESTIONS

Evaluate each of the following questions. Are they acceptable as they stand? If not, how can they be improved?

a. Questionnaire on Gasoline Use

1. How many major oil company credit cards do you now have?
   a. 1–3
   b. 4–6
   c. None

2. Do you *usually* do business with the same service station?
   a. Yes
   b. No
3. Do you have repair work done at your service station?
   a. Yes
   b. No

b. Survey of Customers

Write a number in the blank beside each statement indicating how accurate each statement is in describing the primary qualities of a sales representative.

1	2	3	4	5
Very inaccurate	Somewhat inaccurate	Neutral	Somewhat accurate	Very accurate

__1. Positive attitude.
__2. Don't promise anything that can't be delivered.
__3. Mental agility (common sense).
__4. Ability and willingness to help you solve your problems.
__5. Communication skills.
__6. Energetic.
__7. Ability to follow directions.

19–5 DESIGNING QUESTIONS FOR AN INTERVIEW OR SURVEY

Submit either a one- to three-page questionnaire or questions for a 20- to 30-minute interview *and* the information listed below for the method you choose.

Questionnaire

1. Purpose(s), goal(s)
2. Subjects (who, why, how many)
3. How and where to be distributed
4. Any changes in type size, paper color, etc., from submitted copy
5. Any details not evident from the submitted copy

6. Rationale for order of questions, kinds of questions, wording of questions
7. References, if building on questionnaires by other authors

Interview

1. Purpose(s), goal(s)
2. Subject (who and why)
3. Proposed site, length of interview
4. Rationale for order of questions, kinds of questions, wording of questions, choice of branching or probing questions
5. References, if building on questions devised by others

19–6 GATHERING INFORMATION FOR A CONGRESSWOMAN

You're an aide to Congresswoman Cheryl Granacki. Congresswoman Granacki has received a letter from a constituent complaining that, although his car prominently displays his Handicapped Parking card, he received a $79 ticket for parking in a handicapped space in another state which does not, apparently, recognize out-of-state handicapped plates or cards. The constituent wants the Congresswoman to introduce a bill which would require all states to recognize every other state's handicapped plates and cards.

"Before I introduce a bill," Ms. Granacki says, "I want some information. Please find out how many states in fact do not honor other states' handicapped plates and cards. Also find out how many handicapped plates and cards are issued in each state and for the whole nation. You'll probably have to settle for numbers that are two or three years old."

As your instructor directs,

a. Brainstorm a list of places which might have the information Ms. Granacki wants.
b. Get the information Ms. Granacki has asked for.
c. Write an informal report presenting your information and recommending whether a national law seems necessary or desirable.

Presenting Information in Reports

QUESTIONS

- What is the difference between formal and informal reports?
- What three elements should a purpose statement contain?
- What are ways to organize information in reports?
- How do you set up headings?

A report is a communication from someone who has information
to someone who wants to use that information.

C. A. Brown
c. 1950

Many kinds of documents are called "reports." In some organizations, a report is a long document that contains numerical data. In others, one- and two-page memos are called "reports." A short report to a client may use letter format. **Formal reports** contain formal elements such as a Title Page, a Transmittal, a Table of Contents, and a List of Illustrations. **Informal reports** use letter or memo format. But all reports, whatever their length or degree of formality, provide the information that people in organizations need to make plans and solve problems.

Whether you write formal reports as part of your job will depend on where you work. In a consulting firm, a report may be the only tangible thing that the client receives for a $5 million job. Formal reports are also common in government. However, formal reports are less common in private businesses. In some companies, no one ever writes full formal reports with all the report parts.

Chapter 22 explains how to set up the formal elements. This chapter discusses aspects that all reports share: solving problems, adapting the report for the audience, and organizing information.

Many organizations have names for specific kinds of reports. Depending on where you work, you may encounter some of the following report labels:

Progress and **interim reports** record the work done so far and the work remaining on a project.

Quarterly reports document a plant's productivity and profits for the quarter.

Annual reports record an organization's accomplishments during the past year and provide financial data.

Audit reports document and interpret the facts revealed during an audit.

Trip reports share what the author learned at a conference or during a visit to a customer or supplier.

Closure reports document research that is not economically or technically feasible for new products under current conditions.

Make-good or **pay-back reports** calculate the point at which a new capital investment will pay for itself.

Scouting reports identify the strengths and weaknesses of a potential recruit or an opposing team and recommend whether to bid for the recruit or recommend strategies for beating the opponent.

Reports can also be called **information reports** if they collect data for the reader but do not recommend action and **recommendation reports** if they recommend action or a solution. Government reports are frequently information reports. After an airplane crash, for example, the Federal Aviation

Administration files a report analyzing the cause of the crash. Some government and most business reports recommend a course of action.

UNDERSTANDING AND SOLVING REPORT PROBLEMS

Understanding the problem you are analyzing or trying to solve is the first step in writing a good report. A report that solves the wrong problem is of no use to the organization.

Sometimes the people who assign reports see the results of the problem but do not themselves understand it. A unit of the U.S. armed services hired a group of business writing professors to rewrite a huge manual. The professors were told, "Make it clear enough so that the lowest-level enlisted people can understand it." But when the professors visited the bases, they found that the lowest-level enlisted people never looked at the manual. When these people had questions, they asked their supervisors. The real problem, the professors realized, was to create a manual in which supervisors could find answers quickly.[1]

How you define the problem shapes the solutions you find. For example, suppose that a manufacturer of frozen foods isn't making money. If the problem is defined as a marketing problem, the researcher may analyze the product's price, image, advertising, and position in the market. But perhaps the problem is really that overhead costs are too high because of poor inventory management, or that an inadequate distribution system doesn't get the product to its target market. Defining the problem accurately is essential to finding an effective solution.

All but the simplest problems have many possible causes. For example, workers in less developed countries traditionally have been less productive than workers in developed nations. If the problem were defined as one of motivation, a manager might concentrate on incentive programs. If the problem were defined as one of cultural differences, managers might be sent to training programs to understand their subordinates better. But two studies by the World Bank suggested that physical health was a major cause: parasitic infections led to iron deficiencies and to malnutrition. With this understanding of the problem, companies offered subsidized lunches and free medical treatment at a company-owned infirmary. Productivity has risen dramatically.[2]

ORGANIZING INFORMATION IN LONG REPORTS

As you plan your report, formulate a statement of your purposes. A good purpose statement must make three things clear:

- The organizational problem or conflict.
- The specific technical questions which must be answered to solve the problem.
- The rhetorical purpose (to explain, to recommend, to request, to propose) which the report is designed to achieve.

The following purpose statement has all three elements. The report's audience is the superintendent of Yellowstone National Park.

> Current management methods keep the elk population within the carrying capacity of the habitat, but require frequent human intervention. Both wildlife

A Good Report Is a Set of Facts, Intelligently Analyzed*

During my years at McKinsey [a consulting firm], we did a prodigious amount of work that we liked to call "strategy." . . . A typical strategy presentation might contain fifty to a hundred pages of charts, graphs, and exhibits, and ten or so pages of recommendations. Most of our recommendations were essentially the same: Raise prices; lower costs; find out what's profitable and what is not; do more of the former and less of the latter. My first reaction was to be amazed that clients would pay us for advice like that. Either they were foolish or we had them fooled. Then it dawned on me that the "strategy" wasn't what they were buying. It was the set of facts, intelligently analyzed.

---

* Quoted from Robert H. Waterman, *The Renewal Factor* (New York: Bantam Books, 1987), 122.

Writing the Report for the Reader*

Reports should be written for the readers who will use them. But many writers write reports for themselves. The document reflects the writer's process, not the reader's needs.

In one company, a young employee comparing the economics of two proposed manufacturing processes gave his logic and his calculations in full and only then gave his conclusion. But his superiors didn't want to wade through eight single-spaced pages; they wanted his recommendation up front.

Another employee assumed that because he had spent a long time working on a report, he should record his actions in detail. The resulting report was 75 pages. His supervisor told him the report was unusable. "Cut it to five pages; put the data in an appendix."

Another company was asked to examine a building that had problems with heating, cooling, and air circulation. The client who owned the building wanted to know how to solve these problems in a way that would be energy-efficient and would pay for itself.

The consultant submitted a detailed report which began with a physical description of the building, listed the problems, examined the possible solutions in detail (with long and rigorous number crunching), and finally recommended a solution. The consultant was charging $30,000 for the answer, so a report was needed, but not the kind of report he submitted. The client worked in the building and didn't need to be reminded of the floor plan. Instead, the client wanted quick answers to three questions: Can we do it? What will it cost? When will it pay for itself? The report could have been three pages with a seven-page appendix showing the payback figures.

conservation specialists and the public would prefer methods that controlled the elk population naturally. This report will compare the current short-term management techniques (hunting, trapping and transporting, and winter feeding) with two long-term management techniques, habitat modification and the reintroduction of predators. The purpose of this report is to recommend which techniques or combination of techniques would best satisfy the needs of conservationists, hunters, and the public.

Most sets of data can be organized in several logical ways. Choose the way that makes your information easiest for the reader to understand and use. If you were filing correspondence, for example, it would be just as logical to file by recipient or by date as by subject, but it would be far easier to find documents later on if they were filed by subject. If you were compiling a directory of all the employees at your plant, alphabetizing the last name would be far more useful than listing people by height, social security number, or length of service with the company, although those organizing principles might make sense in other lists for other purposes.

The following five guidelines will help you choose the arrangement that will be the most useful for your reader:

1. **Process your information before you present it to your reader.** The order in which you become aware of information usually is not the best order to present it to your reader.
2. **When you have lots of information, group it into three to seven categories.** The average person's short-term memory can hold only seven chunks, though the chunks can be of any size.[3] By grouping your information into seven categories (or fewer), you make your report easier to read.
3. **If possible, arrange ideas in a logical progression.** Logical patterns help the reader know what to expect and thus speed reading. They also may make your ideas themselves seem more logical.
4. **Work with the reader's expectations, not against them.** Present ideas in the overview in the order in which you will discuss them.
5. **Consider the way the document will be used.** Reports are rarely read straight through from start to finish. Use layout and physical design to make it easy for readers to find the sections that interest them and to understand what they read.

Patterns of Organization for Reports

The best way to organize a report depends upon the subject matter, the reader's probable response to the information in the report, how the reader will use that information, and your own purposes. The following patterns frequently appear in reports:

1. Comparison/contrast.
2. Problem-solution.
3. Elimination of alternatives.
4. General to particular or particular to general.
5. Geographic or spatial.

* Based on James Paradis, David Dobrin, and Richard Miller, "Writing at Exxon ITD: Notes on the Writing Environment of an R&D Organization," in *Writing in Nonacademic Settings*, ed. Lee Odell and Dixie Goswami (New York: Guilford Press, 1985), 300–2 and on Michael L. Keene, *Effective Professional Writing* (Lexington, MA: D.C. Heath, 1987), 292–93, augmented by conversation with the author, May 17, 1988.

PATTERN A: USE ALTERNATIVES FOR MAIN CATEGORIES

Alternative 1	Opening a New Store on Campus
Criterion A	Cost of Renting Space
Criterion B	Proximity to Target Market
Criterion C	Competition from Similar Stores
Alternative 2	Opening a New Store Downtown
Criterion A	Cost of Renting Space
Criterion B	Proximity to Target Market
Criterion C	Competition from Similar Stores
Alternative 3	Opening a New Store in the Suburban Mall
Criterion A	Cost of Renting Space
Criterion B	Proximity to Target Market
Criterion C	Competition from Similar Stores

PATTERN B: USE CRITERIA FOR MAIN CATEGORIES

Criterion A	Cost of Renting Space for the New Store
Alternative 1	Cost of Campus Locations
Alternative 2	Cost of Downtown Locations
Alternative 3	Cost of Locations in the Suburban Mall
Criterion B	Proximity to Target Market
Alternative 1	Proximity on Campus
Alternative 2	Proximity Downtown
Alternative 3	Proximity in the Suburban Mall
Criterion C	Competition from Similar Stores
Alternative 1	Competing Stores on Campus
Alternative 2	Competing Stores Downtown
Alternative 3	Competing Stores in the Suburban Mall

FIGURE 20.1
TWO WAYS TO ORGANIZE A COMPARISON/CONTRAST REPORT

6. Functional.
7. Chronological.

Any of these patterns can be used for a whole report or for only part of it. Let's discuss each of them briefly.

1. **Comparison/Contrast.** Many reports use comparison/contrast sections within a larger report pattern. Comparison/contrast can also be the purpose of the whole report. In a **feasibility study,** for example, you evaluate two or more possible alternatives and recommend one of them. (Doing nothing is always one alternative.)

There are two ways to organize your discussion of the alternatives. You can take up each alternative in turn (Pattern A in Figure 20.1), or you can take up each criterion in turn (Pattern B).

Using the alternatives for the main categories is better when

- One alternative is clearly superior. When one alternative is much better, organizing by alternatives shortens the report.

- The criteria are hard to separate. If the criteria interact, organizing by alternatives is easier and more accurate.

- The reader will intuitively grasp the alternative as a whole rather than as the sum of its parts. If the reader sees the choices as indivisible, organizing by alternatives makes the report more useful for the reader.

Myths about Reports*
Contrary to popular belief,

1. The person who asks for the report is not necessarily the primary audience.

2. The audience may not be experts in the field.

3. The audience may not understand the report-writer's assignment.

4. The audience may not be looking forward to reading the report.

5. Few people in the audience will read the whole report carefully.

6. The author of the report may not be available to answer questions if the report is incomplete or unclear.

7. The report will be filed and may be used years later.

---

* Based on J. C. Mathes and Dwight W. Stevenson, *Designing Technical Reports: Writing for Audiences in Organizations* (Indianapolis: Bobbs-Merrill, 1976), 10.

Using the criteria for the main categories is better when

- **The superiority of one alternative to another depends on the relative weight assigned to various criteria.** Perhaps Alternative 1 is better if we are most concerned about Criterion A, cost, but worst if we are most concerned about Criterion B, proximity to target market. Organizing by alternatives allows readers to apply their own weights to each criterion.
- **The criteria are easy to separate.** When there is no apparent relationship among criteria, organizing by criteria may make the division neater.
- **The criteria can easily be grasped individually.** If the reader sees the choices in terms of competing criteria, organizing by criteria makes the report more useful for the reader.

A variation of Pattern A is the *pro and con pattern*. In this pattern, under each specific heading, give the arguments for and against that alternative. A report recommending new plantings for a university quadrangle uses the pro and con pattern:

> Advantages of Monocropping
>   High Productivity
>   Visual Symmetry
> Disadvantages of Monocropping
>   Danger of Pest Exploitation
>   Visual Monotony

When you have several alternatives, give the advantages and disadvantages in the same order for all of them. Whatever information comes second will carry more psychological weight. This pattern is least effective when you want to deemphasize the disadvantages of a proposed solution, for it does not permit you to "sandwich" the disadvantages between neutral or positive material.

2. Problem-Solution. Identify the problem; explain its background or history; discuss its extent and seriousness; identify its causes. Discuss the factors (criteria) which affect the decision. Analyze the advantages and disadvantages of possible solutions. Conclusions and recommendations can go either first or last, depending on the preferences of your reader. This pattern works well when the reader is neutral.

A report recommending ways to eliminate solidification of a granular bleach during production uses the problem-solution pattern:

> Recommended Reformulation for Vibe Bleach
> Problems in Maintaining Vibe's Granular Structure
>   Solidifying during Storage and Transportation
>   Customer Complaints about "Blocks" of Vibe in Boxes
> Why Vibe Bleach "Cakes"
>   Vibe's Formula
>   The Manufacturing Process
>   The Chemical Process of Solidification
> Modifications Needed to Keep Vibe Flowing Freely

3. Elimination of Alternatives. After discussing the problem and its causes, discuss the *impractical* solutions first, showing why they will not work. End with the most practical solution. This pattern works well when the solutions

the reader is likely to favor will not work, while the solution you recommend is likely to be perceived as expensive, intrusive, or radical.

A report on toy commercials eliminates alternatives:

Criticisms of TV Ads Directed at Children

The Effect of TV Ads on Children
   The Number of TV Ads Children See
   The Ages of Children Most Susceptible to Advertisers
   Children's Ability to Interpret TV Toy Ads

Camera Techniques Used in TV Advertisements
   Camera Movements
   Camera Angles
   Numbers of Shots and Cuts
   Transitions between Shots
   Special Effects

Current TV Ads for Toys

Alternative Solutions to Problems in TV Toy Ads
   Leave Ads Unchanged
   Mandate School Units on Advertising
   Allow the Industry to Regulate Itself
      The Success of Self-Regulation on Network TV
      Problems with Self-Regulation on Cable TV
   Mandate FTC Authority to Regulate TV Ads Directed at Children

4. General to Particular and Particular to General. General to particular starts with the problem as it affects the organization or as it manifests itself in general and then moves to a discussion of the parts of the problem and solutions to each of these parts. Particular to general starts with the problem as the audience defines it and moves to larger issues of which the problem is a part. Both are good patterns when you need to redefine the reader's perception of the problem in order to solve it effectively.

The directors of a student volunteer organization, VIP, have defined their problem as "not enough volunteers." After studying the subject, the writer is convinced that problems in training, supervision, and campus awareness are responsible for a high dropout rate and a low recruitment rate. The general to particular pattern helps the audience see the problem in a new way:

Why VIP Needs More Volunteers
   Need to Expand Prison Concern and Recreation Projects
   Need to Replace Graduating Seniors

Why Some VIP Volunteers Drop Out
   Inadequate Training
   Inadequate Supervision
   Feeling that VIP Requires Too Much Time
   Feeling that the Work Is Too Emotionally Demanding

Why Some Students Do Not Volunteer
   Feeling that VIP Requires Too Much Time
   Feeling that the Work Is Too Emotionally Demanding
   Preference for Volunteering with Another Organization
   Lack of Knowledge about VIP Opportunities

---

* Based on Janice LaRouche, "I'm Stuck in a Dead-End Job," *Family Circle,* March 24, 1987, 121.

Report Your Way to a Better Job*

Reports can show that a person in a too small job is ready for better things.

Joan was hired by a computer company to search current publications for references to the company's business: articles on rival firms, on customer attitudes toward computers, on the hiring conditions within the computer industry. It wasn't long before she realized that in this company, being a business librarian offered no room for advancement.

Joan decided to expand her job description. Instead of just sending files of clippings to the departments that used her services, she wrote reports summarizing the data. The receivers were delighted because she was saving them time.

Her second step was to meet with the people who got her reports to ask them what they hoped to accomplish and what sorts of information they needed. Now she was able to target her reports to her colleagues' needs. People in each unit began to think of her as part of their groups; they began to invite her to meetings discussing the projects she was researching.

As a member of the various groups within the company, Joan now had the information she needed to take a third step: drafting the report for the ultimate audience, for the primary decision-maker rather than for the immediate gatekeeper. For example, if the sales department wanted information for a proposal to a client, she presented her information in a sales proposal. If the president wanted material for a speech, she arranged her information in a speech outline.

When the director of business communications resigned, Joan (not the director's assistant) was perceived to be the obvious candidate for the job. She persuaded the company to combine the business library and the communications department into one unit which she would head. She now had even more responsibility than the person she was "replacing."

Using Visuals in Reports

Visuals in reports should tell a story, not just decorate the page. Use a title for the visual that makes its point clear. To test whether your title is specific enough, ask whether you could use the same title if the data told a different story. "Relation of Ad Creativity to Sales" doesn't tell us whether creative ads move merchandise. A better title for the visual would be "Creative Advertising Leads to Higher Sales."

Visuals must be honest. A visual communicates quickly. The quick impression the reader gets must be accurate.

Visuals should be free from chartjunk—meaningless decoration. Avoid the temptation to use all of your computer's capabilities to add cross-hatching, background, and little pictures. Simple visuals tell your story more clearly and more forcefully.

Always refer to each visual in the report. If you're not able to place the visual on the page where you discuss it, tell the reader where to find it: "See Figure 2 on page 10."

See Chapter 11 for a review of visuals and principles for presenting numerical data.

VIP's Training Program
  General Orientation for Volunteers
  Training Programs for Specific Projects
  Ways to Improve VIP's Training Program
VIP's Supervision of Volunteers
  Current Supervision Available
  Where Supervision Is Needed Most
  Ways to Improve VIP's Supervision of Volunteers
Time Demands on VIP Volunteers
  Current Time Demands in Specific Projects
  Ways to Increase Flexibility of Volunteer Hours
Emotional Demands on VIP Volunteers
  Projects in Which the Emotional Stress Is Greatest
  Ways to Provide More Emotional Support for VIP Volunteers
Campus Awareness of VIP
  Current Awareness among Undergraduate Students
  Ways to Increase Awareness among Undergraduate Students
Ways to Increase Volunteer Commitment and Motivation
  Providing More Information about Community Needs and VIP Services
  Assigning Duties to Volunteers
  Recognizing Volunteers

5. **Geographic or Spatial.** In a geographical or spatial pattern, you discuss problems and solutions by units by their physical arrangement. Move from office to office, building to building, factory to factory, state to state, region to region, etc.

A report on campus remodeling uses a spatial pattern of organization:

Remodeling and Renovations Needed in Bricker Hall
  Repairing Walls and Partitions
  Replacing Carpeting
  Painting
Remodeling and Renovations Needed in Denney Hall
  Building Walls and Partitions
  Painting
  Replacing Desks
  Rewiring
Remodeling and Renovations Needed in Smith Laboratory
  Repairing Walls and Partitions
  Painting
  Replacing Tables and Desks
  Replacing Lecterns
  Rewiring

6. **Functional.** In functional patterns, you discuss the problems and solutions of each functional unit. For example, a report on a new plant might divide data into sections on the costs of land and building, on the availability of personnel, on the convenience of raw materials, etc. A government report might divide data into the different functions an office performed, taking each in turn.

A strategy report for a political party uses a functional pattern of organization:

Current Makeup of the House and Senate
Congressional Seats Open in 1992
  Seats Held by a Democratic Incumbent
    Races in Which the Incumbent Has a Commanding Lead
    Races in Which the Incumbent Is Vulnerable
  Seats Held by a Republican Incumbent
    Races in Which the Incumbent Has a Commanding Lead
    Races in Which the Incumbent Is Vulnerable
  Seats Where No Incumbent Is Running
Senate Seats Open in 1992
  Seats Held by a Democratic Incumbent
    Races in Which the Incumbent Has a Commanding Lead
    Races in Which the Incumbent Is Vulnerable
  Seats Held by a Republican Incumbent
    Races in Which the Incumbent Has a Commanding Lead
    Races in Which the Incumbent Is Vulnerable
  Seats Where No Incumbent Is Running

7. Chronological. A chronological report records events in the order in which they happened or are planned to happen. Many progress reports are organized chronologically:

Work Completed in October
Work Planned for November

Making Your Organizational Pattern Clear to the Reader

The purpose of organization is to help your reader. If the reader can't figure out how your material is organized, the pattern you're using, however ingenious, isn't working. You can use both words and layout to make your organization clear.

Using Words to Make Your Organization Clear. Whenever your message is long, offer a summary or overview early in the message. The Table of Contents of a report serves as an overview; you may also want to provide an overview in the first few paragraphs of the report, or in the first paragraph of a new section of the report. (Remember to list items in the order in which you will discuss them.) Give enough information so that readers can turn directly to the portion of your report in which they are most interested.

Transition words and phrases, signposts, and internal summaries help readers know that they're still on track. In a short memo, an occasional transition will be all you'll need. If you're writing a long report, explicit signposts or summaries from time to time are a good idea.

There are economic advantages, too.
An alternative to this plan is . . .
The second factor . . .
These advantages, however, are found only in A, not in B or C.

Using Layout to Make Your Organization Clear. Headings, indented lists, and outlining can indicate each idea's level of importance.

Winston Churchill on Report Style*
[During World War II, Prime Minister Winston Churchill sent the following memo to the War Cabinet:]

To do our work, we all have to read a mass of papers. Nearly all of them are far too long. This wastes time while energy has to be spent looking for essential points.

I ask my colleagues and their staffs to see to it that their Reports are shorter.

(i) The aim should be Reports which set out the main points in a series of short, crisp paragraphs.

(ii) If a Report relies on detailed analysis of some complicated factors, or on statistics, these should be set out in an Appendix.

(iii) Let us have an end to . . . wooly phrases [that] are mere padding, which can be left out altogether or replaced with a single word. Let us not shrink from using the short expressive phrase, even if it is conversational.

* Quoted from Winston S. Churchill to the War Cabinet, August 1940, Public Record Office, in David W. Ewing, *Writing for Results in Business, Government, and the Professions* (New York: John Wiley, 1974), 372.

FIGURE 20.2
FIVE LEVELS OF HEADINGS IN A SINGLE-SPACED DOCUMENT

FIRST-LEVEL HEADINGS   *Center*
Bold or underline
Full capital letters

First-level headings are used for the titles of short documents and for chapter titles within long documents. Center them, using full capital letters. If you're using a word processor, use boldface type.

Second-Level Headings   *Center*
Bold or underline
Regular capital letters

Second-level headings introduce divisions within major points. The first letter of each major words in the heading is capitalized; the heading is either underlined or put in bold type; it is centered on the page. In a single-spaced document, triple space between the previous text and the heading; double space between the heading and the text which follows. In a double-spaced document, double space twice between the previous text and the heading; double space either once or twice between the heading and the following text.

When you do not need five levels of division, you may use "second-level headings" for the major divisions (Roman numerals in an outline) of the report.

Left Margin
Third-Level Headings   *Bold or underline*
Regular capitals

Third-level headings are flush with the left-hand margin and are either underlined or put in bold. The first letters of the first word and of other major words are capitalized; all other letters are lower case. In a single-spaced document, triple space between the previous text and the heading; in a double-spaced document, double space twice before the heading. In both, double space between the heading and the text which follows.

In a report using second-level headings for the Roman numerals, third-level headings would indicate capital letter points. Third-level headings are usually used for the main headings in memos.

At ¶ Indentation Bold or underline
Followed by a period

Fourth-level headings. Fourth- and fifth-level headings will normally appear only in a very long or complicated report. Fourth-level headings use the normal paragraph indentation, if any, are underlined or put in bold, and are followed by a period. (Some authorities recommend capitalizing the first letters of all major words and following the headings with a period and a dash--two hyphens.) Double space between previous text and the heading. The paragraph begins on the same line on which the heading is placed.

At ¶ Indentation Bold or underline

Fifth-level headings are integral parts of the first sentence of the first paragraph about a topic. They are underlined or set in bold. Since they are part of the paragraph, only the first letter of the first word is capitalized and only the spacing normal between paragraphs is used between previous text and the heading.

Headings are single words, short phrases, or complete sentences which indicate the topic in each section. A heading must cover all of the material under it until the next heading. For example, under the heading "Cost of Tuition," one could discuss only the cost of tuition, not the cost of books or of room and board. You can have just one paragraph under a heading or several pages. Since headings are designed to help the reader, if you do have several pages between headings you may want to consider using subheadings. Use subheadings only when you have two or more divisions within a main heading.

Topic headings focus on the structure of the report. As you can see from the following example, topic headings give very little information.

Recommendation
Problem
   Situation 1
   Situation 2
Causes of the Problem
   Background
   Cause 1
   Cause 2
Recommended Solution

Informative or **talking heads,** in contrast, tell the reader what to expect. Informative heads, like those in the examples in this chapter, provide an overview of each section and of the entire report:

Recommended Reformulation for Vibe Bleach
Problems in Maintaining Vibe's Granular Structure
   Solidifying during Storage and Transportation
   Customer Complaints about "Blocks" of Vibe in Boxes
Why Vibe Bleach "Cakes"
   Vibe's Formula
   The Manufacturing Process
   The Chemical Process of Solidification
Modifications Needed to Keep Vibe Flowing Freely

Headings must be parallel, that is, they must use the same grammatical structure. Subheads must be parallel to each other but do not necessarily have to be parallel to subheads under other headings.

Not Parallel:
   Are Students Aware of VIP?
      Current Awareness among Undergraduate Students
      Suggested Improvements
   Ways to Increase Volunteer Commitment and Motivation
      Provide More Information about Community Needs and VIP
      Services
      Assigning Duties to Volunteers
      How to Recognize Volunteers More Effectively
Parallel:
   Campus Awareness of VIP
      Current Awareness among Undergraduate Students
      Ways to Increase Awareness among Undergraduate Students
   Ways to Increase Volunteer Commitment and Motivation
      Providing More Information about Community Needs and VIP
      Services

FIGURE 20.3
ROMAN NUMERAL AND DECIMAL OUTLINES

```
            Roman Numeral Outline                    Decimal Outline


   I.  Main Point                       1.0   First point
       A.  Subpoint under I.                  1.1  Subpoint under 1.0
       B.  Subpoint under I.                  1.2  Subpoint under 1.0
  II.  Main Point                       2.0   Second point
       A.  Subpoint under II.                 2.1  Subpoint under 2.0
           1.  Subpoint under IIA.                 2.1.1  Subpoint under 2.1
               a.  Subpoint under IIA1.                   2.1.1.1  Subpoint under 2.1.1
               b.  Subpoint under IIA1.                   2.1.1.2  Subpoint under 2.1.1
           2.  Subpoint under IIA.                 2.1.2  Subpoint under 2.1
       B.  Subpoint under II.                  2.2  Subpoint under 2.0
       C.  Subpoint under II.                  2.3  Subpoint under 2.0
 III.  Main Point                       3.0   Third point

       etc.                                   etc.
```

Assigning Duties to Volunteers
Recognizing Volunteers

In a very complicated report, you may need up to five levels of headings. Figure 20.2 illustrates one way to set up headings. When you don't need this many levels, pick the headings you find most attractive. Use a lower level for subheadings.

The example in Figure 20.2 shows only one example of each level of heading. In an actual report, however, you would not use a subheading unless you had at least two subsections under the next higher heading.

Whatever the format for headings, avoid having a subhead come immediately after a heading. Instead, some text should follow the main heading before the subheading. (If you have nothing else to say, give an overview of the division.) When you type a document, avoid having a heading or subheading all by itself at the bottom of the page. Instead, have at least one line (preferably two) of type. If there isn't room for a line of type under it, put the heading on the next page. Don't use a heading as the antecedent for a pronoun. Instead, repeat the noun.

In a very long or complicated report, you may want to keep the outline signals with the headings. The heading *9.3 Recognizing Volunteers* clearly indicates the level of importance. Since outline signals indicate logical relationships, don't use them unless those relationships in fact exist. Outlines can use either Roman numerals or decimals.

Whichever form you choose, be consistent within a document. If a number of documents are part of a series, consider using the same organizational pattern for all of them.

SUMMARY OF KEY POINTS

- **Formal reports** contain the formal elements such as a Title Page, Transmittal, Table of Contents and List of Illustrations. **Informal reports** use letter or memo format.

- Use the following guidelines to choose the arrangement that will be the most useful for your reader:
  1. Process your information before you present it to your reader.
  2. When you have lots of information, group it into three to seven categories.
  3. If possible, arrange ideas in logical progression.
  4. Work with the reader's expectations, not against them.
  5. Consider the way the document will be used.

- A good purpose statement must make three things clear:
  - The organizational problem or conflict.
  - The specific technical questions which must be answered to solve the problem.
  - The rhetorical purpose (to explain, to recommend, to request, to propose) which the report is designed to achieve.

- **Comparison/Contrast** patterns discuss similarities and differences. The **pro and con** pattern divides the alternatives and discusses the arguments for and against that alternative. A **problem-solution report** identifies the problem, explains its causes, and analyzes the advantages and disadvantages of possible solutions. **Elimination of alternatives** identifies the problem, explains its causes, and discusses the least practical solutions first, ending with the one the writer favors. **General to particular** begins with the problem as it affects the organization or as it manifests itself in general, then moves to a discussion of the parts of the problem and solutions to each of these parts. **Particular to general** starts with specific aspects of the problem, then moves to a discussion of the larger implications of the problem for the organization. **Geographical or spatial** patterns discuss the problems and solutions by units. **Functional** patterns discuss the problems and solutions of each functional unit. **Chronological** patterns record events in the order in which they happened or are scheduled to happen.

- **Headings** are single words, short phrases, or complete sentences which cover all of the material under it until the next heading. **Informative** or **talking heads** tell the reader what to expect in each section.

- Headings must use the same grammatical structure. Subheads must be parallel to each other but do not necessarily have to be parallel to subheads under other headings.

NOTES

1. Donna Kienzler, conversation with the author, June 10, 1988.

2. Donald A. Ball and Wendell H. McCulloch, Jr., *International Business: Introduction and Essentials,* 2nd ed. (Plano, TX: Business Publications, 1985), 162.

3. George A. Miller, "The Magical Number Seven, Plus or Minus Two: Some Limits on Our Capacity for Processing Information," *The Psychological Review* 63, no. 2 (March 1956): 81–97.

PROBLEMS FOR CHAPTER 20

20–1   ANSWERING A SCHOOL SUPERINTENDENT'S QUESTION

Assume that you're an elementary school teacher or principal and respond to the following memo:

November 1, 19--

To: All Elementary School Teachers and
           Principals
From: Derek Powell, Superintendent of Schools   *DP*
Subject: Making Children Aware of the Religious
           Holidays of Various Faiths

Last December a teacher told me that when she passed out triangles of green construction paper to decorate as Christmas trees, one of her students turned it upside down and made it into a dreidel, a toy top that Jewish children play with during Hanukkah.

This year, please be sure that decorations, lessons, and activities acknowledge not only Christmas but also Hanukkah, and, if appropriate, the holidays of other religions. However, not all teachers have the information necessary to create such lessons and activities.

By November 10th, please send me a brief report on the religion you know best, detailing the information that should be shared about its winter religious holiday. If you have ideas for specific activities which teachers could use, please include them. I will compile the best of these and distribute them to all of you.

Answer the memo.

20–2   WRITING UP A SURVEY

As your instructor directs,

a. Survey 40 to 50 people on some subject of your choice.

b. Team up with your classmates to conduct a survey and write it up as a group. Survey 50 to 80 people if your group has two members, 75 to 120 people if it has three members, 100 to 150 people if it has four members, and 125 to 200 people if it has five members.

c. Keep a journal during your group meetings and submit it to your instructor.

d. Write a memo to your instructor describing and evaluating your group's process for designing, conducting, and writing up the survey. (See Chapter 25 on group dynamics.)

For this assignment, you DO NOT have to take a random sample. Do, however, survey at least two different groups so that you can see if they differ in some way. Possible groups are men and women, business majors and English majors, Greeks and independents, freshmen and seniors, students and townspeople.

As you conduct your survey, make careful notes about what you do so that you can use this information when you write up your survey. If you work with a group, record who does what. Use complete memo format. Your subject line should be clear and reasonably complete. Omit unnecessary words such as *Survey of.* Your first paragraph serves as an introduction, but it needs no heading. The rest of the body of your memo will be divided into four sections with the following headings: Purpose, Procedure, Results, and Discussion.

In your first paragraph, briefly summarize (not necessarily in this order) who conducted the experiment or survey, when it was conducted, where it was conducted, who the subjects were, what your purpose was, and what you found out. You will discuss all of these topics in more detail in the body of your memo.

In your **Purpose** section, explain why you conducted the survey. What were you trying to learn? What hypothesis were you testing? Why did this subject seem interesting or significant?

In your **Procedure** section, describe in detail *exactly* what you did. "The first 50 people who came through the Union on Wed., Feb. 2," is not the same as "The first 50 people who came through the south entrance of the Union on Wed., Feb. 2, and agreed to answer my questions." Explain any steps you took to overcome possible sources of bias.

In your **Results** section, first tell whether your results supported your hypothesis. Use both visuals and words to explain what your numbers show. (See Chapter 11 on how to design visuals.) Process your raw data in a way that will be useful to your reader.

In your **Discussion** section, evaluate your survey and discuss the implications of your results. Consider these questions:

1. What are the limitations of your survey and your results?

2. Do you think a scientifically valid survey would have produced the same results? Why or why not?

3. Were there any sources of bias either in the way the questions were phrased or in the way the subjects were chosen? If you were running the survey again, what changes

would you make to eliminate or reduce these sources of bias?

4. Do you think your subjects answered honestly and completely? What factors may have intruded? Is the fact that you did or didn't know them, were or weren't of the same sex relevant? If your results seem to contradict other evidence, how do you account for the discrepancy? Were your subjects shading the truth? Was your sample's unrepresentativeness the culprit? Or have things changed since earlier data were collected?

5. What causes the phenomenon your results reveal? If several causes together account for the phenomenon, or if it is impossible to be sure of the cause, admit this. Then go on to discuss the claims of rival hypotheses and the reasons one cannot be sure what the cause is.

6. What action should be taken?

The **Discussion** section gives you the opportunity to analyze the significance of your survey. Its insight and originality lift the otherwise well-written memo from the ranks of the merely satisfactory to the ranks of the above-average and the excellent.

The whole assignment will be more interesting if you choose a question which interests you. It does not need to be significant in terms of major political or philosophic problems; a quirk of human behavior that fascinates you will do nicely.

20–3 WRITING AN INFORMATIVE REPORT ABOUT A MAGAZINE

As an assistant to the Media Buyer at a major advertising agency, you help recommend to clients in which magazines they should run print ads. To do that, you need to know not only circulation and ad fees but also the kind of people who read each magazine so that you can match the product and ad strategy to the readership of the magazine.

Since magazines change, you need to update your information every two or three years.

Your boss gives you the following questions to cover in your report and these instructions: "Some of these questions can be answered very briefly; some of them will require pages of analysis with lots of supporting examples. You can rearrange this information if you want to, and you can cover things not on this list. If you

want to omit something that is on it, check with me first to be sure it's OK."

1. **Topics, Tone, and Slant.** What topics are covered in every issue? Which are covered occasionally? Is coverage light, serious, or a mixture? Is there a political or religious slant? Are some topics avoided? Are topics covered superficially or in depth?

2. **Language.** Is the language abstract and complex or simple and down-to-earth? Do titles or articles use puns and alliteration? Quote examples.

3. **Art.** Discuss the use of drawings, photos, cartoons, etc. Does the art help to convey editorial content, or is it just decoration?

4. **Ads.** What sort of things are advertised? Luxury items or necessities? What appeals are used in the ads—to economy, to efficiency, to snobbery, or what? What kinds of products and services are *not* advertised?

5. **Target Audience.** Indicate sex, age, education, income range, and interests.

Write an informal report based on three to six issues of one magazine. Since it is an information report, you will not make any recommendations.

20–4 IDENTIFYING POPULAR SPORTS IN VARIOUS COUNTRIES

You get the following directions from your superior in the advertising agency for which you work:

"Some of our clients are interested in sponsoring sporting events—either buying advertising time on TV broadcasts of sporting events or paying to have their names on the walls of the arenas or stadiums.

Please draw up a list of the most popular sports. For each sport, indicate the season. List the countries in which it is popular and indicate how popular it is in each country. If possible, also give demographic data: are its followers likely to be of a specific age, sex, or socioeconomic class?"

As your instructor directs,

a. Write an informal report analyzing the popularity of a single sport around the world.

b. Write an informal report analyzing the sports that are popular in a specific country or geographic region.

20–5 RECOMMENDING WAYS TO REDUCE UNEMPLOYMENT

You're a member of a joint business-government commission charged with recommending ways to reduce unemployment in your city.

As your instructor directs,

a. Write an informal report documenting the incidence of unemployment in your city. How many people are unemployed? How long, on the average, are they out of work? Why can't they find jobs? Try to get demographic data on age, sex, and education.

b. Write an informal report documenting the kinds and approximate numbers of jobs that exist for unskilled workers in your city.

c. Write an informal report documenting the kinds and approximate numbers of jobs that exist for skilled and professional workers in your city.

d. Recommend to the local high schools or to a local community college the kind of training needed to prepare students to enter the job market in your city.

Hints:

- What agencies in your city would have information about unemployment? If you wanted to talk to some of the people who are unemployed, where could you find them?

- Will reading newspaper ads tell you what jobs are available? What are the limitations of newspaper ads? (See Chapter 26.) How else could you get information on skilled and unskilled jobs? Where could you get a list of the employers in your city?

20–6 IDENTIFYING THE INCIDENCE OF PHONY IDS

Several legislators in your state have introduced a bill which would suspend for one year the driving privileges of anyone convicted of using a falsified ID or an ID that belongs to someone else to buy alcoholic beverages. The legislators hope that this bill will reduce the incidence of underage drinking and of drunk driving.

As your instructor directs,

a. Conduct a survey to estimate how often underage drinkers use falsified or borrowed IDs to buy alcohol in your city.

b. Review the traffic accident reports in your city or your state to determine how many involve underage drinkers.

c. Survey the population as a whole or a group to which you belong to find out people's attitudes toward the proposed law.

Write up the results of your study in an individual or a group report.

Hints:

- Will sales clerks and servers where alcohol is sold be reliable guides to the use of falsified or borrowed IDs?

- Underage drinkers may not want to admit they have used falsified or borrowed IDs, even in an anonymous survey. What tactics could you use to get this information? What are the strengths and weaknesses of less direct tactics (e.g., "Do you know anyone who has purchased alcohol using a falsified or borrowed ID?").

20–7 GATHERING INFORMATION ABOUT FRINGE BENEFITS IN AN INDUSTRY

As a member of a consulting firm, you advise companies about compensation and fringe benefits. Common fringe benefits include payments for time not worked (vacations, sick days, holidays) and company contributions to social security, insurance, workers' compensation, and pension. Less common benefits include free parking, subsidies for education or day care, and profit-sharing plans. High-level employees may receive reimbursement for moving costs, expense allowances, and even club memberships.

As your instructor directs,

a. Write an informal report on the fringe benefits offered by a single organization. Which benefits are extended to everyone? Which benefits are "perks" of employees at higher ranks? What percent of total compensation do fringe benefits represent?

b. Join with other students to write a group report on the fringe benefits offered by several employers in a single field or industry. How much variation is there among employers?

20–8 GATHERING INFORMATION FOR SOJOURNERS ABROAD

You work for a fast-growing telecommunications company which develops, manufactures, and sells computerized telecommunications equipment worldwide. U.S. employees go to other countries to direct joint ventures, to supervise manufacturing, accounting, marketing, and sales, and to train nationals of other countries to take over these functions.

A dent in your profitability comes from the fact that many of the people you send abroad for scheduled stays of two to five years are unable to adapt to another culture and come home much sooner. Relocating an employee and his or her family runs $50,000 to $300,000 depending on the country and the size of the family. Furthermore, it is disruptive to your international ventures to have a constant turnover.

This problem appeared on the agenda of the last meeting of department heads. You said that teaching the employee the language was not enough. Virtually everyone who sojourns abroad experiences culture shock. Furthermore, workers in other countries have different motivations and use different nonverbal behaviors than U.S. managers are familiar with. And training should include the sojourner's family. The employee will have a work environment to provide stability and at least limited familiarity; family members may have more trouble developing a social network.

Now you have been put in charge of gathering information that can be given to employees before they leave for other countries. Pick one country or culture, and write an informal report answering the following questions for it.

1. What is the climate like? How does it differ from what employees are used to?
2. What immunizations are necessary? Will Americans be able to drink the water and eat the food? Are there any supplies or food (e.g., peanut butter) that may not be available?
3. What should a sojourner expect in terms of housing, schools for children, low-cost entertainment, and employment for spouses?
4. What is the exchange rate? What everyday items may be expensive or unavailable in the country? What goods or services may be much less expensive than they are in the United States?
5. What is (are) the dominant religion(s)? How do religious observances affect business life?
6. What everyday behaviors and nonverbal signals differ from the behavior and signals Americans are used to? Are there any typical American behaviors that could offend people in the country?
7. What interesting trips should the family try to take during their sojourn? What sights should they try to see?

Hints:
- In addition to using published sources to get this information, talk to people in your college and in your city who have visited the country, who have lived there, or who are natives of the country.
- See Chapter 23 for some information about nonverbal behaviors in different countries.

20–9 WRITING A SAFETY REPORT

You are Assistant to the Director of Safety and Training. Last week, before she left on vacation, your boss told you, "The monthly injury reports will be in Friday. I want you to write up a report of the month's injuries and summarize the whole quarter. Our injury rates last month were high. If that trend continues, we need to alert the plant managers immediately. In your report, give not only the numerical totals, but also categorize the injuries and tell managers what kinds of safety to stress. Use some graphs: maybe that will help get people's attention."

The reports from each plant came in yesterday.

Spokane
Disabling injuries: 0
Frequency of injuries per million worker hours: 0.0
Worker hours since the last disabling injury: 130,231
Days since the last disabling injury: 422
Disabling injuries last month: 0
Disabling injuries two months ago: 0
Disabling injuries this quarter last year: 1
Specific injuries: None

Houston
Disabling injuries: 3
Frequency of injuries per million worker hours: 62.8
Worker hours since the last disabling injury: 10,522
Days since the last disabling injury: 19
Disabling injuries last month: 2
Disabling injuries two months ago: 4
Disabling injuries this quarter last year: 7
Specific injuries: (1) As the shift was about to end, the employee started walking to the time clock. Her foot slipped off the edge of the driveway and she sprained her ankle. (2) The worker was using a crane to move some material. He wanted to lower the chains and without looking pushed a button. He pushed the UP button by mistake and the block was raised into the hoist housing, The chain fell and struck the employee on the head. His hard hat prevented a serious injury, but a deep laceration still resulted. (3) An office worker tripped over a cable linking a computer to the printer. He sprained his ankle.

Chattanooga
Disabling injuries: 2
Frequency of injuries per million worker hours: 64.5

Worker hours since the last disabling injury: 354
Days since the last disabling injury: 1
Disabling injuries last month: 3
Disabling injuries two months ago: 1
Disabling injuries this quarter last year: 4
Specific injuries: (1) While tarping a trailer, the employee stepped down on an unsupported area of the tarp and fell. He caught his foot on a chain binder and broke his ankle. (2) As a truck driver was hooking up the second end of a box of materials 12′ long, the crane operator hoisted the material to take up the slack. The truck driver's hand got caught between the chain and the crane hook and his middle finger was crushed.

Detroit
Disabling injuries: 0
Frequency of injuries per million worker hours: 0.0
Worker hours since the last disabling injury: 111,920
Days since the last disabling injury: 142
Disabling injuries last month: 0
Disabling injuries two months ago: 0
Disabling injuries this quarter last year: 1
Specific injuries: None

Pittsburgh
Disabling injuries: 5
Frequency of injuries per million worker hours: 72.0
Worker hours since the last disabling injury: 9,863
Days since the last disabling injury: 12
Disabling injuries last month: 2
Disabling injuries two months ago: 0
Disabling injuries this quarter last year: 2
Specific injuries: (1) The employee was returning to the maintenance room after inspecting a construction site. As he stepped over some rebar that had been set for foundation flooring, his heel caught and he fell. His head struck a concrete footer and he suffered a cut over the right eye. In addition, he cut his hand when he tried to break his fall. (2) This loader was attempting to slide four pieces of 2 3/4″ D, 2′ 1″ long steel along hacksaw exit rolls so that he could hook it up. He had one hand on top of the bundle and one hand underneath. As he pulled harder, the bundle fell between the rolls and pinched his hand against the roller. One finger was fractured and three other fingers were severely bruised. (3) This employee was helping to move galvanized sheets from a lift to the scales. One sheet slipped from his grasp and cut his hand. He was not wearing safety gloves. (4) This maintenance worker was welding braces on a slot rack and standing on an eight-inch high step to do so. As she leaned over to weld, she lost her balance and fell against the rack. The fall resulted in bruised ribs and a broken hand.

As your instructor directs,

  a. Write a report to the plant managers, with copies to the executive committee.

  b. Write individual memos to the managers at the plants with the greatest safety problems, recommending actions they should take.

  c. Write individual memos congratulating the managers of the plants without any injuries.

  d. Write an informal report for your boss recommending what safety training or reminder programs your office should conduct.

20–10   INVESTIGATING A LOCAL PROBLEM
Write an information report on a problem that exists on your campus or in your city. The problem can affect a specific organization or the college or town as a whole.

As your instructor directs,

  a. Write an informal informational report explaining the problem and its causes.

  b. Write an informal analytical report examining the cause(s) of the problem and recommending a complete or partial solution.

  c. Write an informal feasibility study recommending whether the organization should undertake a specific course of action.

  d. Present a summary of your conclusions and recommendations orally to the class.

Documents in the Reporting Process

QUESTIONS

- What are the criteria for a good problem statement?
- What is a Request for Proposal (RFP)? How does it affect the proposal?
- How do you write proposals for research projects, sales proposals, and proposals for funding?
- How should a progress report be organized?
- Why should a progress report use positive emphasis?
- Why is it necessary to write closure reports?
- How can an organization produce better annual reports?

It is a bad plan that admits of no modification.
Publilius Syrus
Maxim 469, first century B.C.

The process of writing a report begins with defining a research problem. During the research phase, the writer normally produces at least two documents: a proposal and one or more progress reports. Research that does not merit presentation in a problem-solving report can be recorded in a closure report. And once a year, organizations communicate with their stockholders in an annual report.

DEFINING A RESEARCH PROBLEM

Good report problems grow out of real problems: disjunctions between reality and the ideal, choices that must be made. When you write a report as part of your job, the organization has usually defined the topic for you. To think of problems for class reports, think about problems that face various groups: your community college, college, or university, housing units on campus, social, religious, and professional groups, local businesses, and city, county, state, and federal governments and their agencies. Read your campus and local papers and news magazines; watch the news on TV or listen to it on National Public Radio.

A good statement of a research problem in business or administration meets the following criteria:

1. The problem is
   - Real.
   - Important enough to be worth solving.
   - Narrow but challenging.
   - Possible to solve with the time and resources available.
   - Something you're interested in.
2. The audience for the report is
   - Real.
   - Able to implement the recommended action.
   - One you can get information about.
3. The data, evidence, and facts are
   - Sufficient to document the severity of the problem.
   - Sufficient to prove that the recommendation will solve the problem.
   - Available to *you*.
   - Comprehensible to *you*.

Meg Morgan has shown that groups sometimes create problems which do not really exist. One student group, for example, decided that students were not informed about campus events and that the problem could be solved with a campus radio station. In fact, their university already had a radio station which broadcast, among other things, university announcements. But even with this information, the group was unable to change its problem formulation. As Morgan says, the group "created among group members a problem that did not exist outside the group."[1] To be sure that the problem is real, check your perceptions against those of others, especially people in the organization whose problem you hope to solve.

Often problem statements need to be revised so that they address one well-defined problem. For example, "improving the college experiences of foreign students studying in the United States" is far too broad. First, limit the scope to one specific college or university. The problems of foreign students and the resources to solve those problems will differ dramatically at different schools. Second, narrow the problem. Do you want to increase the social interaction between U.S. and foreign students? Help foreign students find housing? Help them learn English more quickly? Offer social support for spouses? Increase the number of ethnic grocery stores and restaurants? Reduce discrimination? Increase job opportunities in the United States? Third, identify the specific audience which would have the power to implement your recommendations. Depending on the specific topic, the audience might be the Office of International Studies, the residence hall counselors, faculty in a specific department, a service organization on campus or in town, an existing store or employer, or a group of investors.

The problem you pick must be one you can solve in the time available. Six months of full-time (and overtime) work and a team of colleagues might allow you to look at all the ways to make a store more profitable. If you're doing a report in 6 to 12 weeks for a class which is only one of your responsibilities, you need to limit the topic. Rather than looking at all the factors that contribute to profitability, pick just one. Depending on your interests and knowledge, you could choose to examine the prices and styles of clothes a store carried, its inventory procedures, its overhead costs, its layout and decor, or its advertising budget.

PROPOSALS

Researchers seeking funding and companies or consultants wishing to sell a product or service submit proposals to get funding or to get the sale. Students writing reports or theses are also usually asked to submit proposals.

When students write reports or theses individually, the instructor or advisor hopes to approve a proposal for each student. The proposal will be accepted if it shows that you've defined the problem acceptably, have a solid research plan, and can meet the requirements in the time available. However, other sorts of proposals are more competitive. When several students prepare a group report, students will think of different problems, but the group must decide on a single problem to study. Similarly, applications for research funding are often very competitive. The National Science Foundation, for example, funds only one out of every five proposals submitted.[2] Many companies will bid for government or corporate contracts, but in each case, only one proposal will be accepted.

A proposal must answer the following questions convincingly:

- **What problem are you going to solve?**
  Show that you understand the problem and the organization's needs. Define the problem as the audience sees it, even if you believe

A "C" Proposal Earns $167 Million in Profits*

When he was an undergraduate at Yale, Frederick W. Smith wrote an economics paper proposing an independent air-service system to deliver packages. His professor didn't believe that the idea would work. Smith got a "C" on the paper. But Frederick Smith started a delivery service anyway. Federal Express was founded in 1973. In the fiscal year that ended May 30, 1987, Federal Express had over half of the overnight delivery market, took in revenues of $3.18 billion, and earned an operating profit of $167 million.

Not bad for an "average" idea.

---

* Based on Larry Reibstein, "Turbulence Ahead: Federal Express Faces Challenges to Its Grip on Overnight Delivery," *The Wall Street Journal,* January 8, 1988, 1, 8.

The Answer May Be in the RFP *

Again and again, proposal writers waste hours in discussions, telephone calls, and other research, seeking answers which are found, eventually, in the RFP [Request for Proposal] itself. . . .

[A] Department of Agriculture [RFP] called for a variety of publications services. . . . One proposer, invoking the Freedom of Information Act, asked for a list of prices currently charged by the incumbent contractor. Studying the list, he found that it was going to be most difficult to be the low bidder, which he thought he had to be to win the contract.

He was almost at the point of submitting a "no bid," when he decided to study the solicitation package more closely in one final effort to find a strategy for being the low bidder. Concealed (virtually) in a thick appendix of specifications he found his answer.

One of the many items to be priced for the contract was typing double-spaced pages of manuscript. Using the then-standard 8 × 10½ inch paper (now 8½ × 11 inches, as in commercial practice), a typical typing page would normally be about 7 × 9 inches, at the largest. And using the more popular elite or 10-point type this would amount to 27 lines of 84 characters and spaces each, or a grand total of 2,268 keystrokes. The price currently being paid by the Department of Agriculture seemed about right for such a page of draft typing, but it didn't seem possible to cut that.

However, buried among the stack of specifications, this proposer found the customer's own specification for a "page" of typing. It specified a page as 55 characters wide and 18 lines deep, for a total of 990 characters and spaces. That was less than one-half the number he had assumed would represent a typical typed page. The price now being paid for *that* page of typing was quite high. He had little difficulty now in cutting the price and winning the contract.

that the presenting problem is part of a larger problem that must first be solved.

- **How are you going to solve it?**
  Prove that your methods are feasible. Show that a solution can be found in the time available. Specify the topics you'll investigate. Explain how you'll gather data.
- **What exactly will you provide for us?**
  Specify the tangible products you'll produce; explain how you'll evaluate them.
- **Can you deliver what you promise?**
  Show that you have the knowledge, the staff, the facilities to do what you say you will. Describe your previous work in this area, your other qualifications, and the qualifications of any people who will be helping you.
- **What benefits can you offer?**
  In a sales proposal, several vendors may be able to supply the equipment needed. Show why the company should hire you. Discuss the benefits—direct and indirect—that your firm can provide.
- **When will you complete the work?**
  Provide a detailed schedule showing when each phase of the work will be completed.
- **How much will you charge?**
  Provide a detailed budget that includes costs for materials, salaries, and overhead costs.

Government agencies and companies often issue Requests for Proposals, known as **RFP**s. Follow the RFP exactly when you write a proposal. Competitive proposals are often scored by giving points in each category. Evaluators will not say, "Oh, they've discussed what we call *Facilities* under *Qualifications*." Instead, the evaluators look only under the heads specified in the RFP. If information isn't there, the proposal gets no points in that category.

People faced with a stack of proposals are looking for grounds to eliminate as many proposals as possible. Any one of the following can be a sufficient reason to reject the proposal.

- It didn't arrive by the deadline.
- It doesn't follow the instructions in the RFP.
- It isn't specific enough to prove its claims.
- Its budget is unrealistic, suggesting that the proposers don't understand the scope of the job.

Proposals for Class Research Projects

You may be asked to submit a proposal for a report that you will write for a class. Even when the report and the assignment are addressed to a real person in a real organization, your instructor is the audience for the proposal. Your instructor wants evidence that your problem is not too big and not too small, that you understand it, that your methods will give you the information you need, and that you have the knowledge and resources to collect and analyze the data.

Problem 21–4 lists specific topics that your instructor might ask you to cover. Figure 21.1 presents a proposal in response to that assignment for a student report using both original and library research.

* Quoted from Herman Holtz and Terry Schmidt, *The Winning Proposal: How to Write It* (New York: McGraw-Hill, 1981), 90–91.

FIGURE 21.1
A PROPOSAL FOR A STUDENT REPORT

November 5, 1988

To: Kitty O. Locker

From: Deborah Buchmueller

Subject: A Proposal to Evaluate the Use of a Cook-Freeze System
         for Quantity Food Production of Alternative Main Entree
         Selections

For my report, I plan to evaluate the feasibility of a cook-
freeze system for the quantity food production of alternative
main entree selections. The system described will be adapted
to the current needs of the Nutrition Services department at
St. Elizabeth Hospital Medical Center in Youngstown, Ohio.

Problem

Some hospital patients request main entrees that are not on the
lunch or dinner menu for the day. These requests result from
the patients'

- Religious beliefs
- Cultural backgrounds
- Food allergies and intolerances
- Chewing impairment
- Boredom with the menu.

The dietitians encourage these patients to select an alternative
main entree so that they will enjoy their meals and receive the
proper nourishment. The problem is that the entrees are of
poor quality and are unappetizing. Sending meals that the
patients will not eat defeats the intentions of the dietitians.

It is well documented in the medical literature that nutrition
is a primary factor in the recovery from surgery and illness.
Dietitians and physicians are always concerned about patients'
food intake because they want to be sure the patients are getting
the nutrition they need.

My analysis of this problem reveals three contributing factors:

- The variability of the requested entrees.
- The lack of time during meal preparation hours to prepare
  the entrees.
- The recent labor hour reductions.

Due to these factors, the present food production system cannot
incorporate these additional entrees, and poor quality results.
Another system of food production is needed for the preparation
of quality alternative main entree selections.

FIGURE 21.1
(continued)

Kitty O. Locker   2   November 5, 1988

Topics to Investigate

In this report I will describe a cook-freeze system that can be used in this hospital's food service. To accomplish this, I will be considering the following questions:

- How can the hospital determine what entrees to prepare?
- How many different entrees can be produced?
- How many of each entree should be produced at a time?
- What container is best for freezing and reheating?
- Where will the frozen entrees be held?
- What method of reheating will be used?
- What is the best time to produce these entrees?
- Is there any equipment that should be purchased?
- How often will inventory checks be conducted?

The concepts that I will explain include:

- The control of microorganism growth in chilled and frozen foods.
- The qualities of the equipment included in this system.
- The proper food preparation methods to maintain the quality of the frozen foods.
- The method(s) of reheating that are best for specific main entrees.

By addressing these questions and concepts, I will be able to objectively evaluate and possibly recommend the use of a cook-freeze system for the preparation of quality alternative main entree selections.

Audience

The person who is able to implement my recommendation is:

Lisa Gill, Director of Nutrition Services, St. Elizabeth Hospital Medical Center, 1044 Belmont Ave., Youngstown, Ohio 44501

She is knowledgeable in related food service terminology and is very interested in ways of producing quality food items. She will review this report in detail. She will require the approval of the following individuals prior to implementing my recommendation:

Dennis Schaffer, Associate Director, St. Elizabeth Hospital Medical Center, 1044 Belmont Ave., Youngstown, Ohio 44501
Sonia Schultz, Assistant Director, St. Elizabeth Hospital Medical Center, 1044 Belmont Ave., Youngstown, Ohio 44501

They are well aware of the poor quality of the current alternative main entrees, and they would like to see an improvement. They are also very concerned about any additional labor or material

FIGURE 21.1
(continued)

Kitty O. Locker   3   November 5, 1988

expenses. For this audience, I will provide a clear relationship between the problem and my recommendation as a solution.

A fourth person that will be reviewing this report is:

> Carol Hoffman, Administrative Dietitian, St. Elizabeth
>   Hospital Medical Center, 1044 Belmont Ave., Youngstown,
>   Ohio 44501

She is responsible for organizing the food production schedules
and all employee training. She will understand the terminology
and is most concerned with how this system will relieve the
daily frustration of preparing these required items. She will
also be concerned with the production time required for the
quantity preparation of these items. Therefore, I will include
enough details about how this recommendation can easily fit
into their present food production system.

My immediate audience is:

> Kitty O. Locker, Professor, 545 Denney Hall, The Ohio State
>   University, Columbus, Ohio 43210

You are concerned with the clear organization, the writing style,
and a strong content in my report. Since you are not familiar
with the hospital, I will explain a "2-week-cycle menu" and the
daily food production routine. A definition of what "quality"
means in a food service context is necessary.

I will complete my report with an appendix that contains these
definitions and any additional food service terminology that I
may include in my report.

Methods/Procedures

My professional experience and data collection at this hospital
will provide most of the information that I will need to answer
my questions. I have a good understanding of the patients'
needs and the types of alternative main entree selections they
prefer. My production scheduling class has taught me how to
accurately define the best time for production of these items.

Information on the remaining questions and concepts will come
from the following sources:

> 1. Livingston, G. and Chang, C. M. (1979). _Food service
> systems: Analysis, design, and implementation_. New York:
> Academic Press.
>
> 2. Boltman, B. (1978). _Cook-freeze catering systems_.
> London: Applied Science Publishers.
>
> 3. West, B., Wood, L., Harger, V., Shugart, G. (1977).
> _Food service in institutions_. New York: Wiley.

FIGURE 21.1
(continued)

Kitty O. Locker   4   November 5, 1988

In addition to these books, I plan to use the following journal articles:

    1. Mudgett, R. E. (1986). "Microwave properties and heating characteristics of foods." Food Technology, 40, 84.

    2. Edgar, R. (1986). "The economics of microwave processing in the food industry." Food Technology, 40, 106.

Qualifications/Facilities/Resources

I am able to successfully complete this project because I have both the practical and technical experience necessary to view the problem and determine the feasibility of my recommended solution. I am a senior in Food and Nutrition, and I have worked for six summers at this hospital. Last summer as a dietitian intern I

- Helped plan menus according to the capabilities of the food production equipment and employees.

- Conducted recipe standardization for quality food production.

- Observed the importance of the Nutrition Services department in patient care.

- Observed the consistent poor quality products that are being sent to the patients when alternative main entree selections are made.

Since I have remained in touch with the staff, I can obtain further information from the department if it is needed. I also have access to books and periodicals at the OSU library facilities to search for additional information.

If an unexpected snag should develop, I am able to consult Margaret Horvath and Marion Cremer, who are both food service professors that are knowledgeable in this area.

Work Schedule

Outlined below is a schedule of the time allowances and completion dates that I have set up for the activities involved in my project.

FIGURE 21.1
(*concluded*)

Kitty O. Locker   5   November 5, 1988

Activity	Total Time	Date
gathering information	9 hours	11/2/88
analyzing information	10 hours	11/9/88
preparing the progress report	6 hours	11/14/88
organizing information	9 hours	11/11/88
writing the draft	12 hours	11/18/88
revising the draft	6 hours	11/21/88
editing the draft	3 hours	11/23/88
typing the report	7 hours	11/28/88
proofreading the report	1 hour	11/29/88

I will discuss any changes in this schedule with you.

Call to Action

I would like to meet with you, as soon as your schedule permits,
to discuss my research plan and answer any questions you may
have. I welcome any suggestions you may have so that my report
will be clear and accepted as an effective solution to the problem
in this hospital Nutrition Services department. Please thoroughly
review and approve my proposal so that I may begin my report.

Sales Proposals

To sell expensive goods or services, you may be asked to submit a proposal.

Be sure that you understand the buyer's priorities. A phone company lost a $26 million sale to a university because it assumed that the university's priority would be cost. Instead, the university wanted a state-of-the-art system. The university accepted a higher bid.

Don't assume that the buyer will understand why your product or system is good. For everything you offer, show the reader benefits of each feature. (Review Chapter 7 on how to develop reader benefits.) Be sure to present the benefits using you-attitude. Consider using psychological description (Chapter 14) to make the benefits vivid.

Use language appropriate for your audience. Even if the buyers want a state-of-the-art system, they may not want the level of detail that your staff could provide; they may not understand or appreciate technical jargon.

Sales proposals, particularly for complicated systems costing millions of dollars, are often long. Provide a one-page cover letter to present your proposal succinctly. The best organization for this letter is a modified version of the sales pattern in Chapter 16:

1. Catch the reader's attention and summarize up to three major benefits you offer.
2. Discuss each of the major benefits in the order in which you mentioned them in the first paragraph.
3. Deal with any objections or concerns the reader may have.
4. Mention other benefits briefly.
5. Ask the reader to approve your proposal and provide a reason for acting promptly.

Proposals for Funding

If you need money for a new or continuing public service project, you may want to submit a proposal for funding to a foundation, a corporation, a government agency, or a religious agency. In a proposal for funding, stress the needs your project will meet. There are many worthy causes, and no one can fund them all. Why should the agency fund yours? Show how your project helps fulfill the goals of the funding organization.

Every funding source has certain priorities; some have detailed lists of the kind of projects they fund. *The Foundation Directory* indexes foundations by state and city and by field of interest. *The Foundation Grants Index Annual* lists grants of $5,000 or more made by the 425 biggest foundations. Check recent awards to discover foundations that may be interested in your project. *Source Book Profiles* describes 1,000 national and regional foundations.

PROGRESS REPORTS

When you're assigned to a single project that will take a month or more, you'll probably be asked to file one or more progress reports. A progress report reassures the funding agency or employer that you're making progress and allows you and the agency or employer to resolve problems as they arise. Different readers may have different concerns. An instructor may want to know whether you'll have your report in by the due date. A client

* Quoted from Albert Szent-Györgyi, "Dionysians and Apollonians," *Science* 176 (June 2, 1972): 966.

may be more interested in what you're learning about the problem. Adapt your progress report to the needs of the audience.

The following pattern of organization focuses on what you have done and what work remains:

1. **Summarize your progress in terms of your goals and your original schedule.** The agency or employer uses progress reports to make decisions: Should funding on this project continue? Does it require additional resources? Should its focus be revised? In your first paragraph(s), allow the reader to see how your work is going so that he or she can put it into an organizational context.

2. **Under the heading "Work Completed," describe what you have already done.** Provide enough detail to enable the agency or employer to understand your claims in the first paragraph and to appreciate your hard work. Describe any serious obstacles you've encountered and tell how you've dealt with them.

3. **Under the heading "Work to Be Completed," describe the work that remains.** If you're more than three days late (for school projects) or 10 days (for business projects) submit a new schedule. You may want to discuss "Observations" or "Preliminary Conclusions" if you want feedback before writing the final report or if your reader has asked for substantive interim reports.

4. **Either express your confidence in having the report ready by the due date or request a conference to discuss extending the due date or limiting the project.**

The student progress report in Figure 21.2 uses this pattern of organization. Use a straightforward subject line for a progress report:

Subject: Progress on Developing a Marketing Plan for TCBY
Subject: Progress on Group Survey on Campus Parking

If you are submitting weekly or monthly progress reports on a long project, you may want to number your progress reports and give dates for the work completed since the last report and to be completed before the next report.

Make your progress report as positive as you honestly can. You'll build a better image of yourself if you show that you can take minor problems in stride and that you're confident of your own abilities.

Negative: I have not deviated markedly from my schedule, and I feel that I will have very little trouble completing this report by the due date.

Positive: I am back on schedule and expect to complete my report by the due date.

CLOSURE REPORTS

A **closure report** summarizes completed research that does not result in action or recommendation. From the researcher's point of view, a closure report marks a failure or a dead end: a proposed product is too expensive to be profitable; a production process is not yet technically feasible; a new direct mail package is being discontinued because it was less effective than the control package. However, this research needs to be documented so that the organization has a record of what has been tried and why it failed. A few years from now, new technologies, new conditions, or new ideas may make a "failed" idea feasible.

When the Stakes Are High Enough*

A country in the Middle East issued RFPs (Requests for Proposals) for a company to build a brand new university and to build a town in a place where there was no town. The jobs would take five years for the winning firms—and bring five years of profits. To respond to the RFPs, an international architectural firm created a task force which spent three months working almost around the clock to write the proposal. The company had to produce its own paper for the proposal because the Middle Eastern country used the metric scale rather than paper sized in inches. The proposal was bound in leather made from the hides of unborn calves to get perfectly unblemished leather.

The proposal went through so many drafts that at the end the document belonged to the whole group. No sane person would have accepted sole responsibility for such an important document; everyone on the task force wanted to make the proposal perfect.

---

* Based on Betty Evans White, conversation with the author, October 17, 1987.

FIGURE 21.2
A STUDENT PROGRESS REPORT

November 10, 1986

To: Kitty O. Locker

From: David G. Bunnel

Subject: Progress on CAD/CAM Software Feasibility Study for
           the Architecture Firm, Patrick and Associates, Inc.

I have obtained most of the information necessary to recommend
whether CADAM or CATIA is better for Patrick and Associates,
Inc. (P&A). I am currently analyzing and organizing this information and am on schedule.

Work Completed

To learn how computer literate and how computer phobic P&A
employees are, I interviewed a judgment sample of five employees.
My interview with Bruce Ratekin, the director of P&A's Computer-
Aided Design (CAD) Department on November 3 enabled me to determine the architectural drafting needs of the firm. Mr. Ratekin
also gave me a basic drawing of a building showing both two-
and three-dimensional views so that I could replicate the drawing
with both software packages.

I obtained tutorials for both packages to use as a reference
while making the drawings. First I drew the building using
CADAM, the package designed primarily for two-dimensional
architectural drawings. I encountered problems with the iso-
metric drawing because there was a mistake in the manual I was
using; I fixed the problem by trying alternatives and finally
getting help from another CADAM user. Next, I used CATIA, the
package whose strength is three-dimensional drawings, to construct
the drawing. I am in the process of comparing the two packages
based on these criteria: quality of drawing, ease of data entry
(lines, points, surfaces, etc.) for computer experts and novices,
and ease of making changes in the completed drawings.

My analysis of the training people with and without experience
in CAD would need to learn to use each of these packages is
complete. I have also done a preliminary investigation of the
feasibility of P&A's buying both packages.

Work to Be Completed

As soon as he comes back from an unexpected illness that has
kept him out of the office, I will be meeting with Tom Merrick,
the CAD systems programmer for The Ohio State University. I
will ask him about software expansion flexibility for both
packages as well as the costs for initial purchase, installation,
maintenance, and software updates. After this meeting, I will
be ready to begin the first draft of my report.

Whether I am able to meet my deadline will depend on when I am
able to meet with Mr. Merrick. Right now, I am on schedule and
plan to submit my report by the December 1 deadline.

The Post-It Notes® use a "failed" adhesive. The adhesive was developed during a search for a very sticky adhesive. One formula failed all the tests for this special project as well as some conventional tests that 3M uses for all its adhesives. But another 3M employee saw the weak adhesive as a solution to a problem:

> I was singing in the choir in my church. And we would sing for two different services and I would mark the pages with little pieces of paper normally. And sometimes they would fall out between the services—the first service and the second service. . . . I thought what I really need is . . . a book mark that's going to stick to those pages, to the right spot and still not damage the book when I pull them off. . . . I knew that Spence Silver back in our laboratory had just developed an adhesive that would do that. And I made . . . rough samples of the bookmarks. . . . I had also made up some larger sized and found, hey these are really handy for notes.[3]

An adhesive that failed in its original application was a spectacular success in a new and highly profitable product.

Closure reports also allow a firm to document the alternatives it has considered before choosing a final design and to prove its right to copyrights and patents. Dwight W. Stevenson has shown that firms challenged in product liability suits need to be able to document in detail the evaluation process that led to the product design.[4] In another kind of case, the Wells Fargo bank was sued for $480 million in a suit charging that it had misappropriated someone else's idea for a credit card operation. The bank used materials from its archives going back 20 years to prove that it had developed the idea itself.[5]

ANNUAL REPORTS

Whether you're interested in investing in a company or working for it, the annual report is the place to start your research. Many college and university libraries carry copies of companies' annual reports for the past two years. You can also get the current annual report by requesting it directly from the company.

Every firm which sells stock to the public is required by the Securities and Exchange Commission (SEC) to issue an annual report every year summarizing the company's financial position. In the last 15 years, annual reports have increasingly become persuasive and image-building documents. In addition to presenting the required financial data, most companies use lavish color photos and graphics to keep readers interested; most companies try to portray themselves as good corporate citizens; the company's management defends its record. Annual reports have become so popular that many privately held and nonprofit organizations also issue annual reports as a way to build loyalty among employees, clients or customers, and the various publics to which the organization is accountable.

U.S. companies spend an estimated $2 billion a year on annual reports, but many investors feel ill-served by the reports.[6] Geoffrey Cross has shown that poor planning and inadequate analysis sometimes extend unnecessarily the time needed to prepare a report. In one organization, eight people spent 77 days writing the two-page Executive Letter,[7] which is only one component of the annual report.

If you're involved in the preparation of an annual report,

- Agree on the report's purposes and audiences (primary, secondary, and immediate) early in the planning process.

How One Foundation Decides Whom to Fund*

The Kellogg Foundation [in Battle Creek, Michigan] will give away $120 million this year. . . . Preferring straightforward letters, it doesn't even have grant application forms. "We're looking for the germ of a great idea, not someone who's good at grant forms." . . .

The average grant stretches across three years and totals about $300,000, though grants range from roughly $5,000 to $5 million. The foundation makes about 300 grants a year, and at any one time has some 600 to 700 active projects.

It favors grass-roots efforts to help communities—mostly in the U.S. and Latin America. . . .

For instance, Rick Little turned to the Kellogg Foundation as a 19-year-old college dropout, after 155 other foundations rejected his idea. He developed a high-school course to teach practical skills like how to balance a checkbook along with helping kids make responsible decisions in such areas as sex and drugs. . . .

That was in 1977. . . . now his course, called Quest, is being taught to 1.4 million teenagers in 29 countries. Quest International has a $15 million budget, which it raises mostly by selling materials to schools. More important, the program has cut absentee and dropout rates and drug and alcohol use in the schools that offer it, while improving academic performance.

* Quoted from Meg Cox, "Snap, Crackle, Give: How the Kellogg Foundation Decides Who Receives Its Generosity," *The Wall Street Journal*, May 13, 1988, 20R–21R.

The Political Uses of Progress Reports

Progress reports can do more than just report progress. You can use progress reports to

- Enhance your image. Details about the number of documents you've read, people you've surveyed, or experiments you've conducted create a picture of a hard-working person doing a thorough job.

- Float trial balloons. If you want to change the direction of your work, you can use the progress report to try to persuade your boss or funding agency that your time (and their money) would be better spent in different activities. Explain, "I could continue to do X [what you approved]; I could do Y instead [what I'd like to do now]." The detail in the progress report can help back up your claim. Even if the idea is rejected, you don't lose face because you haven't made a separate issue of the alternative.

- Minimize potential problems. As you do the work, it may become clear that implementing your recommendations will be difficult. In your regular progress reports, you can alert your boss or the funding agency to the challenges that lie ahead, enabling them to prepare psychologically and physically to act on your recommendations.

- Allow writers drafting parts of the report that will be signed by someone else (e.g., the Executive Letter) to talk directly with the signer to get a sense of his or her priorities and style.

- Make sure that visuals are accurate as well as attractive. Deliberately misleading visuals are one of the factors that have made so many readers skeptical of annual reports.

- Make the best case possible for management and for the company, but be honest about problems and weaknesses. In the current climate of distrust of annual reports, honesty is the only way to build credibility.

SUMMARY OF KEY POINTS

- A good research problem meets the following criteria:
  1. The problem is real, important, narrow but challenging, possible to solve with the time and resources available, and something that interests you.
  2. The audience for the report is real, able to implement any recommendations you might make, and accessible to you.
  3. The data, evidence, and facts are sufficient to document the severity of the problem, sufficient to prove that the recommendation will solve the problem, and available and comprehensible to you.

- A proposal must answer the following questions convincingly:
  - What problem are you going to solve?
  - How are you going to solve it?
  - What exactly will you provide for us?
  - Can you deliver what you promise?
  - When will you complete the work?
  - How much will you charge?

- In a proposal for a class research project, prove that your problem is the right size, that you understand it, that your method will give you the information you need to solve the problem, and that you have the knowledge and resources.

- Use the following pattern of organization for the cover letter for a **sales proposal.**
  1. Catch the reader's attention and summarize up to three major benefits you offer.
  2. Discuss each of the major benefits in the order in which you mentioned them in the first paragraph.
  3. Deal with any objections or concerns the reader may have.
  4. Mention other benefits briefly.
  5. Ask the reader to approve your proposal and provide a reason for acting promptly.

- In a proposal for funding, stress the needs your project will meet. Show how your project helps fulfill the goals of the funding organization.

- To focus on what you have done and what work remains, organize a **progress report** in this way:
  1. Summarize your progress in terms of your goals and your original schedule.
  2. Under the heading "Work Completed," describe what you have already done.

3. Under the heading "Work to Be Completed," describe the work that remains.

4. Either express your confidence in having the report ready by the due date or request a conference to discuss extending the due date or limiting the project.

- Use positive emphasis in progress reports to create an image of yourself as a capable, confident worker.

- A **closure report** summarizes completed research that does not result in action or recommendation so that the organization has a record of what has been tried and why it failed.

- A firm which sells stock to the public must issue an annual report summarizing the company's financial position. In the last 15 years, annual reports have increasingly become persuasive and image-building documents.

- Use these guidelines in preparing **annual reports**:

  - Agree on audiences and purposes early in the planning process.

  - Give people who will be drafting and designing the report direct access to top management.

  - Make sure that visuals are honest as well as attractive.

  - Make the best case possible for management and for the company, but be honest about problems and weaknesses.

NOTES

1. Meg Morgan, "Case Study Methods and Collaborative Writing," Conference on College Composition and Communication, St. Louis, MO, March 17–19, 1988.

2. John Reed, panel on proposal development, Columbus, OH, November 14, 1985.

3. Art Fry speaking in John Nathan, "In Search of Excellence," (Waltham, MA: Nathan/Tyler Productions, 1985), 9.

4. Dwight W. Stevenson, "The Implications of Product Liability Concerns for Corporate Communication," Business and Technical Writing Teachers' Roundtable, Purdue, IN, October 19–20, 1986.

5. Frederick Rose, "In Wake of Cost Cuts, Many Firms Sweep Their History Out the Door," *The Wall Street Journal*, December 21, 1987, 21.

6. Ned Raynolds, "What Investors Want from the Annual Report," *The Wall Street Journal*, January 18, 1988, 10.

7. Geoffrey A. Cross, "Editing in Context: An Ethnographic Exploration of Editor-Writer Revision at a Midwestern Insurance Company" (Ph.D. diss., Ohio State University, 1988), 95.

* Quoted from Ned Raynolds, "What Investors Want from the Annual Report," *The Wall Street Journal*, January 18, 1988, 10.

How to Make Annual Reports Fit Investors' Needs*

Here are some findings, based on three years of research, concerning investors' specific complaints about annual reports, plus suggestions on how to make an annual report meet investors' needs:

Credibility. Investors complain that annual reports . . . play down negatives. . . . Some investors distrust what they read in annual reports.

Suggestion. . . . Don't try to sugarcoat or play down a bad year. If there are problems, have management take responsibility for solving them. Say what you are doing to solve them—in specifics. . . .

Detail. . . . Investors are eager for more facts in annuals—provided they are relevant.

Suggestion. . . . Go beyond minimum Securities and Exchange requirements in providing information. Communicate the significance of the numbers and details you are providing.

Use clear, appealing graphics and typography to present the mass of financial data required in the back of the report. Select key facts from the required data and highlight them prominently in the early pages of the report.

If you are not sure what information will be most important to investors, survey them to get a clear picture of their needs. . . .

Clarity. Investors criticize companies for using stilted wording and "technicalese" in their annual reports. They want to hear from companies in clear, straightforward language.

Suggestion. Assume your reader is intelligent, but knows nothing about your business or its jargon. Where only technical terms are accurate, define them the first time you use them.

Avoid using long words and convoluted sentences. Paraphrase aloud what you're trying to say, and use those words. Employ the active voice, so that management is portrayed as making things happen, rather than having things happen to it.

EXERCISES AND PROBLEMS FOR CHAPTER 21

21–1 IDENTIFYING THE WEAKNESSES IN PROBLEM STATEMENTS

Identify the weaknesses in the following problem statements. What specifically is the problem? Is it narrow enough? Can a solution be found in a semester or quarter? What organization could implement any recommendations to solve the problem?

After you have identified the weaknesses with the statement here, suggest ways the topic could be limited or refocused to yield an acceptable problem statement.

1. One possible report topic which I would like to investigate would be the differences in women's intercollegiate sports in our athletic conference.

2. To legalize victimless crimes.

3. How can a gullible public be warned against the dangers of medical quackery?

4. The purpose of this report is to reevaluate present teaching and grading methods and suggest possible alternatives.

5. Is solar energy an economical and energy-efficient substitute for traditional methods in agricultural grain drying today and in the future?

6. To determine the usefulness of the library computer system.

7. Reducing the problem of the homeless in our city.

8. How can XYZ university increase minority student enrollment?

21–2 WRITING A PRELIMINARY PURPOSE STATEMENT

Answer the following questions about a topic on which you could write a formal report. (See problem 22–6.)

As your instructor directs,
   a. Be prepared to answer the questions orally in a conference.
   b. Bring written answers to a conference.
   c. Submit written answers in class.
   d. Give your instructor a photocopy of your statement after it is approved.

1. What problem will you investigate or solve?
   a. What is the name of the organization facing the problem?
   b. What is the technical problem or difficulty?
   c. Why is it important to the organization that this problem be solved?
   d. What solution or action might you recommend to solve the problem?

2. Will this report use information from other classes or from work experiences? If so, give the name and topic of the class and/or briefly describe the job. If you will need additional information (that you have not already gotten from other classes or from a job), how do you expect to find it?

3. List the name, title, and business phone number of a professor who can testify to your ability to handle the expertise needed for this report.

4. List the name, title, and business phone number of someone in the organization who can testify that you have access to enough information about that organization to write this report.

21–3 WRITING A RFP

You're director of the student union at your school. In response to student requests for more modern food service, the union has decided to allow one or more private businesses or franchises to set up fast-food service in the union. The businesses you select will get one-year licenses, pay for any remodeling needed, and pay a percentage of their gross profits to the college. You want interested businesses to submit proposals. Depending on the proposals, you will grant one-year licenses to up to five businesses. You reserve the right to accept fewer applications or none at all if the proposals do not seem sound.

You must first write a Request for Proposal (RFP). The RFP must list the information you want in the proposal: information that will enable you to evaluate the applicants and to choose the best ones. You also want to provide some information about the students at your college so that you don't have to spend hours on the phone giving information to hopeful bidders.

Write a Request for Proposal (RFP) that will give you the information you need.

21–4 WRITING A PROPOSAL FOR A STUDENT REPORT

Write a proposal to your instructor to do the research for a formal or informal report. (See problems 20–10 and 22–6.)

The following questions and headings are your RFP; be sure to answer every question and to use the headings exactly as stated in the RFP. Exception: where alternate heads are listed, you may choose one, combine the two ("Qualifications and Facilities"), or treat them as separate headings in separate categories.

(Introductory Paragraph)

In your first paragraph (no heading), summarize in a sentence or two the topic and purposes of your report.

Problem

What organizational problem exists? What is wrong? Why does it need to be solved? Is there a history or background which is relevant?

Feasibility

Are you sure that a solution can be found in the time available?

Topics to Investigate

What do you intend to do? List the questions and subquestions you will answer in your report, the topics or concepts you will explain, the aspects of the problem you will discuss. Indicate how deeply you will examine each of the aspects you plan to treat. Explain your rationale for choosing to discuss some aspects of the problem and not others.

Audience

What person in the organization would have the power to implement your recommendation? List his or her name, job title, and business address. What secondary audiences might be asked to evaluate your report? What audiences would be affected by your recommendation?

For all these audiences, as well as for your immediate audience (your instructor), identify the audience's priorities, biases (if any), interest in and knowledge of your topic. List any terms, concepts, equations, or assumptions which one or more of your audiences may need to have explained. Briefly identify ways in which your audiences may affect the content, organization, or style of the report.

Methods/Procedures

How will you get answers to your questions? Whom will you interview or survey? What published sources will you use? Give the full bibliographic references.

Your *Methods* section should clearly indicate how you will get the information needed to answer the questions in the *Topics to Investigate* section.

Qualifications/Facilities/Resources

Do you have the knowledge and skills needed to conduct this study? Do you have adequate access to the organization? Do you have access to any equipment you will need to conduct your research (computer, books, etc.)? Where will you turn for help if you hit an unexpected snag?

You'll be more convincing if you have already scheduled an interview or have checked out books.

Work Schedule

List both the total time you plan to spend on and the date when you expect to finish each of the following activities:

> Gathering information
> Analyzing information
> Preparing the progress report
> Organizing information
> Writing the draft
> Revising the draft
> Editing the draft
> Typing the report
> Proofreading the report

If you omit any activity, be sure to explain its omission (e.g., you may not need separate typing time if you are composing and revising the report on a word processor).

You may answer this question either in a chart or in a calendar. Indicate total time and completion date for each activity separately. Make it clear that you will meet deadlines for papers and conferences.

Call to Action

In your final section, indicate that you'd welcome any suggestions your instructor may have for improving the research plan. Ask your instructor to approve your proposal so that you can begin work on your report.

21–5 WRITING A SALES PROPOSAL

Assume that you run a food service in town. Respond to the RFP from problem 21–3, and propose to establish an outlet in the student union. In addition to answering the questions in the RFP, be sure to stress your company's strong points: Why should the student union give you one of a limited number of licenses?

21–6 WRITING A PROPOSAL FOR FUNDING FOR A NONPROFIT GROUP

Pick a nonprofit group you care about. Examples include professional organizations, a school sports team, a charitable group, a community organization, a religious group, or your own community college, college, or university.

As your instructor directs,
   a. Check a directory of foundations to find one which makes grants to groups like yours. Brainstorm a list of businesses which might be willing to give money for specific projects. Check to see whether state or national levels of your organization make grants to local chapters.
   b. Write a proposal to obtain funds for a special project your group could undertake if it had the money. Address your proposal to a specific organization.
   c. Write a proposal for operating funds or for money to buy something your group would like to have. Address your proposal to a specific organization.

21-7 WRITING A PROGRESS REPORT

Write a memo to your instructor summarizing your progress on your report.

In the introductory paragraph, summarize your progress in terms of your schedule and your goals. Under a heading titled "Work Completed," list what you have already done. (This is a chance to toot your own horn: if you have solved problems creatively, say so! You can also describe obstacles you've encountered which you have not yet solved.) Under "Work to Be Completed," list what you still have to do. If you are more than two days behind the schedule you submitted with your proposal, include a *revised schedule,* listing the completion dates for the activities that remain.

In your last paragraph, either indicate your confidence in completing the report by the due date or ask for a conference to resolve the problems you are encountering.

21-8 WRITING A PROGRESS REPORT FOR A GROUP REPORT

Write a memo to your instructor summarizing your group's progress.

In the introductory paragraph, summarize the group's progress in terms of its goals and its schedule, your own progress on the tasks for which you are responsible, and your feelings about the group's work thus far.

Under a heading titled "Work Completed," list what has already been done. Be most specific about what you

yourself have done. Describe briefly the chronology of group activities: number, time, and length of meetings; topics discussed and decisions made at meetings.

If you have solved problems creatively, say so! You can also describe obstacles you've encountered which you have not yet solved. In this section, you can also comment on problems that the group has faced and whether or not they've been solved. You can comment on things that have gone well and have contributed to the smooth functioning of the group.

Under "Work to Be Completed," list what you personally and other group members have still have to do. Indicate the schedule for completing the work.

In your last paragraph, either indicate your confidence in completing the report by the due date or ask for a conference to resolve the problems you are encountering.

21-9 EVALUATING ANNUAL REPORTS

Evaluate one or more annual reports. Is the report interesting and easy to read? Does it create a favorable impression of the company? Does it deal effectively with any problems the company faced that year? Consider the following aspects of the report:

* Financial data. What is included? How is it presented? Can a nonaccountant understand it?

* Visuals and layout. Are visuals used effectively? Are they accurate and free from chartjunk? What image do the pictures and visuals create? Are color and white space used effectively?

* Emphasis. What points are emphasized? What points are deemphasized? What verbal and visual techniques are used to highlight or minimize information?

As your instructor directs,
   a. Write a memo to your instructor analyzing the annual report of a company that interests you.
   b. Write a memo to your instructor comparing and contrasting the annual reports of two companies in the same industry.
   c. Join with a small group of students to analyze three or more annual reports. Present your evaluation in an informal group report.
   d. Present your evaluation orally to the class.

Writing the Front Matter in Formal Reports

QUESTIONS

- How do you set up the Title Page, the Table of Contents, and the List of Illustrations?
- Should the title of a report contain the recommendations?
- How should a transmittal be organized?
- What are three kinds of abstracts? What is the relation between sentence and topic outlines and summary and descriptive abstracts?
- What style of writing should an abstract use?
- What subheadings appear in the Introduction? What do you discuss under each of them?

> One writer, for instance, excels at a plan or a title page, another works away at the body of the book, and a third is a dab at an index.
>
> Oliver Goldsmith
> *The Bee*, 1759

Formal reports are distinguished from informal letter and memo reports by their length and by their **front matter**—the items that precede the report itself. The most common pieces of front matter are the Title Page, the Letter or Memo of Transmittal, the Table of Contents, the List of Illustrations, and the Abstract. Less formal reports may have simply a Title Page and a Table of Contents.

TITLE PAGE

The Title Page of a report usually contains four items: the title of the report, whom the report is prepared for, whom it is prepared by, and the release date. Sometimes reports also contain a brief summary or abstract of the contents of the report; some title pages contain decorative art work.

The Title of the Report

The title of the report should be as informative as possible. Like subject lines, report titles are straightforward.

Poor title: New Plant Site

Better title: Why Eugene, Oregon, Is the Best Site for the New Kemco Plant

Poor title: Planting for the Quadrangle

Better title: Why Honey Locusts Are the Best Trees for the New Quadrangle

In many cases, the title will state the recommendation in the report: "Why the United Nations Should Establish a Seed Bank." However, the title should omit recommendations when

- The reader will find the recommendations hard to accept.
- Putting all the recommendations in the title would make it too long.
- The report does not offer recommendations.

If the title does not contain the recommendation, it normally indicates what problem the report tries to solve.

Eliminate any unnecessary words:

Wordy: Report of a Study on Ways to Market Life Insurance to Urban Professional People Who Are in Their Mid-Forties

Better: Ways to Market Life Insurance to the Mid-Forties Urban Professional

The Audience for the Report

The statement of whom the report is prepared for normally includes the name of the person who will make a decision based on the report, his or her job title, the organization's name, and its location (city, state, and zip code). Government reports often omit the person's name and simply give the organization which authorized the report.

The Writer(s) of the Report

If the report is prepared primarily by one person, the *Prepared by* section will have that person's name, his or her title, the organization, and its location (city, state and zip code). In internal reports, the organization and location are usually omitted if the report writer works at the headquarters office.

If several people write the report, government reports normally list all their names, using a separate sheet of paper if the group working on the report is large. Practices in business differ. In some organizations, all the names are listed; in others, the division to which they belong is listed; in still others, the name of the chair of the group appears.

The Release Date

The **release date,** the date the report will be released to the public, is usually the date the report is scheduled for discussion by the decision makers. The report is due four to six weeks before the release date so that the decision makers can review the report before the meeting.

Designing the Title Page

If you have the facilities and time, try using different sizes and styles of type, color, and art work to create a visually attractive and impressive title page. For most reports, however, a plain typed page is acceptable. The format in Figure 22.1 will enable you to create an acceptable title page by typing it only once.

LETTER OR MEMO OF TRANSMITTAL

Use a letter of transmittal if you are not a regular employee of the organization for which you prepare the report; use a memo if you are a regular employee. See Appendix A for letter and memo formats.

The transmittal has several purposes: to transmit the report, to orient the reader to the report, and to build a good image of the report and of the writer. An informal writing style is appropriate for a transmittal even when the style in the report is more formal. An informal writing style helps you create a good image of yourself and enhances your credibility. Personal statements are appropriate in the transmittal, even though they would not be acceptable in the report itself.

Organize the transmittal in this way:

1. **Release the report, noting when and by whom it was authorized and the purpose it was to fulfill.**

   Here is the report you asked for in February on the best ways to market life insurance to urban professionals who are in their mid-forties.

Preparing the Report Cover

Formal reports usually have a cover with the title of the report, the organizational audience, and the name of the writer. Fancy visuals aren't necessary, but do put some care into the cover. With the growing popularity of desktop publishing, more and more readers are becoming used to covers that use graphics and different sizes of type.

Check to see if your audience has any preferences about the physical cover. Some firms want a cover that permits the report to lie flat when it is opened. Some dislike plastic covers because they are too slippery.

Plan your cover before you type the final report so that you can set extra-wide margins to allow for binding or hole punching.

FIGURE 22.1
FORMAT FOR A TITLE PAGE

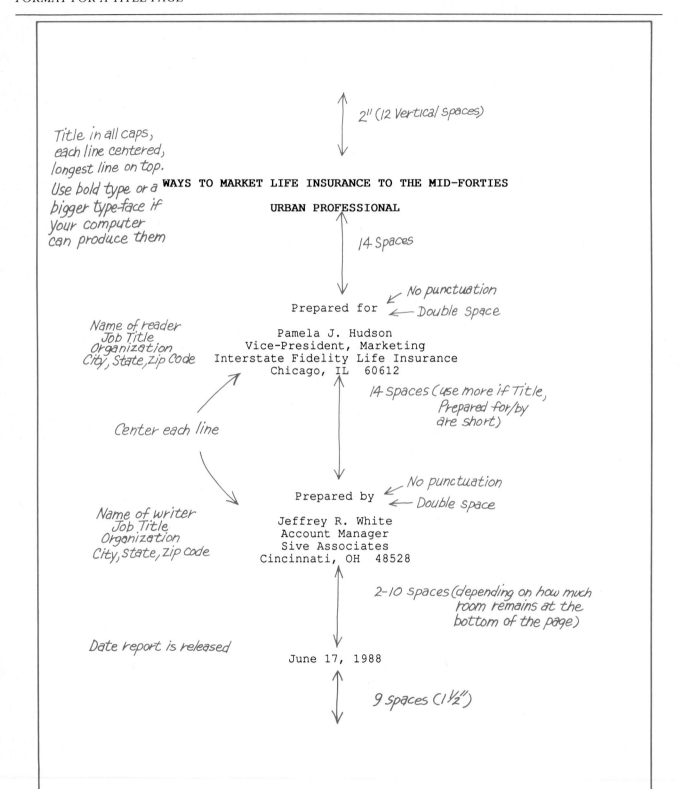

2. **If the recommendation will be easy for the reader to accept, put it early in the transmittal; briefly summarize the reasons for it. If it will be difficult, summarize the findings first and put the conclusion after them.**

> My research shows that advertising in upscale publications and direct mail are the most effective ways to reach this market. Network TV and radio are not cost-efficient for reaching this market. Urban professionals tend to discard general-interest periodicals quickly, but many of them keep upscale periodicals for months or years. Since they are busy, most are already used to shopping by mail and respond positively to well-conceived and well-executed direct mail appeals.

3. **(Optional) Mention any points of special interest in the report. Indicate minor problems you encountered in your investigation and show how you surmounted them. Thank people who helped you.**

> Our surveys showed that most of the people in this group have some life insurance provided as a fringe benefit by their employers. However, this insurance is typically only equal to two years' salary—not enough to provide protection for dependents. Any advertising campaign needs to overcome this group's feeling that they already have the insurance they need. One way to do this would be to encourage them to check to see what their company actually provides and to calculate the cost of their children's expenses until they graduate from college.
>
> Response to our survey was initially only 36%. Insurance is not a topic that people enjoy thinking about. Marcia Nygen and Brian Garbo were very helpful in making phone calls to nonrespondents. Thanks to their persuasive ability, we doubled our response rate to 70%. The information in the report is based on this group.
>
> I'd also like to thank Angela Manning for compiling the census data and Joseph Sanchez for running the statistical tests.

4. **If further research remains, suggest it. If you're interested in doing it, volunteer.**

> Once you decide to use a direct mail campaign, it will be necessary to create control and test packages. Sive would be very happy to undertake this work. As you know, our direct mail division has put together successful packages for a number of clients.

5. **Thank the reader for the opportunity to do the work. If you are doing the report as a consultant or under contract, offer to answer any questions the reader may have about the report itself. Even if the report has not been fun to do, expressing satisfaction in doing the project is expected. Saying that you'll answer questions about the report is a way of saying that you won't charge the reader your normal hourly fee to answer questions (one more reason to make the report clear!).**

> I've enjoyed conducting this research. If you have any questions, just call.

THE TABLE OF CONTENTS

In the Table of Contents, list the headings exactly as they appear in the body of the report. (See Chapter 20 for a discussion of headings.) In a short report, you'll probably list all the levels of headings. In a long report, pick a level and put all the headings at that level and above in the Table of Contents.

All items except the Title Page have a page number. Use lower-case Roman numerals for the front matter; start with Arabic 1 for the Introduction. In the Table of Contents, list the page number on which a section begins. If two or

---

Repetition in Formal Reports

Only a few people read the whole formal report. Most just read the Abstract, the Conclusions, and the Recommendations. Even people who read most of a report are likely to read it at several sittings. Between one reading and the next, they may forget what an earlier part has said.

To communicate with an audience that skips through the report, formal reports are repetitive: they say the same thing several times. For example, the recommendations appear at least twice and usually three times: in the Transmittal, the Abstract, and in the section titled "Recommendations." Sometimes the recommendations are also included in the title. Similarly, the Conclusions section repeats material that has been covered in the report body.

FIGURE 22.2
FORMAT FOR TABLE OF CONTENTS

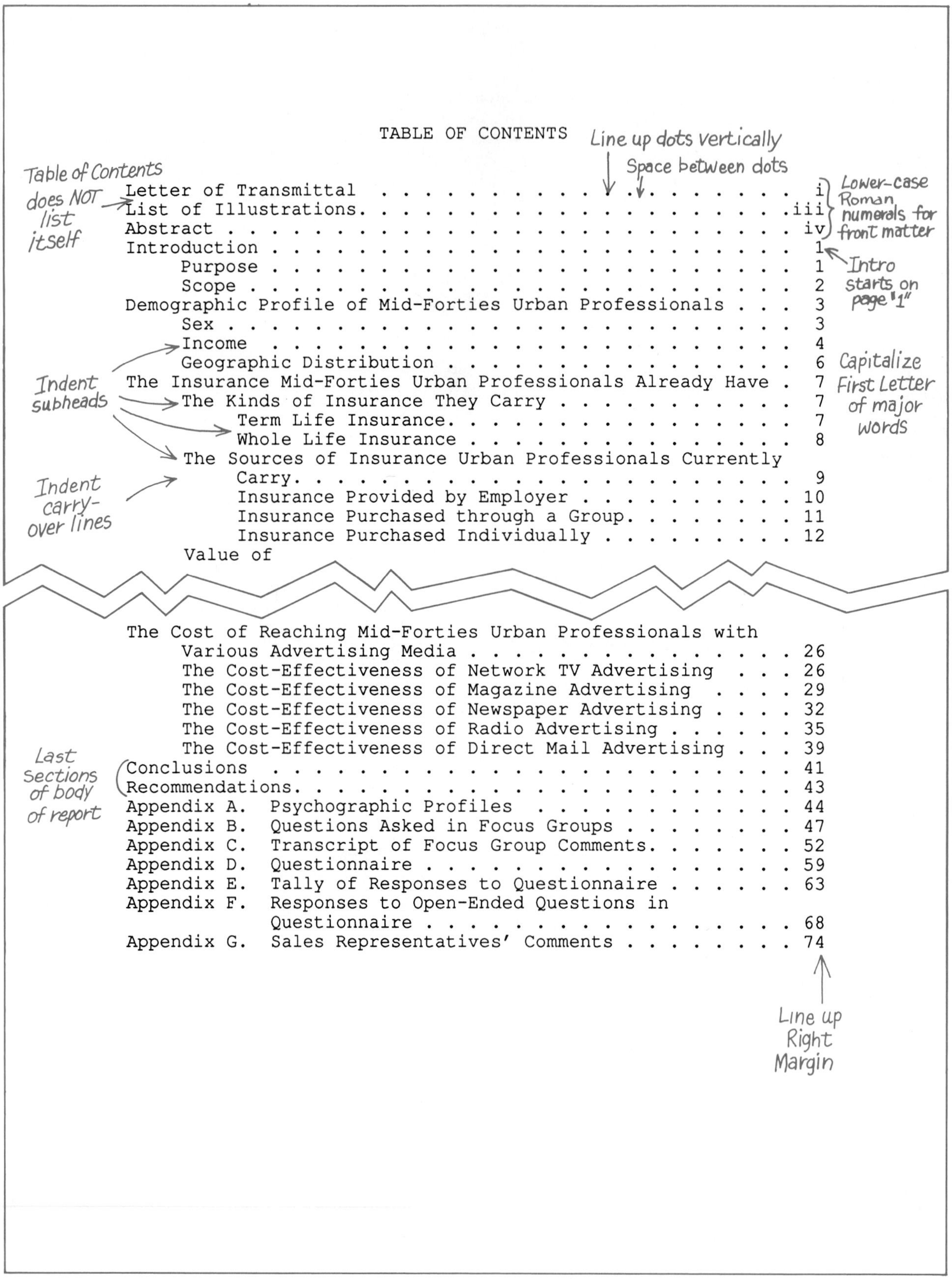

TABLE OF CONTENTS

Letter of Transmittal i
List of Illustrations. iii
Abstract iv
Introduction 1
    Purpose 1
    Scope 2
Demographic Profile of Mid-Forties Urban Professionals . . . 3
    Sex 3
    Income 4
    Geographic Distribution 6
The Insurance Mid-Forties Urban Professionals Already Have . 7
    The Kinds of Insurance They Carry 7
        Term Life Insurance. 7
        Whole Life Insurance 8
    The Sources of Insurance Urban Professionals Currently
        Carry. 9
        Insurance Provided by Employer 10
        Insurance Purchased through a Group. 11
        Insurance Purchased Individually 12
    Value of

The Cost of Reaching Mid-Forties Urban Professionals with
    Various Advertising Media 26
    The Cost-Effectiveness of Network TV Advertising . . . 26
    The Cost-Effectiveness of Magazine Advertising 29
    The Cost-Effectiveness of Newspaper Advertising 32
    The Cost-Effectiveness of Radio Advertising 35
    The Cost-Effectiveness of Direct Mail Advertising . . . 39
Conclusions 41
Recommendations. 43
Appendix A. Psychographic Profiles 44
Appendix B. Questions Asked in Focus Groups 47
Appendix C. Transcript of Focus Group Comments. 52
Appendix D. Questionnaire 59
Appendix E. Tally of Responses to Questionnaire 63
Appendix F. Responses to Open-Ended Questions in
    Questionnaire 68
Appendix G. Sales Representatives' Comments 74

Line up dots vertically
Space between dots
Table of Contents does NOT list itself
Lower-case Roman numerals for front matter
Intro starts on page "1"
Capitalize First Letter of major words
Indent subheads
Indent carry-over lines
Last sections of body of report
Line up Right Margin

FIGURE 22.3
FORMAT FOR LIST OF ILLUSTRATIONS

LIST OF ILLUSTRATIONS

Line up dots → *Space between dots*

Indent carry-over lines

Table 1. Estimated Income of Mid-Forties Urban
Professionals in 1990 4

Figure 1. Mid-Forties Urban Professionals Have High
Discretionary Income 5

Figure 2. Mid-Forties Urban Professionals Are
Concentrated in the Northeast, Midwest, and
Southwest 6

Table 2. Cost of Whole Life Insurance for Men and
Women Ages 35-50 7

Tables, Figures are numbered independently

Table 3. Cost of Term Insurance for Men and Women
Ages 35-50 7

Figure 3. Most Employers Offer Term Insurance
as a Fringe Benefit 10

Table 4. Employer-Provided Term Insurance Covers
Only Two Years' Salary 14

Figure 4. The Percentage of Mid-Forties Urban
Professionals in the Prime-Time Network TV
Audience 23

Capitalize First letters of major words

Line up right margin

---

more headings begin on the same page, the same page number would appear in the Table of Contents. Connect each heading to its page number with a line of leader dots that are lined up vertically. To avoid making the page appear black, space between the dots that lead from the heading to the page number. Notice whether dots in the first line are on even or odd spaces so that you can line up the dots. (This method may not work with proportional spacing in some word-processing programs.) Indent subheads in the Table of Contents.

Note that the Title Page and Table of Contents are not listed in the Table of Contents. The Table of Contents gets page numbers; the Title Page is not numbered. The Introduction is normally called *Introduction*. A separate section is labeled *Recommendation(s)* (use the plural if you have more than one) and is placed at the end of the body. Other materials gathered at the end of the report are called **appendices**. Each Appendix is designated by both a letter and a title.

THE LIST OF ILLUSTRATIONS

A List of Illustrations enables readers to refer to your visuals.

Report visuals comprise both tables and figures. **Tables** are words or numbers arranged in rows and columns. **Figures** are everything else: bar graphs, pie charts, flow charts, maps, drawings, photographs, computer printouts, etc.

Does Material Belong in an Appendix or in the Body of the Report?

Put material in the body of the report if it is crucial to your proof or if it is short. (Something less than half a page won't interrupt the reader.) Anything that a careful reader will want but which is not crucial to your proof can go in an Appendix. Appendices can include

- A copy of a survey questionnaire or interview questions.
- Complete tally of responses to each question in a survey.
- Copy of responses to open-ended questions in a survey.
- A transcript of an interview.
- Computer printouts.
- Previous reports on the same subject.

Different Abstracts for Different Audiences

You may want to change the first sentence of your abstract to fit the audience and the situation. Suppose that you were writing an abstract for John Fielden's article "What Do You Mean I Can't Write?" (*Harvard Business Review*; rpt. in Robert D. Gieselman, *Readings in Business Communication*.) Depending on your purposes in writing the abstract and the audience for which you were writing it, you might begin with any of these three sentences:

- (Thesis sentence to open a summary abstract)

   Executives should use the Written Performance Inventory to give subordinates specific information about which aspects of their writing need to be improved.

- (Purpose statement to open a descriptive abstract)

   This essay presents the Written Performance Inventory, which executives can use to explain to subordinates which aspects of their writing need to be improved.

- (Attention-getter for a mixed abstract)

   When an executive tells a subordinate that he or she can't write, the executive needs to provide specific information about the areas that the subordinate needs to work on.

Tables and figures are numbered independently, so you may have both a "Table 1" and a "Figure 1." In a report with maps and graphs but no other visuals, the visuals are sometimes called "Map 1" and "Graph 1" (and so on). Whatever you call the illustrations, list them in the order in which they appear in the report; give the name of each visual as well as its number.

If the List of Illustrations is short, it can go on the same page as the Table of Contents.

ABSTRACTS AND EXECUTIVE SUMMARIES

An **abstract** or **Executive Summary** tells the reader what the document is about. It **summarizes** the recommendation of the report and the reasons for the recommendation or **describes** the topics the report discusses and indicates the depth of the discussion.

Abstracts may make it unnecessary for you to read the original, if you are interested only in the findings or conclusions and not in the supporting data leading to those conclusions. Second, a good abstract will make it clear whether the original article or report is good enough and relevant enough to deserve reading. Even when the reader goes on to read the proposal or report, the summary gives busy readers an overview of the main points of the document and thereby enables them to read it more quickly.

If you write an article for publication or file for a U.S. patent, you may need to write an abstract to accompany your document. Many professional organizations ask for abstracts of proposed papers to decide which papers to include on the program. Most abstracts are written by the author. Some professional services, like *Chemical Abstracts,* hire writers to prepare abstracts of research conducted by other people.

Summary abstracts present the logical skeleton of the article: the thesis or recommendation and its proof. **Descriptive abstracts** indicate what topics the article covers and how deeply it goes into each topic, but do not summarize what the article says about each topic. **Mixed abstracts** have some characteristics of both summary and descriptive abstracts. They may list all of the topics covered in an article and summarize some of the points about some of the topics.

Summary Abstracts

A summary abstract gives the recommendation in the first paragraph. The rest of the abstract cites the conclusions that led the author to make those recommendations but does not give the specific results of the research which led to those conclusions. Use a summary abstract to give the most useful information in the shortest space.

Reports of experimental research in the sciences use a formal structure which you can use for scientific abstracts: the purpose of the research, its hypothesis; the experimental method; the significant results; the implications for treatment, action, or further research.

To write abstracts of business and government reports, conference papers, and published articles, write a *sentence outline*. Combine the sentences into paragraphs, adding transitions if necessary, and you'll have your abstract.

A **sentence outline** not only uses complete sentences rather than words or phrases but also contains the thesis sentence or recommendation and the points that prove that point. (See Figure 22.5.) The Roman numerals indicate sentences which, together, prove the thesis. The capital letters indicate sentences which prove these main points. Although the outline could have Arabic numbers under each capital letter, an abstract usually gives that level of detail only

FIGURE 22.4
SUMMARY ABSTRACT FOR A BUSINESS REPORT

WAYS TO MARKET LIFE INSURANCE TO THE MID-FORTIES

URBAN PROFESSIONAL

To market life insurance to mid-forties urban professionals, Interstate Fidelity Insurance should advertise in upscale publications and use direct mail.

Network TV and radio are not cost-efficient for reaching this market. This group comprises a small percentage of the prime-time network TV audience and a minority of most radio station listeners. They tend to discard newspapers and general-interest magazines quickly, but many of them keep upscale periodicals for months or years. Magazines with high percentages of readers in this group include <u>Architectural Digest</u>, <u>Bon Appetit</u>, <u>Business Week</u>, <u>Forbes</u>, <u>Golf Digest</u>, <u>Metropolitan Home</u>, <u>Southern Living</u>, and <u>Smithsonian</u>. Therefore ads in these publications can receive repeated exposure. Most urban professionals in their mid-forties are already used to shopping by mail and respond positively to well conceived and well executed direct mail appeals. Direct mail is cost-effective since it can be sent only to people in the target market.

A stratified random sample survey with 1526 responses showed that most of the people in this group have term life insurance provided as a fringe benefit by their employers--not enough to provide adequate protection for dependents. However, this insurance is typically only equal to two years' salary. Supplemental term insurance has been purchased by 42% of this group, often as mortgage insurance. Only 12% of the people in this group own whole life insurance.

In spite of this low level of coverage, a majority feel that they have enough insurance (58%). Even the people who say they would like to have more insurance rank it only fifth in their financial priorities, after saving for college expenses for children, buying a bigger house, taking a vacation, and buying a more prestigious car. Any advertising campaign needs to overcome this group's feeling that they already have the insurance they need. One way to do this would be to encourage them to check to see what their company actually provides and to calculate the cost of their children's expenses through college graduation. Insurance plans that provide savings and tax benefits as well as death benefits might also be appealing.

FIGURE 22.5
SENTENCE OUTLINE

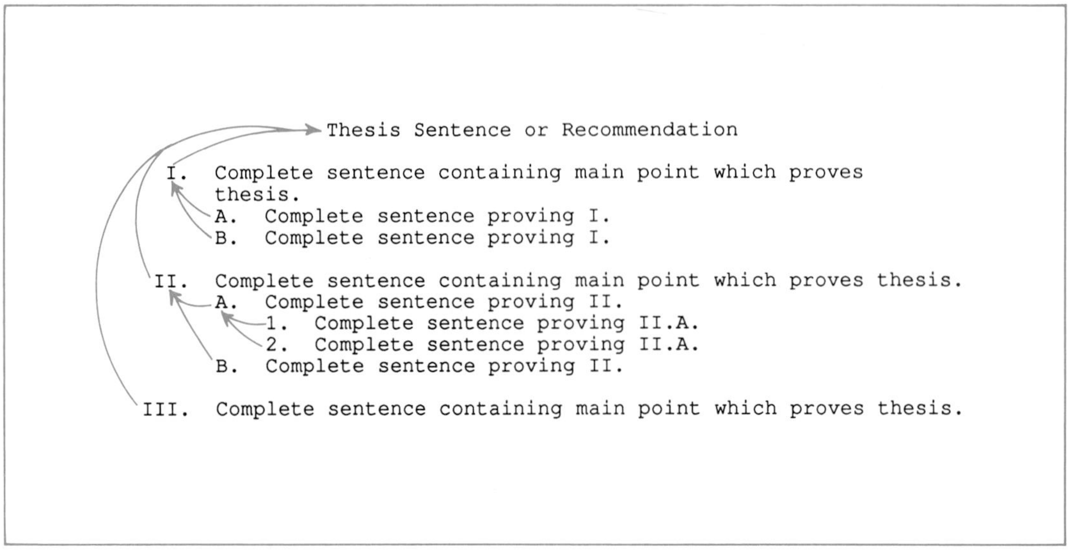

```
                            ➤ Thesis Sentence or Recommendation
        I.  Complete sentence containing main point which proves
            thesis.
            A.  Complete sentence proving I.
            B.  Complete sentence proving I.

       II.  Complete sentence containing main point which proves thesis.
            A.  Complete sentence proving II.
                1.  Complete sentence proving II.A.
                2.  Complete sentence proving II.A.
            B.  Complete sentence proving II.

      III.  Complete sentence containing main point which proves thesis.
```

when it is necessary to convince the reader of the abstract. The abstract in Figure 22.4 can say that mid-forties urban professionals respond positively to good direct mail—a main point that proves the recommendation—without further proof in the abstract.

Sentence outlines usually have only two to five Roman numerals, since the recommendation is usually based on a small number of reasons. Sentence outlines do not contain every part of the report or article. For instance, the introduction of a report or a description of the history in insurance sales or the survey design are not part of the proof, though they are essential parts of the full report. The decision as to whether to include main points which do not prove the thesis is based on the reader's needs.

Descriptive Abstracts

A **descriptive abstract** lists the topics covered in a paper or report but does not specify the recommendations or the reasons for the recommendations. Phrases that describe the paper (*this paper reports, it includes, it summarizes, it concludes*) are marks of a descriptive abstract. An additional mark of a descriptive abstract is that the reader can't tell what the article says about the topics it covers.

Since this report makes recommendations, we can write either both summary and descriptive abstracts of it. However, some documents make many small points which do not prove a main point. Examples would include articles composed of examples or statistical data, answers to a series of questions, and annotated bibliographies. In such cases, a descriptive abstract is the only kind possible. When you have a choice, it is better to write a summary abstract because summaries are more informative and more helpful to the reader.

To write a descriptive abstract, simply list the topics the article covers. If the article is long or complicated, you may want to make a topic outline. Put the words in the outline into complete sentences, and you have a descriptive

**WAYS TO MARKET LIFE INSURANCE TO THE MID-FORTIES
URBAN PROFESSIONAL**

This report recommends ways Interstate Fidelity Insurance could market insurance
to mid-forties urban professionals. It examines demographic and psychographic
profiles of the target market. It discusses how much insurance this group already
has. Survey results are used to show attitudes toward insurance. The report
suggests some appeals that might be successful with this market.

FIGURE 22.6
A DESCRIPTIVE ABSTRACT
FOR A BUSINESS REPORT

abstract. The topic outline can also be used to create the report's Table of
Contents.

Mixed Abstracts

A **mixed abstract** is a hybrid: part summary, part description. Mixed abstracts
exist because many publications care more about length than about purity. If
a publication calls for a 200-word abstract and you send in a 250-word document, it may be cut, but the editor is unlikely to check to see that it is a pure
summary or pure descriptive abstract.

In Figure 22.7, the last sentence summarizes the book's main points, but
the first three sentences, both in form and content, are characteristic of descriptive abstracts.

Mixed abstracts enable you both to comment about the kind of information
("This article contains examples of sentences revised to create you-attitude")
and present the thesis and its proof. Mixed abstracts are also good when the
abstract will appear as a headnote over a journal article. Since the article is
right there, the abstract essentially serves as an advertisement for the article.
Rather than using a pure summary abstract and starting with the thesis, you
may build readership if you start with the purpose or an attention-getter. Mixed
abstracts are often the easiest to write, since you do not have to worry about
the form of the abstract.

FIGURE 22.7
A MIXED ABSTRACT FOR A
BOOK

The Robert Collier Letter Book

Robert Collier

This book was originally published in 1931. The author states that "the
greatest value of a book such as this [is that] it gives … scores of letters, on all
matter of subjects, that have proved highly successful." This book contains
hundreds of examples of sales letters. Chapter 9, "The Six Essentials,"
presents, in essence, Collier's method for successful sales letters: (1) the
opening that gets the reader's interest; (2) the description or explanation of
the product or service; (3) the motive for the reader; (4) the proof or
guarantee to reassure the reader; (5) the "snapper," or penalty, if the reader
does not act; (6) the close that makes it easy for the reader to act.

Source: Gerald J. Alred, Diana C. Reep, and Mohan Limaye, *Business and Technical Writing: An Annotated
Bibliography of Books, 1880–1980* (Metuchen, NJ: Scarecrow, 1981), entry 175.

Format for Abstracts

Abstracts that will be printed or put on microfiche (such as abstracts for articles, theses, and dissertations) should be double-spaced with generous margins. Abstracts that will be photocopied (such as abstracts in reports for business and government) should be single-spaced with double-spacing between paragraphs. Use a single paragraph if the abstract is short (150 words or less). If the abstract is one-half page or longer, it will be easier to read if you divide it into two or more paragraphs. Put the abstract on a page all by itself even if it is very short.

The length of the abstract depends in part on the length of the full document: a 1,600-page report (and many government reports are that long) would need a summary of perhaps 15 to 20 pages. If the report itself is under 100 pages, the abstract can be only one or two pages.

Some agencies have very strict word limits for abstracts; others have *space* limits. While these limits are arbitrary, they are inflexible, so stick to them. If you find that your abstract is much shorter than the limit, you may want to consider adding more information.

Writing Style in Abstracts

A good abstract can be understood by itself, without the original article or reference books. Define terms that may be unfamiliar to the reader, or at least clarify them. Avoid jargon and abbreviations that may not be clear to general readers. Remember the abstracts are read by people who are not experts in the subject area of the article or report.

A good abstract is easy to read, concise, and clear. Edit your abstract carefully to tighten your writing and eliminate any unnecessary words.

Wordy: The author describes two types of business jargon, *businessese* and *reverse gobbledygook*. He gives many examples of each of these and points out how their use can be harmful.

Tight: The author describes and gives examples of two harmful types of business jargon, *businessese* and *reverse gobbledygook*.

It's OK to use direct quotes from an article, or, for a report you author, to use exactly the same words in the abstract and the report. Any duplicate language is *not* put in quotation marks and does *not* need footnotes or other documentation. Use quotation marks or italics for quoted material only if the author uses unusual terminology (see the example immediately above and the Collier abstract) or if a sentence is so unclear that you cannot summarize it and must quote it.

Abstracts generally use a more formal style than other forms of business writing. Avoid contractions. Use second-person *you* only if the article uses second-person; even then, use *you* sparingly.

It is not necessary to follow the organization, wording, or proportions of the original report or article. The abstract usually uses a logical pattern of organization, putting the thesis first, even though the report may use another pattern (a psychological problem-solving pattern, for instance).

THE INTRODUCTION FOR A FORMAL REPORT

The **Introduction** of the report always contains a statement of purpose and scope and may include all the parts in the following list.

- **Purpose.** The Purpose statement identifies the organizational problem the report addresses, the technical investigations it summarizes, and the rhetorical purpose (to explain, to recommend).

- **Scope.** The Scope statement identifies how broad an area the report surveys. For example, Company XYZ is losing money on its line of radios. Does the report investigate the quality of the radios? The advertising campaign? The cost of manufacturing? The demand for radios? A scope statement is necessary so that the reader can evaluate the report on appropriate grounds. If it has been agreed that advertising is not to be included in the scope, then the reader cannot fault a report which looks only at the other factors.

- **Limitations.** Limitations make your recommendations less valid or valid only under certain conditions. Limitations usually arise because time or money constraints haven't permitted full research. For example, a campus pizza restaurant considering expanding its menu may ask for a report but not have enough money to take a random sample of students and townspeople. Without a random sample, the writer cannot generalize from the sample to the larger population.

Many recommendations are valid only for a limited time. For instance, a campus store wants to know what kinds of clothing will appeal to college men. Obviously, the recommendations will remain in force only for a short time: three years from now, styles and tastes may have changed, and the clothes that would sell best now may no longer be in demand.

- **Assumptions.** Assumptions in a report are like assumptions in geometry: statements whose truth you assume, and which you use to prove your final point. If they are wrong, the conclusion will be wrong too.

  For example, to plan cars that will be built five years from now, an automobile manufacturer commissions a report on young adults' attitudes toward cars. The recommendations would be based on assumptions both about gas prices and about the economy. If gas prices radically rose or fell, the kinds of cars young adults wanted would change. If there were a major recession, people wouldn't be able to buy new cars.

  Almost all reports require assumptions. A good report spells out its assumptions so that readers can make decisions more confidently.

- **Methods.** The Methods section explains how you gathered your data. If you conducted a survey, focus groups, or interviews, you need to tell how you chose your subjects, and how, when, and where they were interviewed. (The actual questions are normally put in an appendix at the end of the report, not in the methodology section.) If you have relied heavily on a few library sources, mention them here. Cite these and any other sources appropriately in the text of the report and include a Bibliography or List of Works Cited at the end of the report. Check with your audience before you write the final draft to see how complete the Methods section needs to be.

  Reports based on scientific experiments usually put the Methods section in the body of the report, not in the Introduction.

- **Criteria** or **Standards.** The Criteria section outlines the factors that you are considering and the relative importance of each. If a company is choosing a city for a new office, is the cost of office space more or less important than the availability of skilled workers? Check with your audience before you write the draft to make sure that your criteria match those of your readers.

- **Definitions.** When you know that some members of your primary, secondary, or immediate audience will not understand technical terms, define them. If you have only a few definitions, you can put them in the Introduction. If you have many terms to define, use a **glossary** either early in the report or at the end. If the glossary is at the end, refer to it in the Introduction so that readers know that you've provided it.

SUMMARY OF KEY POINTS

- The Title Page of a report usually contains four items: the title of the report, whom the report is prepared for, whom it is prepared by, and the release date.

- The title of a report should contain the recommendation unless
  - The reader will find the recommendations hard to accept.

A Timetable for Writing Reports

You can write part of the final report even before you finish the research. The following parts can come from your proposal with only minor revisions:

Purpose
Scope
Assumptions
Methods
Criteria
Definitions

The background reading for your proposal can form the first draft of your list of Works Cited.

Save a copy of your questionnaire or interview questions to use as an Appendix. As you tally and analyze the data, prepare an Appendix summarizing all the responses to your questionnaire, your figures and tables, and a complete list of Works Cited. Sometimes appendices are numbered separately so that they can be typed before the final report is ready. The pages in Appendix A would become A-1, A-2, and so on; those in Appendix B would be B-1, B-2, and so on.

After you've analyzed your data, write the Abstract, the body, and the Conclusions and Recommendations. Prepare a draft of the Table of Contents and the List of Illustrations. You can write the Title Page and the Transmittal as soon as you know what your recommendation will be.

Once you have a complete draft, read through the whole report at a single sitting to be sure that it flows well and that there are no inconsistencies. Since few readers will read the report at a single sitting, check to see that each part of the report makes sense alone. Provide introductions and conclusions for each section so that the segments can stand alone if necessary.

Type the final copy of the body of the report so that you can prepare the Table of Contents and the List of Illustrations.

- • Putting all the recommendations in the title would make it too long.
- • The report does not offer recommendations.
- If the title does not contain the recommendation, it normally indicates what problem that the report tries to solve.
- In a short report, list all the headings in the Table of Contents. In a long report, pick a level and put all the headings at that level and above in the Contents.
- Organize the transmittal in this way:
  1. Release the report, noting when and by whom it was authorized and the purpose it was to fulfill.
  2. If the recommendation will be easy for the reader to accept, put it early in the transmittal; briefly summarize the reasons for it. If it will be difficult, summarize the findings first and put the conclusion after them.
  3. (Optional) Mention any points of special interest in the report. Indicate minor problems you encountered in your investigation and show how you surmounted them. Thank people who helped you.
  4. If further research remains, suggest it. If you're interested in doing it, volunteer.
  5. Thank the reader for the opportunity to do the work. If you are doing the report as a consultant or under contract, offer to answer any questions the reader may have about the report itself.
- **Summary abstracts** present the logical skeleton of the article: the thesis or recommendation and its proof. **Descriptive abstracts** indicate what topics the article covers and how deeply it goes into each topic, but do not summarize what the article says about each topic. **Mixed abstracts** have some characteristics of both summary and descriptive abstracts. They may list all of the topics covered in an article and summarize some of the points about some of the topics.
- A summary abstract is based on a sentence outline. A descriptive abstract is based on a topic outline.
- A good abstract is easy to read, concise, and clear. A good abstract can be understood by itself, without the original article or reference books.
- The **Introduction** of the report always contains a statement of purpose and scope. The **Purpose** statement identifies the organizational problem the report addresses, the technical investigations it summarizes, and the rhetorical purpose (to explain, to recommend). The **Scope** statement identifies how broad an area the report surveys. The introduction may also include **Limitations,** problems or factors that limit the validity of your recommendations; **Assumptions,** statements whose truth you assume, and which you use to prove your final point; **Methods,** an explanation of how you gathered your data; **Criteria** or **Standards** used to weigh the factors in the decision; and **Definitions** of terms readers may not know.

EXERCISES AND PROBLEMS FOR CHAPTER 22

22–1 ORGANIZING INFORMATION

Assume that your company is thinking of building a new plant in the West or Southwest. You've been asked to supervise the research and write a report evaluating the strengths and weaknesses, from your company's point of view, of the five sites under consideration: El Paso, Texas; Tucson, Arizona; Salt Lake City, Utah; Eureka, California; and Eugene, Oregon. After conferences with executives at the headquarters office and with several plant managers, you've come up with a long list of criteria on which the locations should be compared. Right now, the list is hard to use for several reasons: it lists items in the order in which they came to your attention: it frequently makes no distinction between levels of importance; some of the items listed are really subsets of other points; the items are not phrased in parallel construction.

A. Organize the list of items.

1. Group similar items together.
2. Combine items into subcategories; group the subcategories into larger categories, and so on as necessary. (If the heading or general category does not appear on the list, you will need to add it.) Some main headings may have more levels of detail (subcategories) than others.
3. Rewrite the categories, subcategories, and items so that they are gramatically parallel.
4. Arrange the categories in the order that seems most useful to the reader.

B. In the process of planning, investigating, and writing a report on the five possible locations, you might prepare several documents: a proposal, instructions for researchers, progress reports, a final report. Name *three* documents in which you could use the organized list you prepared in part A of the assignment.

List of Items to Consider

Available sites—Existing buildings, vacant properties.

How much would existing buildings cost? What is their span width, span height, and crane capacity? How much would it cost to make any necessary conversions?

Property taxes.

Availability of water, gas, electricity, sewer lines, telephones, etc.

Cost of utilities.

Plant operating costs—Existing buildings, new buildings on presently vacant land.

What effect would the proposed plant have on the sales of the nearest existing company plant(s)?

Sales base.

Access to major highways, railroads.

Availability of capital.

Quality of life.

Population.

Climate.

Location.

Labor Base—Numbers, skills, language competency (English, Spanish).

Availability of subcontractors for special jobs.

Vocational training programs in local schools in skills which company needs.

Housing—Quality, availability, cost.

Quality of public schools.

Libraries.

Cultural opportunities—Museums, concerts, theatre.

Entertainment—Sports, movies, night life.

Existing company customers within a 200-mile radius; within a 500-mile radius.

Potential for new customers due to business expansion.

Business climate.

Political climate.

Right-to-work laws.

Zoning ordinances.

Cost of purchasing land and equipment if building on a presently vacant lot.

Cost of new construction.

What equipment would be included in the sales price if we bought an existing building?

Would an existing building offer sufficient potential for expansion?

Are college courses and M.B.A. programs available nearby so that employees can continue their education?

Public parks, pools, playgrounds.

Private recreational facilities and clubs, YMCAs, etc.

Hospitals, health care.

Churches and synagogues.

Stores.

Safety, security—police protection, crime rate.

Population density.

City occupational tax.

Customers in the area presently buying from a competitor.

State and city sales tax.

State and city income tax.

Pollution-control regulations.

Public transportation.

Private schools and colleges.

Physical and economic feasibility.

22-2 WRITING A CONSULTANT'S REPORT

For the past six months, you've been employed full-time as a consultant for Music Revolution, Inc., which is concerned about its financial picture. Sales are declining. It has actually lost money in five of the last eight quarters. Music Revolution has been making turntables for home use since 1967. It was never one of the giants in the field, but for years the stereo component business grew, and Music Revolution earned a good income for its owners. In the last 10 years, however, it has faced intense competition from foreign manufacturers, especially German and Japanese. German and Japanese turntables have a reputation for high quality and are available in a range of prices. Foreign manufacturers have already captured nearly half the domestic market, and their share has risen in each of the last five years. To make matters worse, the market itself is shrinking drastically. With the growing popularity of compact disc players, U.S. sales of traditional turntables last year were 17% lower than the number sold in 1982.

Music Revolution's president, Kent Rahal, has asked you, as a consultant, what to do. After five months of observing Music Revolution's operations, talking to executives, reading trade journals, talking to store owners, and doing some basic market research, you reach these conclusions:

1. The company could reduce its costs by importing parts from Korea, Singapore, and Hong Kong, instead of buying these from U.S. parts manufacturers. Foreign parts are much cheaper and are of equal quality.

2. The tariff on imported turntables is $15^1/_2\%$ on turntables as separate components and $11^1/_2\%$ on turntables built into record players or stereo systems. These rates were established in 1965 after an urgent appeal from domestic stereo manufacturers. The rates they replaced ($7^1/_2\%$ and 5%, respectively) had been in effect since 1948, when, under the general agreement on tariffs and trade, the uniform rate of 30% was reduced. The company could try to persuade Congress to raise the tariff to 30%, but it would not be practical to lobby for an even higher duty. Although some foreign turntables would still undersell American turntables, the higher rate would help all domestic manufacturers. In fact, it would help more than importing parts.

    To obtain a high rate, however, it would be important for manufacturers of parts, complete turntables, and other stereo components to present a united front.

3. Even if the company both imported parts and succeeded in having the tariff raised to 30%, it still could not meet the prices of the German and Japanese manufacturers and the two large American firms which dominate the U.S. turntable market.

4. The stereo market is biggest at the low and the high ends of the price line. The biggest market is for high-quality components; customers are willing to pay high prices to get high quality. A big market also exists for low-priced components and record players. The market for high-quality components is increasingly shifting to compact discs; industry experts predict that by 2000, the demand for high-quality conventional turntables will be only 15% of what it was in 1975. No technological advances are expected which might restore interest in turntables and conventional records for the high-quality market. The market for low-quality turntables should hold steady. It may even grow, if more baby boomers buy inexpensive record players and stereos for their children.

5. Of even more help than a higher tariff would be a quota on imports. Then, even if foreign turntables were cheaper, there would be a limit on the number of turntables that could be imported and the foreign companies could not further increase their market share. Thus, though the total market would continue to decline, Music Revolution could retain its share of this limited market.

    It is not clear whether the President and Congress could be persuaded to impose quotas. Not many workers are employed by turntable manufacturers; there isn't the support for limiting imports of turntables that there is for limiting imports of steel and cars. In any case, a united industry front, including parts manufacturers, would be essential.

6. The company should diversify its manufacturing activities by making products other than turntables. Even if quotas were to prevent foreign manufacturers from obtaining a larger share of the market, there appears to be no way to become profitable by making and selling only turntables. In fact, Music Revolution should consider dropping its turntable line completely and shifting entirely to other products.

7. In the short run, the best opportunities for the company seem to be in inexpensive turntables for children's record players. Few foreign manufacturers have entered this market. An aggressive marketing and advertising campaign would be needed to build brand awareness of Music Revolution's entry in the market.

8. If the company continues to manufacture turntables, it should import some parts. If all American manufacturers did this, there is the risk that domestic companies would stop making parts, leaving the company with no U.S. source of supply. However, the costs saving offsets the risk. The two big American firms already import some parts; their saving contributes to their ability to produce turntables more cheaply than Music Revolution can.

9. The company should try to persuade the industry to press for import quotas. If Congress and the President will not impose quotas, higher tariffs are the next best thing from the industry's point of view.

10. If quotas or higher tariffs are enacted, foreign manufacturers might retaliate by pressuring foreign parts manufacturers to stop selling parts to U.S. manufacturers.

As your instructor directs,

a. Organize the conclusions logically. Some numbered conclusions may deal with two or more topics.

b. Identify the recommendation(s) you must make to management.

c. Identify the best order in which to present the conclusions.

d. Identify the statements in the conclusions which you would have to prove in the report.

e. Identify titles for seven charts, graphs, tables, and appendices you might use in the report.

f. Prepare the following parts of the report:
Title Page
Letter of Transmittal
Table of Contents
List of Illustrations
Summary Abstract

22–3 USING INFORMATION TO WRITE A REPORT TO A SPECIFIC AUDIENCE

Background. You are a consultant who has spent the last three months studying costs for employer-paid health care for state employees. Health care is a major cost for employers, who understandably want to keep the cost as low as possible. Health insurance is an important fringe benefit for employees, who understandably want the program to be as inclusive and as flexible as possible.

Currently your state offers its employees two basic options: Blue Cross/Blue Shield, or participation in a Health Maintenance Organization (HMO). The HMO pays more small bills (e.g., for routine checkups, lab tests, and immunizations), but all medical procedures have to be approved in advance by a physician who is a member of one of the approved HMOs. Blue Cross/Blue Shield has a high deductible that the employee must pay, but the employee can change physicians at any time and never has to pick a doctor from an approved list. Both plans reimburse prescription generic drugs 100% and prescription brand drugs 75%; both cover eye exams and pay part of the cost of corrective lenses; both pay most of the cost of pychological or psychiatric counseling or care; both pay catastrophic expenses.

State employees get the insurance free as one of their fringe benefits. They can insure their spouses and children by paying a monthly fee which is deducted from each paycheck.

In the last three months, you have gathered the available information from neighboring states and from a few private companies which do business in your state. You have read many journals and books. You have interviewed doctors, nurses, psychiatrists, hospice workers, and employees. Your research has produced the following observations and conclusions:

1. Costs are rising rapidly. The cost to the organization for health care insurance has risen 42% in the last two years. The cost to the employee for dependents has risen 63% in the last two years.

2. These costs have risen in spite of major cost containment efforts by hospitals. However, more and more health care takes place outside hospitals—in doctors' offices, in

clinics, and in other out-patient settings. No one has done very much to control these costs: in your state, they rose 49% in the last year—more than offsetting other savings.

3. HMOs cost the employer less. Essentially the HMO gets a fee for each insured person. If the cost is over that, the HMO loses money (and some HMOs have gone broke). But if the cost is less, the HMO makes money. Some people feel that HMOs give poorer care since they have a profit motive.

   Healthier people elect HMOs. In your state, 75% of the employees 50 or younger are in HMOs, while only 22% of the employees 51 and older are in HMOs. But people over 50 have higher health care bills.

4. Thirty-four percent of the state employees are married to spouses who have health care through their own employers. Some of these spouses might be able to insure the state employee as a dependent on their plans. Right now, all employees must participate in the state coverage. It would not be acceptable for someone to opt out of the state plan unless he or she had equal or better coverage elsewhere. However, it would be to the state's advantage to decrease the number of people in the plan. Even if it paid each employee who opted out $200 a year, the state would still save $100 a year for each person who withdrew from the plan.

5. In the last year, 10% of the state's total costs under the health plan went to only three cases: two babies born prematurely with multiple defects, and one person who died of AIDS. Another 15% of the total costs went to 16 cases: a triple heart bypass, two employees on dialysis, a burn victim, two victims of car crashes, one of whom is still in a coma, four babies born with complications, two employees in the early stages of AIDS, and four cancer patients.

6. The best promise for cutting costs lies in *case management*. Case management seeks to identify cases that are likely to be expensive and to suggest alternatives: home rather than hospital care with someone coming in to cook, clean, and administer medications; second opinions; therapy rather than surgery; nursing home care

rather than hospital care, etc. Advocates of case management say that in addition to saving money, the care is often superior. A current AIDS patient wants very much to stay at home. Surgeons are often too quick to assume that surgery is the only way to help someone. Opponents fear that case management will deprive people of the care they need if that care is expensive. Doctors fear that case management will further limit their autonomy. Doctors who are not affiliated with HMOs are particularly opposed to case management.

7. In a survey designed to measure attitudes toward the current health plan, dental care was overwhelmingly what employees would like to see added (45% strongly favor, 33% favor). In questions about current benefits, 32% said they (or their spouses) did not need maternity benefits. No other feature received higher than 14% of respondents saying that they did not need that feature. In questions about where cuts would hurt them least, 38% said, "limit funds for psychological or psychiatric care," 24% said "pay more for prescription drugs," 10% said "higher deductible for hospital bills" and the rest refused to answer.

8. In interviews, a number of employees flatly said that the only reason they continued to work for the state was because of health care benefits. "The salaries are low, and nobody ever gets promoted. If they cut health care, I could make more in private industry." You think that the people who could most easily find other jobs are precisely those the state most wants to keep: the people with the best records.

9. The state has never asked for an analysis of health care costs or for projections for future costs. It is always taken by surprise when the insurance carrier announces an increase. The state has never tried to negotiate special rates with hospitals or with doctors.

10. The insurance carrier would lower its rates to the state if it could refuse to insure people with certain habits or traits, or if it could insure spouses and dependents only if they passed physicals. Employee groups, however, have lobbied loudly against refusing to insure smokers or people who carry genetic markers for disease. State officials have made it clear that they regard

as unethical any policy which might discriminate against Blacks (who are more likely to have high blood pressure), people who use recreational drugs (increasing likelihood of several diseases, including hepatitis and AIDS), or people whose lifestyles put them at higher risks. The Attorney General points out that some categories of discrimination would be illegal as well as unethical.

Situation A. You have been hired by the state government to recommend ways to control the cost of health care. The state is willing to cut benefits if necessary to control costs.

Situation B. You have been hired by the state employees' union to recommend ways the health insurance can be more useful to employees. The union wants to maintain the present level of benefits and expand benefits if possible. The union realizes that if costs continue to rise, benefits are likely to be cut.

Both groups will use your information at contract negotiations, which will start in six weeks.

As your instructor directs,
   a. Organize the conclusions logically.
   b. Identify the recommendation(s) you must make to each group.
   c. Identify the best order in which to present the conclusions.
   d. Identify the statements in the conclusions which you would have to prove in each report.
   e. Identify titles for seven charts, graphs, tables, and appendices you might use in each report.
   f. Prepare the following parts for one of the reports:
      Title Page
      Letter of Transmittal
      Table of Contents
      List of Illustrations
      Summary Abstract

22–4 RECOMMENDING TERMINALS FOR THE LIBRARY

Assume that the library of your community college, college, or university either has already put its card catalog on computers or is planning to do so. You're on a committee charged with recommending which terminals the library should buy to upgrade or to start its Computerized Catalog System (CCS). The committee has been told to consider the following criteria:

- Ease of use
- Compatibility with other library and campus systems
- Capability to accurately show foreign-language characters
- Capacity to handle future changes or upgrades in the CCS
- Capacity to use modems for phone access from other locations.

As your instructor directs,
   a. Prepare a formal report detailing the specifications the terminals will need to meet.
   b. Prepare a formal report recommending the brand and model that your library should buy.

22–5 RECOMMENDING WAYS TO COMBAT ILLITERACY

Federal studies estimate that at least 21 million people over the age of 17 are functionally illiterate: they cannot read job applications, newspapers, or instructions on medicine. The Business Council for Effective Literacy estimates that another 35 to 45 million people have only marginally competent communication skills.

As your instructor directs,
   a. Write a report for the mayor of your city on the extent of the problem in the United States and in your city. Identify the programs already underway to combat illiteracy and recommend what the city should do to help.
   b. Write a report for a major employer in your state on what it can do to support public efforts to combat illiteracy.
   c. Write a report for a company in your state on how it is affected by illiteracy and marginal literacy and whether it should develop programs to help any of its own employees who may be illiterate.

22–6 WRITING A FORMAL REPORT

Study a problem that interests you and write a formal report recommending a solution to the problem. Address your report to the person in the organization who would have the power to approve the recommendation(s) in your report.

Acceptable kinds of reports include

Feasibility Study. Evaluate two or more options that an organization has. Interview people at the organization to identify the criteria by which to evaluate the options. Here, you would recommend which option the organization should adopt. (Remember that to do nothing or to delay action are options, too.)

Problem-Solving Report. Analyze a problem which an organization faces and recommend a way to solve or ameliorate it. Indicate clearly the causes of the problem, the strengths and weaknesses of various solutions, and the degree to which the recommendations would solve the problem.

Analytical Report. Analyze a problem or failure which an organization has had. Here, your report would focus on the cause(s) of a complex problem. You could recommend things the organization should do to avoid repeating the problem in the future, but you would not necessarily prove that those recommendations alone would guarantee success.

As your instructor directs, turn in the following documents:

1. The approved proposal
2. Two copies of the report, including

Cover
Title Page
Letter or Memo of Transmittal
Table of Contents
List of Illustrations
Executive Summary or Abstract
Body (Introduction, all information, Recommendations). Your instructor may specify a minimum length, a minimum number or kind of sources, and a minimum number of visuals
Appendices if useful or relevant

3. Your notes and rough drafts

22–7 WRITING ABSTRACTS

Write both a summary and a descriptive abstract of a journal article. Turn in a copy of the article with your abstracts.

V

ORAL AND NONVERBAL
COMMUNICATION

Nonverbal Communication

QUESTIONS

- What is nonverbal communication?
- Is nonverbal communication easier to interpret than verbal communication?
- What kinds of voices are perceived as being more authoritative?
- What voice qualities connote enthusiasm, energy, and intelligence in the United States?
- What postures and body movements suggest comfort and openness? Which ones suggest discomfort and being closed?
- Can you use gestures to communicate with people whose language you don't know?
- What is "personal space"?
- How are touch and power related in the United States?
- How can different views of time create problems in international business?

Many people believe that the language of gesture is universal. Many people believe that one picture is worth a thousand words, the implication being that what we see is ever so much clearer than what is said. Many people believe that communication means speaking and that misunderstandings only occur with speaking. Many people believe that smiling and frowning and clapping are purely natural expressions. Many people believe that the world is flat.

John C. Condon and Fathi Yousef
An Introduction to Intercultural Communication, 1975

Nonverbal communication—communication that doesn't use words—takes place all the time. Smiles, frowns, who sits where at a meeting, the size of an office, how long someone keeps a visitor waiting—all these communicate pleasure or anger, friendliness or distance, power and status. Face-to-face communication offers multiple nonverbal cues, and phone calls offer limited nonverbal messages through tone of voice and pauses. Even written media offer minimal nonverbal signals through visual impact.

Nonverbal communication can include the following signals:

- **Voice qualities**
  Tone of voice
  Pitch
  Stress
  Volume
- **Body language**
  Posture and movement
  Eye contact
  Facial expressions and emotion
  Gestures
  Greetings
- **Space**
  Personal space
  Touching
  Spatial arrangements
- **Time**
  Waiting and lead time
  Number of things that happen at the same time
- **Miscellaneous**
  Clothing
  Colors
  Age

Most of the time we are no more conscious of interpreting nonverbal signals than we are conscious of breathing. Yet nonverbal signals can be misinterpreted just as easily as can verbal symbols (words). And the misunderstandings can be harder to clear up because people may not be aware of the nonverbal cues that led them to assume that they aren't liked, or respected, or approved.

A young woman took a new idea into her boss, who sat there and glared at her, brows together in a frown, as she explained her proposal. The stare and lowered brows symbolized anger to her, and she assumed that he was rejecting her idea. Several months later, in a casual conversation with another employee she learned that her boss always "frowned" when he was concentrating. The facial expression she had interpreted as anger had not been intended to convey anger at all.

Misunderstandings are even more common when people communicate with people from other cultures or other countries. A white teacher sends two black students to the principal's office because they're "fighting." U.S. whites consider fighting to have started when loud voices, insults, and posture indicate that violence is likely. But the U.S. black culture does not assume that those signs will lead to violence: they are part of nonviolent disagreements.[1] An Arab student assumed that his U.S. roommate disliked him intensely because the U.S. student sat around the room with his feet up on the furniture, soles toward the Arab roommate. Arab culture sees the foot in general and the sole in particular as unclean; showing the sole of the foot is an insult.[2]

Learning about nonverbal language can help us to project the image we want to project and make us more aware of the signals we are interpreting. However, learning what a signal "means" can lead us to stereotype people, rather than seeking and being sensitive to feedback.

While research on nonverbal meanings is extensive, most of it seems to be based on the way symbols are usually interpreted by middle-class white North Americans. The literature on nonverbal communication does not always specify the sex or age of the people involved. Factors such as social status, region, or cultural or ethnic heritage are rarely mentioned, even though anyone who has traveled throughout the United States knows that many differences exist. (For example, older people often prefer to be addressed as "Mr. Selby" or "Mrs. D'Amelio." Younger people may be more comfortable with first names. People from the South are more likely to smile at and speak to strangers on the street than are people from the Northeast.) Finally, research on nonverbal communication in 1960 or 1970 may not apply in 1990. Test the generalizations that follow against your own experience.

VOICE QUALITIES

Voice qualities sometimes convey meaning. Often they are interpreted to indicate credibility and emotion.

Tone of voice refers to the rising or falling inflection that tells you whether a group of words is a question or a statement, whether the speaker is uncertain or confident, whether a statement is sincere or sarcastic. Anyone who has written dialogue with adverbs ("he said thoughtfully") has tried to indicate tone of voice.

When tone of voice and the meaning of words conflict, people "believe" the tone of voice. Jann Davis reports that one person responded to friends' "How are you?" with the words, "Dying, and you?" Most of the friends responded "Fine." Because the tone of voice was cheerful, they didn't hear the content of the words.[3]

Pitch measures whether a voice uses sounds that are low (like the bass notes on a piano) or high. Low-pitched voices are usually perceived as being more authoritative, sexier, and more pleasant to listen to than are high-pitched

---

Buttering Is Different in France*
I grew up in Iowa and I knew what to do with butter: you put it on roastin' ears, pancakes, and popcorn. Then I went to France and saw a Frenchman put butter on radishes. . . . I realized then something I hadn't learned in five years of language study: not only was *speaking* in French different from speaking in English, but *buttering* in French was different from buttering in English. And that was the beginning of cross-cultural understanding.

---

* Quoted from Genelle G. Morain, *Kinesics and Cross-Cultural Understanding,* Language in Education: Theory and Practice, no. 7 (Arlington, VA: Center for Applied Linguistics, 1978), 1.

A Nonverbal Signal May Have Multiple Meanings

Even within a single culture, a specific nonverbal signal may have more than one meaning. For example, fidgeting or using the hands to play with something is usually seen as a sign of nervousness. For a specific individual, however, it may simply be an indication of having extra energy that needs an outlet. Leaning back is sometimes considered to be a sign of emotionally "backing off." In some cases, people may lean back when they're involved but relaxed.

When you're with friends, you can ask the person involved what the behavior means: "You turned away from me just now." In a structured situation, it's probably a good idea to avoid behaviors that have negative stereotypes. In a job interview, for example, an applicant should avoid playing with a tie or jewelry. In a confrontation with a subordinate, a supervisor should avoid leaning back and crossing arms or legs.

voices. Most voices go up in pitch when the speaker is angry or excited; some people raise pitch when they increase volume. Women whose normal speaking voices are high may need to practice projecting their voices to avoid becoming shrill when they speak to large groups.

Stress is the emphasis given to one or more words in a sentence. As the following example shows, emphasizing different words can change the meaning.

I'll give you a raise.
[Implication, depending on pitch and speed: "Another supervisor wouldn't" or "I have the power to determine your salary."]

I'll **give** you a raise.
[Implication, depending on pitch and speed: "You haven't **earned** it" or "OK, all right, you win. I'm saying 'yes' to get rid of you, but I don't really agree," or "I've just this instant decided that you deserve a raise."]

I'll give **you** a raise.
[Implication: "But nobody else in this department is getting one."]

I'll give you **a** raise.
[Implication: "But just one."]

I'll give you a **raise.**
[Implication: "But you won't get the promotion or anything else you want."]

I'll give **you** a **raise.**
[Implication: "You deserve it."]

I'll give you a **raise!**
[Implication: "I've just this minute decided to act, and I'm excited about this idea. The raise will please both of us."]

Speakers who use many changes in tone, pitch, and stress as they speak usually seem more enthusiastic; often they also seem more energetic and more intelligent. Someone who speaks in a monotone may seem apathetic or unintelligent. Nonnative speakers whose first language does not use tone, pitch, and stress to convey meaning and attitude may need to practice varying these voice qualities.

Volume is a measure of loudness or softness. Very soft voices, especially if they are also breathy and high-pitched, give the impression of youth and inexperience. People who do a lot of speaking to large groups need to practice projecting their voices so they can increase their volume without shouting.

In some cultures, it is considered rude to shout; loud voices connote anger and imminent violence. In others, everyday conversations are loud. Edward Hall and William Whyte report that some Arabs discounted Voice of America broadcasts because the signal was so "weak."[4] Arab men who are equals speak loudly by North American standards.

BODY LANGUAGE

In the past 20 years, popular literature has become fascinated with body language. But nonverbal languages differ from each other just as do languages that use words.

Posture and Movement

Posture and body movements connote energy and openness. North American **open body positions** include leaning forward with uncrossed arms and legs, with the arms away from the body. **Closed** or **defensive body positions** include leaning back, sometimes with both hands behind the head, arms and legs crossed or close together, or hands in pockets. As the labels imply, open positions suggest that people are accepting and open to new ideas. Closed positions suggest that people are physically or psychologically uncomfortable, that they are defending themselves and shutting other people out.

People who cross their arms or legs often claim that they do so only because the position is more comfortable. Certainly crossing one's legs is one way to be more comfortable in a chair that is the wrong height. U.S. women are taught to keep their arms close to their bodies and their knees and ankles together. But notice your own body the next time you're in a perfectly comfortable discussion with a good friend. You'll probably find that you naturally assume open body positions. The fact that so many people in organizational settings adopt closed positions may indicate that many people feel at least slightly uncomfortable in school and on the job.

The Japanese value the ability to sit quietly. They may see the U.S. tendency to fidget and shift as an indication of lack of mental or spiritual balance. Even in North America, interviewers and audiences usually respond negatively to nervous gestures such as fidgeting with a tie or hair or jewelry, tapping a pencil, or swinging a foot.

People from different cultures learn to walk differently. Carmen Judith Nine-Curt observes that Caribbean people move the torso as though it was made up of separable parts, while North American Anglos and northern Spaniards carry the torso as if it were one piece.[5] People from one culture often react negatively to another culture's walk. The French see the American walk as "uncivilized."[6] White Americans sometimes see the black male's walk as threatening and the Hispanic walk as sexual, although there is no evidence that these walks carry such meanings in the cultures where people have learned them.

Eye Contact

North American whites see **eye contact** as a sign of honesty. But in many cultures, dropped eyes are a sign of appropriate deference to a superior. Puerto Rican children are taught not to meet the eyes of adults.[7] The Japanese are taught to look at the neck.[8] In Korea, prolonged eye contact is considered rude. The lower-ranking person is expected to look down first.[9]

Arab men in laboratory experiments looked at each other more than did two American men or two Englishmen.[10] Eye contact is so important that Arabs dislike talking to someone wearing dark glasses or while walking side by side. It is considered impolite not to face someone directly. In Muslim countries, women and men are not supposed to have eye contact.

These differences can lead to miscommunication in the multicultural workplace. Superiors may feel that subordinates are being disrespectful when the subordinate is being fully respectful—according to the norms of his or her culture.

Facial Expressions and Emotions

In the United States, smiling varies from region to region. Twenty years ago, Ray Birdwhistell found that "middle-class individuals" from Ohio, Indiana, and Illinois smiled more than did people from Massachusetts, New Hampshire, and Maine, who in turn smiled more than did western New Yorkers. People

What Do Bosses Want?*

When a new manager takes over, people observe and interpret his or her nonverbal behavior.

A new division president always wore his jacket so people thought that he was formal and demanding. He was. He called people to him, rather than going to their offices, and people inferred that he didn't want to waste time with minor people and minor matters. In fact, the man was approachable and a good listener. But it took time to correct the initial misperception based on nonverbal cues.

A boss's working hours communicate expectations. In one office, many people came late and left early. A new general manager was always in the office at 8 A.M. and usually worked past 5 P.M. Nothing was ever said about work hours, but quickly other workers were putting in a full eight-hour day.

Another new division president put a circular table in his office so that sales and manufacturing people couldn't sit on opposite sides of the table. In meetings in the conference room, the president made people in manufacturing, sales, and data processing move their chairs so they wouldn't be seated in "blocks." This president talked a lot about "breaking down barriers" between departments. The nonverbal signals convinced people that he meant what he said.

---

* Based on John J. Gabarro, *The Dynamics of Taking Charge* (Boston: Harvard Business School Press, 1987), 86–88.

The Way You Walk*

In Paris one can recognize Americans two hundred yards away simply by the way they walk. A Belgian student told me that when he returned home after three months at the Harvard Business School, his father was shocked when he saw his son walk from the plane. "You've become an American," were his first words of greeting. "You bounce when you walk!" An American often walks with swinging arms and a rolling pelvis as though moving through a space unlimited by human or physical obstacles.

from cities in southern and border states—Atlanta, Louisville, Memphis, and Nashville—smiled most of all.[11] Some scholars speculate that Northeasterners may distrust the sincerity of Southerners who smile a lot (like former President Jimmy Carter). Students from other countries who come to U.S. universities may be disconcerted by the American tendency to smile at strangers—until they realize that the smiles don't "mean" anything. In Germany, smiles are reserved for friends.[12] The Japanese smile not only when they are pleased or amused but also to say, "That's none of your business" and to cover embarrassment, sadness, and even anger.[13]

The Japanese learn to control their emotions. In situations of strong emotion, it is considered acceptable to smile or laugh, but not to frown or cry. In some U.S. businesses, it is considered acceptable to frown, swear, and yell, but not to cry. Yet both anger and crying may be expressions of the same emotion: frustration at not getting what we want. Most U.S. boys are taught not to cry. Many girls, in contrast, are allowed to cry but told (directly or subtly) not to display anger. As a result of this different upbringing, many American men are uncomfortable when women cry; many American women are uncomfortable when men become angry. Both men and women may be uncomfortable when they see men crying, even though other cultures allow men to cry.

Gestures

Americans sometimes assume that they can depend on gestures to communicate if language fails. But Birdwhistell reported that "although we have been searching for 15 years [1950–65], we have found no gesture or body motion which has the same meaning in all societies."[14] In Bulgaria, for example, people may nod their heads to signify *no* and shake their heads to signify *yes*.[15]

Gestures than mean approval in the United States may have very different meanings in other countries. The thumbs up sign which means "good work" or "go ahead" in the United States and most of Western Europe is a vulgar insult in Greece. The circle formed with the thumb and first finger that means "OK" in the United States is obscene in southern Italy and can mean "you're worth nothing" in France and Belgium.[16]

A member of the audience at a lecture on Puerto Rican gestures in Brooklyn, New York, assumed that shaking the hands up and down in front of the chest, as though shaking off water, was "a sign of mental retardation." The Puerto Rican professor lecturing was horrified: in her culture, the gesture meant "excitement, intense thrill."[17] Studies have found that Spanish-speaking doctors rate the mental abilities of Hispanic patients much higher than do English-speaking doctors. The language barrier is surely part of the misevaluation of English-speaking doctors. Cultural differences in gestures may contribute to the misevaluation. Similarly, Anglo supervisors in the workplace may underestimate the abilities of Hispanics because gestures differ in the two cultures.

SPACE

Personal space is the distance someone wants between him- or herself and other people in ordinary, nonintimate interchanges. Observation and limited experimentation show that most North Americans, North Europeans, and Asians want a bigger personal space than do Latin Americans, French, Italians, and Arabs.

People who prefer lots of personal space are often forced to accept close

---

*   Quoted from Laurence Wylie, *Beaux Gestes: A Guide to French Body Talk* (Cambridge, MA: Undergraduate Press, 1977), xi.

contact on a crowded elevator or subway. In Korea, Jerrold Merchant notes, being touched, pushed, and stepped on is an everyday occurrence; no one says or is expected to say "Excuse me."[18]

Even within a culture, some people like more personal space than do others. One U.S. study found that men occupied more personal space than women did.[19] In many cultures, people who are of the same age and sex take less personal space than do mixed-age or mixed-sex groups. Latin Americans will stand closer to people of the same sex than North Americans would, but North Americans stand closer to people of the opposite sex.[20] Similarly, Laotians of the same sex sit very close together, almost "on top of each other" according to the space norms of the United States. But people of the opposite sex sit at a distance from each other.[21]

Touch

Repeated studies have shown that babies need to be touched to grow and thrive and that older people are healthier both mentally and physically if they are touched. But some people are more comfortable with touch than others. Some people shake hands in greeting but otherwise don't like to be touched at all, except by family members or lovers. Other people, having grown up in families that touch a lot, hug as part of a greeting and touch even casual friends. Each kind of person may misinterpret the other. A person who dislikes touch may seem unfriendly to someone who's used to touching. A toucher may seem overly familiar to someone who dislikes touch.

Studies in the United States have shown that touch is interpreted as power: more powerful people touch less powerful people. When the toucher had higher status than the recipient, both men and women liked being touched.[22]

Most parts of North America allow opposite-sex couples to hold hands or walk arm-in-arm in public but frown on the same behavior in same-sex couples. People in Asia, the Middle East, and South America have the opposite expectation: male friends or female friends can hold hands or walk arm-in-arm, but it is slightly shocking for an opposite-sex couple to touch in public. In Khomeini's Iran, even handshakes between men and women are seen as improper.[23]

Spatial Arrangements

People who don't know each other well may feel more comfortable with each other if a piece of furniture separates them. For example, a group may work better sitting around a table than just sitting in a circle. In North America, a person sitting at the head of a table is generally assumed to be the group's leader. However, one experiment showed that when a woman sat at the head of a mixed-sex group, observers assumed that one of the men in the group was the leader.[24]

Podiums and desks can be used as barricades to protect oneself from other people. One professor normally walked among his students as he lectured. But if anyone asked a question he was uncomfortable with, he retreated behind the podium before answering it.

In the United States, the size, placement, and privacy of one's office connote status. Large corner offices have the highest status. An individual office with a door that closes connotes more status than a desk in a common area. Japanese

It's OK to Smile at a Stranger in the United States*

The following enlightening comments came from international students newly arrived in the United States:

Japanese student:
On my way to and from school I have received a smile by non-acquaintance American girls several times. I have finally learned they have not interest for me; it means only a kind of greeting to a foreigner. If someone smiles at a stranger in Japan, especially a girl, she can assume he is either a sexual maniac or an impolite person.

Arabian student:
When I walked around the campus my first day many people smiled at me. I was very embarrassed and rushed to the men's room to see if I had made a mistake with my clothes. But I could find nothing for them to smile at. Now I am used to all the smiles.

---

* Quoted from Laray M. Barna, "Stumbling Blocks in Intercultural Communication," in *Intercultural Communication*, ed. Larry A. Samovar and Richard E. Porter (Belmont, CA: Wadsworth Publishing, 1985), 331.

How to Summon a Server*

To get someone's attention or to summon a waiter or waitress is often a problem for international travelers. . . . In restaurants in Anglo-Saxon countries, including the United States: Call a waiter or waitress quietly ("Sir," "Miss," "Waiter") or raise a finger to catch their attention, or tilt one's head to one side. Do not snap your fingers.

[In Europe]: Call louder for their attention, or clink a glass or cup with a spoon or your finger ring.

Africa: Knock on the table.

Middle East: Clap your hands.

. . .

Japan: Extend your arm slightly upward, palm down, and flutter your fingers.

Asia and South Pacific: Don't wave your index finger: it's considered uncouth, on the level of calling dogs.

Pakistan and the Philippines: Just say "psssssst!"

Spain and Latin America: Extend your hand, palm down, and rapidly open and close your fingers.

Singapore and Malaysia: To beckon a person, taxi, or waiter/waitress, extend your right hand palm down, keep your fingers together, fold your thumb across your palm or extend it, and wave your hand.

firms, however, see private offices as "inappropriate and inefficient," reports Robert Christopher. Only the very highest executives and directors have private offices in the traditional Japanese company, and even they will also have desks in the common areas.[25]

Japanese homes have much smaller rooms than most U.S. homes. The Japanese use less furniture and arrange it differently: a small table will be in the center of the room. In cold weather, a heater is placed under the table; the table cloth keeps the warm air around the legs and feet of everyone who sits at the table. Even though U.S. homes have more pieces of furniture than the traditional Japanese home, Japanese may see Western rooms as "empty" since Western furniture lines the walls, leaving a large empty space in the middle of the room.[26]

TIME

Organizations in the United States—businesses, government, and schools—keep time by the calendar and the clock. Being on time is seen as a sign of dependability. Other cultures may keep time by the seasons and the moon, the sun, internal body clocks, or a personal feeling that "the time is right."

The U.S. business culture emphasizes the present. Businesses focus on the bottom line for this quarter; consumers use credit to buy things NOW. Japanese businesses, in contrast, emphasize the future; they are willing to forgo profits for years to build market share.[27]

North Americans who believe that "time is money" are often frustrated in negotiations with people who take a much more leisurely approach. Part of the problem is that people in many other cultures want to establish a personal relationship before they decide whether to do business with each other.

The problem is made worse because various cultures mentally measure time differently. Many North Americans measure time in five-minute blocks. Someone who's five minutes late to an appointment or a job interview feels compelled to apologize. If the executive or interviewer is running half an hour late, the caller expects to be told about the likely delay upon arriving. Some people won't be able to wait that long and will need to reschedule their appointments. But in other cultures, 15 minutes or half an hour may be the smallest block of time. To someone who mentally measures time in 15-minute blocks, being 45 minutes late is no worse than being 15 minutes late is to North Americans.

Edward T. Hall points out that different cultures have different lead times. In some countries, you need to schedule important meetings at least two weeks in advance. In other countries, not only are people not booked up so far in advance, but a date two weeks into the future may be forgotten. He advises scheduling appointments only three or four days in advance in Arab countries.[28]

Hall also distinguishes between **monochronic** cultures, where one does only one important activity at a time, and **polychronic** cultures, where people do several things at once. The United States is monochronic. It is impolite to read a book during a meeting, even if much of the meeting does not directly concern the person reading. When U.S. managers feel offended because a Latin American manager also sees other people during "their" appointments, the two kinds of time are in conflict.

According to some scholars, Europeans schedule fewer events in a comparable period of time than do North Americans. Perhaps as a result, Germans and German Swiss see North Americans as too time-conscious.[29]

---

* Quoted from Philip R. Harris and Robert T. Moran, *Managing Cultural Differences* (Houston: Gulf Publishing, 1987), 44.

OTHER NONVERBAL SYMBOLS

Many other symbols can carry nonverbal meanings: clothing, colors, age, and height, to name a few.

In North America, certain styles and colors of clothing are considered more professional and more credible. In his *Dress for Success* and *The Woman's Dress for Success Book* John T. Molloy tells readers what clothes carry nonverbal messages of success, prestige, and competence. In Japan, clothing denotes not only status but also occupational group. Students wear uniforms. Company badges indicate rank within the organization. Workers wear different clothes when they are on strike than they do when they are working.[30]

Colors can also carry meanings in a culture. In the United States, mourners wear black to funerals, while brides wear white. In precommunist China and in some South American tribes, white is the color of mourning. Purple flowers are given to the dead in Mexico.[31] In Korea, red ink is used to record deaths but never to write about living people.[32]

In the United States, youth is valued. Some men as well as some women color their hair and even have face-lifts to look as youthful as possible. In Japan, younger people defer to older people. Americans attempting to negotiate in Japan are usually taken more seriously if at least one member of the team is noticeably gray-haired.

Height connotes status in many parts of the world. Executive offices are usually on the top floors; the underlings work below. Even being tall can help a person succeed. Studies have shown that employers are more willing to hire men over six feet tall than shorter men with the same credentials. Studies of real-world executives and graduates have shown that taller men make more money. In one study, every extra inch of height brought in an extra $600 a year.[33] But being too big can be a disadvantage. A tall, brawny football player complained that people found him intimidating off the field and assumed that he "had the brains of a Twinkie."

SUMMARY OF KEY POINTS

- **Nonverbal communication** is communication that doesn't use words. Nonverbal communication can include voice qualities, body language, space, time, and other miscellaneous matters such as clothing, colors, and age.
- Nonverbal signals can be misinterpreted just as easily as can verbal symbols (words).
- Low-pitched voices are usually perceived as being more authoritative, sexier, and more pleasant to listen to than are high-pitched voices.
- Speakers who use many changes in tone, pitch, and stress as they speak usually seem more enthusiastic; often they also seem more energetic and more intelligent.
- North American **open body positions** include uncrossed arms and legs, with the arms away from the body. **Closed** or **defensive body positions** include arms and legs crossed or close together and hands in pockets. As the labels imply, open positions suggest that people are accepting and open to new ideas. Closed positions suggest that people are physically or psychologically uncomfortable, that they are defending themselves and shutting other people out.

* Quoted from Jerry E. Bishop, "Athletes Wearing Black Play More Aggressively," *The Wall Street Journal*, February 29, 1988, 21.

Give Me Room, Lots of Room

When I was in high school, we had to wait about 45 minutes after school for our bus to make its first trip and come back to get us. A group of us always waited together. We'd put our books down on the blacktop and talk.

We always moved away from our books—sometimes 20 or 30 feet away. I finally realized that I kept backing up. The others moved in closer, and I backed up some more. I needed more personal space than they did.

And the Bad Guys Wore Black*

Black uniforms make football and hockey players appear—and act—meaner, according to a study by two Cornell University psychologists.

Penalty records of 28 National Football League teams from 1970 to 1986 showed that all five teams that wore predominately black uniforms were among the 12 most penalized teams. Similarly, the three most penalized teams in the National Hockey League in those 17 years wore black. When the Pittsburgh Penguins switched to black-and-gold from blue in 1979–80 . . . their average penalty time per hockey game went to 12 minutes from eight minutes.

This prompted the psychologists to launch a series of experiments on the effects of black uniforms. Groups of football fans and referees were shown either of two videotapes of a staged football play. In one tape the defensive team wore black while in the other tape the defenders wore white. Those who saw the black-uniform team rated the defenders as far more aggressive and "dirty" than those who watched the white-cloth defenders making the same moves. . . .

A black uniform may make others think a person is more aggressive or "mean" and, as a result, the person becomes more aggressive, the psychologists speculate.

Walk On By*

My first victim was a woman—white, well dressed, probably in her early twenties. I came upon her late one evening on a deserted street in Hyde Park, a relatively affluent neighborhood in an otherwise mean, impoverished section of Chicago. As I swung onto the avenue behind her, there seemed to be a discreet, uninflammatory distance between us. Not so. She cast back a worried glance. To her, the youngish black man—a broad six feet two inches with a beard and billowing hair, both hands shoved into the pockets of a bulky military jacket—seemed menacingly close. After a few more quick glimpses, she picked up her pace and was soon running in earnest. Within seconds she disappeared into a cross street.

That was more than a decade ago. I was 22 years old, a graduate student newly arrived at the University of Chicago. . . . It was clear that she thought herself the quarry of a mugger, a rapist, or worse. Suffering a bout of insomnia, however, I was stalking sleep, not defenseless wayfarers. . . . I was surprised, embarrassed, and dismayed all at once. . . .

I began to take precautions to make myself less threatening. I [now] move about with care, particularly late in the evening. I give a wide berth to nervous people on subway platforms during the wee hours, particularly when I have exchanged business clothes for jeans. . . . And on late-evening constitutionals along streets less traveled by, I enjoy what has proved to be an excellent tension-reducing measure: I whistle melodies from Beethoven and Vivaldi and the more popular classical composers. Even steely New Yorkers hunching toward nighttime destinations seem to relax, and occasionally they even join in the tune. Virtually everybody seems to sense that a mugger wouldn't be warbling bright, sunny selections from Vivaldi's *Four Seasons*. It is my equivalent of the cowbell that hikers wear when they know they are in bear country.

- No gesture has a universal meaning across all cultures. Gestures which signify approval in North America may be insults in other countries, and vice versa.

- **Personal space** is the distance someone wants between him- or herself and other people in ordinary, nonintimate interchanges.

- Studies in the United States have shown that touch is interpreted as power; more powerful people touch less powerful people.

- North Americans who believe that "time is money" are often frustrated in negotiations with people who want to establish a personal relationship before they decide whether to do business with each other or who measure time in 15- or 30-minute increments rather than the five-minute intervals North Americans are used to.

- In **monochronic** cultures, people do only one important activity at a time. The United States is monochronic. In **polychronic** cultures, people do several things at once.

NOTES

1. Thomas Kochman, *Black and White Styles in Conflict* (Chicago: University of Chicago Press, 1981), 44–45.

2. Laray M. Barna, "Stumbling Blocks in Intercultural Communication," in *Intercultural Communication,* ed. Larry A. Samovar and Richard E. Porter (Belmont, CA: Wadsworth Publishing, 1985), 331.

3. A. Jann Davis, *Listening and Responding* (St. Louis: C. V. Mosby, 1984), 43.

4. Edward T. Hall and William Foote Whyte, "Intercultural Communication: A Guide to Men of Action," *Human Organization* 19, no. 1 (Spring 1960): 7.

5. Carmen Judith Nine-Curt, "Hispanic-Anglo Conflicts in Nonverbal Communication," in *Perspectivas Pedagogicas,* ed. I. Abino et al. (Universidad de Puerto Rico, 1983), 235.

6. Laurence Wylie, *Beaux Gestes: A Guide to French Body Talk* (Cambridge, MA: Undergraduate Press, 1977), xi.

7. Marjorie Fink Vargas, *Louder than Words* (Ames: Iowa State University Press, 1986), 47.

8. Michael Argyle, *Bodily Communication* (New York: International University Press, 1975), 89.

9. Jerrold J. Merchant, "Korean Interpersonal Patterns: Implications for Korean/American Intercultural Communication," *Communication* 9 (October 1980): 65.

10. Argyle, 92.

11. Ray L. Birdwhistell, *Kinesics and Context: Essays on Body Motion Communication* (Philadelphia: University of Philadelphia Press, 1970), 30–31.

12. Edward T. Hall and Mildred Reed Hall, *Hidden Differences* (Hamburg, West Germany: Stern Magazine, 1983), 47.

13. Jack Seward, *The Japanese* (New York: William Morrow, 1972), 37.

14. Birdwhistell, 81.

15. Foseco Minsep, *The Business Traveller's Handbook: How to Get Along with People in 100 Countries* (Englewood Cliffs, NJ: Prentice-Hall, 1983), 30.

16. Paul Ekman, Wallace V. Friesen, and John Bear, "The International Language of Gestures," *Psychology Today* 18, no. 5 (May 1984): 64.

17. Nine-Curt, 234.

18. Merchant, 65.

19. Baxter, 1970, reported in Marianne LaFrance, "Gender Gestures: Sex, Sex-Role, and Nonverbal Communication," in *Gender and Nonverbal Behavior,* ed. Clara Mayo and Nancy M. Henley (New York: Springer-Verlag, 1981), 130.

20. Nine-Curt, 238.

21. Khamdi Amnatvong, interview with the author, Columbus, OH, August 1987.

* Quoted from Brent Staples, "Just Walk On By," *Ms.,* September 1986, 54, 88.

22. Brenda Major, "Gender Patterns in Touching Behavior," in *Gender and Nonverbal Behavior,* ed. Clara Mayo and Nancy M. Henley (New York: Springer-Verlag, 1981), 26, 28.

23. "Minor Memos," *The Wall Street Journal,* February 12, 1988, 1.

24. Natalie Porter and Florence Gies, "Women and Nonverbal Leadership Cues: When Seeing Is Not Believing," in *Gender and Nonverbal Behavior,* ed. Clara Mayo and Nancy M. Henley (New York: Springer-Verlag, 1981), 48–49.

25. Robert C. Christopher, *Second to None: American Companies in Japan* (New York: Crown Publishers, 1986), 102–03.

26. John Condon and Keisuke Kurata, *In Search of What's Japanese about Japan* (Tokyo: Shufunotomo Company, 1974), 77.

27. Christopher, 166–67.

28. Edward Twitchell Hall, *Hidden Differences: Doing Business with the Japanese* (Garden City, NY: Anchor-Doubleday, 1987), 25.

29. Lawrence B. Nadler, Marjorie Keeshan Nadler, and Benjamin J. Broome, "Culture and the Management of Conflict Situations," in *Communication, Culture, and Organizational Processes,* ed. William B. Gudykunst, Lea P. Stewart, and Stella Ting-Toomey (Beverly Hills: Sage Publications, 1985), 103.

30. Argyle, 90.

31. Mary Ritchie Key, *Paralanguage and Kinesics* (Metuchen, NJ: Scarecrow Press, 1975), 23.

32. Fred Hitzhusen, conversation with the author, January 31, 1988

33. Lisa Davis, "The Height Report: A Look at Stature and S·   *Columbus Dispatch,* January 19, 1988, E1, *New York Times* Special Featur·

EXERCISES AND PROBLEMS FOR CHAPTER 23

23–1 OBSERVING NONVERBAL COMMUNICATION

Observe nonverbal communication in one or more of the following situations:

1. Watch a TV show or a movie with the sound turned off. How much of the plot can you infer from nonverbal behavior?

2. Watch a professor or teaching assistant conducting class. Judging simply from nonverbal cues, how comfortable does the instructor seem to be with the material and the students? What nonverbal devices does the instructor use to emphasize points? To maintain the students' interest?

3. Watch the nonverbal behavior of students in a class. What cues suggest that students are paying attention? What cues suggest inattention? Based on nonverbal cues, what things are happening in addition to learning?

4. Sit in the waiting room of a doctor's office or a police station. What can you infer about people's problems from their posture?

As your instructor directs,
a. Share your results orally with a small group of students.
b. Present your findings orally to the class.
c. Summarize your findings in a memo to your instructor.
d. Join with other students in your class to write a group report.

23–2 DELIBERATELY VARYING YOUR OWN NONVERBAL BEHAVIOR

Deliberately change your own nonverbal behavior in one or more of the following ways. Unobtrusively, keep track of what you do and of the response you receive.

1. At the library, which seat do you normally take at an empty table? When one other person is at the table? Try taking a seat right next to someone at a table, even if other chairs are empty. How does the person respond to your closeness? How comfortable are you? What does this suggest about personal space in the library?

2. Vary aspects of your own nonverbal behavior when you're with your friends or family: standing further away or closer than you normally would, wearing different kinds of clothing than you normally wear, smiling more or less than you normally do, etc. How do others react to the changes?

3. Deliberately send nonverbal signals that say, "I'm very interested in what you're saying" to
a. An instructor.
b. A fellow student giving an oral presentation.
c. A family member.
d. A date.
Are your positive signals the same in these different situations?

As your instructor directs,
a. Share your findings orally with a small group of students.
b. Present your findings orally to the class.
c. Summarize your findings in a memo to your instructor.
d. Join with other students in your class to write a group report.

23–3 LEARNING ABOUT THE NONVERBAL BEHAVIOR OF ANOTHER CULTURE

Answer the following questions about nonverbal behavior in a specific country or culture. Use books, watch films, and interview people who have visited the country or are natives of the culture.

Body Language

1. What are acceptable ways for men to stand, sit, or squat during business meetings? What are acceptable ways for women to stand, sit, or squat?

2. What gestures have specific meanings in this culture?

3. Are people encouraged to show emotions? What emotions are acceptable for men to show in business situations? What emotions are acceptable for women to show in business situations? Do men and women show the same emotion in the same way? Is one sex considered more emotional than the other?

4. How would you greet
a. A new acquaintance to whom you are being introduced for the first time?

b. Someone you know slightly?

c. Your boss?

d. Someone who is a very good friend?

Would the answers change if the person were opposite-sex rather than same-sex?

Space

5. How close would men stand to other men? How close would women stand to other women? How close would men and women stand to each other? (Is the distance the same depending on whether the people are business colleagues, friends, or relatives?)

Time

6. How late could a person be to a business meeting before he or she would be considered rude?

7. During an appointment with one person, would it be polite to answer a phone call from someone else? To admit other people to the office who had different questions or concerns?

Miscellaneous

8. What would you wear to
   a. School (as a student)?
   b. A professional job?
   c. An informal party with people you don't know well?
   d. A formal party, dinner, or dance?
   How acceptable would it be to wear something different from what other people were wearing?

9. Are any colors or styles of clothing considered masculine or feminine? Young or old? Rich or poor?

10. Do middle-aged people in the culture prefer to look their age, look as young as possible, or look as old as possible?

As your instructor directs,

a. Share your results orally with a small group of students.

b. Present your findings orally to the class.

c. Summarize your findings in a memo to your instructor.

d. Join with other students in your class to write a group report.

Making Oral Presentations

QUESTIONS

- What purpose(s) does a speaker have in an oral presentation?
- How do oral presentations and written messages differ? What do they both do?
- What are the four components of an effective presentation?
- How do you plan a strategy for your presentation?
- How much information should you give your audience?
- How should you organize a presentation? How can you make the organization easy for the audience to follow?
- How should you deliver your talk?
- How can you be effective if you have to read a speech?
- How can you conquer stage fright?
- How should you handle questions from the audience?

Speak the speech, I pray you, . . . trippingly on the tongue. . . . do not saw the air too much with your hand, thus, but use all gently. . . .

William Shakespeare
Hamlet, 1603

amlet's advice about how to deliver the lines of a play applies to making oral presentations, too. Words need to come forth smoothly; gestures need to seem natural. But making a good oral presentation is more than just good delivery: it also involves developing a strategy that fits your audience and purpose, having good content, and organizing material effectively.

We can subdivide these categories into specific components of effective presentations:

Strategy

- Adapting ideas to audience's areas of acceptance, experience, and interests
- Using a strong opening and close
- Using visual aids or other devices to involve audience

Content

- Using specific, vivid supporting material and language
- Providing rebuttals to counterclaims or objections

Organization

- Providing an overview of main points
- Signposting main points in body of talk

Delivery

- Making direct eye contact with audience
- Using a conversational style
- Using voice and gestures effectively

The choices you make in each of these areas are affected by your purposes, the audience, and the situation.

PURPOSES IN ORAL PRESENTATIONS

Oral presentations can have the same three basic purposes that written documents have: to inform, to persuade, and to build goodwill. Like written messages, most oral presentations have more than one purpose.

Informative presentations inform or teach the audience. Training sessions in an organization are primarily informative. Secondary purposes may be to persuade new employees to follow organizational procedures, rather than doing something their own way, and to help them appreciate the organizational culture.

Persuasive presentations motivate the audience to act or to believe. Giving information and evidence is an important means of persuasion. In addition, the speaker must build goodwill by appearing to be credible and sympathetic to the audience's needs. The goal in many presentations is a favorable vote or decision. For example, speakers making business presentations may try to persuade the audience to approve their proposals, to adopt their ideas, or to buy their products. Sometimes the goal is to change behavior or attitudes or to reinforce existing attitudes. For example, a speaker at a junior high school assembly may try to persuade students not to use drugs. A speaker at a meeting of factory workers may stress the importance of following safety procedures. A speaker at a church meeting may talk about the problem of homelessness in the community and try to build support for community shelters for the homeless.

Goodwill presentations entertain and validate the audience. In an afterdinner speech, the audience wants to be entertained. Heavy technical information, serious problems, and challenges to the audience's initial position would be out of place. Presentations at sales meetings may be designed to stroke the audience's egos and to validate their commitment to organizational goals.

CHOOSING THE BEST CHANNEL

Sometimes your boss or circumstances will dictate whether you use writing or an oral presentation to convey your message. Sometimes you'll use both channels: written proposals and reports are almost always accompanied by oral presentations. But sometimes you may be able to choose which channel to use.

A written message makes it easier to

- Present extensive or complex financial data.
- Present many specific details of a law, policy, or procedure.
- Minimize undesirable emotions.

Oral messages make it easier to

- Use emotion to help persuade the audience.
- Focus the audience's attention on specific points.
- Answer questions, resolve conflicts, and build consensus.
- Modify a proposal that may not be acceptable in its original form.
- Get immediate action or response.

Oral and written messages have many similarities. In both, you should

- Adapt the message to the specific audience.
- Show the audience how they benefit from the idea, policy, service, or product.
- Overcome any objections the audience may have.
- Use you-attitude and positive emphasis.
- Use visuals to clarify or emphasize material.
- Specify exactly what the audience should do.

PLANNING A STRATEGY FOR YOUR PRESENTATION

A **strategy** is your plan for reaching your specific goals with a specific audience. Some strategic choices are common to all presentations; some vary depending on audience, purpose, and message.

---

*We're Running a Little Late . . .**
A story is told of the late Judge Vincent, one of several speakers on a banquet program years ago in Chicago. Although he had expected to be called upon shortly after eleven, it was almost two o'clock in the morning when the poor man's turn came. The toastmaster, the late Mayor Moses Handy, is reported to have introduced his Honor as follows:

"And now we come to the final speaker on this remarkable program. I would be only too happy to give him the laudatory introduction he so richly deserves, but because of the lateness of the hour, I do not wish to deprive the speaker of one moment of his allotted time, nor the ladies and gentlemen of the audience of a moment of their enjoyment. I shall therefore content myself with saying that Judge Vincent will now give his address."

The Judge arose and said, "My address is 2137 Calumet Avenue. Thank you and good night."

---

* Quoted from Steve Allen, *How to Make a Speech* (New York: McGraw-Hill, 1986), 82.

Busy People Want Facts, Not Frills*
Presenting technical information to
an audience of nonspecialists calls
for careful organizing. We usually
have a short time to explain complicated information, and every word
has to count. . . .

We strive for clarity in a number
of ways. First and most important,
we explain our research in terms
that our listeners care about. . . .
Instead of talking out the ins and
outs of new technologies themselves, we explain how these technologies will affect subjects like
unemployment, educational needs,
and international trade—the real
concerns of our clients, the senators
and representatives. We keep this in
focus by working backwards. First,
we ask ourselves what questions our
listeners will want to have answered. Will changing regulations
cause consumer telephone bills to
go up or down? . . . Will growing
uses of automation decrease jobs?
. . .

We also keep our talks clear and
brief by ruthlessly weeding out any
material that doesn't relate to the
four or five key points we're trying
to make. . . . We have to remember
that our listeners don't care a great
deal about the details of our professions: they're busy people who want
key facts and recommendations
without any frills, or even much
background, as long as they are
confident the background exists.

In all oral presentations, you must simplify what you want to say. Identify
the one idea you want the audience to take home. Simplify your supporting
detail so it's easy to follow. Simplify visuals so they can be taken in at a glance.
Simplify your words and sentences so they're easy to understand.

An oral presentation needs to be simpler than a written message to the same
audience. Readers don't need to hold ideas in their heads. If they forget a
point, they can turn back to it and reread the paragraph. Headings, paragraph
indentation, and punctuation provide visual cues to help readers understand
the message. Listeners, in contrast, must remember what the speaker says.
Whatever they don't remember is lost. Even asking questions requires the
audience to remember which points they don't understand.

Analyze your audience for an oral presentation just as you do for a written
message. If you'll be speaking to co-workers, talk to them about your topic
or proposal to find out what questions or objections they have. If you haven't
met your audience, ask the person who arranged the talk to tell you as much
as possible about the audience: How much do they already know about your
topic? How important is it to them? What opinions and values do they have?

Think about the physical conditions in which you'll be speaking. Will the
audience be tired at the end of a long day of listening? Sleepy after a big meal?
Will the group be large or small? The more you know about your audience,
the better you can adapt your message to the audience.

Adapting Your Ideas to the Audience

Measure the message you'd like to send against where your audience is now.
If your audience doesn't particularly care about your topic, or if listeners will
be skeptical or hostile, you need to present the part of your message which
the audience will find most interesting and easiest to accept.

Don't seek a major opinion change in a single oral presentation. If the
audience has already decided to hire some advertising agency, then a good
presentation can convince them that your agency is the one to hire. But if
you're talking to a small business which has always done its own ads, limit
your purpose. You may be able to prove that an agency can earn its fees by
doing things the owner can't do and by freeing the owner's time for other
activities. A second presentation may be needed to prove that an ad agency
can do a *better* job than the small business could do on its own. Only after
the audience is receptive should you try to persuade the audience to hire your
agency rather than a competitor.

Make your ideas relevant to your audience by linking what you have to say
to their experiences and interests. Showing your audience that the topic affects
them directly is the most effective strategy. When you can't do that, at least
link the topic to some everyday experience.

> When was the last time you were hungry? Maybe you remember being hungry
> while you were on a diet, or maybe you had to work late at a lab and didn't
> get back to the dorm in time for dinner.
>
> Speech about world hunger to an audience of
> college students

Planning a Strong Opening and Close

The beginning and end of a presentation, like the beginning and end of a
written document, are positions of emphasis. Use those key positions to interest

---

* Quoted from Fred W. Weingarten, Program Manager, U.S. Congress Office of Technology
Assessment, in Ronald B. Adler, *Communicating at Work* (New York: Random House, 1987),
297.

the audience and emphasize your key point. You'll sound more natural and more effective if you talk from notes but write out your opener and close in advance and memorize them. (They'll be short: just a sentence or two.)

Consider using one of the four modes for openers that appeared in Chapter 16: startling statement, narration or anecdote, questions, or quotation. The more you can do to personalize your opener for your audience, the better. Recent events are better than things that happened long ago; local events are better than events at a distance; people they know are better than people who are only names.

1. Startling Statement

Twelve of our customers have cancelled orders in the past month.

This presentation to a company's executive committee went on to show that the company's distribution system was inadequate and to recommend a third warehouse located in the southwest.

2. Narration or Anecdote

A mother was having difficulty getting her son up for school. He pulled the covers over his head.

"I'm not going to school," he said. "I'm not ever going again."

"Are you sick?" his mother asked.

"No," he answered. "I'm sick of school. They hate me. They call me names. They make fun of me. Why should I go?"

"I can give you two good reasons," the mother replied. "The first is that you're 42 years old. And the second is *you're the school principal.*[1]

This speech to a seminar for educators went on to discuss "the three knottiest problems in education today." Educators had to face those problems; they couldn't hide under the covers.

3. Question

Are you going to have enough money to do the things you want to when you retire?

This presentation to a group of potential clients discussed the value of using the services of a professional financial planner to achieve one's goals for retirement.

4. Quotation

According to Towers Perrin, the profits of Fortune 100 companies would be 25% lower—they'd go down $17 billion—if their earnings statements listed the future costs companies are obligated to pay for retirees' health care.

This presentation on options for health care for retired employees urged executives to start now to investigate options to cut the future cost.

Humor in the Opener. Your opener should interest the audience and establish a rapport with them. Some speakers use humor to achieve those goals. However, most humor puts someone down. An inappropriate joke can turn the audience against the speaker. Never use humor that's directed against the audience. The following quip, used in a speech to the Economic Club of Detroit, puts down the very audience the speaker is trying to put at ease:

I must confess that I was a trifle daunted by the prospect of addressing an organization called "The Economic Club of Detroit." But then I recalled a def-

---

Making Financial Presentations*

When you present financial information to management, follow these guidelines:

- Limit the presentation to information the audience needs and wants.
- Use the data to tell a story. Point out trends and aberrations from the norm.
- Use several simple visuals rather than one complicated one.
- In your visuals, use words rather than numbers when possible: *54 million* instead of *54,000,000.* Round off figures to two numbers. Use *520,000* rather than *519,607* unless the precise number is crucial.
- Use normal business language. Keep accounting jargon to a minimum. Define any terms that your audience won't understand.
- Make the presentation interesting. Financial presentations in particular have a reputation for being boring.

---

* Based on Martha Jewett and Rita Margolies, eds., *How to Run Better Business Meetings: A Reference Guide for Managers* (New York: McGraw-Hill, 1987), 179–84.

inition of an economist given by a professor of mine at Amherst many years ago. "An economist is someone who deals with numbers but doesn't have the personality to be an accountant."[2]

Maybe an economist could get away with saying that. But it's deadly for someone who isn't part of a group to criticize it.

In contrast, speakers who can make fun of themselves almost always succeed:

It's both a privilege and a pressure to be here.[3]

Humor isn't the only way to set an audience at ease. Smile at your audience before you begin; let them see that you're a real person and a nice one.

Options for Your Close. The end of your presentation should be as strong as the opener. For your close, you could do one or more of the following: (1) restate your main point; (2) refer to your opener to create a frame for your presentation; (3) end with a vivid, positive picture; (4) tell the audience exactly what to do to solve the problem you've discussed.

Using Visuals and Other Devices to Involve the Audience

Plan ways to involve your audience as you speak. People's minds will wander; you need to provide hooks to bring them back in.

Visuals for oral presentations need to be simple. Break a complicated point down into several visuals. In a written message, you'd use visuals only to clarify or emphasize material. In an oral presentation, in addition to these visuals, most audiences also accept decorative visuals. **Decorative visuals** illustrate the speaker's points and make them more memorable.

Check to make sure that your visuals are accurate both literally and by implication. The visual in Figure 24.1 is misleading: the arrow makes it appear that computers comprise not 50% but nearly 100% of sales. A reader who takes the time to examine a visual on paper can tell whether it presents the data accurately. But an audience which sees a slide for 60 seconds or less doesn't have a chance to subject the visual to scrutiny.

One study showed that presenters using overhead transparencies were perceived as "better prepared, more professional, more persuasive, more credible, and more interesting" than speakers who did not use visuals. They were also more likely to persuade a group to adopt their recommendations.[4] A study comparing the use of different kinds of visuals found that presenters using slides appeared more professional, but presenters using overhead transparencies seemed more interesting. Colored overhead transparencies were most effective in persuading people to act.[5]

Visuals work only if the technology they depend on works. When you give presentations in your own office, check the equipment in advance. When you make a presentation in another location or for another organization, arrive early so that you'll have time not only to check the equipment but also to

---

* Based on John C. Condon, "Introduction: A Perspective for the Conference," *Intercultural Encounters with Japan: Communication—Contact and Conflict,* ed. John C. Condon and Mitsuko Saito (Tokyo: Simul Press, 1974), 3 and John C. Condon and Fathi Yousef, *An Introduction to Intercultural Communication* (Indianapolis: Bobbs-Merrill, 1975), 25.

† Quoted from A. T. Pilley, in Masumi Muramatsu, "Symposium on Conference Interpreting and Problems in Translation," *Intercultural Encounters with Japan: Communication—Contact and Conflict,* ed. John C. Condon and Mitsuko Saito (Tokyo: Simul Press, 1974), 220.

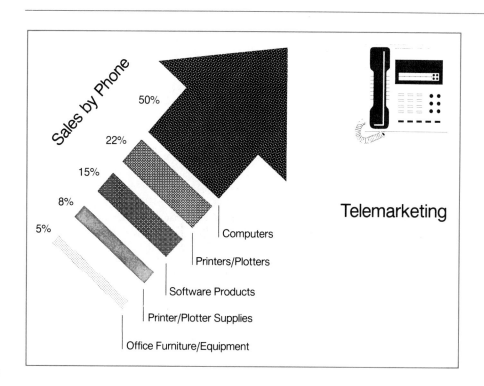

FIGURE 24.1
A MISLEADING VISUAL

track down a service worker if the equipment isn't working. Be prepared with a backup plan to use if you're unable to show your slides or videotape.

You can also involve the audience by asking people to raise their hands or to stand up. A speaker who was trying to raise funds used the simple act of asking people to stand to involve them, to create emotional appeal, and to make a statistic vivid:

> [A speaker] was talking to a luncheon club about contributing to the relief of an area that had been hit by a tornado. The news report said that 70% of the people had been killed or disabled. The room was set up ten people at each round table. He asked three persons at each table to stand. Then he said, ". . . You people sitting are dead or disabled. You three standing have to take care of the mess. You'd need help, wouldn't you?[6]

In an informative presentation, link the points you make to the knowledge your audience has. Show the audience that your information answers their questions or solves their problems. Show them how it will help them do their jobs. When you explain the effect of a new law or the techniques for using a new machine, use specific examples that apply to the decisions they make and the work they do.

If your content is detailed or complicated (as it may be, for example, in a training session), give people a written outline or handouts. The written material both helps the audience keep track of your points during the presentation and serves as a reference after the talk is over.

We Tried to Plan for Everything*
[Two advertisers from Ogilvy and Mather] visited a remote Caribbean island to make a pitch for their tourism business. . . . [We were told that our film projector was too heavy for the small plane on the last leg of the trip.]

The film projector at the Ministry of Tourism chewed up our film and spit it out in the middle of the presentation, so we turned to our slides. "Now," Charlie said, "I want to show you what we have done for our client, TWA." He pressed a button, and there was the photo of a TWA 747, upside down.

---

* Quoted from Jane Maas, *Adventures of an Advertising Woman* (New York: St. Martin's Press, 1986), 80.

"As Someone Famous Probably
Once Said . . . "*

A speaker or writer should never
trust his memory to give him an accurate quote or attribution. For example, Delta Airlines has a radio
commercial that begins, "Mark
Twain said, 'Everybody talks about
the weather but nobody does anything about it.'" . . . It was actually
Charles Dudley Warner, a friend of
Mark Twain and editor of the
Hartford Courant, who made the
statement. . . .

Leo Durocher, baseball manager
of the 1940s and '50s, supposedly
said, "Nice guys finish last." Durocher got tired of denying he ever
said it. Actually, sportswriter Jimmy
Cannon wrote the phrase in a story
discussing Durocher's philosophy.

Another sports great, Vince Lom-
bardi, became coach of the Green
Bay Packers in 1959. I can remember on several occasions a quotation
being attributed to him: "Winning
is not everything; it's the only
thing." Imagine my surprise when I
was watching "Trouble Along the
Way," a 1953 John Wayne movie
about college football that played
on television recently. In the movie,
Wayne is a tough coach. One of his
colleagues quotes the Wayne character as saying, "Winning isn't
everything; it's the only thing."

Such examples prove that the origin of any quote should be re-
garded with suspicion until it is
proven. Cautious writers and speakers may, therefore, wish to take the
advice of George Bernard Shaw: "I
often quote myself; it adds spice to
my conversation."

CHOOSING INFORMATION TO INCLUDE IN A PRESENTATION

Choose the information that is most interesting to your audience and that answers the questions your audience will have. Limit your talk to three to five main points. In a long presentation (20 minutes or more) each main point can have subpoints. Your content will be easier to understand if you clearly show the relationship between each of the main points. Turning your information into a story also helps. For example, a controller might turn charts of financial data into the following story:

> The increase in sales income is offset by an increase in manufacturing costs. A breakdown of manufacturing costs shows that the cost of material is out of line. A further breakdown shows that the costs of materials for product #503 tripled last month. An analysis of the three shifts shows that the cost of materials jumped 800% on the second shift. Now, the problem is to find out why the second shift uses so much more material than the other shifts making the same product.[7]

Back up each point with solid support. Statistics and numbers can be convincing if you present them in ways that are easy to hear. Simplify numbers by reducing them to two significant digits.

Hard to hear:	If the national debt were in pennies, it would take 17,006,802,720 people, each carrying 100 pounds of pennies, to carry all of our debt.
Easier to hear:	If the national debt were in pennies, it would take 17 billion people, each carrying 100 pounds of pennies, to carry all of our debt.[8]

Quotations or appeals to authority can work, as long as you cite authorities whom your audience genuinely respects. Often you'll need to paraphrase a quote to put it into simple language that's easy to understand.

Demonstrations can prove your points dramatically and quickly. During the investigation of the *Challenger* disaster, the late physicist Richard Feynman asked for a glass of water. When it came, he put a piece of the space shuttle's O-ring into the cold water. After less than a minute, he took it out and pinched it with a small clamp. The material kept the pinched shape when the clamp came off. The material couldn't return to its original shape.[9] A technical explanation could have made the same point: the O-ring couldn't function in the cold. But the demonstration was fast and easy to understand. It didn't require that the audience follow complex chemical or mathematical formulas. In an oral presentation, seeing is believing.

To be convincing, you must answer the audience's questions and objections. In an oral presentation, you can do that straightforwardly:

> Some people think that working women are less reliable than men. But the facts show that women take fewer sick days than men do.

However, don't bring up negatives or inconsistencies unless you're sure that the audience will think of them. If you aren't sure, save your evidence for the question phase. If someone does ask, you'll have the answer.

---

*   Quoted from Kenneth L. Calkins, "'As Someone Famous Probably Once Said . . . ,'" *The Wall Street Journal*, January 7, 1988, 16.

ORGANIZING YOUR INFORMATION

Most presentations use a direct pattern of organization, even when the goal is to persuade a reluctant audience. In a business setting, the audience is in a hurry and knows that you want to persuade them. Be honest about your goals, and then prove that your goal meets the audience's needs too.

In a persuasive presentation, start with your strongest point, your best reason. If time permits, give other reasons as well and respond to possible objections. Put your weakest point in the middle so that you can end on a strong note. Sometimes the best way to convince your audience is to show them that the other obvious alternatives won't work. When the other alternatives are eliminated, your solution is easier to accept.

Make your organization clear to your audience. A reader who misses a point can reread a paragraph, but listeners can't. Furthermore, written documents can use headings, paragraphs, lists, and indentations to signal levels of detail. In a presentation, you have to provide more explicit clues to the structure of your discourse. These clues help a careful listener follow what you say; they enable someone who's missed one point to get back on track for the next point.

Early in your talk—perhaps immediately after your opener—provide an **overview of the main points** you will make.

> First, I'd like to talk about who the homeless in Columbus are. Second, I'll talk about the services The Open Shelter provides. Finally, I'll talk about what you—either individually or as a group—can do to help.

An overview provides a mental peg that hearers can hang each point on. It also can prevent someone's missing what you are saying because he or she wonders why you aren't covering a major point which you've saved for later.[10]

Offer a clear signpost as you come to each new point. A **signpost** is an explicit statement of the point you have reached. Choose wording that fits your style. The following statements are four different ways that a speaker could use to introduce the last of three points:

- Now we come to the third point: what you can do as a group or as individuals to help homeless people in Columbus.
- So much for what we're doing. Now let's talk about what you can do to help.
- You may be wondering, what can I do to help?
- As you can see, the Shelter is trying to do many things. We could do more things with your help.

DELIVERING AN EFFECTIVE PRESENTATION

Audiences want the sense that you're talking directly to them and that you care that they understand and are interested. They'll forgive you if you get tangled up in a sentence and end it ungrammatically. They won't forgive you if you seem to have a "canned" talk that you're going to deliver no matter who's in the audience or how they respond. You can convey a sense of caring to your audience by making direct eye contact with them and by using a conversational style.

Organizing Presentations for the Chinese*

While American communicators are trained to develop a message with an introduction, central point, body, and conclusion, Chinese may have a different structure to a message.

KI	(an introduction offering an observation of a concrete reality.)
SHO	(tell a story.)
TEN	(shift or change in which a new topic is brought into the message.)
KETSU	(gathering of loose ends, a "nonconclusion.")
YO-IN	(a last point to think about, which does not necessarily relate.)

The audience, then, is allowed to draw its own conclusion; a central point is not presented in such a structure.

---

* Quoted from Andrew D. Wolvin and Caroline Gwynn Oakley, *Listening* (Dubuque, IA: Wm. C. Brown, 1985), 35.

Finding Your Best Speaking Voice*
Each person's voice has an optimum pitch or key. . . . Soprano and tenor voices, for example, have higher optimum pitches than contralto and bass voices. The best speaking voice has the optimum pitch as its center. . . .

The optimum pitch can be located by following these directions: (1) close your ears with your fingers and hum up and down the scale until you find the pitch where the hum sounds loudest or most vibrant to you. This pitch will be near your optimum pitch. (2) Sing down the scale as far as you can go without forcing. Call this note *do* and sing up the scale to *sol*. This note will be near you optimum pitch. (3) If you have a piano, locate the lowest note you can produce and also your highest falsetto note. Your optimum pitch will be approximately one fourth of the distance from your lowest note.

Using Eye Contact

Look directly at the people you're talking to. In one study, speakers who looked more at the audience during a seven-minute informative speech were judged to be better informed, more experienced, more honest, and friendlier than speakers who delivered the same information with less eye contact.[11] An earlier study found that speakers judged "sincere" looked at the audience 63% of the time, while those judged "insincere" looked at the audience only 21% of the time.[12]

The point in making eye contact is to establish one-to-one contact with the individual members of your audience. People want to feel that you're talking to them. Looking directly at individuals also enables you to be more conscious of feedback from the audience, so that you can modify your approach if necessary.

Developing a Good Speaking Voice

People will enjoy your presentation more if your voice is easy to listen to. To find out what your voice sounds like, tape record it. Also tape the voices of people on TV or on campus whose voices you like and imitate them. In a few weeks, tape yourself again.

When you speak to a group, talk loudly enough so that people can hear you easily. If you're using a microphone, adjust your volume so you aren't shouting. When you speak in an unfamiliar location, try to get to the room early so you can check the size of the room and the power of the amplification equipment. If you don't have time to try out a few sample sentences before the audience arrives, ask early in your talk, "Can you hear me in the back of the room?"

Vary your volume, pitch, and speed. Sound energetic and enthusiastic. If your ideas don't excite you, why should your audience find them exciting?

The bigger the group is, the more slowly you need to speak and the more carefully you need to **enunciate**, that is, voice all the sounds of each word. Sound takes time to travel through a large room. Careful enunciation helps the audience hear what you say.

Using Notes

Unless you're giving a very short presentation, you'll probably want to use notes. Even experts use notes. The more you know about the subject, the greater the temptation to add relevant points that occur to you as you talk. Adding an occasional point can help to clarify something for the audience, but adding too many points will destroy your outline and put you over the time limit.

Put your notes on cards: they're easier to hold than large, flimsy sheets of paper. Most speakers like to use 4" by 6" or 5" by 7" cards because they hold more information. Your notes need to be complete enough to help you if you go blank, so use long phrases or complete sentences. Under each main point, jot down the evidence or illustration you'll use. Indicate where you'll refer to visuals.

Look at your notes infrequently. Most of your gaze time should be directed to members of the audience. Hold your notes high enough so that your head doesn't bob up and down like a yo-yo as you look from the audience to your notes and back again.

---

*   Quoted from George W. Fluharty and Harold R. Ross, *Public Speaking* (New York: Barnes & Noble, 1981), 162–63.

Reading a Speech

Giving a presentation from notes is almost always more effective than reading a speech. Read a speech only if you have a tight, inflexible time limit or if you are speaking about a controversial subject and want to be sure that you don't say anything that could later be used against you. In other situations, even if you must give a written paper to the press or to the conference organizers, it's still better to talk from an outline.

If you must read a speech,

- Use short who-does-what sentences with simple words. Write your speech in oral style, not written style.
- Triple-space your text so you can find your place easily.
- Type the text only half way down the page, so you don't bob your head up and down as you look from the audience to the text and back again.
- Mark your text with colored pens to indicate phrasing, speed, volume, and places to pause for a breath.
- Carry the text to the podium in a thin box so the audience isn't dismayed by the thick sheaf of papers that results from triple-spacing and using only half the page.
- As you read, make a special effort to vary pitch, volume, and speed so you sound as if you're thinking as you speak.

Dealing with Fear

The Book of Lists claims that more people fear giving oral reports than they fear anything else—even snakes.[13]

To calm your nerves as you prepare to give an oral presentation,

- Be prepared. Analyze your audience, organize your thoughts, prepare visual aids, practice your opener and close, check out the arrangements.
- Use only the amount of caffeine you normally use. More or less may make you jumpy.
- Avoid alcoholic beverages.
- Use positive emphasis to relabel your nerves. Instead of saying, "I'm scared," try saying, "My adrenaline is up." Adrenaline sharpens your reflexes and helps you do your best.

HANDLING QUESTIONS

Welcome the chance to answer questions. Treat questions as opportunities to give more detailed information than you had time to give in your presentation. People need to have their anxieties and fears answered before they can endorse your proposal. Sometimes their fears may make their questions sound more hostile than the people themselves are.

Prepare for questions by listing every fact or opinion you can think of that challenges your position. Many of these will come from your initial analysis when you asked people how they felt about your idea. Treat each objection

Dealing with Interruptions*

A presentation can be interrupted.

If the interruption is minor, humor can release the audience's tension. The microphone went dead while Robert Orben, former White House humor writer, was giving a speech. When its power was restored, Orben said, "For a while there I was beginning to feel like Marcel Marceau."

If the interruption is major, a more serious comment is called for. At 5 A.M., a speaker was awakened by the fire alarm in her hotel. She headed down the stairs, only to be turned back by a hotel staffer telling guests that everything was under control. As she looked at her hands, she realized that all she had with her were her room key, her passport, and her wedding ring.

While she was speaking to 250 people later that morning, the alarm sounded again. She told the audience where the exits were and said, "You may stay or leave—but I'm leaving." Again it was a false alarm. When everyone reconvened, she told about her early morning exit, the three things that she wanted to save then, and her feeling of responsibility for the lives of the audience. "Let us hope the few minutes we lost from this session renew in us a sense of what we cherish most in our lives and in our work. Now let us get back to business."

* Based on Roy Alexander, *Power Speech: Why It's Vital to You* (New York: AMACOM, 1986), 195 and Margaret McAuliffe Bedrosian, *Speak Like a Pro* (New York: John Wiley, 1987), 136–37.

Being Interviewed by the Press*

CEOs and community leaders are frequently interviewed by the press. To appear your best on camera, on tape, or in a story,

• Try to find out in advance why you're being interviewed and what information the reporter wants.

• Practice answering possible questions in a single sentence. A long answer is likely to be cut for TV or radio news.

• Talk slowly. You'll have time to think, the audience will have more time to understand what you're saying, and a reporter taking notes will record your words more accurately.

seriously and try to think of a way to deal with it. If you're talking about a controversial issue, you may want to save one point for the question period, rather than making it during the presentation. Speakers who have visuals to answer questions seem especially well prepared.

During your presentation, tell the audience how you'll handle questions. If you have a choice, save questions for the end. In your talk, answer the questions or objections that you expect your audience to have. Don't exaggerate your claims so that you won't have to back down in response to questions later.

During the question period, don't nod your head to indicate that you understand a question as it is asked. Audiences will interpret nods as signs that you agree with the questioner. Instead, look directly at the questioner. As you answer the question, expand your focus to take in the entire group.

If the audience may not have heard the question or if you want more time to think, repeat the question before you answer it. Link your answers to the points you made in your presentation. Keep the purpose of your presentation in mind, and select information that advances your goals.

If a question is hostile or biased, rephrase it before you answer it. "You're asking whether. . . . " Or suggest an alternative: "I think there are problems with both the positions you describe. It seems to me that a third solution which is better than either of them is. . . . "

Occasionally someone will ask a question which is really designed to state the speaker's own position. Respond to the question if you want to. Another option is to say, "I'm not sure what you're asking" or even "That's a clear statement of your position. Let's move to the next question now." If someone asks about something that you already explained in your presentation, simply answer the question without embarrassing the questioner. No audience will understand and remember 100% of what you say.

If you don't know the answer to a question, say so. If your purpose is to inform, write down the question so that you can look up the answer before the next session. If it's a question to which you think there is no answer, ask if anyone in the room knows. When no one does, your "ignorance" is vindicated. If an expert is in the room, you may want to refer questions of fact to him or her. Answer questions of interpretation yourself.

At the end of the question period, take two minutes to summarize your main point once more. (This can be a restatement of your close.) Questions may or may not focus on the key point of your talk. Take advantage of having the floor to repeat your message briefly and forcefully.

SUMMARY OF KEY POINTS

• **Informative presentations** inform or teach the audience. **Persuasive presentations** motivate the audience to act or to believe. **Goodwill presentations** entertain and validate the audience. Most oral presentations have more than one purpose.

• A written message makes it easier to present extensive or complex information and to minimize undesirable emotions. Oral messages make it easier to use emotion, to focus the audience's attention, to answer questions and resolve conflicts quickly, to modify a proposal that may not be acceptable in its original form, and to get immediate action or response.

*   Based on James L. Graham, "What to Do When a Reporter Calls," *IABC Communication World*, April 1985, 15.

- In both oral and written messages, you should
  - Adapt the message to the specific audience.
  - Show the audience how they benefit from the idea, policy, service, or product.
  - Overcome any objections the audience may have.
  - Use you-attitude and positive emphasis.
  - Use visuals to clarify or emphasize material.
  - Specify exactly what the audience should do.
- An oral presentation needs to be simpler than a written message to the same audience.
- Adapt your message to your audience's areas of acceptance, experience, and interests.
- Use the beginning and end of the presentation to interest the audience and emphasize your key point.
- Using visuals makes a speaker seem more prepared, more interesting, and more persuasive.
- Use a direct pattern of organization. Put your strongest reason first.
- Limit your talk to three to five main points. Early in your talk—perhaps immediately after your opener—provide an **overview of the main points** you will make. Offer a clear signpost as you come to each new point. A **signpost** is an explicit statement of the point you have reached.
- Convey a sense of caring to your audience by making direct eye contact with them and by using a conversational style.
- To calm your nerves as you prepare to give an oral presentation,
  - Be prepared. Analyze your audience, organize your thoughts, prepare visual aids, practice your opener and close, check out the arrangements.
  - Use only the amount of caffeine you normally use. More or less may make you jumpy.
  - Avoid alcoholic beverages.
  - Relabel your nerves. Instead of saying, "I'm scared," try saying, "My adrenaline is up." Adrenaline sharpens your reflexes and helps you do your best.
- Read a speech only if you have an inflexible time limit or if you are speaking about a controversial subject and want to be sure that you don't say anything that could later be used against you.
- Treat questions as opportunities to give more detailed information than you had time to give in your presentation. Link your answers to the points you made in your presentation.
- Repeat the question before you answer it if the audience may not have heard it or if you want more time to think. Rephrase hostile or biased questions before you answer them.

NOTES

1. Ray Alexander, *Power Speech: Why It's Vital to You* (New York: AMACOM, 1986), 156.
2. Edward N. Ney, Chairman and President, Young & Rubicam, The Economic Club of Detroit, April 19, 1982; quoted in *The Executive Speaker* advertising flyer.
3. Robert S. Mills, conversation with the author, March 10, 1988.

4. "A Study of the Effects of the Use of Overhead Transparencies on Business Meetings," Wharton Applied Research Center, reported in Martha Jewett and Rita Margolies, eds., *How to Run Better Business Meetings: A Reference Guide for Managers* (New York: McGraw-Hill, 1987), 109–10.

5. University of Minnesota/3M Study, reported in Jewett and Margolies, 115.

6. Edward J. Hegarty, *Humor and Eloquence in Public Speaking* (West Nyack, NY: Parker Publishing, 1976), 204.

7. Based on Jewett and Margolies, 183–85.

8. The comparison is taken from Jim Martin, "National Debt: Pennies to Heaven," *The Wall Street Journal,* February 22, 1988, 18.

9. Andy Rooney, "World Has Lost Mental Magician," Tribune Media Syndicate, *Columbus Dispatch,* February 22, 1988, 7A.

10. Some studies have shown that previews and reviews increase comprehension; other studies have found no effect. For a summary of the research see Kenneth D. Frandsen and Donald R. Clement, "The Functions of Human Communication in Informing: Communicating and Processing Information," *Handbook of Rhetorical and Communication Theory,* ed. Carroll C. Arnold and John Waite Bowers (Boston: Allyn & Bacon, 1984), 340–41.

11. S. A. Beebe, "Eye Contact: A Nonverbal Determinant of Speaker Credibility," *Speech Teacher* 23 (1974): 21–25; cited in Marjorie Fink Vargas, *Louder than Words* (Ames: Iowa State University Press, 1986), 61–62.

12. J. Wills, "An Empirical Study of the Behavioral Characteristics of Sincere and Insincere Speakers," Ph.D. diss, University of Southern California, 1961; cited in Marjorie Fink Vargas, *Louder than Words* (Ames: Iowa State University Press, 1986), 62.

13. D. Wallechinsky et al., *The Book of Lists* (New York: Bantam Books, 1977), 469.

EXERCISES AND PROBLEMS FOR CHAPTER 24

24–1 DECIDING WHETHER TO USE AN ORAL OR A WRITTEN MESSAGE

In each of the following situations, would an oral presentation or a written message be more effective? Why?

a. You want to persuade your organization to buy the hardware and software for desktop publishing so that the Communications Department can produce the company newsletter. Although an up-front investment of $20,000 will be needed, it should pay for itself in three years. The executive committee must approve all major expenditures.

b. You want to persuade your organization to change the way new employees are taught about safety and company procedures. Your proposal will affect every department. The directors of Personnel and of Education and Training are worried that a change would be difficult to implement and make more work for them. The director of Safety favors your idea, feeling that it would reduce on-the-job accidents. The director of Quality Control will support your proposal if it reduces the number of defective parts. Supervisors wonder whether their authority will be increased or reduced.

c. You want to teach employees how to improve their listening skills.

d. You want to teach new employees how to fill out expense vouchers.

e. You want to tell parents in your school district about the new redistricting plan. District lines are controversial; the new plan has been the subject of speculation and of impassioned letters to the newspaper editor even though you have not yet announced it.

f. You want to tell the members of a synagogue about the city's shelter for the homeless. You hope that at a minimum they will support tax dollars being spent on the shelter; ideally, you'd like individuals to donate money or time.

g. You want to tell employees that now they can be reimbursed for tuition and books for courses that enable them to do their current jobs more effectively or for courses that would prepare them for higher-level jobs in the company. Employees have been asking for a program like this for some time.

h. You want to persuade the day care center on whose Board of Directors you serve to revise its fee schedule so that fees are based on parents' ability to pay.

i. You want to persuade the City Council to reduce the speed limit in your subdivision.

24–2 WRITING OPENERS AND CLOSES

Write three possible openers and three possible closes for a presentation on one of the following:

a. The best class you've taken so far
   (1) For an audience of students in your field
   (2) For an audience of faculty interested in improving education
   (3) For a committee choosing "The Best Instructor" Award

b. An evaluation of a stock for investment
   (1) For brokers recommending investments to clients
   (2) For an investment club of people interested in the stock market
   (3) For an organization that is investing its pension fund

c. The results of your own research
   (1) For the group that would have the power to implement your recommendations
   (2) For an audience of your classmates
   (3) For an alumni association meeting

24–3 MAKING A SHORT ORAL PRESENTATION

As your instructor directs, make a short (two- to five-minute) presentation on one of the following topics:

a. Describe the best course you've taken so far. What made it a good course? Should everyone try to take it?

b. Describe the best teacher you've had so far. What made the instructor good? Would every student agree with your evaluation?

c. Describe a sport or extracurricular activity that you enjoy. Why do you like it? Should others try it too?

d. Evaluate a stock as an investment. Describe your criteria for evaluation. Should investors buy now? Why or why not?

e. Make a short presentation based on another problem in this book.

1–2   Introduce yourself to the class.

1–5   Describe your experience in and knowledge of business.

9–6   Explain a technical term in your field.

9–8   Discuss the business slang used in a particular organization.

12–3   Make a presentation to "employees" announcing a new suggestion system.

12–11   Explain an accounting concept to your class.

15–3   Persuade students in your class to use the services of the writing skills lab on campus.

16–2   Evaluate a sales letter.

17–2   Evaluate a fund-raising letter.

19–6   Discuss the status of handicapped parking in your state.

21–4   Persuade the "appropriate group" to allow you to undertake research on a topic.

24–5   Evaluate an oral presentation.

24–6   Evaluate the way a speaker handled questions.

26–1   Tell the class in detail about one of your accomplishments.

26–4   Discuss an organization you'd like to work for.

C–21   Persuade students in your class to use the campus recreation facilities.

24–4 MAKING A LONGER ORAL PRESENTATION

As your instructor directs, make a 5- to 12-minute presentation on one or more of the following. For each, use visuals to make your talk effective.

a. Use another problem in this book as the basis for your presentation.

1–1   Report on the writing done by someone in business or administration.

3–2   Compare two software programs.

3–4   Report on the use of electronic mail on your campus.

5–1   Describe the composing process(es) of a writer in business or administration.

5–3   Describe your own composing process(es).

6–4   Analyze the students in your college.

6–7   Analyze the employees in a place where you've worked.

9–9   Discuss the kinds of changes you make as you edit your own papers.

9–10   Report on the readability levels of your papers, a textbook, a set of instructions, or a newspaper article.

11–3   Evaluate the visuals in three issues of a newspaper or magazine.

12–5   Make a presentation to "The Board of Directors" persuading them to require that all written materials produced by the organization use nonsexist language in all written materials produced by the company.

14–15   Make a presentation to "business people" to persuade them to adopt a school.

20–2   Summarize the results of a survey you have conducted.

20–5   Discuss the kind of training needed to prepare students to enter the job market in your city.

22–6   Summarize the results of your research.

26–5   Summarize what you learned in an information interview.

29–1   Discuss the kinds of questions currently being asked of job applicants in campus interviews at your school.

29–2   Summarize what you learned by interviewing an interviewer.

C–8   Describe an organization's communication environment.

24–5 EVALUATING ORAL PRESENTATIONS

Evaluate an oral presentation given by a classmate or given by a speaker on your campus. Use the following categories:

Strategy

1. Adapting ideas to audience's area of acceptance, experience, and interests

2. Using a strong opening and close

3. Using visual aids or other devices to involve audience

Content

4. Using specific, vivid supporting material and language

5. Providing rebuttals to counterclaims or objections

Organization

6. Providing an overview of main points

7. Signposting main points in body of talk

Delivery

8. Making direct eye contact with audience

9. Using a conversational style
10. Using voice and gestures effectively

As your instructor directs,
a. Fill out a form indicating your evaluation in each of the 10 areas.
b. Share your evaluation orally with the speaker.
c. Write a memo to the speaker evaluating the presentation. Send a copy of your memo to your instructor.

24–6 EVALUATING THE WAY A SPEAKER HANDLES QUESTIONS

Listen to a speaker talking about a controversial subject. (Go to a talk on campus or in town, or watch a speaker on a TV show like "Face the Nation" or "60 Minutes.") Observe the way he or she handles questions.

About how many questions does the speaker answer?

What is the format for asking and answering questions?

Are the answers clear? Responsive to the question?

Something that could be quoted without embarrassing the speaker and the organization he or she represents?

How does the speaker handle hostile questions? Does the speaker avoid getting angry? Does the speaker retain control of the meeting? How?

If some questions were not answered well, what (if anything) could the speaker have done to leave a better impression?

Did the answers leave the audience with a more or less positive impression of the speaker? Why?

As your instructor directs,
a. Share your evaluation with a small group of students.
b. Present your evaluation formally to the class.
c. Summarize your evaluation in a memo to your instructor.

24–7 SIMPLIFYING MATERIAL FOR AN ORAL PRESENTATION

Take an annual report or other extensive financial data.

As your instructor directs,
a. Give a three- to five-minute presentation based on some part of the data.
b. Create three visuals that make the data easier to understand.

Interpersonal and Group Dynamics

QUESTIONS

- How can you become a more effective listener? What kinds of responses block communication?
- How can differences in conversational style lead to miscommunication?
- What are steps in resolving conflicts?
- What are nondefensive ways to respond to criticism?
- How does a speaker use you-attitude in a conflict?
- What phases does a group go through? What kinds of communication are needed in each phase?
- What makes student groups successful in completing class assignments?
- How can a group minimize the danger of groupthink?
- How can meetings be made more productive?

Small groups are, quite simply, the basic organizational building blocks of excellent companies.

Thomas J. Peters and Robert H. Waterman, Jr.
In Search of Excellence, 1982

I n most jobs, the ability to get along with other people and to work in groups is crucial to success. **Interpersonal communication** is communication that focuses on the relationships between people. Interpersonal skills such as listening and dealing with conflict are used in one-to-one interchanges, in groups, and in personal relationships. These skills will make you more successful on the job, in social groups, and in community service and volunteer work.

Some people seem to develop good interpersonal and group skills without conscious thought or training. But other people pick up strategies that are not fully effective. Read what the experts have to say about effective interpersonal skills and group dynamics. Try out some of the suggestions in your job, in classroom groups, and in your personal life. Practice will make even new skills second nature so that they're available to you to help you succeed.

LISTENING

Listening on the job or in everyday life may be more difficult than listening in classes. In the first place, in class you're encouraged to take notes. But you can't whip out a notepad every time your boss speaks. Many classroom lectures are well organized, with signposts and repetition of key points to help hearers follow. But informal conversations usually wander. A key point about when a report is due may be sandwiched in among statements about other due dates for other projects. Finally, in a classroom you're listening primarily for information. In interchanges with friends and co-workers, you need to listen for feelings, too. Feelings of being rejected or overworked need to be dealt with as they arise. But you can't deal with a feeling unless you are aware of it.

As you saw in Chapter 4, to receive a message, the receiver must first perceive the message, then decode it (that is, translate the symbols into meaning), and then interpret it. In interpersonal communication, **hearing** denotes perceiving sounds. **Listening** means decoding and interpreting them correctly.

Some listening errors happen because the hearer wasn't paying enough attention to a key point. After a meeting with a client, a consultant waited for the client to send her more information which she would use to draft a formal proposal to do a job for the client. It turned out that the client thought the next move was up to the consultant. The consultant and the client had met together, but they hadn't remembered the same facts. To avoid the kind of error caused by inattention,

- Be conscious of the points you need to know. During a conversation, listen for answers to your questions.
- At the end of the conversation, check your understanding with the other person. Especially check who does what next.

- After the conversation, write down key points that affect deadlines or how work will be evaluated.

Many listening errors are errors in interpretation. In 1977 when two Boeing 747 jumbo jets ran into each other on the ground in Tenerife, the pilots seem to have heard the control tower's instructions. The KLM pilot was told to taxi to the end of the runway, turn around, and wait for clearance. But the KLM pilot didn't interpret the order to wait as an order he needed to follow. The Pan Am pilot interpreted *his* order to turn off at the "third intersection" to mean the third *unblocked* intersection. He didn't count the first blocked ramp, so he was still on the main runway when the KLM pilot ran into his plane at 186 miles an hour. The planes exploded in flames; 576 people died.[1]

To reduce listening errors caused by misinterpretation,

- Don't ignore instructions you think are unnecessary. Before you do something else, check with the order giver to see if in fact there is a reason for the instruction.
- Consider the other person's background and experiences. Why is this point important to the speaker? What might he or she mean by it?
- Paraphrase what the speaker has said, giving him or her a chance to correct your understanding.

Listening to people is an indication that you're taking them seriously. **Acknowledgment responses**—nods, "uh huh's," smiles, frowns—help carry the message that you're listening. However, listening responses vary in different cultures. Research has found that U.S. whites almost always respond nonverbally when they listen closely, but that U.S. blacks respond with words rather than nonverbal cues. This difference in response patterns may explain the fact that some whites think that blacks do not understand what they are saying. Studies in the mid-1970s showed that white counselors repeated themselves more often to black clients than to white clients.[2] One may speculate that black supervisors may miss verbal feedback when they talk to white subordinates who only nod.

In **active listening,** receivers actively demonstrate that they've heard and understood a speaker by feeding back either the literal meaning or the emotional content or both. Other techniques in active listening are asking for more information and stating one's own feelings.

Instead of simply mirroring what the other person says, many of us immediately respond in a way that analyzes or attempts to solve or dismiss the problem. People with problems need first of all to know that we hear that they're having a rough time. Figure 25.1 lists some of the responses that block communication and possible active responses. Ordering, threatening, preaching, and interrogating all tell the other person that the speaker doesn't want to hear what he or she has to say. Judging and name-calling attack the other person. Praising feels like empty flattery and distances the person who has a problem. Interpreting the problem labels it and denies the other person's uniqueness. Minimizing the problem suggests that the other person's concern is misplaced. Even advising shuts off discussion. Giving a quick answer minimizes the pain the person feels and puts him or her down for not seeing (what is to us) the obvious answer. Even if it is a good answer from an objective point of view, the other person may not be ready to hear it. And sometimes, the off-the-top-of-the-head solution doesn't address the real problem.

Do You Hear What I Hear?*

In Center Harbor, Maine, local legend recalls the day some 10 years ago when Walter Cronkite steered his boat into port. The avid sailor, as it's told, was amused to see in the distance a small crowd of people on shore waving their arms to greet him. He could barely make out their excited shouts of "Hello Walter, Hello Walter."

As his boat sailed closer, the crowd grew larger, still yelling, "Hello Walter, Hello Walter." Pleased at the reception, Cronkite tipped his white captain's hat, waved back, even took a bow.

But before reaching dockside, Cronkite's boat abruptly jammed aground. The crowd stood silent. The veteran news anchor suddenly realized what they'd been shouting: "Low water, low water."

---

* Quoted from Don Oldenburg, "What You Hear Isn't Always What You Get," *Columbus Dispatch*, April 12, 1987, 1C.

FIGURE 25.1

BLOCKING RESPONSES
VERSUS ACTIVE LISTENING

1. Ordering, directing, commanding
   "I don't care how you do it. Just get that report on my desk by Friday."

   Possible active response: Paraphrasing content
   "You're saying that you don't have time to finish this report by Friday."

2. Warning, threatening
   "If you can't do this job, I'll get somebody who can."

   Possible active response: Asking for information or clarification
   "Could you finish it if you had help on part of it?"

3. Preaching
   "You should know better than to air the department's problems in a general meeting."

   Possible active response: Mirroring feelings
   "It sounds like the department's problems really bother you."

4. Interrogating
   "Why didn't you *tell* me that you didn't understand the instructions?"

   Possible active response: Stating one's own feelings
   "I'm frustrated that the job isn't completed yet, and I'm worried about getting it done on time."

5. Judging, criticizing, blaming
   "Look at this section you wrote. It's terrible. Spelling errors . . . typos . . . parts of it don't even make sense."

   Possible active response: Offering to solve the problem together
   "We need to fix the typos and spelling errors and revise some parts of this. What's the best way to get the revisions made in the time we have?"

6. Name-calling, shaming
   "That remark just shows what a male chauvinist you are."

   Possible active response: Stating one's own feelings
   "I get angry when people suggest that women don't belong in the workplace. It makes me feel that I have to prove myself all the time, when I'd rather just concentrate on doing my job."

7. Praising, buttering up
   "You're smart. I'm sure you'll figure out a way to solve this problem."

   Possible active response: Asking for information or clarification
   "What parts of the problem seem most difficult to solve?"

8. Interpreting, psychoanalyzing
   "You just have a problem with authority figures, don't you?"

   Possible active response: Paraphrasing content
   "Are you saying that Jim shouldn't be supervising our work so closely?"

9. Minimizing the problem
   "You think *that's* bad. You should see what *I* have to do this week."

   Possible active response: Mirroring feelings
   "You feel overwhelmed right now, don't you?"

10. Advising, giving suggestions or solutions
    "Well, why don't you try listing everything you have to do and seeing which items are most important."

    Possible active response: Offering to solve the problem together
    "Is there anything I could do that would help?"

Source: The 10 responses that block communication are adapted from a list of 12 in Thomas Gordon and Judith Gordon Sands, *P.E.T. in Action* ([New York:] Wyden, 1976), 117–18.

Active listening takes time and energy. Even people who are skilled active listeners can't do it all the time. Furthermore, as Thomas Gordon and Judith Gordon Sands point out, active listening works only if you genuinely accept the other person's ideas and feelings. Active listening can reduce the conflict that results from miscommunication, but it alone cannot reduce the conflict that comes when two people want apparently inconsistent things or when one person wants to change someone else.[3]

CONVERSATIONAL STYLE

Deborah Tannen uses the term **conversational style** to denote our conversational patterns and the meaning we give to them: the way we show interest, politeness, appropriateness.[4] Your answers to the following questions reveal your own conversational style:

- How long a pause tells you that it's your turn to speak?
- Do you see interruption as rude? Or do you say things while other people are still talking to show that you're interested and to encourage them to say more?
- Do you show interest by asking lots of questions? Or do you see questions as intrusive and wait for people to volunteer whatever they have to say?

Tannen concludes that the following features characterize her own conversational style:

Fast rate of speech
Fast rate of turntaking
Persistence—if a turn is not acknowledged, try again
Marked shifts in pitch
Marked shifts in volume
Preference for storytelling
Preference for personal stories
Tolerance of, preference for simultaneous speech
Abrupt topic shifting

Different conversational styles are not better or worse than each other, but people with different conversational styles may feel uncomfortable without knowing why. A subordinate who talks quickly may be frustrated by a boss who speaks slowly. People who talk more slowly may feel shut out of a conversation with people who talk more quickly. Someone who has learned to make requests directly ("Please pass the salt") may be annoyed by someone who uses indirect requests ("This casserole needs some salt"). In the workplace, conflicts may arise because of differences in conversational style. Thomas Kochman claims that blacks often use direct questions to criticize or accuse.[5] If Kochman is right, a black employee might see a question ("Will that report be ready Friday?") as a criticism of his or her progress. One supervisor might mean the question simply as a request for information. Another supervisor might use the question to mean "I want that report Friday."

Daniel N. Maltz and Ruth A. Borker believe that differences in conversational style may be responsible for the miscommunication that often occurs in male-female conversations. Certainly conversational style is not the same for all men and for all women, but research has found several common patterns in the U.S. cultures studied so far. For example, researchers have found that women are much more likely to nod and to say "yes" or "mm hmm" than men are. Maltz and Borker hypothesize that to women, these symbols mean simply, "I'm listening; go on." Men, on the other hand, may decode these symbols as "I agree" or at least "I follow what you're saying so far." A man who receives nods and "mms" from a woman may feel that she is inconsistent

Assertiveness May Be a Matter of Conversational Style*

Rachel regularly led training groups with a male colleague. He always did all the talking, and she was always angry at him for dominating and not giving her a chance to say anything. After hearing me talk about conversational style, she realized what was going on. He would begin to answer questions from the group while she was still waiting for a slight pause to begin answering. And when she was in the middle of talking, he would jump in—but always when she had paused. So she tried pushing herself to begin answering questions a little sooner than felt polite, and not to leave long pauses when she was talking. The result was that she talked a lot more, and the man was as pleased as she was. Her supervisor complimented her on having become more assertive.

Whether or not Rachel actually became more assertive is debatable. In a sense she did. What is crucial is that she solved her problem with a simple and slight adjustment of her way of speaking, without soul-searching, self-analysis, external intervention, and—most important—without defining herself as having an emotional problem or a personality defect: unassertiveness.

---

* Quoted from Deborah Tannen, *That's Not What I Meant!* (New York: William Morrow, 1986), 177–78.

FIGURE 25.2
DIFFERENT RULES FOR
CONVERSATIONS

	Men's Conversations	Women's Conversations
Interpretation of questions	See questions as requests for information.	See questions as way to keep a conversation flowing.
Relation of new comment to what last speaker said	Do not require new comment to relate explicitly to last speaker's comment. Ignoring previous comment is one strategy for taking control.	Expect new comments to acknowledge the last speaker's comment and relate directly to it.
View of aggressiveness	See aggressiveness as one way to organize the flow of conversation.	See aggressiveness as directed at them personally, as negative, and as disruptive to a conversation.
How topics are defined and changed	Tend to define topics narrowly and shift topics abruptly. Interpret statements about side issues as effort to change the topic.	Tend to define topics gradually, progressively. Interpret statements about side issues as effort to shape, expand, or limit the topic.
Response to someone who shares a problem	Respond to person who shares a problem by offering advice, solutions.	Respond to person who shares a problem by offering solidarity, reassurance. Share problems to establish sense of community.

Source: Daniel N. Maltz and Ruth A. Borker, "A Cultural Approach to Male-Female Miscommunication," in *Language and Social Identity*, ed. John J. Gumperz (Cambridge: Cambridge University Press, 1982), 213.

and unpredictable if she then disagrees with him. A woman may feel that a man who doesn't provide any feedback isn't listening to her.[6]

Figure 25.2 lists other differences between men's and women's conversational styles which may also lead to miscommunication.

Understatement and Exaggeration

Closely related to conversational style is the issue of understatement and overstatement. The British have a reputation for understatement. Someone good enough to play at Wimbledon may say he or she "plays a little tennis." Many people in the United States exaggerate. An American businessman negotiating with a German said, "I know it's impossible, but can we do it?" The German saw the statement as nonsensical: by definition, something that is impossible cannot be done at all. The American saw "impossible" as merely a strong way of saying "difficult" and assumed that with enough resources and commitment, the job could in fact be done.[7]

Compliments

The kinds of statements that people interpret as compliments and the socially correct way to respond to compliments also vary among cultures. The statement "You must be really tired" is a compliment in Japan since it recognizes the other person has worked hard. The correct response is "Thank you, but I'm OK." An American who is complimented on giving a good oral presentation will probably say "Thank you." A Japanese, in contrast, will apologize: "No, it wasn't very good."[8]

Statements that seem complimentary in one context may be inappropriate in another. For example, women in business are usually uncomfortable if male colleagues or superiors compliment them on their appearance: the comments suggest that the women are being treated as visual decoration rather than as contributing workers.

Silence

Silence also has different meanings in different cultures and subcultures. Some Americans have difficulty doing business in Japan because they do not realize that silence almost always means that the Japanese do not like the Americans' ideas. Muriel Saville-Troike reports that during a period of military tension, Greek traffic controllers responded with silence when Egyptian planes requested permission to land. The Greeks intended silence as a refusal; the Egyptians interpreted silence as consent. Several people were killed when the Greeks fired on the planes as they approached the runway.[9]

Different understandings of silence can prolong problems with sexual harrassment in the work place. Women sometimes use silence to respond to comments they find offensive, hoping that silence will signal their lack of appreciation. But some men may think that silence means appreciation or at least neutrality.

CONFLICT RESOLUTION

Conflicts are going to arise in any group of intelligent people. Yet many of us feel so uncomfortable with conflict that we pretend it doesn't exist. However, unacknowledged conflicts rarely go away: they fester, making the next interchange more difficult. Dealing successfully with conflict requires both attention to the issues and to people's feelings.

The first step in conflict resolution is to **make sure that the people involved really disagree.** Sometimes someone who's under a lot of pressure may explode. But the speaker may just be venting anger and frustration; he or she may not in fact be angry at the person who receives the explosion.

Check to see that everyone's information is correct. Sometimes different conversational styles, differing interpretations of symbols, or faulty inferences create apparent conflicts when in fact no real disagreement exists. During a negotiation between a U.S. businessman and a Balinese businessman, the Balinese man dropped his voice and lowered his eyes when he discussed price. The U.S. man saw the low voice and breaking of eye contact as an indication of dishonesty. But the Balinese believe that it is rude to mention price specifically. He was embarrassed, but he wasn't lying.[10]

Similarly, misunderstanding can arise from faulty assumptions. A minor but annoying problem for U.S. students studying in Colombia is the issue of hot water for showering. Colombians turn off the water heater in the morning after everyone has bathed; washing later in the day is done with cold water. But U.S. students, accustomed to having hot water all day long, assume that the Colombians never use hot water.

> One night the señora said to me, "Do you prefer cold showers at night? . . . All the family takes showers in the morning." All I thought was, "That's great, just great, what could be better than crawling out of a warm bed into an icy cold shower!" . . . I began to wonder if my señora had been hinting that I should take a warm shower rather than just saying the family bathed in the morning. Well, I checked up and sure enough it was a fact that there was hot water in the mornings. I had just assumed that they never bathed in hot water since they didn't use hot water to wash the dinner dishes.[11]

If checking out the meaning shows that disagreement is real, the second step in resolving conflict is to **discover the needs each person is trying to meet.** Sometimes determining the real needs makes it possible to see a new solution.

Questions: Challenges or Requests for Information?*

The storeroom at a chemical laboratory was run by Mr. Beto, a nonnative speaker of English. The director of the company received repeated complaints from chemists who had to get supplies from the storeroom; they said they could never get a straight answer from Mr. Beto. . . .

I suggested [Mr. Beto] tape-record an on-the-job conversation. . . . I could see immediately that he wasn't giving enough information to the chemist, who consequently had to question him (and did so with increasing impatience) in an attempt to find out what he needed to know. Mr. Beto also noticed that he was being asked a lot of questions, but he interpreted them differently. He said this was what he was up against—people were always grilling him because they doubted he knew what he was doing. . . .

Whereas the chemists were thinking of their questions simply for the message value—trying to get information—he was responding to the metamessage—questioning his competence.

I didn't try to explain any of this to Mr. Beto. Instead, I made a recommendation that proceeded from his assumptions. I suggested that he short-circuit people's attempts to undermine his position by volunteering in advance all the information they could possibly ask questions about. . . . The director of the company later reported that the problem was solved: "People say he's speaking English now."

---

* Quoted from Deborah Tannen, *That's Not What I Meant!* (New York: William Morrow, 1986), 184–85.

Following morning report I began
my nursing rounds. At the end of
the hall I noticed Dr. D., and as
soon as he saw me he started yelling
about something that had happened
on the night shift. Fortunately, I
hadn't worked the night shift and
had a good night's sleep instead. I
knew that Dr. D. wasn't angry at
me, but I also knew that he was upset about something that happened
earlier. Finally he slowed down, and
I said, "I know that you're not angry at me, but if it helps, it's okay."

He stopped short, as if he had
just realized where he was and what
he was doing. Tears filled the corner
of his eyes. Slowly he reached into
his hip pocket and took out his
handkerchief. After wiping his eyes
and blowing his nose he returned
the handkerchief to his pocket. "I'm
sorry," he said. "I'm okay now.
Two of my favorite patients died
last night." He turned and walked
down the hall to see the rest of his
clients.

I have often wondered what
would have happened if I had taken
his anger literally or personally. I
have also wondered how many people have allowed me to vent my dis-
placed anxiety before it exploded
onto someone more vulnerable,
such as the client.

Solve the Real Problem†

Consider the story of two men
quarreling in a library. One wants
the window open and the other
wants it closed. They bicker back
and forth about how much to leave
it open: a crack, halfway, three
quarters of the way. No solution
satisfies both.

Enter the librarian. She asks one
why he wants the window open:
"To get some fresh air." She asks
the other why he wants it closed:
"To avoid the draft." After thinking
a minute, she opens wide a window
in the next room, bringing in fresh
air without a draft.

The **presenting problem** which surfaces as the subject of dissension may or may not be the real problem. For example, a worker who complains about the hours he's putting in may in fact be complaining not about the hours themselves but about not feeling appreciated. A supervisor who complains that the other supervisors don't invite her to meetings may really feel that the other managers don't accept her as a peer. Sometimes people have trouble seeing beyond the presenting problem because they've been taught to suppress their anger, especially toward powerful people. One way to tell whether the presenting problem is the real problem is to ask, "If this were solved, would I be satisfied?" If the answer is *no*, then the problem that presents itself is not in fact the real problem. Solving the presenting problem won't solve the conflict. Keep probing until you get to the real conflict.

A key step in resolving conflict is to **search for alternatives.** Sometimes people are locked into conflict because they see too few alternatives. Indeed, they may see only two polarized choices. Robert Moran tells the story of a large U.S. high-technology company which was having trouble in the Japanese market. At a meeting called to discuss the problem, the president wrote two alternatives on the board: "GET OUT" and "MAKE THEM DO WHAT WE WANT." Moran suggested a third alternative: "LEARN TO WORK WITH THE JAPANESE."[12]

Responding to Criticism

Conflict is particularly difficult to resolve when someone else criticizes or attacks us directly. When we are criticized, our natural reaction is to defend ourselves—perhaps by counterattacking. The counterattack prompts the critic to defend him- or herself. The conflict escalates; feelings are hurt; issues become muddled and more difficult to resolve.

Just as resolving conflict depends upon identifying the needs each person is trying to meet, so dealing with criticism depends upon understanding the real concern of the critic. Constructive ways to respond to criticism and get closer to the real concern include paraphrasing, checking for feelings, checking inferences, and buying time with limited agreement.

Paraphrasing.   To **paraphrase**, repeat in you own words the verbal content of the critic's message. The purposes of paraphrasing in response to criticism are (1) to be sure that you have heard the critic accurately; (2) to let the critic know what his or her statement means to you; and (3) to communicate the feeling that you are taking the critic and his or her feelings seriously.

Criticism:	You guys are stonewalling my requests for information.
Paraphrase:	You think that we don't give you the information you need quickly enough.

Checking for Feelings.   When you check the critic's feelings, you identify the emotions that the critic seems to be expressing verbally or nonverbally. The purposes of checking feelings are (1) to try to understand the emotions the criticism produces for the critic; (2) to try to understand the importance of the criticism for the critic; and (3) to try to get at ideas and feelings which the

---

critic may not be articulating but which may actually be more important than the voiced criticism.

Criticism:	You guys are stonewalling my requests for information.
Feeling check:	You sound pretty angry.

Always *ask* the other person if you are right in your perception. Even the best reader of nonverbal cues is sometimes wrong.

Checking for Inferences. When you check the inferences you draw from criticism, you identify the implied meaning of the verbal and nonverbal content of the criticism, taking the statement a step further than the words of the critic to try to understand *why* the critic is bothered by the action or attitude under discussion. The purposes of checking inferences are (1) to identify the real (as opposed to the presenting) problem; and (2) to communicate the feeling that you care about resolving the conflict.

Criticism:	You guys are stonewalling my requests for information.
Inference:	Are you saying that you need more information from our group?

Inferences can be faulty. In the above interchange, the critic might respond, "I don't need *more* information. I just think you should give it to me without my having to file three forms in triplicate every time I want some data."

Buying Time with Limited Agreement. Buying time is a useful strategy for criticisms that really sting. When you buy time with limited agreement, you avoid escalating the conflict (as an angry statement might do) but also avoid yielding to the critic's point of view. To buy time, restate the part of the criticism which you agree to be true. (This is often a fact, rather than the interpretation the critic has made of that fact.) *Then let the critic respond, before you say anything else.* The purposes of buying time are (1) to allow you time to think when a criticism really hits home and threatens you, so that you can respond to the criticism rather than simply reacting defensively; and (2) to suggest to the critic that you are trying to hear what he or she is saying.

Criticism:	You guys are stonewalling my requests for information.
Limited agreement:	It's true that the cost projections you asked for last week still aren't ready.

DO NOT go on to justify or explain. A "yes, but . . . " statement is not a time buyer.

You-Attitude in Conflict Resolution

You-attitude means looking at things from the audience's point of view, respecting the audience, and protecting the audience's ego. The *you* statements that many people use when they're angry attack the audience; they do not illustrate you-attitude. Instead, substitute statements about your own feelings. In conflict, *I* statements show good you-attitude!

---

* Quoted from Edward Twitchell Hall and Mildred Reed Hall, *Hidden Differences: Doing Business with the Japanese* (Garden City, NY: Anchor-Doubleday, 1987), 112–13.

Being Strong Means Being Able to Say You're Sorry*

Once, while we were staying at one of Tokyo's finest hotels, we sent a telex to our office in New Mexico. After some time, it became clear that the telex had not been delivered. In trying to discover what had happened, where the slip-up had occurred, our only point of contact was the hotel telex office. Foreseeing chances for misunderstanding, and mindful of all the foreigners we had seen and heard raising their voices and pounding on desks, we made our approach with caution and trepidation, in a low-key manner, accompanied by a Japanese friend to do the talking. Even so, the clerk thought we were accusing him of error. He became visibly distressed, and nothing we said reassured him. . . . What to do? First, even though the New Mexico telex office was the culprit, we apologized. Then, conferring with our Japanese intermediary, we asked if a gift would help. The gift did not have to be expensive, since it was the gesture that was important. The next day a small present, appropriately wrapped, was presented during a quiet time of the morning so there would be no distractions. The man's injured ego was repaired and good relations were reestablished.
. . .

When this sort of incident occurs (and it will if you stay long enough) there are three things to remember: (1) the Japanese transaction rules have been violated (even though inadvertently); (2) the person of superior status is obliged to set things to right; (3) establishing who is to blame is irrelevant; what is wrong is that someone is upset, and that is what must be corrected.

It is a waste of time to try to fix blame, which Americans almost inevitably do as part of our confrontational, litigious style. What matters in Japan is to repair the damage, to make people feel good again, to establish harmony. Being able to show contrition, to say that one is sorry when the other person is upset, is vital.

FIGURE 25.3

COMMUNICATION ACTIVITIES
AND PHASES OF GROUP
DEVELOPMENT

Phase	Events during Phase	Communication Activities during Phase	Focus
Orientation	Group meets. Members decide how to relate to each other. Group tries to define task.	Members make tentative comments, seek information. Statements skip from one topic to another. Members agree more with each other than in any other phase.	Interpersonal and procedural.
Formation	Members begin to specialize. Leader emerges. Group develops strategy, objectives, and procedures to meet goals.	Conflict emerges as leader and strategy are chosen. Positions are stated clearly; ambiguity decreases. Members argue with each other.	Procedural, some interpersonal and informational.
Coordination	Group finds, organizes, and interprets information; examines its assumptions. Group considers alternatives but no one advocates a specific conclusion.	Information flows freely but prompts questions, trial interpretations and solutions. Comments include diagnosis, explanation, and substantiation. Conflict is accepted as part of the effort to find the best solution.	Informational, some procedural and interpersonal.
Formalization	Group makes and formalizes decision.	Members compliment and congratulate each other.	Procedural and interpersonal.

Source: Based on Thomas J. Knutson, "Communication in Small Decision-Making Groups: In Search of Excellence," *Journal for Specialists in Group Work* 10, no. 1 (March 1985): 31–33.

Not you-attitude:	You never do your share of the work.
You-attitude:	I feel that I'm doing more than my share of the work on this project.
Not you-attitude:	You schedule too many meetings.
You-attitude:	It seems to me that I'm always in meetings. I don't feel that the meetings are a good use of my time, and I want to attend fewer of them.
Not you-attitude:	Even you should be able to run the report through a spelling checker.
You-attitude:	I'm not willing to have my name on a report with so many spelling errors. I did lots of writing, and I don't think I should have to do the proofreading and check the spelling, too.

GROUP INTERACTIONS

Groups can focus on three different dimensions. **Informational** messages focus on content: the problem, data, and possible solutions. **Procedural** messages focus on method: how will the group make decisions? Who will do what? When will assignments be due? **Interpersonal** messages focus on people, promoting friendliness, cooperation, and group loyalty. Thomas Knutson notes that different kinds of communication will dominate during the four stages of the life of a task group: orientation, formation, coordination, and formalization.[13] See Figure 25.3.

During **orientation,** when members meet and begin to define their task, groups need to develop some sort of social cohesiveness and to develop procedures for meeting and acting. Although there is less conflict during orientation than at any later stage, some tension always exists in a new group. Interpersonal and procedural comments reduce that tension. Insistence on information in this first stage can hurt the group's long-term productivity.

During **formation**, conflicts almost always arise when the group chooses a leader and defines the problem. Several studies have shown that leaders are likely to talk a lot—even to argue—and to respond nonverbally to other members in the group.[14] Successful leaders make the procedure clear so that each member knows what he or she is supposed to do. Interpersonal communication is needed to resolve the conflict that surfaces during this phase. Successful groups analyze the problem carefully before they begin to search for solutions.

Coordination is the longest phase and the phase during which most of the group's work is done. While procedural and interpersonal comments help maintain direction and friendliness, most of the comments need to deal with information. Good information is essential to a good decision. Conflict occurs as the group debates alternate solutions.

In **formalization**, the group seeks consensus. The success of this phase determines how well the group's decision will be implemented. In this stage, the group seeks to forget earlier conflicts.

Characteristics of Successful Student Groups

A case study of six student groups completing class projects found that students in successful groups were not necessarily more skilled or more experienced than students in less successful groups. Instead, successful and less successful groups communicated differently in three ways.[15]

First, in the successful groups, the leader set clear deadlines, scheduled frequent meetings, and dealt directly with conflict that emerged in the group. In less successful groups, members had to ask the leader what they were supposed to be doing. The less successful groups met less often, and they tried to pretend that conflicts didn't exist.

Second, the successful groups listened to criticism and made important decisions together. Perhaps as a result, everyone in the group could articulate the group's goals. In the less successful groups, a subgroup made decisions and told other members what had been decided.

Third, the successful groups had a higher proportion of members who worked actively on the project. The successful groups even found ways to use members who didn't like working in groups. For example, one student who didn't want to be a team player functioned as a free-lancer for her group, completing assignments by herself and giving them to the leader. The less successful groups had a much smaller percentage of active members and each had some members who did very little on the final project.

Peer Pressure and Groupthink

In a series of experiments in the 1950s, Solomon Asch showed the influence of peer pressure. Subjects "in a perception experiment" were shown a large card with a line and asked to match it to the line of the same length on another card. It's a simple test: people normally match the lines correctly almost 100% of the time. However, in the experiment, all but one of the people in the group

Everybody Needs a Cheering Section*

Not long ago, there were two junior officers in the Dutch Navy who made a pact. They decided that when they were at the various navy social functions, they would go out of their way to tell people what a great guy the other guy was. They'd appear at cocktail parties or dances and say, "What an unbelievable person Charlie is. He's the best man in the Navy." Or, "Did you hear about the brilliant idea Dave had?"

They revealed this pact to the public the day they were both made admirals—the two youngest admirals ever appointed in the Dutch Navy.

Humor Can Defuse Tense Situations†

When he was president of Chrysler, Eugene Cafiero traveled to England to talk with workers at a troubled plant there. Ushered in to meet the burly unionists, he was confronted with a man who loudly proclaimed, "I'm Eddie McClusky and I'm a Communist." The Chrysler executive extended his hand and said, "How do you do. I'm Eugene Cafiero and I'm a Presbyterian." A burst of laughter clears the air.

---

* Quoted from Terence E. Deal and Allan A. Kennedy, *Corporate Culture: The Rites and Rituals of Corporate Life* (Reading, MA: Addison-Wesley Publishing, 1982), 95.

† Quoted from Walter Kiechel III, "Executives Ought to Be Funnier," *Fortune*, December 12, 1983, 208.

Jim is the only black on an engineering staff. Manuel is the single Hispanic on a college history faculty. Nora is the one female member of a commercial sales staff. Beth is the only person under 30 in an editorial group. Tom is the lone male nurse on the pediatrics floor of a hospital. Peter, confined to a wheelchair, is the only handicapped computer programmer at a bank. . . .

No longer are religion and politics the primary social dividers among people at work. Today, lifestyle, age, sexual orientation, and all sorts of other facets can also mark you as "different."

If you do stand out in some way from the people you work with, social discomfort can interfere with your work effectiveness. . . .

There are steps you can take to promote an easy, pleasant interaction. . . .

- Take the initiative to be friendly. . . .
- Explain some facets of yourself, if necessary. . . .
- Forge bonds with similar people in other work groups. . . .
- Ultimately, focus on the work.

had been instructed to give false answers for several of the trials. When the group gave an incorrect answer, the focal person accepted the group's judgment 36.8% of the time. When someone else also gave a different answer—even if it was another wrong answer—the focal person accepted the group's judgment only 9% of the time.[16]

The experimenters varied the differences in line lengths, hoping to create a situation in which even the most conforming subjects would trust their own senses. But some people continued to accept the group's judgment, even when one line was seven inches longer than the other.

Irving Janis terms this pressure groupthink. **Groupthink** is the tendency for groups to put such a high premium on agreement that they directly or indirectly punish dissent. As a result, groups ignore the full range of alternatives, seek only information that supports the positions they already favor, and fail to prepare contingency plans to cope with foreseeable setbacks. Groupthink, Janis believes, led to U.S. public policy fiascoes such as the decision to launch the Bay of Pigs invasion. A business suffering from groupthink may launch a new product which senior executives support but for which there is no demand. The best correctives to groupthink are to consciously search for additional alternatives, to test one's assumptions against those of a range of other people, and to protect the right of people in a group to disagree.[17]

EFFECTIVE MEETINGS

Meetings take a significant part of every manager's week. Unfortunately, many people attend meetings that they feel are unproductive. A survey in one organization found that respondents judged only 62% of the meetings they attended to be effective.[18] **Formal meetings** are run under strict rules, like the rules of parliamentary procedure summarized in *Robert's Rules of Order*. Motions must be made formally before a topic can be debated. Each point is settled by a vote. **Minutes** record each motion and the vote on it. Formal rules help the meeting run smoothly if the group is very large or if the agenda is very long. **Informal meetings** are run more loosely. Votes may not be taken if most people seem to agree. Minutes may not be kept. Informal meetings are better for team building and problem solving.

Planning the agenda is the foundation of a good meeting. Many groups put first routine items on which agreement will be easy. If there's a long list of routine items, save them till the end or dispense with them in an omnibus motion. An **omnibus motion** allows a group to approve many items together. It's important to schedule controversial items early in the meeting, when people's energy level is high, and to allow enough time for a full discussion. Giving a controversial item only half an hour at the end of the day or evening makes people suspect that the leaders are trying to manipulate them.

Pay attention to people and process as well as to the task at hand. At informal meetings, a good leader observes nonverbal feedback and invites everyone to participate. If conflict seems to be getting out of hand, a leader may want to focus attention on the group process and ways that it could deal with conflict, before getting back to the substantive issues.

If the group doesn't formally vote, the leader should summarize the group's consensus after each point. At the end of the meeting, the leader must summarize all decisions and remind the group who is responsible for implementing or following up on each item. If no other notes are taken, someone should record the decisions and assignments.

*   Quoted from Auren Uris and Jane Bensahel, "How to Cope with Being Different," *Los Angeles Times*, January 12, 1981, IV.2.

SUMMARY OF KEY POINTS

- **Interpersonal communication** is communication that focuses on the relationships between people.
- In interpersonal communication, **hearing** denotes perceiving sounds. **Listening** means decoding and interpreting them correctly.
- To avoid listening errors caused by inattention,
  - Be conscious of the points you need to know. During a conversation, listen for answers to your questions.
  - At the end of the conversation, check your understanding with the other person. Especially check who does what next.
  - After the conversation, write down key points that affect deadlines or how work will be evaluated.
- To reduce listening errors caused by misinterpretation,
  - Don't ignore instructions you think are unnecessary. Before you do something else, check with the order giver to see if in fact there is a reason for the instruction.
  - Consider the other person's background and experiences. Why is this point important to the speaker? What might he or she mean by it?
  - Paraphrase what the speaker has said, giving him or her a chance to correct your understanding.
- In **active listening,** receivers actively demonstrate that they've heard and understood a speaker by feeding back either the literal meaning or the emotional content or both.
- **Conversational style** denotes our conversational patterns and the way we show interest, politeness, and appropriateness.
- To resolve conflicts, first make sure that the people involved really disagree. Next, check to see that everyone's information is correct. Discover the needs each person is trying to meet. The **presenting problem** which surfaces as the subject of dissension may or may not be the real problem. Search for alternatives.
- Constructive ways to respond to criticism include paraphrasing, checking for feelings, checking inferences, and buying time with limited agreement.
- Use statements about your feelings to own the problem and avoid attacking the audience. In conflict, *I* statements are good you-attitude!
- A case study of six student groups completing class projects found that successful groups had leaders who set clear deadlines, scheduled frequent meetings, and dealt directly with conflict that emerged in the group; had an inclusive decision-making style; and a higher proportion of members who worked actively on the project.
- **Groupthink** is the tendency for groups to put such a high premium on agreement that they directly or indirectly punish dissent. The best correctives to groupthink are to consciously search for additional alternatives, to test one's assumptions against those of a range of other people, and to protect the right of people in a group to disagree.
- To make meetings more effective,
  - Allow enough time to discuss controversial issues.

Computers Can Keep a Meeting on Track*

With a small to medium-sized investment ($1,000 to $4,000) for a special projector, a personal computer can be turned into a large-screen "intelligent chalkboard" that can dramatically change the texture and effectiveness of a meeting.

At the typical computer-supported meeting, someone is designated to "take notes" on the computer as the participants speak. Key points made by the speakers are dutifully typed into the computer (and onto the screen) as they talk. Everyone at the meeting hears—and sees—the discussion.

Something very subtle and important soon happens. People watching this flow of comments on the screen begin to say things like, "Hey, this point relates to something that was said earlier," or "Wait a second. Doesn't that contradict what you said 10 minutes ago? . . . Let's see." With the tap of a few keys, the screen scrolls back to the desired spot on this list of ideas. . . .

Digressions become more obvious because you can see that they're not connected to anything. By contrast, the quiet but important points assume their rightful positions on this "meetings map." . . .

Participants meeting in this environment often pay more attention to the points displayed on the screen than to the individual making the point. What's on the screen is treated as a creation of the group—not personal property. This technique apparently filters out some of the "duelling egos" mentality that infests too many meetings.

---

* Quoted from Michael Schrage, "Put Those Ideas up against the Wall," *The Wall Street Journal*, December 7, 1987, 22.

International Meetings and Negotiations*

Successful international business depends in part on understanding that expectations for meetings and negotiating styles vary from country to country.

U.S. parliamentary procedure allows new business to be introduced at a meeting. The Japanese, however, don't like surprises. Someone who wants to propose a new idea should introduce it in one-to-one meetings. Only after everyone involved has had a chance to evaluate the idea should it come up for a vote.

Americans expect people to contribute throughout the meeting. Someone who has an alternate proposal is expected to suggest it early enough to permit everyone to examine it. But Indonesians present new ideas near the close of a meeting so that they won't appear to be seeking attention for themselves.

In an effort to limit meetings, Americans sometimes agree on the main points, leaving the details to be worked out later by a small group. Greeks involved in international negotiations want to work out the details in public, at the meeting, no matter how long it takes. They may see a proposal to give the details to a subcommittee as an attempt to take advantage of them.

Americans working on joint ventures overseas often try to focus on the business details to avoid differences in philosophy. But the Chinese want agreement on basic principles before they go on to anything specific. Some Americans have quickly agreed on principles, only to find that the principles then governed the specifics. And most Americans find that the Chinese negotiating style requires more time.

- Pay attention to people and process as well as to the task at hand.
- If you don't take formal votes, summarize the group's consensus after each point. At the end of the meeting, summarize all decisions and remind the group who is responsible for implementing or following up on each item.

NOTES

1. For a full account of the accident, see Andrew D. Wolvin and Caroline Gwynn Coakley, *Listening*, 2nd ed. (Dubuque, IA: Wm. C. Brown, 1985), 6.

2. Molefi Asante and Alice Davis, "Black and White Communication: Analyzing Work Place Encounters," *Journal of Black Studies* 16, no. 1 (September 1985): 87–90.

3. Thomas Gordon with Judith Gordon Sands, *P.E.T. in Action* ([New York:] Wyden, 1976), 83.

4. Deborah Tannen, *That's Not What I Meant!* (New York: William Morrow, 1986).

5. Thomas Kochman, *Black and White Styles in Conflict* (Chicago: University of Chicago Press, 1981), 103.

6. Daniel N. Maltz and Ruth A. Borker, "A Cultural Approach to Male-Female Miscommunication," in *Language and Social Identity*, ed. John J. Gumperz (Cambridge: Cambridge University Press, 1982), 202.

7. Vincent O'Neill, "Training the Multi-Cultural Manager," Sixth Annual EMU Conference on Languages and Communication for World Business and the Professions, Ann Arbor, MI, May 7–9, 1987.

8. Akihisa Kumayama, comment during discussion, Sixth Annual EMU Conference on Languages and Communication for World Business and the Professions, Ann Arbor, MI, May 7–9, 1987.

9. Muriel Saville-Troike, "An Integrated Theory of Communication," in *Perspectives on Silence*, ed. Deborah Tannen and Muriel Saville-Troike (Norwood, NJ: Ablex, 1985), 10–11.

10. Jeffrey A. Fadiman, "Intercultural Invisibility: Deciphering the 'Subliminal' Marketing Message in Afro-Asian Commerce," Sixth Annual Conference on Languages and Communication for World Business and the Professions, Ann Arbor, MI, May 7–9, 1987.

11. Raymond L. Gordon, *Living in Latin America* (Lincolnwood, IL: National Textbook, 1974), 41.

12. Philip R. Harris and Robert T. Moran, *Managing Cultural Differences*, 2nd ed. (Houston: Gulf, 1987), 78.

13. Thomas J. Knutson, "Communication in Small Decision-Making Groups: In Search of Excellence," *Journal for Specialists in Group Work* 10, no. 1 (March 1985): 28–37. The next four paragraphs summarize Knutson's analysis.

14. Beatrice Schultz, "Argumentativeness: Its Effect in Group Decision-Making and Its Role in Leadership Perception," *Communication Quarterly* 30, no. 4 (Fall 1982): 374–75 and Dennis S. Gouran and B. Aubrey Fisher, "The Functions of Human Communication in the Formation, Maintenance, and Performance of Small Groups," in *Handbook of Rhetorical and Communication Theory*, ed. Carroll C. Arnold and John Waite Bowers (Boston: Allyn & Bacon, 1984), 640.

15. Nance L. Harper and Lawrence R. Askling, "Group Communication and Quality of Task Solution in a Media Production Organization," *Communication Monographs* 47, no. 2 (June 1980): 77–100.

16. Solomon F. Asch, "Opinions and Social Pressure," *Scientific American* 193, no. 5 (November 1955): 31–35.

17. Irving I. Janis, *Victims of Groupthink: A Psychological Study of Foreign-Policy Decisions and Fiascoes* (Boston: Houghton Mifflin, 1972), 10–11, 196–99.

18. William L. Williams, Elaine Biech, and Malcolm P. Clark, "Increased Productivity through Effective Meetings," *Technical Communication* 34, no. 4 (November 1987): 265.

---

* Based on Richard W. Brislin, Kenneth Cushner, Craig Cherrie, and Mahealani Yong, *Intercultural Interactions* (Beverly Hills, CA: Sage Publications, 1986), 182, 185; Edward T. Hall, *The Silent Language* (New York: Fawcett, 1959), 10–11; Lucian Pye, *Chinese Commercial Negotiating Style* (Boston: Oegeschlager, Gunn & Hain, 1982), 40–42.

EXERCISES AND PROBLEMS FOR CHAPTER 25

25–1 LISTENING TO FEELINGS AND IDEAS

Go around the room for this exercise. Let the first student read the first statement out loud (with feeling, as though it were something that really bugged you). The next student will offer limited agreement. The third student will offer a paraphrase of the statement. The fourth student will identify the feelings that may be behind the statement. The fifth student will offer inferences. The next student will read the next statement, and so on.

1. Whenever I say something, the group just ignores me.
2. I've done more than my share of work on this project. But the people who have been freeloading are going to get the same grade I've worked so hard to earn.
3. I can't believe you don't have your part done. Don't you realize that this assignment counts 20% of our course grade? You're killing all of us!
4. I've had 16 job interviews, but I haven't got an offer yet.
5. These companies just want somebody slick. Their judgments are really superficial. I mean, how much can you learn about someone in 30 minutes?
6. My dad is going to kill me if I don't have a job lined up when I graduate.
7. They just don't pay me enough here for all the work I do.
8. I've got better qualifications than Sue does, but *she's* the one who got the promotion.
9. This company doesn't care about quality. Grind it out, cut corners, get it done by the deadline. People don't understand that good work takes time.
10. People complain about government, but they won't do anything to improve it. Do they come to hear a candidate talk? No! Lots of them don't even vote.

25–2 TAKING "MINUTES" OF CLASS

As your instructor directs, have two or more people take minutes of each class meeting for a week. Compare the accounts of the same meeting.

To what extent do they agree on what happened?

Does one contain information missing in other accounts?

Do any accounts disagree on a specific fact?

How do you account for the differences you find?

25–3 INTERVIEWING WORKERS ABOUT LISTENING

Interview someone who works in an organization about his or her on-the-job listening. Possible questions to ask include the following:

- Whom do you listen to as part of your job? Your superior? Subordinates (how many levels down)? Customers or clients? Whom else?
- How much time a day do you spend listening?
- What people do you talk to as part of your job? Do you feel they hear what you say? How do you tell whether or not they're listening?
- In what ways is good listening important to this field?
- Do you know of any problems that came up because someone didn't listen? What happened?
- What do you think prevents people from listening effectively? What advice would you have for someone on how to listen more accurately?

As your instructor directs,

a. Share your information with a small group of students in your class.
b. Present your findings orally to the class.
c. Present your findings in a memo to your instructor.
d. Join with other students to present your findings in a group report.

25–4 NOTING PAUSES AND TURN TAKING

Tape record a class session, a conversation among good friends, and a conversation among people who don't know each other well. (Ask the permission of the leader or group before you tape.) Use a watch with a second hand to help answer the following questions for each situation:

- If someone doesn't answer a question immediately, how long does the speaker wait before he or she rephrases the question, calls on someone, or answers it?

- How long after one person pauses do other speakers wait before they begin talking? Is that time about the same for all people in the group, or do some people wait longer than others?

- Is there simultaneous or overlapping speech? Do all people in the group do about the same amount of overlapping, or do some do more than others?

- When someone overlaps or interrupts, is the effect to support the first speaker and encourage him or her to continue? Or do some group members overlap or interrupt so they can get the floor or change the subject?

- For each of the above questions, do you see differences between men and women? Among people with different ages or status? Among people with different ethnic or national backgrounds?

As your instructor directs:
a. Share your findings with a small group of other students.
b. Present your findings orally to the class.
c. Present your findings in a memo to your instructor.
d. Join with other students to write a group report presenting your findings.

25–5 UNDERSTANDING SILENCE IN VARIOUS CULTURES

Study silence in a culture. Use books and articles; talk to people who have visited the country and natives of it. Consider the following questions:

- What role does silence play in religious observances and secular rituals?

- What do proverbs say about silence (e.g., "The way your eyes look can say more than your mouth"—Japanese; "Man becomes wise through the ear"—Farsi; "Who asks does not wander"—Serbo-Croatian)? Are the proverbs in that culture consistent, or do they suggest different values about silence (e.g., "The squeaky wheel gets the grease" versus "Silence is golden")?

- Are certain kinds of people (children, women, subordinates) expected to be silent more often than other groups of people?

- Does silence mean that someone agrees or disagrees with what has been said?

- If two people stand near each other in an office or at a party but don't talk much, is it

more likely that they know each other very well or very little?

As your instructor directs,
a. Share you findings with a small group of other students.
b. Present your findings orally to the class.
c. Present your findings in a memo to your instructor.
d. Join with other students to write a group report presenting your findings.

25–6 ANALYZING PHONE CONVERSATIONS

a. Analyze the conversation recorded in problem 14–11. What parts are clear, complete, correct, efficient, and friendly? What parts could be improved?

b. Record a phone conversation in which you give or ask for information. (Be sure to ask the other person's permission.) How much of the conversation was devoted to socializing? How much to the task? Were there any places where communication broke down? What seemed to cause the breakdowns?

c. Assume that you've been invited for an office visit to a firm you'd like to work for. You need to call the company to find out about your travel arrangements and the interview schedule. Make notes for a phone conversation.

25–7 NEGOTIATING YOUR OWN ROLES*

Your political party comes to you, a successful person in your field, and asks you to run for state office. The party will start you out with about 50% of the estimated costs and will help you raise the rest. The incumbent is retiring and you stand a good chance of winning the election. You realize that you have a lot to give to government and feel you could contribute a great deal if elected.

You're married; your spouse also has a career. Your spouse and children (ages 10 and 15) agree that you'd be a good candidate. Your family already hires a cleaning service that comes in once a week, but you, your spouse, and children share responsibility for lots of chores.

Before deciding to accept your party's nomination, what things would you want to negotiate with the party? With your employer? With your spouse? With your children? What changes would you be willing to make? What is your bottom line?

*Based on a problem by Sarah Weddington, "Learning the Art of Negotiation," Urbana, IL, October 30, 1982.

25–8 MANAGING CONFLICT BETWEEN SUPERVISORS AND SUBORDINATES

Ray Chaudurhi, director of manufacturing, is concerned about the most recent organizational development meeting with the supervisors at his plant.

"The supervisors want to reestablish their authority as supervisors. They feel they don't have 'control' of the hourly workers. They want my authority to assert their authority. But I think this will get into win/lose dynamics and not really solve the problem."

a. What is the problem? How could you find out?

b. What strategies would you suggest that Ray try out? Make your suggestions as specific as possible.

25–9 NEGOTIATING A POLICY ON SMOKING

You're a partner in a large consulting firm. Some people who work in the firm urge that smoking be completely banned in all common areas. Other people favor less stringent restrictions. Still others oppose any limits at all.

Use the background information your instructor gives you and negotiate a settlement with other students in the class.

After your group reaches agreement, answer the following questions:

- How does each member of the group feel about the solution?
- Does each member of the group feel that his or her opinions were respected? What sorts of statements in the group showed respect or disrespect?
- What things happened in the discussion that made finding a solution more difficult? What things helped the group find a solution?

25–10 EXPERIENCING CLOSED AND OPEN GROUPS

Let three people stand up and talk together in front of the class. A fourth person will come up to the group and try to join it. If your social security number ends in an even number, observe what the newcomer does and says. If your social security number ends in an odd number, observe what the group does and says.

Situation a. The group makes it easy for the newcomer to join.
Situation b. The group rejects the newcomer and tries to keep the original group unchanged.

After each situation, discuss the following questions:

- What did the newcomer do to try to join the group? How did the newcomer adjust his or her strategy when the group was closed? Did the newcomer succeed in joining the group?
- What did the group do to welcome the newcomer? What did it do to reject the newcomer?

Ask the following questions of the newcomer and the group members:

- How did it feel to be accepted? How did it feel to be rejected?
- How did it feel to welcome the newcomer? How did it feel to shut the newcomer out?

25–11 ANALYZING THE DYNAMICS OF A GROUP

Analyze the dynamics of a task group of which you are a member. Questions to consider include the following:

- Who was the group's leader? How did the leader emerge? Were there any changes in or challenges to the original leader?
- Describe the contribution each member made to the group, and the roles each person played.
- Did any members of the group officially or unofficially drop out? Did any one join after the group had begun working? How did you deal with the loss or addition of a group member, both in terms of getting the work done and in terms of helping people work together?
- What things did your group do to build trust and loyalty?
- What planning did your group do at the start of the project? Did you stick to the plan or revise it? How did the group decide that revision was necessary?
- How did your group make decisions? Did you vote? Reach decisions by consensus?
- What problems or conflicts arose? Did the group deal with them openly? To what extent did they interfere with the group's task?
- Evaluate your group both in terms of its task and in terms of the satisfaction members felt. How did this group compare with other task groups you've been part of? What made it better or worse?

As your instructor directs,

a. Discuss these questions with the other group members.

b. Present your findings orally to the class.

c. Present your findings in an individual memo to your instructor.

d. Join with the other group members to write a collaborative memo to your instructor.

25–12 INTERVIEWING WORKERS ABOUT THE MEETINGS THEY ATTEND

Interview someone who works for an organization about the meetings he or she attends as part of the job. Possible questions to ask include the following:

- About how many job-related meetings do you attend a week or a month? For each, briefly explain the length, the number of people who attend, and the purpose(s).

- Do you usually get an agenda in advance? Are you told what the purpose of the meeting is?

- Do the meetings usually start on time? Do they usually accomplish the objectives? Is it clear who is to do what after the meeting?

- What makes a meeting productive? What percentage of the meetings you attend are productive?

- What things do you find frustrating or annoying about meetings?

- How often do these annoying or frustrating things happen?

- What advice would you have about how to improve meetings?

As your instructor directs,

a. Share your information with a small group of students in your class.

b. Present your findings orally to the class.

c. Present your findings in a memo to your instructor.

d. Join with a small group of students and present your findings in a group report.

PART

VI

JOB HUNTING

How to Find the Job You Want

QUESTIONS

- When should you start job hunting?
- How do you decide what you want to do?
- How do you learn which fields offer the most potential?
- How do you find out which organizations have job openings?
- Should you apply to blind ads in the newspaper?
- How do you tap into the hidden job market?
- How can you and your spouse find jobs in the same geographical area?

> The person who gets hired is not necessarily the one who can do
> the job best; but, the one *who knows the most about how to get
> hired.*
>
> Richard Nelson Bolles
> *What Color Is Your Parachute?*, 1988

E ven people who get the first job easily need to know how to search for a job. Recent statistics show that the average college graduate stays only five years with the company he or she originally joins.[1] A large number of people not only switch employers but also switch fields at least once in their lives.[2] If you know how to go about the job search systematically, you can use those steps not only to find your first full-time job but also to move on or up later in life.

Take control of the job search process. The secret is to decide what you most want in a job and then to find the firm where you can get it. The payoff will be a job that rewards you for doing what you do best.

This chapter discusses the first four steps in the job search:

1. Evaluate your strengths and interests.
2. Analyze the job market.
3. Study the organizations you're interested in working with.
4. Identify the organizations that are hiring.

Chapter 27 discusses résumés, Chapter 28 will help you write an application letter, and Chapter 29 discusses strategies for job interviews, follow-up letters, and handling job offers.

A TIME LINE FOR JOB HUNTING

Informal preparation for job hunting should start soon after you arrive on campus. Join extracurricular organizations on campus and in the community: they'll increase your knowledge and provide a network for learning about jobs. Find a job that gives you experience. Note which courses you like—and why you like them. If you like thinking and learning about a subject, you're more likely to enjoy a job in that field.

Formal preparation for job hunting should begin a full year *before you begin interviewing.* Visit the campus placement office to see what services it provides. Ask friends who are on the job market about their experiences in interviews; find out what kinds of job offers they get. Check into the possibility of getting an internship or a co-op job that will give you relevant experience the summer before you interview. Think about more education, to decide if you want to job hunt next year or if you'd rather get another degree first.

Job hunting takes time. Richard E. McCollum, president of a career-management firm, says, "In the $20,000 to $25,000 range, you really do need at least three months. At higher levels, $50,000 and above, six months; at $80,000 to $90,000, nine months; over $100,000 we're talking a full year—with all kinds of exceptions, of course, depending on your specialty and the market."[3]

The year you interview, register with your placement office early. If you plan to graduate in the spring, prepare your résumé and buy two interview suits early in the fall. Initial campus interviews occur from October to February for May or June graduation. In January or February, write to any organization you'd like to work for that hasn't interviewed on campus. From February to April, you're likely to visit one or more offices for a second interview.

Try to have a job offer lined up *before* you get the degree. People who don't need jobs immediately are more confident in interviews and usually get better job offers. If you do have to job hunt after graduation, plan to spend at least 30 hours a week on your job search. The time will pay off in a better job that you find more quickly.

EVALUATING YOUR STRENGTHS AND INTERESTS

Each person could do several jobs happily. Personality and aptitude tests can tell you what your strengths are, but they won't say, "You should be a __." You'll still need to answer questions like these:

- What achievements have given you the most satisfaction? *Why* did you enjoy them? That common thread is a good foundation for a career.
- Would you rather have firm deadlines or a flexible schedule? Do you like working alone, or would you rather be in an office where you can learn from people and interact with them? Do you want specific instructions and standards for evaluation, or are you comfortable with more freedom and uncertainty? How comfortable are you with pressure? How much challenge do you want?
- Are you willing to take work home? To travel? How important is money to you? Prestige? Time to spend with family and friends?
- Where do you want to live? What features in terms of weather, geography, cultural and social life do you see as ideal?
- Is it important to you that your work achieve certain purposes or values? Would you prefer working for an organization whose products or services met certain ethical standards? Do you see work as just a way to make a living, or must your work satisfy other needs too? Which ones?

After you've done this brainstorming, make a list of *everything you'd like in your ideal job.* Then, to see which points are really important to you, do a forced choice. In a **forced choice**, you compare each item against every other one. If you could only have one of the two, which would you prefer? Mark that item. Repeat until you've made a choice between each of the possible pairs. Then count the number of times you've chosen each item. The things you've chosen most often are the ones that matter: they're the ones you should look for in your job.

Figure 26.1 is the list that one woman produced. The items are numbered in the order in which they occured to her. To find out what's truly important and what's nice but not necessary, Shelley can do a forced choice. If she had to choose between a high income and living in a medium-sized city, which would she prefer? Counting up the number of times she chooses each factor will tell her what she really wants.

Problem 26–2 provides a chart that you can use to make your own forced choice.

Be a Successful Job Hunter!*
A degree alone doesn't guarantee you a good job. A study by the Administrative Management Society revealed some of the things that prevent college graduates from finding good jobs. Don't repeat the mistakes that others have made. Instead be a successful job hunter.

- **Make lots of contacts; schedule lots of interviews.** Not every contact will produce an interview; not every interview produces a job offer. Increasing the number of contacts and interviews increases the number of job offers.
- **Adapt your approach to the individual employer.** Many students use the same approach for all potential employers. Adapting the strategy to the employer sets you apart from other applicants and increases the chances of a job offer.
- **Take control of the process.** Many job hunters are fairly passive. Employers prefer motivated, active, aggressive candidates.
- **Polish your communication and interpersonal skills.** Even though every college offers courses in these areas, many graduates have poor communication and interpersonal skills. The lack of skills makes it harder to present their qualifications effectively. The lack of skills is also a drawback in itself, since so many jobs require communicating and working with people in addition to specific technical skills.
- **Investigate the hidden job market.** Don't rely just on advertised openings. Use the techniques in this chapter to tap into the hidden job market.

Based on Steven R. Dzubow, "Entering the Job Market," *Journal of College Placement* 45, no. 3 (Spring 1985): 49–50.

FIGURE 26.1
SHELLEY'S LIST FOR A
FORCED CHOICE

1. High income
2. Medium-sized city
3. Near mountains
4. Cost of living not too high
5. Opportunity for advancement
6. Nonsexist environment
7. "Name" company
8. Company that isn't making weapons
9. Lots of open land nearby
10. Medium amount of pressure— someplace where I'm challenged, but not panicked
11. Minimal travel as part of job
12. Good ballet company in town
13. Town with parks, civic services
14. Lots of interaction with other people
15. In the same town where Gordon's working, just in case we stay together
16. Company that will encourage me to get a master's degree and even pay for it
17. City with good bus system, so I don't have to buy a car right away
18. Opportunity to be a vice president by the time I'm 40
19. Not have to work weekends

How to Get an Internship

Some companies advertise internships just as they advertise job openings. To learn about posted openings, check your placement office or the following books:

Community Jobs

Storming Washington: An Intern's Guide to National Government

The Student Guide to Mass Media Internships

The Student Guide to Summer Employment in Business

Summer Employment Directory of the U.S.

You may also be able to persuade an organization to create an internship just for you, particularly if you're willing to work for minimum wage or for free to get experience.

Smaller companies may be more willing to create internships than huge ones. In a small company, you may be also able to get a wider variety of experience.

Check with the alumni or fundraising office on campus to see whether any alumni of your school work at the organization where you'd like an internship.

Once you've identified a company, set up a referral interview or use the pattern of organization for a prospecting letter described in Chapter 28. Stress your enthusiasm and your ability to learn.

ANALYZING THE JOB MARKET

Once you know what is most important to you, analyze the job market to see where you could find what you want. For example, Peter's greatest interest is athletics, but he isn't good enough for the pros. Studying the job market might suggest several alternatives. He could teach sports and physical fitness as a high school coach or a corporate fitness director. He could cover sports for a newspaper, a magazine, or a TV station. He could go into management or sales for a professional sports team, a health club, or a company that sells sports equipment.

To learn about the general business climate, read the business sections of newspapers and news magazines. Read trade journals and industry directories (see Figure 26.2) to find out about trends, challenges, and problems within an industry. Go to your college library (the business library, if your university has several libraries) to get these materials. Begin to read *The Wall Street Journal*, if you aren't already doing so. The index inside the second section lists the companies discussed in that day's issue. Check to see which trade journals are published in your field and read the one that's most appropriate for you.

Think about the industry's prospects. What industries seem to be thriving? Which are endangered? What qualities seem necessary for survival?

Learning about a Specific Organization

Many placement offices have notebooks with extensive information about a number of corporations. This recruiting literature will paint the company in the most positive light possible, so don't make it your only source of information. However, recruiting brochures have information about training programs and career paths for new hires—crucial information which general directories are unlikely to have.

Check out the company's annual report at your library, or write to the company for a copy if your library doesn't have one. Note: only companies whose stock is publicly traded are required to issue annual reports. In this day of mergers and buy outs, many companies are owned by other companies. The parent company is sometimes the only one to issue an annual report.

Check the indexes of *The Wall Street Journal* and of trade journals to locate stories about specific companies.

Check directories for your field to get facts and figures on the companies you're interested in. Figure 26.3 lists a few of the directories available. The information in these books ranges from net worth, market share, and principal products to the names of officers and directors.

Advertising Age	*Discount Store News*	*Nation's Restaurants*	
American Banker	*Electric Power Monthly*	*Personnel*	
Automotive News	*Financial Analysts Journal*	*The Practical Accountant*	
Aviation Week	*Graphic Arts Monthly*	*Real Estate Today*	
Beverage Industry	*Grocery Marketing*	*Television/Radio Age*	
Canadian Business	*Internal Auditor*	*Training and Development Journal*	
CPA Practitioner	*International Advertiser*	*Travel Agent*	
Datamation	*Modern Materials Handling*	*Women's Wear Daily*	
Direct Marketing	*National Electronics*	*Variety*	

FIGURE 26.2
EXAMPLES OF TRADE JOURNALS

Information Interviews

To find out whether you'd like a specific kind of job, conduct information interviews. In an **information interview** you talk to someone who works in the area you hope to enter to find out what the day-to-day work involves and how you can best prepare to enter that field. Problem 26–5 lists specific questions you could ask in an information interview.

An information interview can accomplish several purposes:

- Let you know whether or not you'd like the job.
- Give you specific information about the job and the organization that you can use to present yourself effectively in your résumé and application letter.
- Create a good image of you in the mind of the interviewer.

If you present yourself positively, the interviewer may remember you when openings arise. An information interview may eventually lead to a job offer.

Too many students go into interviews with only the foggiest idea of what they'd be doing if they were hired. Over half the 1,500 graduates hired by one big public accounting firm had quit by the end of the second year. They'd gone into public accounting with visions of advising executives and entrepreneurs. Instead, some of them were spending 12 hours a day, seven days a week, inside bank vaults counting securities. The turnover cost the account-

GENERAL DIRECTORIES

Directory of Corporate Affiliations
Dun's *Million Dollar Directory*
Standard & Poor's Register of Corporations, Directors and Executives
Thomas Register of American Manufacturers

SPECIALIZED DIRECTORIES AND RESOURCE BOOKS

Accounting Firms and Practitioners
California Manufacturers Register
Directory of American Firms Operating in Foreign Countries
Directory of Hotel and Motel Systems
Directory of Management Consultants
Directory of New England Manufacturers
Franchise Annual: Handbook and Directory
O'Dwyer's Directory of Public Relations Firms
The Rand McNally Bankers Directory
Thomas Grocery Register
Standard Directory of Advertisers ("Red Book")
Who's Who in Direct Marketing Creative Services
Television Factbook

FIGURE 26.3
WHERE TO GET INFORMATION ABOUT COMPANIES

Charles E. (Chuck) Morris, vice president and director of Black and Hispanic marketing for Coca-Cola USA . . . is alarmed that so many young Blacks entering the corporate world think they must deny their Blackness to succeed. . . . "When I'm competing one on one, it's performance that counts. Do not deny your cultural heritage. Don't try to be White. I've been working in corporate America for 19 years, and those of us who don't forget who we are, are the achievers—the Joe Blacks [Greyhound Corp.], the Thomas Shropshires [Miller Brewing], the Clarence Finleys [Burlington Industries], the H. Naylor Fitzhughs [Pepsi-Cola] and the Herb Wrights [Philip Morris]. They have not assimilated. . . .

"But in order to get to the top, you must pay a heavy price. No single attribute will get you there. Brains, degrees, performance, support groups, community involvement, and some luck are all involved."

Balance Your Personal and Your Professional Lives†

First Boston's president and CEO, Peter Buchanan, tries to set the example. He tries to pay as much attention to his family as to his work. "It must be a macho thing to work until eleven o'clock every night. I've heard that one of our competitors tells you the firm comes first in your life, and then your family. I think that's *appalling*. It comes around later to hurt the firm. Granted, there is no way we can take the pressure off if a client wants to start a merger the day before Thanksgiving. But I take my vacations every year. I go skiing for two weeks and leave instructions that I'm not to be called." His attitude pervades the firm; the recruiting brochure talks about the need to balance one's personal and professional life. Buchanan emphasizes: "If people here don't think their family comes first, I don't want to hear it." No wonder one third of Yale's graduating class this year signed up to interview with First Boston.

ing firm $7.5 million.[4] No one calculated the cost—financial and personal—to the accountants themselves.

Information interviews are useful both for young people preparing for their first full-time jobs and for people who are thinking about changing careers.

HOW TO FIND OUT WHO'S HIRING

Your placement office can tell you which organizations regularly come to your campus to interview students. Local bankers can tell you which businesses in town are expanding. Even in a generally depressed area, one or more companies will be doing well. Be sure to consider small local companies as well as huge national and multinational corporations. According to Richard Bolles, two-thirds of all new jobs are in organizations with 20 or fewer employees.[5]

If you're interested in government employment, check with your placement office to learn the dates of Civil Service exams. Also talk to someone in the agency you'd like to join to find out how hiring works in that specific agency.

Which Ads to Answer

Newspaper ads often list openings that don't require a four-year college degree. Major newspapers—*The New York Times,* the *Los Angeles Times,* the *Chicago Tribune*—are also worth checking if you're trying to relocate. But few classified ads ask for new college graduates. Ads in *The Wall Street Journal* (reprinted in the *National Business Employment Weekly*) normally list advanced positions, not entry-level ones.

The problem with newspaper ads is that some of them do not represent real jobs and some of them are misleading. A study several years ago showed that only 15% of the employers in San Francisco hired anyone through want ads in a typical year.[6] **Blind ads,** which do not list the company's name, are sometimes misleading. One job hunter responded to an ad for Public Relations/Counseling. The job was for someone to market prepaid funeral arrangements.[7]

Ads in professional or trade journals may be worth following up. However, some of these publications have a long lead time, so the position may have opened weeks or even months before the issue reaches readers' hands. If you want to respond to one of these, do so immediately. You might even want to phone first to see that the job is still open and to ask some basic questions about the organization.

Tapping into the Hidden Job Market

A great many jobs are never advertised—and the number rises the higher on the job ladder you go. Some of these jobs are created especially for a specific person. These unadvertised jobs are called **the hidden job market.** Referral interviews offer the most systematic way to tap into these jobs. **Referral interviews** are interviews you schedule to learn about current job opportunities in your field. Sometimes an interview that starts out as an information interview turns into a referral interview.

* Quoted from Lynn Norment, "How to Succeed in Corporate America," *Ebony* 42 (August 1987): 52.

† Quoted from Robert H. Waterman, *The Renewal Factor* (New York: Bantam Books, 1987), 242–43.

A referral interview should

- Give you information about the opportunities currently available in town in the area you're interested in.
- Refer you to other people who can tell you about job opportunities.
- Enable the interviewer to see that you could make a contribution to his or her organization.

The goal of a referral interview is to put you face-to-face with someone who has the power to hire you. That usually means the president of a small company, the division vice president or branch manager of a big company, the director of the local office of a state or federal agency. None of these people will talk to you if you ask directly for a job, since no one likes to say *no*. However, many people will give you advice—advice about whether your résumé can be improved, advice about useful leads.

You start by scheduling interviews with people you know who may know something about that field—professors, co-workers, neighbors, friends. Your purpose in talking to them is (ostensibly) to get advice about improving your résumé and about general job-hunting strategy and (really) to get **referrals** to other people. In fact, go into the interview with the names of people you'd like to talk to. If the interviewee doesn't suggest anyone, say, "Do you think it would be a good idea for me to talk to ____?" The person will probably give you good advice: if the answer is *no*, you might indeed be wasting your time if you tried to talk to that person.

Then, armed with a referral from someone you know, you call Mr. or Ms. Big and say, "So-and-so suggested I talk with you about job-hunting strategy." If the person says, "We aren't hiring," you say, "Oh, I'm not asking *you* for a job. I'd just like some advice from a knowledgeable person about the opportunities in banking [or image consulting, or freelancing, or whatever] in this city." If this person doesn't have the power to create a position, you seek more referrals at the end of *this* interview. (You can also polish your résumé, if you get good suggestions.)

Even when you talk to the person who could create a job for you, you *do not ask for a job*. But to give you advice about your résumé, the person has to look at it. When a powerful person focuses on your skills, he or she will naturally think about the problems and needs in that organization. When there's a match between what you can do and what the organization needs, that person has the power to create a position for you.

Some business people are cynical about information and referral interviewing. Prepare as carefully for these interviews as you would for an interview when you know the organization is hiring. Think in advance of good questions; know something about the general field or industry; try to learn at least a little bit about the specific company.

Always follow up information and referral interviews with personal thank-you letters. Use specifics to show that you paid attention during the interview, and enclose a copy of your revised résumé.

TWO-CAREER JOB HUNTING

Finding two professional or managerial jobs in the same geographic area requires creativity, hard work, and patience.

Most couples seem to use one of three basic strategies:

a. One spouse accepts a job. (One factor in the decision to accept the job may be whether the area offers opportunities for the other

Information Interviewing Leads to a Job Offer*

As a senior at St. Mary's College in Notre Dame, Indiana, Joan Grabowski couldn't decide whether to pursue a career in music (her major) or business (her minor), so she . . . contacted several successful members of the South Bend, Indiana, business and fine arts communities for informational interviews.

One of the people she approached was the manager of the South Bend Symphony. "We had an excellent talk . . . [but] I never planned on seeing her again."

Nevertheless, Grabowski followed up this meeting . . . by sending a note of thanks, along with a copy of her résumé. Eight months later, just before graduation, the manager called and offered Grabowski the job of assistant manager, overseeing an annual budget of $500,000. She jumped at the chance. . . .

After two years with the South Bend Symphony, Grabowski decided it was time to move on. . . . As an active member of various professional organizations, which she joined at her own expense, Grabowski drew upon her list of professional contacts to restart the informational interview process that had won her first job.

"I was very bold about it. . . . I called people . . . in major symphony orchestras whom I had met however casually . . . and said, 'Hi, I admire you, you've been an inspiration to me; would you have the time to sit down and talk to me?' And in every case they were just so pleased that I had called them up."

Grabowski . . . was referred to the manager of the symphony orchestra in Forth Worth, Texas, which led to a job there as executive assistant manager, overseeing a budget this time of close to $3 million.

* Quoted from American Express, "Networking," *Newsweek on Campus*, August 23, 1985, n.p.

How do people get into careers in global finance?

For Michael Goodson, a Japanese securities analyst at First Boston Corp. in New York, the path was an assignment as a Mormon missionary to Japan. "As a missionary, I was dealing in concepts, showing people that my ideals and values are worth listening to. I'm doing the same now."

After graduating from college with an English major, R. Stephen Wunsch spent eight years climbing mountains in the United States, the United Kingdom, and East Germany. "I didn't have anything on my résumé except for rock climbing." In a rock-climbing class he taught on weekends, he met someone in the bond trading department of Kidder, Peabody & Co. in New York. Wunsch is now a vice president in Kidder's financial futures department.

Dagmar Bottenbruch, a European equities analyst for First Boston, explains European companies to U.S. investors. A Harvard MBA plus fluency in German and English opened doors for her.

International finance requires a knowledge of international markets and international languages and cultures—a combination that few candidates have. As a result, many companies are willing to teach the intricacies of securities to people who already understand the intricacies of another culture.

spouse.) Then the other spouse looks for a job in the geographic area.

b. Both spouses job hunt simultaneously. They weigh the offers that come in. They may accept a pair of offers in the same city. They may take the best offer that either of them receives and have the spouse then limit the job hunt in that city.

c. The couple decides in advance on a geographic area. Both limit their job-hunting to that area.

The method you'll choose will depend on the job opportunities available in your field and what you and your partner feel is best for your relationship.

If you're doing an out-of-town job search, check directories to get the names and addresses of employers. Then use the strategies outlined in Chapter 28 to write "prospecting" letters. If you're particularly interested in a city, follow up the letter with a phone call (at your expense). Few people will respond unless they have an opening. But most people will spend 20 minutes on the phone, and their advice can help you learn how easy it might be to find a second job in that city if one of you is offered a position there.

Once you're in the city where you've decided to live, embark on an aggressive campaign of referral interviews. Ask colleagues where the employed spouse works for names of people who might know something about job strategy in the other spouse's field.

SUMMARY OF KEY POINTS

- Informal preparation for job hunting should start soon after you arrive on campus. Formal preparation for job hunting should begin a full year before you begin interviewing. The year you interview, register with your placement office early.
- Think about the things you have enjoyed most. What do these activities have in common? That common thread is a good foundation for a career.
- Use a **forced choice** to distinguish between what would be nice to have in a job and what's necessary to your success and happiness.
- Use business publications and trade journals to study the industry you hope to enter.
- Use directories, recruiting literature, and annual reports to learn about specific organizations you're interested in working with.
- Newspaper ads are not a good source for jobs for new college graduates. **Blind ads,** which do not list the company's name, produce even fewer job offers.
- Information and referral interviews can help you tap into the **hidden job market**—jobs that are not advertised. In an **information interview** you find out what the day-to-day work involves and how you can best prepare to enter that field. **Referral interviews** are interviews you schedule to learn about current job opportunities in your field.
- Two-career couples should use prospecting letters (described in Chapter 28) for out-of-town job hunting and referral interviews for in-town jobs.

* Based on Peter Gumbel, "Who Gets These Jobs Anyway?" *The Wall Street Journal,* September 18, 1987, 13D.

NOTES

1. Sterling Institute, Washington, DC, cited in Sandra E. La Marre and David M. Hopkins, "The New Employee of the Eighties," *Journal of College Placement*, Fall 1982, 31.

2. Between January 1982 and January 1983, 9.7% of all workers in the United States changed occupations. The most career changes occured among workers 16 to 24 years old (21.7%) and workers ages 35 to 44 (11.7%; U.S. Department of Labor, Bureau of Labor Statistics, "News," March 1, 1984, 1, 4). An earlier study found that 39% of the adult male population changed occupations at least once between 1965 and 1970 (Dixie Sommers and Alan Eck, "Occupational Mobility in the Labor Force," *Monthly Labor Review*, January 1977, 3–26).

3. John Stoltenberg, "Job Hunting in the Work Jungle," *Working Woman*, April 1987, 96.

4. Theodore Cohn and Roy A. Lindberg, *Practical Personnel Policies for Small Business* (New York: Van Nostrand Reinhold, 1984), 72.

5. Richard Nelson Bolles, *What Color Is Your Parachute? A Practical Manual for Job-Hunters & Career Changers* (Berkeley, CA: Ten Speed Press, 1988), 45.

6. Olympus Research Corporation, *A Study to Test the Feasibility of Determining Whether Classified Ads in Daily Newspapers Are an Accurate Reflection of Local Labor Markets and of Significance to Employers and Job Seekers* (Salt Lake City: Olympus Research Corporation, 1973); quoted in Bolles, *What Color Is Your Parachute?*, 19.

7. Allen Fishman, "Misleading Ads Anger Applicants," *Columbus Dispatch*, September 6, 1987, 4C. Tribune Media Services.

Could You Get a Message to the President?*

[A team of researchers at MIT showed that] anyone in the U.S.—sending messages exclusively through personal acquaintances—could reach anyone else in the U.S. in six steps, at a maximum, and that anyone in the world could reach anyone else in the world in fourteen steps. . . .

I ask my class how many steps they would have to go through to get a message to the president of the United States using only a network of face-to-face communication among people who knew and trusted each other. . . . After we have discussed the process for a while, two things usually happen. One, some students begin to think of other "influential" people whom either their friends or family know well; or two, some of the students who . . had at first thought that they were very far removed from anyone in positions of political influence suddenly remember someone they know, who knows someone, who knows someone else.

Use Every Contact†

It happened in a sociology class in a small college. The vice-president of a local company finished his guest lecture. Members of the class asked a few questions then drifted out of the room. One woman approached the speaker. "I'm graduating next month. I enjoy people. I think I have the imagination and persistence to be a good sales representative. I'm interested in a job like that with a company like yours."

The v-p took out his business card. "Write to me. Remind me of your qualifications and that you met me here. I'll set up an interview."

After graduation, five students who had heard the v-p speak tried for sales-rep positions with his company. Naturally, they applied through the personnel department. That summer the company hired only one new sales rep—the woman who had spoken to the v-p.

* Quoted from Marshall R. Singer, *Intercultural Communication* (Englewood Cliffs, NJ: Prentice-Hall, 1987), 149–51.

† Quoted from Miriam Marcus, "Your First Job: How to Find a Good One," *The Working Woman Success Book* (New York: Ace, 1981), 36–37.

EXERCISES AND PROBLEMS FOR CHAPTER 26

26-1 ANALYZING YOUR ACCOMPLISHMENTS

List the 10 accomplishments that give you the most personal satisfaction. These could be things that might go on a résumé but they can also be things that other people wouldn't notice. They can be things you've done recently or things you did as a child.

Answer the following questions for each accomplishment:

1. What skills or knowledge did you use?
2. What personal traits did you exhibit?
3. What about this accomplishment makes it personally satisfying to you?

As your instructor directs,

  a. Share your answers with a small group of other students.

  b. Summarize your answers in a memo to your instructor.

  c. Present your answers orally to the class.

26-2 MAKING A FORCED CHOICE

On another sheet of paper, list the criteria you'd like in a job. Number each item. Then compare each pair.

If you have 12 items or fewer, you can use the Forced Choice Chart below to record your preferences. If you have more than 12 items, make a new chart so that each number will be compared with every other number.

On the chart below, mark the number in each pair that corresponds with the item you'd choose if you could only have one of them. Then count how many times you've marked *1*, how many times you've marked *2*, etc. The items that you mark most often are the features you should try to find in a job.

FORCED CHOICE CHART

1/2	1/3	1/4	1/5	1/6	1/7	1/8	1/9	1/10	1/11	1/12
2/3	2/4	2/5	2/6	2/7	2/8	2/9	2/10	2/11	2/12	
3/4	3/5	3/6	3/7	3/8	3/9	3/10	3/11	3/12		
4/5	4/6	4/7	4/8	4/9	4/10	4/11	4/12			
5/6	5/7	5/8	5/9	5/10	5/11	5/12				
6/7	6/8	6/9	6/10	6/11	6/12					
7/8	7/9	7/10	7/11	7/12						
8/9	8/10	8/11	8/12							
9/10	9/11	9/12								
10/11	10/12									
11/12										

Number of times I've chosen

1 _____	5 _____	9 _____
2 _____	6 _____	10 _____
3 _____	7 _____	11 _____
4 _____	8 _____	12 _____

26-3 GATHERING INFORMATION ABOUT INDUSTRIES

Use six recent issues of a trade journal to report on three to five trends, developments, or issues that are important in an industry.

As your instructor directs,

  a. Share your findings with a small group of other students.

  b. Summarize your findings in a memo to your instructor.

  c. Present your findings orally to the class.

  d. Join with a small group of other students to write a report summarizing the results of this research.

26-4 GATHERING INFORMATION ABOUT SPECIFIC ORGANIZATIONS

Gather printed information about a specific organization, using one or more of the following methods:

- Read the company's annual report.
- Pick up relevant information at the Chamber of Commerce.
- Read articles in trade publications and *The Wall Street Journal* that mention the organization (check the indexes).
- Get the names and addresses of its officers from a directory.
- Read recruiting literature provided by the company.

As your instructor directs,

  a. Share your findings with a small group of other students.

  b. Summarize your findings in a memo to your instructor.

  c. Present your findings orally to the class.

  d. Join with a small group of other students to write a report summarizing the results of this research.

26–5 CONDUCTING AN INFORMATION INTERVIEW

Interview someone working in a field you're interested in. Questions you could ask include the following:

- Tell me about the papers on your desk. What are you working on right now?
- How do you spend your typical day?
- Have your duties changed a lot since you first started working here?
- What do you like best about your job? What do you like least?
- What do you think the future holds for this kind of work?
- How did you get this job?
- What courses, activities, or jobs would you recommend to someone who wanted to do this kind of work?

As your instructor directs,

a. Share the results of your interview with a small group of other students.

b. Write up your interview in a memo to your instructor.

c. Present the results of your interview orally to the class.

d. Write to the interviewee thanking him or her for taking the time to talk to you.

Chapter

27

Résumés

CHAPTER OUTLINE

How Employers Use Résumés

Guidelines for Résumés
Emphasis
Details
Writing Style

Kinds of Résumés

What to Include in a Résumé
Title of the Document
Name, Address, and Personal Information
Career Objective
Education
Honors and Awards
Experience
Activities
References

Typing and Duplicating the Résumé

Designing a Résumé: One Student's Process

Sample Résumés

Summary of Key Points

QUESTIONS

- How do employers use résumés?
- How long should your résumé be?
- How can you emphasize the points that make you look good?
- What writing style should you use in your résumé?
- What are the two basic kinds of résumés? Which kind is best for you?
- What should a résumé include?
- How does someone who hasn't done much fill up a résumé?
- Do you need to get your résumé professionally printed?

Whenever I advertise to fill a good job, I'm inundated with résumés. I'd like to read them all, but frankly, I don't have the time. Sometimes my assistant spends hours just sorting them into piles—those I should definitely read, borderline cases, and résumés which will get immediate form rejections. You'd be amazed at how many qualified people never make it past my assistant's desk because their résumés are sloppy or unclear.

Phyllis Hammond, Personnel Director of a
medium-sized midwestern publishing firm, 1980

A résumé is a persuasive summary of your qualifications for employment. If you're on the job market, having a résumé makes you look well organized and prepared. If you have a job you're happy with, having an up-to-date résumé makes it easier to take advantage of unpredictable opportunities which may come up for an even better job. If you're several years away from job hunting, preparing a résumé now will make you more conscious of what to do in the next two or three years to make yourself as attractive a candidate as possible. Writing a résumé is also an ego-building experience: the person who looks so good on paper is you!

HOW EMPLOYERS USE RÉSUMÉS

Understanding how employers use résumés will help you construct a résumé that works for you.

1. **Employers use résumés to decide whom to interview.** (The major exceptions are on-campus interviews, where the campus placement office has policies that determine who meets with the interviewer.) Since résumés are used to screen out applicants, omit anything that may create a negative impression.

2. **The search committee skims résumés.** Companies often get 50 to 100 résumés a day even when they have not advertised positions; a company that advertises an opening may get 50 to 500 applicants for a single position. A résumé gets a quick glance, 30 to 60 seconds at most. Only the résumés that pass the "skim test" are read more closely. Use layout and immediate visual impact to highlight your credentials.

3. **Employers assume that your letter and résumé represent your best work.** Neatness, accuracy, and freedom from typographical errors are essential.

4. **Interviewers usually reread your résumé before the interview to refresh their memories.** They'll ask about anything that raises questions or looks interesting. Be ready to offer fuller details about everything on your résumé.

5. **After the search committee has chosen an applicant, it submits the applicant's résumé to people in the organization who must approve the appointment.** These people may have different backgrounds and areas of expertise. Spell out acronyms. Explain Greek-letter

honor societies, unusual job titles, or organizations that may be unfamiliar to the reader.

GUIDELINES FOR RÉSUMÉS

A one-page résumé is sufficient, but do fill the page. Less than a full page suggests that you do not have very much to say for yourself.

If you use more than one page, the second page should have at least 10 to 12 lines. Use a second sheet and staple it to the first so that readers who skim see the staple and know that there's more. Leave less important information for the second page. Put your name and *Page 2* or *Cont.* on the page. It's likely that the reader will remove the staple, and it's possible that the pages will be separated. If that happens, you want the reader to know who the qualifications belong to and that the second page is not your whole résumé.

A three-page résumé for someone who's 21 looks pretentious. If you've done a great many things, combine similar small items and omit less important items to keep your résumé to two pages.

Emphasis

Emphasize the things you've done that (a) are most relevant to the position for which you're applying; (b) show your superiority to other applicants; (c) are recent.

The employer is looking for someone to fill a specific job. Show that you're qualified by giving details on course projects, activities, and jobs where you've done similar work. Be brief about jobs that simply show dependability. To prove that you're the best candidate for the job, emphasize items that set you apart from other applicants: promotions, honors and achievements, experience with computers or other relevant equipment, foreign languages, and so on.

Community college graduates may include high school jobs, activities, and honors if they need them to fill the page. As a new college graduate, include information about high school only when

- You began working in high school for a company which you continued to work for during and/or after college;
- You are applying for a job in a small town and grew up in a small town (the fact that you graduated from a small town high school can be a tactful way to show that you can survive in a town without a movie theatre);
- You had *major* honors in high school (awarded to only one person in your school);
- You went to a high school known for its strong academic programs and did well; or
- You were valedictorian or salutatorian of your high school graduating class.

When you're 25 or older, include information about high school only if you need it to show geographical flexibility. Focus on achievements in the last three to five years, not honors that are 10 years old. Whatever your age at the time you write a résumé, you want to suggest that you are now the best you've ever been.

You may include full-time work after high school before you returned to college. If the jobs you held then were low-level ones, present them briefly or combine them:

27.1   1980–87   Part-time and full-time jobs to support family

---

How Long Should a Résumé Be?

Repeated surveys show that employers prefer one-page résumés (probably because they have to read so many of them).

Employment counselors approve either one- or two-page résumés, whichever best highlights the candidate's skills. Even a three-page résumé may be necessary for an older applicant with extensive relevant experience. Two- and three-page résumés should have the most important information on the first page, since that is all the employer will see in the "skim test."

A résumé for a college teaching position—usually called a *Vita* or *Curriculum Vitae*—can be as long as necessary to list all the candidate's publications. Professors with a great many publications, however, usually list only the 10 or so most important ones, adding "plus over 300 articles in [names of journals]."

Résumés for high positions (Board of Directors, Cabinet members) are long, covering every aspect of the candidate's career, current position, and areas of expertise.

Three Rules for Better Résumés*

1. Be realistic.

   Lynn's résumé listed her career objective as "public relations director within a large business organization." No large business is going to give that job to a 20-year-old new college graduate. Right now, she should look for an entry-level job where she can get experience in public relations. A small company as well as a big company could provide that experience.

2. Use layout to emphasize key points.

   Marie's two internships are superb preparation for a career in broadcasting. But she's buried them in the middle of the page. Even worse, she's presented her responsibilities in long paragraphs which look uninviting. Listing her duties vertically, using bullets, or using the two-margin format would allow her to highlight her qualifications.

3. Relate your experience to the job you want.

   Jack is an older-than-average student earning a B.A. in biology who wants to be a pharmaceutical sales representative. His paid jobs have been selling woodstoves, serving subpoenas, waiting tables, mowing lawns, and working on an oil rig. Using a chronological résumé makes his work history look directionless and suggests that he has no relevant experience for the job he wants. But a skills résumé could focus on persuasive ability (selling stoves), initiative and persistence (serving subpoenas), and technical knowledge (courses in biology and chemistry).

You can emphasize material by putting it at the top or the bottom of a page, by giving it more space, and by setting it off with white space. The beginning and end—of a document, a page, a list—are positions of emphasis. When you have a choice (e.g., in a list of job duties), put less important material in the middle, not at the end, to avoid the impression of "fading out."

Weak order:	Coordinated weekly schedules, assigned projects to five staff members, evaluated their performance, submitted weekly time sheets.
Emphatic order:	Coordinated weekly schedules and submitted weekly time sheets. Assigned projects to five staff members and evaluated their performance.

You can also emphasize material by presenting it in a vertical list, by using a phrase in a heading, and by providing details.

Details

Details convince the reader and separate you from other applicants. Tell how many people you trained or supervised, how much money you budgeted or raised. Describe the aspects of the job you did.

Too vague:	Sales Manager, *The Daily Collegian*, University Park, PA, 1988–89. Supervised staff; promoted ad sales.
Good details:	Sales Manager, *The Daily Collegian*, University Park, PA, 1988–89. Supervised 22–member sales staff; helped recruit, interview, and select staff; assigned duties and scheduled work; recommended best performer for promotion. Motivated staff to increase paid ad inches 10% over previous year's sales.

Omit details that add nothing to a title, that are less impressive than the title alone, or that suggest a faulty sense of priorities (e.g., listing minor offices in an organization that tries to give everyone something to do). Either use strong details or just give the office or job title without any details at all.

Writing Style

Without sacrificing content, be as concise as possible.

Wordy:	Member, Meat Judging Team, 1986–87 Member, Meat Judging Team, 1987–88 Member, Meat Judging Team, 1988–89 Captain, Meat Judging Team, 1988–89
Tight:	Meat Judging Team, 1986–89; Captain 1988–89

Wordy:	Performed foundation load calculations
Tight:	Calculated foundation loads

Résumés normally use phrases and sentence fragments. Complete sentences are acceptable if they are the briefest way to present information. To save space and to avoid sounding arrogant, never use *I* in a résumé. *Me* and *my* are acceptable if they are unavoidable or if using them reduces wordiness.

Verbs or gerunds (the *ing* form of verbs) create a more dynamic image of

---

* Based on LeAne Rutherford, "Five Fatal Résumé Mistakes," *Business Week's Guide to Careers* 47, no. 3 (Spring/Summer 1986): 60–62.

you than do nouns. In the revisions below, the nouns, verbs, and gerunds used to list the job duties are in bold type.

Nouns: Chair, Income Tax Assistance Committee, Milledgeville, GA, 1987–88. Responsibilities: **recruitment** of volunteers; flyer **design, writing,** and **distribution** for **promotion** of program; **speeches** to various community groups and nursing homes to advertise the service.

Verbs: Chair, Income Tax Assistance Committee, Milledgeville, GA, 1987–88. **Recruited** volunteers for the program. **Designed, wrote,** and **distributed** a flyer to promote the program; **spoke** to various community groups and nursing homes to advertise the service.

Gerunds: Chair, Income Tax Assistance Committee, Milledgeville, GA, 1987–88. Responsibilities included **recruiting** volunteers for the program; **designing, writing,** and **distributing** a flyer to promote the program; and **speaking** to various community groups and nursing homes to advertise the service.

Note that the items in the list must be in parallel structure. See Chapter 9 for a review of parallelism.

KINDS OF RÉSUMÉS

There are two kinds of résumés: chronological and skills. A **chronological résumé** summarizes what you did in a time line (starting with the most recent events and going backwards in **reverse chronology**). It emphasizes degrees, job titles, and dates. It is the traditional résumé format. Use a chronological résumé when

- Your education and experience are a logical preparation for the position for which you're applying.
- You have impressive job titles, offices, or honors.

A **skills résumé** emphasizes the skills you've used, rather than the job in which or the date when you used them. Use skills résumé when

- You lack impressive job titles, offices, or honors.
- Your education and experience are not the usual route to the position for which you're applying.
- You want to combine experience from paid jobs, activities or volunteer work, and courses to show the extent of your experience in administration, finance, speaking, etc.
- Your recent work history may create the wrong impression (e.g., it has gaps, shows a demotion, shows job-hopping, etc.).

The two kinds differ slightly in the information they include; they have major differences in how that information is organized. You may assume that the advice in this chapter applies to both kinds of résumés unless there is an explicit statement that the two kinds of résumés would handle a category differently.

But I Haven't Done Anything! *

Some students have trouble coming up with details. "I've never been sales manager of my college paper. I've never really done anything." That's too negative. *Everybody* has done *something*. How have you spent the last five years? Use the warm-up exercises in problems 27–1, 27–2, and 27–3 to get started.

One woman's job experience consisted of being a part-time sales clerk in the lighting department of a department store—not a very prestigious job and not one that had important-sounding job duties. But the things she'd done told a different story.

She had gathered data and undertaken research. Because at first she couldn't answer customers' questions, she went to the library to read about lighting, vision, and energy consumption. She visited competitors and noticed their products and displays.

She had demonstrated creativity. In August, she rigged up a mannequin to look like a student—slouched in a chair, holding a textbook and a pop bottle, surrounded by clothes, a football, and a guitar. On the table was a lamp positioned to provide good study light with a sign, "At least he won't ruin his eyes."

She had developed a successful persuasive strategy. The store sold four times as many lamps that August as it ever had, including the month before Christmas.

* Based on John L. Munschauer, *Jobs for English Majors and Other Smart People* (Princeton, NJ: Peterson's Guides, 1986), 36–37.

Omit Personal Data on Résumés

There are two big reasons to omit personal data: it takes up space that could be used to showcase your achievements, and it may work against you.

Marital status, number of children. Anyone who is divorced should omit this information, even if you have dependents. More and more companies now prefer single men for entry-level jobs. Whatever a woman's status, it can be used as a reason to screen her out. Employers may be afraid that a single woman will quit when she gets married; they may be afraid that a married woman will quit to have children or to follow her husband when his career demands a move.

Height, weight. Americans like height: if you're a tall male, the numbers make you look good. If you're 5′8″, you probably look more impressive in person than those numbers sound on paper. Women should omit this category. A woman who's 5′10″ sounds like an Amazon; one who's 5′2″ sounds too fragile for the business world. The only exceptions would be jobs with minimum height requirements (police, flight attendant) or jobs where your height and weight help show that you meet the job's fitness demands (e.g., physical education teacher).

Health. If you say it's only "good," they'll wonder what's wrong with you. If you're handicapped, omit HEALTH in the résumé and discuss your ability to surmount any restrictions in the letter. Make sure your letters of reference testify to your ability to do the job.

Religion. Whatever you are, somebody somewhere is prejudiced against it. Instead, include leadership roles, volunteer work, and paid jobs in religious organizations under EXPERIENCE, ACTIVITIES, and COMMUNITY SERVICE.

WHAT TO INCLUDE IN A RÉSUMÉ

Although the résumé is a factual document, its purpose is to persuade. In a job application form or an application for graduate or professional school, you answer every question even if the answer is not to your credit. In a résumé, you cannot lie, but you can omit anything which does not work in your favor.

Résumés commonly contain the following information. The categories marked with an asterisk are optional.

> *Title of Document
> Name, Address, and Phone Number
> *Career Objective
> Education
> Experience
> *Honors
> *Activities
> *References

You may choose other titles for these categories and add categories that are relevant for your qualifications: COMPUTER SKILLS, FOREIGN LANGUAGES.

EDUCATION and EXPERIENCE always stand as separate categories, even if you have only one item under each head. Combine other headings so that you have at least two long or three short items under each heading. For example, if you're in one honor society, two social clubs, and on one athletic team, combine them all under ACTIVITIES AND HONORS.

If you have more than seven items under a heading, consider using subheadings. For example, a student who had a great many activities might divide them into STUDENT GOVERNMENT, OTHER CAMPUS ACTIVITIES, and COMMUNITY SERVICE.

Put your strongest categories near the top and at the bottom of the first page. If you have impressive work experience, you might want to put that category first after your name, put EDUCATION in the middle of the page, and put your address at the bottom.

Title of the Document

The reader can tell that the document is a résumé, so you don't need a title. Just center your name at the top of the page. If you do use the word RÉSUMÉ, remember that it is a French word and retains the accents over both *é*'s both in full capital letters and in lower case. You will have to add these by hand, unless your typewriter or word processor printer has accent marks or a strongly slanting apostrophe. (On word processors, use a required backspace or an overstrike key to get the accent over the *é*.)

Name, Address, and Personal Information

Use your full name, even if everyone calls you by a nickname. You may use an initial rather than spelling out your first or middle name.

If you are a student, give an address where you can be reached during vacation periods as well as your campus address. If you are employed, give your office as well as your home address.

Give a complete phone number, including the area code. If you don't have a phone, try to make arrangements with someone to take messages for you—employers usually call to schedule interviews and make job offers.

FIGURE 27.1
WAYS TO SET UP NAME AND ADDRESS

Name in Upper Left-Hand Corner, Two Addresses

```
John David Rahal

                          Résumé


Campus Address                     Permanent Address
    403 West College Street            3693 Sycamore Lane
    West Lafayette, IN  47907          South Bend, IN  46529
    (219) 555-7493                     (219) 555-3258


Education
    Bachelor of Science in Industrial Management, May 1989, Purdue
    University (West Lafayette, IN)
```

Name Centered, Used as Title of Document; One Address

```
                  Elizabeth Montgomery Heurta

                       14546 Mallard Drive
                  Northridge, California  91324
                        (213) 555-1693

Experience
    Account Manager, Gilmer Advertising, Los Angeles, CA, 1983-
        present.  Service accounts for the California Travel Bureau
        and the California Office of Economic Development.
        Supervise seven account administrators for the following
        accounts:
            K-Mart              Coca-Cola Bottlers
            Blue Shield         The Los Angeles Times
            Pacific Bell        The Parade of Roses
            La-Z-Boy
```

Emphasize your name by setting it off from the rest of the résumé, either putting it in the top left-hand corner or centering it as the title of the document. (See Figure 27.1.) If you use only one address, consider centering it under your name. If you use two addresses (office and home, until _____/after _____) set them up side by side to balance the page visually.

Questions about age, marital status, race, sex, and health are illegal. If an applicant lists this information, some large companies cut it off so that they

Punctuating Your Résumé

In **dates**, use figures for the day and year. The month is normally spelled out. Modern punctuation uses a comma before the year only when you give both the month and the date:

May 1, 1967
  but
Summers 1988–89
October 1988
Fall 1986

Use a hyphen to join inclusive dates:

August–March 1988 or write out
  August to March 1988
1987–91
'87–'89

If you use numbers for dates, do not space before or after the slash: 10/88–5/89.

Phone Numbers: Either put the area code in parentheses (best), space, then put the number OR separate the area code by a hyphen.

(217) 555-1234 or 217-555-1234

Addresses: Use a comma after the city before the state. It is OK to use either Post Office (two letter, full caps, no period) or traditional abbreviations for the state. Be consistent throughout the résumé. Space two or three times, then type the zip code.

Urbana, IL   61801
Wheaton, Illinois   60187
Morton, Ill.   61550

cannot be accused of discriminating. If you decide to include personal data, keep it brief and deemphasize it, perhaps by using only one line for it.

27.2   Age: 22   Height: 6′1″   Weight: 160   Marital Status: Single

A **picture** is also optional; it cannot be required. There are three **advantages of using a photo**. (1) It is an unobtrusive way of indicating your race and sex. (2) It can disarm possible prejudice if you have a strongly ethnic name but look "melting-pot American." (3) It takes up space, and thus is a way to "pad" if you don't have enough to fill up a page. Even if you want to use a photo to achieve one of these three goals, use one only if the picture makes you look intelligent as well as attractive.

For most people, the **disadvantages of using a photo** outweigh the advantages. (1) Research shows that attractive-looking women are perceived to be less qualified than plainer women or men with the same credentials.[1] (2) The interviewer may be subconsciously disappointed when you don't look like your picture (few people do). (3) Most people seem more attractive in person than they appear in a still photograph, and unattractive people—of either sex—are likely to be judged negatively.

Career Objective

CAREER OBJECTIVE statements should sound like the job descriptions an employer might use in a a job listing. Keep your statement brief—two or three lines at most. Tell what you want to do, what level of responsibility you want to hold.

Ineffective career objective:	To offer a company my excellent academic foundation in hospital technology and my outstanding skills in oral and written communication
Better career objective:	Hospital and medical sales requiring experience with state-of-the-art equipment

Good CAREER OBJECTIVES are hard to write. If you talk about entry-level work, you won't sound ambitious; if you talk about where you hope to be in five or 10 years, you won't sound as though you're willing to do entry-level work. A CAREER OBJECTIVE is essential only when you're changing fields. When you're applying for a job that is a natural outgrowth of your education and experience, you can omit this category and specify the job you want in your cover letter.

Often you can avoid writing a CAREER OBJECTIVE statement by putting the job title or field under your name or in the opposite corner:

Joan Larson Ooyen	Terence Edward Garvey	David R. Lunde
Marketing	Technical Writer	Corporate Fitness Director

Note that you can use the field you're in even if you're a new college graduate. To use a job title, you should have some relevant work experience.

If you use a separate heading for CAREER OBJECTIVE, put it immediately after personal data, *before* the first major heading.

Education

EDUCATION can be your first major category if you've just earned (or are about to earn) a degree, if you have a degree which is essential or desirable for the position you're seeking, or if you can present the information briefly. Save EDUCATION for a later page if you lack a degree that other applicants may have or if you need all of page 1 for another category.

Under EDUCATION, include information about your undergraduate and graduate degrees. Do include junior colleges or transferring from one branch campus to another if you have room. Don't include transfers from one college to another within the same university (e.g., from Engineering to Business). Include summer school if you took courses to fit in extra electives or to graduate early but not if you were making up a course you flunked during the year. Include study abroad, even if you didn't earn college credits. If you got a certificate for foreign study, give the name and explain the significance of the certificate.

Highlight proficiency in foreign or computer languages by using a separate category if you have at least three short or two long entries to put under it.

Professional certifications can be listed under EDUCATION or in a separate category.

If your GPA is good, include it. Because grade point systems vary, specify what your GPA is based on: *3.4/4.0* means 3.4 on a 4.0 scale. If your GPA is under 3.0 on a 4.0 scale, use words rather than numbers: *B− average*. If your GPA isn't impressive, calculate your average in your major and your average for your last 60 hours. If these are higher than your overall GPA, consider using them.

There are two basic options for presenting your educational information. Whichever option you choose, use **indented format** (examples 27.3–27.5), in which items that are logically equivalent begin at the same space, with carryover lines indented three spaces. Because it emphasizes dates rather than degrees, use the **two-margin format** or **block** (see example 27.9) only if you plan to leave school without earning a degree.

Option I. List in reverse chronological order (most recent to earliest) each degree earned, field of study, date, school, city, state of any graduate work, short courses and professional certification courses, college, junior college or school from which you transferred.

27.3   Master of Accounting Science, May 1990, Arizona State University,
        Tempe, AZ
        Bachelor of Arts in Finance, May 1988, New Mexico State University,
        Las Cruces, NM
        Plan to sit for the C.P.A. exam November 1990

27.4   B.S. in Personnel Management, June 1989, Georgia State University, Milledgeville,
        GA
        A.S. in Office Management, June 1987, Georgia Community College,
        Atlanta, GA

Option II. After giving the basic information (degree, field of study, date, school, city, state) about your degree, list courses, using short descriptive titles rather than course numbers. Use a subhead like *Courses Related to Major* or *Courses Related to Financial Management* which will allow you to list all the courses (including psychology, speech, and business communication) which will help you in the job for which you're applying. Don't say *Relevant Courses*, as that implies that all your other courses were irrelevant.

27.5   B.S. in Management, May 1990, Illinois State University, Normal, IL
        G.P.A.: 3.8/4.0
        Courses Related to Management:
            Personnel Administration   Business Decision-Making
            Finance   Use of Computers in Business
            Management I and II   Marketing
            Accounting I and II   Legal Environment of Business
            Business Report Writing   Business Speaking
        Salutatorian, Niles Township East High School, June 1986, Niles, Illinois

---

Punctuating Your Résumé
(*continued*)

In line (indented) format for references, use a comma to separate lines. Use three to five spaces after zip code before phone number.

Professor Richard E. Ziegler,
Assistant Head, Department
of Accountancy, University
of Illinois, Urbana,
IL   61801   (217) 333-4343

Degrees: Periods are optional after degrees. If you use periods, don't space between letter, periods.

A.S. in Office Administration
B.S. in Accountancy
M.B.A.
J.D.
Ed.D. in Business Education

Education: Use commas to separate elements:

Bachelor of Science in Business
Administration, May 1988,
University of Illinois at Urbana-
Champaign

Options: University of Illinois,
Urbana, IL
University of Illinois (Urbana,
Illinois)

Use the same form for city, state of all schools. If you continue information about education on the same line, put a period after state. Otherwise, no punctuation.

B.S. in Education, June 1988,
Ohio State University, Columbus, OH. Undeclared minor in business.

But . . .

B.S. in Education, June 1988,
Ohio State University, Columbus, OH

Experience: Use commas to separate items. Put a period after the date, before other details about the job (responsibilities, etc.):

Job title, name of organization,
city, state, dates. Other
information.

Join Honor Societies

Sometimes students who are invited to join national honor societies such as Phi Beta Kappa and Phi Kappa Phi decline the invitation. Students may not have the money to pay the initiation fee, and the society may not seem like a very big honor.

That's a mistake.

People continue to list national honorary societies which they joined in college no matter how old they are. Not everyone is admitted; your membership can stand you in good stead 10 or 20 years from now.

Pay the fee (borrow it from your parents if you have to) and join the honor society.

This option doesn't tell the reader much, since many other students have taken the same combination of courses. But listing courses is an unobtrusive way to "pad" if you don't have quite enough to fill up a page. It may also be good if you've taken an unusual combination of courses which uniquely qualifies you for the position for which you're applying.

Honors and Awards

It's nice to have the word HONORS in a heading where it will be obvious even when the reader skims the résumé. If you have fewer than three honors and therefore cannot justify a separate heading, consider a heading ACTIVITIES AND HONORS to get that important word in a position of emphasis.

Include the following kinds of entries in this category:

* Listings in recognition books (e.g., *Who's Who in the Southwest*).
* Academic honor societies. Specify the nature of Greek-letter honor societies so the reader doesn't think they're just social clubs.
* Fellowships and scholarships, including honorary scholarships for which you received no money and fellowships which you could not hold because you received another fellowship at the same time.
* Awards given by professional societies.
* Major awards given by civic groups.
* Varsity letters; selection to all-state or all-America teams; finishes in state, national, or Olympic meets. (These could also go under ACTIVITIES but may look more impressive under HONORS. Put them under one category or the other—not both.)

Omit honors like "Miss Congeniality" which work against the professional image you want your résumé to create.

As a new college graduate, try to put HONORS on page 1. In a skills résumé, put HONORS on page 1 if they're major (e.g., Phi Beta Kappa, Phi Kappa Phi). Otherwise, save them till page 2—EXPERIENCE will probably take the whole first page.

Experience

You may use other headings if they work better: WORK EXPERIENCE, SUMMER AND PART-TIME JOBS, MILITARY EXPERIENCE, MARKETING EXPERIENCE, ACHIEVEMENTS RELATED TO CAREER OBJECTIVE.

What to Include.   Under this section, include the following information for each job you list: position or job title, organization, city and state (no zip code), dates of employment, and other details, such as full- or part-time status, job duties, special responsibilities or the fact that you started at an entry-level position and were promoted. Include unpaid jobs and self-employment if they provided relevant skills (e.g., supervising people, budgeting, planning, persuading).

If as an undergraduate you've earned a substantial portion of your college expenses, say so in a separate sentence either under EXPERIENCE or in the section on personal data. (Graduate students are expected to support themselves.)

27.6 These jobs paid 40% of my college expenses.

27.7 Paid for 65% of expenses with jobs, scholarships, and loans.

Note that a complete sentence is acceptable if it does not use *I*.

Ways to Set up Experience. Indented format emphasizes job titles.

27.8 EXPERIENCE
<u>Engineering Assistant,</u> Sohio Chemical Company, Lima, Ohio, Summer 1986. Originally hired as a laboratory technician, Summer 1985; promoted following year. As laboratory technician, tested waste water effluents for compliance with Federal EPA standards. As engineering assistant, helped chemists design a test to analyze groundwater quality and seepage around landfills. Presented weekly oral and written progress reports to Director of Research and Development.
<u>Veterinary Assistant,</u> Animalcare, Worthington, Ohio, June 1983–September 1984. Full-time during summers; part-time during senior year of high school. Cared for and fed animals, assisted veterinarians as needed, and entered information on an IBM AT computer using Enable.

Two-margin or **block format** emphasizes *when* you worked. Don't use two-margin format if your work history has gaps.

27.9 EXPERIENCE

Summers, 1987–88	Repair worker, Bryant Heating and Cooling, Providence, Rhode Island.
1986–87	Library Clerk, Boston University Library, Boston, Massachusetts. Part-time during school year.
Summer, 1986	Delivery person, Domino's Pizza, Providence, Rhode Island.
1985–86	Food Service Worker, Boston University, Boston, Massachusetts. Part-time during school year.

Choosing Headings for Skills Résumés. In a skills résumé the subheadings under EXPERIENCE will be the *skills* used or the *aspects* of the job you are applying for, rather than the title or the dates of the jobs you've held (as in a chronological résumé). For entries under each skill, combine experience from paid jobs, unpaid work, classes, activities, and community service.

Use headings that reflect jargon of the job for which you're applying: *logistics* rather than *planning* for a technical job; *procurement* rather than *purchasing* for a job with the military. A job description can give you ideas for headings. Possible headings and subheadings for skills résumés include

Administration	Communication:
Alternates or Subheadings:	Alternates or Subheadings:
Budgeting	Conducting Meetings
Coordinating	Editing
Evaluating	Fund-Raising
Implementing	Interviewing
Negotiating	Oral Skills
Planning	Negotiating
Keeping Records	Persuasion
Scheduling	Proposal Writing
Solving Problems	Report Writing
Supervising	

Many jobs require a mix of skills. Try to include the skills that you know will be needed in the job you want. For example, one study identified the six top communication skills for jobs in finance and in management.[2] Applicants who had experience in some of these areas could list them as well as subject-related skills and knowledge.

Finance	Management
Listening	Listening
Advising	Motivating
Building Relationships	Advising
Exchanging Routine Information	Building Relationships
Giving Feedback	Persuading
Persuading	Instructing

You need at least three subheadings in a skills résumé; six or seven is not uncommon. Give enough detail under each subheading so the reader will know what you did. Put the most important category from the reader's point of view first.

In a skills résumé, list your paid jobs under WORK HISTORY or EMPLOYMENT RECORD near the end of the résumé. List job title, employer, city, state, and dates. Omit details about what you did if you have already used them under EXPERIENCE.

Activities

Employers are very interested in your activities if you're a new college graduate. If you've worked for several years after college and/or have an advanced degree (MBA, JD), you can omit ACTIVITIES and perhaps include PROFESSIONAL ACTIVITIES AND AFFILIATIONS or COMMUNITY AND PUBLIC SERVICE, if you have strong credentials in these areas. If you went straight from college to graduate school but have an unusually strong record under ACTIVITIES, include this category even if all the entries are from your undergraduate days.

Include the following kinds of items under ACTIVITIES:

- Volunteer work. Include important committees and leadership roles.
- Membership in organized student activities. Include important subcommittees, leadership roles. Include minor offices only if they're directly related to the job for which you're applying or if they show growing responsibility (you held a minor office one year, a bigger office the following year). Include so-called major offices (e.g., vice president) even if you did very little. Provide descriptive details if (but only if) they help the reader realize how much you did and the importance of your work.
- Participation in organized activities which require talent or responsibility (e.g., choir, freshman orientation).
- Participation in varsity, intramural, or independent athletics. However, don't list so many sports that you appear not to have any time to study.
- Social clubs, if you held a major leadership role or if social skills are important for the job for which you're applying.
- Religious organizations if you held a major leadership role or if you're applying for a church- or synagogue-related job.

Major leadership roles may look more impressive if they're listed under EXPERIENCE instead of under ACTIVITIES.

* Based on Phil Elder, "The Trade Secrets of Employment Interviews," Association for Business Communication Midwest Convention, Kansas City, MO, May 2, 1987.

References

Including references anticipates the employer's needs and removes a potential barrier to your getting the job. If you want to limit your résumé to one page, you can omit this category. Don't, however, say "References Available on Request"; no job applicant is going to refuse to supply references. If you don't want your current employer to know you're job hunting, omit the category in the résumé and say in the letter, "If I become a finalist for the job, I will supply the names of current references."

When you list references, include at least three, usually no more than five, never more than six. As a college student or a new graduate, include at least one professor and at least one employer. Personal or character references are less impressive than people who can talk about some aspect of your work. If you're changing jobs, include your current superior.

For each reference, list name, title or position, organization, city, state and zip code, and business phone number. Use courtesy titles (*Dr., Mr., Ms.*) for all or for none. By convention, all faculty with the rank of assistant professor or above may be called *Professor*. If you want to list teaching assistants, omit titles for all references.

References whom the reader knows are by far the most impressive. In a skills résumé, choose references who can testify to your abilities in the most important skills areas.

Include the name and address of your placement office if you have written recommendations on file there.

Ways to Set up References.   References presented in line format in an indented résumé will look like this:

27.10   REFERENCES
  Thomas Elgee, Professor of Community Health, University of Northern
   Colorado, Greely, CO 80639 (303) 351-1111.
  Maria Roderiques, Assistant Dean of Students, University of Northern
   Colorado, Greely, CO 80639 (303) 351-2222.
  Elizabeth Tormei, Professor of Women's Studies, University of Northern
   Colorado, Greely CO 80639 (303) 351-3333.
  Matthew J. Kohl, Director, Brethren Community Services, Eugene, CO 80689
   (303) 726-4444.
  Amy Wilson, Director, Rape Crisis Center, Denver, CO 80203
   (303) 555-5555.

Presenting references in this way takes the minimum amount of space. If you have slightly more room, double-space between the names of references. A two-margin format takes up even more space and can help you fill a page.

27.11   REFERENCES

Thomas Elgee	Elizabeth Tormei
Professor of Community Health	Professor of Women's Studies
University of Northern Colorado	University of Northern Colorado
Greely, CO 80639	Greely, CO 80639
(303) 351-1111	(303) 351-3333
Maria Roderiques	Matthew J. Kohl
Assistant Dean of Students	Director
University of Northern Colorado	Brethren Community Services
Greely, CO 80639	Eugene, CO 80689
(303) 351-2222	(303) 726-4444

    Amy Wilson
    Director
    Rape Crisis Center
    Denver, CO 80203
    (303) 555-5555

I Can't List My Boss as a Reference: I Was Fired!*

Some companies require candidates to fill out job application forms listing each employer and then contact a sample of the employers. What can you do if you know a former employer doesn't like you—or worse, if you were fired?

Phil Elder, an interviewer for an insurance company, suggests calling that person and saying something like this: "Look, I know you weren't pleased with the job I did at _____. I'm applying for a job at _____ now and the personnel director may call you to ask about me. Would you be willing to give me the chance to get this job so that I can try to do things right this time?"

All but the hardest of heart, says Elder, will give you one more chance. You won't get a glowing reference, but neither will the statement be so damning that no one is willing to hire you.

---

* Based on Phil Elder, "The Trade Secrets of Employment Interviews," Association for Business Communication Midwest Convention, Kansas City, MO, May 2, 1987.

Employment in Japan*

In Japan, students compete to get into the best universities because the best employers look only at graduates from those universities.

Graduates are hired into the company, not into a specific job. Employees can expect to be trained to work in several areas of the organization.

"Lifetime" employment covers men till they are 55 years old. (When the system was introduced in 1912–26, the life expectancy of Japanese men was only 44 years. Now, most Japanese men live past 55.) Men from powerful companies may be sent to one of the company's subsidiaries, so their employment can continue past 55. Men who work for a less powerful employer are out on their own.

Women made up a third of the Japanese work force in 1980, but only 20% of all working women had permanent jobs. The rest could be laid off if their employers needed to cut expenses.

TYPING AND DUPLICATING THE RÉSUMÉ

Experimenting with different layouts is easy if you're using a word processor. If you must use a regular typewriter, you may want to cut up the typed sections and move them around on the page or use lines of XXXXXXXs to get spacing down without worrying about typing. Even if you have someone else (friend or paid typist) type it for you, *you* will still need to work out the spacing in advance. You cannot expect the typist to do it for you.

Big blocks of type will create the visual effect of a second, larger margin. If you use the indented format, use a *small* outside margin (about $^3/_4''$) so that you'll have no more than $1^1/_2''$ (sides) or $2''$ (top) between the edge of the page and the start of most of your type.

Type your résumé on standard $8^1/_2 \times 11''$ paper (never legal size). If possible, use a carbon (one-time-only) ribbon, since it makes a cleaner, darker impression.

Duplicate your résumé on 20-lb. bond paper (paper with 20-25% cotton content). White paper is standard; pale cream or pale beige is acceptable if you want a more modern look.

It is not necessary to have your résumé printed; photocopying on good quality bond paper will do. Having your résumé printed suggests that you're applying for lots of jobs—which is OK when you're getting a degree, but which you may not want to suggest when you change jobs later. If you choose to have your résumé printed, be sure to specify all the details of layout and design so that your résumé looks good on the page; be prepared to go through (and pay for) several drafts until you get the printed copy the way you want it.

If you want to send an individually typed résumé, use a word processor or a repetitive typewriter. Corrections don't show up on photocopies, but they do on the original page, and résumés must appear to be error-free.

DESIGNING A RÉSUMÉ: ONE STUDENT'S PROCESS

This section is a story about how one student created a résumé.

Two months before graduation, Allyson hadn't yet written a résumé or begun to job hunt. When she was required to turn in a résumé for a business communication class, Allyson decided to pay a résumé service to do one for her. She was convinced that she couldn't write a good résumé. Her instructor suggested she come in for a conference first: she could always go to the service later if she felt she needed to.

Allyson explained why writing her résumé was so difficult: "I don't feel that I've done a lot in the past four years. I'm not in a sorority, I haven't held any offices in anything, and although I've had a lot of job experience, none of it's been related to the career that I've chosen."

Allyson brought a résumé draft to the conference. The résumé was basically a chronological one, though it did have a section called ACHIEVEMENTS (Figure 27.2). Since people sometimes dismiss their job experience if the job title isn't impressive, the instructor asked Allyson to describe exactly what she'd done for each job.

The answers weren't encouraging. Allyson's "babysitting" was actually house management and child care. But while caring for three small children (six months, two years, and seven years) demonstrated responsibility, the instructor didn't think it would be easy to convince corporate America that the experience

Based on William V. Ruch, *Corporate Communications: A Comparison of Japanese and American Practices* (Westport, CN: Quorum Books, 1984), 4, 31, and 58.

FIGURE 27.2
ALLYSON'S FIRST RÉSUMÉ DRAFT

```
Education

    OSU   BA Advertising 1988
    Harvard   summer 1986
        Journalism, legal writing,
        Creative writing program

    Core classes:
        Copywriting, promotional strategies
        magazine writing, graphics, media planning


Experience

    1987-88        Babysitting--Everyday

    1987           Babysitting  Mother's Helper  N.J.

    1986           Harvard Student Agency

    1985-1981      Garson and Associates Law Firm
                   Law Clerk
                   research on medical malpractice suits.


Achievements:     --asked to write for Sundial
                  --asked to do advertising for The Locker Room
                    and revise menu
                  --Wrote a Promotional Strategies Campaign for
                    a restaurant chain and it won 1st place in
                    a contest among 17 groups.
```

was relevant. The Harvard name looked impressive, but her work there had been changing beds and cleaning rooms for conference guests.

Her five summers of work at the law firm sounded more promising. The last summer, she redid the entire file system, and did it more quickly than people expected her to. But she wasn't reorganizing the file system; she was just putting the materials in order and in new folders. The medical malpractice research was better: she went to the library, formulated medical and legal questions, and searched for answers. The information she found helped the firm win a $7 million out-of-court settlement. Not bad for a sophomore in college. But Allyson was in advertising and wanted to go into copywriting, not market research. The experience was certainly worth putting on her résumé, but the kind of thinking she'd done as a law clerk wasn't the kind of thinking she needed to demonstrate to an ad agency.

Advice from a Retiring CEO*

[Excerpts from an interview with Douglas E. Danforth, chairman and chief executive of Westinghouse Electric Corporation, just before his retirement]

Let's say you were graduating from college [this spring]. What would you do?

I think I'd try to spend 10 years with the best company I could find, that I could learn the most from—not necessarily the biggest—and then I would become an entrepreneur.

Why?

For the average individual who has the drive, the education and the willingness to gamble, you probably have a greater chance at success earlier than going through the corporate system. . . . And much of the wealth in the country isn't by CEOs like me. It's Joe Dry Cleaners, who has 10 different stores, owns a boat in Fort Lauderdale and a Ski Chalet in Colorado.

For the young person who is choosing the corporate career path, would you advise staying with one company or moving around?

If one is too restricted in the disciplines he is exposed to, then he should stay five or eight years, then try another. But if he has the latitude—to move from one function, or one department, or division, [to] another—then he can gain as much experience in one company as he can in two or three.

So the instructor moved to the next category, asking Allyson to explain what each of the items under ACHIEVEMENTS meant. *The Sundial* was a student satirical humor magazine that would be published beginning the next fall. The editor had called Allyson, asking her to submit an article; he had gotten her name from Allyson's Magazine Writing teacher. Allyson planned to revise an article on "Commuter Flights" that her teacher had liked.

The Locker Room was a new restaurant in town where Allyson had had dinner. Its menu was poorly written. For example, it said that the restaurant "had a long history." In fact, the restaurant was brand-new: the *building* was old. Allyson went up to the owner, told him several of the things that were wrong with the menu, and offered to rewrite it. The owner told her he'd pay her for doing that and also invited her to submit ideas for ads.

The instructor was impressed. The whole anecdote might work in a job application letter, while the résumé could highlight the fact that Allyson had written menu and advertising copy for a real business (not a class). "What you need," the instructor said, "is a skills résumé."

"Are skills résumés very common?"

"Not as common as chronological résumés. I don't think everyone knows about them. And they're a little harder to write. You can write a chronological résumé just by going through the list and remembering what you've done under EDUCATION, under EXPERIENCE, and so on. You can almost fill in the blanks: the job title, the organization, the city and state, the dates. And some of the companies you pay to do résumés just take your fill-in-the-blank answers and print them out on good laser printers. With a skills résumé, you think about the skills you'd need in the job you want to have, the skills the employer is looking for, and show how you've used those skills in what you've already done. A skills résumé lets you take things from classes, from paid jobs, from volunteer work and put them all together."

"How do employers feel about skills résumés?"

"There isn't any good research. One survey asked employers which they'd rather get, and more people said, 'the traditional résumé.' But that's just because they know where to look for things on the traditional résumé. Nobody's ever done research taking the same qualifications, presenting them in two different ways, and seeing which way got more interviews or more job offers. I know people who've gotten jobs using skills résumés.

"You want a résumé that immediately says 'WOW' to the employer. People always get more résumés than they want to deal with. To survive the cut, a résumé has to stand out. Even if you have an interview first and the interviewer just looks at your résumé to remember who you are, you want the résumé to have the same punch that you had in person. You're going to come across well in interviews. But the résumé has to be able to stand by itself."

Allyson smiled. "Before we go any further, let me tell you what I'm working on now. Tomorrow I'm going to interview Charlotte Witkind and write it up for my Magazine Writing class. I met her at an event cosponsored by Thurber House and The Columbus School for Girls. She had on blue earrings with the New York Yankees logo in diamonds, which I recognized because I just bought my boyfriend a New York Yankees watch. So I asked her if she liked the Yankees. She said she had just bought into the team. We have to interview someone interesting for Magazine Writing, so I called her and asked if I could interview her. My teacher thinks maybe I can sell the interview to *Ms.* or to another magazine."

*   Quoted from Timothy D. Schellhardt, "Retiring Westinghouse Chief Executive Talks of Issues Facing Firms and Managers," *The Wall Street Journal*, December 30, 1987, 15.

"That's great! Right now, just put that you've written a profile on Ms. Witkind. And in your job application letter (not your résumé), say that your professor has recommended that you submit it to *Ms*. OK. What's the last item here?"

Allyson described the promotional strategy she'd done as part of a class project. In response to the instructor's questions, she was able to be detailed, and the details were impressive. She also remembered other things that, like the Charlotte Witkind interview, weren't in her draft at all.

The next step was to answer two questions: "What do you want to do? What do you think the employer is looking for?" Allyson replied, "I want to get a job as a copywriter in Cleveland. It's the 10th biggest market, and I'd rather work as a copywriter in a smaller market than have to start as a secretary at a New York agency. I think the agencies want someone who shows creativity, who has a strong personality, who isn't afraid to take risks."

"Then your résumé needs to show that. And it can. You're coming across as a self-starter, a problem-solver. When you actually write your résumé, use the language of your field. *Problem solver* is a positive term in most fields, but it may or may not be right for advertising. Given what you've done, you could have headings for WRITING EXPERIENCE, CREATING ADS, PLANNING PROMOTIONAL CAMPAIGNS, RESEARCH, and SPEAKING, with a list of items under each one. If you wanted to, you could also have a heading like PERSONAL CHARACTERISTICS, with adjectives like 'Self-Starter,' 'Problem-Solver,' 'Creative,' 'Competitive' and an anecdote for each. That *is* a bit gimmicky. You shouldn't do it if all the information is under the skills headings.

"And your résumé is going to make you look qualified. Highly qualified. Other students are going to read it and say, 'But she has done so much. *I* haven't done anything.' They're going to feel just the way you felt when you said you hadn't done much in the last four years. But you *have* done a lot. You'll look great in your résumé. Anyone can, who understands the options and who puts in the time and energy."

Allyson still had some work ahead of her, tinkering with headings, deciding what details to use, and experimenting with layout. The final product (Figure 27.3) is worth the work.

SAMPLE RÉSUMÉS

A good résumé makes the person look highly qualified. Yet the people whose résumés are shown here are students just like you (and like Allyson!). Adopt wording or layout if it's relevant to your own situation, but don't be locked into the forms here. You've got different strengths; your résumé will be different, too.

In Figure 27.4, Dyanne Allen uses a chronological résumé because she has traditional honors and awards to put on it. Indented format for her activities allows her to emphasize the offices she's held. She explains one group that some readers may not know about. She shifts to two-margin (block) format for her jobs to emphasize the fact that she's held jobs since high school. The jobs themselves aren't very impressive, but the two-margin format de-emphasizes the job title.

In Figure 27.5, Steve Zajano uses the indented format throughout. Putting EXPERIENCE first helps him compete with job applicants with four-year degrees but less (and less relevant) experience.

FIGURE 27.3
ALLYSON'S SKILLS RÉSUMÉ

ALLYSON KARNES

195 W. Ninth   6782 Fenwick Drive
Columbus, OH 43210   Solon, OH 44121
(614) 555-3498   (216) 555-6182

CAREER OBJECTIVE

This is really Allyson's philosophy—and it's one an agency will appreciate.

To write creative headlines and print ads that make people remember the
product

She presents herself as a fellow professional

EDUCATION

B.A. in Advertising, June 1988, The Ohio State University, Columbus, OH.
   Core courses: Copywriting, promotional strategies, magazine writing,
       graphics, media planning

Double spaces here to emphasize "Harvard" name →

Harvard University Creative Writing Program, Summer 1986, Boston, MA.
   Courses in journalism and legal writing (graduate course)

EXPERIENCE CREATING ADS

Led the team that developed the winning promotional strategy for Max &
Erma's Restaurants
● Developed idea for theme for a year's campaign of ads

Details visually lend weight, even when reader skims

● Wrote copy for radio spots, magazine ads, and billboards. One bill-
   board ad had the headline "Multiple Choice" and boxes for
   hamburgers, chicken, and salads--with all the boxes checked.
● Presented creative strategy to Max & Erma's CEO and the Head of
   Advertising
● Strategy won first place from among 17 proposals

Wrote more than 15 ads for Copywriting class, including
● Ad for cordless phone: "Isn't It Time to Cut the Cord?"

Gives details of wording to demonstrate her creativity

● Slogan for Ohio University's Springfest Jamboree: "In Short, It
   Jams"
● Billboard for Columbus Boys' School: "Who Said It's Lonely at the
   Top?"

Wrote ads and revised menu for The Locker Room (restaurant)

OTHER WRITING EXPERIENCE

Wrote profile on Charlotte Witkind, part owner of the New York Yankees
Wrote "Commuter Flights" (humor)
Wrote more than 30 magazine articles as part of courses at Harvard
   University and Ohio State
Wrote legal briefs as part of course at Harvard University
Wrote summary of research on $7 million medical malpractice case for
   Garson and Associates

At bottom of page (a position of emphasis)

FIGURE 27.3 (continued)

Allyson Karnes

Saves less important material for page 2

Page 2

The city and state here allows reader to identify Gloria Solomon under "References"

EMPLOYMENT HISTORY

1987-88   Child care and house management, Worthington, OH. Part-time
               daily during school year.

Summer   Mother's Helper, Princeton, NJ. Cared for six-month-old baby;
  1987   cared for all three children when parents were away on week-
               ends.

Summer   Maid, Harvard Student Agency, Boston, MA. Part-time while
  1986   attending Harvard University Creative Writing Program.

Adds second line to avoid emphasizing word "Maid"

Summers   Law Clerk, Garson and Associates, Cleveland, OH. Did
1981-85   independent research in medical malpractice case which the
               firm used to reach a $7 million out-of-court settlement for
               the client.

REFERENCES

Paula DiPerna   H. Thomas Hubbard
Thurber Writer in Residence   Department of Journalism
The Ohio State University   The Ohio State University
Columbus, OH 43210   Columbus, OH 43210
(614) 555-6200   (614) 555-6200

David M. Becher, Partner   Gloria Solomon
Garson and Associates   8774 Thorne St.
Cleveland, OH 44139   Worthington, OH 43085
(216) 555-3200   (614) 555-8943

Samuel T. Tennenbaum
Director, Harvard University Creative Writing Program
Harvard University
Boston, MA 02163
(617) 555-4700

Portfolio Available Upon Request

Dyanne Lynn Allen

Campus Address
  218 Curtis Hall
  Greensboro, NC 27411
  (919) 555-2300

Permanent Address
  2500 Anderson Drive, Apt. 503
  Raleigh, NC   27698
  (919) 555-7865

Education
  B.S. in Administrative Services, May 1989, North Carolina Agricultural and
    Technical State University (Greensboro, NC)
    Grade Point Average in Major: 3.6/4.0

(Grade Point in major is higher than overall GPA)

Honors
  Alpha Lambda Delta Honor Society
  Alpha Kappa Mu Honor Society
  Honor Roll every semester

Activities
  Alpha Kappa Alpha Sorority
    Secretary, 1988-89
    Leaders' Council, 1988-89
    Philanthropic Chair, 1987-88
    Pledge Class President, 1985-86
  Angel Flight (speak before schools and civic groups to promote interest in the
    Air Force and aerospace)
  A&T Gospel Choir

Vertical listing emphasizes offices

She's also in "Celestial Beings" in Angel Flight, but omits that detail to create a professional image

Employment

All her jobs are low level, so she uses two-margin (block) format to deemphasize job titles.

1986-Present	Food Service Worker, Williams Cafeteria, North Carolina Agricultural and Technical State University, Greensboro, NC. Part-time during school year.
Summer 1988	Administrative Assistant, Employee Benefits, AT&T, Greensboro, NC. Compiled statistics on employee status; used AT&T Unix computer to process benefit claims; helped conduct exit interviews.
Winter Break 1985, Summer 1986	Secretary, Raleigh Temporary, Raleigh, NC. Filled in as a temporary replacement for secretarial positions in 14 different business and government offices.
1983-85	Sales Clerk, Sears Roebuck, Raleigh, NC. Part-time during junior and senior years of high school; full-time during summers.

Uses details where they help

Uses detail to suggest familiarity with many office layouts and procedures.

References
  Dr. Meada Gibbs, Chairperson, Department of Business Education and
    Administrative Services, North Carolina Agricultural and Technical State
    University, Greensboro, NC 27411 (919) 555-4000
  Dr. Willard R. Bagwell, Professor of Business Administration, North Carolina
    Agricultural and Technical State University, Greensboro, NC 27411   (919)
    555-4352
  Ms. Marian Follman, Director of Employee Benefits, AT&T, Greensboro, NC 27401
    (919) 555-7000

Puts supervisor from her only responsible job at bottom of page to highlight fact that she does have a business reference

FIGURE 27.5
A CHRONOLOGICAL RÉSUMÉ USING INDENTED FORMAT

Steven W. Zajano

921 South Seventh Street
Cambridge, Ohio 43725
(614) 555-4715

WORK EXPERIENCE

Vertical layout emphasizes experience even when reader skims

Groundskeeper, Muskingum College, New Concord, Ohio, 1983-present.
  Duties included
  * Maintaining campus grounds, athletic fields, and equipment
  * Performing electrical, plumbing, and carpentry as needed

Crew Leader, Seneca National Fish Hatchery, Senecaville, Ohio, 1982-1983.
  Started as Young Adult Conservation Corps (YACC) member; promoted to crew
  leader after five months.
  Duties as crew leader included
  * Maintaining hatchery facilities
  * Planning work activities and schedules for 12 YACC workers

Puts this last so the space after it emphasizes it

Uses parallel structure for all duties

Landscaper, R.G.'s Landscaping Service, Canton, Ohio, Summer 1982.
  Duties included
  * Maintaining existing lawns
  * Landscaping and establishing new lawns

Farm Worker, Hanover Stud Horse Farm, Canal Fulton, Ohio, 1980-82.
  Duties included
  * Maintaining tractors and mending fences
  * Baling hay and straw
  * Caring for thoroughbred racing horses

Puts most interesting duty last where it stands out

ACTIVITIES AND INTERESTS

  Boy Scout Troop, Cambridge, Ohio (Leader)
  Bus Ministry, Cambridge United Christian Church
  Hunting, fishing, camping, swimming, hiking

Some readers may respond negatively. But this ministry is an important part of Steve's life, and he wants to suggest that he isn't just interested in outdoor recreational pursuits.

EDUCATION

  Associate of Applied Sciences, June 1989, Hocking Technical College,
    Nelsonville, Ohio
    Specialization: Recreation and Wildlife Management

REFERENCES

  James Heidler, Grounds Supervisor, Muskingum College, Cambridge, Ohio 43725
    (614) 555-5024

  Richard Jordet, YACC Program Director, Seneca National Fish Hatchery,
    Bytesville, Ohio 43723 (614) 555-5541

  Gerald Sagan, Professor of Recreation and Wildlife Management, Hocking
    Technical College, Nelsonville, Ohio 43765 (614) 555-3492

SUMMARY OF KEY POINTS

- Employers skim résumés to decide whom to interview. Employers assume that the letter and résumé represent your best work. Interviewers normally reread the résumé before the interview. After the search committee has chosen an applicant, it submits the résumé to people in the organization who must approve the appointment.

- A résumé must fill at least one page visually.

- To emphasize key points, put them in headings; list them vertically; provide details.

- Résumés use sentence fragments punctuated like complete sentences. Items in the résumé must be concise and parallel. Verbs and gerunds create a dynamic image of you.

- A **chronological résumé** summarizes what you did in a time line (starting with the most recent events, and going backwards in **reverse chronology**). It emphasizes degrees, job titles, and dates. Use a chronological résumé when
    - Your education and experience are a logical preparation for the position for which you're applying.
    - You have impressive job titles, offices, or honors.

- A **skills résumé** emphasizes the skills you've used, rather than the job in which or the date when you used them. Use a skills résumé when
    - You lack impressive job titles, offices, or honors.
    - Your education and experience are not the usual route to the position for which you're applying.
    - You want to combine experience from paid jobs, activities or volunteer work, and courses to show the extent of your experience in administration, finance, speaking, etc.
    - Your recent work history may create the wrong impression (e.g., it has gaps, shows a demotion, shows job-hopping, etc.).

- Résumés commonly contain the applicant's name, address, and phone number, education, and experience. Activities, honors, and references should be included if possible. A title, personal data, and career objective are optional.

- To fill the page, list courses, use a picture, and list references vertically.

- If you don't have room for everything, use the information that is relevant to the job you want, is recent (last three years), and shows your superiority to other applicants.

- Résumés do not need to be professionally printed. Run out the résumé with a dark ribbon; have it photocopied onto good quality bond paper.

NOTES

1. Richard D. Arvey and James E. Campion, "The Employment Interview: A Summary and Review of Recent Research," *Personnel Psychology* 35 (1982): 302.

2. Vincent S. Di Salvo and Janet K. Larsen, "A Contingency Approach to Communication Skill Importance: The Impact of Occupation, Direction, and Position," *Journal of Business Communication* 24, no. 3 (Summer 1987): 13.

EXERCISES AND PROBLEMS FOR CHAPTER 27

27–1 REMEMBERING WHAT YOU'VE DONE

Use the following list to jog your memory about what you've done. For each, give three or four details as well as a general statement.

Describe a time when you

1. Set a goal and achieved it even though doing so was not easy.

2. Used facts and figures to gain agreement on an important point.

3. Identified a problem which a group or organization faced and developed a plan for solving the problem.

4. Made a presentation or a speech to a group.

5. Won the goodwill of people whose continued support was necessary for the success of some long-term project or activity.

6. Interested other people in something that was important to you and persuaded them to take the actions you wanted.

7. Helped deal constructively with conflict in a group.

8. Demonstrated creativity.

9. Evaluated a situation to decide where to put your best efforts to achieve the greatest rewards.

10. Determined what you needed to know to solve a problem, gathered the necessary information, and applied it successfully.

27–2 DEVELOPING ACTION PHRASES

Use 10 of the following verbs to write action statements describing what you've done in paid or volunteer work, in classes, in extra-curricular activities, or in community service.

analyzed	directed	managed	reviewed
budgeted	earned	motivated	revised
built	edited	negotiated	saved
chaired	examined	observed	simplified
coached	evaluated	organized	sold
collected	helped	persuaded	spoke
conducted	hired	planned	started
coordinated	increased	presented	supervised
counseled	interviewed	produced	trained
created	introduced	recruited	translated
designed	investigated	reported	wrote
developed	led	researched	

27–3 EVALUATING CAREER OBJECTIVE STATEMENTS

None of the following career objective statements is effective. What is wrong with each statement as it stands? Which statements could be revised to be satisfactory? Which should be dropped entirely?

1. To use my acquired knowledge of accounting to eventually own my own business

2. A progressively responsible position as a TECHNICAL WRITER where education and ability would have valuable application and lead to advancement

3. To work with people responsibly and creatively, helping them develop personal and professional skills

4. A position in international marketing which makes use of my specialization in marketing and my knowledge of foreign markets

5. To obtain a challenging management or related position with advancement leading to greater responsibilities in upper management

27–4 EVALUATING THE EXPERIENCE SECTIONS OF RÉSUMÉS

Evaluate each of the following experience sections for graduating college seniors. What impression does each section give? Should the student modify grammar, word choice, style, format, or white space? What specific revisions would you suggest?

1. Experience: May 1988–Present: Commercial Loans Department. Duties include using Compaq and IBM PC to reconcile loan and payment accounts for six member banks on a daily basis, as well as the examination of paid notes for return to customers.

2. Experience

December 1985– July 1983 Marketing Assistant
Sea Education Association
Woods Hole, MA

My primary responsibility at SEA was to develop a dBase II data management system to track student inquiries. I also helped to coordinate on-campus recruiting and evaluate marketing strategies. I worked full-time during the summers and breaks and part-time during the school year. With this job I paid approximately 50% of my expenses.

3. EXPERIENCE

7/87-present   **Boston Financial Data Services**, Quincy, Ma.
<u>Computer operator</u> in a banking/mutual funds environment. Includes two VAX 11/750 minicomputers and one VAX 11/785 running in cluster mode under VMS and two NCR 8200 mini-computers under IMOS.
  - Responsibility for remote telecommunications via a 56k leased line utilizing 3780 and HASP protocols.
  - Maintain and document hardware and software problems and resolve data transmission problems.
  - Train new personnel in VAX/VMS regarding production jobs. Provide journals, reports, and data as needed for in-house users.
  - Experienced with IBM PC-XT.

August 1984
to
November 1987   **Occidental Life Insurance Co., San Francisco, CA.**
Organized and paid medical and dental claims, verified eligibility, corresponded with claimants, medical service providers and insurance companies.

4. COMPUTER EXPERIENCE

LANGUAGES: Pascal, BASIC, LOGO, MACRO, LISP (in process)
HARDWARE: IBM PC, VAX 11/780, IBM Displaywriter, EPSON QX-16
SOFTWARE: VAX/VMS, Multimate, LOTUS, VALDOCS 2, PC DRAW

27–5 DECIDING WHICH KIND OF RÉSUMÉ TO USE

In each of the following situations, will a chronological or a skills résumé make the applicant look stronger? How much and what kind of detail should the applicant provide? Briefly defend your choice.

1. Gene Di Salvo wants to leave his job as an auditor and find a position in personnel.

2. Ron Oliver has been steadily employed for the last six years, but most of the jobs have been low-level ones.

3. Adrienne Barcus was an assistant department manager at a clothing boutique. As assistant manager, she was authorized to approve checks in the absence of the manager. Her other duties were ringing up sales, cleaning the area, and helping mark items for sales.

4. Lois Heilman has been a clerk-typist in the Alumni Office. As part of her job, she developed a schedule for mailings to alumni, set up a merge system, and wrote two of the letters that go out to alumni. The merge system she set up has cut in half the time needed to produce letters.

5. As a co-op student, Stanley Greene spends every other term in a paid job. He now has six semesters of job experience in television broadcasting. During his last co-op he was the assistant producer for a daily "morning magazine" show. As assistant producer, he scheduled guests, helped choose stories, and kept budget records.

27–6 REVISING A RÉSUMÉ

Thomas Wilber has almost nothing on his résumé, and as a result he looks minimally qualified. His CAREER OBJECTIVES [sic] tells any nongovernment employer not to waste time with him; it doesn't work even for government jobs since it suggests that he doesn't want a government job now.

Tom knows his résumé isn't good, but he claims he doesn't have anything to add. "If I take out the OBJECTIVE, my résumé will be even emptier. I don't plan to take the CPA exam. I really didn't do much with my internship. They had me do a lot of go-fer work. I only kept records for small accounts—I didn't get to work on payroll or budgeting or taxes or even major vendors and customers. I haven't done anything else. I was just a member of the management club, not an officer or on any committee. I know we're not supposed to put in high school activities, but can I list just one thing under ACTIVITIES? I was just on the yearbook staff, not an editor or anything."

Suggest some brainstorming questions that Tom can ask, additional information he could provide, and a format that would show him to better advantage.

THOMAS W. WILBER

529 Randolph Drive
Apartment 418
New Orleans, Louisiana   70167
(504) 555-3948

CAREER OBJECTIVES:
To use my training in Accounting to eventually work in a position with the government.

EDUCATION:
1985–89   B.S. in Accounting, The University of Nebraska.
G.P.A. of 3.4 of a possible 4.0.

1981–85   Long High School, New Orleans, Louisiana

EMPLOYMENT:
1987–88   Accounting Intern, Myers Manufacturing, Lincoln, Nebraska. Helped keep books, handled small accounts.

1986–87   Sales Clerk, Plum's Sporting Goods,
            Lincoln, Nebraska. Worked with public,
            helped take inventory, worked with
            Manufacturers' Representatives.

EXTRA-CURRICULAR ACTIVITIES:
    High School—Yearbook Staff
    College—Management Club

REFERENCES:
    Available upon request.

27–7 WRITING A RÉSUMÉ

As your instructor directs, write a résumé based either upon what you have already done or including things you hope to do before you get your degree.

    a. Write a chronological résumé.

    b. Write a skills résumé.

Chapter

28

Job Application Letters

CHAPTER OUTLINE

QUESTIONS

- How do job application letters differ from résumés?
- What are the two kinds of job application letters? How are they alike in content and organization? How do they differ?
- What do you put in the first paragraph of each kind of letter?
- How do you demonstrate a knowledge of the position and the company without lecturing the reader?
- How do you show that you're unique?
- How assertive should you be in the last paragraph?
- Is it OK to use relatives' names? What about other kinds of name-dropping?
- How do you apply you-attitude and positive emphasis in a job application letter?
- How long should the letter be?

> A letter intended as an application for employment . . . should, if possible, contain something that will catch the eye of the receiver, and distinguish your communication from the mass of replies always evoked by an advertisement. . . . If you have anything to mention that you think will tell in your favour—previous employment in an eminent house—acquaintance with foreign languages—experience of foreign and colonial trade—state it. . . . Remember that . . . neatness of style and graceful penmanship are all but indispensable to success.
>
> *The Young Clerk's Manual, or Counting House Assistant*, 1848

Today, job letters in the United States are written using word processors rather than quill pens. But the need to be neat and persuasive hasn't changed in almost 150 years.

The purpose of a job application letter is to get an interview. If you get a job through interviews arranged by your campus placement office or through contacts, you won't need to write a letter. However, if you want to work for an organization that isn't interviewing on campus, or later when you change jobs, you probably will need to write a letter. And much of the research that helps you write a good letter is essential for interviewing.

HOW JOB LETTERS DIFFER FROM RÉSUMÉS

Enclose a copy of your résumé with your application letter. Although the two documents overlap slightly, they differ in several ways:

- A résumé is adapted to a position. The letter is adapted to the needs of a particular organization.
- The résumé summarizes all your qualifications. The letter shows how your qualifications can help the organization meet its needs, how you differ from other applicants, and that you have some knowledge of the organization.
- Business résumés can be two to three pages for experienced applicants. The letter should be only one to two pages.
- The résumé uses short, parallel phrases and sentence fragments. The letter uses complete sentences in well-written paragraphs.

Since the résumé doesn't have to be adapted to a specific company, most job applicants find it easier to write the résumé first and then to write the job application letter after they've done some more research. See Chapter 26 for suggestions about how to get information about a company.

To get the name of the person who should receive the letter, check the ad, call the organization, or consult the directories listed in Chapter 26. An advantage of calling is that you can find out what courtesy title a woman prefers and get current information. A directory which went to press months ago will not include recent promotions.

CONTENT AND ORGANIZATION

You can include only a limited number of points in your letter. Choose those which are

- Major requirements of the job for which you're applying.
- Points that separate you from other applicants.
- Points that show your knowledge of the organization.
- Qualities that every employer is likely to value: the ability to write and speak effectively, to solve problems, to get along with people.

Two different hiring situations call for two different kinds of application letters. Write a **solicited letter** when you know that the company is hiring: you've seen an ad, you've been advised to apply by a professor or friend, you've read in a trade publication that the company is expanding. This situation is analogous to a direct request in persuasion: you can indicate immediately that you are applying for the position. Sometimes, however, the advertised positions may not be what you want, or you may want to work for an organization which has not announced that it has openings in your area. Then you write a **prospecting letter.** (The metaphor is drawn from prospecting for gold.)

Prospecting letters help you tap into the **hidden job market,** the jobs that are never advertised. In some cases, your prospecting letter may arrive at a company which has decided to hire but which has not yet announced the job. In other cases, companies create positions to get a good person who is on the market. Even in a hiring freeze, jobs are sometimes created for specific individuals.

In both solicited and prospecting letters you should

- Address the letter to a specific person.
- Indicate the specific position for which you're applying.
- Be specific about your qualifications.
- Show what separates you from other applicants.
- Show a knowledge of the company and the position.
- Refer to your résumé (which you would enclose with the letter).
- Ask for an interview.

The following discussion first gives patterns for the two kinds of letters and then follows the job letter from beginning to end. The two kinds of letters are discussed separately where they differ and together where they are the same.

How to Organize Solicited Letters

When you know the company is hiring, organize your letter in this way:

1. **State that you're applying for the job** (phrase the job title as your source phrased it). Tell where you learned about the job (ad, referral, etc.). Briefly show that you have the major qualifications required by the ad: a degree, professional certification, job experience, etc.

    If you have several qualifications, summarize them briefly in the same order in which you plan to discuss them in the letter. This

> **Write French Application Letters by Hand***
>
> If you're applying for a job in France, write the application letter by hand. French companies use handwriting analysis to evaluate job applicants.

---

* Based on Iris I. Varner, "A Comparison of American and French Business Communication," Association for Business Communication International Convention, Atlanta, GA, October 15–17, 1987.

Toot Your Own Horn!*

Some people find it hard to write good application letters because they've been taught not to brag about their achievements. "Good work speaks for itself," they think.

Unfortunately, in American business, good work needs a megaphone to be heard. A *Wall Street Journal* survey of executives who'd been fired showed that 83% of them made no special effort to tell their superiors about their own good work. Another study showed that successful executives devoted about half their time to paperwork and the other half to self-promotion and office politics.

In job hunting, employers expect applicants to volunteer information about their interest in and qualifications for the job. No employer is going to say, "She probably really wants this job but just didn't want to appear too eager," or "He probably has done a lot more than this letter says but he didn't want to seem stuck up." Instead, employers will assume that the résumé and letter represent the best possible case you can make.

umbrella sentence or paragraph then covers everything you will talk about and serves as an organizing device for your letter.

28.1 I have a good background in standard accounting principles and procedures and a working knowledge of some of the special accounting practices of the oil industry. I also have practical experience in the oil fields: I've pumped, tailed rods, and worked as a roustabout.

28.2 My business experience, experience using DeVilbiss equipment, and communication skills qualify me to be an effective part of the sales staff at DeVilbiss.

28.3 I feel that I have the creative eye, artistic ability, and experience needed to contribute to McLean Design.

2. **Develop your major qualifications in detail.** Be specific about what you've done; relate your achievements to the work you'd be doing in this new job. Remember that readers know only what you tell them. This is not the place for modesty!

3. **Develop your other qualifications, even if the ad doesn't ask for them.** (If the ad asks for a lot of qualifications, pick the most important three or four.) Show what separates you from the other applicants who will also answer the ad. Demonstrate your knowledge of the organization.

4. **Ask for an interview; tell when you'll be available to be interviewed and to begin work.** End on a positive, forward-looking note.

How to Organize Prospecting Letters

When you don't have any evidence that the company is hiring, you cannot use the pattern for solicited letters. Instead, organize your letter this way:

1. **Catch the reader's interest.**

2. **Create a bridge between the attention-getter and your qualifications.** Focus on what you know and can do. Since the employer is not planning to hire, he or she won't be impressed with the fact that you're graduating.

    If you have several qualifications to discuss, summarize these briefly in the same order in which you plan to discuss them in the letter.

3. **Develop your strong points in detail.** Be specific. Relate what you've done in the past to what you could do for this company. Show that you know something about the company. Identify the specific niche you want to fill.

4. **Ask for an interview and tell when you'll be available for interviews.** (Don't tell when you can begin work.) End on a positive, forward-looking note.

*   Based on Charlene Mitchell and Thomas Burdick, *The Right Moves: Succeeding in a Man's World without a Harvard MBA* (New York: Macmillan, 1985), 43.

First Paragraphs of Solicited Letters

When you know that the firm is hiring, announcing that you are applying for a specific position enables the firm to route your letter to the appropriate person, thus speeding consideration of your application. Identify where you learned about the job: "the position of junior accountant announced in Sunday's *Dispatch*"; "William Paquette, our placement director, told me that you are looking for. . . ."

Note how the following paragraph picks up several of the characteristics of the ad:

> Ad: Business Education Instructor at Shelby Adult Education. Candidate must possess a Bachelor's degree in Business Education. Will be responsible for providing in-house training to business and government leaders. . . . Candidate should have at least six months' office experience. Prior teaching experience not required.

> Letter: I am interested in your position in Business Education. I will receive a Bachelor of Science degree from North Carolina A & T University in December. I have two years' experience teaching word-processing and computer accounting courses to adults and have developed leadership skills in the North Carolina National Guard.

Good word choices can help set you letter apart from the scores or even hundreds of letters the company is likely to get in response to an ad. The following first paragraph of a letter in response to an ad by Allstate Insurance Company shows a knowledge of the firm's advertising slogan and sets itself apart from the dozens of letters that start with "I would like to apply for. . . ."

> The Allstate Insurance Company is famous across the nation for its "Good Hands Policy." I would like to lend a helping hand to many Americans as a financial analyst for Allstate, as advertised in the *Chicago Tribune*. I have a Bachelor of Science degree in Accounting from Iowa State University and I have worked with figures, computers, and people.

Note that the last sentence forecasts the organization of the letter, preparing for paragraphs about the student's academic background and (in this order) experience with "figures, computers, and people."

First Paragraphs of Prospecting Letters

In a prospecting letter, asking for a job in the first paragraph is dangerous: unless the company plans to hire but has not yet announced openings, the reader is likely to throw the letter away. Instead, catch the reader's interest. Then in the second paragraph you can shift the focus to your skills and experience, showing how they can be useful to the employer.

Here are some effective first paragraphs and the second paragraphs which provide a transition to the writer's discussion of his or her qualifications:

- First two paragraphs of a letter to the Director of Publications of Standard Oil:

---

* Quoted from John L. Munschauer, *Jobs for English Majors and Other Smart People* (Princeton, NJ: Peterson's Guides, 1986), 78.

What's Wrong with Job Letters?*

To find out about the effectiveness of letters and résumés, I visited corporations and asked employment managers for their comments. "Here," said one employment manager, as he picked up an eighteen-inch stack of letters and handed it to me. "This is my morning's mail. Read these letters and you'll have your answer.

"... Unfortunately, you'll get through the pack in a half hour, because a glance will tell you that most are not worth reading."

It was hard to believe that the letters could be that bad, but he was right. The typical letter was an insult. Among the letters that I did not finish reading was one on onion-skin paper, in very light type—it must have been the fifth carbon in the typewriter. It began:

> Dear Sir:
>
> I am writing to the top companies in each industry and yours is certainly that. I want to turn my outstanding qualities of leadership and my can-do abilities to. . . .

Enough of that. Also the applicant hadn't even bothered to type in the employment manager's name, which he could easily have found in the *CPC Annual* or in Peterson's Job Guide.

The next letter was written in pencil on notepaper. There may have been an Einstein behind that one, but I can't imagine anyone taking the time to find out. Many other letters were smudged and messy. . . .

Five letters, only five letters in that pile of hundreds, were worth reading.

Relating What You've Done to the Job*

The letter continued...

> As I looked into publishing, it occured to me that of all the things I have done, the one I could most closely relate to the field was, strangely enough, an experience I had as a baby-sitter.

Immediately, he had the editor's full attention. How could baby-sitting fit in with publishing? During the summer of his junior year in college he had taken a job as a sailing instructor, tutor, and companion for the children of a wealthy family.... While the parents were on a cruise, the governess suffered a stroke, sending the cook into a tizzy, the maid into tears, and the chauffeur and gardener into the local bar. Only the student could cope, and he took charge and managed the estate for the rest of the summer.

In his letter of application he described the crisis, and subsequent problems he had faced, and told how he had met them. Then he related those experiences to the problems that he had learned editors, advertisers, printers, and others encounter in the publishing industry.

> Americans are probably more concerned with the preservation of oil reserves right now than they have ever been. Some are even beginning to walk instead of riding. If scarcity of resources makes us use them more carefully, perhaps it would be a good idea to announce that words are in short supply. If people used them more carefully, internal communications specialists like you would have fewer headaches because communications jobs would be done right the first time.
>
> I have worked for the last six years improving my communications skills, learning to use words more carefully and effectively. I have taught Business Communication at a major university, worked for two newspapers, completed a Master's Degree in English, and would like to contribute my skills to your internal communications staff.

- First two paragraphs of a letter applying to be a computer programmer for an insurance company:

> Computers alone aren't the answer to demands for higher productivity in the competitive insurance business. Merging a poorly written letter with a data base of customers just sends out bad letters more quickly. But you know how hard it is to find people who can both program computers and write well.
>
> My education and training have given me this useful combination. I'd like to put my associate's degree in computer technology and my business experience writing to customers to work in State Farm's service approach to insurance.

Questions work well only if the answers aren't obvious. One student used the following paragraph in his first draft:

> Do you think that training competent and motivated operating personnel is a serious concern in the nuclear power industry?

If the reader says *yes*, the question will seem dumb. If the reader says *no*, the student has destroyed his common ground. In the next draft, the student revised the first paragraph to read:

> Competent and motivated operating personnel are just as important to the safe and efficient operation of a nuclear power plant as is high quality equipment.

This paragraph gave him an easy transition into talking about himself as a competent, motivated person.

Showing a Knowledge of the Position and the Company

A good letter will be adapted not only to the position for which you're applying but also to the specific company you're writing to. No company will be flattered to receive a letter which sounds as though the writer picked the company's name out of a phone book. If you could substitute another inside address and salutation and send out the letter without any further changes, it isn't specific enough.

The following paragraphs use the writer's knowledge of the company.

- A letter to Bendix Home Appliances uses information that the student got from information in the campus Placement Office about employees and market share.

---

* Quoted from John L. Munschauer, *Jobs for English Majors and Other Smart People* (Princeton, NJ: Peterson's Guides, 1986), 75–76.

> Coursework in business communication has taught me how to write reports that meet the needs of readers. I can use this knowledge to summarize the trends that show up in the Saturday Night Reports that your dealers submit....
>
> A minor in personnel management plus public-relations study has taught me that trends are manifestations of human motives and human feelings, and not just cold numbers. My attention to this fact will enable me to interpret retailers' reports concretely—to keep that 30 cents of every washing-machine dollar clinking into Bendix tills.

- A letter to Coopers and Lybrand's Minneapolis office uses information which the student learned in a referral interview with a partner in an accounting firm. Because the reader will know that Herr Wollner is a partner in the Berlin office, the student does not need to identify him.

> While I was studying in Berlin last spring, I had the opportunity to discuss accounting methods for multinational clients of Coopers and Lybrand with Herr Fritz Wollner. We also talked about the communication problems among Coopers and Lybrand's international offices.
>
> Herr Wollner mentioned that the increasing flow of accounting information between the European offices—especially those located in Germany, Switzerland, and Austria—and the American offices of Coopers and Lybrand is causing many communication problems because of poor translations and misunderstandings. My fluency in German enables me to translate accurately; and my study of communication problems in Speech Communications, Business and Professional Speaking, and Business and Technical Writing will help me see where messages might be misunderstood and choose words which are more likely to communicate clearly.

- A letter to Peat, Marwick, Mitchell & Co. uses information which the student learned in a summer job.

> As an assistant accountant for Pacific Bell during this past summer, I worked with its computerized billing and record-keeping system, *BARK*. I had the opportunity to help the controller revise portions of the system, particularly the procedures for handling delinquent accounts. When the Peat, Marwick, Mitchell *&* Co. audit team reviewed Pacific Bell's transactions completed for July, I had the opportunity to observe your *System 2170*. Several courses in computer science allow me to appreciate the simplicity of your system and its objective of reducing audit work, time, and costs.

One or two specific details usually are enough to demonstrate your knowledge. Be sure to use the knowledge, not just repeat it. Never present the information as though it will be news to the reader. After all, the reader works for the company and knows much more about it than you do.

Showing What Separates You from Other Applicants

Your knowledge of the company separates you from other applicants. You can also use coursework, an understanding of the field, and experience in jobs and extra-curricular events to show that you're unique.

Gimmicks in Job Application Letters*

Gimmicks have an uneven record in job application letters.

A straightforward explanation of your credentials often works best. A woman applying for a foreign correspondent's job sent *The Wall Street Journal* a letter written partly in Chinese. She did not get the job.

Some gimmicks fail because they don't tell enough about the candidate. One résumé set up as a "balance sheet" looked cute, but gave no information about the job hunter's qualifications.

Some gimmicks fail because they've been around too long, like letters in bottles, letters cut up into jigsaw puzzles, and letters that include a nut and shout, "Advertising is a tough nut to crack."

But gimmicks that seem genuinely creative can work. A New York ad agency hired a would-be copywriter who drew up a résumé in the form of a menu, with early experiences as appetizers and hobbies as desserts.

Gimmicks that relate to the job can also be effective. A student who wanted a drafting job printed his letter in large, legible letters on a blueprint specification form.

An architecture student had a box hand-delivered to the president of an architecture firm. When the box was opened, a cardboard house popped up. The letter started out, "I can design larger buildings, using other materials."

- This student uses both coursework and summer jobs to set herself apart from other applicants:

> My college courses have taught me the essential accounting skills required to contribute to the growth of Monsanto. Since you recently adopted new accounting methods for fluctuations in foreign currencies, you will need people knowledgeable in foreign currency translation to convert currency exchange rates. In two courses in international accounting, I compiled simulated accounting statements of hypothetical multinational firms in countries experiencing different rates of currency devaluation. Through these classes, I acquired the skills needed to work with the daily fluctuations of exchange rates and at the same time formulate an accurate and favorable representation of Monsanto.
>
> A company as diverse as Monsanto requires extensive record-keeping as well as numerous internal and external communications. Both my summer jobs and my coursework prepare me to do this. As Office Manager for the steamboat *Julia Belle Swain*, I was in charge of most of the bookkeeping and letter writing for the company. I kept accurate records for each workday, and I often entered over 100 transactions in a single day. In business and technical writing I learned how to write persuasive letters and memos and how to present extensive data in reports in a simplified style that is clear and easy to understand.

- This student uses her sorority experience and knowledge of the company to set herself apart from other applicants in a letter applying to be Assistant Personnel Manager of a multinational firm:

> As a counselor for sorority rush, I was also able to work behind the scenes as well as with the prospective rushees. I was able to use my leadership and communication skills for group activities for 70 young women by planning numerous activities to make my group a cohesive unit. Helping the women deal with rejection was also part of my job. Not all of the rushees made final cuts, and it was the rush counselor who helped put the rejection into perspective.
>
> This skill could be helpful in speaking to prospective employees wishing to travel to Saudi Arabia. Not all will pass the medical exams or make the visa application deadlines in time, and the assistant manager tells these people the news. An even more delicate subject to handle is conveying news of a death of a relative or employee to those concerned. My experience with helping people deal with small losses gives me a foundation to help others deal with more severe losses and deeper grief.

In your résumé, you may list activities, offices, and courses. In your letter, give more detail about what you did and show how that experience will help you contribute to the employer's organization more quickly.

When you discuss your strengths, don't exaggerate. No employer will believe that a new graduate has a "comprehensive" knowledge of a field. Indeed, most employers believe that six months to a year of on-the-job training is necessary before most new hires are really earning their pay. Specifics about what you've done will make your claims about what you can do more believable and ground them in reality.

---

* Based on "Look at Me," *The Wall Street Journal*, March 30, 1976, 1 and personal communication, Francis W. Weeks, 1985.

The Last Paragraph

In the last paragraph, indicate when you'd be available for an interview. If you're free any time, you can say so. But it's likely that you have responsibilities in class and work. If you'd have to go out of town, there may be only certain days of the week or certain weeks that you could leave town for several days. Use a sentence that fits your situation.

28.4 I could come to Albany for an interview any Wednesday or Friday.

28.5 I'll be attending the Oregon Forestry Association's November meeting and will be available for interviews there.

28.6 I could come to Memphis for an interview March 17–21.

If you're writing a prospecting letter to a firm that's more than a few hours away by car, say that you'll be in the area the week of such-and-such and could stop by for an interview. Companies pay for follow-up visits but not for first interviews. A company may be reluctant to ask you to make an expensive trip when it isn't yet sure it wants to hire you.

Should you wait for the employer to call you, or should you call the employer to request an interview? In a solicited letter, it's safe to wait to be contacted: you know the employer wants to hire someone, and if your letter and résumé show that you're one of the top applicants, you'll get an interview. In a prospecting letter, call the employer. Because the employer is not planning to hire, you'll get a higher percentage of interviews if you're aggressive.

End the letter on a positive note that suggests you look forward to the interview and that you see yourself as a person who has something to contribute, not as someone who just needs a job.

I look forward to discussing with you ways in which I could contribute to The Limited's continued growth.

WRITING STYLE AND TONE

In a letter of application, use a smooth, tight writing style. Use the technical jargon of the field, but avoid businessese and stuffy words like *utilize, commence,* and *transpire* (for *happen*).

Unless you're applying for a creative job in advertising, use a conservative style: few contractions, no sentence fragments, clichés, or slang. However, you still want a lively, energetic style that makes you sound like a real person. *The Underground Grammarian* cites the following letter as one whose pompous diction almost wholly obscures the fact that it was written by a real person:

> Enclosed is my personal résumé for your review and consideration for a position which may be available at the present time or in the foreseeable future.
>
> Throughout my successful management career, I have always strived to excel and to utilize initiative and resourcefulness to improve efficiency and quality control.
>
> I have always been cited for superior interpersonal skills and my ability to interface at all management levels.
>
> I ask only the opportunity to interview with your very fine organization and further present my diverse professional and personal attributes.[1]

Name-Dropping

Name-dropping can work, if you follow the following (usually unwritten) rules:

1. Never refer to your relatives or spouse. If you found out from a relative that the company is hiring, simply say "I understand that you're hiring. . . ." rather than "My brother told me that. . . ."

2. Refer only to people the reader is likely to know and think well of.

3. Refer only to people who think well of you and who can say something specific about you.

4. Use someone's name only if he or she has given you permission to do so.

"Bruce Jorgenson suggested that I write to you" can be an extremely effective opener if the statement is true, if the reader thinks well of Jorgenson, and if Jorgenson will say good things about you if the reader talks to him. Strangers will often read your letter out of courtesy to someone they do know, whose name you invoke judiciously and accurately.

Words like *utilize* and *interface* are only part of the problem. More serious problems are the total absence of specifics (this "successful" person fails to point to a single concrete achievement) and the total lack of adaptation to a specific company. Indeed, the letter reads like a form letter sent, unchanged, to dozens or even hundreds of companies.

Word Choice and Connotations

Avoid words that can be interpreted sexually. A model letter distributed by the placement office at a midwestern university included the following sentence:

I have been active in campus activities and have enjoyed good relations with my classmates and professors.

One young woman incorporated this sentence in a letter she mailed out. The recipient circled the sentence and then passed the letter around in the office (and did not invite the woman for an interview). That's not the kind of attention you want your letter to get!

Positive Emphasis

Be positive. Don't plead ("Please give me a chance") or apologize ("I cannot promise that I am substantially different from the lot"). Most negatives should be omitted entirely in the letter.

Avoid word choices with negative connotations. Note how the following revisions make the writer sound more confident:

Negative: I have learned an excessive amount about writing through courses in journalism and advertising.

Positive: Courses in journalism and advertising have taught me to recognize and to write good copy. My profile of a professor was published in the campus newspaper; I earned an "A+" on my direct mail campaign for the American Dental Association to persuade young adults to see their dentists more often.

"Excessive" suggests that you think the courses covered too much—hardly an opinion likely to endear you to an employer.

Negative: You can check with my references to verify what I've said.

Positive: Professor Hill can give you more information about the program in industrial distribution management.

"Verify" suggests that you expect the employer to distrust what you've said.

Negative: I am anxious to talk with you about the opportunities for employment with Arthur Andersen.

Positive: I look forward to talking with you about opportunities at Arthur Andersen.

"Anxious" suggests that you're worried about the interview.

You-Attitude

Unsupported claims may sound overconfident, selfish, or arrogant. Create you-attitude by describing exactly what you have done and by showing how that relates to what you could do for this employer.

*   Quoted from Cynthia Crossen, "Spotting Value Takes Smarts, Not Sight, Laura Sloate Shows," *The Wall Street Journal*, December 10, 1987, 1, 14.

Not you-attitude:	An inventive and improvising individual like me is a necessity in your business.
You-attitude:	Building a summer house-painting business gave me the opportunity to find creative solutions to challenges. At the end of the first summer, for example, I had nearly 10 gallons of exterior latex left, but no more jobs. I contacted the home economics teacher at my high school. She agreed to give course credit to students who were willing to give up two Saturdays to paint a house being renovated by Habitat for Humanity. I donated the paint and supervised the students. I got a charitable deduction for the paint and hired the three best students to work for me the following summer. I could put these skills in problem solving and supervising to work as a personnel manager for Burroughs.
Not you-attitude:	A company of your standing could offer the challenging and demanding kind of position in which my abilities could flourish.
You-attitude:	Omit.
Not you-attitude:	I want a job with your company.
You-attitude:	I would like to apply for Procter & Gamble's management trainee program.

Remember that the word *you* refers to your reader. Using *you* when you really mean yourself or all people can insult your reader by implying that he or she still has a lot to learn about business:

| Not you-attitude: | Running my own business taught me that you need to learn to manage your time. |
| You-attitude: | Running my own business taught me to manage my time. |

Since you're talking about yourself, you'll use *I* in your letter. Reduce the number of *I*'s by revising some sentences to use *me* or *my.*

Under my presidency, the Agronomy Club . . .

Courses in media and advertising management gave me a chance to . . .

My responsibilities as a summer intern included . . .

In particular, avoid beginning every paragraph with *I.* Begin sentences with prepositional phrases or introductory clauses:

As my résumé shows, I . . .

In my coursework in media and advertising management, I . . .

While I was a summer intern in the Mayor's office, I . . .

Paragraph Length and Unity

Keep your first and last paragraphs fairly short—preferably no more than four or five typed lines. Vary paragraph length within the letter; it's OK to have one long paragraph, but don't use a series of eight-line paragraphs.

When you have a long paragraph, check to be sure that it covers only one subject. If it covers two or more subjects, divide it into two or more paragraphs. If a short paragraph covers several subjects, consider adding a topic sentence to provide paragraph unity.

FORMAT AND MECHANICS

Employers faced with a two-foot high stack of job applications may use the physical appearance of the letter to weed out candidates. Make sure your format, mechanics, spelling, and typing create a good impression for you.

Format

As a new graduate, you won't have letterhead to use for your job letter. Modified-block format creates the best visual balance when you do not have a letterhead. Review Appendix A on format. Note that your return address does not include your name or phone number. If you want to include your phone number in the letter (it will be in the attached résumé), you can mention it in the last paragraph of the letter or line it up under your typed name in the signature block.

If you use letterhead, you can use either block or modified-block format.

Paper and Ribbon

Use good quality bond paper for your letter—preferably 25% cotton content (or more), at least 16 lb. weight, watermarked, but *not* erasable—erasable smudges easily. Use the same color that you use for your résumé: white or very pale cream or beige.

Make sure your typewriter or printer ribbon is fairly new. If possible, use a carbon (one-time-only) ribbon for the darkest, sharpest impression.

Typing the Letter

Your letter must be *completely* free from typographical errors. It should also be fairly free from obvious corrections. If you're using a regular typewriter to type your letter, try to use a ribbon with a correcting tape that lifts off the ink of mistakes you make; if you must use correction fluid, make sure that it's well thinned and work slowly and carefully, using only a small amount of fluid, to avoid a big blob where the error was. If you have access to a word processor or a repetitive typewriter, you can correct your text before it is run out so that the final copy is perfect.

If you are going to send out several similar letters, use (or pay a typist who has) a word processor or repetitive typewriter. Not only are the time and cost far lower, but you won't need to proof the whole copy of each letter since no new errors will be introduced as the repeated copy is run out for each letter. You *do* need to proof the parts of the letter that are revised. In particular, check the reader's name and the first paragraph to see that these are correct.

Always type each letter individually. Never have letters printed, photocopied, or mimeographed. Such signs that the letter is part of a mass mailing, sent indiscriminantly to many firms, create a negative impression and make it unlikely that your letter will be read at all.

Length

Most books on job hunting advise you to keep your letter to one page. Certainly a shorter letter looks easier to read. If your draft runs more than a page, consider using elite type and smaller margins or tightening your prose to see if you can fit the letter on one page. However, if you need more than a page,

FIGURE 28.1

516 Montgomery Court
Columbus, Ohio 43210
December 7, 198-

Dr. Phillip Code, Director
Ohio Department of Development
International Trade Division
P. O. Box 1001
30 E. Broad Street
Columbus, Ohio 43266-0101

Dear Dr. Code:

Umbrella statement summarizes his qualifications

I am interested in the position of International Trade Manager announced in the September 14 issue of the Wall Street Journal. With my combination of college training, international and domestic work experience, and fluency in Japanese, I can help the State of Ohio continue to develop an increased balance of trade with Japan and other Pacific Basin countries.

Details would be useful here

I will receive my Bachelor of Science degree in Business Administration with a concentration in International Business and my Bachelor of Arts degree in Japanese Language from The Ohio State University in June. In obtaining these degrees, I have gained a strong knowledge of international business and have honed my Japanese reading, writing, and speaking skills. With this background, I can function effectively as an international trade manager without the need of an expensive and cumbersome interpreter or a large staff of advisors.

Smooth reference to his résumé

He could do more to show he understands trade shows

As my résumé shows, I have both domestic and international work experience. I worked full-time as an engineering cooperative intern at Armco, Inc.'s Special Materials Division for five quarters. Through my work experience with this Middletown, Ohio-based company, I learned how companies in Ohio are affected by the United States's trade with foreign countries. As you know, Armco's primary product is steel, and the company has faced stiff competition from Japanese and South Korean steel producers. Through my engineering internship at Armco, I also learned a lot about the technical aspects of manufacturing, and so I can also represent Ohio companies well at trade shows.

Matt was in Japan as a Mormon missionary. He doesn't want to talk about religion in this letter, but should provide more details to prove the claims in this ¶

Matt could strengthen his letter by developing this

I lived and worked in Japan from July, 1984 to January, 1986. While there, I learned how to read, write, and speak Japanese. In my work in Japan, I met with area business and civic leaders to build goodwill and increase their understanding of the organization I represented. These experiences have given me the skills and understanding of how to conduct myself well in these types of situations, in both English and Japanese. Also, I am already accustomed to Japanese modes of transportation and communication, laws, cultural norms, and social customs, which will help me to avoid the all-too-frequent errors of American business people in Japan.

Since I live in Columbus, I am available for an interview at your convenience. I look forward to talking with you about ways I can help Ohio increase its exports to Japan.

Sincerely,

Matthew A. Miller

Matthew A. Miller

FIGURE 28.2

Room 1410
The Towers
409 E. Chalmers
Waltham, MA 02254
March 1, 19--

Robert H. Catanga
Senior Accountant
IBM Corporation
1717 Central
Boston, MA 02103

Tracey has only coursework and one part-time job. But by being specific about what she's done in class and on the job, she creates a positive impression.

Dear Mr. Catanga:

I am applying for the position in your Accounting Department announced in the fall bulletin at Bentley College. I will receive a Bachelor of Science degree in accountancy from Bentley this spring and plan to take the CPA exam in December.

Many courses provide practice with simulated cases— you may be able to use Tracey's strategy too.

My courses in the accountancy curriculum at Bentley have given me not only the necessary theoretical background but also extensive practical experience. I have worked many in-class cases and problems, including the preparation of simulated accounting records for hypothetical firms.

These true-to-life cases gave me the opportunity to deal with interpreting all sorts of data in order to prepare and complete accurate and proper financial statements. For instance, I've learned to determine the appropriate measure for assets and liabilities, the proper depreciation methods for the useful lives of machinery and equipment, and the best methods of matching revenues with expenditures. These I could then analyze and compare to past statements in order to identify and evaluate trends and recommend ways that the business could be run more efficiently.

This paragraph is weak. Tracey needs to do some more research on IBM so she can be more specific

Fighting off the computer clones depends in part on keeping the differential between IBM PCs and the clones small enough that customers are willing to pay the difference. I can help your staff present the information about costs and revenues that IBM needs to keep its prices competitive and its profits strong.

Shows she understands what a corporate accountant does.

Courses in speech communication and business writing have taught me how to communicate with various business audiences. This means that I would be able to provide financial statements that could be easily read and followed by those not in the Accounting Department. In this way, accounting information could quickly and understandably be related to management needs.

My three years of experience working for Allstate Insurance Company have also given me the opportunity to make decisions and show responsibility. Although I was hired merely as a part-time typist, my supervisor put a lot of trust in me and

FIGURE 28.2 *(continued)*

Only a part-time job, but she gets a lot of mileage out of it!

charged me with many duties outside the job of a typist. My supervisor frequently asked for my opinions and recommendations on various matters, such as in ways to speed up production and to get work done more efficiently. In fact, I developed a procedure for making out arbitration reports which saved so much time that I was asked to teach it to the other employees in my department.

Nice allusion to inclusion of IBM in In Search of Excellence

The enclosed résumé summarizes my qualifications. I would like to make an appointment for an interview any Tuesday or Thursday afternoon. I can begin work in June and look forward to discussing with you ways in which I can help IBM continue its tradition of excellence.

Sincerely,

Tracey McKenna

Tracey McKenna

Encl.

FIGURE 28.3

426 Catalpa Lane
Libertyville, Illinois 60043
February 28, 198-

Mr. William Raffel
Executive Vice-President
Smith, Badofsky, & Raffel
444 North Michigan Avenue
Chicago, Illinois 60611

Dear Mr. Raffel:

This isn't news, but it's to the reader, interesting. Short and interesting. The reader will probably go on to #2.

The fragments are a calculated risk. They'll probably work to an ad agency

Directing traffic. Assisting circulation. Dealing with unruly audiences. They're all in a day's work for police officers and media planners.

My marketing background has shown me how advertising fits into the promotion part of the marketing mix. In addition, as my résumé shows, I have held a position that involved using the above steps to run ad campaigns for a theatre.

I will receive my Bachelor of Science degree in Marketing from the University of Illinois at Urbana-Champaign in May. In obtaining this degree, I have acquired a working knowledge of several aspects of advertising, including media strategy, planning, selection, and placement.

Uses course work to show she can do the job

Good use of knowledge about agency

My familiarity with Chicago media will help me place ads for the 75% of your clients who operate in the Chicagoland area. In my media planning course, I formulated actual media plans using Chicago-based media such as the <u>Chicago Tribune</u>, which has the lowest billing rate and is, therefore, the most cost efficient. These plans, made under usual time restrictions, allowed me to take actual desired GRP's and obtain pinpoint results for reach and frequency.

With this experience, I am prepared to help you make large-scale media plans for your ad campaigns with Merrill Chase Art Galleries, Rogers and Hollands' Jewelers, and newly-acquired Plywood Minnesota.

Separates herself from other applicants

Good use of industry-specific jargon

This would be even stronger if she could show that ads contributed to increased ticket sales.

Many students have developed simulated media plans for classes. I've done the real thing. As an assistant manager of a theatre, I gained practical experience in placing advertisements in newspapers. With a very tight budget, ads had to be placed carefully. I dealt with both flat and open rates, rate differentials, and most importantly, I determined the SAU sizes and costs for placing each ad in each paper. This should give me a head start with dealing with print media plans. I'm very much interested in dealing with the newly-developed Satellite Facsimile (Sat-Fax) space-age system that SBR has been looking into.

More Knowledge of Company

With 50% growth since SBR's founding in 1980, and 12 new clients in the last 4 months alone, SBR is one of the fastest growing agencies. I'd like to grow with you. Could we set up an appointment for an interview the week of March 14? I look forward to an opportunity to meet with you to discuss ways I can help provide the sophisticated media planning your clients expect from SBR.

Forward looking ending

Sincerely yours,

Kimberly Shavell

Kimberly Shavell

use it. The extra space gives you room to be more specific about what you've done and to add details about the experience you have that separates you from other applicants. Even though few employers say that they *want* longer letters, they will read them *if* the letter is well written and *if* the applicant establishes early in the letter that he or she has credentials which the company needs.

Always use at least one full page. A short letter throws away an opportunity to be persuasive; it may also suggest that you have little to say for yourself or that you aren't very interested in the job.

SAMPLE JOB APPLICATION LETTERS

Your letter needs to reflect your personality as well as your qualifications. Even a good phrase loses its impact if it appears in 30 of the letters on an employer's (or instructor's) desk. Use the sample letters in Figures 28.1–28.3 to get ideas, but write an original letter.

SUMMARY OF KEY POINTS

- Résumés differ from letters of application in the following ways:
  - A résumé is adapted to a position. The letter is adapted to the needs of a particular organization.
  - The résumé summarizes all your qualifications. The letter shows how your qualifications can help the organization meet its needs, how you differ from other applicants, and that you have some knowledge of the organization.
  - Business résumés can be two to three pages for experienced applicants. The letter can be only one to two pages.
  - The résumé uses short, parallel phrases and sentence fragments. The letter uses complete sentences in well-written paragraphs.
- When you know that a company is hiring, send a **solicited job letter.** When you want a job with a company that has not announced openings, send a **prospecting job letter.** In both letters, you should
  - Address the letter to a specific person.
  - Indicate the specific position for which you're applying.
  - Be specific about your qualifications.
  - Show what separates you from other applicants.
  - Show a knowledge of the company and the position.
  - Refer to your résumé (which you would enclose with the letter).
  - Ask for an interview.
- Organize a solicited letter in this way:
  1. State that you're applying for the job and tell where you learned about the job (ad, referral, etc.). Briefly show that you have the major qualifications required by the ad. Summarize your qualifications in the order in which you plan to discuss them in the letter.
  2. Develop your major qualifications in detail.
  3. Develop your other qualifications. Show what separates you from the other applicants who will also answer the ad. Demonstrate your knowledge of the organization.
  4. Ask for an interview; tell when you'll be available to be interviewed and to begin work. End on a positive, forward-looking note.

- Organize a prospecting letter in this way:
  1. Catch the reader's interest.
  2. Create a bridge between the attention-getter and your qualifications. Summarize your qualifications in the order in which you plan to discuss them in the letter.
  3. Develop your strong points in detail. Relate what you've done in the past to what you could do for this company. Show that you know something about the company. Identify the specific niche you want to fill.
  4. Ask for an interview and tell when you'll be available for interviews. End on a positive, forward-looking note.

- Use your knowledge of the company, your coursework, your understanding of the field, and your experience in jobs and extra-curricular activities to show that you're unique.

- Don't repeat information that the reader already knows; don't seem to be lecturing the reader on his or her business.

- In the last paragraph of a prospecting letter, take the responsibility for calling the reader to schedule an interview.

- Never use relatives' names in a job letter. Using other names is OK if the reader knows them and thinks well of them, if they think well of you and will say good things about you, and if you have permission to use their names.

- Use positive emphasis to sound confident. Use you-attitude by supporting general claims with specific examples and by relating what you've done to what the employer needs.

- Use at least a full page. It's desirable to limit your letter to one page, but use up to two pages if you need them to showcase all your credentials.

NOTE

[1]   Quoted in "The Disappearance of Everybody," *The Underground Grammarian* 8, no. 7 (November 1984): 1.

EXERCISES AND PROBLEMS FOR CHAPTER 28

28–1 ANALYZING FIRST PARAGRAPHS OF PROSPECTING LETTERS

All of the following are first paragraphs in prospecting letters written by new college graduates. Evaluate the paragraphs on these criteria:

- Is the paragraph likely to interest the reader and motivate him or her to read the rest of the letter?
- Does the paragraph have some content that the student can use to create a transition to talking about his or her qualifications?
- Does the paragraph avoid asking for a job?

1. For the past two and one-half years I have been studying turf management. On August 1, 19___, I will graduate from _____Uni-versity with a B.A. in Ornamental Horticul-ture. The type of job I will seek will deal with golf course maintenance as an assistant superintendent.

2. Ann Gibbs suggested that I contact you.

3. Each year, the Christmas shopping rush makes more work for everyone at Wie-boldt's, especially for the Credit Depart-ment. While working for Wieboldt's Credit Department for three Christmas and sum-mer vacations, the Christmas sales increase is just one of the credit situations I became aware of.

4. Whether to plate a two-inch eyebolt with cadmium for a tough, brilliant shine or with zinc for a rust-resistant, less expensive finish is a tough question. But similar questions must be answered daily by your salesmen. With my experience in the electro-plating industry, I can contribute greatly to your constant need of getting customers.

5. I will be a May graduate from _____Uni-versity. On the recommendation of the for-mer chairman of the board of your com-pany, George Powell, I focused my studies in finance, majoring in insurance.

6. As a graduating advertising student, I read the February 7, 19___ issue of *Ad Age*. In that issue, Mr. Blair Vedder, your company president, stated that unlike some firms, the Needham, Harper & Steers Agency feels a person with an advertising degree can be quite helpful to an ad agency.

7. What a set of tractors! The new 8430 and 8630 diesels are just what is needed by to-day's farmer with his ever-increasing acreage. John Deere has truly done it again.

8. Prudential Insurance Company did much to help my college career, as the sponsor of my National Merit Scholarship. Now I think I can give something back to Prudential. I'd like to put my education, including a B.S. degree in finance from _____ University, to work in your investment department.

9. Since the beginning of Delta Electric Con-struction Co. in 1963, the size and profits have grown steadily. My father, being a stockholder and vice-president, often dis-cusses company dealings with me. Although the company has prospered, I understand there have been a few problems of misman-agement. I feel with my present and future qualifications, I could help ease these problems.

10. You can't afford to let programmers "hack" at a program until they find a solution.

28–2 REVISING SENTENCES FROM APPLICATION LETTERS

Each of the following sentences appeared in the draft of a job letter. Revise them to improve grammar, style, you-attitude, and positive emphasis. You may need to cut or to add information.

1. As my résumé demonstrates, I have the blend of knowledge necessary to help Mead remain on top. Since Mead's start in 1846, the company has become an international organization with 17,000 employees and over 100 mills, plants, and distribution centers scattered among 40 countries.

2. My education provides me with a back-ground that is necessary for success in a lab. I understand when a procedure doesn't work because I can often determine why, and correct it.

3. Work at General Motors has give me hands-on experience in the areas of em-ployee training and recruitment. While working in the human resource office my duties included analysis of training pro-grams, determining their effectiveness, and

to help implement tracking employees' ability to perform required tasks.

4. My present occupation has required me to verify and make payment on merchandise invoices, regulate $200,000 worth of inventory, collect and deposit up to $15,000 in cash.

5. Communication skills are a major part of the entire selling process and are used throughout the selling cycle in presenting yourself clearly, concisely, and convincingly.

6. Included in my résumé are the courses in Finance which earned me a fairly attractive grade average.

7. I have a strong college background in finance and investment but realize that I lack the experience in the real world.

8. During the summer months I hold two jobs. The first is with [name of company], and the second is with [name of college].

9. My work experience includes a supervising position, part ownership in a business, and management skills.

10. Please give me a chance to show you that I can do the work.

28–3 APPLYING FOR A SCHOLARSHIP

Apply for a partial scholarship from a professional organization related to your field.

As your instructor directs,
a. Identify real scholarships and use the real directions.
b. Assume that the organization is composed of local business and professional people; scholarships are available to students in any field. The directions say,

Submit a short (maximum one typed, single-spaced page) statement explaining why we should support your education. We are not necessarily interested in students with the highest grades; we will give equal consideration to students who are surmounting difficulties to continue their education and to students who are making full use of the opportunities available to them.

28–4 WRITING A SOLICITED LETTER

Write a letter of application in response to an announced opening. Assume that you are a senior and add infor-

mation about things you will do between now and your senior year. **Turn in a copy of the listing.** If your instructor directs, **submit a résumé with the letter.**

You may use any of the following options.

a. Respond to an ad in a newspaper, in a professional journal, or listed with the placement office. Be sure that you are fully qualified for the job.
b. Take a job description and assume that it represents a current opening.
c. If you have already worked somewhere, you may assume that your employer is asking you to apply for full-time work after graduation. Be sure to write a fully persuasive letter.
d. Respond to one of the listings below. Use a reference book to get the name and address of the person to whom you should write.

1. Atlantic Richfield Company is hiring an **assistant auditor.** Minimum 12 hours of accounting. Work includes analysis and evaluation of operating and financial controls and requires contact with many levels of Company management. Because Internal Auditing is considered a training ground for future managers, multiple career paths are available to successful auditors. Extensive travel (50%) required through the United States along with some international work. Effective written and oral communication skills a must, along with sound decision-making abilities. Divisions recruiting: Corporate Internal Auditing; ANACONDA Aluminum Company; ARCO Transportation Company. Locations: Los Angeles (Hdqtrs.), Dallas, Philadelphia, Denver, Chicago.

2. A member of Congress in your state wants an **office manager** for a local office in your state and a **staff member** for the Washington, DC office. The office manager will answer constituent questions, write press releases, assist with travel and appearances, record contributions, and recruit and supervise volunteer staff. Good oral and interpersonal skills a must; political and financial skills helpful. The staff member in Washington will answer mail, help with political research, and draft bills and reports. Good writing and research skills a must; interpersonal skills and political savvy helpful.

3. The Extension Service in your state wants an **Extension and 4-H Youth Leader** to provide overall leadership in the development

of an effective long-range educational program for all youth. Duties include recruiting, training, and motivating volunteer leaders.

4. The Federal Trade Commission wants a **computer specialist** to provide end-user support to FTC staff and to manage the Information Center. Must be familiar with IBM-compatible microcomputers and VAX minicomputers. Ability to write programs and patches a plus.

5. Price Waterhouse is hiring **audit trainees.** Travel to client locations to perform compilations and audits; evaluate internal controls as required. Assist in writing reports and memos on findings. Jobs at all U.S. locations; write directly to office you wish to join.

6. Nieman-Marcus is hiring **executive development program trainees.** After completing 10-week training programs, trainees will become assistant buyers. Prefer people with strong interest and experience in retailing.

7. Procter & Gamble is looking for **sales management trainees**—any major. An intensive sales training program leading to sales management. After training will have personal selling responsibility for major accounts, will manage sales plans and presentations, will analyze business results and recommend action.

8. Exxon has openings for **employee relations personnel.** All majors. Responsible for a broad range of areas, such as compensation and benefits, manpower training, training and development, employee selection and placement, and EEO (Equal Employment Opportunities). Overseas placement possible.

9. Your state wants **assistant international trade managers** for offices in London, Paris, Tokyo, Hong Kong, and Buenos Aires. Duties include promoting state exports, promoting the state as a site for foreign business investment and branch plants, and representing the state to government officials. Candidate should know language and culture of target country. Knowledge of state and state businesses a plus.

10. Leo Burnett USA is hiring **assistant account executives.** You will be assigned to a major client account, and will help develop strategies for marketing and advertising, with specific assignments in one of the following: creative, media, research, or production.

28–5 **WRITING A PROSPECTING LETTER**
Pick a company you'd like to work for and apply for a specific position. Assume that you are a senior and add information about things you will do between now and your senior year. If your instructor directs, **turn in a résumé** with the letter.

Address your letter to the president of a small company, the area vice-president, or the branch manager of a large company. Use directories to get the name and address of the person with the power to create a job for you.

Job Interviews, Follow-Up Letters, and Job Offers

QUESTIONS

- How do you develop an interview strategy?
- What should you wear to the interview?
- What should you take to the interview?
- What should you write down during or after the interview?
- Should you "be yourself" at the interview?
- What's the best way to handle stress or sexist questions?
- What communication behaviors do successful interviewees exhibit?
- What kinds of answers do interviewers want?
- What goes in a follow-up letter after an interview?
- How should you handle job offers?

> Before the interview, do as much research on yourself as you
> would before you bought a car or stereo set. Know who you are
> and what you really want to do. Be prepared to talk for at least
> three hours about yourself and your interests.
>
> Irv Pfeiffer, IBM's Manager of Corporate
> College Relations and Recruiting—Midwest, 1984

Y ou may be able to get a job without writing a letter of application; if you're a new graduate, you may be able to use the data sheet designed by your placement office and avoid writing a résumé. But almost everyone has to go through interviews to be offered a position. Job interviews are scary, even when you've prepared thoroughly. But when you are prepared, you can harness the adrenaline to work for you, so that you interview well and get the job you want.

DEVELOPING AN INTERVIEW STRATEGY

Develop an overall strategy based on your answers to these three questions:

1. **What about yourself do you want the interviewer to know?** Pick two to five points that represent your strengths for that particular job. These facts may be achievements, character traits (like enthusiasm), experiences that qualify you for the job and separate you from other applicants, the fact that you really want to work for this company, etc.

   Then at the interview, listen to every question to see if you could make one of your key points as part of your answer. If the questions don't allow you to make your points, bring them up at the end of the interview.

2. **What disadvantages or weaknesses do you need to minimize?** Expect that you may be asked to explain weaknesses or apparent weaknesses in your record: age, sex, physical disabilities, lack of experience, so-so grades, and gaps in your record.

   Plan how to deal with these issues if they arise. See the suggestions later in this chapter under "Stress Interviews" and "Answering Twenty Interview Questions."

3. **What do you need to know about the job and the organization to decide whether you want to accept this job if it is offered to you?** Plan the criteria on which you will base your decision (you can always change the criteria). Use the criteria you developed in doing the forced choice in problem 26–2 and plan questions which will elicit the information you'll need to rank each offer.

TAKING CARE OF THE DETAILS

Inappropriate clothing or being late can cost you a job. Put enough time into planning details so that you can move on to substantive planning.

Personal space is the distance someone wants between himself or herself and other people in ordinary, non-intimate interchanges. Personal space varies from one culture to another and among people in the same culture (Chapter 23).
Cameramann International, Ltd.

Gabe Palmer/Mug Shots

Journalism Services

Jay Nadelson/The Stock Market

*Greetings vary in different cultures. U.S. business people shake hands.
Japanese business people bow (Chapter 23).*
Mary Elenz Tranter

*The size, placement, decor, and privacy of an
office connote status (Chapter 23).*
Both photos by Craig Hammell/The Stock Market.

Presenters who use overhead transparencies are perceived to be more prepared, more persuasive, and more interesting than speakers who don't use visuals (Chapter 24). To avoid blocking the screen, stand beside it, not in front of it.
Randy Duchaine/The Stock Market

The bigger the group you're addressing, the more slowly you need to speak. Sound takes time to travel through a large room (Chapter 24).
Courtesy of The National PTA

Think of ways to involve your audience during the presentation (Chapter 24).
Richard Gross/The Stock Market

When you answer questions, link your answers to points you made in the presentation (Chapter 24).
Michael Philip Manheim/
The Stock Market

Dealing successfully with conflict requires attention both to the issues and to people's feelings (Chapter 25).
Kenji Kerins

Active listening takes time and effort (Chapter 25).
Walter Hodges/TSW/Click

An open group welcomes newcomers. A closed group shuts them out (Chapter 25).
Both photos by Kenji Kerins

Check the job listings and information about companies at the placement office in your community college, college, or university (Chapter 26).
Both photos by William Kniest/Courtesy of Patricia Kirchherr, Director of Placement and Co-op College of Lake County

In an information interview you learn about day-to-day work in a specific job and how to prepare for it. Information interviews can also help you tap into the hidden job market—jobs that are not advertised (Chapter 26).
Michael J. Hruby

A company that advertises an opening may get 50 to 500 applications for a single position. An effective résumé and letter can help you get past the first cut to the interview stage (Chapters 27 and 28).
Brent Jones

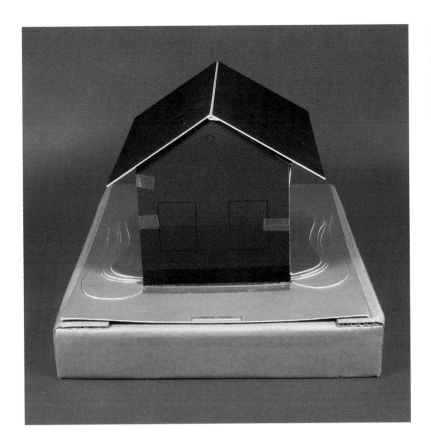

An architecture student's job letter was hand-delivered to the firm he wanted to join. When the box was opened, a cardboard house popped up. The letter started, "I can design larger buildings, using other materials" (Chapter 28).
Michael J. Hruby

Successful job interviewees use the company name during the interview, back up their claims with specific details, and ask specific questions about the industry and the company (Chapter 29).
Gabe Palmer/Mug Shots

During a second interview at a company's office or plant, you may be asked to take a psychological or skills tests, you'll get a tour, and you'll have interviews with many different people (Chapter 29).
Both photos by Michael J. Hruby

What to Wear

If you're interviewing for a managerial or professional position, wear a business suit. Women should wear a skirted suit rather than a pants suit. Dress for the position that's two levels above the one for which you're applying: you'll look like someone who's successful rather than someone who's struggling.

Looking "good" is less important than looking businesslike. Women are more likely to make poor choices here, since women dress differently for work and for leisure. Don't look like you're going to a party or a dance. Don't wear anything sexy. You want the interviewer to evaluate you as a potential peer, not as a date. One male interviewer reported that a woman interviewee's open-toed sandals distracted him; he felt that she was dressed inappropriately. If current fashions are sexy, it might be better to dress more conservatively—unless, of course, you're applying for a job in the fashion industry.

What kind of suit should you wear? If you've got good taste and a good eye for color, follow your instincts. If fashion isn't your strong point, read John Molloy's *Dress for Success* (men's clothes) and *The Woman's Dress for Success Book*. The strength of Molloy's books is that they're based on research about how businessmen (yes, men, since they still make most of the decisions) perceive clothes, rather than on personal preferences. Perhaps the best suggestion in the books is his advice to visit expensive stores, noting details—the exact shade of blue in a suit, the number of buttons on the sleeve, the placement of pockets, the width of lapels—and then go to stores in your price range and buy a suit that has the details found on more expensive clothing.

Choose comfortable shoes. You may do a fair amount of walking during the office visit or plant trip.

Take care of all the details. Check your heels to make sure they aren't run down; make sure your shoes are shined. Have your hair cut or styled conservatively. Jewelry and makeup should be understated. Personal hygiene must be impeccable.

What to Bring to the Interview

Bring extra copies of your résumé. If your campus placement office has already given the interviewer a data sheet, present the résumé at the beginning of the interview: "I thought you might like a little more information about me."

Bring something to write on and something to write with.

Bring copies of your work: an engineering design, a copy of a memo you wrote on a job or in a business writing class, an article you wrote for the campus paper. You don't need to present these unless the interview calls for them, but they can be very effective: "Yes, I have done a media plan. We had a fixed budget and used real figures for cost and rating points, just as I'd do if I joined Needham, Harper, and Steers."

Bring the names, addresses, and phone numbers of references if you didn't put them on your résumé. Bring complete details about your work history and education, including dates and street addresses, in case you're asked to fill out an application form.

If you can afford it, buy a briefcase to carry these items. At this point in your life, an inexpensive vinyl briefcase is acceptable.

Dressing for Success for Women and Men*

Interviews with dozens of executives, both male and female, found that most would be shocked to see miniskirts on female executives. Indeed, the consensus seems to be that . . . it still isn't acceptable to look too feminine—or too sexy or too cute—in corporate America. . . .

"Looking extremely feminine gives the message that you need to be taken care of," says Brenda York, president of the Academy of Fashion and Image Consultants in McLean, Va. . . .

A female candidate for a job involving labor negotiation at a large Los Angeles savings-and-loan association arrived in a blue and pink flowery dress with "little flouncy sleeves" and a "little lace collar," says Patricia Benninger, a vice president of human resources there.

The dress "turned off all the credibility she could have built up during the interview," says Ms. Benninger. "My feelings were, She doesn't know the job." The outfit, she adds, said that the woman was "someone who could be easily persuaded," and that "this person couldn't stand up to toughness.". . .

"The biggest mistake [men make] is not fitting in or wearing something that says 'blue collar,'" says John T. Molloy. . . .

Consider the hapless applicant for a $150,000-a-year position as a vice president and general manager of a large Midwestern company. . . . [The applicant] had taken off his suit jacket and had on a short-sleeved shirt with a pocket protector. . . . [The employer said the applicant] "just wouldn't fit in when standing up in front of the directors and making a presentation.". . .

Martha Heiberg, director of personnel at Ticor Title Insurance in Los Angeles, says one man applying for a job made the mistake of wearing suede slip-on shoes. "The two people who talked to him said, 'I couldn't hire him because he was wearing bedroom slippers,'" she says. "They liked him otherwise."

---

* Quoted from Kathleen A. Hughes, "Businesswomen's Broader Latitude in Dress Codes Goes Just So Far" and "Male Executives Also Suffer for Their Sartorial Mistakes," *The Wall Street Journal*, both September 1, 1987, 29.

Persistence Pays Off*

The interview was a disaster. She was awkward and inarticulate. All she could say was that she really wanted to work for the company, but she could not say what she could offer in return. She was turned down flat.

As she interviewed more, she got the hang of it and began to get some job offers, but her first interview gnawed at her. It had been for the job she really wanted. Figuring that she had one zero from that company and that two zeroes would not be worse than one, she called on the employer again, explained that when she had been there before it had been her first interview and that she had really not known how to handle herself. She told the employer that she really felt she had something to offer and asked if she could have another interview.

The employer was impressed. He liked persistence. The fact that the candidate had come back demonstrated a real interest in the company. A second interview was granted and the young woman got the job.

Note-Taking

You need to write down

- The name of the interviewer (or all the people you talked to, if it's a group interview or an office visit).
- What the interviewer seemed most interested in about you.
- Any negative points that came up that you need to counter in your follow-up letter.
- Answers to your questions about the company.
- When you'll hear from the company.

The easiest way to get the interviewer's name is to ask for his or her card. In some cases, you can make all the notes you need on the back of the card.

Some interviewers say that they respond negatively to applicants who take notes during the interview. However, if you have several interviews back-to-back or if you know your memory is terrible, do take brief notes during the interview. That's better than forgetting which company said you'd be on the road every other week, and which interviewer asked that *you* get in touch with him or her.

PRACTICING FOR THE INTERVIEW

Rehearse everything you can: put on the clothes you'll wear and practice entering a room, shaking hands, sitting down, and answering questions. Ask a friend to interview you. Saying answers out loud is surprisingly harder than saying them in your head.

Some campuses have videotaping facilities so that you can watch your own sample interview. Videotaping is more valuable if you can do it at least twice, so you can modify behavior the second time and check the tape to see whether the modification works.

DURING THE INTERVIEW

Your interviewing skills will improve with practice. If possible, schedule a few interviews with other companies before your interview with the company that is your first choice. However, even if you're just interviewing for practice, you must still do all the research on that company. If interviewers sense that you aren't interested, they won't take you seriously and you won't learn much from the process.

How to Act

Should you "be yourself"? There's no point in assuming a radically different persona. If you do, you run the risk of getting into a job that you'll hate (though the persona you assumed might have loved it). Furthermore, as interviewers point out, you have to be a pretty good actor to come across convincingly if you try to be someone other than yourself. On the other hand, all of us have several selves: we can be lazy, insensitive, bored, slow-witted, and tongue-tied, but we can also be energetic, perceptive, interested, intelligent, and articulate. Be your best self at the interview.

Interviews can make you feel vulnerable and defensive. To counter this,

---

* Quoted from John L. Munschauer, *Jobs for English Majors and Other Smart People* (Princeton, NJ: Peterson's Guides, 1986), 159–60.

review your accomplishments—the things you're especially proud of having done. You'll make a better impression if you have a firm sense of your own self-worth.

Every interviewer repeats the advice that your mother probably gave you: sit up straight, don't mumble, look at people when you talk. It's good advice for interviews. If you smoke, don't smoke at all in an initial interview, and ask if it's OK to smoke during a plant trip before you light up. Be aware that many people respond negatively to smoking.

Office visits which involve meals and semisocial occasions call for sensible choices. When you order, choose something that's easy and unmessy to eat. Eat a light lunch, with no alcohol, so that you'll be alert during the afternoon. At dinner or an evening party, decline alcohol if you don't drink. If you do drink, accept just one drink—you're still being evaluated, and you can't afford to have your guard down. Women should be aware that some men respond negatively to women who drink hard liquor.

Parts of the Interview

Every interview has an opening, a body and a close.

In the **opening** (two to five minutes), good interviewers will try to set you at ease. Some interviewers start with easy questions about your major or interests. Others open by telling you about the job or the company. If this happens, listen so you can later bring up points which show that you can do the job or contribute to the company that's being described.

Limited research suggests that the outcome of an interview is determined in the first four minutes.[1] Even though this research is not conclusive, you want your first impression to be positive. You control many of the things that create a first impression: what you wear, your posture, your handshake, and what you say.

The **body** of the interview (10 to 25 minutes) is an all-too-brief time for you to highlight your qualifications and find out what you need to know to decide if you want to accept a plant trip. Expect questions that give you an opportunity to showcase your strong points and questions that probe any weaknesses evident from your résumé. (You were neither in school nor working last fall. What were you doing?) Normally the interviewer will also try to sell you on the company and give you an opportunity to raise questions.

You need to be aware of time so that you can make sure to get in your key points and questions: "We haven't covered it yet, but I want you to know that I. . . ." "I'm aware that it's almost 10:30. I do have some more questions that I'd like to ask about the company."

In the **close** of the interview (three to five minutes), the interviewer will usually tell you what happens next: "We'll be bringing our top candidates out for plant trips in February. You should hear from us in three weeks." One interviewer reports that he gives applicants his card and tells them to call him. "It's a test to see if they are committed, how long it takes for them to call, and whether they even call at all."[2]

Close with an assertive statement. Depending on the circumstances, you could say: "I've certainly enjoyed learning more about General Electric." "I hope I get a chance to visit your Phoenix office. I'd really like to see the new computer system you talked about." "This job seems to be a good match between what you're looking for and what I'd like to do."

* Quoted from The Catalyst Staff, *Marketing Yourself, The Catalyst Women's Guide to Successful Résumés and Interviews* (New York: G. P. Putnam's Sons, 1980), 96.

Confidence Pays Off*

A senior was looking for a government job—unsuccessfully, though she couldn't put her finger on why, so she copped out and decided to go to graduate school. This decision left her with the summer free, so she decided to try to find an unpaid internship in government. Everyone she approached about such a position welcomed her with open arms, and to her amazement, she was offered *two paid jobs.*

She realized that when she had been looking before, she was in a sense begging psychologically; she had felt desperate, and that was how she showed herself to the interviewers. She did not present herself in a positive way. But when she was looking for an internship, she really felt she was offering something of value. It turned out that she took one of those jobs and changed her mind about graduate school.

The Interview Process

The interview process can have several parts:

- The initial interview—sometimes on campus, sometimes at the company's office—lasting 20 minutes to one hour.

- A second interview at the company's office or plant—an office visit or plant trip—lasting a full day or a day and a half. You may be asked to take various psychological or skills tests; you'll have interviews with many different people.

- Follow-up letters or conversations after the initial interview and after the plant trip.

- The conversation, often a phone call, in which the job offer is made.

Stress Interviews

A stress interview deliberately puts the applicant under stress. The stress may be physical: the interviewer may blow smoke in the interviewee's face, suggest a chair where the light is in the interviewee's eyes, even offer a chair which rocks because one of its legs has been sawed off. If this happens, be assertive: move to another chair or tell the interviewer that the behavior bothers you.

More often, the stress is psychological. A group of interviewers fire rapid questions. A single interviewer probes every weak spot in the applicant's record and asks questions which elicit negatives. If you get questions that put you on the defensive, **rephrase** them in less inflammatory terms, if necessary, and then **treat them as requests for information.**

> Q: Why did you major in physical education? That sounds like a pretty Mickey Mouse major.
>
> A: You're asking whether I have the academic preparation for this job. I started out in physical education because I've always loved sports. I learned that I couldn't graduate in four years if I officially switched my major to business administration because the requirements were different in the two programs. But I do have 21 hours in business administration and 9 hours in accounting. And my sports experience gives me practical training in teamwork, motivating people, and management.

Silence can also create stress. One woman walked into her scheduled interview to find a male interviewer with his feet up on the desk. He said, "It's been a long day. I'm tired and I want to go home. You have five minutes to sell yourself." Since she had planned the points she wanted to be sure interviewers knew, she was able to do this. "Your recruiting brochure said that you're looking for someone with a major in accounting and a minor in finance. As you may remember from my résumé, I'm majoring in accountancy and have had 12 hours in finance. I've also served as treasurer of a local campaign committee and have worked as a volunteer tax preparer through the Accounting Club." When she finished, the interviewer told her it was a test: "I wanted to see how you'd handle it."

Another variety of stress interview asks you to do—on the spot—the kind of thing the job would require. At one university, Joel Bowman and Bernadine Branchaw report, a student was seated in front of a computer, handed a copy of Lotus 1–2–3, and told to "do something with it."[3] At another school, an interviewer for a sales job handed applicants a ballpoint pen and said, "Sell me this pen."

Sexist interviews are a special variety of stress interviews. Although questions about marriage and children are illegal, they occasionally are asked. An interview can also be categorized as sexist if the interviewer implies that an applicant can't do the job because she's female: "You're a woman and you're short. You'd be working with tall men in this job. How would you handle them?"

Although you're within your rights to say, "I don't think that question is legal," a low-key response is more likely to lead to a job offer. Respond as you would to a stress question: **rephrase the question and treat it as a legitimate request for information.**

> Q: Aren't you just looking for a husband?
>
> A: You may be asking whether I'll stay with you long enough to justify the expense of training me as a staff accountant. Well, I'm not promising to work for you the rest of my life, just as you're not

FIGURE 29.1

THE COMMUNICATION BEHAVIORS OF SUCCESSFUL INTERVIEWEES[4]

	Unsuccessful Interviewees	Successful Interviewees
Statements about the position	Had only vague ideas of what they wanted to do; changed "ideal job" up to six times during the interview.	Specific and consistent about the position they wanted; were able to tell why they wanted the position.
Use of company name	Rarely used the company name.	Referred to the company by name four times as often as unsuccessful interviewees.
Knowledge about company and position	Made it clear that they were using the interview to learn about the company and what it offered.	Made it clear that they had researched the company; referred to specific brochures, journals, or people who had given them information.
Level of interest, enthusiasm	Responded neutrally to interviewer's statements: "OK," "I see." Indicated reservations about company or location.	Expressed approval of information provided by the interviewer nonverbally and verbally: "That's great!" Explicitly indicated desire to work for this particular company.
Picking up on interviewer's cues	Gave vague or negative answers even when a positive answer was clearly desired ("How are your math skills?").	Answered positively and confidently—and backed up the claim with a specific example of "problem-solving" or "toughness."
Use of industry terms and technical jargon	Used almost no technical jargon.	Used technical jargon: "point of purchase display," "NCR charge," "two-column approach," "direct mail."
Use of specifics in answers	Gave short answers—10 words or less, sometimes only one word; did not elaborate. Gave general responses: "fairly well."	Supported claims with specific personal experiences, comparisons, statistics, statements of teachers and employers.
Questions asked by interviewee	Asked a small number of general questions.	Asked specific questions based on knowledge of the industry and the company. Personalized questions: "What would my duties be?"
Control of time and topics	Interviewee talked 37% of the interview time, initiated 36% of the comments.	Interviewee talked 55% of the total time, initiated subjects 56% of the time.

promising to employ me for the rest of my life. How long I stay will depend upon whether my assignments continue to be interesting and challenging and whether I can advance.

Sometimes interviewers who do not ask sexist questions still have reservations about offering jobs to women. You may want to set at rest the interviewer's fears by bringing up the subject yourself: "You may have noticed that I'm married. My husband is a dentist and could relocate if the company wanted to transfer me."

ANSWERING TWENTY INTERVIEW QUESTIONS

First interviews seek to screen out less qualified candidates rather than to find someone to hire. Negative information will hurt you less if it comes out in the middle of the interview and is preceded and followed by positive information. If the interviewer asks a question as you're on your way out which you blow,

Nonverbal Communication During the Interview*

Be aware of the research on nonverbal signals, especially body language. Signs that denote interest include leaning forward, facing a person squarely, looking him or her in the eye, and using hand motions. Crossed legs or arms are sometimes a sign of distance, defensiveness, or resistance. Piling papers in a neat stack and looking at a watch are almost always signs that the person is trying to bring the interview to an end.

In a 1977 experiment, candidates' application form, facts, and words were held constant, but their nonverbal behaviors varied. Smiles, eye contact, gestures, and posture accounted for 40% of the variation in interviewer ratings.

don't leave until you've said something positive—perhaps restating one of the points you want the interviewer to know about you.

As Figure 29.1 shows, successful applicants use different communication behaviors than do unsuccessful applicants. In addition to practicing the content of questions, try to incorporate the tactics listed there.

The following questions frequently come up at interviews. Do some unpressured thinking before the interview so that you'll be able to come up with answers that are responsive, honest, and paint a good picture of you. Choose answers which fit your qualifications and your interview strategy.

1. **Tell me something about yourself.**
    Don't launch into an autobiography. Instead, use this as a chance to state the things about yourself that you want the interviewer to know.

2. **Tell me a story.**
    Pick a story that illustrates one of your strong points. Use some of the anecdotes you developed in problem 27–1. Or ask the interviewer, "What would you like me to tell you a story about?"

3. **What makes you think you're qualified to work for this company? or, I'm interviewing 120 people for two jobs. Why should I hire you?**
    This question may feel like an attack. Use it as an opportunity to state your strong points: your qualifications for the job, the things that separate you from other applicants.

4. **What two or three accomplishments have given you the greatest satisfaction?**
    Pick accomplishments that you're proud of, that create the image you want to project, and that enable you to share one of the things you want the interviewer to know about you.

5. **Why do you want to work for us?**
    Even if you're interviewing just for practice, make sure you have a good answer—preferably two or three reasons why you'd like to work for that company.

6. **What college subjects did you like best and least? Why?**
    This question may be an icebreaker; it may be designed to discover the kind of applicant they're looking for. If your favorite class was something outside your major, prepare an answer that shows that you have qualities that can help you in the job you're applying for: "My favorite class was a seminar in the American novel. We got a chance to think on our own, rather than just regurgitate facts; we made presentations to the class every week. I found I really like sharing my ideas with other people and presenting reasons for my conclusions about something."

7. **What is your class rank? Your grade point? Why are your grades so low?**
    If your grades aren't great, be ready with a nondefensive explanation. If possible, show that the cause of low grades now has

---

* Based on Milton D. Hakel, "Employment Interviewing," in Kendrith M. Rowland and Gerald R. Ferris, eds., *Personnel Management* (Boston: Allyn & Bacon, 1982), 140.

been solved or isn't relevant to the job you're applying for: "My father almost died last year, and my schoolwork really suffered." "When I started, I didn't have any firm goals. Once I discovered the field that was right for me, my grades have all been 'Bs' or better." "I'm not good at multiple choice tests. But you need someone who can work with people, not someone who can take tests."

8. **What have you read recently? What movies have you seen recently?**

These questions may be icebreakers; they may be designed to probe your intellectual depth. The semester or quarter you're interviewing, read at least one book or magazine (regularly) and see at least one movie that you could discuss at an interview.

9. **Show me some samples of your writing.**

Many jobs require the ability to write well. Employers no longer take mastery of basic English for granted, even if the applicant has a degree from a prestigious university.

The year you're interviewing, go through your old papers and select the best ones, retyping them if necessary, so that you'll have samples if you're asked for them.

If you don't have samples at the interview, mail them to the interviewer immediately after the interview.

10. **Where do you see yourself in five years?**

Employers ask this question to find out if you are a self-starter or if you passively respond to what happens. You may want to have several scenarios for five years from now to use in different kinds of interviews. Or you may want to say, "Well, my goals may change as opportunities arise. But right now, I want to. . . ."

11. **What would you see as the ideal job for you? What criteria are you using to evaluate the companies you're interviewing with?**

Employers may ask this for a variety of reasons: to see how active a role you're taking in the job search process, to ascertain your interests, to see what you're looking for so they can better sell the job and company to you.

12. **What have you done to learn about this company?**

An employer may ask this to see what you already know about the company (if you've read the recruiting literature, the interviewer doesn't need to repeat it). This question may also be used to see how active a role you're taking in the job search process and how interested you are in this job.

13. **What major problem have you encountered and how did you deal with it?**

Any manager or professional will have to solve problems. The interviewer will be less interested in the specific solution than in the process you used to solve problems. Thus a difficult problem that you approached well but did not completely solve may be a

* Based on Caroline Bird, *Everything a Woman Needs to Know to Get Paid What She's Worth* (New York: David McKay, 1973), 127.

Why Do You Want to Work for Us?*

Lester Korn, an executive recruiter, reports that one woman blew a chance at an important job because when she was asked "Why do you want to work for us?" she said, "Because you are the third largest company in your field in the state of Illinois"—and it was the *second largest.*

What Are Your Goals?*

One person, looking back on a highly successful job campaign that netted seven offers, made this comment about questions relating to goals and plans:

> When I was looking for a job, I was asked the same question in one way or another about a dozen times. I answered that I could not be that analytical about my goals and ambitions. I told them that I had always been a good student and that I enjoyed being with bright and active people. I did well in primary and secondary school and in college. When I did well, opportunities opened up for me. I told them that I hoped to get a job with a good employer and do my best there just as I had done in school, and that I expected further opportunities to open up, although specifically where or when I don't know. I found what I wanted in education by working hard and contributing, and I expect more of the same of work. I do not worry about career goals.

better example to choose than a problem where an off-the-top-of-the-head solution worked.

14. **What adjectives would you use to describe yourself?**

    Use only positive ones. Plan a concrete example to illustrate each choice.

15. **What are your interests outside work? What extracurricular activities have you been involved in?**

    While it's desirable to be well-rounded, naming 10 interests is a mistake: the interviewer may wonder when you'll have time to work.

    If you mention your fiancé, spouse, or children in response to this question ("Well, my fiancé and I like to go sailing"), it is perfectly legal for the interviewer to ask follow-up questions ("What would you do if your spouse got a job offer in another town?"), even though the same question would be illegal if the interviewer brought up the subject first.

16. **What is your greatest strength?**

    Employers ask this question to give you a chance to sell yourself and to learn something about your values. Pick a strength related to work, school, or extra-curricular activities: "I'm good at working with people." "I really can sell things." "I'm good at solving problems." "I learn quickly." "I'm reliable. When I say I'll do something, I do it."

17. **What is your greatest weakness?**

    Avoid negatives which may suggest that you're not promotable, even if they aren't related to the entry-level job you're interviewing for: generating ideas, working with people, and so forth. Use a work-related negative, even if something in your personal life really is your greatest weakness. This isn't the place for unrelieved honesty. There are five basic strategies for answering this question:

    a. Discuss a weakness that can also be seen as positive:

       Well, I tend to get impatient when people don't follow through with what they've said they'll do.

    b. Discuss a weakness which is not related to the job you're being considered for—and end your answer with a positive which *is* related to the job:

       [For a creative job in advertising:] I don't like accounting. I know it's important, but I don't like it. I'd even rather hire someone to do my taxes. I'm much more interested in being creative and working with people, which is why I find this position interesting.

       [For a job in administration:] I don't like selling products. I hated selling cookies when I was a Girl Scout. I'd much

*   Quoted from John L. Munschauer, *Jobs for English Majors and Other Smart People* (Princeton, NJ: Peterson's Guides, 1986), 26.

rather work with ideas—and I really like selling the ideas that I believe in.

[For a job in architecture:] I hate fund-raising. It always seemed to me if people wanted to give, they would anyway. I'd much rather have something to offer people which will help them solve their own problems and meet their own needs.

c. Discuss a weakness which the interviewer already knows from your résumé:

I've never had a chance to work in a brokerage firm. However, my summer jobs at a bank have given me an introduction to the financial world, and of course I've had lots of courses in investments.

d. Discuss a weakness which you are working to improve:

In the past, I wasn't a good writer. But last term I took a course in business writing that taught me how to organize my ideas and how to revise. I may never win a Pulitzer Prize, but now I'm a lot more confident that I can write effective reports and memos.

e. Discuss a work-related weakness:

I procrastinate. Fortunately, I work well under pressure, but a couple of times I've really put myself in a bind.

This strategy can backfire, of course. But strategies *a* through *d* are so widely known that occasionally an interviewer will respond to one of them, "That's not a weakness. What really *are* your weaknesses?" If you use strategy *e*, some interviewers will give you points for honesty and for knowing yourself.

18. **Have you ever been fired? Why?**
Be honest; avoid blaming or bad-mouthing your former employer. If the firing was your fault, try to show that you've learned from the situation and have corrected the problem.

19. **What are your salary requirements?**
Give the interviewer a range using odd increments: "I'd expect to make between $28,300 and $31,900." As you say this, *watch the interviewer.* If he or she has that blank look we use to hide dismay, you may have asked for much more than the company was planning to offer. Quickly continue, ". . . depending, of course, on fringe benefits and how quickly I could be promoted. However, salary isn't the most important criterion for me in choosing a job, and I won't necessarily accept the highest offer I get. I'm interested in going somewhere where I can get good experience and use my talents to make a real contribution."
Prepare for this question by finding out from your placement

* Quoted from John L. Munschauer, *Jobs for English Majors and Other Smart People* (Princeton, NJ: Peterson's Guides, 1986), 28–29 and William Lareau, *Inside Track: A Successful Job Search Method* (Piscataway, NJ: New Century, 1985), 157.

The Same Answer Can Get Different Responses*

One job hunter I knew named O'Brian looked a recruiter straight in the eye and said, "As for my goals, they are to become president of your company in not too many years." The recruiter called him arrogant and told him to see a counselor. That same day O'Brian was asked again about his vocational plans by another recruiter and gave the same self-assured answer. This recruiter was delighted. As he said later, "All day long, I'd been asking students what they wanted to be in our company some day, and I'd been getting evasive or self-effacing answers. Then O'Brian came along. He is smart and knows what he is after. He is the candidate I want."

A friend of mine was once asked the hackneyed old saw, "And where do you expect to be in three years?" The friend, who should have known better (and does now), replied with the also hackneyed but dangerous, "I expect to be sitting in your chair." . . . The interviewer was shocked. His face got white, and he asked my friend, "Where will I be if you get my job?" The guy was dead serious; he planned to be in the job for a long time and had never thought of moving anywhere. We all laughed when we heard the story, but my friend didn't ever hear from them again.

Behind the Scenes with a Big Eight Recruiter*

For bringing back the best, and nothing but the best, there's no one to touch Don Kipper. Based in Los Angeles, this 15-year veteran at Ernst & Whinney, one of the field's top companies, faces a rigorous schedule.

His typical day runs from 8:30 A.M. to about 5 P.M. He will interview 14 candidates, and take only an hour for lunch. . . . Every half hour he will interview a different candidate. . . . What he looks for is "persistence, self-confidence, verbal skills, an ability to answer questions clearly and concisely. Can you think on your feet?" . . .

Yet he doesn't see the campus interview as his top source for candidates. "Those are the dark horses," the ones he hasn't already met for one reason or another at the "proper functions." He's always on campus, officially and unofficially at the honor societies, cocktail parties and the like. He takes an active interest in student affairs and uses it to scoop his rivals on the best potential executives. Once identified, they are invited straight into the corporate office.

The luckiest are the ones invited to an Ernst & Whinney management training seminar. . . .

Kipper is active in campus workshops, helping students improve their interviewing skills. Although claiming not to be a stress interviewer he recognizes their existence, and if you attend one of his sessions, chances are you'll get a couple of real stinkers thrown at you. One unfortunate recently got Kipper's face three inches from his, demanding, "You were drunk last night. After that, why should I waste my time talking to you?" Like many good recruiters, the man has eyes in the back of his head. . . .

His advice? "Get involved with the extracurricular campus activities. That's where you'll get discovered."

office the salaries students got last year. One study showed that male BA and MBA candidates expected to start at salaries 16.5% higher than the salaries women BA and MBA candidates expected.[5] Research will help you know what a job is worth so that you get what you deserve.

20. **What questions do you have?**

This gives you a chance to cover things the interviewer hasn't brought up; it also gives the interviewer a sense of your priorities and values. Don't focus on salary, fringe benefits, or how hard you'll have to work. Better questions are

- What would I be doing on a day-to-day basis?
- What kind of training program do you have? If, as I'm rotating among departments, I find that I prefer one area, can I specialize in it when the training program is over?
- How do you evaluate employees? How often do you review them? Where would you expect a new trainee (banker, staff accountant) to be three years from now?
- What happened to the last person who had this job?
- How are interest rates (a new product from competitors, imports, demographic trends, government regulation, etc.) affecting your company?
- This sounds like a great job. What are the drawbacks?

Of course, you will get questions that aren't on this list, and you won't be able to anticipate every oddball question you may get. (One interviewer asked students, "What vegetable would you like to be?" Another asked, "If you were a cookie, what kind of cookie would you be?"[6]) Check with other people who have interviewed recently to find out what questions are being asked in your field at your community college, college, or university.

AFTER THE INTERVIEW

What you do after the interview can determine whether or not you get the job. One woman wanted to switch from banking, where she was working in corporate relations, to advertising. The ad agency interviewer expressed doubts about her qualifications. Immediately after leaving the agency, she tracked down a particular book the interviewer had mentioned he was looking for but had been unable to find. She presented it to him—and was hired.[7]

Follow-Up Letters

Many people feel that a follow-up letter is optional after a first interview. However, so few candidates write one that it will certainly separate you from other applicants and may well help you get a second interview. A letter after an office visit is essential to thank your hosts for their hospitality as well as to send in receipts for your expenses. Both letters should

- Remind the interviewer of what he or she liked in you.
- Counter any negative impressions that may have come up at the interview.

---

* Quoted from Martin John Yate, "The Life of a Recruiter," *Columbus Dispatch,* November 18, 1986, F1.

- Use the jargon of the company and refer to specific things you learned during your interview or saw during your visit.
- Be enthusiastic.
- Refer to the next move, whether you'll wait to hear from the employer or whether you want to call to learn about the status of your application.

See Figure A.4 in Appendix A for a sample follow-up letter.

Be sure that the letter is well written and free from apparent typos. One employer reports,

> I often interviewed people whom I liked, . . . but their follow-up letters were filled with misspelled words and names and other inaccuracies. They blew their chance with the follow-up letter.[8]

Handling Job Offers

Some employers offer jobs at the end of the office visit. In other cases, you may wait for weeks or even months to hear. Employers almost always offer jobs orally. You must say something in response immediately, so it's good to plan some strategies.

If your first offer is not from your first choice, express your pleasure at being offered the job, but do not accept it on the phone. "That's great! I assume I have two weeks to let you know?" Then *call* the other companies you're interested in. Explain, "I've just got a job offer, but I'd rather work for you. Can you tell me what the status of my application is?" Nobody will put that information in writing, but almost everyone will tell you over the phone. With this information, you're in a better position to decide whether to accept the original offer.

Companies routinely give applicants two weeks to accept or reject offers. Some students have been successful in getting those two weeks extended to several weeks or even months. Certainly if you cannot decide by the deadline, it is worth asking for more time: the worst the company can do is say *no*. If you do try to keep a company hanging for a long time, be prepared for weekly phone calls asking you if you've decided yet.

Make your acceptance contingent upon a written job offer confirming the terms. That letter should spell out not only salary but also fringe benefits and any special provisions you have negotiated. If something is missing, call the interviewer for clarification: "You said that I'd be reviewed for a promotion and higher salary in six months, but that isn't in the letter." You have more power to resolve misunderstandings now than you will after six months or a year on the job.

When you've accepted one job, let the other places you visited know that you're no longer interested. Then they can go to their second choices. If you're second on someone else's list, you'll appreciate other candidates' removing themselves so the way is clear for you.

SUMMARY OF KEY POINTS

- Develop an overall strategy based on your answers to these three questions:
  1. What two to five facts about yourself do you want the interviewer to know?

Bargaining for Benefits*

Benefits bargaining goes hand-in-hand with salary negotiation. If you list the benefits you care about, then your recruiter should be able to determine which ones the company can provide. . . .

Don't expect the sky to be the limit. But remember, what you don't ask for, you don't get. If discussing financial details under pressure with strangers disturbs you, bring a written list of your requirements with you. Make sure your recruiter pins down when your salary reviews will take place and what the minimum increase will be. . . .

A Fortune 500 or other megaoperation is likely to offer:

- **Extensive insurance and retirement plans.** . . .
- **Bonuses.** These are based either on company performance in the marketplace (you bargain for a percentage) or on personal goals (in which case, you should tag the bonuses to the successful completion of predetermined projects).
- **Special perks.** These can include child-care compensation, free financial advice from experts, membership dues for clubs and associations, tuition reimbursement, spouse's travel expenses and a company car, among others.
- **Relocation coverage.** . . .

Small companies are likely to offer:

- **Stock grants.** In lieu of cash benefits, many privately held companies give you stock. The more profitable the company the greater your chances are for substantial gain. . . .
- **Extra salary for a personally managed benefit plan in cases where the company doesn't provide one.** . . .
- **Simplified employee pension plans (SEPs).**

---

* Quoted from Warren Kalbacker, "Beyond Salary: Bargaining for Benefits," *Working Woman*, April 1987, 112.

You Can't Anticipate Everything*

"So, tell me, why do they make man-hole covers round?"

The tall and intimidating partner at the prestigious McKinsey & Company posed the question to a young woman interviewing for a consulting position. She had prepared for and rehearsed over a hundred typical interview questions, but she hadn't anticipated this one. She looked at him suspiciously but no, he wasn't joking. She realized that if she couldn't give him the right answer she would probably not get the job. So in the end, her education and hard work all pivoted on one question.

She paused and then answered. A hint of satisfaction appeared on the interviewer's face. And the woman knew she had the job. . . .

The answer to the question . . . :

If man-hole covers were square or rectangular, when being opened the cover could inadvertently be turned at an angle and fall through the opening. A circular cover can never fall through, no matter how it is turned.

2. What disadvantages or weaknesses do you need to overcome or minimize?
3. What do you need to know about the job and the organization to decide whether you want to accept this job if it is offered to you?

- Wear a business suit to the interview. Try to dress for the position that's two levels above the one for which you're applying. John Molloy's books can help you choose appropriate interview clothing.
- Bring an extra copy of your résumé, something to write on and write with, and copies of your work to the interview.
- Record the name of the interviewer, what the interviewer liked about you, any negative points that came up, answers to your questions about the company, and when you'll hear from the company.
- Rehearse in advance everything you can. Ask a friend to interview you. If your campus has videotaping facilities, watch yourself on tape so that you can evaluate and modify your interview behavior.
- Be your best self at the interview.
- In a **stress** interview, the interviewer deliberately creates physical or psychological stress. Change the conditions that create physical stress. Meet psychological stress by rephrasing questions in less inflammatory terms and treating them as requests for information.
- Successful applicants know what they want to do, use the company name in the interview, have researched the company in advance, back up claims with specifics, use technical jargon, ask specific questions, and talk more of the time.
- As you practice answers to questions you may be asked, choose answers that fit your qualifications and your interview strategy.
- A follow-up letter after an interview should
  - Remind the interviewer of what he or she liked in you.
  - Allay any negative impressions that may have come up at the interview.
  - Use the jargon of the company and refer to specific things you learned during your interview or saw during your visit.
  - Be enthusiastic.
  - Refer to the next move you'll make.
- If your first offer isn't from your first choice, call the other companies you're interested in to ask the status of your application.

NOTES

1. The study, a doctoral dissertation by Springbett in 1958, involved 20 interviews by eight different interviewers. It has not been replicated. Another study by Hakel, Leonard, and Siegfried in 1972 showed that evaluations changed during the course of the interview. Milton D. Hakel, "Employment Interviewing," in Kendrith M. Rowland and Gerald R. Ferris, eds., *Personnel Management* (Boston: Allyn & Bacon, 1982), 136–37.
2. The Catalyst Staff, *Marketing Yourself* (New York: G. P. Putnam's Sons, 1980), 179.
3. Joel P. Bowman and Bernadine P. Branchaw, "Taking the Byte Out of Computer Training," *CommShare* 1 (Spring 1988) [3].
4. Based on research reported in Lois J. Einhorn, "An Inner View of the Job Interview: An Investigation of Successful Communicative Behaviors," *Communication Education* 30 (July 1981): 217–28.

* Quoted from Charlene Mitchell and Thomas Burdick, *The Right Moves: Succeeding in a Man's World without a Harvard MBA* (New York: Macmillan, 1985), 79, 90n.

5. Brenda Major and Ellen Konar, "An Investigation of Sex Differences in Pay Expectations and Their Possible Causes," *Academy of Management Journal* 27, no. 4 (1984): 182.

6. Donna Stine Kienzler, letter to Ann Granacki, April 6, 1988.

7. *Marketing Yourself,* 101.

8. Ray Robinson quoted by Dick Friedman, "The Interview as Mating Ritual," *Working Woman,* April 1987, 107.

EXERCISES AND PROBLEMS FOR CHAPTER 29

29–1 INTERVIEWING JOB HUNTERS

Talk to students at your school who are interviewing for jobs this term. Possible questions to ask them include the following:

- What field are you in? How good is the job market in that field this year?
- How long is the first interview with a company, usually?
- What questions have you been asked at job interviews? Were you asked any stress or sexist questions? Any really oddball questions?
- What answers seemed to go over well? What answers bombed?
- At an office visit or plant trip, how many people did you talk to? What were their job titles?
- Were you asked to take any tests (skills, physical, drugs)?
- How long did you have to wait after a first interview to learn whether you were being invited for an office visit? How long after an office visit did it take to learn whether you were being offered a job? How much time did the company give you to decide?
- What sources did you use to track down job leads? How many contacts did you make with companies? (Count all letters, résumés, and phone calls, as well as any walk-in visits.) How many interviews did you get? How many job offers? Which kinds of sources produced the highest percentage of interviews and offers?
- What advice would you have for someone who will be interviewing next term or next year?

As your instructor directs,
  a. Summarize your findings in a memo to your instructor.
  b. Report your findings orally to the class.
  c. Join with a small group of students to write a group report describing the results of your survey.

29–2 INTERVIEWING AN INTERVIEWER

Talk to someone who regularly interviews candidates for entry-level jobs. Possible questions to ask include the following:

- How long have you been interviewing for your organization? Does everyone on the

management ladder at your company do some interviewing, or do people specialize in it?

- Do you follow a set structure for interviews? What are some of the standard questions you ask?
- What are you looking for? How important are (1) good grades, (2) leadership roles in extra-curricular groups, or (3) relevant work experience? What advice would you give to someone who doesn't have any of these?
- What are the things you see students do that create a poor impression? Think about the worst candidate you've interviewed. What did he or she do (or not do) to create such a negative impression?
- What are things that make a good impression? Recall the best student you've ever interviewed. Why did he or she impress you so much?
- What proportion of first interviews generally result in office visits or plant trips?
- How does your employer evaluate and reward your success as an interviewer?
- What do you like best about interviewing? What do you like least?
- What advice would you have for someone who still has a year or so before the job hunt begins?

As your instructor directs,
  a. Summarize your findings in a memo to your instructor.
  b. Report your findings orally to the class.
  c. Join with a small group of students to write a group report describing the results of your survey.
  d. Write to the interviewer thanking him or her for taking the time to talk to you.

29–3 PREPARING AN INTERVIEW STRATEGY

Based on your analysis in problems 26–1, 26–2, 26–3, 27–1, and 27–2 prepare an interview strategy.

1. List two to five things about yourself that you want the interviewer to know before you leave the interview.
2. Identify any weaknesses or apparent weaknesses in your record and plan ways to explain them or minimize them.

3. List the points you need to learn about an employer to decide whether to accept an office visit or plant trip.

As your instructor directs,

a. Share your strategy with a small group of other students.

b. Describe your strategy in a memo to your instructor.

c. Present your strategy orally to the class.

29–4 PREPARING QUESTIONS TO ASK EMPLOYERS

Prepare a list of questions to ask at job interviews.

1. Prepare a list of three to five general questions to apply to most employers in your field.

2. Prepare two to five specific questions for the three companies you are most interested in.

As your instructor directs,

a. Share the questions with a small group of other students.

b. List the questions in a memo to your instructor.

c. Present your questions orally to the class.

29–5 PREPARING ANSWERS TO QUESTIONS YOU MAY BE ASKED

Prepare answers to each of the 20 interview questions listed in this chapter and to any other questions that you know are likely to be asked of job hunters in your field or on your campus.

As your instructor directs,

a. Write down the answers to your questions and turn them in.

b. Conduct mini-interviews in a group of five students. In the group, let student A be the interviewer and ask five questions from the list. Student B will play the job candidate

and answer the questions, using real information about Student B's field and qualifications. Student C will evaluate the content of the answer. Student D will observe the non-verbal behavior of the interviewer (A); student E will observe the nonverbal behavior of the interviewee (B).

After the mini-interview, let students C, D, and E share their observations and recommend ways that B could be even more effective.

Then switch roles. Let another student be the interviewer and ask five questions of another interviewee, while new observers note content and nonverbal behavior. Continue the process until everyone in the group has had a chance to be "interviewed."

29–6 WRITING A FOLLOW-UP LETTER AFTER A CAMPUS INTERVIEW

Write a follow-up letter for a campus interview. Relate your strong points to facts about the company that came out in the interview; minimize any negatives that you think may remain; show that you paid attention to what the interviewer said; be enthusiastic about the job and the company.

If you are not interviewing this term, make up the details of the interview so that you can be specific in your letter.

29–7 WRITING A FOLLOW-UP LETTER AFTER AN OFFICE VISIT OR PLANT TRIP

Write a follow-up letter after an office visit or plant trip. Thank your hosts for their hospitality; relate your strong points to things you learned about the company during the visit; allay any negatives that may remain; be enthusiastic about the company; and submit receipts for your expenses so you can be reimbursed.

If you are not interviewing this term, use the names, addresses, and facts in problem 14–8 as the basis for your letter.

APPENDICES

Formats for Letters and Memos

QUESTIONS

- What is the difference between letters and memos?
- What are the three standard letter formats? How do they differ from each other? What are the advantages of each?
- How big should the margins be?
- Where should the address go on an envelope?
- What is the standard memo format? How do you set it up on the page?
- How do you set up the second page of a letter or memo?
- What are the Post Office abbreviations for states and provinces?

> When it comes to arranging the various parts of a business letter on the page, there is no one form that might be called "best."... What that format is to be depends on the judgment and good taste of the individual responsible. It may be dictated by the [person] who writes the letters, in other cases, by company regulation.
>
> L. E. Frailey
> *Handbook of Business Letters,* 1948

Letters normally go to people outside your organization; **memos** go to other people in your organization. In very large organizations, corporate culture determines whether people in different divisions or different locations feel close enough to each other to write memos. Letters and memos do not necessarily differ in length, formality, writing style, or pattern of organization. However, letters and memos do differ in format. **Format** means the parts of a document and the way they are arranged on the page.

FORMATS FOR LETTERS

Most writers choose one of three letter formats: **block** (see Figure A.1), **modified block** (see Figure A.2), or the **Administrative Management Society Simplified** format, also called **AMS Simplified** (see Figure A.3). Many organizations adopt a single format which all writers must use.

The three formats differ in these ways:

- **Placement of the date and signature block.** Block and AMS Simplified line up the date and the writer's name at the left margin. Modified block format moves the date and signature block over to the right one-half or two-thirds of the way on the page.
- **Paragraph indentation.** Neither block nor AMS Simplified ever indents paragraphs. Paragraph indentation is optional in modified block. Since some people feel that indented paragraphs make a letter look more personal, companies often used modified block format with indented paragraphs when they write to consumers.
- **Use of salutation and close.** Both block and modified block use a salutation and a complimentary close. AMS Simplified omits both the salutation and the close entirely.

  Use the same level of formality in the **salutation,** or greeting, as you would in talking to someone on the phone: *Dear Glenn* if you're on a first-name basis, *Dear Mr. Helms* if you don't know the reader well enough to use the first name.

  Some writers feel that the AMS Simplified format is better since the reader is not *Dear.* Omitting the salutation is particularly good when you do not know the reader's name or do not know which courtesy title to use. (For a full discussion on nonsexist salutations and salutations when you don't know the reader's name, see Chapter 8.) However, readers like to see their names. Since the AMS

Northwest Hardware Warehouse

100 Freeway Exchange   **Provo, UT 84610**   **(801) 555-4683**

Date and signature Block lined up at left margin

↕ 2-6 spaces, depending on length of letter

June 20, 1988

↕ 2-4 spaces

Mr. James E. Murphy, Accounts Payable   *Title could be on a separate line*
Salt Lake Equipment Rentals
5600 Wasatch Boulevard
Salt Lake City, Utah 84121 *← Zip code on same line*

1"–1½"

Dear Jim: *← Colon in mixed punctuation*

Use first name in salutation if you'd use it on the phone

If I does NOT have a heading

The following items totaling $393.09 are still open on your account.

Invoice #01R-784391 *← Underline or Bold*

After the bill for this invoice arrived on May 14, you wrote saying that   *5/8"–1"*
the material had not been delivered to you. On May 29, our Claims
Department sent you a copy of the delivery receipt signed by an employee
of Salt Lake Equipment. You have had proof of delivery for over three
weeks, but your payment has not yet arrived.

Please send a check for $78.42.

Triple-space before each new heading

Single-space paragraphs, Double-space between paragraphs

Voucher #59351

The reference line on your voucher #59351, dated June 11, indicates that
it is the gross payment for invoice #01G-002345. However, the voucher
was only for $1171.25, while the invoice amount was $1246.37. Please
send a check for $75.12 to clear this item.

Voucher #55032

Voucher #55032, dated June 15, subtracts a credit for $239.55 from the
amount due. Our records do not show that any credit is due on this
voucher.

Please send either an explanation or a check to cover the $239.55
immediately.

Total Amount Due

Please send a check for $393.09 to cover these three items and to bring
your account up to date.

2-3 Spaces

Sincerely, *← Comma in Mixed punctuation*

3-4 Spaces

Neil Hutchinson
Credit Representative

Headings are optional in letters

cc: Joan Stottlemeyer, Credit Manager

Leave bottom margin of 3-6 spaces — more if letter is short

MODIFIED BLOCK FORMAT ON LETTERHEAD (MIXED PUNCTUATION)

Bay City
Information Systems

2-6 spaces depending on length of letter.

September 14, 1989

Line up date with signature block ½ or ⅔ of the way over

2-4 spaces

1"-1½"

Ms. Mary E. Arcas
Personnel Director
Cyclops Communication Technologies
1050 South Sierra Bonita Avenue
Los Angeles, CA 90019 *Zip code on same line*

Dear Ms. Arcas: *Colon in mixed punctuation*

5/8"-1"

Indenting paragraphs is optional in Modified Block

Enclosed is the evaluation form you asked me to fill out for Colleen Kangas. Let me add a little information here. Colleen was hired as a clerk typist by Bay City Information Systems on April 4, 1986 and was promoted to Administrative Secretary on August 1, 1987. At her review in June, I recommended that she be promoted again. She is an intelligent young woman with good work habits and a good knowledge of computer software.

Single-space paragraphs

As an Adminstrative Secretary, Colleen not only handles routine duties such as processing time cards, ordering supplies, and entering data, but also screens calls for two marketing specialists, answers basic questions about Bay City Information Systems, compiles the statistics I need for my monthly reports, and investigates special assignments for me. In the past eight months, she has investigated freight charges, inventory department hardware, and microfiche files. I need only to give her general directions: she has a knack for tracking down information quickly and summarizing it accurately.

Double-space between paragraphs

Although the department's workload has increased during the year, Colleen manages her time so that everything gets done on schedule. She is consistently poised and friendly under pressure. Her willingness to work overtime on occasion is particularly remarkable considering that she has been going to college part-time ever since she joined our firm.

At Bay City Information Systems, Colleen uses XyWrite and Paradox software. She tells me that she has also used WordPerfect and Lotus 1-2-3 in her college classes.

If Colleen were staying in San Francisco, we would want to keep her. She has the potential both to become an Executive Secretary or to move into line or staff work, especially once she completes her degree. I recommend her highly.

2-3 spaces

Comma in mixed punctuation

Sincerely,

Headings are optional in letters

3-4 spaces

Jeanne Cederlind

Jeanne Cederlind

↕ 2-4

Encl.: Evaluation Form for Colleen Kangas

Leave at least 3-6 spaces—
More if letter is short

Line up signature block with date

4500 HOLLOWAY AVENUE • SAN FRANCISCO, CA 94132 • (415) 555-2000

578

McFarlane
Memorial
Hospital

1500 Main Street
Iowa City, IA 52232
(319) 555-3113

Everything lined up at left margin

↑ *2-4*

August 24, 1988

↓ *2-4*

1" – 1½"

Melinda Hamilton
Medical Services Division
Health Management Services, Inc.
4333 Edgewood Road, NE
Cedar Rapids, IA 52401

↓ *3*

Subject in capital letters

REQUEST FOR INFORMATION ABOUT COMPUTER SYSTEMS   *No Salutation*

We're interested in upgrading our computer system and would like to talk   *⅝" – 1"*
to one of your marketing representatives to see what would best meet our
needs. We will use the following criteria to choose a system:

List lined up at left margin

1. Ability to use our current software and data files.

2. Price, pro-rated on a three-year expected life.

3. Ability to provide auxiliary services, e.g., controlling inventory
    of drugs and supplies, monitoring patients' vital signs, processing
    insurance forms.

4. Freedom from down time.

Double-space between ¶'s   Triple-space between paragraphs and list

Do not indent paragraphs

McFarlane Memorial Hospital has 50 beds for acute care and 75 beds for
long-term care. In the next five years, we expect the number of beds to
remain the same while out-patient care and emergency room care increase.

Could we meet the first or the third week in September? We are eager to
have the new system installed by Christmas if possible.

← No close. No need to sign

Writer's name in full caps

HUGH PORTERFIELD
Controller

↕ *2-4 spaces*

Headings are optional in letters

Encl.: Specifications of Current System
        Data Bases Currently in Use

↕ *2-4 spaces*

cc: Rene Seaburg

*Leave at least 3-6 spaces —
More if letter is short*

Subject Lines for Letters and Memos

Both letters and memos can have subject lines. Subject lines are required in memos; they are optional in letters.

Good subject lines are

- Specific enough to differentiate this message from others on the same subject, but broad enough to cover everything in the message.
- Concise (usually no more than 7 to 10 words).
- Appropriate for your purposes and the response you expect from your reader.

When you have good news, put it in the subject line.

When your information is neutral, summarize it concisely in the subject line.

When your information is negative, put the subject—but not the negative aspect—in the subject line.

When you have a request that will be easy for the reader to grant, put either the subject of the request or a direct question in the subject line.

When you must persuade a reluctant reader, do not put your request or even the topic in the subject line. Instead, use a common ground or a reader benefit.

For examples of subject lines in each of these situations, see Chapters 12, 13, and 14.

Simplified omits the reader's name in the salutation, writers who use this format but who also want to be friendly often try to use the reader's name early in the body of the letter.

Sincerely and *Yours truly* are standard **complimentary closes.** When you are writing to people in special groups or to someone who is a friend as well as a business acquaintance, you may want to use a less formal close. Depending on the circumstances, the following informal closes might be acceptable: *Yours for a better environment, Cordially, Thank you!,* or even *Ciao.*

In **mixed punctuation,** a colon follows the salutation and a comma follows the close. In a sales or fund-raising letter, it is acceptable to use a comma after the salutation to make the letter look like a personal letter rather than like a business letter. In **open punctuation,** omit all punctuation after the salutation and the close. Mixed punctuation is traditional. Open punctuation is faster to type.

- **Use of a subject or reference line.** AMS Simplified always uses a subject line. A subject or reference line is optional in block and modified block formats.

  A **subject line** tells what the letter is about. A **reference line** refers the reader to the number used on the previous correspondence this letter replies to, or the order or invoice number which this letter is about. Very large organizations, like the IRS, use numbers on every piece of correspondence they send out so that it is possible quickly to find the earlier document to which an incoming letter refers.

- **Signature.** The writer always signs his or her name in block and modified block formats. AMS Simplified omits the signature (though it retains the typed name).

- **Writer's typed name.** The writer's name is typed using regular capital letters in block and modified block formats. The name is typed in full capital letters in AMS Simplified format.

All three formats single-space paragraphs and double-space between them. Single-spaced paragraphs create better visual appeal in a typed page. Some writers double-space rough drafts to make revisions easier. Reports may be either single- or double-spaced depending on the audience and on the conventions of the organization for which the report is prepared.

Each of the three formats has advantages. Both block and AMS Simplified can be typed quickly since everything is lined up at the left margin. Block format is the format most frequently used for business letters; readers expect it. Modified block format creates a visually attractive page by moving the date and signature block over into what would otherwise be empty white space. Modified block is a traditional format; readers are comfortable with it.

The examples of the three formats in Figures A.1–A.3 show one-page letters on company letterhead. **Letterhead** is preprinted stationery with the organization's name, logo, address, and phone number. Figures A.4–A.5 show how to set up block or modified block format when you do not have letterhead.

Although not every example uses the same devices to provide visual impact, all three formats can use headings, lists, and indented sections for emphasis.

You can save time by adopting standard side margins. Use at least 1″ to 1 1/2″ on the left and 5/8″ to 1″ on the right. If your letterhead extends all the way across the top of the page, set your margins even with the ends of the letterhead for the most visually pleasing page. The top margin should be three to six lines under the letterhead, or 2″ down from the top of the page if you

6-12 spaces from top of page

Single spaced

405 West College, Apt. 201
Thibodaux, LA 70301
April 2, 1989

2-6 spaces

1" - 1½"

Mr. Robert Land, Account Manager *← could put title on separate line*
Sive Associates
378 Norman Boulevard
Cincinnati, OH 48528

2-4 spaces

Dear Mr. Land ○ *No punctuation in open punctuation*

After visiting Sive Associates last week, I'm even more sure that writing direct mail is the career for me.

Single-space paragraphs

I've always been able to brainstorm ideas, but sometimes, when I had to focus on one idea for a class project, I wasn't sure which idea was best. It was fascinating to see how you make direct mail scientific as well as creative by testing each new creative package against the control. I can understand how pleased Linda Hayes was when she learned that her new package for Smithsonian beat the control.

Seeing Kelly, Luke, and Gene collaborating on the Sesame Street package gave me some sense of the tight deadlines you're under. As you know, I've learned to meet deadlines, not only for my class assignments, but also in working on Nicholls' newspaper. The award I won for my feature on the election suggests that my quality holds up even when the deadline is tight!

Double-space between paragraphs

Thank you for your hospitality while I was in Cincinnati. You and your wife made my stay very pleasant. I especially appreciate the time the two of you took to help me find information about apartments that are accessible to wheelchairs. Cincinnati seems like a very liveable city.

I'm excited about a career in direct mail and about the possibility of joining Sive Associates. I look forward to hearing from you soon!

Sincerely ○ *No punctuation in open punctuation*

Gina Focasio

Gina Focasio

Writer's phone number → (504) 555-2948

P.S. My expenses totalled $424. Enclosed are receipts for my plane fare from New Orleans to Cincinnati ($357), the taxi to the airport in Cincinnati ($20), and the bus from Thibodaux to New Orleans ($47).

Encl.: Receipts for Expenses

3-6 spaces - more if letter is short

6-12 Spaces

11408 Brussels Ave. NE
Albuquerque, NM 87111 } *Single spaced*
November 5, 1988

2-6 Spaces

1" - 1½"

Mr. Tom Miller, President
Miller Office Supplies Corporation
P.O. Box 2900
Lincolnshire, IL 60197-2900

Subject: Invoice No. 664907, 10/29/88 ← *Subject line is optional in Block and Modified Block*

Dear Mr. Miller ○ *No punctuation in Open punctuation*

Indenting paragraphs is optional in Modified Block

My wife, Caroline Lehman, ordered and received the briefcase listed on page 71 of your catalog (881-CD-L-9Q-4). The catalog said that the Leatherizer, 881-P-4, was free. On the order blank she indicated that she did want the Leatherizer and marked "Free" in the space for price. Nevertheless, the bill charged us for the Leatherizer.

5/8" - 1"

Please remove the $3.19 charge for the Leatherizer from our bill. The total bill was for $107.53, and with the $3.19 deducted, I assume the correct amount for the bill should be $104.34. I have enclosed a check for $104.34.

Please confirm that the charge has been removed and that our account for this order is now paid in full.

Sincerely ○ *No punctuation in open punctuation*

3-4 spaces

William T. Mozing
William T. Mozing

2-4 Spaces

Encl.: Check for $104.34

Line up signature block with date

FIGURE A.6

SECOND PAGE OF A 2-PAGE LETTER, BLOCK FORMAT (MIXED PUNCTUATION)

Plain paper for 2nd page

3–6 spaces

Stephanie Voght   **2**   August 10, 1988

Center

3 spaces

campus life, including football and basketball games, fraternities and sororities, clubs and organizations, and opportunities for volunteer work. The tape stresses the diversity of the student body and the very different lifestyles that are available at State.

Triple-space before each new heading

Scheduling the Videotape   *Bold or underline*

To schedule your free showing, just fill out the enclosed card with your first, second, and third choices for dates, and return it in the stamped, self-addressed envelope. Dates are reserved in the order that requests arrive. Send in your request early to increase the chances of getting the date you want.

Same margins as page 1

"Life at State College" will be on its way to give your high school students a preview of the college experience.

Sincerely,   *Comma in mixed punctuation*

3–4 spaces

Michael L. Mahler
Director of Admissions

2–4 spaces

Encl.: Reservation Form

cc: R. J. Holland, School Superintendent
     Jose Lavilla, President, PTA Association

aren't using letterhead. If your letter is very short, you may want to use bigger side and top margins so that the letter is centered on the page.

To eliminate typing the reader's name and address on an envelope, some organizations use envelopes with cut-outs or windows so that the **inside address** (the reader's name and address) on the letter shows through and can be used for delivery. If your organization does this, adjust your margins, if necessary, so that the whole inside address is visible.

When a letter runs two or more pages, use letterhead only for page 1. For the remaining pages, use plain paper that matches the letterhead in weight, texture, and color.

Figures A.6–A.8 show how to set up the second page of a two-page letter.

Many letters are accompanied by other documents. Whatever these documents may be—a multipage report or a two-line note—they are called **enclosures,** since they are enclosed in the envelope. The writer should refer to the enclosures in the body of the letter: "As you can see from my résumé, ..."

FIGURE A.7

SECOND PAGE OF A 2-PAGE LETTER, MODIFIED BLOCK FORMAT (MIXED PUNCTUATION)

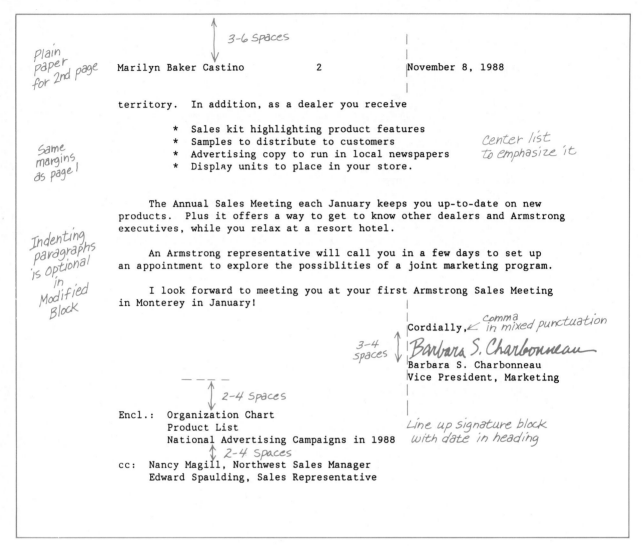

The enclosure line reminds the person who seals the letter to include the enclosures.

Sometimes you write to one person but send copies of your letter to other people. If you want the reader to know that other people are getting copies, list their names on the last page. The abbreviation *cc* originally meant *carbon copy* but now means *computer copy*. Other acceptable abbreviations include *pc* for *photocopy* or simply *c* for *copy*. You can also send copies to other people without telling the reader. Such copies are called **blind copies.** Blind copies are not mentioned on the original; they are listed on the copy saved for the file with the abbreviation *bc* preceding the names of people getting these copies.

You do not need to indicate that you have shown a letter to your superior or that you are saving a copy of the letter for your own files. These are standard practices.

FIGURE A.8
SECOND PAGE OF A 2-PAGE LETTER, AMS SIMPLIFIED FORMAT

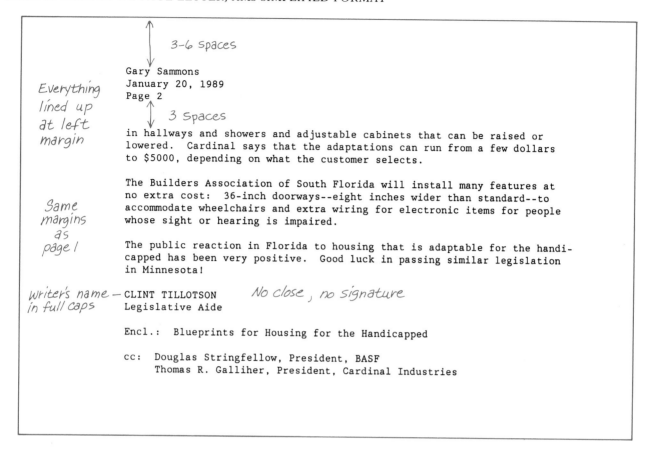

ALTERNATE FORMAT FOR LETTERS THAT ARE NOT INDIVIDUALLY TYPED

Merge functions in word-processing programs allow you to put in a reader's name and address even in a form letter. *If you use a specific name in the salutation, also use the reader's name and address in the inside address.*

If you cannot afford to type each reader's name and address individually on the page, you have two options. The first option is to omit the inside address and use a generic salutation: "Dear Voter." Figure A.9 illustrates this option. The second option is to omit the salutation and use the space where it and the inside address normally go for a benefit or attention-getter. Figure A.10 illustrates this option.

TYPING ENVELOPES

Business envelopes need to put the reader's name and address in the area that is picked up by the Post Office's Optical Character Readers (OCRs). Use side margins of at least 1″. Your bottom margin must be at least $^5/_8$″ but no bigger than $2^1/_4$″.

IPC
INDIANOLA **C** PRESBYTERIAN CHURCH

1970 WALDECK AVENUE, COLUMBUS, OHIO 43201-1593
TELEPHONE (614) 294-3796

Cable Address: *ECCLESIA*, Columbus, Ohio

July 9, 1986

Use singular, not plural,
since each person reads the letter
individually

Dear Indianola Member:

What Adult Education classes would you like to attend at Indianola this year?

Many ideas have been suggested, both by a special brainstorming committee of Indianola members and by the Adult Education Committee. Now, we'd like to develop classes on the topics that most people want to attend.

On the enclosed survey, please indicate **whether you yourself would come** to a class on each topic. We'll use answers to plan classes for the whole year, so mark as many as you'd like to come to. (Answer only for yourself, not for what might be a good class for other Indianolans. Every church member is getting this questionnaire.)

Bold for emphasis

We need your response by **Sunday, July 27.** Please bring your survey to church (give it to a Committee member or leave it in the church office) or mail it to

          Ms. Kitty O. Locker   *Address centered for*
          3749 Dort Place   *emphasis, visual variety*
          Columbus, OH 43227.

Since some people are out of town during the summer, your response is particularly important to us so we can plan classes for September.

Please take a few minutes soon--today, if you can--to circle the topics that interest you. Your prompt response will help us develop Adult Education programs to better meet the needs and interests of the congregation. Thanks!

Sincerely,

Kitty O. Locker

Kitty O. Locker
Adult Education Committee

                                              Signature block
                                              lined up with date,
Adult Education Committee: Gail Amnatvong, Chair   *printing on letterhead*
                           Agnes Kinschner
                           Kitty Locker
                           Victor Makari
                           Lance Shreffler

COMPUTER
SUPPORT
CORPORATION

2215 Midway Road
Carrollton, Texas 75006
(214) 661-8960
Telex: 284831 CSCTX UR
Fax: (214) 661-1096

"Johnson Box" used for emphasis, visual variety

```
* * * * * * * * * * *
* Five FREE Libraries *
*  Worth Up to $615!  *
* * * * * * * * * * *
```

Date omitted so letter can be sent out unchanged.

Johnson Box visually substitutes for date

Attention-Getter visually substitutes for inside address, salutation

No Other Business
Graphics Software Can
Match the Versatility &
Flexibility of Diagraph!

Let us prove to you that Diagraph is a breakthrough in business graphics software.

Use Diagraph to turn your ideas, concepts, plans, and data into organization charts, signs, flow charts, diagrams, forms, and maps. Diagraph comes with a money-back guarantee. Use it for 30 days and we're certain that you will have discovered so many uses for Diagraph that you won't want to part with it.

And now you have two choices: Diagraph/500 for only $99 or Diagraph/2000 for $395.

Diagraph/500 files are fully compatible with Diagraph/2000 so you can upgrade to Diagraph/2000 at any time. What's more, the cost of Diagraph/500 is credited towards your purchase of Diagraph/2000.

See the enclosed data sheet for additional information or call us today to see how the power of Diagraph can enhance everything you write!

Sincerely,

4 spaces

Gail McCannon

Gail McCannon
Director, Customer Services

Signature block lined up with Johnson Box

Initials of writer

GM:ec *← Initials of typist*

Encl.

P.S. As an added incentive, if you purchase Diagraph/2000 before November 30, 1987, you can select five Diagraph libraries, worth up to $615, **absolutely free.** Call for more details.

Reader benefit saved for a P.S. People's eyes drop to P.S., which they read before returning to rest of letter

↑ 6-12 spaces

plain paper

Lined up

Everything lined up at left

Double Space

October 7, 1987

To: Annette T. Califero

From: Kyle B. Abrams *KBA* Writer's initials, added in ink

Subject: A Low-Cost Way to Reduce Energy Use   Capitalize first letter of each major word in subject line

2 spaces   3 spaces

No heading for paragraph 1

As you requested, I've investigated low-cost ways to reduce our energy costs. Reducing the building temperature on weekends is a change that we could make immediately, that would cost nothing, and that would cut our energy use by about 6%.

Triple-space before each new heading

The Energy Savings from a Lower Weekend Temperature ← Underline or Bold

Single space paragraphs, double space between paragraphs

Lowering the temperature from 68° to 60° from 8 p.m. Friday evening to 4 a.m. Monday morning could cut our total consumption by 6%. It is not feasible to lower the temperature on weeknights because a great many staff members work late; the cleaning crew also is on duty from 6 p.m. to midnight. Turning the temperature down for only four hours would not result in a significant heat saving.

Turning the heat back up at 4 a.m. will allow the building temperature to be back to 68° by 9 a.m. Our furnace already has computerized controls which can be set to automatically lower and raise the temperature.

How a Lower Temperature Would Affect Employees   Capitalize first letter of each major word of heading

Do not indent paragraphs

A survey of employees shows that only 7 people use the building every weekend or almost every weekend. Eighteen percent of our staff have worked at least one weekend day in the last two months; 52% say they "occasionally" come in on weekends.

People who come in for an hour or less on weekends could cope with the lower temperature just by wearing warm clothes. However, most people would find 60° degrees too cool for extended work. Employees who work regularly on weekends might want to install space heaters.

Action Needed to Implement the Change

Would you also like me to check into the cost of buying a dozen portable space heaters? Providing them would allow us to choose units that our wiring can handle and would be a nice gesture towards employees who give up their weekends to work. I could have a report to you in two weeks.

We can begin saving energy immediately. Just authorize the lower temperature, and I'll see that the controls are reset for this weekend.

Memos are initialed by To/From/Subject block

Headings are optional in memos

FIGURE A.12
MEMO ON MEMO LETTERHEAD

Kimball, Walls, and Morgenstern
———— Interoffice Memorandum ————

Double-space

Date: March 15, 1988

To: Annette T. Califero

From: Kyle B. Abrams *KBA* *Writer's initials added in ink*

Subject: The Effectiveness of Reducing Building Temperatures on Weekends *Capitalize first letter of each major word*

2 Spaces

3 Spaces

Margin lined up with items in To/From/Subject to save typing time

Reducing the building temperature to 60° on weekends has cut energy use by 4% compared to last year's use from December to February and has saved our firm $22,000.

This savings is particularly remarkable when you consider that this winter has been colder than last year's, so that more heat would be needed to maintain the same temperature.

Fewer people have worked weekends during the past three months than during the preceding three months, but snow and bad driving conditions may have had more to do with keeping people home than the fear of being cold. Five of the 12 space heaters we bought have been checked out on an average weekend. On one weekend, all 12 were in use and some people shared their offices so that everyone could be in a room with a space heater.

Fully 92% of our employees support the lower temperature. I recommend that we continue turning down the heat on weekends through the remainder of the heating season and that we resume the practice when the heat is turned on next fall.

Headings are optional in memos

Most businesses use envelopes that already have the return address printed in the upper left-hand corner. When you don't have printed envelopes, type your name (optional), your street address, and your city, state, and zip code in the upper left-hand corner. Since the OCR doesn't need this information to route your letter, exact margins don't matter. Use whatever is convenient and looks good to you.

FORMAT FOR MEMOS

Memos omit both the salutation and the close entirely. Memos never use indented paragraphs. Subject lines are required; headings are optional. Each

plain paper for second page

↕ *3-6 spaces*

Dorothy N. Blasingham   2   February 18, 1988

↕ *3 spaces*   *center*

before the summer vacation season begins.

Triple-space before each new heading

Orientation for New Hires *Bold or underline*

Same margins as page 1

With a total of 16 full-time and 34 part-time people being hired either for summer or permanent work, we'll need at least two and perhaps three orientation sessions. We'd like to hold these the first, second, and third weeks in June. By May 1, we should know how many people will be in each training session.

Would you be free to conduct training sessions on how to use our computers on June 8, June 15, and June 22? If we need only two dates, we'll use June 8 and June 15, but please block off the 22nd too in case we need a third session.

Memos are initialed by To/From/Subject block

plain paper for second page

↕ *3-6 spaces*

Jonathan Yates
May 12, 1988
Page 2

↕ *3 spaces*

than last year.

Single-space paragraphs, double-space between paragraphs

Same margins as page 1

Students who accepted out-of-state jobs did even better. The median salary offered for out-of-state jobs was $28,300. Regional medians ranged from $23,100 in the Southeast to $31,600 in the Southwest:

Region	Median Salary
Northeast	$29,700
Southeast	$23,100
Midwest	$25,800
Northwest	$24,200
Southwest	$31,600

However, many students prefer to accept jobs in-state, even if the starting salary is not quite as high. Almost half of the students who received out-of-state offers declined them.

We have not yet heard from 15% of the students who registered with us. I'll send postcards to the nonrespondents urging them to fill out the questionnaire before they leave for the summer. I'll use all of the surveys that are in by June 15 to compile the evaluation report on the Placement Center which is due August 1.

heading must cover all the information until the next heading. Never use a separate heading for the first paragraph.

Figure A.11 illustrates the standard memo format typed on a plain sheet of paper. Note that the first letters of the reader's name, the writer's name, and the subject phrase are lined up vertically. Note also that memos are usually initialed by the *To/From* block. Initialing tells the reader that you have proofread the memo and prevents someone's sending out your name on a memo you did not in fact write.

Some organizations have a special letterhead for memos. When *Date/To/From/Subject* are already printed on the form, the date, writer's and reader's names, and subject are set at the main margin to save typing time. (See Figure A.12).

Some organizations alter the order of items in the *Date/To/From/Subject* block. Some organizations ask employees to sign memos rather than simply initialing them. The signature goes below the last line of the memo, starting half way over on the page, and prevents anyone's adding unauthorized information.

If the memo runs two pages or more, set up the second and subsequent pages in either of the ways shown in Figures A.13 or A.14.

STATE AND PROVINCE ABBREVIATIONS

States with names of more than five letters are frequently abbreviated in letters and memos. The Post Office abbreviations, listed in Figure A.15, use two capital letters with no punctuation.

Using Computers to Personalize Letters

Computers allow you to merge a form letter with a data base containing names and addresses to create individually typed personalized letters.

When you use a computer to create letters, be sure to proofread the parts that are personalized. If a field is typed incorrectly in the data base, the merged letter will have errors.

A prestigious California university sent a graduate school acceptance to "Dear Champaign, IL 61820."

A job applicant mailed a letter to "Dear Victorian Literature" applying for a position teaching "Arnold Shapiro."

The student's admittance was still good. The job applicant was cut.

FIGURE A.15
POST OFFICE ABBREVIATIONS FOR STATES, TERRITORIES, AND PROVINCES

State Name	Post Office Abbreviation	State Name	Post Office Abbreviation	Territory	Post Office Abbreviation
Alabama	AL	Missouri	MO	Guam	GU
Alaska	AK	Montana	MT	Puerto Rico	PR
Arizona	AZ	Nebraska	NE	Virgin Islands	VI
Arkansas	AR	Nevada	NV		
California	CA	New Hampshire	NH	**Province Name**	**Post Office Abbreviation**
Colorado	CO	New Jersey	NJ	Alberta	AB
Connecticut	CT	New Mexico	NM	British Columbia	BC
Delaware	DE	New York	NY	Labrador	LB
District of	DC	North Carolina	NC	Manitoba	MB
Columbia		North Dakota	ND	New Brunswick	NB
Florida	FL			Newfoundland	NF
		Ohio	OH	Northwest	NT
Georgia	GA	Oklahoma	OK	Territories	
Hawaii	HI	Oregon	OR	Nova Scotia	NS
Idaho	ID	Pennsylvania	PA	Ontario	ON
Illinois	IL	Rhode Island	RI	Prince Edward	PE
Indiana	IN			Island	
		South Carolina	SC	Quebec	PQ
Iowa	IA	South Dakota	SD	Saskatchewan	SK
Kansas	KS	Tennessee	TN	Yukon Territory	YT
Kentucky	KY	Texas	TX		
Louisiana	LA	Utah	UT		
Maine	ME				
		Vermont	VT		
Maryland	MD	Virginia	VA		
Massachusetts	MA	Washington	WA		
Michigan	MI	West Virginia	WV		
Minnesota	MN	Wisconsin	WI		
Mississippi	MS	Wyoming	WY		

Writing Correctly

QUESTIONS

- Can you rely on a computer grammar checker to catch any mistakes you make?
- How can you fix common grammatical errors in a draft?
- How do you punctuate sentences to avoid comma splices, run-on sentences, and sentence fragments?
- How do you use punctuation within sentences?
- How and when do you use special punctuation marks?
- How should numbers and dates be written?
- How can you tell apart words that are often confused?
- What do you do if you find an error while you're proofreading a typed paper?

Grammar is an obscure, esoteric body of ridiculous rules carefully formulated to torture students and cause neurotic insecurity among adults.

Robert L. Webb
Grammar for People Who Wouldn't Have to Worry About It If They Didn't Have Children, 1964

T oo much concern for correctness at the wrong stage of the writing process can backfire: writers who worry about grammar and punctuation when they're writing a first or second draft are more likely to get writer's block. Wait till you have your ideas on paper to check your draft for correct grammar, punctuation, typing of numbers and dates, and word use. Use the proofreading symbols at the end of the chapter to indicate changes needed in a typed copy.

Most writers make a small number of grammatical errors repeatedly. Most readers care deeply about only a few grammatical points. Keep track of the feedback you get (from your instructors now, from your supervisor later) and put your energy into correcting the errors you make that bother the people who read what you write. A command of standard grammar will help you build the credible, professional image you want to create with everything you write.

This chapter begins with a discussion of four grammatical issues: agreement, case, and dangling and misplaced modifiers. The section on punctuating sentences shows you how to use periods, semicolons, and commas to avoid comma splices, run-on sentences, and sentence fragments. The section on punctuation within sentences covers apostrophes, colons, commas, dashes, hyphens, parentheses, and periods. The section on special punctuation covers marks used to quote material or for emphasis: quotation marks, square brackets, ellipses, and underlining. Next, the chapter defines 40 pairs of words that are often confused and shows how to use them correctly. The last section shows you how to make changes in a typed draft when you proofread.

USING GRAMMAR

With the possible exception of spelling, grammar is the aspect of writing that writers seem to find most troublesome. Faulty grammar is often what executives are objecting to when they complain that college graduates or MBAs "can't write."

Computerized **grammar checkers** are software programs which flag errors and doubtful usage in a passage so that you can correct them. Some of the best known are *Grammatik, Punctuation and Style, RightWriter,* and *Electric Webster.* As these programs are updated, they are likely to get better. In 1988, they're no substitute for human editing. Reviewing these and other programs in 1986 for *PC Magazine,* Robin Raskin reported,

> The style analyzer programs missed more [errors] than they found. . . . They flagged only the more obvious mistakes. They paid no attention whatever to context and left the bulk of error-flagging to human editors.[1]

Donald H. Cunningham's 1988 review of *RightWriter* was more positive, but he admitted, "Running RightWriter does not substitute for eagle-eyed editing."[2]

Agreement

Subjects and verbs agree when they are both singular or both plural.

Incorrect: The accountant s who conducted the audit was recommended highly.

Correct: The accountants who conducted the audit were recommended highly.

Subject-verb agreement errors often occur when other words come between the subject and the verb. Edit your drafts by finding the subject and the verb of each sentence.

American usage treats company names and the words *company* and *government* as singular nouns. British usage treats them as plural:

Correct (United States): State Farm Insurance trains its agents well.

Correct (Great Britain): Lloyds of London train their agents well.

Use a plural verb when two or more singular subjects are joined by *and*.

Correct: Larry McGreevy and I are planning to visit the client.

Use a singular verb when two or more singular subjects are joined by *or, nor,* or *but.*

Correct: Either the shipping clerk or the superintendent has to sign the order.

When the sentence begins with *Here* or *There,* make the verb agree with the subject which follows the verb.

Correct: Here is the booklet you asked for.
Correct: There are the blueprints I wanted.

Note that some words which end in "s" are considered to be singular and require singular verbs.

Correct: A series of meetings is planned.

When a situation doesn't seem to fit the rules, or when following a rule produces an awkward sentence, revise the sentence to avoid the problem entirely.

Problematic: The plant manager in addition to the sales represenative (was, were?) pleased with the new system.

Better: The plant manager and the sales representative were pleased with the new system.

Problematic: None of us (is, are?) perfect.
Better: All of us have faults.

Errors in **noun-pronoun agreement** occur if a pronoun is of a different number or person than the word it refers to.

Incorrect: All ☐drivers☐ of leased automobiles are billed $100 if damages to ☐his☐ automob☐ile☐ are caused by a collisi☐on.☐

Correct: All <u>drivers</u> of leased automobiles are billed $100 if damages to <u>their</u> automob<u>iles</u> are caused by colli<u>sions</u>.

Incorrect: A ☐manager☐ has only ☐yourself☐ to blame if things go wrong.

Correct: As a manager, <u>you</u> have only <u>yourself</u> to blame if things go wrong.

The following words require a singular pronoun:

everybody	neither
each	nobody
either	a person
everyone	

Correct: <u>Everyone</u> should bring <u>his or her</u> copy of the manual to the next session on changes in the law.

If the pronoun pairs necessary to avoid sexism seem cumbersome, avoid the terms in this list. Instead, use words which take plural pronouns or use second-person *you*.

Use *who* and *whom* to refer to people and *which* to refer to objects. *That* can refer to anything: people, animals, organizations, and objects.

Correct: The new <u>Executive Director</u>, <u>who</u> moved here from Boston, is already making friends.

Correct: The <u>information which</u> she wants will be available tomorrow.

Correct: This confirms the <u>price that</u> I quoted you this morning.

Case

Case refers to the grammatical role a noun or pronoun plays in a sentence. Figure B.1 identifies the case of each personal pronoun.

Use **nominative** pronouns for the **subject** of a clause.

Correct: Shannon Weaver and <u>I</u> talked to the customer, <u>who</u> was interested in learning more about integrated software.

Use **possessive** pronouns to show who or what something belongs to.

Correct: Enable, <u>whose</u> cost is reasonable, will exactly meet <u>her</u> needs.

Use **objective** pronouns as **objects** of verbs or prepositions.

Correct: When you send in the quote, thank <u>her</u> for the courtesy she showed Shannon and <u>me</u>.

Use **reflexive** and **intensive** pronouns to refer to or emphasize a noun or pronoun that has already appeared in the sentence.

Correct: I <u>myself</u> think the call was a very productive one.

Do not use reflexive pronouns as subjects of clauses or as objects of verbs or prepositions.

Incorrect: Elaine and ☐myself☐ will follow up on this order.

Incorrect: He gave the order to Dan and ☐myself☐.

	Nominative (Subject of Clause)	Possessive	Objective	Reflexive/ Intensive
Singular				
1st person	I	my, mine	me	myself
2nd person	you	your, yours	you	yourself
3rd person	he/she/it	his/hers/its	him/her/it	himself/herself/itself
	one/who	one's/whose	one/whom	oneself/(no form)
Plural				
1st person	we	our, ours	us	ourselves
2nd person	you	your, yours	you	yourselves
3rd person	they	their, theirs	them	themselves

FIGURE B.1
THE CASE OF THE PERSONAL PRONOUN

Incorrect: Thank you for the courtesies you showed Clint and myself.

Correct: Elaine and I will follow up on this order.

Correct: He gave the order to Dan and me.

Correct: Thank you for the courtesies you showed Clint and me.

Note that the first-person pronoun comes after names or pronouns that refer to other people.

Dangling Modifier (DM)

Modifiers are words or phrases which give more information about the subject, verb, or object in a clause. A modifier **dangles** when the word it modifies is not actually in the sentence.

Incorrect: Confirming our conversation, the truck will leave Monday.
[The speaker is doing the confirming. But this sentence says that the truck confirmed the conversation.]

Incorrect: At the age of eight, I began teaching my children about American business.
[This sentence says that the author was eight when he or she had children who could understand business.]

Correct a dangling modifier in one of these ways:

- Recast the modifier as a subordinate clause.

   Correct: As I told you, the truck will leave Monday.

   Correct: When they were eight, I began teaching my children about American business.

- Revise the main clause so its subject can be modified by the now-dangling phrase.

   Correct: Confirming our conversation, I have scheduled the truck to leave Monday.

   Correct: At the age of eight, my children began learning about American business.

Whenever you use a verb or adjective that ends in *ing,* check to see which word in the main clause it modifies. Modifiers used as introductory phrases **must** modify the grammatical subject of your sentence.

Misplaced Modifier (MM)

A **misplaced modifier** appears to modify another element of the sentence than the writer intended.

Incorrect: May I please have your reply to this recommendation with the action you plan to take or reasons for not adopting this recommendation by February 26.

Correct a misplaced modifier by moving it closer to the word it modifies or by adding punctuation to clarify your meaning.

Correct: By February 26, may I please have your reply to this recommendation with the action you plan to take or your reasons for not adopting the recommendation?

Correct: May I please have your reply to this recommendation, with the action you plan to take—or your reasons for not adopting this recommendation—by February 26?

If a modifier modifies the whole sentence, use it as an introductory phrase or clause; follow it with a comma.

PUNCTUATING SENTENCES

A **sentence** is a statement together with words added to the statement. A **main clause** is a complete statement. A **subordinate** or **dependent clause** is not a complete statement and cannot stand by itself.

Main Clauses:
   Your order will arrive Thursday.
   He dreaded talking to his supplier.
   I plan to enroll for summer school classes.
Subordinate Clauses:
   if you place your order by Monday
   because he was afraid the product would be out of stock
   so that I can graduate next spring

Using the correct punctuation will enable you to avoid three major sentence errors: comma splices, run-on sentences, and sentence fragments.

Comma Splice (CS)

A **comma splice** or **comma fault** occurs when two main clauses are joined only by a comma (instead of by a comma and a coordinating conjunction).

Incorrect: The contest will start in June, the date has not been set.

Correct a comma splice in one of the following ways:

- If the ideas are closely related, use a semicolon rather than a comma. If they aren't closely related, start a new sentence.

  Correct: The contest will start in June; the exact date has not been set.

- Add a coordinating conjunction.

  Correct: The contest will start in June, but the exact date has not been set.

- Subordinate one of the clauses.

Correct: Although the contest will start in June, the date has
          not been set.

Remember that **the following conjunctions do not make clauses dependent or subordinate.** When you use them, you do not have a complex sentence and cannot join the clauses with a comma.

however
therefore
nevertheless
moreover

Run-on Sentence (RO)

A **run-on sentence** strings together several main clauses using *and, but, or, so,* and *for.* Run-on sentences and comma splices are *mirror faults.* A comma splice uses *only* the comma and omits the coordinating conjunction, while a run-on sentence uses *only* the coordinating conjunction and omits the comma.

Correct a short run-on sentence by adding a comma.

Incorrect: The deadline for filing income tax returns is April 15 but
            anyone can get a four-month extension by filing Form
            4868.

Correct: The deadline for filing income tax returns is April 15, but
          anyone can get a four-month extension by filing Form
          4868.

To fix a long run-on sentence, separate it into two or more sentences. Consider subordinating one or more of the clauses.

Incorrect: We will end up with a much smaller markup but they use
            a lot of this material so the volume would be high so try
            to sell them on fast delivery and tell them our quality is
            very high.

Correct: Although we will end up with a much smaller markup,
          volume would be high since they use a lot of this material.
          Try to sell them on fast delivery and high quality.

Sentence Fragment (Frag)

In a **sentence fragment,** a group of words that is not a complete sentence is punctuated as if it were a complete sentence. Sentence fragments can be used to save space in résumés and to give ads and direct mail the effect of spontaneous speech, but they are not acceptable in other kinds of business and administrative writing.

Incorrect: Observing these people, I have learned two things about
            the program. The time it takes . The rewards it brings .

To fix a sentence fragment, either add whatever parts of the sentence are missing or incorporate the fragment into the sentence before it or after it.

Correct: Observing these people, I have learned that the program is
          time-consuming but rewarding.

Remember that **the following conjunctions make clauses dependent and subordinate.** When you use them, you **do** have a complex sentence; the clause of which they are a part cannot stand alone as a complete sentence.

after	if
although, though	when, whenever
because, since	while, as
before, until	

Incorrect: We need to buy a new computer system. Because our current system is obsolete .

Correct: We need to buy a new computer system because our current system is obsolete.

PUNCTUATION WITHIN SENTENCES

The good business and administrative writer knows how to use the following punctuation marks: apostrophes, colons, commas, dashes, hyphens, parentheses, periods, and semicolons.

Apostrophe

1. Use an apostrophe in a contraction to indicate that a letter has been omitted.

   We're trying to renegotiate the contract.
   The '80s were years of consolidation for our company.

2. Use an apostrophe with a noun to indicate possession.

   The corporation's home office is in Houston, Texas.

   Apostrophes to indicate possession are especially essential when part of the sentence is "understood."

   This year's sales will be higher than last year's.

   When a word already ends in an *s*, add only an apostrophe to make it possessive.

   The meeting will be held at New Orleans' convention center.

   With many terms, the placement of the apostrophe indicates whether the noun is singular or plural.

   Incorrect: The program should increase the participant's knowledge. [Implies that only one participant is in the program.]

   Correct: The program should increase the participants' knowledge. [Many participants are in the program.]

   Note that possessive pronouns (e.g., *his, ours*) usually do not have apostrophes. The only exception is *one's*.

   The company needs the goodwill of its stockholders.
   His promotion was announced yesterday.
   One's greatest asset is the willingness to work hard.

3. Use an apostrophe to make plurals that could be confused for other words.

   I earned A's in all my business courses.

However, other plurals do not need apostrophes.

Computer prices are expected to continue to fall in the 1990s.

Enclosed is a list of the jobs accepted by this year's class of M.B.A.s.

Colon

1. Use a colon to separate a main clause and a list which explains the last element in the clause. The items in the list are specific examples of the word that appears immediately before the colon.

Please order the following supplies:
   Printer ribbons
   Computer paper (20-lb. white bond)
   Bond paper (25-lb., white, 25% cotton)
   Company letterhead
   Company envelopes.

When the list is presented vertically, capitalize the first letter of each item in the list. When the list is run in with the sentence, you don't need to capitalize the first letter after the colon.

Please order the following supplies: printer ribbons, computer paper (20-lb. white bond), bond paper (25-lb., white, 25% cotton), company letterhead, and company envelopes.

Do not use a colon when the list is grammatically part of the main clause.

Incorrect: The rooms will have coordinated decors in earthtones such as: rust, sand, putty, etc.

Correct: The rooms will have coordinated decors in earthtones such as rust, sand, putty, etc.
   or
Correct: The rooms will have coordinated decors in a variety of earthtones: rust, sand, putty, etc.

If the list is presented vertically, some authorities suggest introducing the list with a colon even though the words preceding the colon are not a complete sentence.

2. Use a colon to join two independent clauses when the second clause explains or restates the first clause.

Selling is simple: give people the service they need, and they'll come back with more orders.

Comma

1. Use commas to separate the main clause from an introductory clause, the reader's name, or words which interrupt the main clause. Note that commas both precede and follow the interrupting information.

R. J. Garcia, the new Sales Manager, comes to us from the Des Moines office.

Use commas if the phrase is extra information which is not needed to identify the noun it modifies. You'll use extra commas when you use proper names since they identify specific people, companies, and things.

Sue Decker, who wants to advance in the organization, has signed up for the company training program in sales techniques.

Do not use commas to set off information which is crucial to the meaning of the sentence.

Anyone <u>who wants to advance in the organization</u> should take advantage of on-the-job training.

Do not use commas to separate the subject from the verb, even if you would take a breath after a long subject.

Incorrect: Laws requiring anyone collecting $5000 or more on behalf of another person to register with the state, apply to schools and private individuals as well as to charitable groups and professional fund-raisers.

Correct: Laws requiring anyone collecting $5000 or more on behalf of another person to register with the state apply to schools and private individuals as well as to charitable groups and professional fund-raisers.

2. Use a comma after the first clause in a compound sentence if the clauses are long or if they have different subjects.

This policy eliminates all sick leave credit of the employee at the time of retirement, and payment will be made only once to any individual.

Do not use commas to join independent clauses without a conjunction. Doing so produces comma splices.

3. Use commas to separate items in a series. Using a comma before the *and* or *or* is not required by some authorities, but using a comma always adds clarity. The comma is essential if any of the items in the series themselves contain the word *and.*

The company pays the full cost of hospitalization insurance for eligible employees, spouses, and unmarried dependent children under age 23.

Dash

Use dashes to emphasize a break in thought.

Ryertex comes in 30 grades—each with a special use.

To type a dash, use two hyphens with no space before or after.

Hyphen

1. Use a hyphen to indicate that a word has been divided between two lines.

Attach the original receipts for lodging, transportation, and registration fee.

Divide words only at syllable breaks. If you aren't sure where the syllables divide, look up the word in a dictionary. When a word has several syllables, divide it after a vowel or between two consonants.

Correct: sepa-rate
government

Don't divide words of one syllable (e.g., *used*); don't divide a two-syllable word if one of the syllables is only one letter long (e.g., *acre*).

2. Use hyphens to join two or more words used as a single adjective.

Order 5 ten- or twelve-foot lengths.

> The computer-prepared income and expense statements will be ready
>   next Friday.

The hyphen prevents misreading. In the first example, five lengths are needed,
not lengths of five, ten, or twelve feet. In the second example, without the
hyphen, the reader might think that *computer* was the subject and *prepared*
was the verb.

Parentheses

1. Use parentheses to set off words, phrases, or sentences used to explain or
comment on the main idea.

> For the thinnest Ryertex (.015″) only a single layer of the base mate-
>   rial may be used, while the thickest (10″) may contain over 600
>   greatly compressed layers of fabric or paper. By varying the fabric
>   used (cotton, asbestos, glass, or nylon) or the type of paper, and by
>   changing the kind of resin (phenolic, melamine, silicone, or epoxy),
>   we can produce 30 different grades.

Punctuation goes outside the second parenthesis when the punctuation applies to the whole sentence. It goes inside when it applies only to the words
in the parentheses.

> Please check the invoice (a copy is attached) to see if credit should be
>   issued.
> Please check the invoice to see if credit should be issued. (A copy of
>   the invoice is attached.)

2. Use parentheses for the second of two numbers presented both in words
and in figures.

> Construction must be completed within two (2) years of the date of
>   the contract.

Period

1. Use a period at the end of a sentence. Leave two spaces before the next
sentence.

2. Use a period after some abbreviations. When a period replaces a person's
name, leave one space after the period before the next word. In other
abbreviations, no space is necessary.

> R. J. Tebeaux has been named vice president for marketing.
> The U.S. division plans to hire 300 new M.B.A.s in the next year.

Semicolon

1. Use semicolons to join two independent clauses when they are closely related.

> We'll do our best to fill your order promptly; however, we cannot
>   guarantee a delivery date.

It would be equally correct to use a period instead of a semicolon and begin
the next clause with a capital letter. Using a semicolon suggests that the two
ideas are very closely connected. Using a period and a new sentence implies
nothing about how closely related the two sentences are.

2. Use semicolons to separate items in a series when the items themselves contain commas.

> The final choices for the new plant are El Paso, Texas; Albuquerque, New Mexico; Salt Lake City, Utah; Eureka, California; and Eugene, Oregon.

> Hospital benefits are also provided for certain specialized care services such as diagnostic admissions directed toward a definite disease or injury; normal maternity delivery, Caesarean section delivery, or complications of pregnancy; and in-patient admissions for dental procedures necessary to safeguard the patient's life or health.

SPECIAL PUNCTUATION MARKS

Quotation marks, square brackets, ellipses, and underlining are necessary when you use quoted material.

Quotation Marks

1. Use quotation marks around the names of brochures, pamphlets, and magazine articles.

> Enclosed are thirty copies of our pamphlet "Saving Energy."
> You'll find articles like "How to Improve Your Golf Game" and "Can You Keep Your Eye on the Ball?" in every issue.

In American punctuation, periods and commas go inside quotation marks. Colons and semicolons go outside. Question marks go inside if they are part of the material being quoted.

2. Use quotation marks around words to indicate that the term is not necessarily one you agree with.

> These "pro-business" policies actually increase corporate taxes.

3. Use quotation marks around words that you are discussing as words.

> Forty percent of the respondents answered "yes" to the first question.
> Use "Ms." as a courtesy title for a woman unless you know she prefers another title.

It is also acceptable to underline such words instead of using quotation marks.

4. Use quotation marks around words or sentences that you quote from someone else.

> "The Fog Index," says its inventor, Robert Gunning, is "an effective warning system against drifting into needless complexity."

Extended quotes, or numbers of short quotes, such as a list of comments on a questionnaire, are normally indented on both the left and the right. Indenting sets them off from the rest of the text, so quotation marks are not needed.

Square Brackets

Use square brackets to add your own additions to or changes in quoted material.

> According to Senator Smith, "These measures [in the new tax bill] will increase the deficit."

If your typewriter or printer does not have square brackets, put them in by hand. Parentheses are not an acceptable substitute.

Ellipses

Ellipses are spaced dots. In typing, use three spaced periods for an ellipsis. When an ellipsis comes at the end of a sentence, us a dot immediately after the last letter of the sentence for a period. Then add three spaced dots. Two spaces follow the last of the four dots.

1. Use ellipses to indicate that one or more words have been omitted in quoted material.

> *The Wall Street Journal* notes that Japanese magazines and newspapers include advertisements for a "$2.1 million home in New York's posh Riverdale section . . . 185 acres of farmland [and] . . . luxury condos on Manhattan's Upper East Side."

2. In advertising and direct mail, use ellipses to imply the pace of spoken comments.

> If you've ever wanted to live on a tropical island . . . cruise to the Bahamas . . . or live in a castle in Spain . . .
> . . . you can make your dreams come true with Vacations Extraordinaire.

Underlining

1. Underline the names of newspapers, magazines, and books.

> The Wall Street Journal
>
> Fortune
>
> The Wealth of Nations

Titles of brochures and pamphlets are put in quotation marks.
If you have a printer which does italic typeface, you may use italics instead of underlining for titles.

2. Underline words to emphasize them.

> Here's a bulletin that gives you, in handy chart form, workable data on over 50 different types of tubing and pipe.

If you have a printer which has a bold typeface, you may use bold to emphasize words.

WRITING NUMBERS AND DATES

Spell out **numbers** from one to nine. Use figures for numbers 10 and over in most cases. Always use figures for amounts of money.
    Spell out any number that appears at the beginning of a sentence.

Fifty students filled out the survey.
We polled 50 students about their shopping preferences.

When two numbers follow each other, use words for the smaller number, figures for the larger number.
    In **dates,** use figures for the day and year. The month is normally spelled out. Modern punctuation uses a comma before the year only when you give both the month and the date:

May 1, 1968
  but
Summers 1987–89
October 1986
Fall 1990

No punctuation is needed in military or European usage, which puts the date before the month: 16 March 1989.

Use a hyphen to join inclusive dates:

August–March, 1989 or write out August to March, 1989
1986–90
'87–'89

If you use numbers for dates, do not space before or after the slash:

10/88–5/89.

WORDS THAT ARE OFTEN CONFUSED

Pity the poor investor who wrote asking his broker to buy *bouillon* rather than *bullion*. He wanted gold, and he got chicken broth. Here's a list of words that are frequently confused. Master them, and you'll be well on the way to using words correctly.

1. accede/exceed
   accede: to yield
   exceed: to go beyond, surpass
      I accede to your demand that we not exceed the budget.
2. accept/except
   accept: to receive
   except: to leave out or exclude; but
      I accept your proposal except for point 3.
3. access/excess
   access: the right to use; admission to
   excess: surplus
      As supply clerk, he had access to any excess materials.
4. adept/adopt
   adept: skilled
   adopt: to take as one's own
      She was adept at getting people to adopt her ideas.
5. advice/advise
   advice: (noun) counsel
   advise: (verb) to give counsel or advice to someone
      I asked him to advise me but I didn't like the advice I got.
6. affect/effect
   affect: (verb) to influence or modify
   effect: (verb) to produce or cause; (noun) result
      He hoped that his argument would affect his boss' decision, but so far as he could see, it had no effect.

      The tax relief effected some improvement for the citizens whose incomes had been affected by inflation.
7. affluent/effluent
   affluent: (adjective) rich, possessing in abundance

effluent: (noun) something that flows out
  Affluent companies can afford the cost of removing pollutants from the effluents their factories produce.

8. a lot/allot
  a lot: many (informal)
  allot: divide or give to
  A lot of players signed up for this year's draft. We allotted one first-round draft choice to each team.

9. amount/number
  amount: (use with concepts which cannot be counted individually but can only be measured)
  number: (use when items can be counted individually)
  It's a mistake to try to gauge the amount of interest he has by the number of questions he asks.

10. attributed/contributed
  attributed: was said to be caused by
  contributed: gave something to
  The rain probably contributed to the accident, but the police officer attributed the accident to driver error.

11. between/among
  between: (use with only two choices)
  among: (use with more than two choices)
  This year the differences between the two candidates for president are unusually clear.

  I don't see any major differences among the candidates for the city council.

12. cite/sight/site
  cite: (verb) to quote
  sight: (noun) vision, something to be seen
  site: (noun) location, place where a building is or will be built
  She cited the old story of the building inspector who was depressed by the very sight of the site for the new factory.

13. complement/compliment
  complement: (verb) to complete, finish; (noun) something which completes
  compliment: (verb) to praise; (noun) praise
  The compliment she gave me complemented my happiness.

14. compose/comprise
  compose: to make up, to create
  comprise: to consist of, to be made up of, to be composed of
  The city council is composed of 12 members. Each district comprises an area 50 blocks square.

15. confuse/complicate/exacerbate
  confuse: to bewilder
  complicate: to make more complex or detailed
  exacerbate: to make worse
  Because I missed the first 20 minutes of the movie, I didn't understand what was going on. The complicated plot exacerbated my confusion.

16. describe/prescribe
  describe: to list the features of something, to tell what something looks like
  prescribe: to specify the features something must contain

The law prescribes the priorities for making repairs. This report describes our plans to comply with the law.

17. do/due
    do: (verb) to act or make
    due: (adjective) scheduled, caused by
    The banker said she would do her best to change the due date.
    Due to the computer system, the payroll can be produced in only two days for all 453 employees.

18. elicit/illicit
    elicit: (verb) to draw out
    illicit: (adjective) not permitted, unlawful
    The reporter could elicit no information from the Senator about his illicit love affair.

19. eminent/immanent/imminent
    eminent: distinguished
    immanent: dwelling within tangible objects
    imminent: about to happen
    The eminent doctor believed that death was imminent. The eminent minister believed that God was immanent.

20. fewer/less
    fewer: (use for objects which can be counted individually)
    less: (use for objects which can be measured but not counted individually)
    There is less sand in this bucket; there are probably fewer grains of sand, too.

21. forward/foreword
    forward: ahead
    foreword: preface, introduction
    The author looked forward to writing the foreword to the book.

22. good/well
    good: (adjective, used to modify nouns; as a noun, means something that is good)
    well: (adverb, used to modify verbs, adjectives, and other adverbs)
    Her words "Good work!" told him that he was doing well.

    He spent a great deal of time doing volunteer work because he believed that doing good was just as important as doing well.

23. i.e./e.g.
    i.e.: (*id est*—that is) introduces a restatement or explanation of the preceding word or phrase
    e.g.: (*exempli gratia*—for the sake of an example; for example) introduces one or more examples
    Although he had never studied Latin, he rarely made a mistake in using Latin abbreviations, e.g., *i.e.*, etc., because he associated each with a mnemonic device (i.e., a word or image used to help one remember something). He remembered *i.e.* as *in effect,* pretended that *e.g.* meant *example given,* and used *etc.* only when *examples to continue* would fit.

24. imply/infer
    imply: to suggest, to put an idea into someone's head
    infer: to deduce, to get an idea out of something
    She implied that an announcement would be made soon. I inferred from her smile that it would be an announcement of her promotion.

25. it's/its
    it's: it is, it has
    its: belonging to it
    >It's clear that a company must satisfy its customers to stay in
    >business.

26. lie/lay
    lie: to recline; to tell a falsehood (never takes an object)
    lay: to put an object on something (always takes an object)
    >He was laying the papers on the desk when I came in, but they
    >aren't lying there now.

27. moral/morale
    moral: (adjective) virtuous, good; (noun: morals) ethics, sense of
    >right and wrong
    morale: (noun) spirit, attitude, mental outlook
    >Studies have shown that coed dormitories improve student
    >morale without harming student morals.

28. objective/rationale
    objective: goal
    rationale: reason, justification
    >The objective of the meeting was to explain the rationale
    >behind the decision.

29. personal/personnel
    personal: individual, to be used by one person
    personnel: staff, employees
    >All personnel will get personal computers by the end of the
    >year.

30. precede/proceed
    precede: (verb) to go before
    proceed: (verb) to continue; (noun: proceeds) money
    >Raising the money must precede spending it. Only after we
    >obtain the funds can we proceed to spend the proceeds.

31. principal/principle
    principal: (adjective) main; (noun) person in charge; money lent
    >out at interest
    principle: (noun) basic truth or rule, code of conduct
    >*The Prince,* Machiavelli's principal work, describes his
    >principles for ruling a state.

32. quiet/quite
    quiet: not noisy
    quite: very
    >It was quite difficult to find a quiet spot anywhere near the
    >floor of the stock exchange.

33. regulate/relegate
    regulate: to control
    relegate: to put (usually in an inferior position)
    >If the federal government regulates the size of lettering on
    >country road signs, we may as well relegate the current
    >signs to the garbage bin.

34. respectfully/respectively
    respectfully: with respect
    respectively: to each in the order listed
    >When I was introduced to the Queen, the Prime Minister, and
    >the court jester, I bowed respectfully, shook hands politely,
    >and winked, respectively.

FIGURE B.2
PROOFREADING SYMBOLS

Symbol	Meaning
e	delete
e̸	insert a letter
¶	start a new paragraph here
stet	stet (leave as it was before the marked change)
tr ↰	transpose (reverse)
lc	lower case (don't capitalize)
≡	capitalize
⊏	move to left
⊐	move to right
#	leave a space
⌒	close up
‖	align vertically

35. simple/simplistic
    simple: not complicated
    simplistic: watered down, oversimplified
       She was able to explain the proposal in simple terms without
          making the explanation sound simplistic.

36. their/there/they're
    their: belonging to them
    there: in that place
    they're: they are
       There are the plans, designed to their specifications, for the
          house they're building.

37. to/too/two
    to: (preposition) function word indicating proximity, purpose,
          time, etc.
    too: (adverb) also, very, excessively
    two: (adjective) the number 2
       The formula is too secret to entrust to two people.

38. unique/unusual
    unique: sole, only, alone
    unusual: not common
       I believed that I was unique in my ability to memorize long
          strings of numbers until I consulted the *Guinness Book of
          World Records* and found that I was merely unusual:
          someone else had equalled my feat in 1983.

39. verbal/oral
    verbal: using words
    oral: spoken, not written
       His verbal skills were uneven: his oral communication was ex-
          cellent, but he didn't write well. His sensitivity to nonverbal
          cues was acute: he could tell what kind of day I had had just
          by looking at my face.

FIGURE B.3
MARKED TEXT

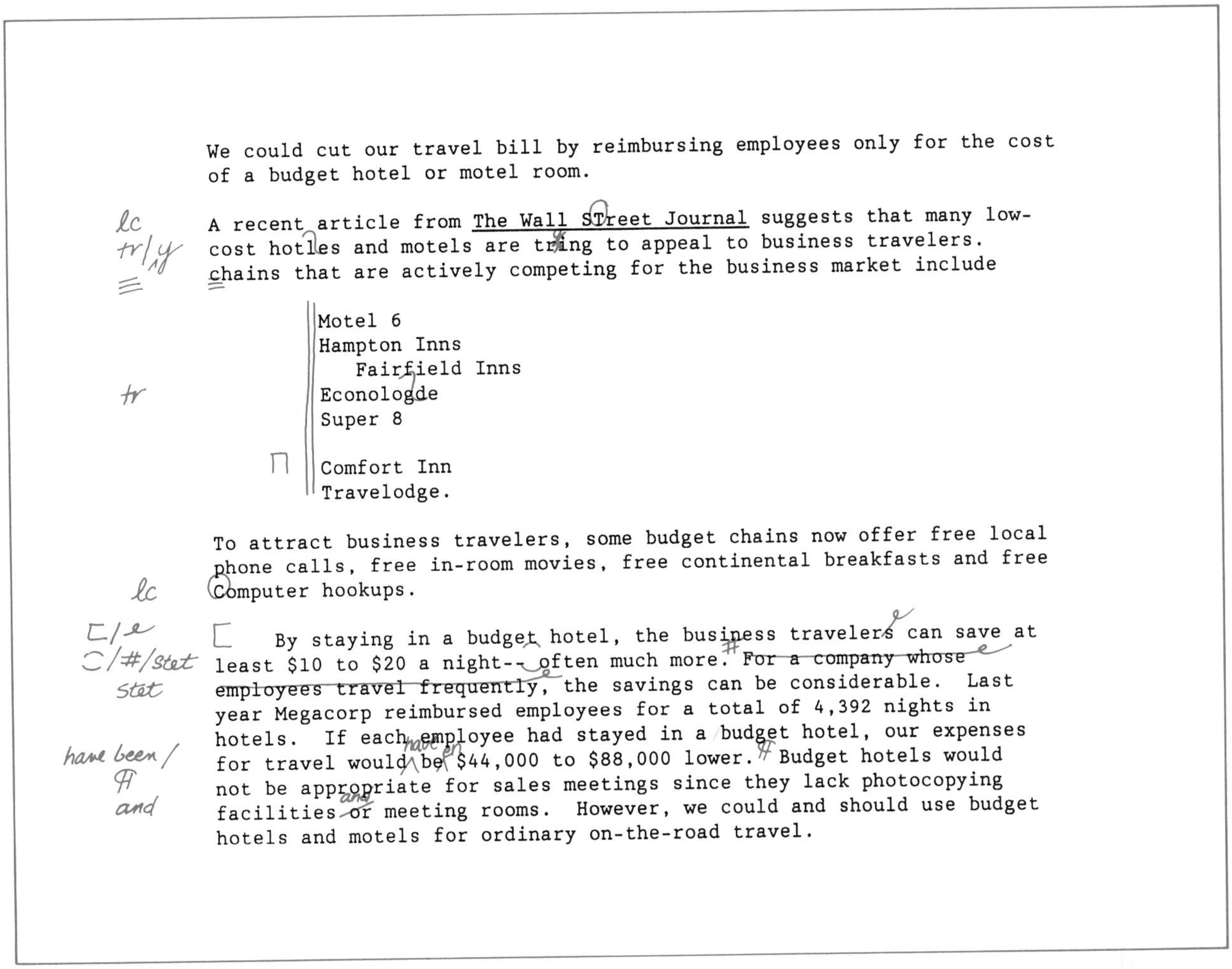

We could cut our travel bill by reimbursing employees only for the cost
of a budget hotel or motel room.

lc
tr/y
A recent article from The Wall Street Journal suggests that many low-
cost hotles and motels are tring to appeal to business travelers.
chains that are actively competing for the business market include

tr
Motel 6
Hampton Inns
     Fairfield Inns
Econologde
Super 8

Comfort Inn
Travelodge.

To attract business travelers, some budget chains now offer free local
phone calls, free in-room movies, free continental breakfasts and free
lc
Computer hookups.

C/e
C/#/stet
stet
By staying in a budget hotel, the business travelers can save at
least $10 to $20 a night--often much more. For a company whose
employees travel frequently, the savings can be considerable. Last
year Megacorp reimbursed employees for a total of 4,392 nights in
hotels. If each employee had stayed in a budget hotel, our expenses
have been/
#
and
for travel would be $44,000 to $88,000 lower. Budget hotels would
not be appropriate for sales meetings since they lack photocopying
facilities or meeting rooms. However, we could and should use budget
hotels and motels for ordinary on-the-road travel.

---

40. your/you're
     your: belonging to you
     you're: you are
          You're the top candidate for promotion in your division.

PROOFREADING SYMBOLS

Use the proofreading symbols in Figure B.2 to make corrections when you no
longer have access to a typewriter. Figure B.3 shows how the symbols can be
used to correct a typed text.

NOTES

1. "Analyzing the Analyzers," *PC Magazine* 5, no. 10 (May 27, 1986): 200.
2. Donald H. Cunningham, review of *RightWriter, The Technical Writing Teacher* 15, no. 1
    (Winter 1988): 86.

EXERCISES AND PROBLEMS FOR APPENDIX B

B-1 PROVIDING PUNCTUATION
Provide the necessary punctuation in the following sentences. Note that not every box requires punctuation.

1. The system☐s☐ user☐friendly design☐ provides screen displays of work codes☐ rates☐ and client information.

2. Many other factors also shape the organization☐s☐ image☐ advertising☐ brochures☐ proposals☐ stationery☐ calling cards☐ etc☐☐

3. Charlotte Ford☐ author of☐ ☐Charlotte Ford☐s☐ ☐Book of Modern Manners☐☐ says☐ ☐Try to mention specifics of the conversation to fix the interview permanently in the interviewer☐s☐ mind and be sure to mail the letter the same day☐☐ before the hiring decision is made☐☐

4. What are your room rates and charges for food service☐

5. We will need accommodations for 150 people☐ five meeting rooms☐ one large room and four small ones☐ coffee served during morning and afternoon breaks☐ and lunches and dinners.

6. The Operational Readiness Inspection☐ which occurs once every three years☐ is an intense☐ realistic☐ exercise☐ which evaluates the National Guard☐s☐ ability to mobilize☐ deploy☐ and fight.

7. Most computer packages will calculate three different sets of percentages☐ row percentages☐ column percentages☐ and table percentages☐

8. In today☐s economy☐ it☐s almost impossible for a firm to extend credit beyond it☐s regular terms.

9. The Department of Transportation does not have statutory authority to grant easements☐ however☐ we do have authority to lease unused areas of highway right☐of☐way.

10. The program has two goals☐ to identify employees with promise☐ and to see that they get the training they need to advance.

B-2 PROVIDING PUNCTUATION
Provide the necessary punctuation in the following sentences. Note that not every box requires punctuation.

1. To reduce secretaries☐ overtime hours☐ the office should hire part☐time secretaries to work from 5 to 9 P.M.

2. Since memberships can begin at any time during the year☐ all member☐s☐ dues are recognized on a cash basis when they are received.

3. I would be interested in working on the committee☐ however☐ I have decided to do less community work so that I have more time to spend with my family.

4. One of the insurance companies☐ American Family Corp☐☐ Columbus☐ GA☐ said it hopes to persuade the FASB to reconsider the rule.

5. The city already has five☐ two☐hundred☐bed hospitals.

6. Students run the whole organization☐ and are advised by a Board of Directors from the community.

7. I suggest putting a bulletin board in the rear hallway with all the interviewer☐s☐ pictures on it.

8. ☐Most black businesses just get enough money to open the doors☐☐ says Mr. Quinn☐ adding ☐that the $10,000 or so of savings he used to start up simply wasn☐t☐ enough☐☐

9. Otis Conward Jr☐☐ who grew up in this area☐ now heads the Council for Economic Development.

10. Volunteers also participate in a one☐on☐one pal program.

B-3 EDITING FOR GRAMMAR AND USAGE
Revise these sentences to correct errors in grammar and usage.

1. A team of 85 researchers around the world are conducting the study.

2. Confirming our phone conversation earlier today, the new equipment will be tested under simulated working conditions.

3. The new information does not alter my conclusion to include it now will make the report unduly bulky and destroy its structural unity.

4. Two basketball players announced they will

attend Indiana State University next season during the weekend.

5. To get a random sample of students, I took random samples of residence hall floors, fraternities, sororities, and apartments. A representative from each living unit helped distribute these and wait for them to fill them out before picking them up.

6. A writer should first define their purpose and then their audience before you physically start to write the paper.

7. One should list the functions one will use most. Before deciding on a word processing program.

8. No system of internal control is perfect, there will always be limitations inherent in the system.

9. Neither of my parents graduated from college; my mother is the most educated of the two.

10. Many technical analysts, which were selling the market short two days ago, are now bullish.

B-4 EDITING FOR GRAMMAR AND USAGE
Revise the following sentences to eliminate errors in grammar and usage.

1. On many items our prices are lower than our competition.

2. A random sample of motorists were picked for the survey.

3. The control sheet originates in the EDP Department presently prepared by Renee Simms.

4. Hunters are required to attend an orientation seminar where light refreshments will be served.

5. When you call on a customer, one should first learn as much as possible about them in advance.

6. Work of an architectural firm organized as a partnership is performed in the name of the partnership, this means that all partners are jointly liable for the work of any one of them.

7. Steps to be taken before April 1st would include urging our sources to ship everything possible before March 29th, delivery of ma-

terials to our customers by the 30th, and if there is a strike and our drivers continue to work, to choose truck routes that would avoid known trouble spots.

8. While working as a receptionist, my duties included answering phones, typing, and filing.

9. If you have any questions, call Ralph Metcalf or myself.

10. People in higher management have usually held line rather than staff positions. Though staff work can be satisfying and is crucial to the organization.

B-5 EDITING FOR GRAMMAR AND USAGE
Revise the following sentences to eliminate errors in grammar and usage:

1. If a group member doesn't complete their assigned work, it slows the whole project down.

2. Our phones are constantly being used. Not only for business calls, but also for personal calls.

3. Todd drew the graphs after him and I discussed the ideas for them.

4. Originally a group of four, a member dropped out after the first meeting due to a death in the family.

5. Our group met seven times outside of class, we would have met even more if we could have found times when we could all get together.

6. There has also been suggestions for improving the airflow in the building.

7. I didn't appreciate him assuming that he would be the group's leader.

8. With people like yourself giving gifts, the 4-H program will be able to survive and grow.

9. Volunteers need a better orientation to Planned Parenthood as a whole, to the overall clinic function, and to the staff there is also a need to clarify volunteer responsibilities.

10. Children are referred to the Big Brother/Big Sister program by their school social workers, often from underprivileged homes.

B-6 CHOOSING THE CORRECT DENOTATION

Choose the right word for each sentence.

1. The audit revealed a small (amount, number) of errors.

2. I do not think that the fact that I surveyed only business students (affected, effected) the survey's results.

3. In her speech, she (implied, inferred) that the vote would be close.

4. We need to redesign the stand so that the catalog is eye-level instead of (laying, lying) on the desk.

5. (Their, There, They're) is some evidence that (their, there, they're) thinking of changing (their, there, they're) policy.

6. The settlement isn't yet in writing; if one side wanted to back out of the (oral, verbal) agreement, it could.

7. In (affect, effect), we're creating a new department.

8. This is a somewhat (unusual, unique) type of equipment.

9. During the training program, new employees learn about the department and (its, it's) procedures.

10. We have (fewer, less) lost items with our new inventory program.

B-7 CHOOSING THE CORRECT DENOTATION

Choose the right word for each sentence.

1. The author (cites, sights, sites) four reasons for computer phobia.

2. The error was (do, due) to inexperience.

3. (Your, you're) doing a good job motivating (your, you're) subordinates.

4. One of the basic (principals, principles) of business communication is "Consider the reader."

5. I (implied, inferred) from the article that interest rates would go up.

6. Working papers generally are (composed, comprised) of (1) working trial balance, (2) assembly sheets, (3) adjusting entries, (4) audit schedules, and (5) audit memos.

7. Eliminating time clocks will improve employee (moral, morale).

8. The (principal, principle) variable is the trigger price mechanism.

9. (Its, It's) (to, too, two) soon (to, too, two) tell whether the conversion (to, too, two) computerized billing will save as much time as we hope.

10. Formal training programs (complement, compliment) on-the-job opportunities for professional growth.

B-8 CHOOSING THE CORRECT DENOTATION

Choose the right word for each sentence.

1. The costs should be allocated (among, between) the two subsidiaries.

2. The lease should be written and signed by all parties. (Oral, verbal) agreements can lead to misconceptions and leave you with no written evidence if there is a dispute.

3. Several customers have asked that we carry more campus merchandise, (i.e., e.g.,) pillows and mugs with the college seal.

4. Diet beverages have (fewer, less) calories than regular drinks.

5. The firm will be hiring new (personal, personnel) in the next year.

6. They fear that a strike is (eminent, immanent, imminent).

7. We have investigated all of the possible solutions (accept, except) adding a turning lane.

8. Although the final specifications haven't been drawn up, we could (preceed, proceed) with the first stage of installation.

9. The law (regulates, relegates) the distribution of funds to each county.

10. The proposed (cite, sight, site) is convenient to both rail and road transportation.

B-9 TRACKING YOUR OWN MECHANICAL ERRORS

Keep track of the mechanical errors (grammar, punctuation, word use, and typos) in each of your papers. Use the following questions to analyze them:

- How many different errors are marked on each paper?
- Which three errors do you make most often?
- Is the number of errors constant in each paper, or does the number increase or decrease during the term?

As your instructor directs,

a. Correct each of the mechanical errors in one or more papers.

b. Deliberately write two new sentences in which you make each of your three most common errors. Then write the correct version of each sentence.

c. Write a memo to your instructor discussing your increasing mastery of mechanical correctness during the semester or quarter.

d. Briefly explain to the class how to avoid one kind of error in grammar, punctuation, or word use.

Additional Exercises and Problems

C–1 MAKING ETHICAL CHOICES

Answer two questions about each of the following actions. (1) Do you consider the action ethical, unethical, or a gray area? (2) Would you do this, refuse to do it, or do it but feel uncomfortable about doing it?

1. Calling in sick so you can stay home to care for your sick child.

2. Preparing advertising for a product that's inferior to and cheaper than the leader in the product category.

3. Taking home office supplies (e.g., pens, markers, calculators, etc.) for personal use.

4. Inflating your evaluation of a subordinate because you know that only people ranked "excellent" will get pay raises.

5. Telling your secretary to tell callers that you're "in conference" while you take an after-lunch nap.

6. Taking long lunch hours on occasion because everyone does it.

7. Making personal long distance calls on the company phone.

8. Not offering a promotion to a married woman because you feel the travel required at the new level would interfere with her home life.

9. Not offering a promotion that will require moving to a married man because you feel his wife could not find a job comparable to her current job in the new town.

10. Agreeing to write direct mail for a candidate whom you believe to be inferior to the incumbent who is running for re-election.

11. Accepting a job to write direct mail for an organization you loathe, and then deliberately doing less than your best work.

12. Coming in to the office in the evening to use the company's word processor and computer for personal projects.

13. Designing an ad campaign for a cigarette brand.

14. Working as an accountant for a company that makes or advertises cigarettes.

15. Working as a manager in a company which exploits its nonunionized hourly workers.

16. Using computerized personalization to make the reader of a direct mail letter think that the letter is a personal one just to him or her.

17. Writing copy for a company's annual report hiding or minimizing the fact that it pollutes the environment.

18. "Padding" your expense account by putting on it charges you did not in fact pay for.

19. Writing a subscription letter for a sex magazine that glamorizes rape, violence, and sadism.

20. Doing the taxes of a client who publishes a sex magazine that glamorizes rape, violence, and sadism.

21. Telling a job candidate that the company "usually" grants cost-of-living raises every six months, even though you know that the company is losing money and plans to cancel cost-of-living raises for the next year.

22. Laughing at the racist or sexist jokes a client makes, even though you find them offensive.

23. Refusing to hire a black sales representative because you know that some of your customers are prejudiced against blacks.

24. Reading *The Wall Street Journal* on company time.

25. Minimizing the negative effects of a policy in a memo explaining the policy to subordinates.

C–2 RECOMMENDING A CANDIDATE FOR AN OVERSEAS ASSIGNMENT

In most companies, the Director of Human Resources has little to say about job assignments at the executive level. But after some bad experiences with American managers who couldn't handle international assignments, your company has agreed that you would evaluate the candidates for each overseas assignment. The Vice President for each area still has the final voice, so you must explain your criteria and show convincingly why the candidate you support is indeed the best.

You need to recommend someone to begin a three-year term as Manager of Asian Marketing. The Asian division is your company's fourth-largest in terms of sales; the company feels that with the right person, this market can grow dramatically in the next five years.

You don't know any of the finalists for the position, so you must rely on the summary data you have been given.

1. **Rachel A. Diamond,** 48, white, single. Employed by the company for 20 years. Harvard MBA. Speaks French and German. Formerly, Manager of Canadian Marketing for the company; very successful. Excellent technical knowledge, good managerial skills, excellent communication skills, acceptable interpersonal skills. Excellent health; excellent emotional stability. Children ages 22, 18, and 15.

2. **Scott Robert Greers,** 41, white, single. Employed by the company for eight years. University of Minnesota MBA. Formerly in the Buenos Aires office as a staff person; successful. Speaks Spanish. Acceptable technical knowledge, good managerial skills, excellent communication skills, excellent interpersonal skills. Excellent health; good emotional stability. No children.

3. **Adam X. Fong,** 34, of Chinese descent, married. Employed by the company for 11 years. Stanford MBA. Does not speak any foreign language. Has not worked abroad. A "boy wonder" who helped increase sales by 20% in his U.S. region. Good technical knowledge, excellent managerial skills, acceptable communication skills, excellent interpersonal skills. Excellent health; good emotional stability. Wife speaks Japanese. Wife is a college professor of political science who hopes to get an appointment at a university in Japan or China. Children ages 6 and 4.

4. **Amanda Fuentes,** 42, of Hispanic descent, married. Employed by the company for 14 years. University of Texas MBA. Speaks French, Spanish, Korean, and some Japanese. Has not worked abroad, but as liaison with the international marketing staff has written monthly summary reports for all international divisions. Excellent technical knowledge, acceptable managerial skills, excellent communication skills, excellent interpersonal skills. Excellent health; excellent emotional stability. Husband is an executive at another U.S. company; the couple plans to commute every six weeks. No children.

5. **Bill Evans,** 46, black, married. Employed by the company for 22 years. Howard University MBA. Speaks Farsi and Hebrew. Formerly manager of Middle East Marketing for the company; very successful. Excellent technical knowledge, good managerial skills, good communication skills, excellent interpersonal skills. Good health; excellent emotional stability. Wife teaches fourth grade, does not plan to seek paid employment in the Orient. Children ages 14 and 10.

Write a memo to Lawrence Vandiver, Vice President for Marketing, explaining your criteria and ranking the candidates.

C–3 RECRUITING VOLUNTEERS TO SERVE AS BIG BROTHERS AND BIG SISTERS

Big Brothers and Big Sisters help children who need adult attention and role models. Each Big Brother or Big Sister is paired with a child of the same sex, aged 6 to 12, and is urged to meet with the child at least twice a month. No specific activities are required. In the past, volunteers have taken the children to sports events, helped them with homework, gone to museums or shopping, played in the park, and just talked.

While the community has a successful program, this year barely half the children who have asked for a Big Brother or a Big Sister have gotten one. And you'd particularly like more minority volunteers and more men.

As your instructor directs,
   a. Write a letter to students in your college or university persuading them to volunteer.
   b. Write a letter to business people in the community persuading them to volunteer.
   c. Make a three- to five-minute presentation to students persuading them to volunteer.
   d. Make a three- to five-minute presentation to business people persuading them to volunteer.
   e. Write a press release about the need for volunteers.

C–4   WRITING TO A CLIENT WHO IS EVADING TAXES

As an independent CPA, you do tax work for a number of individuals and small businesses. One of your clients is Claire Ross, a college professor who owns three apartment buildings in town and has income from several stocks and two mutual funds. This year, when you were preparing Professor Ross's taxes, you found almost by accident that she did not report income from consulting work she did for the local Board of Realtors this year and last year. You asked her if she did any other paid consulting; she said, "It varies from year to year." You pointed out that the income from these jobs was taxable and had to be declared, and asked Professor Ross for information on her income from these jobs. You noted that in addition to including the information on this year's return, you wanted the information about last year (when you also prepared her taxes) so you could file an amended return and pay the extra tax due.

Professor Ross flatly refused to give you the information. She said that the companies paying her didn't file any forms with the IRS, so no one can prove she was paid (a statement that could be true, if the amounts were small enough), and that she already pays 28% of her income in taxes. (That is true.) She claimed the amount she earned from consulting was "so small that it wouldn't make any difference anyway." (That could be true, but you doubt it.) You can't make up information for a client's tax return, so you finally prepared the returns based on the information you did have.

Now you need to send Professor Ross a bill for your services. You have spent 46 hours on Professor Ross's taxes, at $120 an hour. Professor Ross knows what your fee structure is, but this year her taxes took much longer

to do than usual, so your bill is higher—a surprise that will be an unpleasant one. You will also bill her for $18.35 in photocopying charges and $32.58 in long distance bills related to determining the sales prices of various bonds so you could calculate profits and losses on transactions in her mutual funds.

Should you repeat your concern that she is suppressing income? Should you remind her that the deliberate failure to report income is considered fraud and is punishable by very high fines and even carries the possibility (remote) of a jail sentence? Should you refuse to do Professor Ross's taxes next year if she isn't going to be honest? Should you threaten to report her to the IRS, and if you make that threat, should you carry it out?

As your instructor directs,
   a. Write a letter to Professor Ross.
   b. Write a memo for your files describing what has happened.
   c. Write a letter to the IRS.

C–5   PERSUADING HIGH SCHOOL STUDENTS TO COME TO A SUMMER PROGRAM

To make money and use their facilities year-round, many colleges and universities offer special summer programs for high school students or retired people. Participants commute from their homes or stay in dorms; they use campus facilities. Each session is taught by professors assisted by graduate students and high school teachers. Occasionally college credit is available, but usually the courses are just designed for personal enrichment and fun.

As your instructor directs,

   a. Write a form letter to go to high school teachers, coaches, and counselors telling them about one of the sessions and urging them to encourage interested students to apply.
   b. Write a two-page letter directly to high school students. Assume that you have a list of people who have indicated interest; now you want them actually to apply to one of the three camps you offer.
   1. Computer Camp. (Second week in June or second week in July.) Categories: beginning PC (IBM and Apple); PC software (word processing, spreadsheet, and data base programs); programming beginning and advanced (PASCAL, FORTRAN, BASIC, ASSEMBLER). Cost: $300 resident, $225 commuter.
   2. Marching Band Clinic. (Third week in June.) Categories: band (practicing music; marching

steps and patterns); auxiliary units—drum majors, baton twirlers, drill teams, flag corps, precision dance lines—(designing routines and costumes). Open to entire units and to individuals. Cost: $325 resident, $250 commuter.

3. Sports Camp. [You pick the sport.] (Fourth week in June or July.) Open to students grades 6 to 12 who wish to prepare for competition in this sport. Stresses conditioning, drills, strategy, and rules. Cost: $400 resident; $325 commuter.

C–6 RESPONDING TO A CUSTOMER COMPLAINT

You place cards on each table in your restaurant, inviting patrons to evaluate their dining experience. Patrons may turn in the cards when they leave or mail them in later. Today you received this evaluation:

Were you greeted pleasantly? Yes

How would you rate food quality and preparation? Good

What entrée items did you order? Filet mignon and lobster

Was service efficient? Yes

Would you recommend this restaurant to other people? No

Name of waiter/waitress: Don't remember

Date of visit: Time: 7:30 P.M.

Name: Susan Northrop

Address: Cranston Advertising
           400 State Street
           [Your town]

Additional Comments: I brought a client here— the waiter gave *him* the check. It was very embarrassing. I'll never bring a business guest here again. Come into the 20th century. Do you *really* think the man always pays?

You called the Chamber of Commerce and found out that Cranston Advertising was the third biggest agency in the city. You certainly don't want to be blacklisted by the advertising community.

Write a letter to Susan Northrop, apologizing for what happened and reestablishing goodwill.

C–7 WRITING A COVER LETTER FOR A QUESTIONNAIRE

Each year, your college gives an "Excellence in Teaching" award. To be eligible, instructors must be nominated by one or more students. However, as chair of the

selection committee you want to hear from a representative sampling of students in addition to the student who nominated the instructor. Therefore, you get each instructor's rosters for the last two years and write to a random sample of students, asking them to evaluate the instructor. You provide a five-page questionnaire that takes about 30 minutes to complete and a self-addressed, stamped envelope. To avoid embarrassing anyone who is nominated but who does not win an award, you want students to refrain from telling anyone about the questionnaire.

Write a cover letter to accompany the questionnaire. Persuade students to take the time to evaluate the instructor and to keep the information confidential.

Hints:
- How quickly do you need a response? How busy are students right now?
- What would motivate students to take the time to complete the questionnaire? What obstacles might keep them from doing so? Can you overcome or minimize the obstacles?

C–8 ANALYZING THE COMMUNICATION ENVIRONMENT OF AN ORGANIZATION

Describe and evaluate the communication environment of an organization of which you've been a part.

Possible organizations would include a business where you've worked, your living unit on campus, a club to which you belong, your community college, college, or university, your church or synagogue, a class you've taken. If you choose a large organization, limit your analysis to the part(s) of it you know best.

In the opening paragraph (which you should write after you've written the middle section), summarize your conclusion in a sentence or two.

In the body of your memo, first describe the organization and your role in it. Your description should emphasize those factors which might affect the organization's communication: size, hierarchical versus democratic structure, leadership styles, etc. External factors, such as the ease with which the organization is able to fulfill its purpose, may also be relevant in some cases.

Next, describe the kinds of communication you observed in the organization. Include informal channels— the grapevine—as well as such formal channels as memos, letters, announcements, speeches, etc. Include communication with people outside the organization only if you were able to observe it. Identify the purpose(s) of the communicative acts you observed: to request or give information, to persuade someone to act, to build goodwill, to satisfy someone's ego, etc. You may want to note the direction of communication: was it all downward (from a boss to subordinates), or was there also upward (from subordinate to boss) and lateral (among peers) communication?

The meat of your memo will be your evaluation of the communication you observed. The criteria you choose may vary with the organization you discuss. Possible questions to consider include the following:

- Did the communicative acts fulfill their purpose(s)?
- Was communication clear, or did confusion sometimes result?
- Did informal channels help or hinder formal communication?
- Was one kind of communication (downward, for instance) significantly better or worse than other kinds?
- Did communication help or hinder the group's fulfillment of its purpose?
- Were there obvious trouble spots or weak links in the communication process?

Cite one or two examples of specific communicative acts to illustrate your points. Be sure to give enough information so that someone who wasn't there will be able to understand your example and see how it proves your main point.

In your last paragraph, you may either (gracefully) restate your main point or offer suggestions of ways communication in that organization could be improved. Any suggestions should grow out of your evaluation; they should not seem to be "new points" to the reader.

C–9 ANNOUNCING A CHANGE IN ACCOUNT EXECUTIVES

You're manager of the branch office of a major brokerage firm. One of your account executives, Peter Mayes, is leaving your firm. He was not working out well, and several of his clients had complained to you about him. Some of them had even transferred their accounts to other brokerage firms.

Cynthia Waters is being assigned Peter's remaining clients. Ideally, you'd like each of the clients to schedule an appointment with her, partly to review their investment portfolios, and partly just so they get to know her. But you know most people would be reluctant to schedule an appointment, which they would see simply as sales pressure.

Draft a letter to go to those clients, telling them that Cynthia will be their new account executive. You'll use individually typed form letters. Direct this one to Ms. Marilyn Snyder, 402 Rolling Hills, in your city. You want to build confidence in your firm.

C–10 INVITING CONTESTANTS TO AN AWARDS BANQUET

Every year, the Society for Technical Communication has contests to recognize the best technical art and technical writing its members produce. Judges fill out a detailed evaluation sheet on each entry. Awards are made at four levels: distinguished, excellent, merit, and achievement. Entries winning awards at the two highest levels are forwarded to the National Competition. In addition, a special award is made to the entry judged "Best in Show."

You are this year's chair of your chapter's Writing Competition. By one standard, the competition has been a great success: 192 entries—up from 148 last year— were submitted in the 17 categories (brochure, consumer manual, technical article, annual report, etc.) Your six judges have evaluated the entries and decided upon the awards.

The problem: your judges gave only 95 awards (last year, with 148 entries, there were 115 awards), and many of these were at lower levels. Normally, at least one entry in each category is termed "distinguished," but your judges gave only eight such awards.

Awards are presented at the annual banquet. If you tell people in advance whether or not they got awards, a lot may not come. If you don't warn them that this year's judges were tough, there are going to be a lot of angry people at the banquet.

Write to the entrants. You may write one letter to all, or compose one letter for those who did get some award and another for those who got nothing. You may enclose the evaluation sheets now or send them later. Give the entrants full information about the banquet and persuade them to attend.

Here is the information about the banquet: entries will be on display; awards will be made; there will be a speaker. January 23 (or June 23) at 6 P.M. Reservations to be made with Banquet Coordinator Kevin Meyers, Dwayne Electronics. (Pick an address for the hotel and an office address and phone for Kevin.) Deadline 5 P.M., January 13 (or June 13). Tickets $35 each. Entrants must pay for themselves and their guests.

C–11 SELLING BIRTHDAY CAKES

To raise money to put yourself through school, you've decided to bake and sell birthday cakes. You've had a cake-decorating class and can make letters, flowers, festoons, etc. You decide to offer chocolate, white, and yellow cakes with either white or chocolate icing in two sizes: 6″ by 9″ sheet cake for $10.95 or 10″ by 13″ sheet cake for $17.95.

1. Identify the best central selling point for each of the following target audiences:

Parents or guardians
Roommates
Boyfriends or girlfriends

2. What target audience(s) can you reach? Can you get students' home addresses? Do you have to pay for the list?

3. People may be reluctant to order a cake and send a check months before a birthday. How can you best get your message to people when they're thinking about birthdays? How much lead time do you need? What information do you need?

4. You could sell cakes for other occasions, too: graduation, engagements, honors, etc. How could you tap into these markets?

As your instructor directs,
a. Write a message for the target audience of your choice.

b. Write a memo to your instructor explaining why you chose (1) the target audience, (2) the length of the message, (3) the channel for the message.

c. Write a press release about your business for the local paper.

C–12 SOLVING THE PROTECTIVE CLOTHING PROBLEM

You are plant manager at a processing plant where workers must wear goggles and hard hats. You issue one pair of goggles and one hard hat to each person as he or she is hired. Everyone is expected to bring the goggles and hat to work each day. You have a few extra goggles and hats, and in the past have lent them to people who forgot theirs. However, more and more people seem to be "forgetting." The problem is a serious one. People can't work without protective clothing, and when they don't work, your production schedule is destroyed. You don't have lockers for individual employees; in the past, people have claimed that they left hats at work and someone else "swiped them."

You could buy lockers and force people to keep their goggles and hats at work. The cost of lockers and remodeling to make room for them would cut into the profit your plant is expected to make this quarter. Since the quarter's profit is the major criterion on which you're evaluated, you're not eager to do that.

You're within your rights under the contract to make people go home to get the clothing and to dock them for the time they miss. However, when you have sent people home in the past, some of them have been gone for up to three hours. It's a big city, and some of your workers live on the other side of town, but some of them may be in no hurry to get back. But the uncertainty of knowing when they'll be back isn't good for your production schedule.

What are your options? What are the advantages and disadvantages of each? Decide what to do, and write the appropriate message(s) to the plant workers.

C–13 STRAIGHTENING OUT A CONVERSION PROBLEM

You are branch manager of a large bank which has offices throughout the state. For years, each branch processed the checks written on its accounts. Two months ago, the bank switched to a centralized check processing system. Now, all checks are sent to the division headquarters (which happens to be 200 miles away) and are processed there. Then the cancelled checks are sent to you; you send them out to each checking account customer. The new system will save the bank a great deal of money because it will reduce the number of people needed at each branch and because it will enable the bank to earn 8 to 24 hours' interest on the funds withdrawn from checking accounts to pay check obligations. Given the large sums of money involved, the interest is expected to be considerable.

However, the system is not working. Last month, the monthly statements arrived, but none of the cancelled checks came. You didn't include an explanation in statements and were deluged with phone calls asking what had happened. Now the cancelled checks are finally arriving (though some still aren't here).

As your instructor directs,
a. Write a form letter to checking account customers, to serve as a transmittal letter with the cancelled checks and to rebuild goodwill.

b. Write a memo to Division Headquarters explaining the problem and asking that it be resolved quickly.

c. Write a script for a phone call to Division Headquarters.

d. Write answers to the hostile questions you expect when you are interviewed about the problem by the reporter from the local TV station's "Consumer Watchdog" show.

C–14 TELLING RESIDENTS TO REMOVE JUNK CARS FROM THEIR PROPERTY

The City Council wants to get rid of junk cars sitting on several properties within the city limits. It is unclear whether people are working on these cars, saving them till they become antiques, or just avoiding the hefty fee the city dump charges to accept a junk car, but the cars are definitely an eyesore.

In the Council debate, Seymour Wray pointed out

that the town has an ordinance stating "No property owner in a residential zone shall have more than two vehicles visible from the road; no more than one of these shall be parked on the road. No vehicle without a current license and registration shall be parked or stored on any property in a residential zone." Carla Altschul said that provision didn't solve the problem. "Couldn't someone who was willing to keep paying the registration and license fees keep the car? The ordinance doesn't say anything about how the car looks." Ann Gell-Mann reminded the group of another ordinance which states, "No property owner in a residential zone shall maintain his or her property in such a condition as to create an eyesore, a health hazard, or a public nuisance." George Mineta noted that some people have cars which they still drive which look pretty bad: dented, rusting, with trim hanging loose or replacement fender panels in another color than the original. Everyone agreed that the intent was to get rid of the junked cars that are just sitting on people's lots; if someone is driving the car, the Council wouldn't intervene. As mayor, you do not vote on the Council unless there is a tie. Here, agreement was unanimous.

The "eyesore" ordinance gives an offender 14 days to remove the eyesore after the date of an official warning. If, 14 days after the warning, the eyesore remains, the city has the power to correct it, bill the property holder for the work and fine him or her $50. If the bill and fine are not paid within 30 days, they are added to the property tax bill.

As your instructor directs,
   a. Write a letter to go out to the people who have junk cars on their lots. Assume that the city has a computer which can fill in the name and address of the property owner and any other specifics you want to include in the letter.
   b. Write a press release about the Council's decision to enforce the ordinance.

Hint:
   • Should you be legalistic, quoting directly from the ordinance(s)? Are these persuasive or negative messages? How can you maintain goodwill? You don't want people to fight against you when you come up for reelection.

C–15 NOTIFYING NOMINEES OF ELECTION RESULTS
In addition to its officers, the Association for Business Communication (ABC) has a Board of Directors. Terms are staggered so that a portion of the Board is elected each year. Association Bylaws require that the ballot name twice as many nominees as the number of available seats; write-in votes are also possible. Ballots are mailed to the entire membership; the ballot has a 100-word biographical statement supplied by each nominee. The nominees with the highest numbers of votes win. This year, eight nominees ran for four positions.

Assume that you're ABC's Executive Director and notify the nominees of the results.

Hints:
   • Should you write one form letter to everyone? (Of course, the form letters would be individually typed and would have the recipient's name in the inside address and salutation.) Would it be better to write one letter to the winners and a second letter to the losers? Totally different letters to everyone?

Would the following circumstances change the message(s) you'd write?

   a. This year, you disagree violently with the results of the popular vote. You're a member of the Association as well as Executive Director, so you have one vote, but you can't influence the results. The two people whom you believe to be the best nominees of the bunch both were among the losers.
   b. This year, three of the losers have lost before—two once each, and one person four times! (The nominating committee frequently renominates losing candidates; since there are twice as many nominees as seats on the Board, and since the nominating committee tries to nominate only good people, many good people will lose.) You know that all three of these people very much want to be on the Board of Directors and are going to be bitterly disappointed that the membership has rejected them—again.
   c. This year's election produced a tie for fourth place. The Bylaws specify that the current Board breaks any ties. The Bylaws are available to any interested member. There was considerable discussion about the Bylaws when they were revised extensively two years ago, but it's very likely that few of the nominees (and fewer of the general membership) are aware of the provisions for handling ties in election votes.

C–16 URGING EMPLOYEES TO HANDLE ROUTINE CALLS COURTEOUSLY
You are manager of the local power company. A recent market survey about people's plans for appliances, larger homes, etc. also had some questions about recipients'

attitudes toward the company. On the 7-point "friendly . . . unfriendly" scale, you came out at 2.1—with 1 being the lowest score possible.

Most people never see anyone from the company; their only contact with you is through monthly bills, ads, and phone calls. You do get a lot of calls. Many of these calls are about routine matters: when bills are due, whether people can delay payment, how to handle payment when they're away for extended periods of time, how to tell if there's a gas leak, how to relight a furnace in the fall, how the budget payment system works. Workers answer these questions over and over and over again. They may get impatient explaining something for the 10th time, or answering a question that was already answered in an enclosure with the bill. But the caller asks because he or she needs to know. To the worker, the caller is just one more faceless voice; to the caller, the worker is the company.

Write a memo to your staff urging them to be patient and friendly when they answer questions.

Hints:

- In your town, does the power company have a monopoly, or do gas and electricity compete for customers? How might competition affect your message?
- What specifically do you want your staff to do? How could they achieve your general goals?
- How can the job be made more interesting for workers?

C–17 RESPONDING TO A FRIEND WHO HAS USED YOU AS A REFERENCE WITHOUT PERMISSION

You're active in community groups and have served for several years on the Board of Directors of Roundhouse, a live-in facility for runaways and other teens in conflict with their families. Today you receive the following letter from Jim Wyatt, who served a one-year term on the Board three years ago. You liked Jim while you were working with him on the Board. He did a good job as a member of a subcommittee you chaired. You even went to a party at his house. However, you haven't seen him since he left the Board two years ago. The letter is typed and photocopied, with your name written in by hand after the "Dear."

Dear

I have recently applied to Buckman Laboratories, Inc., Memphis, TN, for a position as sales representative. This family-owned company manufacturers and

---

markets various biologicals and chemicals for water treatment and other processes for numerous industries.

I expect to employ the knowledge learned in the fields of construction, manufacturing and processing, and medical sales to support this highly technical product line.

Your name has been listed as a reference and it is likely that Buckman Laboratories will contact you by letter or telephone with a short questionnaire. Your prompt response will be greatly appreciated.

If you have any questions, please contact me at the telephone below. Thank you for your cooperation.

Respectfully,
Jim C. Wyatt
555–2538

cc: Buckman Laboratories, Inc.

You remember that (at least when you knew him), Jim was a sales representative for a company selling medical supplies to hospitals; you don't have any evidence about how good a sales representative he was. He and his wife had literally built their house themselves, so you know he does have some practical experience in construction. Does he know anything about manufacturing and processing? Maybe, but you don't have any evidence of it.

Jim has been rude in not asking you in advance whether you'd be willing to serve as a reference for him. He's been even ruder in writing—not calling—to inform you. However, you did like him as a person, and you don't want to sabotage his job hunting.

As your instructor directs,

a. Write a letter to Jim or make notes for a phone conversation.

b. Joellen Schaffer, Director of Personnel at Buckman, writes to you: "Your name has been listed as a reference for James C. Wyatt. Please give us any information you have that may be relevant." Write a letter to Buckman.

C–18 GIVING A CUSTOMER LESS THAN SHE WANTS

You are a Consumer Relations Specialist for East India Spices. You've received a letter from (Mrs.) Naomi Gallion complaining that she made a stew using the recipe printed on a bottle of East India garlic powder, measuring carefully, but that the stew was "inedible." She wants a refund for the bottle, $3.36.

You know that there was a problem with a batch of labels that had a typographical error calling for twice the proper amount of garlic powder. However, that was two years ago. Mrs. Gallion either used a bottle that she's had for a long time, or she bought it from a store that is selling outdated spices. Many people do keep spices for a long time, especially if they've bought a large jar of a spice they use rarely. But spices should be used within six months of the date on the label.

You aren't willing to send Mrs. Gallion a refund, but in the interest of corporate goodwill, you will send her a coupon for a free .45 oz. jar of East India garlic powder (estimated retail value $1.95).

Write the letter.

C–19 TELLING AN EMPLOYEE ABOUT HER PENSION BENEFITS

You're Director of Employee Benefits for a Fortune 500 company. Today, you received the following memo:

To: [Your Name]

From: Michelle Jagtiani

Subject: Getting My Retirement Benefits

Next Friday will be my last day here. I am leaving [name of company] to take a position at another firm.

Please process a check for my retirement benefits, including both the deductions from my salary and the company's contributions for the last six years. I would like to receive the check by next Friday if possible.

You have bad news for Michelle. Although the company does contribute an amount to the retirement fund equal to the amount deducted for retirement from the employee's paycheck, employees who leave with less than 10 years of employment get only their own contributions. Michelle has worked for the company for almost seven years. Michelle will get back the money that has been deducted from her own pay, plus 4 1/2% interest compounded quarterly, but that is all she gets. Her payments and interest came to just over $12,000; the amount could be higher based on her last paycheck. Furthermore, since the amounts deducted were not considered taxable income, she will have to pay income tax on the money when she receives it.

You cannot process the check until after her resignation is effective, so you will mail it to her. You have her home address on file; if she's moving, she needs to let you know where to send the check. Processing the check may take two to three weeks.

Write a memo to Michelle.

C–20 SELLING SPORTS VIDEOS

You've started a business which you think has excellent potential: Sports Images, Incorporated. You've bought up the video rights for high school football and basketball regular season and championship games in your state and for your college's football and basketball regular season games.

The high school regular season games are mostly from tapes made by teams for their own scouting and review; some of the tapes don't have very good quality; all are in black and white. You have tapes for some schools going back to the 1940s. The boys' state championship games were filmed for TV coverage and go back to the 1950s. Quality is good; they're in color after 1973. You have girls' basketball state tournaments dating from 1975; you have girls' basketball regular season games from 1971.

The college games include both those filmed for TV and some filmed by the team for scouting and review. You have all the men's regular season games starting in 1948 and all the women's basketball regular season games starting in 1974. The games filmed for TV are in color after 1968; all of the games filmed for the teams' use are in black and white.

A full season is available in either VHS or Beta cassettes for $49.95 a season. You accept VISA and Discovery credit cards. Persons requesting high school games should check first to see if their school and year are available.

You've run an ad in the local paper with some success. But not everyone who played high school and college ball in your area still lives there. Each school has records of team members and coaches; some of the schools also have list of cheerleaders and band members. You can get current addresses for many of these people from the alumni association. Pick a target audience and write a one- to three-page letter urging people to order (for college games) or to call or send in a card to find out if the games they want are available (for high school games).

C–21 PERSUADING STUDENTS AND FACULTY TO USE CAMPUS RECREATION FACILITIES

Your boss, the Campus Director of Recreation, tells you to write a letter to go to all new and current students and faculty, telling them about the recreation facilities (buildings and programs) available on campus and persuading them to use them.

As your instructor directs,
   a. Prepare a brochure for one or more parts of the campus recreation program.
   b. Give a five- to seven-minute presentation on the campus recreation program to "a living unit on campus."
   c. Pick a target audience and write a letter persuading people in it to use the campus facilities.
   d. Write a press release about a specific recreation event.

Hints:
   • Even with a narrowly defined audience, you still need to stress several different benefits. Develop at least three to five of these in detail using psychological description.

   • Be sure to overcome people's objections. People may think that the racquetball courts are always taken, that they won't be able to swim laps because too many other people will be playing in the water, or that the facilities are reserved for classes. Faculty and older students may think that they'll look out of place among hundreds of 20-year-olds.

   • The people to whom exercise is essential are already getting it. How can you convince people who are "too busy" to make time for the formal and informal exercise you offer?

   • Use real information about the facilities, tournaments, lectures, counseling, coaching, and programs available on your campus.

C–22 ASKING FOR AN OFFICE WORKER
You're accounting manager for a medium-sized hospital. You supervise a staff of five people who bill patients and insurance companies, make out payroll checks, and write checks to pay for supplies, utilities, lab work which you send out, etc.

In addition to doing accounting work, you make bank deposits, get signatures on checks, and go to the Post Office to get the postage meter refilled—low-level jobs that someone else could do. They really wouldn't take that long—not more than 15 hours a month. However, the 15 hours aren't neatly divided into four hours every week. Some weeks you have little of this work to do; once a month you spend a whole day making deposits.

You talk to your staff to see if anyone has unused time. It turns out they're overworked, too, and have duties they'd like to get rid of. One of them spends a lot of time dealing with taxicab companies and overnight delivery companies. The person assigned to order, check, unpack, and distribute supplies feels that this time-con-

suming work is a waste of his college degree. They all say that they spend hours every month waiting in line at the copier.

There seems to be enough work for a half-time person (perhaps a college student?). The person would need to be reliable and, if he or she deposits money, bondable, but none of the duties require any particular knowledge or skill. At first, the person wouldn't save you time because you'd need to train him or her, but after just a week or two, having an assistant would really help.

As your instructor directs,
   a. Write a memo to the Administrative Director of the hospital, Wayne Mobin-Udin, asking for a half-time office worker.
   b. Write a job description for the position.

Hints
   • Every hospital in the country is trying to keep down costs. Your unit is functioning now without this extra person. How will delegating all these duties to an office worker enable your staff to improve the hospital's cash flow?

C–23 GETTING RECOMMENDATIONS FOR NEW SENIOR CPAs
Normally, senior CPAs at your Big Eight accounting firm "come up through the ranks." However, your firm is short-handed. You've been the subject of a favorable article in *Fortune*, which may partly account for the fact that you've just signed four new major clients, with several more companies considering you for their auditors.

Even before the influx of new business, last tax season was exhausting for partners, staff, and clerical help. You'd like to add a few senior CPAs to your audit staff by December 31. You'll advertise in the appropriate journals and papers, but you realize that your current staff members may also have suggestions. In addition, you want to allay fears. Staff accountants may be afraid that the hiring of senior accountants will slow their own career advancement. However, if the firm's business continues to grow, there will be ample room for everyone. You don't intend to hire outside people every year.

You're prepared to pay $1,000 to any employee who refers someone to you who is hired by December 31. Candidates must have excellent qualifications. They should have public accounting experience, either with a Big Eight firm or with a smaller CPA firm. Someone formerly with a CPA firm who is now working within a company would be acceptable. Naturally, you would not want one of your people to contact someone working with another CPA firm—large or small—unless that person had already indicated that he or she wanted to leave the current employer. And accountants on the staffs of companies you now audit should not be approached under any circumstances.

Write a memo to your professional staff, explaining your plans to hire additional senior accountants and asking them to help you locate qualified people. They should give the names of possible candidates to Pamela Jannot, Director of Personnel Management.

C-24 CLARIFYING THE TERMS OF A JOB OFFER

Last week, you got a job offer from your first choice company, and you accepted it over the phone. Today, the written confirmation arrived. The letter specifies the starting salary and fringe benefits you had negotiated. However, during the office visit, you were promised a 7% raise in six months. The job offer says nothing about the raise. You do want the job, but you want it on the terms you thought you had negotiated.

Write to your contact at the company, Frank Dunbar.

C-25 NEGOTIATING WITH YOUR EMPLOYER

You work part-time as a word-processing operator at a securities firm in town to help pay for your college expenses. You're scheduled to work from 5 P.M. to 8 P.M. Monday through Friday nights. However, you almost always have to work until 10 P.M. and sometimes have been there until 2 A.M. To make matters even worse, you don't know until you get to work how late you'll be, which makes it difficult to schedule homework and dates. You have morning classes, and when you work so late you don't have time to do your best work on assignments.

Your boss is a procrastinator. He often works late himself finishing correspondence and reports which always have to be on someone's desk at 9 A.M. the next day. You've tried explaining that you need a regular schedule and that you have work of your own to do, but he didn't seem to take your problems very seriously, and nothing has changed. You like the pay, the work conditions (but not the hours!), and the chance to work in a securities firm. You don't want to find another job. You do want your boss to be willing to recommend you when you graduate.

Develop a strategy to improve the situation.

As your instructor directs,
   a. Describe your strategy in a memo to your instructor.
   b. Team up with another student to role-play a discussion between you and your boss.

Hints:
   • What are the problems here?
   • What options do you have? Think of as many as possible.
   • Analyze your boss. What are his needs? Is there any way both of you can get what you want? Think of as many ways as possible and evaluate each of them.

C-26 WARNING EMPLOYEES ABOUT ROBBERIES

You're the manager of a store that stays open 24 hours. You want to warn employees about the danger of robberies, but you don't want them to become so scared that they quit or that they frighten customers.

You want employees to remember to take cash to the bank between 5 and 6 P.M. so that there is less in the register. Employees working after 10 P.M. should stay close to the floor during their breaks so that no one is left totally alone. If an armed robbery does occur, employees should cooperate with the robber, move slowly, and do as they are told. Employee safety is more important than the money. Employees should cooperate with the police and report any suspicious behavior. They should call the police if something is suspicious. Someone who is nervous may want to ask the police to make regular checks or to have a pre-arranged signal with other workers.

You've taken some precautions against thefts: the store is well lit and has large front windows so that a cruising police car could see any sign of trouble.

Prepare an announcement that will get workers' attention and make your points without unduly frightening people.

C-27 BRINGING IN MORE VISITORS AND NEW MEMBERS TO A CHURCH, SYNAGOGUE, OR TEMPLE

Your church, synagogue, or temple wants to bring in more visitors and to recruit more new members. Last year's New Member Outreach Committee compiled the following suggestions:

1. Use a series of mailings, since one letter may not be enough. Keep each letter short. Maybe have each letter list members who live near the recipient—one of them can sign it. Give the phone numbers too—people will be more willing to come if they know somebody.

2. Give people directions or a map. Tell them what time services start and where to park.

3. Need to have a separate mailing to recruit college students.

4. Have two different follow-up letters—one to use if the people did come after the first or second letter, one to use if they didn't.

5. We should tell them what we offer besides weekly worship.

As your instructor directs,

a. Write a series of four one-page letters to go to new residents.

b. Write a one-page flyer to be distributed to freshmen during orientation.

c. Write a letter to new graduate students who have been referred to you by their home church or synagogue.

d. Write a report recommending to the church, synagogue, or temple what changes it could make to be more appealing to visitors and new members.

e. Write a report recommending a marketing strategy that your church, synagogue, or temple could use to recruit new members.

Hints:

• What kind of neighborhood is your church, synagogue, or temple in? What kinds of people move in? How diverse are they? What are their needs and interests?

• You have no way of knowing whether new residents are of your faith or interested in religion at all, but in general, is belonging to a community of faith important to people near you? If it isn't, is there any way you could persuade them to at least visit you once?

• You'd like people to come to you, but the most important thing is that they find someplace to worship.

• Are there many synagogues or churches of your denomination in the area? Are people likely to go to a specific place of worship just because it is close? Would they drive half an hour to worship?

• How would you characterize your church, synagogue, or temple? What are your strengths? To what sorts of people do you appeal? What do you have to offer?

C–28 URGING THAT A DECISION BE REVERSED

You are Sales Manager of a company that makes industrial blowers used to circulate air in power plants, steel mills, coal mines, cement plants, and the like. For years you have had 40% of the power plant market, but less than 10% of other industrial markets. In the last

five years, new power plant construction has dropped sharply, cutting into your profits deeply. Industry analysts predict that power plant construction will not rise significantly in the '90s. Your only hope for a turnaround is to dramatically increase penetration into the other industrial markets.

As a cost-cutting measure, your president has announced a hiring freeze and has put a $3,000-a-month ceiling on travel expenses for each department. The cuts have received extensive press coverage in your town; the president is being portrayed in the media as a white knight who is curbing past excesses to make the company lean and mean for modern times. The metaphor is mixed, but it's good PR. The president is delighted by all the publicity and has begun seeking out speaking engagements to spread his philosophy.

You know the company has to cut costs, but you think it is penny-wise and pound-foolish to apply this policy equally to all departments. You have only two sales representatives who know anything about the non-power plant market. They have been sharing their expertise with fellow workers, but they don't know all the market segments, and they don't know all the customers even within the areas they cover. Besides, you feel, they should be out selling, not at home talking. You might as well have training meetings: with a limit of $3,000 a month for all travel, most of your sales representatives stay home most of the time anyway. But how are they going to sell—especially to new customers—if they don't visit potential customers?

You would like to hire three new sales representatives, each with experience in one industrial market. And you want to require your sales representatives to be on the road *at least* three days a week—no matter what the travel bills are. You feel that a knowledgeable, aggressive sales force is the key to sales, market share, and cash flow.

As your instructor directs,

a. Write a memo to the president, Remington Fairlamb Davis, IV, urging him to reverse his decision and approve the changes you want to make.

b. Role-play a meeting with the president in which you try to get him to approve the changes you want to make.

c. Prepare a presentation for the executive committee, persuading them to grant an exception for your department so that you can make the changes you want to make.

C–29 PLACATING AN ANGRY DONOR

Six months ago you accepted a position with a major charitable group in your town as Director of Giving. In that time, you've revamped the organization's direct mail fund-raising letters and started three new programs: follow-up letters to nondonors, letters persuading donors to increase their gifts or to make a monthly pledge, and meetings with wealthy people in town to try to persuade them to make major gifts.

You have been very successful. As a result of your efforts, the charity has raised enough money in the last six months not only to meet its goals for that time but also to pay off part of a deficit that was outstanding when you were hired. (The group, like many charities, had been operating in the red or on the edge of solvency for years.)

You are now in the middle of the group's Annual Campaign—a fund-raising drive that has, in the past, brought in 90% of the donations for the year. This year, you hope to increase the actual dollar giving to the Annual Campaign while at the same time reducing the percentage (since you have increased other kinds of giving).

In the mail yesterday morning was an angry letter:

> I have received a letter from [name of charity] expressing regret that I am not a donor for this year and urging me to contribute. I *am* a donor. I sent you a $100 check after I received your first letter three weeks ago. If you cannot keep decent records, I am not sure that you deserve my continued support. There are many worthwhile groups, and some of them seem to be better run than yours is.
>
> Please send me an apology and confirmation that you have received my check.
>
> Sincerely,
> [signed]
>
> (Mrs.) Marjorie Hamilton Humphreys

You have set up a system to send a second letter two or three weeks after the first arrives. A thank-you letter goes to people who have made gifts; a "we still need you" letter goes to people who have not yet given, trying to persuade them to make a gift. Evidently Mrs. Humphreys got the second letter instead of the first.

You're not sure how the mistake happened. Indeed, you're not sure that Mrs. Humphreys' check has been processed. The checks that came in through last Friday have already been deposited. But it's crucial to retain Mrs. Humphreys' good will. Only 38% of your donors give $100 or more a year. You're trying to raise that percentage, but in the meantime, you want to retain the donors you do have in that category.

Write a letter to Mrs. Humphreys.

Hints:
- Pick a charitable organization you're familiar with. The bad experience with her donation

seems to have expanded into a global distrust of the group. What can you do to persuade Mrs. Humphreys that your group deserves her support—and to build a foundation of goodwill for the future requests you'll make of her?
- How long would it take to find out if Mrs. Humphreys' check is being processed? Does the bank charge for this information?

C–30 ANSWERING THE PHONES BEFORE AND AFTER STATED WORK HOURS

You're Plant Manager of the Dallas office of a major manufacturing organization which has plants in 28 cities across the mainland United States. Office hours are 8:15 A.M. to 4:45 P.M. (These unusual hours, designed to help employees avoid the worst of the commuting rush, are standard in all the plants.) Today at 8:15 sharp you got a phone call from Jeff Ogden, Sales Manager in the Rochester office.

> "I called your office 10 minutes ago and was told by the person who answered the phone, 'We don't open till 8:15.' Now I work for the company and I'll call back. But what about a customer? OK, I got my time zones mixed up. But most places open at 8 or 9, not 8:15. I bet you get lots of calls between 8 and 8:15 and between 4:45 and 5—I know we do. If your people are going to answer the phone, they should be polite and take care of the caller's request. The experience really annoyed me—and I *like* this company. What effect would it have on someone to whom we were just another brand?"

As your instructor directs,
- a. Prepare a pep talk for the staff meeting next week to solve the problem.
- b. Prepare notes for discussion at the staff meeting on the best way to solve the problem.
- c. Write a memo to all employees to solve the problem.
- d. Write a memo to all the other plant managers reminding them about the problem, especially as it affects calls across time zones.
- e. Write a follow-up note to Jeff, telling him what you've done.

Hints:
- What are your options? Should you tell people not to answer the phone outside of regular hours? What are the disadvantages of doing that? Should you get some sort of answering machine? Can you get one big enough to store all messages a company could receive? How much would it cost? Is it feasible to pay some-

one to work an extra half hour a day or to stagger work times so that some people start at 8 and some people work till 5? The people who worked during those 15-minute periods between "normal" hours and your hours wouldn't be able to answer all possible questions. What should you ask them to do?

- What are the advantages in deciding on a solution to this problem and trying to persuade everyone to make the necessary changes? What are the advantages in asking the group to solve the problem? Which should you do?

C–31 GETTING MORE FOR YOUR DEPARTMENT

For some time now, it's seemed to you that your department isn't getting its fair share of the good things your organization provides. Your people seem to have to work harder and longer than do people in other departments to get promoted; requests from other departments seem to be filled more readily than your requests. You have to justify every request for money at great length; from what you've seen, other departments get by with much briefer justifications—and still get far more of what they ask for.

As your instructor directs,

a. Write a statement identifying one possible cause for this problem, outlining the changes (in perception or reality) that would be needed to solve it, and listing the various messages that could be used to solve it. For each message indicate the channel you'd use, the timing (consider the first message as day 1), your purposes and audience, and the general strategy you'd employ.

b. Write or deliver one or more of the messages described in *a.*

Hints:

- Pick a unit in an organization you know well. How necessary is your department to the organization's goals? Is your department's contribution obvious? Direct or indirect?

- A possible objection from management is that your people aren't as good, your requests are less essential, your projects have lower priority. How can you overcome that objection? Have the management personnel you must convince ever worked in your department? Do they have a clear idea of what you do? Do they have a realistic understanding of the difficulties you face?

- Do management personnel like you personally? If you decided that your department was

suffering because of a personality conflict between you and higher management, what would your options be? What should you do?

C–32 RESOLVING A PERSONNEL DILEMMA

You're the president of a medium-sized company that manufactures equipment used in oil drilling. With the drop in crude oil prices, demand for your equipment has dropped; the company has lost substantial sums in each of the last six years. You've already done the obvious things to save money, like reducing waste and replacing retiring employees with cheaper entry-level workers. You've also had to do some unpleasant things, like giving minimal pay raises, not replacing all employees who leave, and deferring scheduled maintenance.

An internal audit now recommends that you combine the jobs of Production Engineer and Line Supervisor. The most important aspects of the two jobs could be done by one person. Combining the two jobs would save the company $100,000 a year (salary, benefits, and taxes for social security, unemployment, and workers' compensation).

The current Line Supervisor is Edward Donnelly, a 54-year-old married man with two grown children. Ed has worked for the company for 23 years (longer than you have, in fact) and is third in terms of seniority. He has a high school education. He has taken an occasional night school class, but his knowledge of current technology is limited. The Production Engineer is Charles Gupta, a 35-year-old married man with one school-age child. Chuck has worked for the company for three years. He has a master's degree in Industrial Engineering and stays current with the field by attending professional meetings and reading professional journals. Chuck is the clear choice to fill the new position.

You have to tell Ed that his services are no longer needed, but you also need to decide how to handle his benefits. Laying Ed off would be cheapest: you'd have to give him two weeks' notice, but after two weeks your obligation to him would be over.

A second alternative would be to "offer" Ed early retirement. That might be kinder to his ego. Since Ed has not yet worked the 25 years required to receive full pension benefits, his retirement stipend would be small— only 40% of the full benefit amount. However, retired employees continue to be covered by the company's health plan for a year after retirement, so he'd have health insurance.

A third alternative would be to offer Ed early retirement and at the same time "buy up" the 20 months that remain until his 25-year anniversary. This alternative would cost the company $12,000 immediately, but it would entitle Ed to the full pension benefits he'd receive if he retired after 25 years of service.

Make a decision, and communicate it to Ed.

Hints:

- What are the financial implications for Ed? Under the laws of your state, could he receive unemployment compensation if he is laid off? If he did, would that exceed the partial pension payment?

- Your message is going to drastically restrict Ed's freedom. How can you help to re-establish a sense of freedom? Why is it important for you to minimize psychological reactance?

- Should you give the news to Ed orally or write to him? If it's oral, should you call him into your office or visit him on his turf? Even if you tell him orally, you'll still need to write a message to have a record.

C–33 SAYING *NO* TO THE CEO

You're in charge of scheduling the retirement banquet for Martha Rowland, who at the age of 67 is retiring as Correspondence Supervisor.

Martha has worked for your company for 40 years and has been in charge of the centralized clerical staff for 30 years. She supervised the installation of a central dictation system in 1963, the purchase of repeating typewriters in 1974, the installation of a dedicated word processing system in 1981, the purchase of PCs in 1983, and the installation of a local area network (LAN) with electronic mail in 1986. She understands and is interested in the equipment used to process information, and she's also good at dealing with people. Her staff are fiercely loyal to her. Though some of them have only high school degrees, they produce excellent work under her tutelage. The managers, supervisors, and sales people whose work is typed in the centralized unit respect her. She isn't tolerant of writers who blame transcriptionists for their sloppy diction or handwriting, and she's been known to lecture staff members for whom everything "has to be done in an hour," but she always tries to accommodate genuine rush jobs and emergencies. Hers is a difficult job, and she has done it superbly.

You expect most of the 300 people who work in your office to come to her retirement banquet. Since many people will bring a guest, the total could easily run to 400 people. You've been visiting hotels, restaurants, and caterers and asking senior staff members in the organization for suggestions on where to hold the banquet. You only wanted suggestions. But one person has taken it upon himself to make reservations—at a place which would be political suicide to use.

In your in-basket this morning was a note from Everett Downing, the company's President and CEO, saying that he had reserved the whole dining room at the Juniper Club for the last Friday evening next month. The Juniper Club is an elegant, exclusive club which counts as members many of the most powerful men in town—but only the men. Women are allowed as luncheon or dinner guests, but they may not join. You think it is ironic to hold Martha's banquet at a place that would exclude her and most of her subordinates.

Furthermore, several of your mid-level managers—men as well as women—have been urging that the company do more to hire and promote women and minorities. For years your company, like so many American businesses, expected that all its managers and executives would be white males. That has changed, but many of the older people (some of them in high places) still haven't figured out what "all the fuss is about." Although your company's record on affirmative action is better than that of some companies, your company has had one suit for sex discrimination (settled out of court) and some complaints of sexual harassment. You have no desire to create a major scandal by scheduling a company function at a club which discriminates on the basis of sex (or indeed on any other basis).

Let Everett Downing know why you do not think the Juniper Club is an appropriate place to hold Martha Rowland's retirement banquet.

Hints:

- Should you phone Everett, make an appointment to see him, or write him a memo?

- How well do you know Everett? Are you on a first-name basis with him? Does he even know who you are? How many organizational levels intervene between you and him?

- What are your own views on affirmative action and clubs that refuse to admit a specific class of people, whether the exclusion is based on sex, race, religion, or some other factor? Should you talk about your own views? Will you look as though you are spineless if you imply that the possibility of an outcry is your only reason for rejecting his suggestion?

- Should you cancel the reservation? Offer to cancel it for him? Ask him to cancel it himself?

C–34 RECOMMENDING WAYS THE COLLEGE BOOKSTORE CAN INCREASE SALES

You are co-owner of Redwood Market Research (RMR) which you and a friend founded two years ago. Most of your clients are local, but you've had a few statewide jobs and even three out-of-state contracts.

The college bookstore has hired you to see how it could increase sales to students and faculty. After three weeks of intense work, you've gathered the information which follows. Now you have to write a report for Henry Paxton, the Director of the Student Union. The Student

Union owns the bookstore and determines its policies. In some cases, the information you have is incomplete. You may add what you know about students and faculty on your campus, but your report must distinguish between recommendations that are just based on your own ideas and those that are supported by the research you have done.

Initial Questions

You started by brainstorming the following questions:

Who are the bookstore's competitors? Does it have a monopoly on textbooks?

What products does the bookstore carry now? How much room does it have to add new products? (Presumably it must still carry texts for classes.)

What sorts of products would students and faculty like to buy that they can't now get at the bookstore?

Why do people go to other stores to buy products that the bookstore sells? Are its hours convenient? Prices competitive? Shelves well-stocked? Sales people competent? Is there enough parking?

Would more or better advertising help? What sorts of advertising does the bookstore do now? What do its competitors do?

You gathered information three ways: interviews with bookstore employees, observation of the bookstore and its competitors, and a questionnaire mailed to students and faculty.

Interviews with Bookstore Employees

You told one of your employees to interview the manager and at least two of the employees to find out their perceptions of (1) the bookstore's competitors, (2) what current items bring in the most money, (3) how much space could be made for new merchandise, and (4) the improvements they would like to see implemented. Your employee gave you the following summary:

1. Interview with Karen Sweeney, manager. Karen has been manager for three years, has worked at the bookstore eight years. She says that Walton's also carries texts and gets about 45% of the textbook sales. In terms of supplies (paper, calculators, etc.), the college store's competitors are Walton's and the Campus Drug Store. (Apparently it carries all kinds of things, not just drugs and sundries.) Several stores on campus carry insignia clothing and merchandise. She thinks this is a lucrative market and would like to carry more of such items. In terms of paperback books (not texts), the store has a small selection which doesn't sell well. Faculty tend to buy supplies and paperbacks off campus. Space is tight: if they add much, they'll have to drop something they now carry. Doesn't want to add product lines that require expertise to sell; most employees are students.

2. Interview with John Laskey, stock clerk. John has worked in the bookstore part-time for 18 months. He says the store is a real zoo at the beginning of each term. The store doesn't hire enough employees. During the rush when classes start, shelves aren't restocked frequently enough, students have to wait in line for up to an hour to pay for their books, and students have trouble finding the books they need. The shelves are marked, but the overall plan isn't clear to people who don't know the bookstore well. He would like to see many more people hired just for the rush at the beginning of the term, and a few more people hired at the end of each term to help with book buy-backs and restocking the shelves for the next term. He says it might be hard to find people for the end of the term because people are busy with papers and exams and don't want to work then. Indeed, lots of the employees the bookstore does have try to cut back on their hours then.

3. Interview with Cheryl Englehart, cash register clerk. Mrs. Englehart has worked full-time in the bookstore for four years. She agrees that check-out lines at the beginning of each term are a disaster, but points out that there are times during the term when the cash register clerks don't have anything to do. She isn't sure that hiring people just for the beginning of the term would work. "The computer cash registers are complicated; not just anyone can use them." (I'm not sure she's right.) She notes that during the term, people seem to come in for one or two items they've forgotten rather than for a list of several things. The store does offer book covers, wastebaskets, and desk lamps with the college logo; these are good sellers and often are impulse purchases.

Observation

You told one of your employees to compare products and sample prices at the book store and at two of its competitors near campus. The employee gave you the following information:

The prices on items that all three stores carry are comparable. The bookstore has higher prices on calculators because it offers more sophisticated calculators; on models that both the college bookstore and Walton's carry, the price is within $1.

Both the college bookstore and Walton's stock texts for all classes. All three stores carry basic supplies: paper, pencils, pens, notebooks and report covers, etc. Their selection of items other than texts and basic supplies varies widely:

	College Bookstore	Walton's Bookstore	Campus Drug Store
Selection of reference books			
Job hunting	good	good	good
Dictionaries, style sheets	good	good	—
Selection of paperback books			
Science fiction	a few	good	good
Murder mysteries	—	good	good
Best sellers	a few	good	a few
Other fiction	some	—	—
Other nonfiction	—	good	—
Items with insignia or logos			
Clothing	—	good	good
Office supplies	a few	good	good
Gift items	a few	good	good
Greeting cards	—	good	good
Magazines	—	good	good
Candy and snacks	—	good	good

One thing that I observed was that the college bookstore looks pretty crowded. Walton's has an airier feel, probably because the ceilings are higher. (I think the aisles are just as close together.) It's interesting to me that the Campus Drug Store is really dingy. It looks like an oversized mom-and-pop store, but evidently it's very successful. Both the college bookstore and Walton's have lockers for people to use while they're in the stores.

Questionnaire

You constructed the following questionnaire which two employees then conducted by phone. You helped them construct a template to take a systematic random sample based on the *Student Telephone Directory* published by the college. You chose 150 numbers and instructed your employees to make two call-backs to any number that did not answer. The final tally is based on 113 responses.

Bookstore Service Survey

The following questionnaire is designed to allow us to give you better service. All responses will be kept confidential.

Please evaluate each of the following areas on a scale of 1 to 5, where 1 is the lowest score, and 5 is the highest score possible.

1. Availability of coursebooks
   low 1 2 3 4 5 high
2. Availability of used books
   low 1 2 3 4 5 high
3. Availability of supplies
   low 1 2 3 4 5 high
4. Availablity of general reading books
   low 1 2 3 4 5 high
5. Availability of reference books
   low 1 2 3 4 5 high
6. Selection of merchandise
   low 1 2 3 4 5 high
7. Friendliness of staff
   low 1 2 3 4 5 high
8. Knowledge of staff
   low 1 2 3 4 5 high
9. Appearance of store
   low 1 2 3 4 5 high
10. Convenience of shopping here
    low 1 2 3 4 5 high
11. Quality of merchandise
    low 1 2 3 4 5 high
12. Prices
    low 1 2 3 4 5 high
13. General opinion of store
    low 1 2 3 4 5 high
14. When you know that you could get something either at the college bookstore or at another store, where would you be more likely to buy it? (If answer is "the college bookstore":) What do you like about the bookstore? (If answer is "another store":) Why do you like the other store better?
15. What changes would you like to see the bookstore make?
16. What additional products would you like to see the bookstore carry?
17. Do you have any additional comments or suggestions?

Thank you!

Tally of Responses to Questionnaire

Questions 1–13: average of 113 responses, where 1 = low, 5 = high.

Q1. 3.4

Q2. 3.3

Q3. 4.3

Q4. 2.6

Q5. 3.6

Q6. 1.5

Q7. 2.5

Q8. 1.9

Q9. 3.2

Q10. 2.6

Q11. 2.9

Q12. 3.1

Q13. 3.2

Q14.   Buy it at the College Bookstore: 32%

Reasons: Close.

Saves time.

On my way to class.

I have a friend who works there.

Buy it at Walton's: 42%

Reasons: Better selection.

I can charge things.

Closer to where I live.

I like to browse to see what's new.

I can buy everything I need at one stop—the college bookstore only carries part of what I buy.

Buy it at the Campus Drug Store: 26%

Reasons: Better selection.

I like to look at the magazines.

I can get everything I need in one stop.

I like the owners.

Responses to Open-Ended Questions on Questionnaire

Changes Needed

Have free parking.

Get in more books. Last summer I had to come back three times before I could get one of the books I needed for a class.

It takes too long to pay for books.

Personnel are snobs.

Bring down prices a bit and you'll see me much more often!

I can't find the books I want. And the staff don't seem to know where things are, either.

Products Desired

Carry sweatshirts, T-shirts, and shorts with campus logos.

I'd like to be able to buy inexpensive gifts.

Why don't you carry more books? I really like science fiction.

I would buy greeting cards there if you carried them.

Additional Comments

Books are much too expensive. I spent $100 on books for my classes this term, and I'm going to school part-time.

There's no place to park.

Why don't you stay open later? I usually shop on Saturdays.

I think there is already too much junk in this town tempting students to spend money on things they don't need. I hope you won't add Garfield posters and beer steins. We don't need any more of them.

Tell the college to lower tuition and fees and the campus stores to lower their prices. Everybody here is trying to gouge us. I am not made of money!

I would like to see you stock nice things I could buy for gifts for friends.

Why don't you sell computers and software?

Assignment

Write a formal report recommending any changes the bookstore should make.

GLOSSARY

A

Abstract or **Executive Summary** A summary of a report, specifying the recommendations and the reasons for them.

Acknowledgment Responses Nods, smiles, frowns, and words that let a speaker know you are listening.

Active Listening Feeding back the literal meaning or the emotional content or both so that the speaker knows that the listener has heard and understood.

Active Verb A verb which describes the action of the grammatical subject of the sentence.

Adjustment The response to a claim letter. If the company agrees to grant a refund, the amount due will be adjusted.

Administrative Management Society (AMS) Simplified Letter Format Letter format which omits the salutation, the complimentary close, and the writer's signature; uses a subject line; lines up everything at the left margin; and puts the writer's typed name in full capital letters.

Alliteration A sound pattern occurring when several syllables begin with the same sound.

Allness The semantic error of assuming it is possible to know or communicate everything that is important about a topic.

Annual Report A report distributed to stockholders and other audiences summarizing the firm's financial performance and achievements during the year; a document with informative, persuasive, and goodwill purposes.

Areas of Acceptance Positions close to the audience's own beliefs, any one of which they could easily accept.

Areas of Noncommitment Positions on which the audience has no preconceived beliefs.

Areas of Rejection Positions which the audience will not consider.

Argument The reasons or logic offered to persuade the audience.

Assumptions Section in the Introduction of a report listing statements which are not proven, but on which the recommendations are based.

B

Bar Graph A visual consisting of parallel bars or rectangles which represent specific sets of data.

Blind Ads Job listings which do not list the company's name.

Blindering Imposing limits that do not exist in reality.

Block Format (1) A letter format in which inside address, date, and signature block are lined up at the left margin. (2)

A format for résumés in which dates are listed in one column and job titles and descriptions in another. This format emphasizes work history.

Body Language Nonverbal communication conveyed by posture and movement, eye contact, facial expressions, and gestures.

Boilerplate Language from a previous document that a writer includes in a new document. Writers use boilerplate both to save time and energy and to use language which has already been approved by the organization's legal staff.

Branching Question Question that sends respondents who answer differently to different parts of the questionnaire. Allows respondents to answer only those questions which are relevant to their experience.

Bridge In Toulmin logic, the general principle which authorizes making the step between the claim and the evidence in an argument.

Buffer A neutral or positive statement designed to allow the writer to bury, or buffer, the negative message.

Build Goodwill To create a good image of yourself and of your organization—the kind of image that makes people want to do business with you.

Bullets Large round dots that set off items in a list. When you are giving examples, but the number is not exact and the order does not matter, use bullets to set off items.

Businessese A kind of jargon including unnecessary words or "deadwood." Some words were common two or three hundred years ago but are no longer part of spoken English. Some have never been used outside of business writing. All of these terms should be omitted.

Business Slang Terms that have technical meanings but which are used in more general senses. Used sparingly, these terms are appropriate in job application letters and in messages for people in the same organization, who are likely to share the vocabulary.

Buying Time with Limited Agreement Agreeing with the small part of a criticism which one does accept as true.

Bypassing Miscommunication that occurs when two people use the same symbol to mean different things.

C

Centralized Dictation System A system in which employees dictate messages into desk or handheld units or over the phone. The messages are received in a centralized unit where transcriptionists type them into word-processing equipment.

Central Selling Point A super reader benefit, big enough to motivate readers by itself, but also serving as an umbrella to cover other benefits and to unify the message.

Chain The body of a direct mail letter, providing the logical and emotional links that move readers from interest to the action the writer wants.

Channel The physical means by which a message is sent. Written channels include memos, letters, and billboards. Oral channels include phone calls, speeches, and face-to-face conversations.

Channel Overload The inability of a channel to carry all the messages that are being sent.

Chartjunk Decoration which is irrelevant to a visual and which may be misleading.

Checking for Feelings Identifying the emotions which the previous speaker seems to be expressing verbally or nonverbally.

Checking for Inferences Trying to identify the unspoken content or feelings implied by what the previous speaker has actually said.

Choice or **Selection** The decision to include or omit information in a message.

Chronological Résumé A résumé which lists what you did in a time line, starting with the most recent events and going backwards in reverse chronology.

Citation Attributing a quotation or other idea to a source in the body of the report.

Claim In Toulmin logic, the part of an argument that the speaker or writer wants the audience to agree with.

Claim Letter A letter seeking a replacement or refund.

Clear A message whose audience gets the meaning the writer or speaker intended.

Closed or **Defensive Body Position** Keeping the arms and legs crossed and close to the body. Suggests physical and psychological discomfort, defending oneself, and shutting the other person out.

Closed Question Question with a limited number of possible responses.

Closure Report A report summarizing completed research that does not result in action or recommendation.

Cognitive Dissonance Having two ideas which conflict. The theory of cognitive dissonance explains that people will resolve dissonance by deciding that one of the ideas is less important, by rejecting one of the ideas, or by constructing a third idea which has room for both of the conflicting ideas.

Collaborative Writing Working with other writers to produce a single document.

Collection Series A series of letters asking customers to pay for goods and services they have already received. Early letters in the series assume that the reader intends to pay; final letters threaten legal action if the bill is not paid.

Comma Splice or **Comma Fault** Using a comma to join two independent clauses. To correct, use a semicolon, subordinate one of the clauses, or use a period and start a new sentence.

Common Ground Values and goals that the writer or speaker and audience share.

Communication Theory A theory explaining what happens when we communicate and where miscommunication can occur.

Complaint Letter A letter that challenges a policy or tries to get a decision changed.

Complete A message which answers all of the audience's questions. The audience has enough information to evaluate the message and act on it.

Complimentary Close The words after the body of the letter before the signature.

Conflict Resolution Strategies for getting at the real issue, keeping discussion open, and minimizing hurt feelings so that people can find a solution which feels good to everyone involved.

Connotation The emotional colorings or associations that accompany a word.

Convenience Sample A group of subjects who are easy to get.

Conversational Style Conversational patterns such as speed and volume of speaking, pauses between speakers, whether questions are direct or indirect. When different speakers assign different meanings to a specific pattern, miscommunication results.

Coordination The third stage in the life of a task group, when the group finds, organizes, and interprets information and examines alternatives and assumptions. This is the longest of the four stages.

Correct A message whose information is accurate and which is free from errors in punctuation, spelling, grammar, word order, and sentence structure.

Credibility The audience's response to the source of the message; believability.

Cutaway Drawings or **Schematic Diagrams** Line drawings which depict the hidden or interior portions of an object.

D

Daisy Wheel Printer A computer printer that functions like a fast typewriter. A wheel with a slight resemblance to a daisy spins around and the petal with the appropriate letter hits the ribbon.

Data Base A computer program which organizes data in categories which the user can then manipulate to get the information he or she needs.

Decision Trees A branching chart of sequential questions with different paths depending on the answer to each question, designed to allow users to find the best solution quickly.

Decode To extract meaning from symbols.

Decorative Visual A visual which makes the speaker's points more memorable but which does not convey numerical data.

Dedicated Word Processors Machines that can do only word processing.

Defensive Body Position Keeping the arms and legs crossed and close to the body. Suggests physical and psychological discomfort, defending oneself, and shutting other people out.

Demographic Characteristics Measurable features of an audience that can be counted objectively: age, sex, race, education level, income, etc.

Denotation A word's literal or "dictionary" meaning. Most common words in English have more than one denotation. Context usually makes it clear which of several meanings is appropriate.

Dependent Clause A group of words containing a subject and a verb but which cannot stand by itself as a complete sentence.

Descriptive Abstract A listing of the topics an article or report covers which tells how thoroughly each topic is treated but which does not summarize what is said about each topic.

Descriptors Words describing the content of an article used to permit computer searches for information on a topic.

Direct Mail A form of direct marketing which uses letters to ask for an order, inquiry, or contribution directly from the reader.

Direct Request A pattern of organization which makes the request directly in the first and last paragraphs.

Documentation Providing full bibliographical information so that interested readers can go to the original source of material used in a report.

Document Design The process of writing, organizing, and laying out a document so that it can be easily used by the intended audience.

Dot Matrix Printer A computer printer which uses a pattern of dots to form each letter.

E

Editing Checking the draft to see that it satisfies the requirements of good English and the principles of business writing. Unlike revisions, which can produce major changes in meaning, editing focuses on the surface of writing.

Ego-Involvement The emotional commitment the audience has to its position.

Elimination of Alternatives A pattern of organization for reports which discusses the problem and its causes, the impractical solutions and their weaknesses, and finally the solution the writer favors.

E-mail or **Electronic Mail** A mail system that uses computer terminals to bypass paper. Messages are composed on a computer screen; the recipient reads the message on screen. E-mail requires that both sender and receiver have computer terminals and that both be on the same E-mail system.

Emotional Appeal Making the audience want to do what the writer or speaker asks.

Empathy The ability to put oneself in someone else's shoes, to *feel with* that person.

Encode To put ideas into symbols.

Enunciate To voice all the sounds of each word while speaking.

Evaluating In the writing process, measuring the draft against your goals and the requirements of the situation and audience. Anything produced during each stage of the writing process can be evaluated, not just the final draft.

Evidence In Toulmin logic, facts or data which the audience already accepts.

Executive Summary A summary of a report, specifying the recommendations and the reasons for them.

Expectancy Theory A theory which argues that motivation is based on the expectation of being rewarded for performance and the importance of the reward.

Extensionalism Inspecting and responding to reality itself.

External Documents Documents that go to people in another organization.

External Report Report written by a consultant for an organization of which he or she is not a permanent employee.

Extrinsic Benefits Benefits which are "added on"; they are not a necessary part of the product or action.

F

Facsimile or **Fax Machine** Machine that can send a copy of a document to another location in less than a minute. Fax machines may be stand-alone machines or part of a computer.

Fact In semantics, a statement that you yourself have verified.

Feasibility Study A report which evaluates two or more possible alternatives and recommends one of them. Doing nothing is always one alternative.

Feedback The receiver's response to a message.

Figure Any visual that is not a table.

Five W's and H Questions that must be answered early in a press release: who, what, when, where, why, and how.

Flesch "Reading Ease Scale" A readability formula which determines reading ease (measured on a 0 to 100 scale) by subtracting multiples of average words per sentence and average syllables per word from 206.835.

Flow Chart A chart representing each subprocess and decision point in a process.

Forced Choice A choice in which each item is ranked against every other item. Used to discover which of a large number of criteria are crucial.

Form Letter A letter which is sent unchanged or with only minor modifications to a large number of readers.

Formalization The fourth and last stage in the life of a task group, when the group makes and formalizes its decision.

Formal Meetings Meetings run under strict rules, like the rules of parliamentary procedure summarized in *Robert's Rules of Order*.

Formal Report A report containing formal elements such as a title page, a transmittal, a table of contents, and an abstract.

Format The parts of a document and the way they are arranged on a page.

Formation The second stage in the life of a task group, when members choose a leader and define the problem they must solve.

Foundation In Toulmin logic, a statement proving the truth of a bridge.

Freewriting A kind of writing uninhibited by any constraints. Freewriting may be useful in overcoming writer's block, among other things.

Frozen Evaluation An assessment which does not take into account the possibility of change.

G

Gathering Physically getting the background data you need. It can include informal and formal research or simply getting the letter to which you're responding.

General Semantics The study of the ways behavior is influenced by the words and other symbols used to communicate.

General Slang Words or phrases such as *awesome, heavy,* or *at the end of my rope* which are sometimes used in conversations and in presentations, but which are not appropriate in business and administrative writing since they appear sloppy or imprecise.

Gerund The *-ing* form of a verb; grammatically, a verb used as a noun.

Getting Feedback Asking someone else to evaluate your work. Feedback is useful at every stage of the writing process, not just during composition of the final draft.

Goodwill Ending Shift of emphasis away from the message to the reader. A goodwill ending is positive, personal, and forward-looking and suggests that serving the reader is the real concern.

Goodwill Presentation A presentation which entertains and validates the audience.

Grammar Checker Software program that flags errors or doubtful usage.

Grid System A means of designing layout by imposing columns on a page and lining up graphic elements within the columns.

Groupthink The tendency for a group to reward agreement and directly or indirectly punish dissent.

Gunning "Fog Index" A readability formula which determines level of education necessary for comprehension by multiplying average words per sentence by percentage of difficult words by .4.

H

Hard Copy The paper copy of what is recorded on a word processor.

Hardware The computer and other equipment necessary for computer technology.

Headings Words or short phrases which group points and divide your letter, memo, or report into sections.

Hearing Perceiving sounds.

Hidden Job Market Jobs that are never advertised but which may be available or may be created for the right candidate.

Hidden Negatives Words that are not negative in themselves, but become negative in context.

Histogram A bar graph using pictures, asterisks, or points to represent units of data.

Hook The action close of a direct mail letter, which harnesses the motivation you have created and turns it into action.

I

Immediate Audience The audience which assigns the message and routes it to other audiences. Most immediate audiences choose which messages to send on; they serve as gatekeepers.

Impersonal Construction A sentence which attributes actions to inanimate objects, designed to avoid placing blame on a reader.

Indented Format A format for résumés in which items that are logically equivalent begin at the same horizontal space, with carry-over lines indented three spaces. Indented format emphasizes job titles.

Independent Clause A group of words which can stand by itself as a complete sentence.

Inference A statement which has not yet been verified, but whose truth or falsity could be established, either now or in the future.

Infinitive The form of the verb which is preceded by *to.*

Inform To explain something or tell the audience something.

Informal Meetings Loosely run meetings in which votes are not taken on every point.

Informal Report A report using letter or memo format.

Information Interview An interview in which you talk to someone who works in the area you hope to enter to find out what the day-to-day work involves and how you can best prepare to enter that field.

Information Overload The inability of a human receiver to process all the messages he or she receives.

Information Report A report that collects data for the reader but that does not recommend action.

Informative or **Talking Heads** Headings which are detailed enough to provide an overview of the material in the sections they introduce.

Informative Message Message to which the reader's basic reaction will be neutral.

Informative Presentation A presentation which informs or teaches the audience.

Instructions Step-by-step information about how to perform actions that one person does.

Intensionalism An unconscious response to a symbol rather than reality.

Internal Documentation Providing information about a source in the text itself rather than in footnotes or endnotes.

Internal Documents Documents written for other employees in the same organization.

Internal Reports Reports written by employees for use only in their organization.

Interpersonal Communication Communication between people that focuses on feelings and relationships.

Interpret To determine the significance or importance of a message.

Intrinsic Benefits Benefits which come automatically from using a product or doing something.

J

Jargon There are two kinds of jargon. The first kind is the specialized terminology of a technical field. The second is Businessese, outdated words which do not have technical meanings and which are not used in other forms of English.

Judgment or **Opinion** A statement which can never be verified, since it includes terms that cannot be measured objectively.

Judgment Sample A group of subjects whose views seem useful.

Justified Margins Margins which end evenly on the right side of the page.

K

Key Words or **Descriptors** Words describing the content of an article used to permit computer searches for information on a topic.

L

Laser Printer A computer printer that uses electrophotography to produce images. Laser printers are faster than both daisy wheel and dot matrix printers and produce sharp, easy-to-read letters.

Lead An attention-getting statement opening a press release.

Letterhead Stationery with the organization's name, logo, address, and telephone number printed on the page.

Limit Boundary placed on a claim which cannot be made with 100% certainty.

Limitations Problems or factors that limit the validity of the recommendations of a report.

Line Graph A visual consisting of lines which show trends or which allow the viewer to interpolate values between the observed values.

Listening Decoding and interpreting sounds correctly.

M

Mailing List The list of names and addresses to which a direct mail letter is sent.

Main or **Independent Clause** A group of words which can stand by itself as a complete sentence.

Maslow's Hierarchy of Needs Five levels of human need posited by Abraham H. Maslow. They include physical needs, the need for safety and security, for love and belonging, for esteem and recognition, and for self-actualization.

Merge Program A computer software program which allows the user to combine a form letter with a list of names and addresses to produce individually typed, personalized letters.

Methods Section The section of a report or survey describing how the data was gathered.

Mirror Question Question which paraphrases the content of the answer an interviewee gave to the last question.

Mixed Abstract An abstract which has characteristics of both summary and descriptive abstracts: it contains the thesis or recommendation and proof, but also contains statements about the article or report.

Mixed Punctuation Using a colon after the salutation and a comma after the complimentary close in a letter.

Modem A device which can be attached to a computer and which translates computer signals into signals which can be carried over phone lines.

Modified Block Format A letter format in which the inside address, date, and signature block are lined up with each other $1/2$ or $2/3$ of the way over on the page.

Monochronic Culture Culture in which people do only one important activity at a time.

Myers-Briggs Type Indicator A scale which categorizes people on four dimensions: introvert–extrovert; sensing–intuitive; thinking–feeling; and perceiving–judging.

N

Negative Message A message in which basic information conveyed is negative; the reader is expected to be disappointed or angry.

Noise Any physical or psychological interference in a message.

Nonsexist Language Language that treats both sexes neutrally, that does not make assumptions about the proper gender for a job, and that does not imply that men are superior to or take precedence over women.

Nonverbal Communication Communication that does not use words.

Normal Interview A job interview with some questions that the interviewer expects to be easy, some questions that present an opportunity to showcase strong points, and some questions that probe any weaknesses evident from the résumé.

O

Omnibus Motion A motion which allows a group to vote on several related items in a single vote. Saves time in formal meetings with long agendas.

Open Body Position Keeping the arms and legs uncrossed and away from the body. Suggests physical and psychological comfort and openness.

Open Punctuation Using no punctuation after the salutation and the complimentary close.

Open Question Question with an unlimited number of possible responses.

Opinion A statement which can never be verified, since it includes terms that cannot be measured objectively.

Organization As a characteristic of messages, the order in which ideas are arranged in a message.

Orientation The first stage in the life of a task group, when members meet and begin to define their task.

Original or **Primary Research** Research which gathers new information.

Originator The person who sent the original message recorded and processed by a centralized dictation unit.

P

Package The outer envelope and everything that goes in it in a direct mailing.

Parallel Structure Putting words or ideas that share the same role in the sentence's logic in the same grammatical form.

Paraphrase To repeat in your own words the verbal content of what the previous speaker said.

Passive Verb A verb which describes action done to the grammatical subject of the sentence.

Perception The act of seeing, hearing, tasting, smelling, touching.

Performance Appraisals Supervisors' written evaluations of their subordinates.

Persona (1) The "author" or character who allegedly writes a letter; (2) the voice that a writer assumes in creating a document.

Personal Space The distance someone wants between him- or herself and other people in ordinary, non-intimate interchanges.

Personalized Letter A form letter which is adapted to the individual reader by including the reader's name and address and perhaps other information.

Persuade To motivate and convince the audience to act.

Persuasive Presentation A presentation which motivates the audience to act or to believe.

Pictograph or **Histogram** A bar graph using pictures, asterisks, or points to represent units of the data.

Pie Chart A circular chart whose sections represent percentages of a given quantity.

Planning All the thinking done about a subject and the means of achieving your purposes. Planning takes place not only when devising strategies for the document as a whole, but also when generating "miniplans" that govern sentences or paragraphs.

Polarization A logical fallacy which argues that there are only two possible positions, one of which is clearly unacceptable.

Polychronic Culture Culture in which people do several things at once.

Population The group a researcher wants to make statements about.

Positive Emphasis Focusing on the positive rather than the negative aspects of a situation.

Positive or **Good News Message** Message to which the reader's reaction will be positive.

Post Office Abbreviations Two-letter abbreviations for states and provinces.

Prepositions Words that indicate relationships, for example, *with, in, under, at.*

Presenting Problem The problem which surfaces as the subject of disagreement. The presenting problem is often not the real problem.

Press Release Message which packages information about a company which the writer would like announced in local or national media.

Primary Audience The audience who will make a decision or act on the basis of a message.

Primary Research Research which gathers new information.

Pro and Con Pattern A pattern of organization for reports which presents all the arguments for an alternative and then all the arguments against it.

Probe Question A follow-up question designed to get more information about an answer or to get at specific aspects of a topic.

Problem-Solving Persuasion A pattern of organization which describes a problem which affects the reader before offering a solution to the problem.

Procedural Messages Messages that focus on the methods a group uses.

Procedures Information about how to perform actions that involve several different people at various stages.

Process of Writing What people actually do when they write. Most researchers would agree that the writing process can include eight parts: planning, gathering, writing, evaluating, getting feedback, revising, editing, and proofreading.

Product of Writing The final written document.

Progress Report A statement of the work done during a period of time and the work proposed for the next period.

Proofreading Checking the final copy to see that it's free from typographical errors.

Proposal A document proposing that the writer undertake research on a topic or provide a product or service for a specific fee.

Prospecting Letter A job application letter written to companies which have not announced openings but where you'd like to work.

Psychographic Data Human characteristics which are qualitative rather than quantitative: values, beliefs, goals, and lifestyles.

Psychological Description Description of a product or service in terms of reader benefits.

Psychological Reactance Phenomenon occurring when a reader reacts to a negative message by asserting freedom in some other arena.

Purpose Statement A paragraph in a report summarizing the organizational problem the report addresses, the technical investigations it summarizes, and the rhetorical purpose of the report (to explain, to recommend).

Q

Questionnaire List of questions for people to answer in a survey.

R

Ragged Right or **Unjustified Margins** Margins which do not end evenly on the right side of the page.

Random Cluster Sample A random sample of subjects at each of a random sample of locations. This method is faster and cheaper when face-to-face interviews are required.

Random Sample A sample for which each person of the population theoretically has an equal chance of being chosen.

Reader Benefits Benefits or advantages that the reader gets by using the writer's services, buying the writer's products, following the writer's policies, or adopting the writer's ideas. Reader benefits can exist for policies and ideas as well as for goods and services.

Rebuttal The refutation of a counter-argument.

Recommendation Report A report that recommends action.

Referral Interview Interviews you schedule to learn about current job opportunities in your field and to get referrals to other people who may have the power to create a job for you. Useful for tapping into unadvertised jobs and the hidden job market.

Request To ask the audience to take an easy or routine action.

Request for Proposal or **RFP** A statement of the service or product that an agency wants; a bid for proposals to provide that service or product.

Respondents The people who fill out a questionnaire.

Response Rate The percentage of subjects receiving a questionnaire who agree to answer the questions.

Résumé A persuasive summary of your qualifications for employment.

Revising Making changes in the draft: adding, deleting, substituting, or rearranging. Revision can be changes in single words, but more often it means major additions, deletions, or substitutions, as the writer measures the draft against purpose and audience and reshapes the document to make it more effective.

RFP A statement of the service or product that an agency wants; a bid for proposals to provide that service or product.

Rhyme Repetition of the final vowel sounds, and if the words end with consonants, the final consonant sounds.

Rhythm The repetition of a pattern of accented and unaccented syllables.

Rule of Three The rule explaining that when a series of three items are logically parallel, the last will receive the most emphasis.

S

Salutation The greeting in a letter: "Dear Ms. Smith."

Sample The portion of the population a researcher actually studies.

Saves the Reader's Time A message whose style, organization, and visual impact helps the reader to read, understand, and act on the information as quickly as possible.

Schematic Diagrams Line drawings which depict the hidden portions of an object.

Scope Statement A statement in a report specifying the subjects the report covers and how broadly or deeply it covers them.

Secondary Audience The audience affected by the decision or action. These people may be asked by the primary audience to comment on a message or to implement ideas after they've been approved.

Secondary Letters Additional letters in a direct mail package. Often on smaller paper, these letters may be to readers who have decided not to accept the offer, from people who have benefited from the charity in the past, and from recognized people corroborating the claims made in the main letter.

Secondary Research Research retrieving data someone else gathered.

Semantic Triangle A triangle without a base, a graphic portrayal of the idea that people provide the only connection between words and things.

Semantics or **General Semantics** The study of the ways behavior is influenced by the words and other symbols used to communicate.

Sentence Outline An outline using complete sentences which lists the sentences that prove the thesis and the points proving each of those sentences. A sentence outline is the basis for a summary abstract.

Sexist Interview A stress interview in which questions are biased against one sex. Many sexist questions mask a legitimate concern. The best strategy is to respond as you would to a stress question: rephrase it and treat it as a legitimate request for information.

Signpost An explicit statement of the place that a speaker or writer has reached: "Now we come to the third point."

Simple Random Sample A random sample generated by using a list of all members of a population and a random digit table.

Simplified Letter Format Letter format which omits the salutation, the complimentary close, and the writer's signature; uses a subject line; lines everything up at the left margin; and puts the writer's typed name in full capital letters.

Skills Résumé A résumé organized around the skills you've used, rather than the date or the job in which you used them.

Software A computer program, usually sold on a disk, which performs a specific task.

Solicited Letter A job letter written when you know that the company is hiring.

Spreadsheet A computer program which sets up financial or other formulas and allows the user to change variables to see how they would affect the outcome.

Star The attention-getting opener of a direct mail letter.

Stereotyping Putting similar people or events into a single category, even though significant differences exist.

Strategy A plan for reaching your specific goals with a specific audience.

Stratified Random Sample A sample generated by first dividing the sample into the same proportion of subgroups as exists in the population and then taking a random sample for each subgroup. This method enables a researcher to be sure that all important subgroups are included in the sample.

Stress Emphasis given to one or more words in a sentence.

Stress Interview A job interview which deliberately puts the applicant under stress, physical or psychological. Here it's important to change the conditions that create physical stress and to meet psychological stress by rephrasing questions in less inflammatory terms and treating them as requests for information.

Strong Verbs Verbs which help to convey information forcefully or more clearly than verb strings or nouns.

Structured Interview An interview which follows a detailed list of questions prepared in advance.

Subject Line The title of the document, used to file and retrieve the document. A subject line tells readers why they need to read the document and provides a framework in which to set what you're about to say.

Subjects The people studied in an experiment, focus group, or survey.

Subordinate or **Dependent Clause** A group of words containing a subject and a verb but which cannot stand by itself as a complete sentence.

Success Consciousness Projecting a tone of confidence in yourself, your products or services, or your organization.

Summary Abstract The logical skeleton of an article or report, containing the thesis or recommendation and its proof.

Survey A method of getting information from a large group of people.

Systematic Random Sample A random sample generated by setting up a template for a random entry on a page, choosing a random interval, and then taking the name at that entry on every page at the interval. A systematic random sample is often used when the researcher has a phone book.

T

Table Numbers or words arrayed in rows and columns.

Target Audience The audience one tries to reach with a mailing: people who are likely to be interested in buying the product, using the service, or contributing to the cause.

Teaser Copy Words written on the envelope to get the reader's attention and persuade him or her to open the envelope.

Teleconferencing Telephone conference calls among three or more people in different locations and video conferences where one-way or two-way TV supplements the audio channel.

Telephone Tag Making and returning telephone calls repeatedly before the two people are on the line at the same time.

Telex Messages are keyed in on a special machine which translates the keystrokes into a code. Incoming messages are decoded by the machine and printed on paper. Telex messages are common in international business communication.

10-K Report A report filed with the Securities and Exchange Commission summarizing the firm's financial performance; an informative document.

Thank-You Letter A letter thanking someone for helping you.

Threat A statement, explicit or implied, that someone will be punished if he or she does something.

Tone The implied attitude of the author toward the reader and the subject.

Tone of Voice The rising or falling inflection that indicates whether a group of words is a question or a statement, whether the speaker is uncertain or confident, whether a statement is sincere or sarcastic.

Topic Outline An outline listing the main points and the subpoints under each main point. A topic outline is the basis for the table of contents of a report.

Topic Sentence A sentence that introduces or summarizes the main idea in a paragraph. A topic sentence may be either stated or implied, and it may come anywhere in the paragraph.

Toulmin Logic A model, developed by Stephen Toulmin, useful in planning and in presenting arguments.

Transmit To send a message.

Transmittal A memo or letter explaining why something is being sent.

Trip Report A report of a visit to a client or of a conference in which the writer shares findings and impressions with others in the organization.

Truncated Code Symbols such as asterisks which turn up other forms of a key word in a computer search.

Truncated Scales Graphs with part of the scale missing.

Two-Margin or **Block Format** A format for résumés in which dates are listed in one column and job titles and descriptions in another. This format emphasizes work history.

Type Fonts The style of type. Each font has a design for each letter, number, and symbol.

U

Umbrella Sentence or Paragraph A sentence or paragraph listing in order the topics which following sentences or paragraphs will discuss.

Unity A piece of writing that has only one idea or topic.

Unjustified Margins Margins which do not end evenly on the right side of the page.

Unstructured Interview An interview based on three or four main questions prepared in advance and other questions which build on what the interviewee says.

V

Verbal Communication Communication that uses words; may be either oral or written.

Vested Interest The emotional stake readers have in something if they benefit from keeping things just as they are.

Vicarious Participation An emotional strategy in fund-raising letters based on the idea that donating money allows readers participate in work they are not able to do personally by having someone else do it on their behalf.

Visual Impact The visual "first impression" you get when you look at a page.

Voice Mail A mail system that uses telephones to bypass paper. Voice mail allows a sender to leave a message in his or her own voice using a push-button telephone. Various numbers on the phone allow the sender to record a message, play it back, or send it. To record a message, the sender simply speaks into the phone; to hear recorded messages, one listens just as one would to a regular phone call.

Volume The loudness or softness of a voice or other sound.

W

Weak Verbs Verbs composed of a form of the verb *to be* plus a noun.

White Space The empty space on the page. White space emphasizes material that it separates from the rest of the text.

Wild Card or **Truncated Code** Symbols such as asterisks which turn up other forms of a key word in a computer search.

Wordiness Taking more words than necessary to express an idea.

Word Processing A method of capturing the keystrokes of typing so that a document can be revised or reformatted without retyping the parts that are unchanged.

Writing The act of putting words on paper or on a screen, or of dictating words to a machine or a secretary.

Y

You-Attitude A style of writing which looks at things from the reader's point of view, emphasizes what the reader wants to know, respects the reader's intelligence, and protects the reader's ego. Using *you* probably increases you-attitude in positive situations. In negative situations or conflict, avoid *you* since that word will attack the reader.

INDEX